# Access 97 Macro & VBA Handbook

## Susann Novalis

SYBEX®

**San Francisco • Paris • Düsseldorf • Soest**

Associate Publisher: Amy Romanoff
Acquisitions Manager: Kristine Plachy
Acquisitions & Developmental Editor: Melanie Spiller
Editor: Brenda Frink
Technical Editor: Helen Feddema
Book Designers: Catalin Dulfu and Inbar Berman
Graphic Illustrator: Inbar Berman
Electronic Publishing Specialist: Dina F Quan
Production Coordinators: Alexa Riggs and Robin Kibby
Indexer: Nancy Guenther
Cover Designer: Design Site
Cover Photographer: David Bishop
Screen reproductions produced with Collage Complete.
Collage Complete is a trademark of Inner Media Inc.

SYBEX is a registered trademark of SYBEX Inc.

The Event Logger database application, provided on the CD and
used in Chapter 2, is from *Access 97 Developer's Handbook*, by Paul
Litwin, Ken Getz, and Mike Gilbert (Sybex, 1997).

TRADEMARKS: SYBEX has attempted throughout this book to
distinguish proprietary trademarks from descriptive terms by
following the capitalization style used by the manufacturer.

Library of Congress Card Number: 96-71017
ISBN: 0-7821-1977-8

Manufactured in the United States of America

10 9 8

## Software License Agreement: Terms and Conditions

a replacement of identical format at no charge by sending the defective media, postage prepaid, with proof of purchase to:

SYBEX Inc.
Customer Service Department
1151 Marina Village Parkway
Alameda, CA 94501
(510) 523-8233
Fax: (510) 523-2373
e-mail: info@sybex.com
WEB: HTTP//:WWW.SYBEX.COM

After the 90-day period, you can obtain replacement media of identical format by sending us the defective disk, proof of purchase, and a check or money order for $10, payable to SYBEX.

## Disclaimer

SYBEX makes no warranty or representation, either expressed or implied, with respect to the Software or its contents, quality, performance, merchantability, or fitness for a particular purpose. In no event will SYBEX, its distributors, or dealers be liable to you or any other party for direct, indirect, special, incidental, consequential, or other damages arising out of the use of or inability to use the Software or its contents even if advised of the possibility of such damage. In the event that the Software includes an on-line update feature, SYBEX further disclaims any obligation to provide this feature for any specific duration other than the initial posting.

The exclusion of implied warranties is not permitted by some states. Therefore, the above exclusion may not apply to you. This warranty provides you with specific legal rights; there may be other rights that you may have that vary from state to state. The pricing of the book with the Software by SYBEX reflects the allocation of risk and limitations on liability contained in this agreement of Terms and Conditions.

## Shareware Distribution

This Software may contain various programs that are distributed as shareware. Copyright laws apply to both shareware and ordinary commercial software, and the copyright Owner(s) retains all rights. If you try a shareware program and continue using it, you are expected to register it. Individual programs differ on details of trial periods, registration, and payment. Please observe the requirements stated in appropriate files.

## Copy Protection

The Software in whole or in part may or may not be copy-protected or encrypted. However, in all cases, reselling or redistributing these files without authorization is expressly forbidden except as specifically provided for by the Owner(s) therein.

*To Rich.*
*This book could not have*
*been written without your*
*support and understanding.*
*Thank you.*

# ACKNOWLEDGMENTS

Thanks to James Kelley, Dean of San Francisco State University's College of Science and Engineering, and Marci Manderscheid, Executive Director, Downtown Center at San Francisco State University, for their continued support of my work with software applications.

Thanks to everyone at Sybex who worked on this book. I especially appreciate the support that Melanie Spiller, Developmental Editor, and Amy Romanoff, Associate Publisher, have given me. Thanks to Editors Brenda Frink, Pat Coleman, June Waldman, Nancy O'Donnell, Toni Logan, Kris Vanberg-Wolff, and Jim Compton for their careful and helpful editing and to Inbar Berman for help with the graphics. Thanks to Dina Quan, Alexa Riggs, and Robin Kibby for turning my manuscript into a book.

Special thanks to Helen Feddema, Technical Editor. Her many comments and suggestions have made this a better book.

Writing a book for a new version of software requires strong support from the vendor. Thanks to Microsoft for including me in the Access 97 beta test program and to Jim Sturms, Jim Lucey, and the other people at Microsoft who answered critical questions. Thanks to the other members of the Access 97 beta test program for great questions, answers, and insightful comments. You are the ones who have taught and continue to teach me about the nuances and undocumented features of this wonderful product.

Thanks to Paul Litwin, Ken Getz, and Mike Gilbert, authors of *Access 97 Developer's Handbook* (Sybex, 1997) for giving me permission to include the Event Logger application on the book's CD-ROM.

And lastly, thanks to my parents, my sons, and especially Rich, for understanding my absence while the passion to create this book overtook me.

# CONTENTS AT A GLANCE

|  |  |  |
|---|---|---|
| *Introduction* | | *xxi* |
| **PART I** | **Preliminaries** | **1** |
| 1 | Automating a Database without Programming | 3 |
| 2 | Getting Started with Objects and Events | 67 |
| 3 | Introducing the Access Object Model | 109 |
| 4 | Communicating with Forms | 149 |
| **PART II** | **Macro Programming** | **197** |
| 5 | Macro Basics | 199 |
| 6 | Dealing with Errors in Macros | 273 |
| 7 | Navigation with Macros | 297 |
| 8 | Data Maintenance with Macros | 339 |
| 9 | Working with Groups of Records Using Macros | 377 |
| **PART III** | **Access VBA Programming** | **435** |
| 10 | The Access Object Model Revisited | 437 |
| 11 | The Data Access Objects | 485 |
| 12 | Mechanics of Procedures I: The Basics | 529 |
| 13 | Mechanics of Procedures II: Using Variables | 587 |
| 14 | Mechanics of Proocedures III: Controlling Execution | 649 |
| 15 | Dealing with Errors in VBA | 689 |
| 16 | Navigation with Access VBA | 737 |
| 17 | Data Maintenance with Access VBA | 803 |
| 18 | Working with Groups of Records Using Access VBA | 847 |
| 19 | Creating and Modifying Database Objects | 911 |
| 20 | Expanding Access | 969 |
| | *Index* | *1026* |

# TABLE OF CONTENTS

*Introduction*                                                              *xxi*

**PART I**   **Preliminaries**                                                **1**

**1   Automating a Database without Programming**                             **3**

Using the Database Wizard                                                      6
   Creating Navigation Paths with Switchboards                  7
   Exploring the Application                                   11
   Examining the Wizard's Work                                 16
Using the Command Button Wizard                                              22
   Creating a Return Path                                      23
Using a Hyperlink to Navigate                                                26
   Storing Hyperlinks as Data in a Table                       28
   Using a Hyperlink as an Unbound Form Control                30
Using the Combo Box Wizard                                                   35
Using the Switchboard Manager                                                39
   Editing a Switchboard                                       41
Controlling the User Interface                                               42
   Setting Startup Properties                                  43
   Protecting Your Application with a Password                  46
   Creating Custom Menus and Toolbars                          48
A Simple Automated Access Application                                        58
   Limitations of the Wizards and Helpers                      59
Taking the Next Step                                                         61
   Two Programming Languages                                   61
   Two Data Languages                                          62
Summary                                                                      63

**2   Getting Started with Objects and Events**                             **67**

Thinking in Objects                                                         68
   What's in a Name?                                           69
   Names in VBA Programming                                    71

What the User Sees 73
Changing Names 73
Describing an Object's Properties 74
Other Property Sheets 78
Lifetime of Objects 85
Manipulating Objects 86
Using Macros 87
Using VBA Procedures 89
The Access Events 91
The Access Programming Model 93
Categories of Events 94
Event Properties of Objects 94
Canceling Default Behavior 101
Getting Hands-on Experience with Events 101
Summary 105

**3    Introducing the Access Object Model    109**

Relating Objects to Each Other 110
Grouping Similar Objects 111
Objects Contain Objects 113
The Architecture of Access 116
The Application Layer 116
The Jet Database Engine 118
Object Hierarchies 120
The Access Application Object Model 123
Application Object 123
The Forms and Reports Collection Objects 123
The Form Object 124
The Report Object 124
The Controls Collection Object 124
The Control Object 124
The Screen Object 126
The VBA-Only Application Objects 126
The Access Visual Basic Object Model 127
The Debug Object 127
The Macro Programming Environment 128
Referring to Objects and Properties by Name 129
Referring to an Object by Name 129

Referring to a Form or Report · · · 130
Using the Immediate Pane to Evaluate an Object Property · · · 131
Referring to a Control · · · 133
Properties That Represent Other Objects · · · 135
Referring to a Subform · · · 135
Referring to Controls on the Active Form or Report · · · 137
Using the Screen Object to Refer to the Active Object · · · 138
Referring to a Field · · · 139
Using the Expression Builder to Create References · · · 141
Summary · · · 146

**4  Communicating with Forms**   **149**

Relating Forms and Controls to Data · · · 151
What Is a Recordset? · · · 152
Record Source for a Form or Report · · · 155
Control Source for a Control · · · 156
Controls without a ControlSource Property · · · 158
One Form–One Record Source Model · · · 159
Using AutoLookup Queries · · · 160
Communication between Controls and Fields · · · 162
Using Calculated Query Fields · · · 163
Using Calculated Form Controls · · · 164
Using an Unbound Control as a Variable · · · 175
Saving a Calculated Result to the Database · · · 177
Controls with Two Data Sources · · · 178
Using a Combo Box to Look Up Information · · · 178
Relations among Forms · · · 183
Synchronizing Two Forms · · · 183
Using the Form/Subform Technique to Synchronize Two Forms · · · 189
Summary · · · 194

**PART II  Macro Programming**   **197**

**5  Macro Basics**   **199**

The Macro Window · · · 200
The Macro Toolbar · · · 203

Macro Actions 205
 Macro Arguments 205
 Setting Values 209
 Duplicating Built-in Commands 214
 Sending Messages 217
 Sending Keystrokes 219
 Displaying Current Data 222
Creating Macros 225
 Using Macro Flow Diagrams 225
 Storing Macros in Macro Groups 226
 Editing in the Macrosheet 228
 The Flow of Macro Execution 229
Running Macros 230
 Running a Macro from the Macro Window 230
 Running a Macro from Any Active Window 230
 Running a Macro from Another Macro 231
 Running a Macro from a Command Bar 232
 Running a Macro from a Shortcut Key 233
 Running a Macro at Startup 234
 Running a Macro from the Debug Window 235
 Running a Macro from a VBA Procedure 237
 Running a Macro by Trapping an Event on a Form or Report 237
 Documenting Macros 239
Manipulating Objects with Macros 241
 Forms Navigation 242
Controlling Macro Program Execution 250
 Conditional Macros 251
 Controlling the Flow of a Macro with Conditions 252
 The Built-in Decision Functions 262
 Macro Loops 264
Summary 270

**6 Dealing with Errors in Macros 273**

Kinds of Macro Errors 274
 Syntax Errors 274
 Run-Time Errors 275
 Logic Errors 277
Troubleshooting 278

Single Stepping Macros 278
Using Breakpoints 279
Printing Macros 279
Using the MsgBox Action to Troubleshoot 281
Using the Debug Window to Troubleshoot 282
Handling Run-Time Errors: Macros versus Visual Basic 286
The Error Code for an Error 287
Using Macro Programming 288
Using Visual Basic Programming 288
A Simple Visual Basic Error Handler for the Error Event 289
Designing to Avoid Macro Errors 292
Exceptional Macro Actions 293
Summary 295

**7   Navigation with Macros                                      297**

Navigation through Controls 298
Moving to a Specific Control on the Active Form 299
Moving to a Specific Control on Another Open Form 302
Moving within a Record 302
Physical Navigation among Records 303
Automating Keystroke Navigation 303
Automating the Default Navigation Buttons and
  Menu Commands 305
Logical Navigation among Records 309
Finding a Specific Record 309
Returning to the Previous Record 317
Remove Navigation Buttons from a Form with
  Logical Navigation 320
Adding Logical Navigation to Another Form 321
Synchronizing Two Forms 323
Adding the Review Button to Another Form 327
Keeping the Forms Synchronized 328
Create a Macro to Keep the Forms Synchronized 330
Synchronizing a Report to a Form 333
Creating a Startup Macro 335
Summary 337

## 8 Data Maintenance with Macros 339

Using Macros to Validate Data 341
Using ValidationRule Properties 341
Checking for Duplicate Primary Key Values 344
Display a Primary Key Violation Form instead of a Message 346
Adding New Records 348
Analyze and Automate the Process 350
Undoing Changes 351
Design a Macro to Test the Dirty Property 351
Saving Changes 353
Date-Stamp a Changed Record 353
Saving a New Record 356
Carrying Values Forward to a New Record 357
Setting the DefaultValue Property 357
To Delete or Not to Delete? 361
Not to Delete 361
To Delete 362
Cascading a Delete 366
Other Ways to Delete a Record 368
Working with Data in Two Open Forms 369
Edit an Existing Record 370
Add a New Record 370
Summary 374

## 9 Working with Groups of Records Using Macros 377

Sorting Records 379
Sorting Interactively 380
Automate the Sort Process 381
Using Query By Form to Find a Group of Records 389
Selecting a Group of Records Interactively 390
Automate the Selection Process 392
Using Multiple Criteria to Select a Group of Records 397
Creating a Second Selection Combo Box 397
Adding a Null Row to a Selection Combo List 400
Synchronizing Two Combo Boxes 405
Creating a Combo Box to Display the First Letter 405
Synchronizing the Second Combo Box Using Query By Form 407

Creating a Macro to Keep the Second Combo Box Synchronized 408
Finding Records to Print 409
Printing a Group of Records Based on the Current Form 410
Using a Custom Dialog to Select Records 415
Create a Filter Query for the Report 418
Creating a Custom Dialog 420
Modifying a Group of Records 426
Using the OpenQuery Action to Run an Action Query 426
Summary 432

**PART III**  **Access VBA Programming**  **435**

**10**  **The Access Object Model Revisited**  **437**

Objects, Properties, and Methods 439
Using the Debug Window 441
Setting Properties 442
Getting Properties 443
Calling Methods 446
Manipulating the Access Application Objects 450
Using the Methods of the DoCmd Object 450
Using Functions and Statements 453
VBA-Only Form and Report Features 453
Referring to Objects in Collections 462
Indexing a Collection by Number 463
The Access Application Object Hierarchy 464
Application Object 464
The Collections 466
Form 466
Report 466
The Module Object 466
Control 468
Screen 473
DoCmd 473
Properties Collection 474
Property 475
The References Collection 475
The Reference Object 476

The Access Visual Basic Objects 476
The Microsoft Office Shared Objects 477
Using the Object Browser 478
Summary 482

**11   The Data Access Objects** **485**

The Data Access Object Hierarchy 489
Types of DAO Objects 493
Types of DAO Properties 493
Using Data Access Objects 495
Referring to Existing Data Access Objects 495
Creating New Data Access Objects 498
Manipulating Data in a Recordset Object 505
The Data Access Object Model 515
DBEngine 516
The Collection Objects 516
Workspace Object 517
Database Object 517
TableDef 518
Field 518
Index 519
Relation 521
Recordset 522
QueryDef 523
Parameter 523
Error 524
Property 524
Container 524
Document 524
User 525
Group 525
Using the Object Browser 525
Summary 526

**12   Mechanics of Procedures I: The Basics** **529**

Data Types 531
Fundamental Data Types 532
Variant Data Type 532

The Object Data Type 538
Procedures and Modules 539
The Access VBA Programming Environment 556
Module View 557
Editing in the Module Window 566
Programming Style 568
The Access VBA Compiler 569
Running Procedures 572
Running Function Procedures 572
Running Sub Procedures 581
Summary 584

## 13 Mechanics of Procedures II: Using Variables 587

Using Variables in Procedures 588
Using Variables to Create Reusable Code 589
Using Variables for Faster Code 594
How Procedures Use Variables 597
Declaring Variables 597
Naming Constants and Variables 599
Specifying a Data Type 599
The Life Cycle of a Variable 601
Procedure-Level Variables 604
Declaring a Variable within the Procedure 604
Declaring a Variable in the Argument List 606
Visibility of Procedure-Level Variables 606
Lifetime of Procedure-Level Variables 609
Passing Data to a Procedure 612
Passing Data to an Event Procedure 624
Module-Level Variables 625
Visibility of Module-Level Variables Created in a Form or
  Report Module 628
Lifetime of Module-Level Variables 629
Summary of Declarations and Data Typing 631
Using Constants 631
Using Intrinsic Constants 632
Creating Your Own Constants 634
Using Arrays 636
Fixed-Size Arrays 637

Dynamic Arrays 640
Using Arrays as Arguments 643
Creating Your Own Data Types 643
Using Custom Data Types as Arguments 645
Summary 646

**14 Mechanics of Procedures III: Controlling Execution 649**

Making Decisions with Conditions 651
If...Then 651
If...Then...Else 653
Select Case 657
Loops for Repetitive Operations 660
For...Next 661
For Each...Next 664
Do...Loop 666
Looping through a Recordset 671
Nesting Control Structures 672
Abbreviating Object References 674
Useful Statements and Functions 676
Using Not to Toggle a Property 677
Exit Statements 678
Timer Function 678
DoEvents Function 679
MsgBox and InputBox Functions 680
SysCmd Function 682
Summary 685

**15 Dealing with Errors in VBA 689**

Avoidable and Unavoidable Errors 691
Avoidable Errors 691
Unavoidable Errors 692
Fatal and Nonfatal Errors 692
Dealing with Unavoidable Errors 693
The Access VBA Compiler 694
Troubleshooting Tools 701
Using Help 702
Suspending Execution 702
Viewing Current Values in the Module Window 710

Using the Debug Window for Debugging 710
Using the Calls Box 715
Printing to the Debug Window from Code 716
Avoiding Bugs 717
Error Handling 719
Error Codes 719
Custom Error Messages 722
Jet and Interface Errors 722
VBA Errors 726
Errors in Called Procedures 734
Summary 735

**16 Navigation with Access VBA 737**

The Form and Its Recordset 740
Interface Navigation 743
Writing Reusable Procedures 744
Form Navigation 747
Synchronizing Two Forms 750
Navigation between Controls 753
Physical Navigation through the Records of a Form 758
Creating Custom Navigation Buttons 759
Finding a Specific Record 768
Using the FindRecord Method of the DoCmd Object 769
Using the ApplyFilter Method of the DoCmd Object 770
Using the RecordsetClone 771
Undoing the Search 773
Working with the Data in the Tables 774
Creating Recordset Variables to Work with the Data 775
Recordset Navigation 779
Finding a Specific Record 785
Using Clones 795
Reading Table Data into an Array 797
Summary 800

**17 Data Maintenance with Access VBA 803**

Maintaining Data Using Forms 804
Toggling a Form between Review and Data Entry Modes 805
Using VBA to Validate Data 807

Using an Event Procedure to Cancel the Default Behavior 810
Changing the Timing of a Validation Test 811
Using the Command Button Wizard for Data Entry Operations 813
Carrying Values Forward to a New Record 823
Working with Data in Two Related Forms 830
Using the NotInList Event to Add a New Row to a Combo List 832
Editing Data in a Recordset 836
Changing a Record 836
Adding a Record 838
Deleting a Record 842
Summary 843

**18 Working with Groups of Records Using Access VBA 847**

Sorting Records in a Form or Report 849
Selecting Groups of Records in a Form or Report 857
Finding a Group of Records Using Query By Form 867
Using a Multi-Select List Box to Filter Records 871
Navigational Techniques of DAO versus Relational
Techniques of SQL 880
Using Stored Queries and SQL Statements 881
Creating New Stored Queries in VBA Procedures 884
Running Select Queries in VBA Procedures 890
Making Bulk Changes to a Recordset with Action Queries 898
Transactions 904
Summary 907

**19 Creating and Modifying Database Objects 911**

Understanding How Access and Jet Create Objects 912
Creating Data Access Objects 916
Creating and Deleting Database Window Objects 917
Creating a Table 918
Linking to an External Table 932
Creating a Form or Report 933
Creating a Module 936
Deleting a Database Window Object 939
Creating Your Own Properties 940
Custom Properties for Data Access Objects 940

Custom Properties for Forms, Reports, and Controls   947
Custom Properties for Forms and Reports   948
Creating Custom Methods for a Form or Report   954
Displaying Multiple Instances of a Form   955
Using the Collection Object   958
Using the New Keyword in a Declaration Statement   958
Using the New Keyword in an Assignment Statement   959
Creating Multiple Instances   962
Example: The Product List and Viewing Product Information   963
Summary   966

**20   Expanding Access   969**

Converting Macros to VBA Procedures   971
Converting Event Macros to Event Procedures   975
Converting Macros to Function Procedures   979
Understanding Library Databases   983
Creating a Library Database   983
Creating a Reference to a Library Database   984
Understanding Dynamic-Link Libraries   987
Using a Type Library   988
Using a Declare Statement   989
The Windows API DLLs   990
Using ActiveX   993
Using ActiveX Controls   994
Installing and Registering an ActiveX Control   996
Inserting an ActiveX Control   998
Setting Properties at Design Time   1001
Using Events   1003
Automation   1006
Learning About an Application's Objects   1008
Using Automation Objects   1012
Summary   1025

*Index*   *1026*

# INTRODUCTION

Microsoft Access is the leading relational database management system for creating database applications on the desktop. Why is Access number one? Two reasons are that Microsoft Access is easy to learn and fun to use. Microsoft has achieved great success in providing a graphical interface environment that makes it as easy as possible for you to learn to use the enormous power available in Access.

If we think of using Access interactively as walking, then learning how to write the programs that automate Access is running, and learning how to put it all together into a custom application is flying. There are several excellent introductory books that help you learn all about walking with Access. A particularly helpful book is *Mastering Access 97* by Alan Simpson and Elizabeth Olson (Sybex, 1997). There are far fewer flying manuals available; one of the best is *Access 97 Developer's Handbook* by Paul Litwin, Ken Getz, and Mike Gilbert (Sybex, 1997). The book you are reading now is the running manual that bridges the gap.

## About Macros and VBA

Microsoft Access provides two sets of tools for automating your database: macro programming and Visual Basic for Applications (VBA) programming. Why two automation tools? Because Microsoft intends Microsoft Access as a database management system for the broadest possible spectrum of computer users.

At one end of the spectrum are people who want to move beyond an interactive database application and pass more of the work to the computer but who have no programming background and are too busy to acquire one. Access macros are the solution for these people. At the other end of the spectrum, developers need the additional power and the ability to deal with errors that VBA provides. In between are people with varying programming backgrounds and experience who may choose to use both tools.

In this book you'll learn the essentials of both macro and Access VBA programming. You'll learn how to deal with errors. You'll learn how to create both macros and procedures for the three basic database operation categories: navigating through the application, maintaining data, and selecting groups of records for specific purposes.

# How This Book Is Organized

*Access 97 Macro & VBA Handbook* is organized into three parts and two appendixes. The first part covers basic concepts that both macro and VBA programming use. The second part, "Macro Programming," and the third part, "Access VBA Programming," are parallel sections. Each starts with the basics of its programming language and moves on to dealing with errors and to writing programs for navigation, for data maintenance, and for selecting groups of records. Part III continues with two more chapters covering VBA-only features. Depending on your programming experience and personal choice, you can go directly to either part after finishing Part I.

Appendix A, "Macro Actions and DoCmd Methods," is an alphabetical list of the 49 macro actions, their action arguments, whether there is a corresponding DoCmd method, additional method arguments, and a description of the action/method. Appendix B, "Glossary," is an alphabetical list of the terms used in the book and their definitions. The two appendixes are on the book's companion CD-ROM. See the readme file for more information.

## Organizing Your Work

Microsoft Access 97 Macros & VBA Handbook is both a reference and a hands-on tutorial. In most chapters, you'll either create a new database from scratch or create a copy of the Northwind sample database. To organize your work:

1. Create a new folder named MacrosVBAHandbook in which to store your example databases.

2. Locate the Samples folder. In a default installation of Microsoft Office 97, the path is C:\Program Files\Microsoft Office\Office\Samples. Drag to your MacroVBAHandbook folder copies of all of the files except Orders.mdb, Orders80.hlp, Orders80.cnt, Solutions.mdb, Soltn80.hlp, and Soltn80.cnt.

Many of the files you copy from the Samples folder are image and other files that the Northwind database uses. These related files must be in the same folder as your working copies of the Northwind database. The files you'll need in the chapters are now readily available in your work folder.

# What's on the CD-ROM

The book's CD-ROM contains answer databases for the book's chapters, an application called Event Logger, a glossary of Access terms, a list of the 49 macro actions, tables referred to in the book, and a text file describing the declaration statements required to use procedures in the dynamic link libraries of the Windows API. To use the CD-ROM, you must have Windows 95 and Microsoft Access 97 installed on your computer.

**Solutions**    The folder named Solutions contains the answer databases for the book's chapters. You can run the answer databases directly from the CD-ROM, or you can copy them to your MacrosVBAHandbook folder. The solutions folder contains the following answer databases:

| | |
|---|---|
| Expenses.mdb | A semi-automated database that the Database Wizard creates and that we modify using the other built-in Access tools in Chapter 1. Chapters 2, 3, and 4 also refer to this database. |
| Northwind_Ch4.mdb | A copy of the Northwind database used in Chapter 4. |
| NorthwindMacros.mdb | A copy of the Northwind sample database that you create and use throughout Part II. |
| Ch12_Examples.mdb | A solutions file you create from scratch in Chapter 12. |
| Northwind_Ch13.mdb | A copy of the Northwind database used in Chapter 13. |
| Northwind_Ch14.mdb | A copy of the Northwind database used in Chapter 14. |
| Ch15_Examples.mdb | A solutions file you create from scratch in Chapter 15. |

| | |
|---|---|
| Northwind_Ch16.mdb | A copy of the Northwind database used in Chapter 16. |
| Northwind_Ch17.mdb | A copy of the Northwind database used in Chapter 17. |
| Northwind_Ch18.mdb | A copy of the Northwind database used in Chapter 18. |
| Northwind_Ch19.mdb | A copy of the Northwind database used in Chapter 19. |
| Northwind_Ch20.mdb | A copy of the Northwind database used in Chapter 20. |

**Tables**    The Tables folder contains the tables referred to in the book. Most of these tables are comprehensive reference tables that you'll want to have available as you write your programs. You can view the tables using the Adobe Acrobat Reader, which is also on the CD-ROM. For instructions, see the file readme.txt.

**Appendixes**    The appendixes folder contains the following files:

| | |
|---|---|
| AppendixA.pdf | Appendix A, "Macro Actions and DoCmd Methods," is an alphabetical list of the 49 macro actions, their action arguments, whether there is a corresponding DoCmd method, additional method arguments, and a description of the action/method. |
| AppendixB.pdf | Appendix B is a glossary of the terms used in the book and their definitions. |

To view the appendixes, you will need to install the Adobe Acrobat Reader (also on the CD-ROM). See the CD-ROM's readme file for instructions.

**Event Logger**    The Event Logger directory contains the file Eventlogger.mdb. This is the Event Logger database application used in Chapter 2 for hands-on experience with events. This application was created by the authors of *Access 97 Developer's Handbook,* who have kindly given permission to include this excellent tutorial database in my book.

## And Finally

The file Win32api.txt, located in the CD-ROM's root directory, describes the declaration statements required to use procedures in the dynamic link libraries of the Windows Application Programming Interface (API). Chapter 20 refers to this file.

# Who Should Read This Book

This is an intermediate-level book about Microsoft Access. You should be familiar with the basic concepts and techniques of interactive Access, including creating a simple Access database complete with related tables, queries, forms, and reports. This book builds on that knowledge and shows you how to automate database operations using macro programming and Access VBA programming. You do not need any prior experience with programming. Although this book is an intermediate-level Access book, it is a beginning-level programming book.

*Access 97 Macro & VBA Handbook* focuses on teaching you the macro and Access VBA programming languages and on showing you how to use these languages to automate individual database operations. For more information on custom application design, that is, on how to incorporate these techniques into the whole of an automated application, see my book *Automating Access with Macros* (Sybex, 1996) for the macros approach and *Access 97 Developer's Handbook* (Sybex, 1997) for the Access VBA approach.

# New Access 97 Features Used in This Book

Access 97 provides several features that were not included in Access 95. The new features covered in this book include Internet features; Command bars; improvements to the Module Editor, the Debug Window, and the Object Browser; lightweight forms and reports; MDE files; the ODBCDirect technology; and additions to the Access Application object model.

# Conventions Used in This Book

This book uses the following conventions: Key combinations that you press are indicated by joining the keys with a plus sign. For example, Shift+F2 indicates that you hold down the Shift key while you press the F2 function key. Sequences of menu commands are indicated by the symbol ➤. For example, File ➤ Close indicates the Close command on the File menu. Words, phrases, and names that you must type or enter are shown in **bold type**. `Monospace type` is used for examples of VBA programming code. Keywords of SQL statements are shown in uppercase (for example, DISTINCTROW).

Chapter 5 suggests using flow diagrams to depict the logic of complicated macros and uses diagram symbols including:

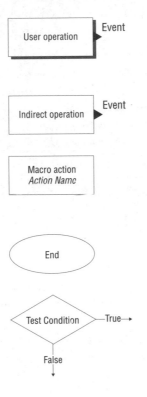

The shadowed operation box with the event triangle indicates the direct user operation that causes the event shown above the event triangle.

The operation box with the event triangle indicates the indirect operation that causes the event shown above the event triangle.

The operation box indicates a single macro action and includes an English phrase to describe the action (the macro action is in italics).

The rounded termination symbol indicates the end of the macro.

The decision diamond indicates branching to one of two alternative sets of actions, depending on the outcome of the test shown in the diamond.

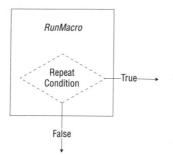

The loop symbol indicates an action that runs another macro repeatedly as long as the test shown in the dashed decision diamond is true.

Although the diagrams in Chapter 5 pertain to macros, you can use the same symbols in flow diagrams to depict the logic of complicated procedures.

# Endnotes

Thank you for selecting this book to help you learn about macro and Access VBA programming. Writing this book has been a wonderful opportunity for me to learn more about programming and to share my insights with you. I hope you enjoy learning from this book. Please send your comments, suggestions, and corrections to me at novalis@sfsu.edu.

**NOTE** Material from the CD may be found on the Sybex Web site at http://www.sybex.com/ in the near future.

# PART I

# Preliminaries

# CHAPTER

## ONE

1

# Automating a Database without Programming

- Using the Database Wizard

- Automating operations with the Command Button Wizard

- Navigating with hyperlinks

- Creating a navigation control center with the Switchboard Manager

- Controlling the user interface

- Creating custom menus and toolbars

**A** *database* is a collection of records and files. To create a database, you need a system that will help you to store, retrieve, and sort your data, as well as analyze and convert it into useful information. If the database is large or complex, you'll probably want to use a commercial computer database application such as Microsoft Access.

One way to create a new Access database is to start from scratch. Access has a terrific set of tools and wizards to help you create a database, including *tables* to store data, *queries* to retrieve and manipulate data, *forms* to enter and view data, and *reports* to print information. But if you stop at this point you'll have taken advantage of only a fraction of the power that Access offers; you'll have used only four of the six database container objects, having left the *macros* and *modules* untouched.

Without macros and modules, a database is *interactive*. In an interactive database the user initiates each individual action the computer carries out by choosing a menu command or by clicking a toolbar button. So in order to perform a task the user has to know which menu commands to use and which sequence to use them in. In an interactive database, the user is the one who supplies the connections between the forms and reports in the database, so in order to perform a task the user must know how the forms and reports are related. In an interactive database, the user has complete control: a knowledgeable user has the power to use the interactive database in productive ways, a less sophisticated user has the power to corrupt the data and damage the database by selecting the wrong command at the wrong time.

In this book you'll learn how to use the macro and module objects to transform your interactive database into an *automated database application*. In automating a database you use the macro and module objects to create lists of instructions, and you arrange to have the computer execute an entire list when a user chooses a custom menu command or clicks a custom command button. A well-designed, fully automated database application can be used by any computer user, even by someone who doesn't know Access. The user doesn't have to know the sequence of steps for a task and doesn't have to know the Access commands. The user needs only to click a single button to execute a complicated task.

Access provides a set of wizards and helpers to assist you with some of the automation. This chapter shows you how to use the helpers to create a partially automated database application. The wizards and helpers use modules, but no macros, in their work and give you a glimpse of what is possible when you automate a database. (Later in the book you'll learn how to duplicate most of the automation routines using macros instead.) This chapter introduces you to some of the helpers including the Database Wizard for creating the first draft of a complete application, two of the control wizards for creating automated command buttons and combo boxes, and the Switchboard Manager for creating road maps to the forms and reports in the application.

Whether or not you use the wizards and helpers to do some of the automation, when you create a fully automated application, you create a custom user interface. The *user interface* is what you see on the screen and how you use the keyboard and mouse to communicate with the computer. In the custom application's user interface, the user clicks command buttons to move between tasks, to perform data entry operations, to find records, and to print reports. The custom user interface is where the user lives in your database application. From the user's perspective, the custom user interface *is* your database application.

**NOTE**    In Access you can't place buttons on tables or queries, so tables and queries are not usually displayed in a custom user interface. Instead, you build the new user interface entirely out of forms and reports because these two objects have been designed to respond to a user clicking a button, selecting a value from a list, or entering a value in a text box

When creating the new interface, you should supply the tools to open forms, perform data entry, locate specific records or groups of records, import data, archive old records, and print reports. You should also provide a choice of paths for navigating through your database, making sure that users always know where they are and how to backtrack along the path.

This chapter shows you how to use the new hyperlink techniques from Internet technology to navigate between database objects. You'll also learn how to use hyperlinks to navigate directly from a form in your application to any document in your computer's file system or in any other computer that is connected to your computer using the Internet's TCP/IP network. At each stage of user interface construction, your goals are to build in ease of use, intuitive understanding, and protection of the application. This chapter shows you how to create custom menus and toolbars so your application provides only the tools and commands that a user needs. You'll learn how to protect your application with a password. You'll learn how to set startup conditions so a user who survives the password test never sees the Database window and is greeted instead by your application's startup form and by custom menus and toolbars. This chapter ends with a preview of macros and VBA, the two programming languages used in Access, and gives you a glimpse of the additional power you'll have when you learn to use them.

# Using the Database Wizard

The Database Wizard can help you to create database applications for 22 different business and personal scenarios as follows:

| | |
|---|---|
| Address Book | Music Collection |
| Asset Tracking | Order Entry |
| Book Collection | Picture Library |
| Contact Management | Recipes |
| Donations | Resource Scheduling |
| Event Management | Service Call Management |
| Expenses | Students and Classes |
| Household Inventory | Time and Billing |
| Inventory Control | Video Collection |
| Ledger | Wine List |
| Membership | Workout |

Once you identify the scenario that is closest to the application you want to create, the wizard, in the usual wizard style, displays a series of screens telling you about the application and soliciting your input. After collecting your choices, the wizard uses the template you selected to create and customize the necessary tables, queries, forms, reports, and modules.

The Database Wizard is able to create both simple and complex databases. Depending on the scenario you choose, the wizard may create several groups of tables. When there are pairs of tables in a many-to-many relationship, the wizard automatically resolves the relationship into a pair of one-to-many relationships by creating a relationship table. The wizard creates simple data entry forms for each table and may even create a form/subform combination to display a one-to-many relationship. The wizard creates summary reports appropriate to the scenario you choose.

# Creating Navigation Paths with Switchboards

After creating the individual data entry forms and summary reports, the wizard automatically creates forms called *switchboards* that provide navigation paths between groups of forms and reports. The wizard creates a *main switchboard* that serves as the control center for the application. The main switchboard has command buttons for each of the basic database tasks. Clicking a button on the main switchboard takes you automatically to a form that you use to perform a database task such as entering data into one of the tables. Clicking a button on the main switchboard may also take you to another switchboard with buttons that take you to other forms, reports, or even other switchboards.

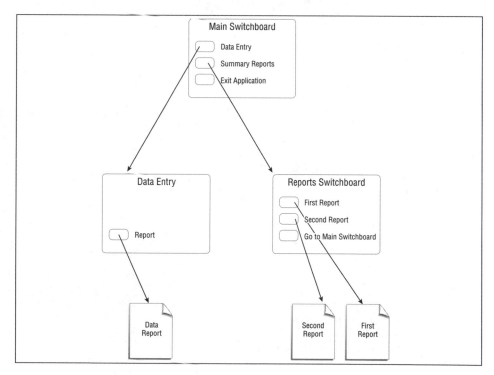

The buttons react when you click them because the wizard has created an individual set of instructions for each button. The wizard writes instructions and stores them in one of two places: either in modules called *standard modules* that are listed as separate objects in the Modules pane of the Database window or in modules called *form modules* and *report modules* that are built into the forms and reports. A form or report module is part of the form or report definition so it is stored as part of the form listed in the Forms pane or the report listed in the Reports pane of the Database window.

To observe the Database Wizard at work, we'll create an application for tracking employee expenses.

1. Start up Access 97 and select the Database Wizard in the opening dialog (see Figure 1.1a). Select the Databases tab in the New dialog and choose Expenses.mdz (see Figure 1.1b). The instructions for each scenario are stored in a template file with the .mdz extension.

---

**FIGURE 1.1:**

Summon the Database Wizard in the opening dialog (a) and select a template for the new database (b).

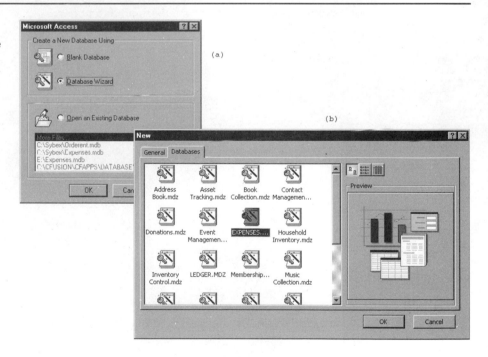

2. In the next dialog, enter Expenses as the name and save the database to the MacroVBAHandbook folder. (If you haven't created this folder, see the Introduction for instructions on setting it up.) Click the Create button to summon the Database Wizard. The wizard's first screen explains the kinds of information the database will manage (see Figure 1.2).

3. The next screen, shown in Figure 1.3, gives you the opportunity to make minor changes in the database. The list box on the left displays the tables to be created; when you click on a table the list box on the right changes to display the fields for the selected table. You can't add new tables or delete tables from the list, but you can add the fields shown in italics. For each table, check the fields you want to add. Check the box at the bottom of the screen to ask the wizard to supply sample data.

4. Specify styles for the forms and reports in the next two dialogs (see Figure 1.4).

5. You can use the next dialog, shown in Figure 1.5a, to enter a title and a bitmap picture. If you added a picture, it would appear on reports that the wizard creates. In the final screen, shown in Figure 1.5b, you can elect to start the database immediately after it is created and to display help. Clicking the Finish button puts the wizard to work. While the wizard toils, a dialog box displays one progress meter showing the overall progress and another progress meter showing the progress in creating a specific object (see Figure 1.5c).

**FIGURE 1.2:**

The Database Wizard explains the kinds of information the database will manage.

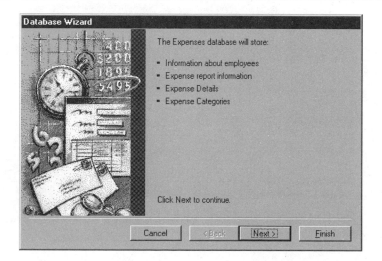

**FIGURE 1.3:**

You can choose to add optional fields to some of the tables and populate the database with sample data.

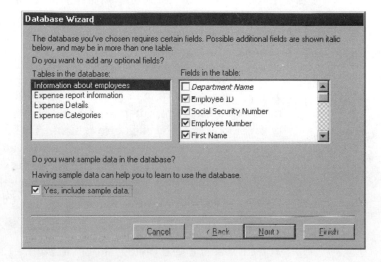

**FIGURE 1.4:**

You can specify styles for forms (a) and reports (b).

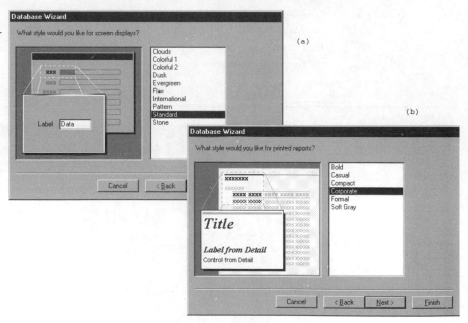

## FIGURE 1.5:

Enter a new title and maybe a bitmap picture (a). After you click Finish in the final screen (b), the wizard starts to work. Progress meters indicate which object is being created (c).

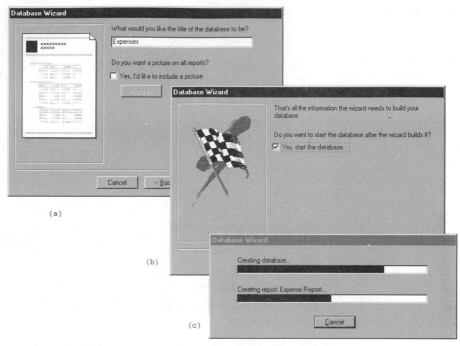

(a)

(b)

(c)

If you watch closely you see that the wizard first flashes a window you may not have seen before; this is a module window where some of the sets of instructions are stored. Next, the wizard creates the tables and relationships, a form named Switchboard, and finally, the forms and reports. The last text that flashes above the lower progress meter states that the wizard is setting database properties. When the job is finished the Main Switchboard is displayed (see Figure 1.6) and the Database window is minimized.

## Exploring the Application

The Main Switchboard is the first stop in navigating through the application; you learn how to use this form as a startup form later in the chapter. The Main Switchboard gives an immediate sense of the main tasks that the application manages. The command buttons direct you to forms for carrying out database tasks or to other switchboards that may branch to still more forms and switchboards. The last two buttons appear on every Main Switchboard that the

FIGURE 1.6:

The Main Switchboard is the central dispatch for the database application.

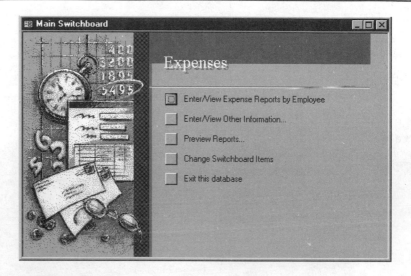

Database Wizard creates. We'll explore the Change Switchboard Items button later in the chapter. Clicking the Exit this database button closes the database without exiting Access.

Take a few minutes to travel to other forms by clicking buttons. After exploring the Expenses application for a while, you observe that some of the forms have buttons that take you to other forms. The buttons on switchboards and the forms provide navigational paths through the application to the various tasks. The overall organization emerges as shown in the *task flow diagram* in Figure 1.7. A task flow diagram displays the underlying sequence, or flow, of the tasks. The directional arrows in the task flow diagram indicate whether a form has a command button that takes you back to a previous form.

The first button on the Main Switchboard takes you to the Expense Reports by Employee form, which has a button that opens the Expense Reports form. Clicking the Preview Report button on the Expense Reports form opens a preview of the Expense Report report. Clicking this sequence of buttons takes you along a one-way path from the Main Switchboard to the Expense Report report (see Figure 1.8). The path is one way because there are no command buttons to take you back to the Main Switchboard; of course, you can use a form's default Close button in its upper-right corner or choose the Close command from the File menu to close the form and return to the previous form. Later we'll make the navigation back to the previous form more obvious by adding command buttons to the forms.

**FIGURE 1.7:**

The task flow diagram for the Expenses application

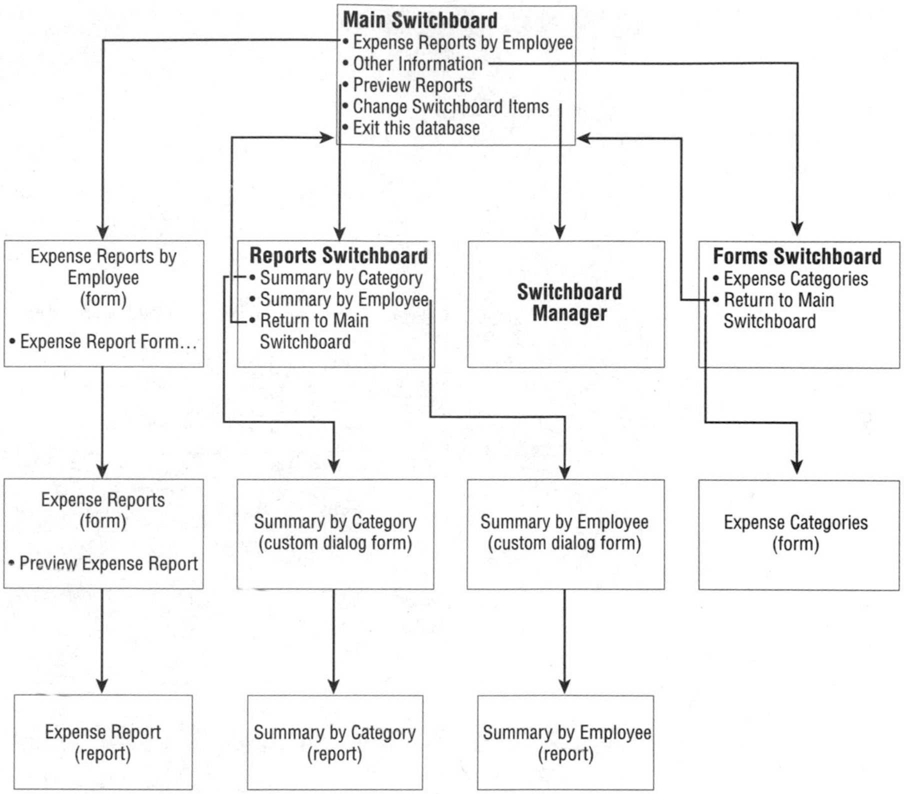

**Main Switchboard**
- Expense Reports by Employee
- Other Information
- Preview Reports
- Change Switchboard Items
- Exit this database

Expense Reports by
Employee
(form)

- Expense Report Form...

**Reports Switchboard**
- Summary by Category
- Summary by Employee
- Return to Main
  Switchboard

**Switchboard
Manager**

**Forms Switchboard**
- Expense Categories
- Return to Main
  Switchboard

Expense Reports
(form)

- Preview Expense Report

Summary by Category
(custom dialog form)

Summary by Employee
(custom dialog form)

Expense Categories
(form)

Expense Report
(report)

Summary by Category
(report)

Summary by Employee
(report)

Notice that when you select an employee in the Expense Reports by Employee form and click the button on the form, the Expense Reports form opens displaying information for the same employee, that is, the opened form is *synchronized* to the form that opened it. If you click into the first form, move to a different employee, and then click back into the second form, you'll see that the two forms remain synchronized. Similarly, when you click the Preview Report button on the Expense Reports form, the report that opens is synchronized to the form that opened it.

The second button on the Main Switchboard takes you to another switchboard called the Forms Switchboard where you have the choice of displaying the Expense Categories data entry form or returning to the Main Switchboard (see Figure 1.9).

**FIGURE 1.8:**

The one-way path from the Main Switchboard to the Expense Reports form (a) and then to the Expense Report report (b).

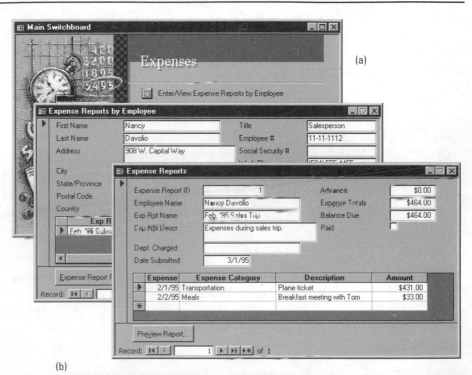

(a)

(b)

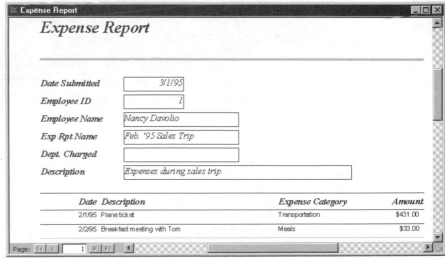

FIGURE 1.9:

The path from the Main Switchboard to the Expense Categories form

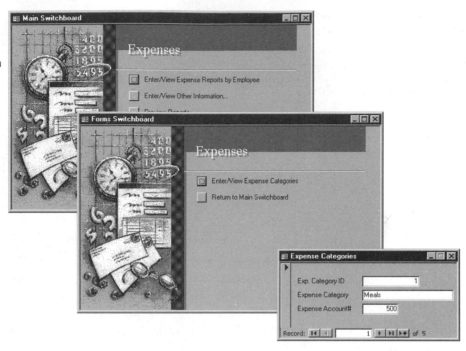

The third button branches to a third switchboard, called the Reports Switchboard, where you can click either of two summary reports or return to the Main Switchboard. Clicking either of the summary report buttons opens a custom dialog form where you enter the beginning and ending dates for a report. Clicking the Review button after entering dates takes you to a preview of a summary report for the specified interval (see Figure 1.10).

The Database Wizard has done more than simply provide navigational paths between forms and reports: the wizard has built a *custom dialog form* for collecting input. In this example, the date interval is the criterion for a parameter query that selects the appropriate records for the summary report (a parameter query that gets its information from a form is using a technique called *Query By Form*, which you'll learn about in Chapters 9 and 18).

**FIGURE 1.10:**

The path from the Main Switchboard to the custom dialog boxes for collecting date input for the summary reports

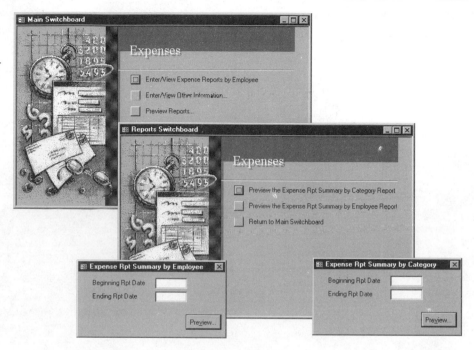

## Examining the Wizard's Work

Let's look behind the scenes to explore how the wizard accomplishes some of its tasks. The Database Wizard uses a number of elementary and advanced techniques. At this point we'll observe what the Wizard has done as a glimpse into some of the techniques you'll be learning to use in your databases.

Restore the Database window and note the following:

- There is only one form called Switchboard, yet we have seen three switchboards in the Expenses example: the Main Switchboard, the Forms Switchboard, and the Reports Switchboard. If you open the Switchboard form in Design view, you see a form with eight command buttons and eight blank labels (see Figure 1.11a). The Database Wizard uses this form for all of the switchboards. Although it isn't obvious, each switchboard is created on-the-fly as a different version of the same form when you click a command button. Clicking the second button on the Main Switchboard converts the form into the Forms Switchboard, and clicking the third button converts the form into the Reports Switchboard. The Wizard has created instructions for converting the form including changing the caption, displaying the correct number of buttons and the correct labels, and empowering the command buttons displayed by each version of the form to carry out their specific tasks.

- In addition to the four data tables, there is a Switchboard Items table. One of the fields in this table, the ItemText field, holds the labels for the buttons on the various switchboards (see Figure 1.11b). The other fields store information for creating the switchboards and making the buttons work. Note that this table is the record source for the Switchboard form.

**FIGURE 1.11:**

Design view of the Switchboard form (a) and the Switchboard Items table that holds the information for creating the switchboards (b)

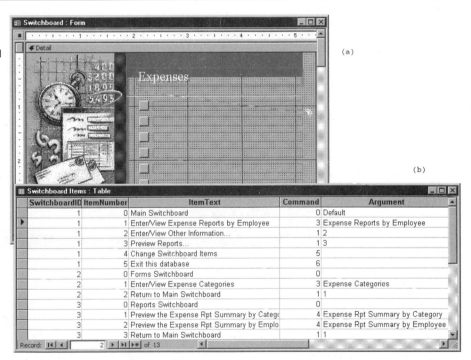

(a)

(b)

| SwitchboardID | ItemNumber | ItemText | Command | Argument |
|---|---|---|---|---|
| 1 | 0 | Main Switchboard | 0 | Default |
| 1 | 1 | Enter/View Expense Reports by Employee | 3 | Expense Reports by Employee |
| 1 | 2 | Enter/View Other Information... | 1 | 2 |
| 1 | 3 | Preview Reports... | 1 | 3 |
| 1 | 4 | Change Switchboard Items | 5 | |
| 1 | 5 | Exit this database | 6 | |
| 2 | 0 | Forms Switchboard | 0 | |
| 2 | 1 | Enter/View Expense Categories | 3 | Expense Categories |
| 2 | 2 | Return to Main Switchboard | 1 | 1 |
| 3 | 0 | Reports Switchboard | 0 | |
| 3 | 1 | Preview the Expense Rpt Summary by Categ | 4 | Expense Rpt Summary by Category |
| 3 | 2 | Preview the Expense Rpt Summary by Emplo | 4 | Expense Rpt Summary by Employee |
| 3 | 3 | Return to Main Switchboard | 1 | 1 |

Record: 2 of 13

- Although the wizard has used the Query By Form technique to select records based on your input in a dialog form, there are no queries listed in the Queries pane. There are, in fact, no queries stored as *saved queries* in the Expenses application. If you've studied the way the Form or Report

Wizards create their objects, you know that these wizards use SQL statements instead of saved queries as the record sources for the forms and reports. Most of the applications that the Database Wizard can create have no stored queries and use only SQL statements directly for RecordSource and RowSource properties.

- There is a single Report Date Range form that the wizard uses for both of the custom dialog forms. The wizard has created instructions to change the caption depending on the button you click in the Reports Switchboard.

- There is a single standard module named Global Code listed in the Modules pane of the Database window. There are no macros listed in the Macros pane.

Let's explore the standard module. Select the Global Code module in the Modules pane of the Database window and click the Design button to display the Module window. What is displayed in the window depends on the Module window option settings on your computer. Most likely, the window opens to the module's first pane (see Figure 1.12), called the Declarations section, where you store directions to Access and "declare" the names of constants, variables, and certain functions that you intend to use in the module. The Declarations section stores two statements for option settings. If you see additional text then you are displaying Full Module View; click the button in the extreme lower-left corner of the window to display Procedure View. You use subsequent module panes to store the sets of instructions.

**FIGURE 1.12:**

The first pane of the Global Code module is the Declarations section.

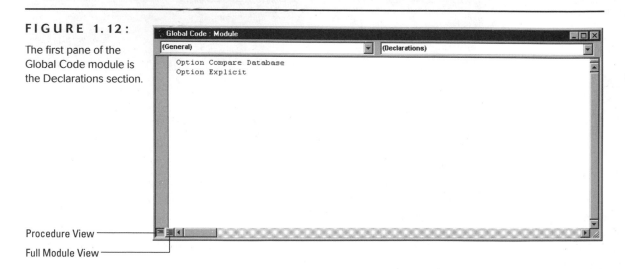

Procedure View

Full Module View

NOTE You can change the default view of the Module window by choosing the Options command in the Tools menu, clicking the Modules tab, and checking or clearing the Full Module View checkbox in the Window Settings. For this chapter, clear the checkbox to display the declarations and the procedures in separate panes.

A module stores instructions written in the Visual Basic for Applications (VBA) programming language. In VBA you write sets of instructions in units called *procedures*. To see the procedures stored in the Global Code module, click the down arrow of the combo box on the right. The combo box list indicates the module has only one procedure called IsLoaded (see Figure 1.13).

Even though we haven't learned about the VBA language, it is obvious that this procedure says nothing about opening forms or reports, not to mention synchronizing them. As I'll discuss later in the book, the Expenses application uses the IsLoaded procedure to determine whether a specified form is open.

**FIGURE 1.13:**

The IsLoaded procedure

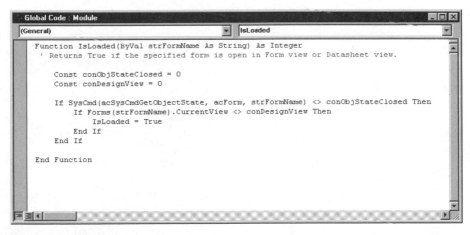

```
Function IsLoaded(ByVal strFormName As String) As Integer
    ' Returns True if the specified form is open in Form view or Datasheet view.

        Const conObjStateClosed = 0
        Const conDesignView = 0

        If SysCmd(acSysCmdGetObjectState, acForm, strFormName) <> conObjStateClosed Then
            If Forms(strFormName).CurrentView <> conDesignView Then
                IsLoaded = True
            End If
        End If

End Function
```

## Exploring the Procedure for a Command Button

We know there must be additional procedures for the command buttons, so we'll explore a button.

1. Open the Expense Reports by Employee form and switch to Design view.

2. Select the Expense Report Form... button and, if necessary, open its property sheet by clicking the Properties button in the toolbar.

An object's property sheet lists all of the properties you can set at design time. (You are in design mode or *design time* whenever the active window is the Design view of one of the six database window objects.) In addition, most objects have properties that aren't listed in the property sheet. (You'll learn about the unlisted properties later.) The full set of an object's properties describes the object fully at a particular moment and is called the object's *state*. Whenever you change a property, you change the object's state. For example, when you click a command button you change its state from unclicked to clicked. In Access, many of an object's changes in state are given special treatment; these particular changes in state are called *events*. When you click a command button, it recognizes the Click event. For each of its events, the object has a corresponding *event property* listed in the Event category of the object's property sheet. In most cases the name of the event property is the word "On" followed by the event's name, for example, the OnClick event property corresponds to the Click event.

3. Click the Event tab. Figure 1.14 shows the 12 event properties for the command button.

**FIGURE 1.14:**

The event properties for a command button

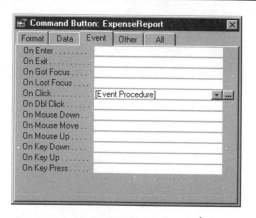

The name of an event property suggests the action that causes the object's state to change; for example, OnMouseDown suggests that when you press a mouse button while the pointer is over the button, the command button recognizes an event called MouseDown. While you can make similar deductions about other event properties and be correct most of the time, it's best to invest some time using online Help to learn the precise definition of each event property. Click the

Help button in the toolbar and then click the event's property box to display help for the event (see Figure 1.15). You'll learn more about specific events and the order of events in Chapter 2.

**FIGURE 1.15:**

Online help for the
MouseDown and
MouseUp events

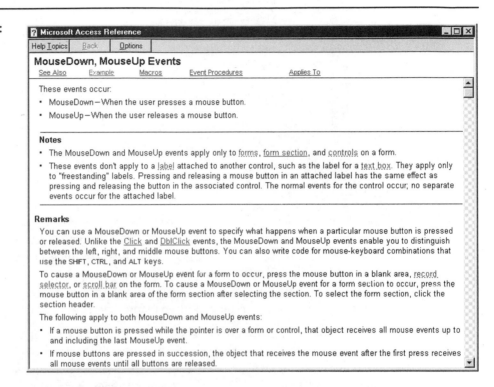

The reason that events are important is that events are programming opportunities. You can create a list of instructions, that is, a *program*, and tell Access to execute the program when an object recognizes one of its events. This programming technique is called *event-driven programming*.

Figure 1.14 shows [Event Procedure] as the setting for the OnClick property. This means that a VBA procedure has been created and assigned to the button's Click event. Access runs the procedure when you click the button. A VBA procedure that runs when an object recognizes an event is an *event procedure*. When you click the Build button at the right of an event property, the Module window opens showing the event procedure (see Figure 1.16).

FIGURE 1.16:

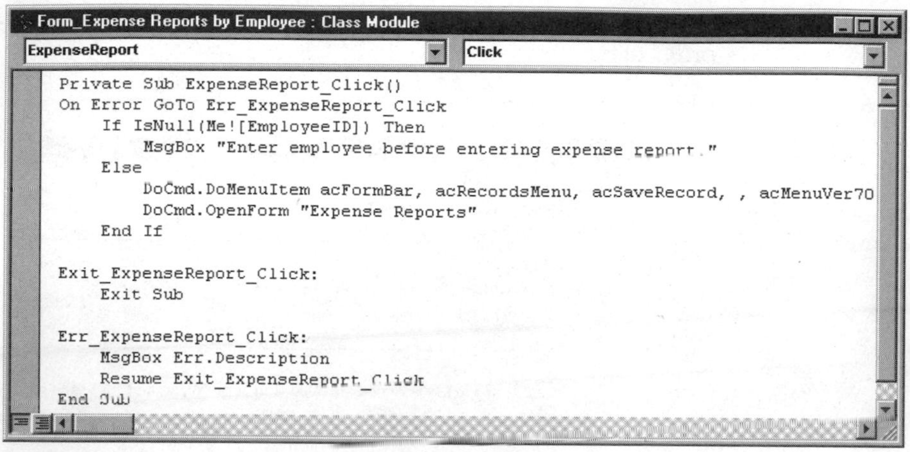

The event procedure
for the OnClick property
of the command button

```
Form_Expense Reports by Employee : Class Module

ExpenseReport                              Click

Private Sub ExpenseReport_Click()
On Error GoTo Err_ExpenseReport_Click
    If IsNull(Me![EmployeeID]) Then
        MsgBox "Enter employee before entering expense report."
    Else
        DoCmd.DoMenuItem acFormBar, acRecordsMenu, acSaveRecord, , acMenuVer70
        DoCmd.OpenForm "Expense Reports"
    End If

Exit_ExpenseReport_Click:
    Exit Sub

Err_ExpenseReport_Click:
    MsgBox Err.Description
    Resume Exit_ExpenseReport_Click
End Sub
```

You'll learn how to create VBA event procedures in Part III. For now, note that the Module window's title bar displays the caption Form_Expense Reports by Employee, which means we are looking at the form module for the Expense Reports by Employee form. Access automatically names a form module for a form using the word Form and the form's name separating the two with an underscore; the general pattern, or syntax, is Form_*formname*. (Similarly, Access automatically names a report module using the syntax Report_*reportname*.)

The Database Wizard creates event procedures for each of the command buttons: some procedures simply open other forms or reports while other procedures also synchronize the form or report to display the matching record. The Database Wizard has created an application that is sufficiently automated that someone who knows Access can navigate through its tasks easily. There is also a way to go before the Expenses application can be described as *fully automated* so someone who doesn't know Access can use it without detailed instruction. The Database Wizard provides a well-designed first draft for the application. Let's explore some of the other Access helpers you can call on to add features that make the application easier to use.

# Using the Command Button Wizard

The task flow diagram in Figure 1.7 shows that the Database Wizard has created a one-way path from the Main Switchboard to the Expense Report by Employee form. We'll call on the Command Button Wizard to create a two-way path. The Command Button Wizard automatically creates a command button and a VBA event procedure for the button's Click event.

1. Open the Expense Reports by Employee form in Design view. If the Control Wizards toolbox button is not pressed, press the button now to activate the Control Wizards.

2. Click the Command Button tool and then click in the form next to the Expense Report Form… button. The wizard's first screen shows a list of six categories of tasks and a list of the actions for each category (see Figure 1.17). This powerful wizard can create procedures for many of the common database operations. Table 1.1 shows the 32 actions you can automate with the Command Button Wizard.

**FIGURE 1.17:**

The Command Button Wizard can automate common database operations.

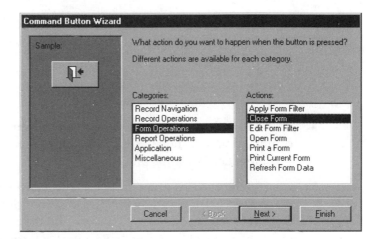

## Creating a Return Path

To make a two-way path between the form and the Main Switchboard, we'll create a command button to close the Expense Reports by Employee form and return to the Main Switchboard.

1. Select the Form Operations category and the Close Form action. Click the Next button.

**TABLE 1.1:**   Operations automated with the Command Button Wizard

| Category | Task |
|---|---|
| Record Navigation | Go to First, Last, Next, Previous Record, Find Record, Find Next |
| Record Operations | Add New Record, Delete Record, Duplicate Record, Print Record, Save, Undo Record |
| Form Operations | Apply Form Filter, Edit Form Filter, Close Form, Open Form, Print a Form, Print Current Form, Refresh Form Data |
| Report Operations | Print Report, Preview Report, Mail Report, Send Report to File |
| Application | Run Notepad, Run MS Word, MS Excel, Quit Application, Run Application |
| Miscellaneous | Print Table, Run Macro, Run Query, AutoDialer |

2.  In the next screen you design the button's appearance. For a consistent look, enter **Return** as a text caption instead of as a picture (see Figure 1.18a). Click the Next button.

3.  The final screen, shown in Figure 1.18b, gives you the opportunity to name the button. Enter **cmdReturn**

4.  Click the Finish button in the last wizard screen. The wizard creates the command button and attaches a VBA procedure to carry out the action you specified. Let's view the procedure.

5.  Click in the OnClick event property and click the Build button to the right of the property box. Figure 1.19 shows the event procedure. The combo box on the left displays the button's name and the combo box on the right displays the name of the event. In Part III you learn about the purpose of each line in the procedure, for now just note that the DoCmd.Close line is the instruction that closes the form.

6.  Save the form, switch back to Form view, and click the new Return button. The form closes and you are returned to the Main Switchboard.

**FIGURE 1.18:**

You can design the button's appearance (a) and give the button a name (b).

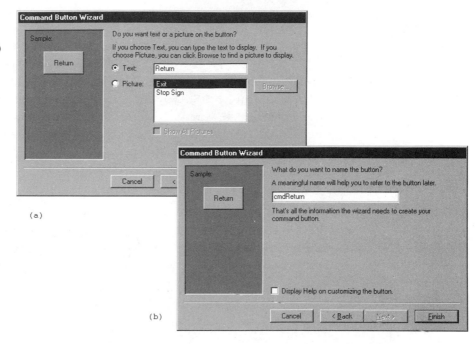

(a)

(b)

**FIGURE 1.19:**

The event procedure to close a form

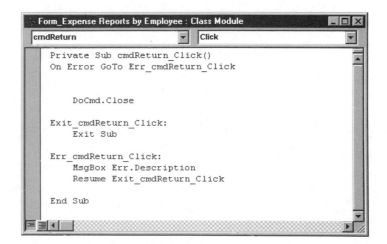

## Naming New Objects

You can use just about any name for an object, and you should give names a great deal of thought. For one thing, it's very inconvenient to change an object's name later if you change your mind. Changing the name of the object itself is easy; for example, you can change the name of a field in a table by opening the table in Design view and changing the Field name. The problem is that Access does not trace through the database to find and update references to the object with the changed name. For example, if you open a form based on a table with a changed field name, Access looks for the original field name (which no longer exists) and displays #Name? in the bound control. Remember: if you change the name of an object, you must find and change the references yourself. (There are some third-party add-ins that you can use to update the references, but Access itself isn't able to update references.) More importantly, naming objects is an opportunity to make your work as an application developer much easier. Chapter 2 discusses *naming standards* that have been adopted by most professional Access developers. You can choose one of these standards or create your own. The reason you use a naming standard is that you can pack a name with useful information. For example, by choosing the name cmdReturn instead of accepting the default (such as Command7) we document that the object is a command button by using the cmd prefix (called a *tag* in naming-standard vocabulary), and we document that clicking the button returns to the previous form by including the word Return as the descriptive part (called the *base name*).

# Using a Hyperlink to Navigate

Hyperlinks are a new Access 97 feature that you can use for navigation. A *hyperlink* is a piece of text, an image, or a command button that you click to jump to another location. In Access, you can use hyperlinks to open and jump to:

- Another object in your database

- Any available file stored in your computer's file system (on your computer or on another computer in your local area network)

- A specified sublocation within any Microsoft Office file, including a bookmark in a Word document, a range in an Excel spreadsheet, a slide in a PowerPoint presentation, or an object in another Access database

- Any available file in your company's private intranet or in the public Internet—if the file is an HTML document, you can jump to a specified sublocation within the document

In order for a hyperlink to work, you must use the correct format to identify the location you want to jump to. For example, to identify a file on an intranet or on the Internet, you use an Internet address, called a *Uniform Resource Locator* (URL). `http://www.microsoft.com/` identifies the home page for the Microsoft Web site on the World Wide Web and `ftp://ftp.microsoft.com` identifies the Microsoft ftp site. To identify a file in your computer's file system, you use a standard format for specifying the path to the file called the *universal naming convention* (unc) path, for example, C:\Program Files\Microsoft Office\Access\Samples\Cajun.htm identifies the HTML document you may have installed as part of Access and C:\Program Files\Microsoft Office\Access\Samples\NWind.mdb identifies the Northwind sample database for Access. The Internet or path address of the file is called the *hyperlink address*. You can specify the location within the Microsoft Office file or an HTML document, called the *hyperlink subaddress*, using the syntax shown in Table 1.2.

When the target of the hyperlink is another object in the current Access database, you don't have to specify the hyperlink address; you need only specify the hyperlink subaddress. For example, if you are working in the Expenses database and want to create a hyperlink with the Expense Categories form as the target, you need only specify the subaddress as Expense Categories or as Form Expense Categories.

If the target of the hyperlink is another object in the Access database you are currently working with, clicking the hyperlink in Access opens the object. A table or query opens in Datasheet view, a form opens in Form view, a report opens in Print Preview, and macros and modules open in Design view. If the target is an

**TABLE 1.2:**   Hyperlink subaddress syntax

| Type of File | Syntax for a Location within the File |
| --- | --- |
| Microsoft Access | The name of a Database window object. If there are several objects with the same name, Access looks up objects in the following order: forms, reports, tables and queries, macros, modules. You can also enter *object type object name*; for example, to specify a report named Suppliers, use the syntax Report Suppliers. |
| Microsoft Word | The name of a bookmark. You must define the bookmark in Word before you can jump to it. |
| Microsoft Excel | The name of a range. Use the syntax *sheet!range*; for example, to specify the target as the L8 cell in the worksheet named Source, use the syntax Source!L8 |
| Microsoft PowerPoint | The number of a slide. For example, to specify the tenth slide, use the syntax 10. |
| HTML document | The Name tag. |

object in another Access database, the current Access window minimizes and a second instance of Access opens and displays the target object. If the target is a file in another Microsoft Office application, the current Access window minimizes, the application opens and displays the target. If the target is a file or document on the intranet or Internet, the Access window minimizes and the browser opens to display the document (your TCP/IP connection must be open when you click the hyperlink).

Access 97 provides two ways to use hyperlinks for navigation: you can store hyperlink addresses in tables and display the hyperlinks in a datasheet or in a form control bound to the hyperlink field, or you can create a hyperlink in an unbound control on a form using a label, a command button, or an image.

## Storing Hyperlinks as Data in a Table

Access 97 provides a new Hyperlink data type for storing hyperlink addresses. For example, in an order entry database application, you can store the Internet addresses for your suppliers just as you store their other contact information and display the addresses in a suppliers form. When you move the mouse pointer over the text box that displays the hyperlink address, the pointer icon changes to a pointing finger and the status bar displays the hyperlink address. Clicking the hyperlink takes you to the hyperlink target.

As an example, we'll add a Hyperlink field to the Employees table for storing the URL for each employee's personal home page.

1.  Open the Employees table in Design view. Click in a blank FieldName cell and enter **HomePage**. Choose Hyperlink from the Datatype combo box. The Hyperlink data type lets you store information in three parts: the first part, *displaytext*, is the text that you want to display in the field, the second part, *address*, is the hyperlink address, and the third part, *subaddress*, is the hyperlink subaddress. The first part is optional. The parts are separated by the pound sign as follows: *displaytext#address#subaddress#*

2.  Save the table and switch to Datasheet view. The easiest way to enter a hyperlink target is to use the Hyperlink toolbar button.

3.  Click the HomePage cell for the first employee and type the text that you want to display. For example, type **Nancy's Page** and then click the Insert Hyperlink button in the toolbar. You can enter the hyperlink address in the Link to File or URL text box and the hyperlink subaddress in the Named Location in File text box (see Figure 1.20). By default, if you entered display text, the Link to File or URL text box displays the protocol `http://` followed by the display text; you'll need to clear the text box before entering the hyperlink address.

4.  Delete the text in the Link to File or URL text box and type in **http://www.microsoft.com/employees/davolio.htm** as the fictitious URL for the home page for the first employee. Click OK. Access displays the hyperlink text in the standard way: the text is shown underlined and blue. The *displaytext* part of the hyperlink information is optional: if you do enter display text in the Hyperlink field, Access shows only the *displaytext* in the cell and does not display the rest of the address; if you omit *displaytext*, Access shows only the hyperlink address.

5.  Click to another record to save the entry and reset the pointer. When you move the pointer back over the cell, the pointer icon changes to a hand with a pointing finger. If we had entered a real URL, clicking the cell would open the browser and display the document.

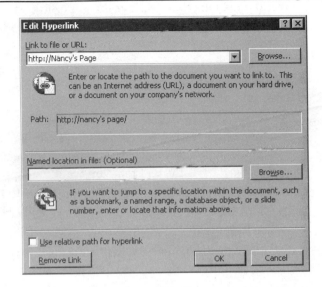

**FIGURE 1.20:**

Using the Insert
Hyperlink dialog to
enter an address
and subaddress

6. To edit the hyperlink, right-click the cell and choose Hyperlink from the shortcut menu. To change the address or subaddress, choose Edit Hyperlink from the fly-out menu to display the Edit Hyperlink dialog, change the address or subaddress, and click OK. You can edit the display text in the Display Text box in the fly-out menu.

7. Click in the Display Text box in the fly-out menu, select the text, Nancy's Page, press Delete to delete the display text, and then press Enter. The cell shows the hyperlink address.

8. Open the Expense Reports by Employee form in Design view. Display the Field List and drag the HomePage field to the form just below the Work Phone text box. Switch to Form view. The hyperlink for each employee's home page is displayed in the HomePage text box control (see Figure 1.21).

## Using a Hyperlink as an Unbound Form Control

When you don't want the hyperlink to change with each record, you can use a label, a command button, or an image to create a hyperlink on a form. For example, when you want to use a hyperlink to navigate from a form to another form or to a report, you create the hyperlink directly on the form. To create an unbound

FIGURE 1.21:

Displaying a bound
hyperlink in a form

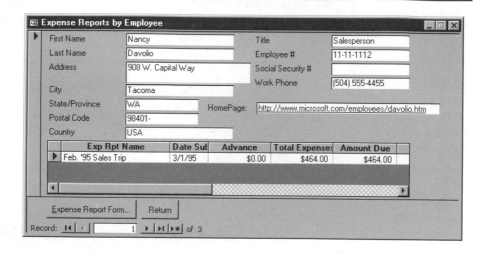

hyperlink, place a label, a command button, or an image on the form. You can use the Caption property of the label or the command button to describe the hyperlink. To create the hyperlink, set the control's HyperlinkAddress and HyperlinkSubAddress properties. To create a hyperlink to another object in the current Access database, leave the HyperlinkAddress property blank.

To explore unbound hyperlinks, create a new unbound form named frmHyperlinks and set the Caption property to Hyperlinks. We'll create a hyperlink for a label that opens and displays another object in the same database, a clickable image hyperlink that opens and displays an object in another Access database, and a command button hyperlink that opens a browser and displays a Web page on the World Wide Web.

## Creating a Label Hyperlink

To create a hyperlink as a label control:

1. Place a label control on the form and set the Caption property to Categories. Click in the HyperlinkSubAddress property in the label's property sheet. Click the Build button at the right of the property box to display the Insert Hyperlink dialog to select the object.

2. Click the Browse button to the right of the Named location in the file combo box. When you leave the Link to File or URL text box blank, Access assumes

you are creating a hyperlink to an object in the current database and displays the Select Location dialog with tabs that list the objects in the current database for each type (see Figure 1.22).

**FIGURE 1.22:**

Use the Select Location dialog to choose the database object.

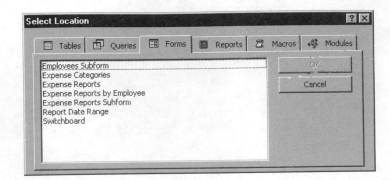

3. Choose the Expense Categories form and click OK. Click OK to close the Insert Hyperlink dialog. Access sets the HyperlinkSubAddress property to Form Expense Categories, creates the hyperlink, and displays the label caption in blue underlined text.

4. Save the form, switch to Form view, and click the label. The Expense Categories form opens.

## Creating a Clickable Image

To create a clickable image,

1. Switch to Design view and choose the Picture command from the Insert menu. Select an image in the Insert Picture dialog. We'll use the dove.wmf file in the Microsoft Office\Clip Art\Popular folder. To resize the image, set the SizeMode property to Stretch, click a corner of the image selection rectangle and drag to the desired size. We'll use this image to create a hyperlink to a form in another Access database.

2. With the image selected, click the Insert Hyperlink button in the toolbar to display the Insert Hyperlink dialog (see Figure 1.23a). Click the Browse button to the right of the Link to File or URL combo box and locate the Northwind.mdb database in the Samples folder. Click the Browse button to the right of the Named location in the file combo box and choose the Product List form in the Select Location dialog (see Figure 1.23b). Close the

Select Location dialog and then close the Insert Hyperlink dialog. Access sets the HyperlinkAddess property to the path to the database file and sets the HyperlinkSubAddress property to Form Product List.

**FIGURE 1.23:**

To create a clickable image, select the image, click the Insert Hyperlink button in the toolbar to display the Insert Hyperlink dialog (a), and set the destination. To create a hyperlink to an object in another Access database, set the Link to File or URL text box to the path to the database and set the Named location in the file text box to the object (b).

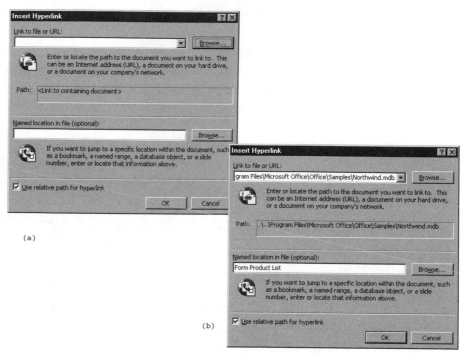

3. Save the form, switch to Form view, and click the image. The current instance of Access minimizes. Another instance of Access opens and displays the Product List form in the Northwind database.

4. Close the second instance of Access and then restore the first instance of Access.

## Creating a Command Button Hyperlink

To create a command button as a hyperlink,

1. Switch to Design view. If necessary, click the Control Wizards button to deselect the wizard, then click the Command Button tool and draw a command button on the form. We'll use this button to create a hyperlink to a Web page on the World Wide Web.

2. Set the Caption property to Microsoft Home Page.

3. Click the HyperlinkAddress property in the command button's property sheet and enter the URL to the Microsoft home page: **http://www .microsoft.com/** When you press Enter, Access creates the hyperlink, changes the button's font color to blue, and underlines the text to indicate a hyperlink.

4. Save the form and switch to Form view (see Figure 1.24). Click the command button. If your Internet connection is open and you have Internet Explorer installed, a new instance of the Internet Explorer starts and, after a delay, displays the Microsoft home page.

**FIGURE 1.24:**

The Hyperlinks form with hyperlinks for a label, an image, and a command button

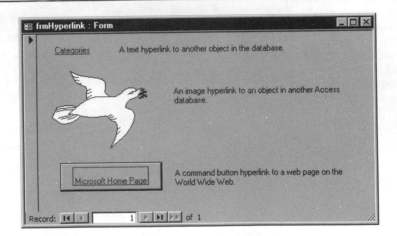

## Changing the Hyperlink Control Type

You can change the control type for the hyperlink. After creating a hyperlink control as one of the three types, in form Design view select the control and choose the Change To command from the Format menu. The fly-out menu displays commands for the other two control types as active commands. Click the type you want to change to. If you change from a label or command button to an image, the Picture property of the image control displays the word, "none" because you haven't selected an image. To insert an image, click the Build button to the right of the Picture property and choose a bitmap image to display. If you change from an image to a label or command button, Access sets the Caption property of the changed control to the value of the HyperlinkAddress property, or, if this property is blank, to the value of the HyperlinkSubAddress property.

## Using the Web Toolbar

When you click hyperlinks to jump to other objects, Access 97 maintains an internal history list of the hyperlink targets you've visited. Access provides a Web toolbar for navigation (see Figure 1.25). You use the Back button to return to the previous hyperlink target and the Forward button to go to the next hyperlink target on the history list (the Forward button can only take you to a target that you have already visited). If you change your mind after activating a hyperlink, you can click the Stop button on the Web toolbar to stop following the link.

**FIGURE 1.25:**

Use the Web toolbar to navigate between hyperlinks.

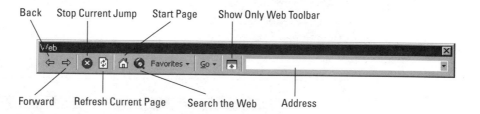

Using images, labels, and command buttons as hyperlinks is an easy way to open and display another object. When you create the hyperlink by setting the HyperlinkAddess and HyperlinkSubAddress properties, you are limited to opening an object and moving to a location within the object and you can't specify additional actions. However, when you click the control to activate the hyperlink, the control recognizes the Click event. If you want to take any other action, such as hiding the form that contains the hyperlink or synchronizing an opened form or report, you can write a program and request that Access run the program when you click the control.

# Using the Combo Box Wizard

The Expense Reports by Employee form in the Expenses database displays a record for each employee. In our example, the Database Wizard supplies only three employees as sample data. With so few employees, finding the record for a specific employee is a simple matter of browsing the records using the navigation buttons at the bottom of the form. With more employees, you need a more efficient way to find a specific employee. The Combo Box Wizard provides the answer. You can use the Combo Box Wizard to create a Lookup combo box. With a Lookup combo box, you select a value from the list and Access automatically locates and displays the corresponding record.

In our example, we'll use the wizard to create a combo box that lists each employee's name in alphabetical order and a procedure that runs when you select a name. The procedure finds and displays the record for the employee that you selected.

1. Open the Expense Reports by Employee form in Design view. If necessary, click the Control Wizards button to activate the wizards (the Control Wizards are activated when the button is pressed in). Click the combo box tool in the toolbox and then click in the form next to the Return button. The first screen asks for the source of the values you want in the combo list (see Figure 1.26).

**FIGURE 1.26:**

You can use the Combo Box Wizard to create a Lookup combo box.

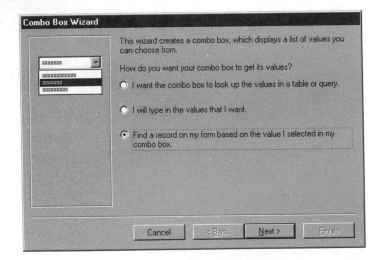

2. Choose the third option to create a Lookup combo box.

3. The next screen displays a list of the fields in the form's underlying record source (see Figure 1.27). Select the EmployeeID, LastName, and FirstName. We'll display only the employees' names in the list, but we'll also select the EmployeeID field because it is the primary key for the Employee table. The wizard creates a VBA procedure that uses the EmployeeID to find the unique record corresponding to the employee's name you choose.

**FIGURE 1.27:**

The Available Fields are the fields in the form's underlying record source.

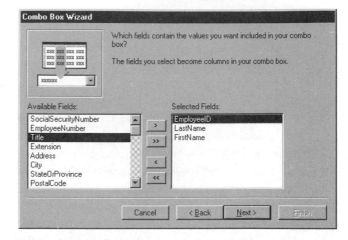

4. You can modify the list's appearance in the next screen (see Figure 1.28a). Be sure to leave the Hide key column checked. Click the Next button. The final screen gives the opportunity to customize the label (see Figure 1.28b). Type **Lookup employee** in the text box.

**FIGURE 1.28:**

Modify the combo box list (a) and customize the label (b).

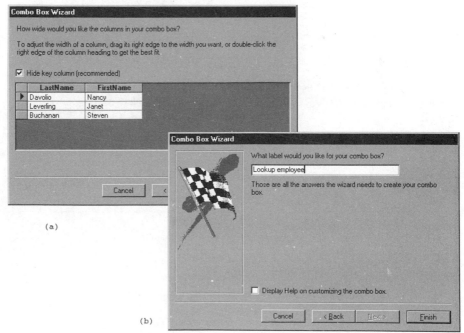

(a)

(b)

**5.** Click the Finish button. The wizard creates the Lookup combo box and attaches the VBA procedure to do the looking up.

To see the procedure, note that the property sheet indicates that an event procedure now exists for the AfterUpdate event (see Figure 1.29a). The property sheet also shows that the wizard has assigned a default name, Combo29, that doesn't help at all in identifying the purpose of this combo box. (It would have been more helpful if the Combo Box Wizard had allowed you to name the control cboEmployee instead.) The BeforeUpdate and AfterUpdate events are trickier than the simple Click event. We'll be more precise about these events in Chapter 2, but for now we'll note that the combo box recognizes the AfterUpdate event the instant after you select an employee's name. Click the Build button to the right of the AfterUpdate property box to view the VBA procedure shown in Figure 1.29b. This procedure *synchronizes* the form to the value displayed in the combo box by finding and displaying the record that matches the combo box. To test the wizard's work, save the form, switch back to Form view, and select an employee's name from the list (see Figure 1.30). The form automatically displays the synchronized record.

---

**FIGURE 1.29:**

The Combo Box Wizard creates an event procedure for the AfterUpdate event (a). The event procedure (b) synchronizes the form's recordset to the combo box value.

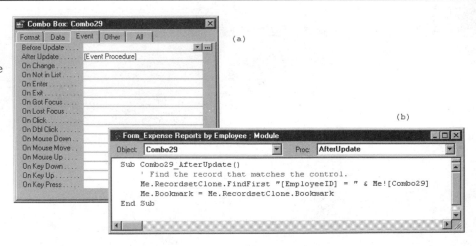

**FIGURE 1.30:**

The customized Expense Reports by Employee form provides a return path and a lookup.

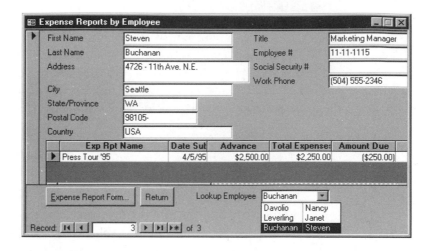

# Using the Switchboard Manager

You can customize a basic application that the Database Wizard creates by adding forms and reports. When you add a new form or report, you can provide a path to it by adding a command button that runs a program or by adding a hyperlink to the appropriate form or to one of the switchboards. To add a button to a switchboard, click the Change Switchboard Items button on the switchboard. Your click summons another Access helper, the Switchboard Manager, shown in Figure 1.31.

**FIGURE 1.31:**

The Switchboard Manager

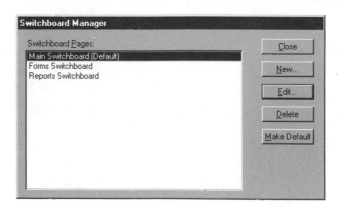

The purpose of the Switchboard Manager is to help you modify the Switchboard form created by the Database Wizard. You can also use the Switchboard Manager to create a new Switchboard form if you started from scratch and didn't use the Database Wizard to create the database. The Switchboard Manager shown in Figure 1.31 lists the three switchboard pages in the Expenses application. The Main Switchboard is shown as the default; the default page is the one that is displayed when you first open the Switchboard form. By clicking the buttons, the Switchboard Manager helps you do the following tasks:

**New** creates a new switchboard page. Click the New button to name the new switchboard (see Figure 1.32a).

**Edit** modifies the buttons on the selected switchboard page. Click the Edit button to display the Edit Switchboard Page dialog (see Figure 1.32b). For the selected page, this dialog displays the labels for the buttons on the page. You can add a new button, change the label of an existing button, delete a button, and move a button up or down in the list.

**Delete** deletes the selected switchboard page.

**Make Default** changes the default to the selected switchboard page.

**FIGURE 1.32:**

Add a new switchboard page (a) or edit an existing page (b).

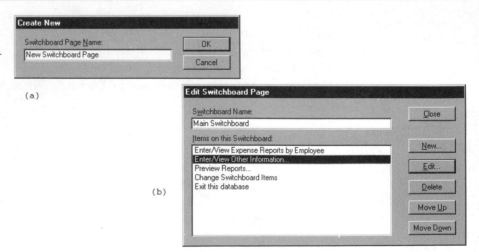

# Editing a Switchboard

We'll change the label for the second button on the Main Switchboard to the slightly more informative Enter/View Expense Information.

1.  With the Main Switchboard selected in the Switchboard Manager dialog, click the Edit button, and select the second item in the list. Click the Edit button on the Edit Switchboard Page dialog to display the Edit Switchboard Item dialog, as shown in Figure 1.33a. Change the label's text in the first box to Enter/View Expense Information.... You can change the button's action by selecting any of the eight actions in the Command combo list (see Figure 1.33b). After you select an action, the third box changes to display appropriate choices. In our case, the command Go to Switchboard takes you to another switchboard page and the third combo box displays the name of the switchboard page, Forms Switchboard.

2.  Click OK to close the Edit Switchboard Item dialog, click Close to close the Edit Switchboard Page dialog, and click Close to close the Switchboard Manager. The Main Switchboard displays the changed label for the second button.

**FIGURE 1.33:**

The Switchboard Manager lets you change the button's label (a) and its action (b).

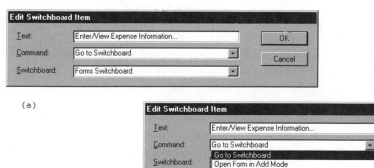

# Controlling the User Interface

After you use the Control Wizards and the Switchboard Manager, your customized application should be easier for you to use, but you still don't want to turn it over to a novice. At this stage, you have designed navigation paths but have not restricted the user to the paths. The complete built-in command environment is exposed: all of the menu commands, shortcut menu commands, toolbar buttons and keyboard shortcuts that are built into Access are available for switching to Design view and changing the design of the application. The Database window is also displayed, though minimized. The novice user has immediate access to the objects that make up your application.

Before turning the application over to a novice, you should protect the application by hiding any commands that could be used to change the application's design and by hiding the Database window. Access provides tools for controlling the user interface and protecting your application; in this section you learn about three of the tools that don't require programming:

- You can control many features of the Access environment by setting startup properties; for example, you can specify whether or not the Database window is displayed when you start up the application, and you can disable the keyboard shortcuts that display the Database window (the F11 or Alt+F1 key combinations). However, without programming you cannot prevent users from pressing the Shift key to bypass your startup property settings when opening a database.

- You can prevent unauthorized entry into a database by defining a password. Simple password security restricts entry into your database but offers no protection after a user who knows the password has opened the database.

- You can replace the built-in menu bars, menus and toolbars with custom versions that include only the commands required for using your application. Without programming you can include built-in commands and commands for opening database objects. However, you must use macro programming in order to create custom commands for running a set of instructions and in order to customize the keyboard.

# Setting Startup Properties

Startup properties dictate how a database application looks when it starts up. Choose the Startup command from the Tools menu to display the Startup dialog and click the Advanced button to display the options (see Figure 1.34).

**FIGURE 1.34:**

You can set most of the startup properties for a database using the Startup dialog.

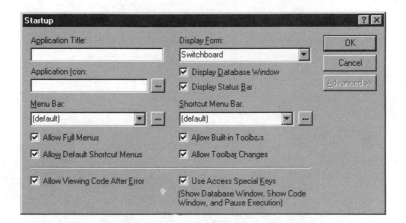

You use the Startup dialog to set the properties shown in Table 1.3. (Table 1.3 is on the CD that came with this book, under Tables\Chapter1.pdf.) The application title and icon settings take effect as soon as you close the Startup dialog. The other settings take effect the next time you open the database. Table 1.4 (on the CD under Tables\Chapter1.pdf), lists the Key Combinations that can be disabled using the Startup dialog.

## Protecting the Application

The simplest and easiest ways to control the commands available to the user are to set startup properties to hide the Database window and prevent the user from displaying the window after starting the database, hide all toolbars and shortcut menus, and replace the built-in menus with an alternate reduced set of built-in menus. The reduced set includes only the commands that are useful when a user is working with a custom database application in views other than Design view and eliminates the menu commands for changing the design of a database object as well as several other menu commands. Figure 1.35 shows the reduced menu bar for Form view. This menu bar doesn't include the View or Tools menus at all and eliminates menu commands on the remaining menus.

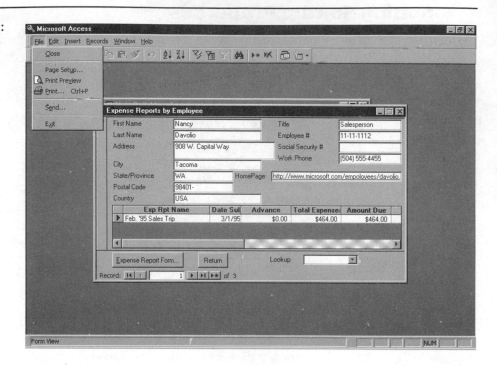

The built-in reduced
Form view menu bar

We'll use the Startup dialog to customize the title bar and protect the application.

1. Choose the Startup command from the Tools menu and click the Advanced button.

2. Set the Application Title property to Expenses.

3. Clear all of the check boxes except the one to display the Status Bar (see Figure 1.36).

4. Click OK. Notice that the application title bar changes to Expenses immediately. In building the Expenses database, the Database Wizard creates a procedure that runs when the Switchboard form first opens and includes statements that redisplay and minimize the Database window. The procedure runs after Access starts the database according to the Startup settings and, therefore, overrides the startup setting to hide the Database window. In the next few steps, we'll modify the procedure to eliminate the statements so that the Database window remains hidden.

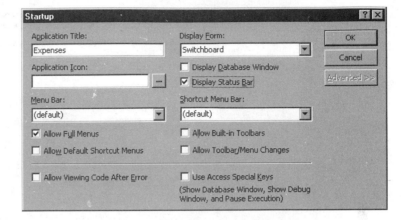

Using the Startup settings to hide the Database window and restrict the available menu, toolbar, and keyboard commands.

5. Open the Switchboard form in Design view. Click in the OnOpen property in the property sheet and then click the Build button to the right of the property box. The Module window opens displaying the event procedure that runs when the form opens. The three lines that begin with 'Minimize the database window are the comment and instructions that display and minimize the Database window.

6. Click to the left of the line that begins with 'Minimize the database window (see Figure 1.37). Drag to select the three lines and then press Delete.

7. Save the changes and close the Switchboard form.

8. Click the Close box in the Database window. Reopen the database by choosing Expenses in the list of recently opened databases in the File menu. The Expenses application opens with the reduced menus, no toolbars, and no shortcut menus.

   With these settings, you won't be able to display the Database window by pressing F11 or Alt+F1 after you start the database. Note however, that you can still bypass the Startup setting by pressing the Shift key when you first open the database. (In Chapter 19 you'll learn how to disable the Shift bypass key as well.)

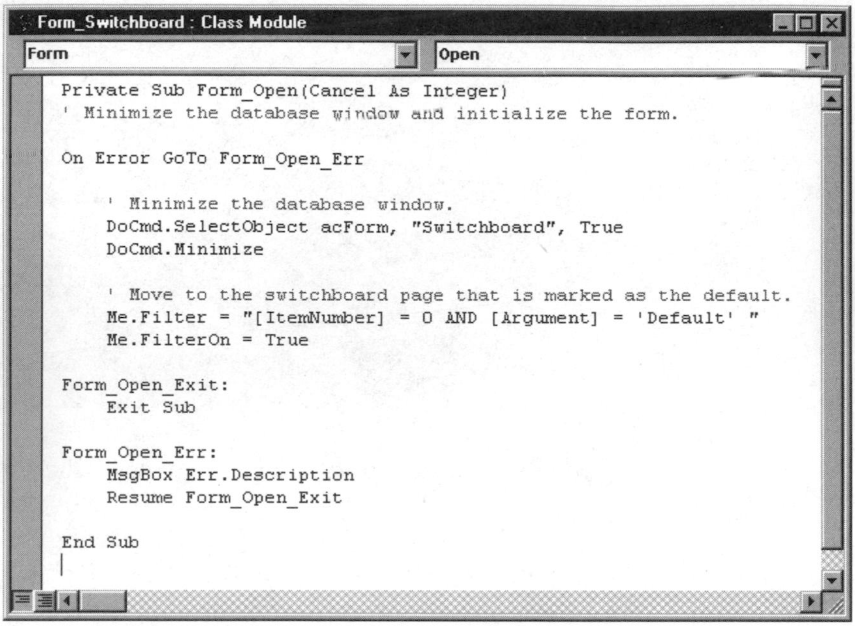

**FIGURE 1.37:**

The instructions to display and minimize the Database window

```
Form_Switchboard : Class Module                                    _ □ ×
Form                          ▼   Open                              ▼
    Private Sub Form_Open(Cancel As Integer)
    ' Minimize the database window and initialize the form.

On Error GoTo Form_Open_Err

    ' Minimize the database window.
    DoCmd.SelectObject acForm, "Switchboard", True
    DoCmd.Minimize

    ' Move to the switchboard page that is marked as the default.
    Me.Filter = "[ItemNumber] = 0 AND [Argument] = 'Default' "
    Me.FilterOn = True

Form_Open_Exit:
    Exit Sub

Form_Open_Err:
    MsgBox Err.Description
    Resume Form_Open_Exit

End Sub
```

# Protecting Your Application with a Password

You can prevent unauthorized people from opening your application by defining a password. Before you can set a password you need to establish exclusive access to the database. A database must be closed before you can specify exclusive mode. When you open a database in exclusive mode you prevent anyone else from opening the database.

1. Close the database by clicking the Exit button in the Main Switchboard.

2. Choose the Open Database command from the File menu; select Expenses, and check the Exclusive option (see Figure 1.38).

3. Press Shift and then click Open. By pressing the Shift key you bypass the startup options.

4. Choose the Security command from the Tools menu and then choose the Set Database Password from the fly-out menu. Use the Set Database Password dialog to set a password (see Figure 1.39a).

**FIGURE 1.38:**

Open a database in exclusive mode before setting a password.

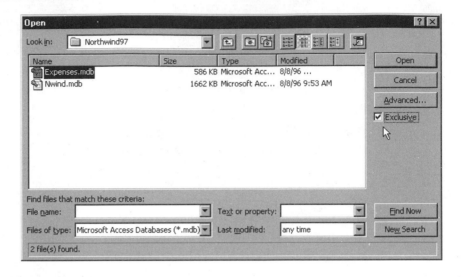

5.  In the Password edit box, type **expenses.** In Access, passwords are case-sensitive.

6.  In the Verify edit box, type **expenses** again and click OK. In the Database window, click the Close box.

7.  Choose Expenses from the list of recently opened databases in the File menu. Enter **expenses** in the Password Required dialog (see Figure 1.39b). The database opens with the reduced set of menus. For the next section we need access to the full menus so we'll restart the database.

8.  Click the Exit this database button. Press the Shift key and choose Expenses from the list of recently opened databases in the File menu. Enter the password and click OK. The database opens with the full set of menus.

**FIGURE 1.39:**

Use the Set Database Password dialog (a) to set a password and the Password Required dialog (b) to gain entry to the password-protected database.

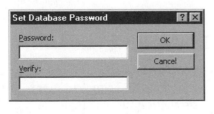

(a)

(b)

**WARNING**   Make sure you record your password somewhere. If you forget or lose your password, you can't open the database.

When you protect a database with a password, you have to enter the password before you can import its objects into another database or compact the database.

While adding a password to a database is an easy way to restrict entry to the database, password protection is very limited:

- Anyone with a disk editor or similar utility program can read your data without opening the database. You can prevent this by encrypting the database. To encrypt a database, close the database and choose the Security command from the Tools menu. Select the database in the Encrypt/Decrypt Database dialog and click OK.

- Anyone who knows the password and has access to the Unset Database Password command can change or clear the password.

A better way to protect your database is to use the user-level security that Access provides. With user-level security you can define users and groups of users and specify different levels of access to data and the database objects. For more information about user-level security, see *Access 97 Developer's Handbook* by Paul Litwin, Ken Getz, and Mike Gilbert (Sybex, 1997).

**NOTE**   To remove password protection, choose the Security command from the Tools menu and then choose Unset Database Password from the fly-out menu. Enter the password in the Unset Password dialog and click OK.

## Creating Custom Menus and Toolbars

We've used the Startup dialog to display a reduced set of menu bars and menu commands and to hide all toolbars and shortcut menus. Although we have achieved some degree of protection for our database, we still haven't made the command environment as helpful as it could be. Menu bars hide their commands: the new user must search through the drop-down menus to learn what commands are available and then remember where the commands are. In addition, the reduced menu bars may not provide the set of commands the user wants. Toolbars are a better way to display the available commands: with toolbar buttons displayed at all times and tooltips displayed as the user browses through the buttons, your application is easier to learn and to use. Most users are familiar with using the right mouse button to display a shortcut menu.

In previous versions of Access, you could customize existing toolbars and create new toolbars without programming by using a Customize dialog to create toolbars by drag and drop; however, creating custom menu bars and shortcut menus required macro programming to create menu macros. The previous versions provided a Menu Builder to help you create the macros for custom menu bars and shortcut menus. Access 97 provides a new way to create custom menu bars, toolbars and shortcut menus. (While Access 97 is able to run menu macros for the sake of backward compatibility with the previous versions, the Menu Builder is no longer available.)

In Access 97 you can edit built-in menu bars, shortcut menus, and toolbars as well as create custom versions using the Customize dialog. Access 97 takes a more uniform approach to the three objects by calling them command bars and by providing common ways to customize them. For example, menu bars can now display menus with command buttons and combo boxes, and toolbars can now display menu names with drop-down menus. While there is enormous flexibility in how you design menu bars, shortcut menus, and toolbars in Access 97, you should probably stick to the standard Windows designs to avoid confusing your users.

To display the Customize dialog, right-click in the toolbar and choose Customize from the shortcut menu (see Figure 1.40).

The Toolbars tab lists both the built-in toolbars and new toolbars that you create. A check in front of an item means that the item is currently displayed. You can display any toolbar by clicking its checkbox. In addition to the toolbars, the list includes Menu Bar as a checked item that represents the menu bar that is currently displayed. Since the menu bar for every view has a View menu with a Toolbars command, you can display the menu bar you want to work with before opening the Customize dialog. The Commands tab displays command categories in the list box on the left (see Figure 1.40b). When you select a category, the list box on the right changes to display the commands in the selected category. The Categories list also includes categories for each of the types of database objects

**FIGURE 1.40:**

Use the Customize dialog to modify existing menu bars, shortcut menus, and toolbars and to create new ones. The dialog has tabs to list the toolbars (a), display most of the built-in commands (b), and display options (c).

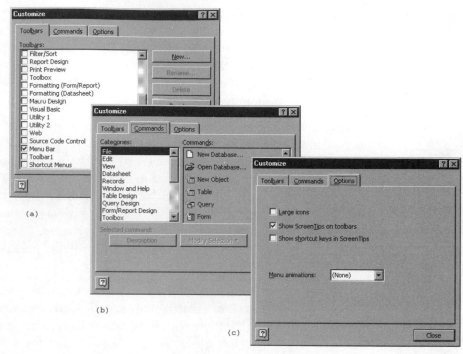

except Modules. If you select one of these categories, for example, All Forms, the list box on the right displays all of the objects of the type. The ActiveX category represents all of the ActiveX controls currently installed and registered on your computer; selecting this category displays the list of your ActiveX controls in the list box on the right. The New Menu item in the Categories list represents a new menu; when you select the New Menu item, the Command list displays the New Menu command that you use to create a new menu.

The Options tab lets you specify additional command bar options such as whether to display screentips on toolbars (see Figure 1.40c).

The list in the Toolbars tab of the Customize dialog includes the Shortcut Menus item, which represents the shortcut menus (see Figure 1.40a). To explore shortcut menus:

1. Click the Shortcut Menus item to display a menu bar with menu items for each of the main categories of shortcut menus (see Figure 1.41a). You can

click on a menu item to display a drop-down menu that lists all of the short-cut menus available in that category.

2. Click the Form category to display the shortcut menus available when a form is the active window (see Figure 1.41b). Note that there are shortcut menus for each of the three form views.

3. Select Form View Record from the list to view the shortcut menu (see Figure 1.41c).

**FIGURE 1.41:**

The menu bar representing the shortcut menus (a), the shortcut menus when a form is active (b), and the Form View shortcut menu(c)

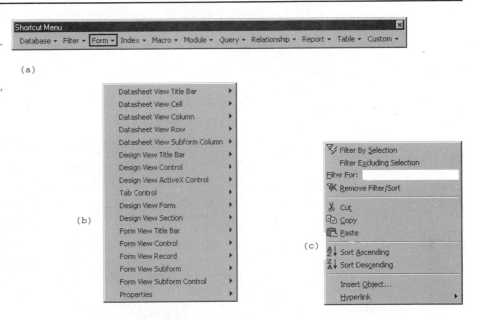

## Customizing a Built-In Command Bar

To customize a built-in command bar, you must display the command bar when the Customize dialog is open. As explained above, you can display any toolbar or any shortcut menu by checking the item in the Toolbars list, but you can only customize the menu bar that is displayed before you open the Customize dialog.

- To remove a command from any command bar, click the command or command button and drag it off the command bar and into the work area.

- To move a command to a new location on a command bar or to move a command from one command bar to another command bar, click the command you want to move and drag it to its new location.

- To copy a command from one displayed command bar to another displayed command bar, press down the Ctrl key and then drag the command to its new location.

- To add a built-in command to a command bar, you can copy the command from another command bar or select the command in the Commands list and drag the command to its new location on a command bar.

- To add a command to open a table, query, form, or report, choose the type in the Categories list, select the object in the Commands list, and drag the object to its new location on a command bar. To add a command that runs a program you have created as a macro, choose All Macros from the Categories list, select the macro you want to run, and drag the macro to its new location on a command bar.

- To undo the changes to a command bar, select the command bar in the Toolbars list in the Customize dialog and click the Reset button. Access displays a message asking you to confirm the reset.

- To modify a toolbar button or menu name, right-click the item to display the shortcut menu shown in Figure 1.42a. You can undo changes to the command, delete the command, or change its name; you can copy, paste, or modify the button image; you can specify the command as text, as an image, as both text and image, or as the default style; you can add a horizontal bar to a menu or a vertical bar to a toolbar to separate commands into groups; and you can display the properties for the command. Clicking the Properties command displays the Control Properties dialog for the selected item. For example, Figure 1.42b shows the dialog for the Copy command on the Edit menu. To run a VBA procedure that you have created as a function procedure (you'll learn about the different kinds of procedures in Part III), you enter the name of the function procedure in the On Action box using the syntax =*functionname*()

**FIGURE 1.42:**

You can modify a command or menu name. Right-click the command with the Customize dialog open to display the shortcut menu (a). Click the Properties command to edit the properties (b).

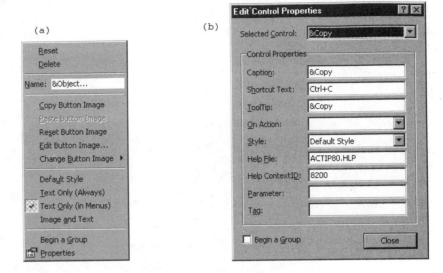

## Creating and Displaying Custom Menu Bars

You can create a new custom menu bar that includes built-in menu commands, commands to open any database window object, and your own custom commands. This section covers creating and displaying new custom menu bars. You can display a custom menu bar in two ways:

- Create an individual custom menu bar and attach it to a specific form or report. The menu bar is displayed whenever the form or report is the active object.

- Create a global menu bar that is displayed in all windows except for those forms and reports that have their own individual custom menu bars.

As an example, we'll create and display a new global menu bar.

1. Choose the Toolbar command from the View menu and then choose Customize, or right-click the menu bar and select Customize from the shortcut menu.

2. Click the New button and type **ExpenseGlobal** in the New Toolbar dialog as the name of the new global menu bar. Click OK. Access creates a small

blank command bar and adds the ExpenseGlobal item to the list of toolbars (see Figure 1.43).

FIGURE 1.43:

Creating a new global menu bar

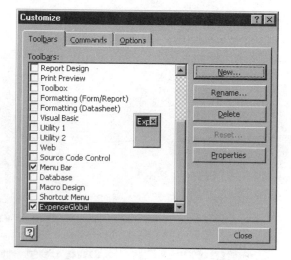

3.  Click the Properties button to display the Toolbar Properties dialog. You use this dialog to specify whether the command bar is a menu bar, a toolbar, or a shortcut menu (choose popup for a shortcut menu). Choose Menu bar in the Type combo box and click Close.

4.  Holding down the Ctrl key, select the File menu name in whatever menu bar you are displaying, drag to the blank command bar, and release. When you drag a menu name, you also drag the drop-down menu. There are several ways to build the menu bar and menus. We'll look at a few techniques in the next steps.

5.  Click the File menu on the new menu bar to display the drop-down menu. One by one, select commands and drag them off the menu; leave only the Close, Save As HTML, Page Setup, Print Preview, Print, and Exit commands.

6.  Pressing the Ctrl key, select the Edit menu name in the displayed menu bar, drag to the right of the File menu in the blank command bar, and release. Click the Edit menu on the new menu bar to display the drop-down menu. One by one, select commands and drag them off the menu; leave only the Undo, Cut, Copy, and Paste commands.

7. Select New Menu from the Categories list in the Commands tab of the Customize dialog. Click the New Menu command in the Commands list and drag to the right of the Edit menu on the new menu bar. Right-click in the menu name (named New Menu by default)and change the name to Forms. Click the new menu name to display the small blank drop-down menu.

8. Choose the All Forms category in the Commands tab of the Customize dialog, select Expense Reports by Employee, and drag it to the drop-down menu for the Forms menu; select Expense Categories and drag it to the drop-down menu.

9. Click the ExpenseGlobal toolbar and drag towards the top of the window to dock the new toolbar below the other toolbars you may be displaying.

10. Select the Toolbars tab and click the Properties button to display the Toolbar Properties dialog. You can use this dialog to allow or prevent menu bar changes. Choose ExpenseGlobal from the combo list and clear all of the check boxes to prevent changing or moving. Click Close and the Customize dialog appears. Click Close again. The global menu bar is finished. You can display the global menu bar by setting one of the startup properties.

11. Choose the Startup command in the Tools menu. Click the down arrow on the Menu Bar combo box. Select the ExpenseGlobal menu bar and click OK. The new menu bar will be displayed the next time you start up the application.

You use exactly the same technique to create an individual menu bar for a form or a report. The only difference between an individual menu bar and a global menu bar is in how you arrange for the menu bar to be displayed. While you specify a global menu bar as a startup property, you specify an individual menu bar for a form or report by setting the form's or report's MenuBar property to the name of the menu bar. When you display a form or report that has its own custom menu bar, Access displays the custom menu bar instead of the custom global menu bar (or the default built-in menu bar if your application doesn't have a global menu bar).

## Creating and Displaying a Custom Shortcut Menu

You can create custom shortcut menus for forms, for reports, and for controls on forms. You can create an individual shortcut menu for each form or report and a global shortcut menu that is displayed whenever the active form or report doesn't have an individual shortcut menu.

As an example, we'll create a simple custom shortcut menu bar that we'll use as a global shortcut menu.

1. Right-click the menu bar and select Customize from the shortcut menu.

2. Click the New button, name the new command bar ExpenseShortcut. Click the Properties button on the Customize dialog, select Popup from the Type list box, click OK, and click the Close button. The small command bar disappears. To build a shortcut menu you must display the Shortcut Menus menu bar.

3. Click in the Shortcut Menus item in the Toolbars list. Click the small black arrow to the right of the Custom menu at the right end of the Shortcut Menus menu bar to display a drop-down list containing the Expense-Shortcut menu (see Figure 1.44a). Click the small black arrow to display a small blank fly-out menu where you can build the new shortcut menu. We'll create the menu by dragging copies of the filter commands from the Form View shortcut menu.

4. Click the Form menu on the Shortcut Menu, click the Form View Title Bar item to display the shortcut menu. Press the Ctrl key and then, one by one, select the Filter by Form, Apply Filter, and Remove Filter/Sort commands and drag them to the ExpenseShortcut custom menu (see Figure 1.44b). (You drag to the small black arrows to display the menus.)

**FIGURE 1.44:**

Creating a custom shortcut menu

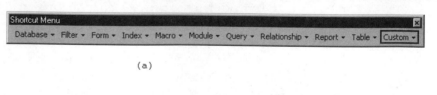

(a)

(b)

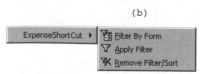

5. Click the Close button to close the Shortcut Menu and the Customize dialog. In the next step, you will specify the ExpenseShortcut menu as the global shortcut menu by setting a startup property.

6. Choose the Startup command from the Tools menu. Select ExpenseShortcut from the Shortcut Menu Bar combo box and click OK. The custom shortcut menu is displayed when you right-click a form the next time you start up the application.

You use exactly the same technique to create an individual shortcut menu for a form, form control, or a report. The only difference between an individual shortcut menu and a global shortcut menu is in how you arrange for the shortcut menu to be displayed. While you specify a global shortcut menu as a startup property, you specify an individual shortcut menu for a form, form control, or report by setting the form's, the control's, or the report's ShortcutMenuBar property to the name of the shortcut menu bar. When you display a form or report that has its own custom shortcut menu bars, Access displays the custom shortcut menu bar instead of the custom global shortcut menu bar (or the default built-in menu bar if your application doesn't have a global shortcut menu bar).

## Creating and Displaying a Custom Toolbar

Although you can display only one menu bar and one shortcut menu bar at a time, you can display any number of built-in and custom toolbars. One simple strategy for providing custom toolbars for your application is to hide all of the built-in toolbars (by clearing the Allow Built-in Toolbars check box in the Startup dialog), display a custom global toolbar, and display custom individual toolbars for forms and reports. You can carry out this simple strategy without programming.

As an example, we'll create a simple global toolbar.

1. Right-click the menu bar and select Customize from the shortcut menu.

2. Click the New button, name the new toolbar ExpenseToolbar (see Figure 1.45a), and click OK. Access adds the new toolbar to the list in the Toolbars tab.

3. From the Edit category in the Commands tab of the Customize dialog, select and drag the Undo, Cut, Copy, and Paste commands. From the Records category, drag the Sort Ascending and Filter by Form commands.

4. Click the title bar of the new toolbar and drag and dock the ExpenseToolbar below the menu bar.

5.  Click the Properties button on the Toolbars tab of the Customize dialog to display the Toolbar Properties dialog (see Figure 1.45b). You use this dialog to allow or prevent menu bar changes. Choose ExpenseToolbar from the combo list and clear the check boxes to prevent customizing, resizing, or moving the toolbar.

6.  Make sure that the Menu Bar and the ExpenseToolbar are the only checked items in the Toolbars list in the Customize dialog. Click the Close button. Figure 1.45c shows the built-in Database window menu bar and the new toolbar.

7.  Click the Close button in the Database window.

**FIGURE 1.45:**

The New Toolbar dialog for naming a custom toolbar (a) and the Toolbar Properties dialog for setting the properties (b) of the new toolbar (c)

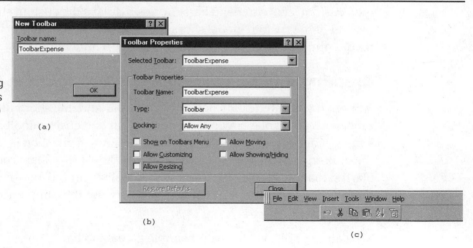

# A Simple Automated Access Application

This chapter has introduced you to many of the tools that you can use to automate a database, to restrict the menu and toolbar commands, and to protect your application without creating programs yourself. We've explored the tools by creating the Expenses application. Let's look at the Expenses application and review its current state.

1.  Choose the File menu and, from the list of most-recently opened databases at the bottom of the File menu, choose Expenses to open the database. Access displays the Password Required dialog.

2. Type **expenses** in the text box and click OK. You must use all lowercase letters; the password is case sensitive and Access won't accept mixed case versions such as Expenses. The Database window is hidden and the global menu bar and custom toolbar are displayed. Click Enter/View Expense Reports by Employee. Right-click in the form to display the custom global shortcut menu.

3. Click the Return button and then click the Exit this database button on the Main Switchboard.

Because the Expenses database has some protection from any design changes, you can comfortably turn it over to someone who doesn't know Access. Keep in mind, though, that the protection measures can still be disabled by pressing Shift when starting the application.

You can continue to use techniques described in this chapter to improve the application. For example, by using the Command Button Wizard, you can make it easy to navigate on two-way paths to all of the application's forms and reports. You can also use the Command Button Wizard to add the other automated tasks in Table 1.1. You can add additional Lookup combo boxes using the Combo Box Wizard. You can add additional forms and reports, and you can use the Switchboard Manager to include the new objects on switchboards. You can create additional custom menu bars, shortcut menus and toolbars to make your application easier to use. Working with only the Access helpers and the various property dialogs such as the Startup dialog and the Customize dialog, you have the power to create fully automated database applications without going any further in this book. Do you need to read any further?

## Limitations of the Wizards and Helpers

The Database Wizard, while very powerful, is able to create only databases based on the templates that come with Access. If your application does not fall into one of the categories of databases the wizard can create, you'll have to build the database from scratch and then use the other wizards and helpers to automate the database. And although it is possible to create a fully automated application with the Access helpers, the applications you can create are still limited in the kinds of operations they can carry out.

For example, an application created with the helpers limits data validation to the kinds of data validation rules you can enter in table field properties and form control properties. The drawbacks are:

- You can use only a single validation rule to validate a record, even though in some cases you might want to carry out a sequence of validation tests.

- If the data entered doesn't satisfy the validation rule, you can display only a single message, even though you might want to display different messages depending on the value that was entered.

The validation tests are performed according to default timing rules. For example, Access tests the validation rules for a control on a form when you try to tab out of the control and tests the validation rules for a record when you try to save the record. Often you'll want to change the timing of the validation tests; for example, Access tests for uniqueness of the primary key value (entity integrity) when you try to save a record, but you may want to test for uniqueness when you tab out of the primary key control instead of waiting until the other data for the record has been entered.

Another example of a database operation you can't do with the helpers is *transaction processing*. A *transaction* is a set of operations that you handle as a single unit; either you carry out all of the operations in the set or you don't carry out any of them. If you begin the transaction and one operation fails, you roll back the previous operations by returning the data to the state it was in before you started the transaction. A good candidate for transaction processing is the archive process: you append records to historical tables and then delete them from the current data tables. Either both operations occur or you don't want either to occur. Access doesn't provide a transaction processing helper.

Additionally, you may want your Access application to be a component in a complex mega-application that includes Excel spreadsheets and Word documents and in which Access, Excel, and Word communicate automatically with each other according to your specific instructions. Or you might want to take advantage of the hundreds of useful procedures in the procedure library that the Windows operating system makes available or the procedures stored in the libraries of other applications (see Chapter 20 for more information on procedure libraries). You can't use the helpers for communication outside of Access.

# Taking the Next Step

This chapter has introduced you to the Access helpers and to several new property dialogs. The rest of this book takes you beyond the helpers. You'll create your own programs to automate a database from scratch using the two automating tools that Access provides: macro programming and Access VBA programming.

## Two Programming Languages

There aren't many commercial applications that offer two automating tools. Even within the Microsoft product array, Access is the only one with two tools. There are two automating tools because Microsoft's first vision of Access was as a desktop database for a wide range of users from novice end users to professional developers. At one end of the range are people who want to move beyond an interactive database application and pass more of the work to the computer but who have no programming background and are too busy to acquire one. Access macros were, and still are, the solution for these people. At the other end of the range, developers need the additional power that VBA provides. In between are people with varying programming backgrounds and experience who may choose to use both tools.

The two automating tools are not independent. You *can* create an automated database application using only macros but not if you want to control the way Access reacts when an unanticipated error occurs. A complex application will require features that only VBA procedures provide, however, a VBA-powered application still requires macros for custom keyboard shortcuts. Both macro and VBA programming use the same set of predefined instructions for carrying out common actions such as opening and closing objects and importing data. The predefined instructions are called *actions* in macro programming and *methods* in VBA.

The remaining chapters of Part I explain the fundamentals that are common to both macro and VBA programming. Part II focuses on macro programming starting with a comprehensive treatment of macro programming basics and then illustrating macro techniques for three categories of essential database operations: navigation, data maintenance, and manipulation of groups of records. Part III does the same for VBA programming.

Both automating tools have advantages and disadvantages and you'll want to understand both tools so you can make the best choice in each situation.

- The macro language is simpler than VBA in its capabilities but easier to learn. The macro window is specially designed to minimize the need to learn syntax rules.

- The VBA language is harder to learn than the macro language, but it is much more powerful. VBA has a long list of features not available in the macro language.

- Usually it is faster to create a simple application using macros. Often, macros are the tool of choice for building prototypes.

- In some circumstances, macros provide the best performance. A new approach in Access 97 is to design some forms and reports using only macros and hyperlinks, thereby improving performance.

- You can easily convert macros to VBA procedures at any time. You can start an application or build a prototype with macros and convert to VBA later if you need the additional power.

## Two Data Languages

In addition to learning about the macro and VBA programming languages, you'll learn about two other languages. The other two languages are not stand-alone programming languages; instead they are special-purpose *data access languages* that you use along with a programming language to specify the data you want to retrieve from or add to the tables. The part of Microsoft Access that you interact with to create and display the database objects is called the Access Application and the part that manages the data in a database is called the Jet database engine, or Jet. The two parts of Access communicate with each other using data access languages.

You've been using one of the data access languages from the beginning of your work with Access, perhaps without being aware of it. Structured Query Language, or SQL (sometimes pronounced "sequel"), is the language that Access uses every time you create a query in query Design view. SQL is also the language that the Form, Report, Combo Box, and List Box Wizards often use to specify record sources and row sources. Both macro and VBA programming use SQL for working with tables and queries.

In Part III you'll learn about the second data language called Data Access Objects, or DAO. The DAO language is used only in VBA programming. You use DAO to write instructions for creating and manipulating the objects that are managed by the Jet database engine including the tables and queries in your database, but also including the objects that Jet uses to restrict access to the data and manage the database. There are two basic roles for DAO: The first role is to give an alternative method for specifying data (although in most cases the SQL method has better performance). The second role is to provide the ability to create and modify database objects as part of VBA procedures. Most of the time you create all of the tables and queries in an application using their Design windows. However, there are times when you prefer to create tables and queries programmatically. For example, you use DAO when you write a VBA procedure that creates a new temporary table as part of an automated data import process.

# Summary

This chapter has introduced you to the tools that you can use to automate a database without doing any programming yourself. The tools rely on setting properties in dialogs and property sheets and on using the wizards and helpers to write programs for you. The wizards have introduced you to the concept of writing a program as either a macro or a VBA procedure and then arranging for Access to run the program automatically when the user takes an action. Following is a summary of the helpers and the concepts we've explored:

- The Database Wizard creates partially automated applications complete with switchboards for navigation, command buttons to open and synchronize forms and reports, and custom dialog boxes that collect user input before selecting records for summary reports.

- The Command Button Wizard creates command buttons with scripts for automating more than 30 simple database tasks.

- The Combo Box Wizard creates lookup combo boxes that automatically look up and display a record that matches the value in the combo box.

- The Switchboard Manager creates and modifies a switchboard form for providing navigation paths to forms, reports, and other switchboards.

- The Startup dialog lets you control how your application starts up and lets you protect your application's design.

- The Customize dialog lets you create custom menu bars, shortcut menus, and toolbars.

- The programming environment in Access is event driven. Certain user actions cause controls, forms, and reports to recognize changes called events. Access runs programs when events occur.

- Two programming languages are used in Access. In macro programming, you create macros stored in macro objects listed in the Macros pane of the Database window. In VBA programming, you create procedures stored either in *standard modules* listed in the Modules pane of the Database window or in *form* or *report modules* that are built into forms and reports. (Access 97 also has another kind of module that you'll learn about called an independent *class module*.)

You are ready to learn about programming in Access. You are ready to use programming to provide the automatic connections between the objects in your database: not only the familiar database window objects, but also additional objects that will be new to you. The next chapter starts you thinking about how objects are designed in Access and about how you can control them with your programs.

# CHAPTER
## TWO

**2**

# Getting Started with Objects and Events

■ Choosing names to document objects

■ Describing an object by setting properties

■ Setting startup, database and security properties and environmental options

■ Manipulating objects

■ Understanding the Access event model

■ Canceling default behavior

**T**his chapter introduces two concepts fundamental in both macro and VBA programming: objects and events.

The first part of the chapter discusses the familiar Database window objects and the not so familiar data access objects. The data access objects are used by a major component of Access, the Jet database engine. It is the Jet database engine that manages the data and that controls who can use each of the Database window objects. When you work interactively with Access, you don't work explicitly with the data access objects; Jet works in the background creating and managing the data access objects automatically. As an example, when you create a new Database window object such as a table, Jet creates a corresponding data access object, called a TableDef object for the table and another data access object called a Document object that stores administrative information about the new table. Also, when you set database and security properties, you are actually working with the data access objects. The chapter explores using properties to describe the characteristics of objects and teaches you how to read, set, and change different categories of properties.

The second part of the chapter introduces *events*, which are triggered by actions. As soon as you interact with an object, you change the object. For example, when you open a form or move the mouse cursor to a text box, your action changes at least one property. Some of the changes that an object experiences are made available as programming opportunities; these special changes are the object's events. Programming in Access consists of writing programs and arranging to have Access run them automatically when events occur. This chapter describes the events that objects recognize. Knowing the precise conditions that trigger events is crucial to both macro and VBA programming.

# Thinking in Objects

Even the simplest Access database has hundreds of items: tables, fields, indexes, relationships, queries, forms, controls, reports, properties, and so on. Each of the items that you create, or that Access creates for you, is an *object*. In Access the word object has a definition, which will evolve as the chapter unfolds. Object is a concept that we'll return to at different times in the book. I like to think of object as an onion with several layers. At the outside layer, you can just think of an object as a "thing" that you can use or change by setting properties in a property sheet or dialog or by running a macro or a VBA procedure. We'll peel away the layers as we go along.

The hundreds of objects in a database need to be organized so that you can make sense out of them. The Database window helps out by displaying the main objects, called the Database window objects, in tabbed panes with separate panes for tables, queries, forms, reports, macros, and modules. You can introduce another level of organization by using an object's name to provide information about the object's type and purpose.

# What's in a Name?

Naming an object is your first opportunity to uniquely identify it. The name you choose can provide no information at all, or it can richly document the object. For example, when you name the controls on a form, you are free to name them numerically, as in Control1, Control2, ..., ControlN. Or, you can include descriptive information within the name and use names such as txtLastName, cmdReturn, or cboCustomerID. The name txtLastName implies that the control is a text box control holding someone's last name; we can easily deduce both the control's type and its purpose from the control's name without knowing the naming codes adopted by the database's author. A name packed with such information is *self-documenting*. Using self-documenting names avoids the need to set up a separate dictionary to define the type and purpose of your objects. You can make up your own naming codes, or you can adopt one created by others. It's up to you, but in any case do adopt a naming standard and take the time to apply it consistently.

## Naming Conventions

Most professional Access developers follow a naming standard based on a style for naming objects called the Hungarian style after the birth country of its inventor, Charles Simonyi.

**NOTE**    Unfortunately, the wizards don't follow the Hungarian naming style. The Northwind sample application that we'll be using throughout this book doesn't follow the Hungarian naming style either, so this book does not practice the consistency rule that it preaches. I decided to use the Northwind database so that you would be working with the same familiar database used in the Access documentation and wouldn't have to take the time to learn a new database. As a result, we'll be using both the given names for existing objects and the Hungarian style names for the new objects that we create.

In the Hungarian naming style, an object's name has four parts:

*[prefix][tag][BaseName][Suffix]*

The name parts have the following meanings:

**BaseName**    The BaseName is the name you would probably use if you weren't following a naming convention. The BaseName is typically one or two words that describe the object's purpose. Capitalize the first letter of each word and don't use spaces. It is preferable to spell out words entirely, but abbreviations are okay if they are long enough to be memorable (or better still, recognizable by someone else trying to understand your work).

**Tag**    The tag refers to the type of the object and is usually three or four lower case letters.

**Prefix**    A prefix modifies the tag and is usually a single lower case letter. A tag may have one or more prefixes to provide additional information about the object's type.

**Suffix**    A suffix modifies the base name. A suffix is usually a single word with the first letter capitalized. A name may have one or more suffixes to provide additional information about how the object is used.

When you name an object, you decide on the base name and the suffix or suffixes. Tags and prefixes, however, are normally selected from standardized lists that you create or adopt.

**NOTE**

The Hungarian style naming standard was first introduced to the Access community by Stan Leszynski and Greg Reddick in their article "Naming Objects in Access: Version 2 of a Proposed Standard" (*Smart Access Journal*, August 1993) and updated in the article "Revisions to the Leszynski-Reddick Naming Standard for Access 2.0" by Leszynski, Reddick, Litwin, and Getz (*Smart Access Journal*, May 1994).

On the disk under Tables\Chapter2.pdf, Table 2.1 lists examples of tags for the Database window objects and Table 2.2 lists examples for controls on forms and reports. See *Access 97 Developer's Handbook* by Paul Litwin, Ken Getz, and Mike Gilbert (Sybex, 1997) for a complete list of commonly used tags.

Here are a examples of how some of the objects in the Northwind database could be renamed using tags:

| Object | Tagged Name |
|---|---|
| Customers table | tblCustomers |
| Customers form | frmCustomers |
| Orders form | frmOrders |
| Orders Subform form | fsfrOrders |
| Customers macro | mfrmCustomers |
| Customer Labels Dialog form | fdlgCustomerLabels |
| Customers and Suppliers by City | quniCustomersSuppliers |
| CustomerID combo box | cboCustomerID |
| PrintInvoice command button | cmdPrintInvoice |

Normally, you don't use prefixes in macro programming. If you are new to programming and are planning to focus on Part II next, then you can skip the next section and come back to it later before continuing on with Part III.

## Names in VBA Programming

An essential difference between macro programming and VBA programming is in their ability to deal with variable information. Suppose you want to keep a count of the number of times you run an operation. To keep track, you define a

Counter variable to store the number representing how many times you run the operation and to increase the Counter by one each time you run the operation. In VBA programming, you define, or *declare*, a variable using a declaration statement in a module; when you declare a variable, VBA sets aside a location in memory to hold the current value. By definition, a *variable* is a temporary storage location in memory that you name and use to hold a value or refer to an object.

In macro programming, you can't write a macro instruction to create a temporary storage location in memory; instead, you simulate a variable by using a control on a form to hold the current value.

## Prefixes for VBA Variables

Chapter 13, "Mechanics of Procedures: Using Variables," deals with VBA variables; you'll learn about storing different types of data, limiting which procedures can "see" a variable (called the variable's *scope*), and limiting the variable's lifetime. Tables 2.3 and 2.4 list examples of the commonly used prefixes for VBA variables; both tables can be found on the CD under Tables\Chapter2.pdf.

## Tags for VBA Object Variables

In VBA programming, you can also define variables to refer to objects such as forms, reports, or controls. These special variables are called *object variables*. Table 2.5, on the CD under Tables\Chapter2.pdf, lists common tags for the VBA object variables.

## Tags for Data Access Objects

Another essential difference between macro and VBA programming is in the way they access the information stored in the database file. When you install Microsoft Access you are actually installing two separate entities. The first part, the Access Application, contains all of the files for working in the Access interface and all of the files for writing and running macro and VBA programs. The second part, the Jet database engine, contains all of the files for managing the database, including defining and manipulating data, enforcing data integrity rules, and controlling who can use the database. In macro programming the connection between the two parts is handled automatically and you can't work directly with Jet. In VBA programming you can work directly with Jet using its own data access objects. Table 2.6, on the CD under Tables\Chapter2.pdf, lists examples of tags for these objects.

# What the User Sees

When you create a custom database application using the techniques in this book, the users see only forms and reports. Users see the form or report caption in the window's title bar and not the coded name you use when you create the application. Make the captions informative, include spaces as appropriate, and avoid using jargon. Here are some examples:

| Object Name | Caption |
|---|---|
| rptMailLabelCust | Mailing Labels: Customers |
| cboCustomerID | Lookup Customer |
| frmCustomers | Customers |

# Changing Names

Unfortunately, Microsoft Access doesn't provide a way to propagate name changes. Whenever you want to change the name of a table, field, control, form, query, and so on, you have to go through all of your tables, queries, forms, reports, macros, and modules and make all of the changes manually. (For VBA modules, the job is made easier with a Replace command.) Without a utility that propagates name changes, a basic Access guideline is "Don't make any name changes!" However, even with careful planning, you may need to change names. For example, when you use the Combo Box Wizard to create a lookup combo box, you don't have the opportunity to name the control; the wizard uses the default name, ComboN where N is a number. Because the default name doesn't identify the purpose of object, it is preferable to change the name to one that follows a naming standard and includes information about both the object's type and its purpose.

**NOTE**   There are a couple of third party utilities that can help you with name changes including Speed Ferret by Black Moshannon Systems (phone: (814)-345-5657) and Find and Replace, a shareware utility by Rich Fisher (http://www.dnai.com/~rfisher). Both utilities install as add-ins and propagate name changes throughout your application. Be very careful when you use any name-changing utility. Because they allow you to make name changes almost too easily, you can make changes that may be difficult to undo if you change your mind. You should always back up your database before using a name-changing utility.

# Describing an Object's Properties

Objects have properties that describe their characteristics. In a sense, an object is the sum of its properties. At any instant, each form, control, field, relation, and so on is uniquely defined by the current values of its properties. The set of current values is stored in memory as the object's *state*.

Objects have two kinds of properties:

**Design-time properties** are properties that you can set when you are working in Design view. They are listed in the object's property sheet.

**Run-time properties** are properties that you can set or read only at run time. They are not listed in the object's property sheet.

> **NOTE**
> In this book we'll use the terms *design time* to refer to the time when you are working in the Design view of an object, the term *run mode* to refer to the time when you are viewing an object in Datasheet view, Form view or Print Preview, and the term *run time* to refer to the time when you are running a macro or a VBA procedure.

## Viewing Design-Time Properties in the Property Sheets

Each Database window object has one or more property sheets listing the properties that you can set at design time. For example, Figure 2.1 shows the Field, Table, and Index property sheets available when you create a table. You set the design-time properties for a field by selecting the field in the upper pane of the Design window and entering property values in the lower pane. A field's design-time properties fall into two tabbed categories: General and Lookup. General properties include data properties such as FieldSize, format properties such as InputMask, and data validation properties such as ValidationRule and Required. You can use the Lookup tab to specify properties for a lookup field. A lookup field makes data entry easier by displaying a list of values in a combo box or list box when you click the field in Datasheet view or click a form control bound to the lookup field. The Lookup properties include data properties such as RowSource and BoundColumn and control design properties such as ListRows.

**FIGURE 2.1:**

The Field Properties, Table Properties, and Indexes property sheets in table Design view

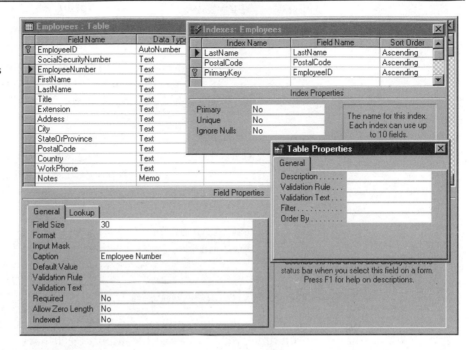

In addition to setting design-time properties using the property sheets, you can change the settings at run time when a macro or a VBA procedure is running. Usually, when you change one of these settings at run time, the change is in effect only during run time. For example, you can use a macro or VBA procedure to change the Caption property of a form, but when you open the form in design time, you can observe that the stored value of the Caption property is not changed.

## Run-Time Properties in Macro and VBA Programming

In addition to the design-time properties listed in their property sheets, most objects have run-time properties that you can set or read only when a macro or a VBA procedure is running. Run-time properties are not listed in an object's property sheet. Here are a few examples.

| Property | Applies To | Description |
|---|---|---|
| Value | controls | Determines or specifies the text contained in a text box control or the text box portion of a combo box control. The Value property can also determine or specify whether a control is selected or which value or option within the control is selected. |
| Painting | forms or reports | Specifies whether a form or report is repainted. (Repaint completes any pending screen updates and redraws the screen.) |
| Text | text box or combo box controls | Sets or returns the text in a text box control or the text box portion of a combo box control. |

## Properties Available Only in VBA

Another important difference between macro and VBA programming lies in the number of run-time properties available. Most objects have a set of run-time properties available only in VBA programming; if you refer to these properties in a macro, you generate an error. Here are a few examples of run-time properties that are available in VBA procedures but not in macros:

| Property | Applies To | Description |
|---|---|---|
| Bookmark | form | Sets a bookmark that uniquely identifies a particular record in the form's underlying recordset. |
| Selected | list box | Selects an item or determines if an item is selected in a list box. |

In Part III you learn about creating your own custom properties using VBA procedures.

Earlier in the chapter, you learned that the data access objects that you use to work directly with the Jet database engine are available only in VBA procedures. There are no Design windows or property sheets for these objects. You set, read, and change their properties by writing statements in VBA procedures.

## Read-Only Properties

Some objects have *read-only* properties, which are properties that you can't set or change. An example of a read-only property is a form's Dirty property; you use the Dirty property to determine if the current record has been modified since it was last saved. Read-only properties are not listed in an object's property sheet. Here are a few more examples of read-only properties:

| Property | Applies To | Description |
|---|---|---|
| Form | form | Refers to the form itself or to the form associated with a subform control. |
| ActiveControl | Screen | Refers to the control that has the focus. |
| Count | Open forms or reports | Determines the number of open forms, the number of open reports, or the number of controls on an open form or report. |
| Me | form or report | Refers to the form or report or to the form or report associated with a subform or subreport where a VBA procedure is currently running (VBA only). |
| CurrentObjectName | any Database window object | Determines the name of the active Database window object. |
| CurrentRecord | form | Identifies the current record being viewed in a form. The value corresponds to the value in the current record number box between the default navigation controls on the form. |
| HasData | form or report | Determines if a form or report is bound to an empty recordset. |

# Other Property Sheets

The Database window objects and the objects they contain have property sheets where you can set their design-time properties as described in the previous section. Access also provides property sheets in the form of dialogs for setting properties of the database you are currently working with, for setting options of the Access environment itself, and for setting security permissions. This section describes the dialogs you can use to set these properties and options. In most cases, you can also set them in VBA procedures, and in one case (the startup properties) you can set them in macros. This section contains more advanced material; you can skip the section for now and come back to it later.

## Setting Startup Properties

Most of the startup properties are displayed in the Startup dialog (see Figure 2.2), available by choosing the Startup command in the Tools menu. When you set startup options in the Startup dialog you are setting properties of the database itself. In Part III you'll learn how to use the Database object, one of the data access objects, to refer to the database so you are actually setting properties of the Database object when you use the Startup dialog. While it is easiest to set startup properties in the Startup dialog, you can also set them using macros or VBA. Part III explains how to set startup properties in macros or VBA.

FIGURE 2.2:

Using the Startup dialog
to set properties of the
Database object

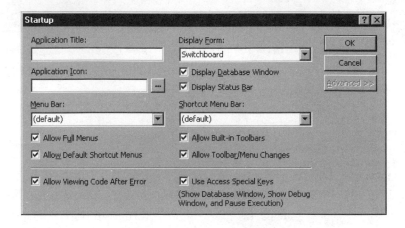

**NOTE**   An important startup property that is not displayed in the Startup dialog is the AllowByPassKey property that enables and disables the Shift key used to bypass startup property settings.

## Setting Database Properties

You set administrative properties for a database in the Database Properties dialog, available by choosing the Database Properties command in the File menu or by right-clicking the database window title bar and selecting Properties from the shortcut menu (see Figure 2.3). The administrative properties of the database are actually properties of several Document objects managed by the Jet database engine. There are five tabbed categories of administrative information. The properties in the General, Statistics, and Contents categories are read-only.

**General** displays the same information that is displayed when you right-click the database's filename in the Windows Explorer and choose the Properties command.

**Statistics** displays administrative information about the date and time the current database was created and the date and time the database was last modified, accessed, and printed.

**Contents** displays a list of names of the Database window objects contained in the database.

The Summary and Custom tabs display properties you can set.

**Summary** displays text boxes in which you can enter summary information (see Figure 2.2a) that allows you to identify and locate a database more easily. The information you enter is stored as a property setting of a data access object called the SummaryInfo Document object.

**Custom** provides the opportunity for you to create custom database properties. Figure 2.2b shows that a custom database property named ReportsDue has been added to the Expenses database. Custom properties become properties of the data access object called the UserDefined Document object.

The Database Properties dialog. The Summary tab (a) and the Custom tab (b) display properties that you can change.

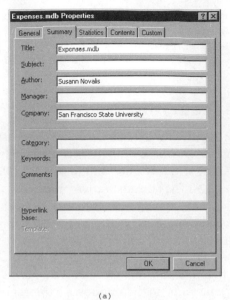

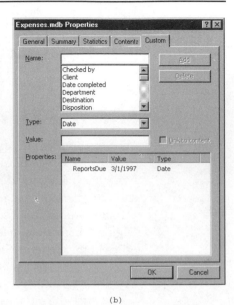

(a)

(b)

Although is it easiest to set the Summary properties and create the Custom properties in the Database Properties dialog, you'll also learn how to set or create them using VBA in Part III.

## Setting Environmental Options

You can shorten development time by customizing your Access working environment. You set Access environmental options in the Options dialog, available by choosing the Options command from the Tools menu (see Figure 2.4). There are ten tabbed categories with more than 60 options you can set.

The environmental options describe characteristics of the Access Application object and seem, at first glance, to be properties of that object. However, the environmental options are given special treatment by being stored in the central information database in Windows 95, called the Registry. The Windows 95 Registry stores both system information and environmental—or configuration—information about individual applications in a hierarchical arrangement. The main folders in the Registry are called *keys*. You can use the Registry Editor (regedit.exe) to view the contents of the Registry (see Figure 2.5). To run the Registry Editor, click Run in the Windows Start menu and type **regedit**.

**FIGURE 2.4:**

Use the Options dialog to set environmental options.

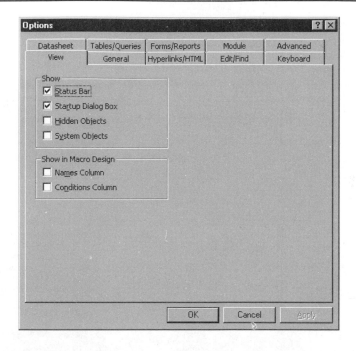

**FIGURE 2.5:**

The Registry Editor displays folders, called keys, containing information about the computer's hardware, peripheral hardware, software settings, and so forth.

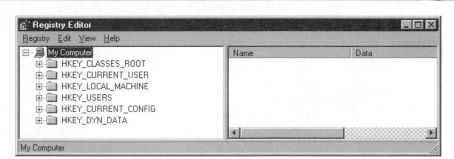

An individual key can contain subfolders called *subkeys* and data items called *value entries*. To view the contents of a key or subkey, double-click the folder icons. The settings for the Access environmental options are stored in the subkey with path

HKEY_CURRENT_USER\Software\Microsoft\Office\8.0\Access\Settings

Figure 2.6 shows the value entries for the options.

FIGURE 2.6:

The environmental options that you set in the Options dialog are stored in the HKEY_CURRENT_USERS key.

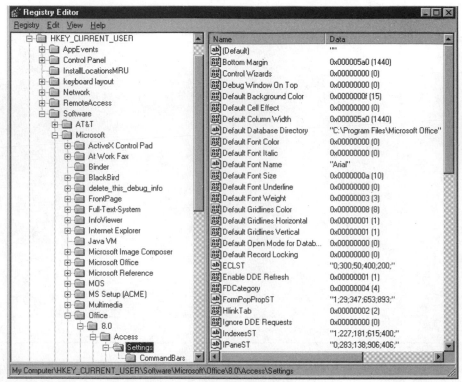

> **NOTE**
>
> **The settings for the Access built-in commands are also stored in the Windows Registry. The command information is stored in the subkey with path HKEY_CURRENT_USER\Software\Microsoft\Office\8.0 \Access\Settings\CommandBars**

Normally, you set the environmental options using the Options dialog; you can also set most of them in VBA. You can use VBA to set the environmental options in all of the panes of the Options dialog except those in the Modules pane. The only option in the Modules pane that you can set using VBA is the Break On All Errors option; you can set the remaining Modules options only in the Options dialog.

**NOTE**  In previous versions of Access the environmental options are stored in a separate database, called the workgroup information file, that is created automatically when you install Microsoft Access. The previous versions use the workgroup information file to store two kinds of information: information about the users and groups that you create and information about the values that a user specifies for the environmental options. Access 97 continues to use the workgroup information file to store users information.

## Setting Security Properties

You secure an application in order to protect its data and the application itself. You protect the application's structure (its tables, queries, forms, and reports) and the programming (macros and modules) from inadvertent changes that could break the application. Security in Access is the responsibility of the Jet database engine. Jet has two security models: database password security and workgroup security.

There are two parts to the workgroup security model: users and permissions. Users have usernames and passwords to identify themselves to Jet as valid users. Each Database window object has a set of permissions, such as ReadData and ModifyDesign. In the workgroup security model, you assign a set of permissions for each object in the database to each user or to each group of users. The two kinds of security information are stored in different locations. The permissions information is stored with the individual database and the users information is stored in the workgroup information file. The Setup program for Microsoft Access installs a default workgroup information file named system.mdw, but you can create a new workgroup information file for each workgroup. (An Access *workgroup* is a group of users in a multi-user environment who share data.)

You can store information about users, groups, and their passwords by choosing the Security command in the Tools menu and then choosing User and Group Accounts command in the flyout menu. Figure 2.7 shows the User and Group Accounts dialog. When you use this dialog you are creating data access objects called the User and Group objects.

**FIGURE 2.7:**

The User and Group Accounts dialog creates users, groups, and their passwords.

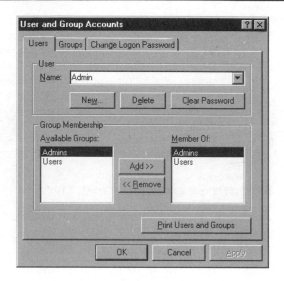

You can specify permissions for each database object in your database in the User and Group Permissions dialog box, available by choosing the Security command in the Tools menu and then choosing the User and Group Permissions command in the flyout menu (see Figure 2.8).

**FIGURE 2.8:**

Use the User and Group Permissions dialog to assign permissions for each object to users and groups.

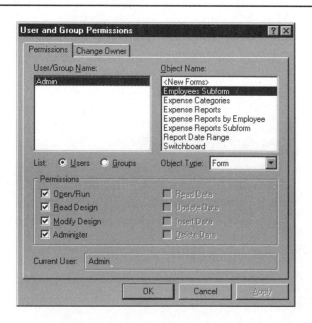

**Using Document and Container Objects to Store Permissions**  Each
Database window object that you create has a corresponding data access object
called a Document object. Jet uses the Document object to keep track of any permissions you have set in the User and Group Permissions dialog, as well as to
keep track of other administrative information, such as when you created the
object and who created it. Each category of Database window object, such as
forms or macros, has a corresponding data access object called a Container object.
Jet uses the Container object to keep track of permissions you have set, as well as
to keep track of administrative information for the category such as its name. (As
a special case, two categories of Database window objects, tables and queries,
have a single Container object named Tables.) The permissions you set are properties of the Document and Container data access objects.

# Lifetime of Objects

An object exists for a time interval called its *lifetime*.

When you create a Database window object and save your work, the object is
saved to the .mdb file; this means that the Database window objects are permanent, or *persistent*, objects. A Database window object's lifetime begins when you
first create it and ends when you delete it from the .mdb file. In contrast, not all of
the objects managed by the Jet database engine are persistent. Some data access
objects including the DBEngine, Error, Workspace, and Recordset objects are temporary, or *non-persistent*, objects and are not saved in the .mdb file. Some temporary objects are created automatically each time the database file is opened; you
create other temporary objects in VBA procedures. Temporary objects exist only
in memory. The lifetime of a temporary object may be as long as the database is
open or may be a shorter time interval. For example, you can create a Recordset
object in a VBA procedure; the object you create lives only while the VBA procedure that created it is running. When the VBA procedure terminates, the
Recordset object ceases to exist.

When you work interactively with Access or when you use macro programming to automate a database, you don't work directly with the data access
objects. However, in Part III you'll learn how to write VBA programs to
control objects that Jet manages; you'll put your programming hands on the
data access objects that Jet constantly creates and destroys.

# Manipulating Objects

When you start up an Access database, the database's objects just sit waiting for you to do something. When you take some action by clicking a mouse button, entering keystrokes, or choosing a menu command, your computer executes programs that manipulate objects. In essence, there are two kinds of programs: the built-in programs that are part of Access and the programs you write yourself. In either case, programs are instructions passed to the computer to do something to your objects or to Access. The built-in programs include programs that run when you choose a built-in menu command or toolbar button; these are the internal programs that make Access work. The programs that you write yourself are the ones that run when you choose a custom menu or toolbar button, click a custom command button, or open a form.

The purpose of programs is to manipulate objects. Programs open and close forms, run queries to select or modify groups of records, print reports, and save changes in data to the database file. Programs start up and close a database, and programs set startup conditions and quit Access.

Another way to separate programs is by where they are stored:

**Programs that are stored as internal components of the objects** are called *methods*. You can ask an object to run one of its methods. Objects have built-in methods, and you can also create your own custom methods.

**Programs that are stored as external components separate from the objects** are called *macros* and *procedures*. You ask Access to run a macro or a procedure to take actions on an object.

**NOTE**  The procedures that you store in a form's or report's module don't fall neatly into one of these categories. The procedures in a form or report module that you designate as *private* can be considered as methods of the form or report while other procedures that you designate as *public* can be considered as external components (even though they are stored with the form or report). See Chapter 19 for more information.

# Using Macros

This section and the next section provide an overview of the ways you manipulate objects in macro programming and in VBA programming. You may find these sections difficult to understand until after you have read some of Parts II and III. You can skip them for now and come back later.

In macro programming, you manipulate objects using individual instructions called *macro actions*. There are about 50 macro actions in Access. The macro actions have been individually optimized for performance. Many of the macro actions are equivalent to menu commands such as Close, others mimic manual user interactions such as SelectObject, and others provide capabilities not available in the user interface such as Beep.

Most of the macro actions are used to manipulate the Database window objects and the objects they contain such as fields, sections, and controls. You use these macro actions to manipulate the objects: for example, to open, close, move, import, export, or delete them. You use one of the macro actions, the SetValue macro action, to change the values of an object's properties. You also use the SetValue action to change the values of fields and controls. Figure 2.9 depicts the way that you use macro actions to manipulate objects.

**FIGURE 2.9:**

Manipulating an object using a macro action. The macro action is stored separately from the object.

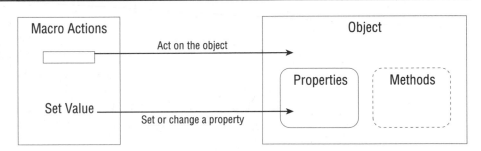

There is no way to create your own custom macro actions. To run more than one macro action at a time, you create a macro. A *macro* is a list of macro actions that runs as a unit.

One reason macro programming is easy to learn is that the instructions you create using macros simulate the instructions you give when you work interactively. In fact the best way to get started writing macros is to work through the interactive steps of an operation and then translate each step into a macro action. When you work interactively, one of the steps you must take is to select the object before you can perform any action on it: you select an open window by clicking into it, you select a control by tabbing to it or clicking into it, you select a record by clicking into its record selector or by choosing one of the Go To... commands in the Edit menu, and so on. Macro programming is *selection-centric* because a macro must establish which object is selected. In macro programming, there are two ways to do so:

- You can use a macro action that selects an object such as the OpenForm, SelectObject, and GoToControl macro actions.

- If the object has already been selected, you can use object properties that refer to the active object such as the ActiveForm and ActiveControl properties.

One of these two things must take place before any action can be performed on the object.

When you use a macro to manipulate an object, there is no way to ask the object to run one of its methods. When you use only macro programming, methods simply are not part of the programming environment: although the internal programs that we call methods exist, they are inaccessible in macro programming. Figure 2.9 shows the methods in a dotted rectangle inside the object to indicate that the methods exist but are not available. In macro programming, your view of objects is simplified: objects in macro programming have no accessible methods and only a limited set of properties.

## Selecting Objects and the Focus

The *focus* is the ability to receive the result of your mouse or keyboard action. Only one control at a time can have the focus. The control that has the focus is called the *active control*. When a control has the focus there is usually some visible indication: for example, the insertion point is in a text box control that has the focus and the caption of a command button that has the focus is enclosed by a dotted rectangle. Some controls, such as labels, lines, rectangles, images, and page breaks, cannot receive the focus. Controls that are capable of receiving the focus have both an Enabled and a Visible property; you must set both of these properties to allow a particular control to receive the focus.

When you click a form, it becomes the *active form*, and the color of its title bar changes to indicate the form's active status. The first control in the form's tab order that can receive the focus becomes the active control. If the form doesn't contain any controls that can receive the focus, the form itself receives the focus.

# Using VBA Procedures

In Access VBA programming, there are basically two ways to manipulate objects.

The first way is similar to macro programming: you take action on the object you want to manipulate by running a program that is external to the object. In Access VBA, the external programs are analogous to macro actions; but, instead of being considered as separate entities as they are in macro programming, the external programs are defined as methods of a special Access VBA object called the DoCmd object. The DoCmd methods correspond to most of the macro actions, so running a DoCmd method in VBA programming is analogous to running a macro action in macro programming. Figure 2.10 depicts using DoCmd methods to manipulate an object.

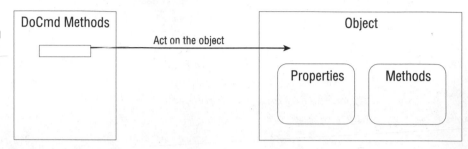

**FIGURE 2.10:**

Using a DoCmd method to manipulate an object in VBA is analogous to using a macro action in macro programming.

Access VBA provides a second way to manipulate an object that lets you work directly with the object and its internal programs; this way is referred to as the *object-enabled approach*. You can use an assignment statement to set or change a property of an object, or you can ask the object to run its own methods. The methods are a set of more than one hundred predetermined actions built into Access as internal components of objects. In VBA programming, your view of an object includes both the set of its properties that define what the object *is* and the set of its methods that define what the object can *do* to itself. Figure 2.11 depicts the object-enabled approach to manipulating an object.

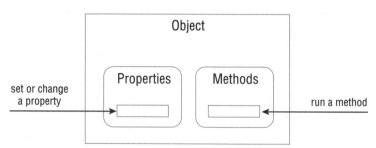

**FIGURE 2.11:**

You can manipulate an object directly in VBA by changing one of its properties with an assignment statement or by running one of its methods.

You can write VBA procedures that are selection-centric. Similar to macros, before manipulating an object, selection-centric procedures must either select the object or recognize that the object is the active object.

The selection can be established using

- methods such as the OpenForm, SelectObject, or GoToControl methods of the DoCmd object and the SetFocus method of the control or form you want to select,

- object properties such as ActiveForm or ActiveControl when the object has already been selected, or

- the Me property when you want to refer to the form or report in which the procedure is running.

You can also write VBA procedures that manipulate objects directly without first selecting them. It is more difficult to learn how to write such *object-centric* procedures because they don't mimic the familiar interactive steps; however, your time and effort is rewarded by procedures that run faster because Access doesn't need to take the time to select the object. In Part III you'll work with examples of both selection-centric and object-centric programming techniques.

# The Access Events

The state of an object is the sum of its characteristics at an instant. An object's state is recorded in memory. When any of the characteristics changes, the state changes. Some of the changes in an object's state are opportunities for you to interrupt the processing that normally follows the change; these changes in state are called *events*. When you open a form, you change the form's state from unopened to opened; this change in state is defined as an event for the form, called the Open event.

**NOTE**    Not all changes in state are events. If you change the color of a form's background, you change the form's state, but this change in state is not defined as an event. You cannot create custom events.

# Four New Events in Access 97

Access 97 defines four new events: Initialize, Terminate, ItemAdded, and ItemRemoved.

The Initialize and Terminate events are recognized by an object called the class module. Class modules are an advanced feature of VBA that you use to create the definition, or blueprint, for a custom object. In Access 95, class modules are used only to create forms and reports. A new feature of Access 97 is the independent class module for creating objects independent of forms and reports. (For example, you can use an independent class module to create an importing process as an object.) After creating the definition and storing it in a class module, you can run a VBA procedure to create a new object in memory, called an instance, based on the definition. A class module recognizes the Initialize event when you create an instance based on the class module. When the new object ceases to exist, the class module recognizes the Terminate event.

The ItemAdded and ItemRemoved events are recognized by another new object called References when you add or remove a reference to the type library of another application or another Access database. (A *type library* is a file that contains descriptions of the objects, properties, and methods in the other application or Access database that you can manipulate using VBA procedures in your Access application.) The ItemAdded and ItemRemoved events require special handling: they occur only when use a VBA procedure to add or remove a reference, you can assign only an event procedure and not a macro to these events, and you must follow a specific syntax (see ItemAdded Event—Event Procedure in online Help for more information).

For each event defined for a form, form control, or report, there is a corresponding event property. An object's event properties are listed in the Event category in the object's property sheet. For example, Figure 2.12 shows the event properties of a form.

**FIGURE 2.12:**

The Event properties category for a form

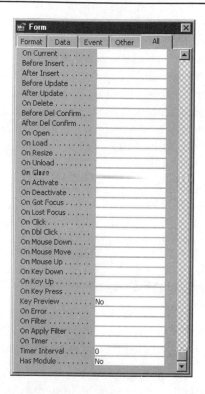

## The Access Programming Model

The Access programming model is an event-driven programming model. You create a macro or VBA procedure that you want Access to run when an object recognizes an event, and you assign the program to the object's event property. When the event occurs, it *triggers* the program, which means that Access runs the assigned macro or VBA procedure. The program that is executed when an event occurs is called an *event handler*; if the program is a macro, it is an *event macro*; if the program is a VBA procedure, it is an *event procedure*.

**NOTE**    In VBA there are two kinds of procedures: function procedures and sub procedures. A sub procedure used as an event handler is commonly referred to as an event procedure while a function procedure used as an event handler is an event function procedure.

When you assign a program to an event property, you are *trapping* the event. When you set an event trap by assigning a program to an event property, you interrupt the default processing that Access would normally carry out following the occurrence of the event. After the program is executed, Access returns to normal processing. For example, you can trap the AfterUpdate event of a lookup combo box by assigning a program for Access to find the record corresponding to the value in the combo box before continuing its normal processing which, in this case, is to stop and wait for your next action. For some events, your program not only interrupts, but can also terminate, the default processing that would normally follow the event.

Access defines events for forms and reports, for sections on forms and reports, and for controls on forms. There are no events defined for tables and queries, and there are no events defined for the data access objects. Access 97 defines two new events for the new References object.

## Categories of Events

There are 43 events defined in Access. One way to organize events is according to what happened to cause the event. Table 2.7, (on the CD under Tables\Chapter2.pdf), lists the events grouped by cause.

The rest of the chapter describes the events in all except the last two categories. The last two categories include the four new events available only in VBA.

## Event Properties of Objects

Because an event is a special change in the state of an object, you can also organize events according to object. Table 2.8 (on the CD under Tables\Chapter2.pdf) shows the events recognized by forms, form sections, form controls, reports and report sections.

### Sequences of Events

When a user, macro, VBA procedure, or the computer does something, typically a sequence of events is recognized by one or more objects. Let's look at some examples.

**Clicking a Mouse Button**  When you click the left mouse button while the mouse pointer is over a control, the control recognizes a sequence of three events as follows:

- MouseDown when you press a mouse button

- MouseUp when you release a mouse button

- Click after you press and release the left mouse button

The control recognizes the MouseDown and MouseUp events regardless of which mouse button you clicked; however, the control recognizes the Click event only if you click the left mouse button.

**Clicking a Command Button**  When the control can receive the focus, additional events are recognized. For example, the simple click of the left mouse button when the mouse pointer is over a command button triggers a sequence of five events recognized by the command button as follows:

- Enter before the command button actually receives the focus from another control on the same form, or is the first control on the form to receive the focus when the form first opens

- GotFocus after the command receives the focus

- MouseDown when you press a mouse button

- MouseUp when you release a mouse button

- Click when you press and then release the left mouse button

A similar sequence of events is recognized by other controls such as text boxes, option buttons, list boxes, and check boxes.

**Changing Text in a Text Box or Combo Box**  You can change text in a text box or in the text box part of a combo box by pressing a key. Not all keystrokes result in sending characters, for example, pressing the Tab or Enter key does not result in sending a character. Windows uses the ANSI character set to relate the keys on the keyboard to characters displayed on the screen. Pressing an ANSI character set key results in sending a character to the text box. If the keystroke changes the text, the text box recognizes the sequence of four events as follows:

- KeyDown when you press any key

- KeyPress when you press a key that sends an ANSI character

- Change when Access recognizes that the contents of a text box or text box portion of a combo box has changed

- KeyUp when you release any key

If the keystroke doesn't change the text, the Change event doesn't occur. If you do change the text and then try to update the control by pressing Enter or by moving to another control or record, what happens next depends on whether the control is a text box or a combo box.

When your keystroke has changed the text in a text box and you take some action to update the control by moving to another control on the form, the text box recognizes two additional events as follows:

- BeforeUpdate when Access recognizes the changed value of the text box and just before updating the changed data to the record buffer

- AfterUpdate when Access recognizes the changed value of the text box and just after updating the changed data to the record buffer

When you change the text in the text box part of a combo box by sending keystrokes and then try to update the control by pressing Enter or by moving to another control or record, Access compares the value to the values in the combo box list. If the value is not on the list, the combo box recognizes the NotInList event. What happens next depends on the setting of the LimitToList property:

- If the LimitToList property is set to Yes, Access cannot accept the change, and the combo box recognizes the Error event. The full sequence is

    KeyDown → KeyPress → Change → KeyUp → NotInList → Error

- If the LimitToList property is set to No, Access updates the combo box control. The sequence of events recognized by the combo box is

    KeyDown → KeyPress → Change → KeyUp → NotInList → BeforeUpdate → AfterUpdate

You can also send keystrokes programmatically using the SendKeys macro action or the SendKeys VBA statement. Sending keystrokes programmatically triggers the same sequence of events as if you had pressed the keys.

# The Update Process

Access uses a two-buffer system to track changes in data: When a record is first displayed, Access places a copy of the data contained in its controls into a temporary storage location called a *record buffer*; when you type a character into a control, Access places a copy of the data you typed into another temporary storage location called a *control buffer*.

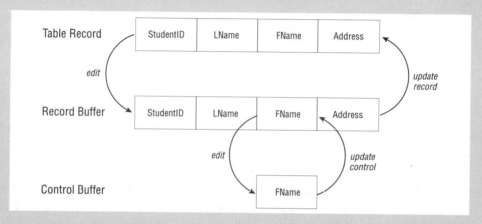

When you try to move out of the control, Access compares the data in the two buffers to determine if you have made any changes.

If you have made a change, the following sequence occurs: the control recognizes the BeforeUpdate event, Access *updates the control* by copying the changed data from the control buffer to the record buffer, and finally the control recognizes the AfterUpdate event. If you haven't changed the data in the control, the control update process doesn't occur.

When you attempt to save the record, Access compares the data in the record buffer with the data stored in the table. If you have made changes to at least one control, the following sequence occurs: the form recognizes the BeforeUpdate event, Access *updates the record* by copying the changed data from the record buffer to the table fields, and the form recognizes the AfterUpdate event. If you haven't changed the data, the record update process doesn't occur.

**Changing the Value of an Option Group**   When you change the value of an option group by clicking an option button, a toggle button, or a check box that is in the option group, the option group recognizes the following sequence:

- BeforeUpdate when Access recognizes the changed value of the option group and just before updating the changed data to the record buffer

- AfterUpdate when Access recognizes the changed value of the option group and just after updating the changed data to the record buffer

- Click immediately after the AfterUpdate event

**Tabbing from One Control to Another Control**   When you tab out of one control into a second control on the same form without making any changes, the two controls recognize the following sequence of events:

- The first control recognizes the Exit event when you leave the control but before it loses the focus.

- The first control recognizes the LostFocus event after the control loses the focus.

- The second control recognizes the Enter event when you go to the control but before it receives the focus.

- The second control recognizes the GotFocus event when the control receives the focus.

If you changed the data in the first control before tabbing out, then the first control recognizes the following two events before the sequence listed:

- The first control recognizes the BeforeUpdate event before the changed data is updated to the record buffer.

- The first control recognizes the AfterUpdate event after the changed data is updated to the record buffer.

**Opening a Form**   When you open a form the form recognizes the following sequence of events:

- Open when you first open the form but before the first record is displayed

- Load after the records are loaded from memory and are displayed

- Resize when the form is first displayed

- Activate when the form receives the focus and becomes the active window (except this event is not recognized if the form receives the focus from another form whose PopUp property is set to Yes or from a window in another application)

- GotFocus when the form has received the focus but only if all controls on the form are disabled or hidden

- Current before the first record becomes the current record

When the form has at least one control that is visible and is enabled, the form doesn't recognize the GotFocus event. Instead, the first visible, enabled control recognizes the following sequence immediately following the form's event sequence:

- Enter just before the control receives the focus

- GotFocus when the control receives the focus

## Timing Is Everything

In the event-driven programming model, you must decide the correct event to trigger a program. When a sequence of events is recognized by one or more objects, you need to select an event that is appropriate for your program. Sometimes you have a choice and selecting any of several events will cause the action to be carried out as you intended. More often, there is only one event that gives the result you want, and your task as the programmer is to determine that single correct event. A good place to start is to search in online help for the topic events, listed alphabetically to display the lists shown in Figure 2.13 and the topic Events, Order of.

In the rest of this section, we'll look at the events recognized by controls on forms, by forms, by reports, and by report sections.

**Events for Controls on Forms**   A control on a form recognizes events when the control gains or loses the focus and when you change the data and the control is updated. Table 2.9 shows the nine focus and data events, and Table 2.10 shows the mouse and keyboard events. (Both tables are on the CD under Tables\Chapter2.pdf.)

**FIGURE 2.13:**

The Events and Event Properties Reference

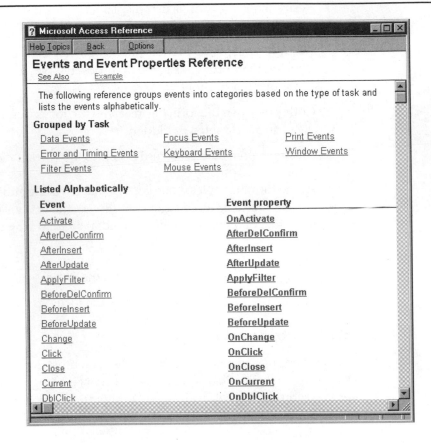

**Events for Forms and Form Sections**  A form recognizes the window and focus events shown in Table 2.11 when you open, close, or resize the form or when the form gains or loses the focus. A form recognizes events when a record gains or loses the focus, when you change the data and the record is updated, when you create a new record or delete an existing record, and when you apply or remove a filter. A form recognizes an event when Access detects an error in the interface or the Jet engine and the form has the focus. Finally, a form recognizes an event when a specified time interval has elapsed. Table 2.12 shows the data and filter events; Table 2.13 shows the Error and Timer events. (All three tables are on the CD under Tables\Chapter2.pdf.)

**Events for Reports and Report Sections**  A report recognizes events when you open or close the report, when the report gains or loses the focus, or when Access detects an error and the report has the focus. Table 2.14 shows the events for reports. Additionally, report sections recognize the events shown in Table 2.15. (Tables 2.14 and 2.15 are on the CD under Tables\Chapter2.pdf.)

## Canceling Default Behavior

After an object recognizes an event, Access carries out default behavior. Sometimes the default behavior is to stop and wait for the next user action. For example, when a command button recognizes the Click event, Access looks to see if you have assigned a macro to the OnClick event; if you have, then Access runs the macro, but if you haven't, Access stops and waits for your next action. Other times, Access goes through a series of default operations either before or after running the macro assigned to the event. For example, when you change the data in a control and then tab to the next control, the changed control recognizes the BeforeUpdate event. In response, the following default behavior occurs:

1. Access updates the control to the record buffer.

2. The changed control recognizes the AfterUpdate event.

3. The changed control recognizes the Exit event.

4. The changed control recognizes the LostFocus event.

5. The next control recognizes the Enter event.

6. The next control recognizes the GotFocus event.

For some events, including the BeforeUpdate event, Access runs the assigned macro or VBA procedure before the default behavior takes place. For these events you can include a step in the macro or procedure to cancel the subsequent default behavior. The events with default behavior that can be canceled are listed in Table 2.16 (on the CD under Tables\Chapter2.pdf). For the events not listed in the table, Access runs the macro *after* carrying out the default behavior so the default behavior can't be canceled.

## Getting Hands-on Experience with Events

The examples of event sequences demonstrate how careful you must be in selecting an event to trigger your programs. Selecting the correct event becomes particularly delicate when you are working with interacting event sequences for two different objects, such as two forms. You don't have to be an event expert to get started with macro and VBA programming; but as your applications become more complex, you'll need to study the event model.

You can get hands-on experience and see events as they occur by working with the EventLogger application included on the book's CD-ROM. The EventLogger application was created by the authors of *Access 97 Developer's Handbook* (Sybex, 1997). (The authors have kindly given permission to include the EventLogger in this book.) The application is an excellent way to understand the complex and subtle event sequences. You can use the application by itself as described below. Additionally, you can incorporate the application into your databases. Chapter 2 of *Access 97 Developer's Handbook* describes how to use the EventLogger application to view events in your own forms and explains the VBA procedures that make the application work.

1. Copy EventLogger.mdb to the MacroVBAHandbook folder on your hard disk. Open the database and open frmLog in Form view (see Figure 2.14). This form logs events as they occur in the form's list box. After logging a group of events you can clear the list box by clicking the Clear button. The events are grouped into seven types as shown below. Check the event types you want to study and clear the check boxes for the other types.

| Event Type | Event |
|---|---|
| Mouse Movement | MouseMove |
| Mouse Click | Click, DblClick, MouseDown, MouseUp |
| Data | AfterDelConfirm, AfterInsert, AfterUpdate, BeforeDelConfirm, BeforeInsert, BeforeUpdate, Change, Current, Delete |
| Keystroke | KeyDown, KeyPress, KeyUp |
| Focus | Activate, Deactivate, Enter, Exit, GotFocus, LostFocus |
| Action | Close, Error, Load, Open, Resize |
| Timer | Timer |

The Event Logger form

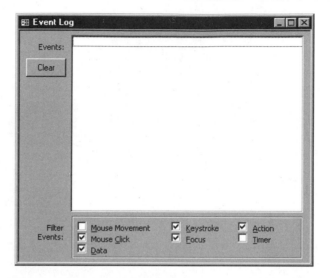

2. Check the Mouse Click, Data, Focus, and Action check boxes.

3. Open the frmEventTest form in Form view. Figure 2.15a shows the Event Test Form as it appears when you first open the form. The form includes a variety of test controls for studying the events associated with a form, a subform, and form controls. Figure 2.15b lists all of the events of the selected types that occurred when you opened the form with the first event at the top of the list. Notice that the subform opens, loads its records, resizes, and recognizes its current event and that then the text box on the subform receives the focus. After the subform events occur, the main form recognizes its events as the form opens, loads its records, resizes, and recognizes the Activate, GotFocus, and Current events. Finally the first control on the main form's tab order that can receive the focus, the txtSample text box, recognizes the GotFocus event.

4. Click the Clear button on the Event Log form and then click the main form's Push Me! command button. Figure 2.16 shows that the Event Test Form recognizes the Activate event and the focus moves first to the main form's text box. When you click the command button, the text box recognizes the Exit event followed by the LostFocus event. The command button recognizes the sequence of events shown in the figure.

**FIGURE 2.15:**

Opening the Event Test Form (a) triggers the set of events shown in the Event Log (b).

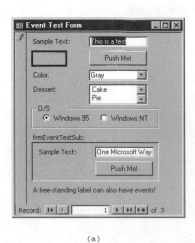
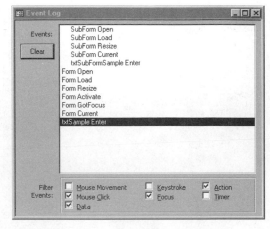

(a)

(b)

**FIGURE 2.16:**

Clearing the Event Log and then clicking the Push Me! button on the main form of the Event Test Form triggers events recognized by the form, the first control that can receive the focus, and then the command button.

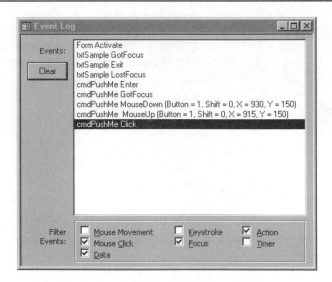

5. Click the Clear button on the Event Log form and then click the subform's Push Me! command button. Figure 2.17 shows that the main form recognizes the Activate event, then the focus moves to the control that last had the focus, the Push Me! command button. The main form's Push Me! command button recognizes a sequence of events and then the main form

recognizes its update events (because the form opened in edit mode). The subform control recognizes the Enter event, the text box on the subform recognizes the Exit event, and then the Push Me! command button on the subform recognizes its sequence of events.

Clearing the Event Log and then clicking the Push Me! button on the subform of the Event Test Form triggers events recognized by the main form and the last control that had the focus on the main form and then by the subform and controls on the subform.

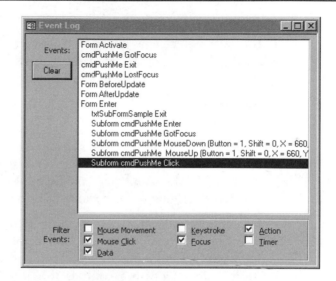

6. Explore the events recognized by the other controls on the Event Test Form. For example, click the Windows NT option button to observe the events recognized by the option buttons and the option group, click the down arrow for the combo box and select another item, edit the text in the text boxes in the main form and the subform, and so on.

# Summary

This chapter has introduced the concept of objects. Here are the important points.

- Adopting a naming convention such as the Hungarian style makes your objects self-documenting by providing information on the object's type and purpose.

- Objects have properties that describe their characteristics. Most Access objects have design-time properties that you can set in property sheets, but there are no property sheets for the data access objects of the Jet database engine. Both Access and Jet objects have run-time properties that you can set or read only when a macro or procedure is running. Some run-time properties are read-only.

- While some properties are available in both macro and VBA programming, there are many properties that you can use only in VBA programming.

- The database itself has properties that you can set using dialog boxes available by choosing menu commands. You can set startup, general database information, and security properties.

- You can set environmental options. Settings are stored in a separate workgroup information database file.

- One difference between the macro and the VBA programming models of an object is that the VBA model has access to the methods of an object and the macro model does not. A method is a built-in program stored internally with the object that you can run to take an action on the object.

- The settings for all of an object's properties define its state at an instant. User, macro, procedure, or computer action can result in changing the state. Some changes in state are called events and are available as programming opportunities. Only form controls, forms, form sections, reports, and report sections recognize events.

- Typically, a single user action triggers a sequence of events. Selecting an appropriate event for a macro or procedure is an important skill.

- Events are the same in both macro and VBA programming (except for the two new ItemAdded and ItemRemoved events that you can trigger and respond to only in VBA).

Now that you know about the object concept, it's time to learn about the specifics of the Access object model. We study the model in two segments. The next chapter focuses on the objects and properties that are available in both macro and VBA programming. In Part III, we return to the object model in order to learn about the objects, properties, and methods that are available only in VBA programming.

**3**

# Introducing the
# Access Object Model

- Relating objects to each other

- Introducing the object hierarchies in Access and Jet

- The Access Application object model

- Referring to objects and properties by name

- Using the Expression Builder to create references

**W**hen you automate a database operation you create instructions that run when an object recognizes an event. You must understand which objects you can write instructions for, the events that an object recognizes, and how to write the instructions. The last chapter introduced you to the concept of an object as a thing that you can use or change by running a macro or a VBA procedure. This chapter focuses on the specific objects: which objects are available, which properties can be changed, how the objects are related to each other, and how you identify an object when you write a program.

The Access object model is large and complex. The purpose of this chapter is to get you started with the model by introducing you to those objects and properties that are available in both macro and VBA programming. In Part III you look more deeply into the model and learn about the additional objects and properties as well as the methods that are available only in VBA programming.

# Relating Objects to Each Other

You are familiar with the Database window objects of interactive Access: the tables, queries, forms, and reports. We'll continue to use the word "object" informally and add a few more objects to our list: table fields, query fields, form controls, and report controls. When you work interactively with Access, you don't have to be concerned with how objects are related to each other; the Access user interface takes care of the relationships for you. However, to create programs that manipulate the objects, you need to understand how objects are related so you can use these relationships to refer to an object in a program.

Understanding groups of objects, whether the objects are people, celestial bodies, or database objects, means understanding how they are tied together in relationships. Two kinds of relationships are obvious: some objects are *similar* to other objects, and some objects *contain* other objects.

# Grouping Similar Objects

It is natural to group objects with similar properties and behaviors together. For example, it is natural to group the forms in a database, to group command buttons, or to group text boxes. A group of similar objects is called a *collection*.

In Access, most of the objects are in collections. For example, a database has a single collection of tables that contains all of the tables in the database; each table has a collection of fields that contains all of the fields you have defined for the table; a database has a single collection of open forms; and each open form has a collection of controls that contains all of the controls you have placed on the form. Access begins the name of each type of object with a capital letter such as Form, Report, Control, and Field objects. Access names a collection by adding the letter "S" to the name of the object type in the collection; for example, the Controls collection of a specific form contains the Control objects placed on the form. Access treats the collection itself as an object; for example, a Controls collection is an object that contains the Control objects for a specific form or report.

Another example of collections involves the distinction between a form that is open and one that is closed. An open form is a Form object and the collection of open forms is the Forms collection. By contrast, a closed form is not a Form object and is not a member of the Forms collection—a closed form is just a closed form. Figure 3.1 depicts the Forms collection for the Expenses application when the Switchboard and the Expense Reports by Employee forms are the only open forms.

Objects that are not in collections are *singular objects*. There is, for example, an object named Application that represents the Access application and an object named DBEngine that represents the Jet database engine. Each of these is a singular object, because Access has only one Application object and the Jet database engine has only one DBEngine object. A collection object is also a singular object; for example, there is only one Forms collection object in the application and each Form in the collection has only one Controls collection. Whether an object is a singular object or is in a collection becomes important when you refer to the object.

**FIGURE 3.1:**

The Forms collection contains the open forms. Each open form has its own Controls collection containing the controls on the form.

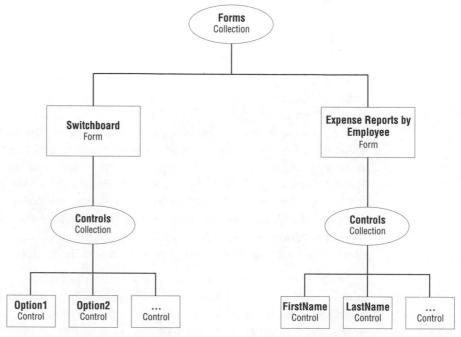

## Classes and Instances

Another way to look at groups of similar objects is to separate the definition of a group from the objects in the group.

We'll use the word *class* to refer to the definition of a group, for example, the class of forms or a class of text boxes. A class is a blueprint for its objects. As a simple example, you can think of table Design view as representing the class of tables. When you create a specific table by defining table fields and setting table properties, you are creating an *instance* of the class.

As another example, the Text Box tool in the toolbox represents the text box class. When you use the text box tool to create a text box with a specific set of properties, you are creating an instance.

*(continued)*

So, when you think of a group of objects with similar properties and behaviors, there are really two parts: the definition of the group, that is, the class, and the objects themselves, that is, the instances.

# Objects Contain Objects

The second important relationship among objects is objects containing other objects. For example, a form contains its controls and a table contains its fields. A table also contains its indexes and each index contains its fields. In general, objects contain objects, which may contain other objects, and so on. The container relationship is a parent and child relationship: an object is the *parent* of the objects it contains, and an object is the *child* of the object that contains it. For example, a form is the parent of the controls it contains, and a control on a form is the form's child.

The different levels of container relationships can be shown as tiers in a hierarchy. For example, let's look at the hierarchy of container relationships for tables. In Access, a table object that you define in table Design view is called a TableDef object and is one of the data access objects managed by Jet. A table contains three collections as follows:

- A table has a Fields collection containing its Field objects as listed in the upper pane of Design view (see Figure 3.2a). Each Field object has a Properties collection containing a Property object for each property listed in the lower pane of Design view.

- A table has an Indexes collection as listed in its Indexes dialog (see Figure 3.2b); each Index in the collection has a Properties collection containing a Property object for each property listed in the lower pane of the Indexes dialog. Each Index has a Fields collection containing the Field objects listed in the upper pane of the Indexes dialog (in this example, each Index object has a single field). Each Field object in an Index has a Properties collection containing Property objects for the Field.

- A table has a Properties collection containing Property objects as listed in the Table Properties dialog (see Figure 3.2c).

**FIGURE 3.2:**

The Field objects for a table and the Property objects for a table Field (a). The Property objects and the Field objects for a table Index (b). The Property objects for a table (c).

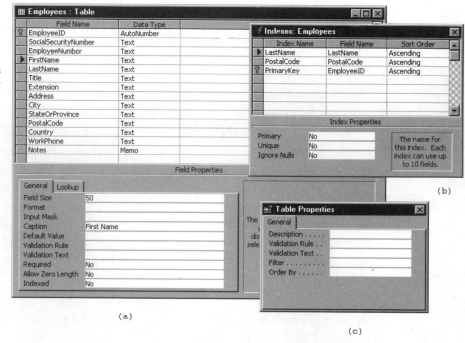

Figure 3.3 shows a partially expanded view of the TableDefs collection for the Expenses database. In this figure, the Employees table is expanded to show its three collections, which are expanded to show some of their members. In each case, one of the collection members is expanded to show its collections, which are expanded to show their members, and so on. The property sheets that you are familiar with in Design view show only the design-time properties; each object also has many run-time properties. The expanded views of container relationships quickly become large and overwhelming; the important concept here is the structure of the hierarchy.

Figure 3.4 is a fully collapsed view of the table hierarchy that focuses on the structure: in this figure, each rectangle represents a collection and a representative member of the collection shown in parentheses. In looking at a collapsed view, keep in mind that each collection can be expanded to show its specific members.

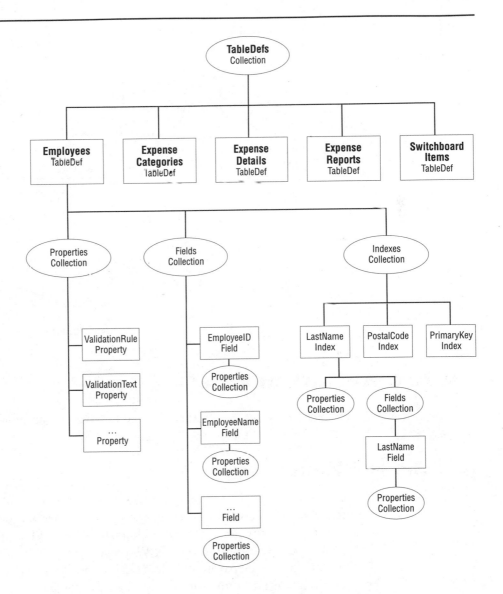

You need to know the container relationships for all of the objects in Access because when you write programs to manipulate the properties and behaviors of an object, you may have to refer to all of the objects that lie along a hierarchical path to the object.

FIGURE 3.4:

The hierarchy of container relationships for tables

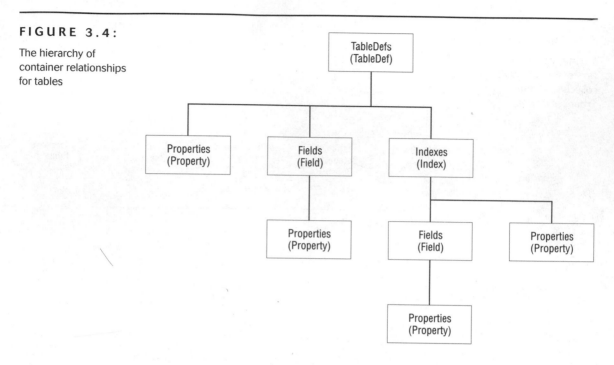

# The Architecture of Access

When you install Access you actually install two major components: the Access Application layer and the Jet database engine.

## The Application Layer

The Application layer consists of all the files necessary to control the user interface and all the files needed for writing and running macros and VBA procedures. The Application layer contains the menu bars, toolbars, and windows for creating and viewing Database window objects. When you create a database interactively, you work directly in the Application layer using the Design windows to create the individual tables, queries, forms, and reports as well as the macros and modules that fuse the objects into an application. Although you use the Application's interface to create all six Database window objects, only forms, reports, and modules are defined as Application objects. The tables and queries you create in the Access interface are Jet data access objects. Macros are not included in either object model because normally you don't write programs to manipulate macros, you write just the macros themselves.

# Library Databases, Add-Ins, and the Workgroup Information File

The Application layer also includes a set of library databases, add-ins, and the workgroup information file.

A *library database* is a collection of database objects and procedures that you can use in any database you create. The convention in Access is to use the .mda and .mde extensions for library databases. You can use the built-in library databases or you can create your own. (You'll learn to create library databases in Chapter 20.) Access comes with five built-in library databases: utility.mda, wzcnf80.mda, wzlib80.mde, wzmain80.mde, and wztool80.mde. You can open any of these as a normal database except for utility.mda. Utility.mda opens automatically when you start Access, so if you try to open it within Access you get a message telling you the file is already open as a library database. If you want to work directly with the utility.mda library database, make a copy of utility.mda under another name, such as myutility.mda, before you open Access; after you open Access, you can open the copy. (A database with the .mde extension contains only a compiled version of code and does not contain a viewable and editable version.)

An *add-in* is a tool designed to accomplish a specific task. Add-ins can make a task easier to carry out or can introduce a new operation that isn't available in the basic product. There are several add-ins that are built-in, and you can also create your own add-ins. There are three kinds of add-ins:

- A *wizard* is a series of dialogs for guiding you through the process of creating an object. You design the object by entering your specifications in the dialogs. After collecting all the required information, the wizard creates the object for you. Examples of wizards include the Table, Query, Form, and Report Wizards. In Chapter 1 we used the Database Wizard and two of the Control Wizards.

*(continued)*

- A *builder* is usually a single dialog for helping you through the process of creating items. There are builders for creating expressions and for setting properties. Later in this chapter we'll use the Expression Builder to create object references. Normally, builders are context sensitive—you summon a builder after selecting a specific property you need help with. For example, when you change one of the color properties, clicking the Build button to the right of the property box summons the Color builder.

- A *menu add-in* is a mini-application that performs some general function. Normally a menu add-in operates on several objects or on the entire application. You summon menu add-ins by selecting the Add-ins command on the Tools menu. Examples of built-in add-ins are the Switchboard Manager, the Database Splitter, the Linked Table Manager, and the Menu Builder. Additionally, the Add-in Manager is a menu add-in that you use to install your own menu add-ins. Several useful third-party utilities, such as the Find and Replace utility for propagating name changes, install as menu add-ins.

The *workgroup information file*, named system.mdw, stores information about the users, groups, and passwords that you set as part of your security model. You can specify security information in dialogs available by choosing the Security command in the Tools menu.

# The Jet Database Engine

The Jet database engine consists of the files necessary to manage your data, to control access to the data in your database file, and to store objects that belong to the Application layer. Jet includes the internal programs for six basic database management functions:

**Data definition and integrity**   With Jet you can create and modify the objects that hold the data. You can use both the interface and VBA programming to create and modify the following Jet objects: databases, tables, fields, indexes, relations, and queries. Jet enforces the entity and referential integrity rules that you specify when you design tables and create relationships.

**Data storage**   Jet uses a method called the Indexed Sequential Access Method (ISAM) to store data in the file system. The basic characteristics of this method are: data is stored in pages of size 2K containing one or more records, records have variable length, and records can be ordered using an index.

**Data retrieval**   Jet provides two ways to retrieve data. One way is to use Jet's powerful query engine, which uses Structured Query Language (SQL) to retrieve data. The second way is to access the data programmatically using the data access objects in VBA procedures.

**Data manipulation**   With Jet you can add new data and modify or delete existing data. You can manipulate data either using the Jet query engine with SQL action queries or using the data access objects in VBA procedures.

**Security**   Jet has two security models, including a database password model for simple password security to the entire database and a workgroup security model in which individual users and groups have permissions to individual database objects.

**Data sharing**   Jet enables multiple users to access and modify data in the same database. Jet locks the data on a given page when a record is being modified by a user: either Jet locks the page as soon as one user starts editing (*pessimistic locking*) and unlocks the page when the editing is completed, or Jet allows multiple users to edit a record and locks the page only when a user tries to save or commit the changes (*optimistic locking*).

## Jet's Evolution

In the first release of Access 1.0 in 1992, Jet 1.0 was packaged as a database management system specifically designed to support Access. For the most part, Jet was hidden; you worked directly with the Application layer and couldn't write programs to manipulate Jet's objects.

Through its versions 1.1, 2.0, 2.5, 3.0, and now 3.5 in Access 97, Jet has evolved into an application-independent database management system. Normally, you use another application such as Access or Excel to run Jet (the

*(continued)*

application that runs Jet is called the *host application*). Jet 3.5 can manage the data created by a large set of applications including Word, Excel, Visual C++, FoxPro, and Visual Basic. Jet itself doesn't recognize the application-specific objects that these applications create. Jet does, however, provide storage for the objects that an application creates. The Access forms, reports, macros, and modules that you create in the Application are stored in your database file. Jet keeps track of such application-specific objects using Document and Container data access objects.

Jet 3.5 provides access to all of its objects through the Data Access Objects (DAO) language. This means that you can arrange for Jet to provide its database management services by writing and running VBA procedures in addition to the usual arrangements for services that you make through the Access interface when you work interactively with Access.

A new feature of DAO 3.5 is that you can establish a direct connection, called *ODBCDirect*, to an ODBC data source managed by another database management program such as Microsoft SQL Server. When you establish a direct connection to the data source, Access doesn't have to load the Jet database engine into memory. ODBCDirect is useful when you need the additional features that the other program can provide. When you use ODBCDirect, the Connection object is similar to the Database object that you use to connect to the Jet database engine. See *Access 97 Developer's Handbook* by Paul Litwin, Ken Getz, and Mike Gilbert (Sybex, 1997) for more information.

## Object Hierarchies

You create macros and VBA procedures to manipulate objects. The objects that are available for manipulation are the built-in objects that the developers of Access and Jet have defined. (You can create your own objects in VBA programming but not in macro programming.) These built-in objects are grouped into their own collections and arranged into separate hierarchies. In each case, the top of the hierarchy is occupied by a singular object: the Application object sits at the top of the Access Application hierarchy and the DBEngine object sits at the top of the Jet engine hierarchy. The upper portion of Figure 3.5 shows the Application hierarchy that you use for programming in VBA. The lower portion of Figure 3.5 shows the Access VBA object hierarchy. Figure 3.6 shows the data access objects in the Jet database engine hierarchy that you use for manipulating the Jet engine using VBA programming. (The figure does not show the Properties collection and Property object contained in each object except for the Error object.) In these figures, singular objects that are not collection objects are shown in ovals. Collection objects are shown in rectangles with objects contained within the collection shown in parentheses.

**FIGURE 3.5:**

The Access Application hierarchy

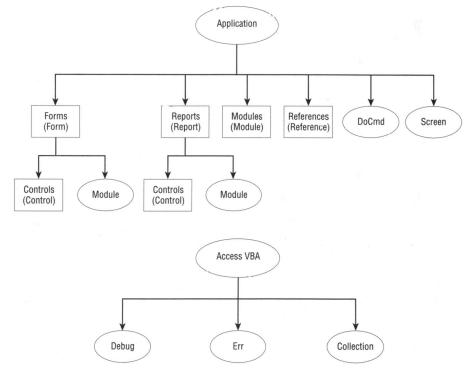

> **NOTE** There is a separate object model for opening a connection to a database using ODBCDirect. See Microsoft Data Access Objects (DAO) in the Contents tab of online Help.

The Jet database engine hierarchy. Each object except the Error object also contains a Properties collection with Property objects for the built-in properties.

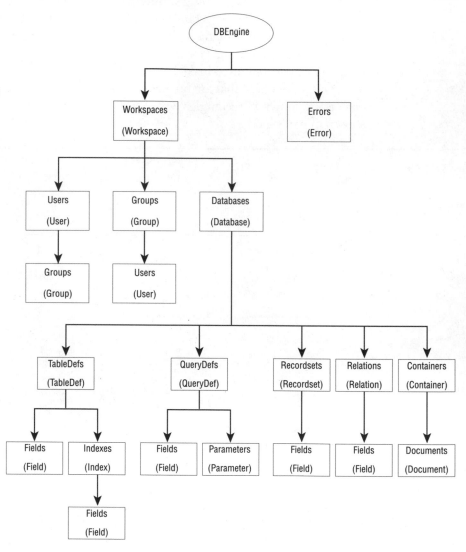

Every data access object except the Error object (and the Connection object in ODBCDirect) has a Properties collection containing separate Property objects for each built-in property. The Access Application hierarchy does not include separate Properties collection and Property objects because properties are treated differently in the Application and in Jet (see Part III for more information).

# The Access Application Object Model

The next section is a reference to the objects and their properties; Parts II and III provide hands-on exercises. Let's take a quick tour of the Access Application object model starting at the top of the hierarchy.

## Application Object

The Application object represents Access itself. The Application object also represents the environment in which macros and VBA procedures run. When you set properties for the Application object, you affect the entire Access environment while those settings are in effect. The properties available in both macro and VBA programming are listed in Table 3.1. Table 3.1 is on the CD under Tables\Chapter3.pdf.

**NOTE**  When you set the Menu Bar and the Shortcut Menu Bar options in the Startup dialog, you are setting the Database object's StartupMenuBar and StartupShortcutMenuBar properties and not the Application's MenuBar and ShortcutMenuBar properties. The difference is that Access uses the properties you set in the Startup dialog when starting up the database. You can set the corresponding Application properties in a macro or VBA procedure that are run after the database starts up (and override the Startup dialog settings).

## The Forms and Reports Collection Objects

When you first open a database, Access creates two collections: Forms is the collection of all open forms and Reports is the collection of all open reports. Access updates each collection as you open and close individual forms and reports. The Forms and Reports collections have the properties shown in Table 3.2 (on the CD under Tables\Chapter3.pdf).

## The Form Object

The Form object refers to a specific open form. Form objects are members of the Forms collection. You can't add or delete a Form object from the Forms collection (except by opening or closing a form). There are more than 100 Form object properties that describe a form's appearance and behavior; you can set about 75 of the properties in the form's property sheet. The property sheet includes the 30 event properties that a form recognizes. Table 3.3 (on the CD under Tables\ Chapter3.pdf) is a list of some of the properties that are particularly useful in both macro and VBA programming; many of these properties are available only in macro and VBA programming and are not listed on the form's property sheet. The list includes the property's data type and how the property can be set.

## The Report Object

The Report object refers to a specific open report. Report objects are members of the Reports collection. You can't add or delete a Report from the Reports collection (except by opening or closing a report). There are more than 100 Report object properties that describe a report's appearance and behavior; you can set about 50 of the properties in the report's property sheet. The list includes the seven event properties that a report recognizes. Table 3.4 (on the CD under Tables\Chapter3.pdf) is a list of some of the properties that are particularly useful in both macro and VBA programming. The list includes the property's data type and how the property can be set. (See Table 10.8 for the VBA-only properties and Table 10.9 for the methods of the Report object.)

## The Controls Collection Object

Each form and each report has a Controls collection object that contains all of the controls on the form or report. The Controls collection has properties shown in Table 3.5 (on the CD under Tables\Chapter3.pdf).

## The Control Object

The Control object represents a control on a form or report. The controls on a form or report belong to the Controls collection for that form or report. You are familiar with the 17 types of built-in controls, including the new Tab Control, that appear on the toolbox (see Figure 3.7). In addition there is a built-in Chart Control that you can add to the toolbox. You can also use custom controls, called ActiveX controls, to provide your application with additional features (see Chapter 20 for more information on custom controls). The Control object represents both built-in and custom controls.

**FIGURE 3.7:**

The built-in controls in the toolbox

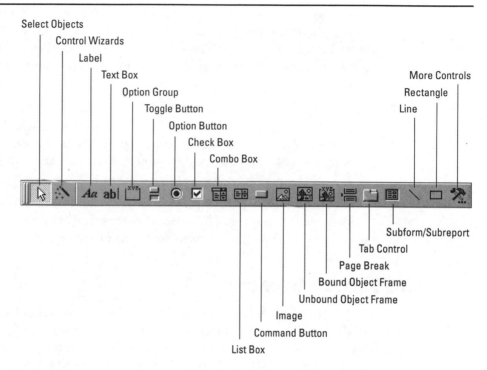

Each type of control has its own set of properties, including event properties for the events that the control recognizes. For some types of controls there is a special property, called the *default property*, that is the most commonly used property for that type of control. The default property is the property that Access assumes when you refer to a control without specifying a property name. For example, when you refer to a text box, Access assumes you are referring to the Value property.

*Data controls* are controls that can hold data and can be bound to table fields. A data control has a ControlSource property to indicate the source of the data. The seven built-in data controls include text boxes, combo boxes, list boxes, check boxes, option buttons, toggle buttons, and option groups. Other controls may be associated with another object such as a form or report; such controls have a SourceObject property to indicate the object or a SourceDoc property to indicate the source of an embedded or linked file. As an example, subform and subreport controls have a SourceObject property that you use to specify the form or report that you want to display in the control. Some controls can display a picture and have a Picture property to indicate the source of the image; for example, command buttons and toggle buttons may display images. Table 3.6 (on the CD under Tables\Chapter3.pdf) lists the built-in controls, their default properties, and whether each control is associated with data, another object or file, or an image.

Each individual type of control has its own set of properties, but all control types share a set of core properties. Table 3.7 (on the CD under Tables\Chapter3.pdf) describes each core control property, the type of value the property can hold, and information about setting or reading the value.

Most controls have numerous additional properties; at the extreme, the Combo Box control has more than 80 properties. Table 3.8 (on the CD under Tables\Chapter3.pdf) lists some of the properties for controls that are particularly important when you create programs to automate an application.

## The Screen Object

The Screen object refers to the particular form, report, or control that currently has the focus or to the control that previously had the focus. By using the Screen object in a macro or VBA procedure, you can refer to the active object without knowing the object's name. Referring to the Screen object does not, however, make the form, report, or control the active object. Table 3.9 (on the CD under Tables\Chapter3.pdf) lists the properties of the Screen object; all properties are read-only and return a reference to the object.

Chapter 2 explains the selection-centric approach to programming, which requires that a macro or VBA procedure establish a connection with an object before performing an action on it. You can use the properties of the Screen object to make the connection to the active object.

## The VBA-Only Application Objects

The Access Application object model includes several objects that are available only in VBA programming. These objects include the DoCmd object, the Module object and the Modules collection, the Reference object and the References collection; you'll learn more about them in Chapter 10.

# The Access Visual Basic Object Model

The Access Visual Basic model provides three objects: the Debug, Err and Collection objects. Only the Debug object is used in macro programming, and only one of its features, the Immediate Window, is used. You'll learn about the other features of the Debug object and two other Visual Basic objects in Chapter 10.

## The Debug Object

The Debug object is an extraordinary object available in both macro and VBA programming. You use the Debug object to send output to a special window called the Debug window. You can display the Debug window when any window is active by pressing Ctrl+G. The Debug window consists of three panes: the lower pane is called the Immediate pane, the upper pane has tabs for the Locals and Watch panes (see Figure 3.8).

**FIGURE 3.8:**

The panes of the Debug window

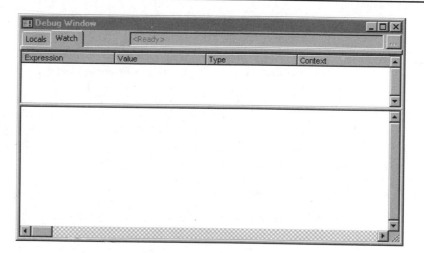

You can use the Immediate pane like a scratch pad to evaluate expressions, view and set the values of properties, and run macros and procedures. The Immediate pane is available in both macro and VBA programming. You can use the Locals pane to view the values of variables that may change when a VBA procedure runs. You can use the Watch pane to view the value of an expression or a variable while a VBA procedure is running. The Locals and Watch panes are available only in VBA.

The Debug object has no properties.

# The Macro Programming Environment

When you create macros, you write instructions that manipulate the Access interface directly. You don't manipulate the Jet database engine directly; instead macros make requests for database management services in the Access interface and rely on Access to arrange for Jet database services in response to the requests. In the macro programming environment, you use a simplified version of the programming objects defined for VBA programming; you use a restricted set of the built-in properties and you don't use the concept of methods at all.

The macro programming environment uses objects from the following sources:

- Three of the collections and objects in the Access object model shown in Figure 3.5: Forms, Reports, and Controls. In macro programming you use the Screen object to refer to the active object and the Immediate pane of the Debug window to evaluate references and expressions and to run macros.

- Three of the objects in the data access object model shown in Figure 3.6. In macro programming you work with the Table (called TableDef in DAO), Query (called QueryDef in DAO), and Field objects. You set properties for all other data access objects using the property sheets and dialogs of the Access interface.

- The macro Database window objects.

- The Customize dialog of the Access interface. You use it to create custom menu bars, shortcut menus, and toolbars.

**NOTE**  The Access Application object hierarchy shown in Figure 3.5 doesn't include macros. Microsoft could define Macros as a collection of Macro objects and a Macro as the object that refers to a macrosheet. Microsoft could define properties and macro actions or VBA methods that would allow you to create and modify macros directly from other macros or VBA procedures. Microsoft just doesn't do this.

# Referring to Objects and Properties by Name

Before manipulating an object in a macro or a VBA procedure, you must identify the object using the Access rules for referring to objects. (While you may use a naming standard to identify and document the objects you create, Access has its own rules for referring to objects that you must follow when you write programs.) There are four ways you can refer to an object. Only one of these methods, referring to an object explicitly by its name, is available in macro programming, so that is the only method we'll discuss in this chapter. We'll examine the other kinds of references in Chapter 10.

**NOTE**  We'll be using the Immediate pane of the Debug window to test and evaluate some of the references, so you'll want to be at your computer to work through this section using the Expenses application we created in Chapter 1. If you didn't work through Chapter 1, follow the steps in that chapter to create the Expenses database now.

## Referring to an Object by Name

One way to refer to an object is to start with the top object in the hierarchy and traverse along the hierarchical path to the object, recording the names of the specific objects and collection objects you encounter as you move along the path. You use the exclamation point (!), or bang, operator and the dot (.) operator to distinguish between steps and between objects and collections as follows:

- Use the bang operator when you are stepping from a collection to one of its members, that is, *collectionname!objectname*

- Use the dot operator when you are stepping from an object to one of its collections, that is, *objectname.collectionname*

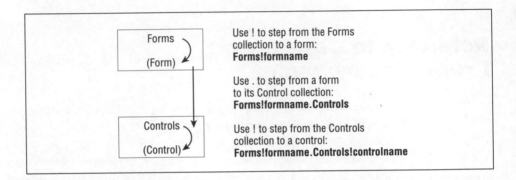

## Referring to a Form or Report

To refer to an open form, say the Switchboard form in the Expenses application, start with the Application object and traverse to the Forms collection and then to the Switchboard form in the collection:

Application.Forms!Switchboard

To refer to an open report, for example, the Expense Report report, start with the Application object and traverse to the Reports collection and then to the Expense Report report in the collection:

Application.Reports![Expense Report]

When an object's name contains spaces, you must enclose the name in square brackets; otherwise, you can omit the square brackets. (Access may enter the square brackets for you.)

You can decrease the length of a reference by using defaults. For example, Access assumes that you are in Access when you refer to objects; this means you don't have to refer explicitly to the Application object and the references become:

Forms!Switchboard

Reports![Expense Report]

These references are still full path references that refer to the specific form or report by name.

### Referring to Form and Report Properties

You use the dot operator to separate an object from a property of the object, that is, *objectname.propertyname*. For example, to refer to the RecordSource property of the Expense Categories form:

Forms![Expense Categories].RecordSource

> **NOTE**  When the name of a property contains more than one word the property sheet displays spaces between the words; for example, the property sheet for a form displays the label for the RecordSource property as Record Source. You have to omit the spaces when you create a reference to a property.

## Using the Immediate Pane to Evaluate an Object Property

You can use the Immediate pane of the Debug object to determine the setting of an object property. Here's how to use the Immediate pane of the Debug window to determine the value of an object property for a form or a report.

1. Press Ctrl+G to open the Debug window.

2. With the form or report open, type **Print** or **?**, followed by the property reference you want to evaluate, and then press Enter. Access evaluates the property reference immediately and displays the value of the property setting in the next line of the Immediate pane.

The Immediate pane executes a single line each time you press Enter. You can use many of the familiar text editing commands in the Immediate pane including the Cut, Copy, Paste, Delete, and Select All commands in the Edit menu. You can edit a line that you have already executed and then press Enter to execute the edited line (Access inserts a new line below the edited line and displays the result of the execution).

Figure 3.9 shows several examples for the Expenses application. Note that when the value is a Yes/No value, such as the value for the NavigationButtons property, Access converts Yes to True and No to False. Also, if no value has been set for the property, Access displays a blank line.

**FIGURE 3.9:**

Using the Immediate window to evaluate the setting of a property

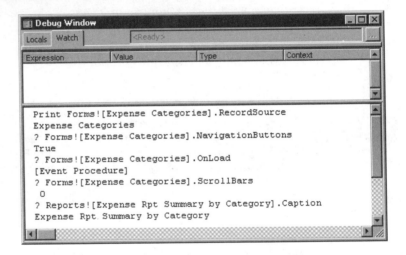

If the property is one that you can set in Design view (design-time property), then the form or report can be open in any view when you evaluate the property. If the property has a value that is determined only when the form or report is in run mode, such as the Dirty property, then the form or report must be in its run mode or else Access displays the error message such as the one shown in Figure 3.10a.

The Immediate pane can display only text values. If you type a reference for an open form such as **?Forms![Expense Reports by Employee]** and then press Enter, Access displays the error message shown in Figure 3.10b. If the form or report is closed when you try to evaluate a property such as ?Forms![Expense Categories] .RecordSource, Access displays the same error message.

**FIGURE 3.10:**

The error messages
when you try to evaluate
a run mode property
when the form or report
is in Design view (a), and
when you try to evaluate
a reference to an object
or a reference to a prop-
erty of a closed form or
report (b)

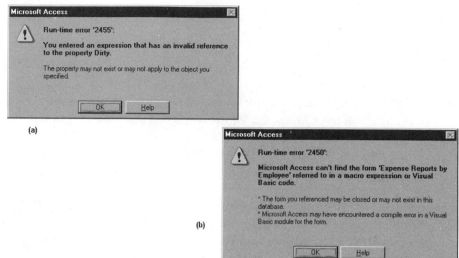

## Referring to a Control

To refer to a control on an open form, you start at the top of the hierarchy with the
Application object, traverse to the Forms collection, step to the specific form,
traverse to the Controls collection, and finally step to the control:

Forms!*formname*.Controls!*controlname*

For example, to refer to the command button named Option1 on the
Switchboard, step along the path first to the Controls collection and then to the
specific control:

Forms!Switchboard.Controls!Option1

However, you can shorten the reference by using defaults. An object can have a
*default collection* that Access assumes when you specify a member of a default
collection without specifying the collection. The Form and Report objects have
the Controls collection as the default collection, so you can omit the reference to
Controls along with the dot and the reference becomes:

Forms!Switchboard!Option1

## Referring to a Control's Properties

To refer to a property of a control, append a dot and the property name to the end of the control reference as follows:

**Forms!*formname*!*controlname*.*propertyname***

For example, to refer to the saved data in the ExpenseCategory text box control on the Expense Categories form, use the Value property:

Forms![Expense Categories]!ExpenseCategory.Value

An object may have a *default property* that Access assumes when you don't explicitly specify a property name. The default property for a text box control is the Value property. Using the defaults, the reference to the saved data in the text box is

Forms![Expense Categories]!ExpenseCategory

> **NOTE**
> The Text property of a text box also refers to the text contained in a text box control. The difference between the Value and Text properties is that the Value property is the value last saved to the field while the Text property is the current value in the active control. If you edited the text box but haven't saved the change, the Text and Value properties contain different values. When you save the record without leaving the text box, the control is updated and the Text and Value properties contain the same data.

To explore the Value and Text properties:

1. Open the Expense Categories form in Form view and change the Expense Category for the first record to Meal.

2. Without saving the record, type each of the following lines and press Enter to evaluate the expression (see Figure 3.11).

    **?Forms![Expense Categories]!ExpenseCategory**

    **?Forms![Expense Categories]!ExpenseCategory.Text**

    **?Forms![Expense Categories]!ExpenseCategory.Value**

**FIGURE 3.11:**

Exploring the Text and
Value properties for a
text box control

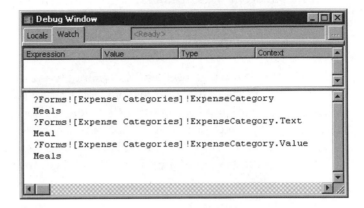

## Properties That Represent Other Objects

Most properties have a text value as their setting; you can display the value in the Immediate window. Some objects have special properties that you can use to refer to another object. For example, a control's Parent property refers to the control's parent object. A label's Parent property refers to the control the label is linked to and a text box's Parent property refers to the form that contains the text box. Table 3.10 (on the CD under Tables\Chapter3.pdf) lists the objects having properties that refer to other objects. (For completeness, this table includes the Me and RecordsetClone properties that are available only in VBA; you learn about these properties in Chapter 10.)

Because these properties refer to an object and not a value, you can't test these references in the Immediate window. For example, you can use the Parent property of a text box to refer to the form itself, but if you type the expression **?Forms![Expense Categories]!ExpenseCategory.Parent** and press Enter, Access displays an error message.

## Referring to a Subform

A common way to display data from two tables is to create forms based on each of the tables, place a subform control on one of the forms, and display the second form within the subform control. In this arrangement, the form containing the subform control is called the *main form* and the form displayed within the subform control is called the *subform*.

To explore the references for a subform, do the following:

1.  Open the Expense Reports by Employee form in Form view. The Name property of the subform control is Employees Subform, so you can refer to the subform control using the reference Forms![Expense Report By Employee]![Employees Subform]. You can evaluate properties of the subform control in the Immediate pane; for example, we'll use the SourceObject property to determine the name of the form displayed in the subform control.

2.  Type **?Forms![Expense Reports by Employee]![Employees Subform].SourceObject** and press Enter. You can refer to the form displayed within the subform control using the Form property of the subform control as follows: Forms![Expense Report By Employee]![Employees Subform].Form. You can evaluate properties of this form in the Immediate pane; for example, we'll evaluate the DefaultView property.

3.  Type **?Forms![Expense Reports by Employee]![Employees Subform].Form.DefaultView** and press Enter. Access displays the integer 2, which represents Datasheet view. You can refer to a control on a form displayed in a subform control by first referring to the form then traversing to the Controls collection and stepping to the specific control. For example, we'll refer to the value in the Total Expenses control on the subform.

4.  Type **?Forms![Expense Reports by Employee]![Employees Subform].Form.Controls![Total Expenses]** and press Enter. Fortunately, you can use defaults to simplify the reference to a control on a subform. The default collection for the subform is the Controls collection, so the first simplification is to omit the reference to the Controls collection.

5.  Type **?Forms![Expense Reports by Employee]![Employees Subform].Form![Total Expenses]** and press Enter. In addition, Access treats the Form property as the default property for the subform control when you are referring to a control on the subform, so you can omit the reference to the Form property.

6.  Type **?Forms![Expense Reports by Employee]![Employees Subform]![Total Expenses]** and press Enter.

The general syntax for referring to a control on a subform is

Forms!*formname*!*subformcontrolname*!*controlname*

Figure 3.12 shows the results of testing these references in the Immediate window.

**FIGURE 3.12:**

Testing references to a subform control and to the form displayed in the subform control in the Immediate pane

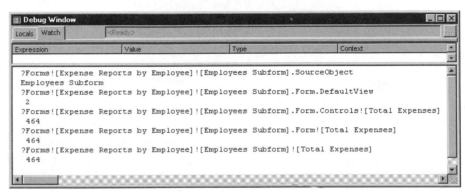

```
?Forms![Expense Reports by Employee]![Employees Subform].SourceObject
Employees Subform
?Forms![Expense Reports by Employee]![Employees Subform].Form.DefaultView
 2
?Forms![Expense Reports by Employee]![Employees Subform].Form.Controls![Total Expenses]
 464
?Forms![Expense Reports by Employee]![Employees Subform].Form![Total Expenses]
 464
?Forms![Expense Reports by Employee]![Employees Subform]![Total Expenses]
 464
```

## Referring to Controls on the Active Form or Report

The references, or *identifiers*, we've been exploring are full path references obtained by starting at the top of the object hierarchy and traversing the path to the object. We've shortened the references by referring to the Application object implicitly and using default collections and default properties. You can also shorten the reference when you want to refer to a control on the active form or the active report. Because Access knows which form is the active form, you can reference the active form implicitly; in other words, you can omit the reference to the active form or report. For example, if Expense Reports By Employee is the active form, you can identify the FirstName text box control using simply

FirstName

or, the Total Expenses control displayed in the Employees Subform control using

[Employees Subform]![Total Expenses]

An identifier that refers to the active form or report implicitly is called the *short syntax* or *unqualified reference,* while an identifier that includes the full hierarchical path (and uses defaults and an implicit reference to the Application object) is called the *fully qualified reference.* Normally, you can use the fully qualified reference without problems, but there are exceptions when you must use the short syntax instead. For example, in Part II we'll see that you must use the short syntax when you use the GoToControl macro action to specify the name of the control on the active object that you want to move the focus to.

You can't test identifiers that refer to the active object when you are working in the Immediate window because the Immediate window is the active window. If you try to test an unqualified reference in the Immediate window, Access displays an error message (see Figure 3.13).

---

**FIGURE 3.13:**

The error message you get when you enter the short reference in the Immediate window

## Using the Screen Object to Refer to the Active Object

Access has a way to uniquely identify the active form, report, or control, or even the control that last had the focus without using the specific names you've given the object. Avoiding specific names is necessary when you create objects that you want to reuse in your application. You can use the properties of the Screen object to identify the active object. For example, to refer to the RecordSource property of the active form, use the reference

    Screen.ActiveForm.RecordSource

and to refer to the Locked property of a control named LastName on the active form, use the reference

    Screen.ActiveForm!LastName.Locked

Additionally, you can refer to the active control on the active form using the Screen object as follows:

Screen.ActiveControl

For example, to refer to the name of the active control, you use the reference

Screen.ActiveControl.Name

As another example, you can refer to the TabIndex property of the control on the active form that previously had the focus using the reference

Screen.PreviousControl.TabIndex

You can use the Screen object in calculated controls on forms, in macros, and in VBA procedures to refer to an object without naming it explicitly.

You can't test references that use the Screen object when you are working in the Immediate window. When you enter a statement in the Immediate window, the Immediate window itself is the active window. If you try to refer to one of the Screen object's properties, such as **?Screen.ActiveControl.Name**, Access displays an error message (see Figure 3.14).

**FIGURE 3.14:**

You can't test references to the Screen object in the Immediate window because the Immediate window is the active window.

## Referring to a Field

Often you need to refer to a field in a table or query. The syntax for the reference depends on whether the table or query is in the underlying record source of an open form.

## Referring to a Field in the Form's Record Source

You can refer to a field in the table or the query that is the record source for the form whether or not the field is bound to a control on the form, using the reference

Forms!*formname*!*fieldname*

For example,

1. Add a DateHired field to the Employees table and enter sample hire dates for each employee. Do not add a control to the Expense Reports by Employee form.

2. Type **?Forms![Expense Reports by Employee]!DateHired** and press Enter. The Debug window displays the sample hire date for the employee.

> **NOTE** By default, when you create a form using a form wizard, the Name property of each control created is the same as the name of the field the control is bound to. Or, when you add a control to a form by dragging a field from the field list, the control inherits the field name. However, the control name and the field name need not be the same.

## Referring to a Field in a Table or Query

When you are designing a query or an SQL statement, you often need to refer to a field in a table or query. In each case, the Field object belongs to the Fields collection of the table or query. The Fields collection is the default collection for tables and queries so you can use the syntax

*tablename*.Fields!*fieldname*  or  *tablename*!*fieldname*

*queryname*.Fields!*fieldname*  or  *queryname*!*fieldname*

However, tables and queries are managed by the Jet database engine, which uses either the dot operator or the bang operator when you step from a collection to one of its members. For example, you can use either Employees!LastName or Employees.LastName to refer to the LastName field in the Employees table.

You can't test table and query references in the Immediate window directly. When you work in the Immediate window, you can use the DLookup() function to test a reference to a field in a table or a query. For example, to look up the first value in the LastName field in the Employees table, type **?DLookup("LastName", "Employees"**) in the Immediate pane and press Enter. Access displays Davolio. See Chapter 4 for more information on the DLookup() function. In Chapter 11 you'll learn how to use the data access objects to retrieve data from tables and queries.

# Using the Expression Builder to Create References

The expressions for referring to properties and controls on forms and subforms can be very complex. Fortunately, Access provides the Expression Builder that helps in creating expressions of any kind, including expressions for query criteria and property settings as well as references for macro and VBA programming. Unfortunately, the Expression Builder is not available in the Immediate pane of the Debug window.

Start the Expression Builder by right-clicking in the location where you want the expression and choosing the Build command from the shortcut menu, or start it by clicking in the location and then clicking the Build button in the toolbar. When you are creating an expression in a property edit box or an argument edit box of a macro action, you can also summon the Expression Builder by clicking the Build button that appears to the right of the edit box. Figure 3.15a shows the Expression Builder dialog. The Expression Builder is context sensitive; the contents displayed in the edit box in the upper pane and in the list boxes in the lower pane depend on where you are when you start the builder.

The lower pane contains three list boxes. The list box on the left contains folders for all of the tables, queries, forms, and reports in your database. There are also folders for built-in functions, constants, operators, common expressions, and custom Visual Basic functions. The set of folders that appears in the first list box depends on where you started the builder; in Figure 3.15, the builder was started from one of the programming windows (a Macro or Module window). Folders that contain other folders have a plus sign; when you click to expand the folder, the plus sign changes to a minus sign. The Forms and Reports folders contain folders for each of your forms and reports and separate folders for the open forms (in the Loaded Forms folder) and for the open reports (in the Loaded Reports folder). If a form with a subform is open when you start the Expression Builder, Access recognizes the relationship between the form and the subform and shows a folder for the subform within the folder for the form. In Figure 3.15b the Forms folder is fully expanded.The figure shows that the Switchboard and the Expense Reports by Employee forms are only open forms and that the builder recognizes the Employees Subform as a subform of the Expense Reports by Employee form.

**FIGURE 3.15:**

Use the Expression Builder to create object references (a). Click the plus sign to expand the Forms folder (b) .

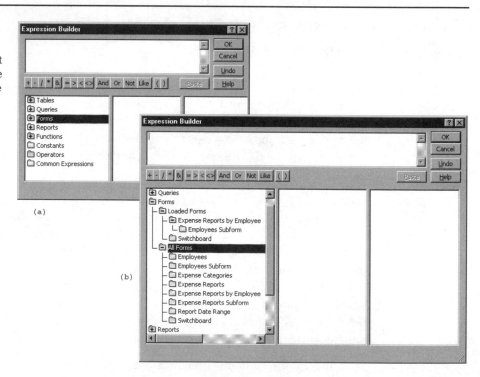

When you select a specific object in the list box on the left, the list box in the center changes to show the objects contained in the selected object. If you select a form, the first item in the center list is <Form> representing the form itself, the second item is <Field List> representing the field list for the table or query that underlies the form, and the remaining items are the controls and sections on the form. When you select an item in the center list box, the list box on the right changes to display the properties of the item you selected. Figure 3.16 shows the choices for the Total Expenses text box on the Employees Subform form. The duplicate names in the center list box correspond to a label and its linked text box, which have the same name on this form.

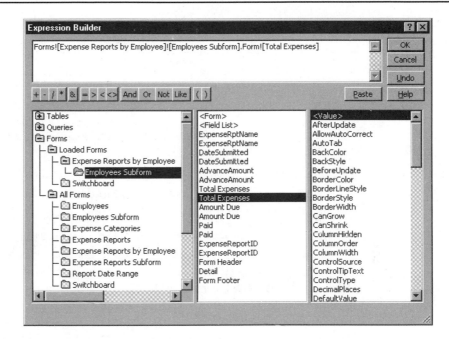

After you have made your choices, click the Paste button. The Expression Builder creates the reference based on your choices and also based on the context where you started the builder and pastes the reference in the edit box in the upper pane. Figure 3.16 shows the qualified reference for the Total Expenses text box (note that the Expression Builder includes the default Form reference). You create expressions in the edit box by pasting references and editing them using the keyboard and the operator buttons in the Builder dialog. In this example, you can edit the reference to delete the Form reference, or you can shorten the reference to the unqualified reference.

To show how the starting location affects the Expression Builder, you can start the builder with the Expense Reports by Employee form as the active object.

1. With the Expense Reports by Employee form in Design view, select the form and click the Build button in the toolbar. Access displays the Choose Builder dialog (see Figure 3.17).

FIGURE 3.17:

The Choose Builder dialog

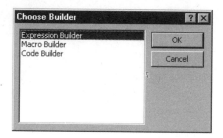

2. Choose the Expression Builder and click OK. The Expression Builder displays a folder for the form as the first folder in the list box on the left and fills the list box in the center with the controls on the form (see Figure 3.18a).

3. Make the choices shown in Figure 3.18b and click the Paste button. The Expression Builder pastes the short reference for the control.

You can also use the Expression Builder to create expressions involving custom functions. Click the Functions folder in the list box on the left to display folders for the built-in functions and for the current database. When you select the current database, the list box in the center displays the standard modules in the current database. When you select a standard module, the list box on the right displays the custom functions stored in the module. When you select a custom function and click the Paste button, the syntax for the function is displayed in the edit box. Figure 3.19 shows the syntax for the IsLoaded function in the GlobalCode standard module in the Expenses database.

**FIGURE 3.18:**

Opening the Expression Builder with a form as the active object (a) allows the Expression Builder to create an unqualified reference (b).

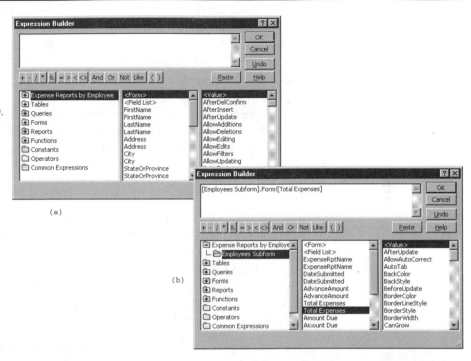

(a)

(b)

**FIGURE 3.19:**

Using the Expression Builder to display the syntax for a custom function

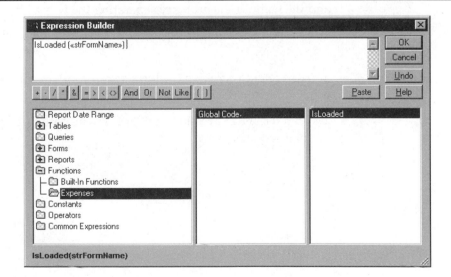

# Summary

This chapter has taken you on an introductory tour of the Access object model that focuses on the objects and properties that are common to both macro and VBA programming. The important points are:

- Objects are related to each other in two ways: they can be similar to other objects or they can contain other objects in a parent-child relationship. The parent-child relationships are used to arrange objects in a hierarchy.

- The Microsoft Access application has two major components each with its own object hierarchy: the Access Application and the Jet database engine.

- In general, to refer to an object in a macro or VBA procedure, you must use a fully qualified reference. To obtain the fully qualified reference you start at the top of the object hierarchy and traverse down to the object, recording the names of all of the collections and objects you step through on the way. In the Access object hierarchy, you use the dot operator to indicate stepping from an object to one of its collections and the exclamation point operator to indicate stepping from a collection to one of its members.

- You can use default collections and properties to shorten references.

- To refer to a property of an object, you include the reference to the object and the name of the property separating the two with the dot operator.

- The properties of the Screen object let you refer to an active object without using its name.

- You can refer to a field in the form's underlying record source even if there is no control on the form that is bound to the field.

- You can use the Expression Builder to create both fully qualified and unqualified references.

# CHAPTER
## FOUR

**4**

# Communicating
# with Forms

- ■ **Relating controls to data**

- ■ **Understanding how controls communicate with each other**

- ■ **Using an unbound control as a variable**

- ■ **Using a combo box to look up information**

- ■ **Synchronizing two forms**

**F**orms play a key role in most Access applications. When you create a fully automated application for others to use, you normally create a custom interface composed entirely of forms and reports. All data entry and data review takes place in forms. Normally, you use the events on forms to trigger the macros and VBA procedures that automate the application. This chapter is devoted to two fundamental form topics: the relationship between a form and the data stored in the database tables and the communication between controls on one or more forms.

The chapter covers several of the more advanced topics in form design including

- Using AutoLookup queries to display information from two or more tables and look up information from one of the tables automatically

- Using calculated query fields

- Using calculated form controls to look up information in other controls on the same form or on another form and to look up information in table and query fields using the DLookup domain aggregate function

- Using unbound form controls to hold temporary values

- Using combo boxes to display records from a table or query as the rows of a mini-datasheet

- Synchronizing two forms by using the built-in form/subform technique

- Synchronizing two forms displayed in separate windows by creating procedures with the Form Wizard

The theme of this chapter is how information is communicated from one element to another element. We'll consider the situations in which Access updates the display automatically and the situations in which you'll need to either update the display interactively or write programs to update the display.

**NOTE**   The examples in this chapter use the Northwind sample database. To follow along, create a fresh copy of Northwind.mdb and save it to the MacroVBAHandbook folder as Northwind_Ch4.mdb. (See this book's Introduction for instructions on setting up this folder.) Open Northwind_Ch4.mdb.

# Relating Forms and Controls to Data

The primary reason for using a relational database to manage information is to minimize the duplication of stored information by storing facts about different subjects in separate tables. If you design a relational database correctly, the only fields that must have duplicated information are the fields that you use to join the tables; the data in all other fields need appear only once. If you change data (such as an address or the spelling of a name), you can make the change in just one place and the changed data is automatically reflected in your queries, forms, and reports. Figure 4.1 shows the tables and the relationships in the Northwind database that comes with Access (we'll be using this sample database throughout the rest of the book). By contrast, in a flat-file database, the same data may appear in fields in many records, for example, each order may duplicate the customer's name and address. In a flat file, changing the data in one record doesn't trigger an automatic change in the other fields with the same data.

**FIGURE 4.1:**

The tables and relationships in the Northwind database

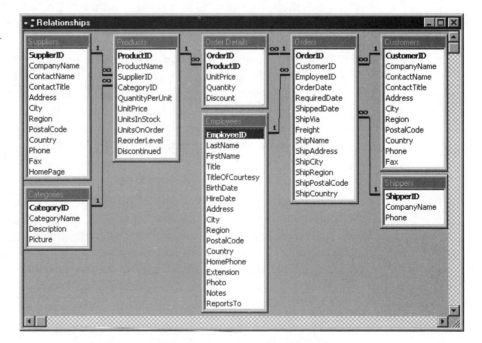

Having data stored in separate tables gives a relational system its power but makes it more difficult when you want to see and use information from different tables simultaneously. Access provides several ways to retrieve data stored in multiple tables.

# What Is a Recordset?

When you open a table, run a stored query, or run an SQL statement, the result is a *recordset* that is created in memory by the Jet database engine. A recordset is the set of records in a table or the set of records produced by running a query or an SQL statement. (Not all queries and SQL statements produce records; recall that the action queries do not produce records when you run them.)

Sometimes the data you want to retrieve is stored in a single table. For example, if you want to review employee addresses, you work with the Employees table. More frequently, the data is stored in several different tables. Suppose you wanted to review the addresses only for the employees who handled orders shipped to Ireland. The shipping information is stored in the Orders tables, so you need to work with fields from both the Employees and the Orders tables. An essential role of the query is to join the data stored in two or more tables. We'll quickly step through creating a new query and review some of the important Access query basics. Figure 4.2a shows the Design view for the new query, named qryEmployeesShipCountry.

**Graphical query design**   When you create a query in query Design view, you add tables with the data you want to retrieve to the upper pane and you drag fields from the tables to the design grid. Add the Orders and Employees tables. Drag ShipCountry from the Orders tables and the name and address fields from the Employees table.

**Relating the tables**   The table relationships you create in the Relationships window are maintained when you add the tables to a query. You can also create new temporary query relationships by modifying the join lines of existing relationships or creating new join lines. Access uses the join lines between fields to match records in the tables and constructs a query row for each set of matching records. The Employees and Orders tables have a one-to-many relationship. The bold join line with the 1 and ∞ symbols at either end indicate that the option to enforce referential integrity has been checked in the Relationships layout.

**Doing calculations**  When creating a query, you can include fields from tables, and you can also create new calculated fields by entering expressions in vacant Field cells in the query design grid. The value in a calculated field is the result of the expression you entered in the Field cell. The value in a calculated field is not saved anywhere in the database and is recalculated each time the query is run. The value in a calculated field is read-only. Replace the LastName and FirstName fields with a calculated field named FullName that concatenates the data in the two fields.

**Limiting and sorting the rows**  You can limit the rows in the query result by entering expressions in the Criteria and Or cells in the query design grid. You can sort the rows by entering sort instructions in the Sort cells. Limit the rows by entering Ireland in the Criteria cell below the Ship-Country field. Sort the FullName calculated field in ascending order.

**Equivalent SQL statements**  When you create a query in query Design view, Access automatically creates a corresponding *SQL statement* that you can observe by changing to SQL view. Figure 4.2b shows the equivalent SQL statement for the qryEmployeesShipCountry query. You can also create queries directly as SQL statements in SQL view. There are queries, called *SQL specific queries*, that can only be created in SQL view and can't be viewed in query Design view. An example of an SQL specific query is the Customers and Suppliers union query in the Northwind database.

**Storing the query**  Whether a query is created in Design view or SQL view, there are two ways to store the query:

- You can save the query as a query object in the database. The saved query is displayed in the Queries pane of the Database window. When you save a query, the Jet database engine analyzes the query and creates an optimized plan for running the query; when you run a saved query, the optimized plan is used.

- You can store the SQL statement as a property setting of another object. For example, if a form is based on a query, you can store the SQL statement as the form's RecordSource property. Each time you open the form, the Jet database engine analyzes the SQL statement, creates an optimized plan on-the-fly, and runs the query.

When you open a table or run a stored query or an SQL statement, Access displays a datasheet as a visual representation of the recordset for your convenience (see Figure 4.3). The recordset itself exists as an object in memory. When you close the datasheet, the recordset ceases to exist.

**FIGURE 4.2:**

The Design view (a) and
the SQL view (b) for a
query

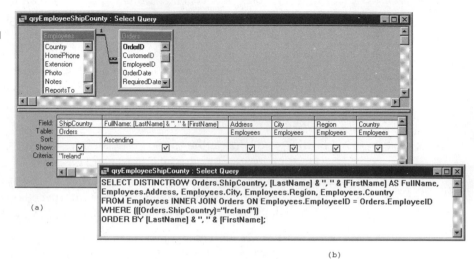

(a)

(b)

**FIGURE 4.3:**

Datasheet view is a
visual representation on
the screen of a recordset
in memory.

| Ship Country | FullName | Address | City | Region | Country |
|---|---|---|---|---|---|
| Ireland | Callahan, Laura | 4726 - 11th Ave. N.E. | Seattle | WA | USA |
| Ireland | Davolio, Nancy | 507 - 20th Ave. E. | Seattle | WA | USA |
| Ireland | Dodsworth, Anne | 7 Houndstooth Rd. | London | | UK |
| Ireland | Dodsworth, Anne | 7 Houndstooth Rd. | London | | UK |
| Ireland | Dodsworth, Anne | 7 Houndstooth Rd. | London | | UK |
| Ireland | Fuller, Andrew | 908 W. Capital Way | Tacoma | WA | USA |
| Ireland | Fuller, Andrew | 908 W. Capital Way | Tacoma | WA | USA |
| Ireland | Fuller, Andrew | 908 W. Capital Way | Tacoma | WA | USA |
| Ireland | King, Robert | Edgeham Hollow | London | | UK |
| Ireland | King, Robert | Edgeham Hollow | London | | UK |
| Ireland | Leverling, Janet | 722 Moss Bay Blvd. | Kirkland | WA | USA |
| Ireland | Leverling, Janet | 722 Moss Bay Blvd. | Kirkland | WA | USA |
| Ireland | Leverling, Janet | 722 Moss Bay Blvd. | Kirkland | WA | USA |

Record: 1 of 19

You can open a table or query directly and display its data in the grid of
Datasheet view. When you open a form or report based on a table or query,
Access sends a request to Jet to open a recordset in memory and then displays the
data from the recordset in the controls of the form or report. When you close the
form or report, the recordset is destroyed automatically. Access handles the
arrangements with Jet and manages the connection between the data and the
form or report for you. When you work interactively you don't need to know the
details of the connection. However, when you automate a database, you often

need to write programs that change the data displayed in a form or report, so it is important that you understand the recordset-to-form or recordset-to-report connection.

## Record Source for a Form or Report

There are two kinds of forms and reports: unbound and bound. When you create a form or report, you use the RecordSource property to specify the source of the data for the form or report. If you leave the RecordSource property blank, the form or report is *unbound;* that is, the form or report has no connection to a recordset.

You can specify the RecordSource property as the name of a table, the name of a saved query, or the name of an SQL statement that produces records; in this case the form or report is *bound* to the specified table, query, or SQL statement, called the *data source* of the form or report. The controls on a bound form or report act like windows into the fields of the recordset. When you open a bound form or report, Jet creates in its memory the recordset corresponding to the specified RecordSource property setting. Figure 4.4 shows the Customers form based on the Customers table. When you open the Customers form Jet creates a recordset based on the Customers table, and the controls on the form display the data in the fields of the first row of the recordset. When you click a navigation button, Access moves to another record and the control displays the data from the corresponding row of the recordset. When you close the form, the recordset ceases to exist.

**FIGURE 4.4:**

When you open the Customers form, Jet opens in memory a recordset based on the Customers table, and the form controls display data from fields of the recordset.

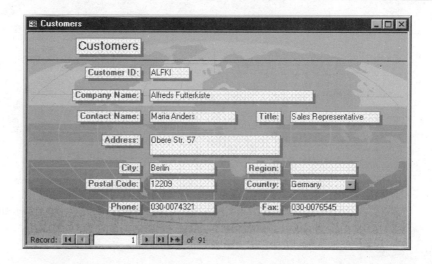

# Control Source for a Control

When you create a data control on a form or report, you use the ControlSource property to specify the source of the control's data. There are two kinds of data controls you can place on a form or report: bound and unbound.

## Bound Controls

If the form or report is bound to a data source, then you can *bind* a control on the form or report to a field in the form's or report's data source, by entering the name of the field in the ControlSource property; the control is called a *bound control* and acts like a window into the specified field. Figure 4.5 depicts the binding of the CompanyName control to the CompanyName field in the form's data source.

**FIGURE 4.5:**

Setting the ControlSource property binds the control to a field in the form's data source.

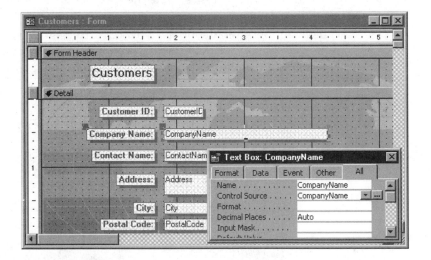

## Unbound Controls

If the ControlSource property is not set to the name of a field in the form's or report's data source, the data control is *unbound*. There are two kinds of unbound controls: either you enter an expression in the ControlSource property, or you leave the property setting blank. When you enter an expression in the ControlSource property, the control is called a *calculated control*. When you open a form with a calculated control, Access automatically uses the expression in the ControlSource property to generate a value and displays the value in the control.

The value displayed in a calculated control is determined by the ControlSource expression, and you can't change the value by typing in the control. By contrast, when you leave the ControlSource property setting blank, there are no editing restrictions; you can enter and edit the value in such controls. Whether the ControlSource property is set to an expression or is left blank, the value displayed in an unbound control exists only while the form is open and ceases to exist when you close the form.

## Controls with Two Sources of Data

The combo box and list box are interesting controls because they can be associated with two different sources of data. A combo box or list box control has a ControlSource property that you can use to specify the source of the control's data. You can bind a combo box or list box to a field in the form's data source or leave the control unbound just like you do with a text box. These controls also have a RowSource property that you use to specify the source of the data displayed in the rows of the list. The source of the data for the rows in the list can be one of four types:

- A table, query, or SQL statement that produces records

- A list of values that you specify

- A list of the field names in a table, query, or SQL statement

- A list of values that you specify using a custom function

When you open a form with a list box or drop down a combo box's list on a form, Access creates the list you specify. If you specify a table, query, or SQL statement, Jet creates a recordset for the list and Access displays fields from the recordset in the rows. This means that a form with a list box or a combo box can be associated with two recordsets: the form's recordset (specified in the form's RecordSource property) and the control's row recordset (specified in the control's RowSource property). For example, in the Orders form shown in Figure 4.6, the subform is associated with two recordsets: the subform's recordset is based on the Order Details Extended query and the Product combo box's row recordset is based on the Products table.

**FIGURE 4.6:**

The combo box control has a dual nature: it can be bound to a field in the form's recordset, and it displays rows from its own row recordset.

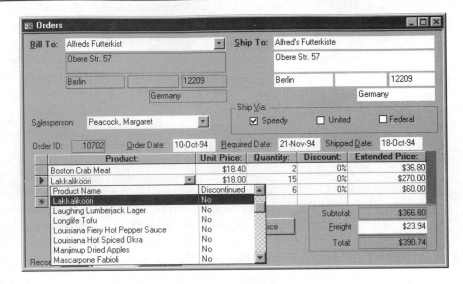

## Controls without a ControlSource Property

There are two kinds of controls without a ControlSource property: controls that aren't associated with data in any way and controls that are associated with data in some way but don't display a specific value. For example, when you place a check box, option button, or toggle button directly on a form, the control has a ControlSource property that you can use to specify the data source for the control. However, when you place one of these controls inside an option group, the control becomes a *subcontrol* and loses its independence. The ControlSource property of each subcontrol is replaced with an OptionValue property, and only the option group control itself has a ControlSource property that you can use to specify the data source for the option group. When you select a checkbox, a toggle button, or an option button in an option group, the value of the option group control equals the OptionValue of the subcontrol you selected (see Figure 4.7).

Another control without a ControlSource property is the Subform/Subreport control. In this case the control doesn't display a value; instead, the Subform/Subreport control displays another form or report. Because the source of the control is another form or report instead of a field, you use the SourceObject property to specify the name of the form or report that the control displays.

**FIGURE 4.7:**

The option button inside an option group passes the value of its Option-Value property to the option group.

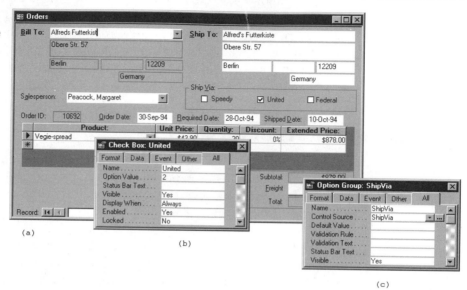

(a)

(b)

(c)

# One Form–One Record Source Model

Access uses the one form–one record source model: a form or a report can have only a single source of data. Through the use of a query or an SQL statement, the form or report can display data from several tables, but only a single table, query, or SQL statement can be entered as the RecordSource property. When the form must be based on data from two tables that are related to each other, you can create a query or an SQL statement for the record source. For example, to display contact information for employees who have customers in Ireland, you can base the form on the qryEmployeesShipCountry query we created earlier.

Depending on the relationship between the tables and how you build the query, the form can appear to be based on two recordsets instead of one. To see how this works, suppose you are creating a form for entering new orders in the Northwind database. The form needs to display customer address information as well as the order information. You can create a query based on the Customers table and the Orders table and then base the form on the query. Because most of your customers are regular customers, you'd like to set up the form so that the customer's address information is entered automatically. You can design the query as an AutoLookup query so as soon as you enter a CustomerID, the query looks up and displays the customer information automatically and you can enter order information into the remaining controls. Because Access fills in the customer information controls automatically and you type the order entry controls yourself, it seems as though the form is based on two data sources: a data source for customer information and a second data source for order information.

## Using AutoLookup Queries

An AutoLookup query is a query based on two tables in a one-to-many relationship that automatically fills in field values from the one table when you enter a value in a join field for a new record. A query is an AutoLookup query when the following four conditions are met:

- Two tables in the query have a one-to-many relationship. The relationship can be a temporary relationship created in the query or can be a permanent relationship created in the Relationship window. (Referential integrity doesn't have to be enforced.)

- The join field on the one side of the relationship has a unique index. This means that the Indexed property for the field is set to Yes (No Duplicates). (The join field does not have to be a primary key.)

- The join field that you add to the query must be from the many side of the relationship. For an AutoLookup query based on the Customers and Orders tables, this means you must include CustomerID from the Orders table and not from the Customers table.

- The value you enter in the join field of a query row must already exist in the join field on the one side. In the example, this means you must enter the CustomerID for an existing customer, that is, you can only enter the CustomerID for a record already saved in the Customers table.

If these conditions are satisfied, when you enter a value in the join field Access automatically looks up the associated values from the table on the one side.

Here are the steps for creating an AutoLookup query:

1. Create a new query based on Customers and Orders.

2.  Drag some fields from Customers to the grid, but do not include CustomerID.

3.  Drag some fields from Orders, including CustomerID.

4.  Switch to Datasheet view and select a customer from the CustomerID combo list. The fields you dragged from the Customers table are filled in automatically.

The Orders form in Northwind uses an AutoLookup query as the record source for the main form. Figure 4.8 shows the automatic lookup of customer information that occurs when you enter a new order. When you select a customer in the Bill To combo box, the customer address information is automatically entered in the Bill To section of the main form. Notice that information is also entered automatically in the Ship To section of the form; the Ship To information is not the result of automatic lookup, however. We'll return to the technique used for the Ship To controls later in this chapter.

**FIGURE 4.8:**

When you select a customer, the AutoLookup query of the main form automatically displays the customer's address in the Bill To section of the form.

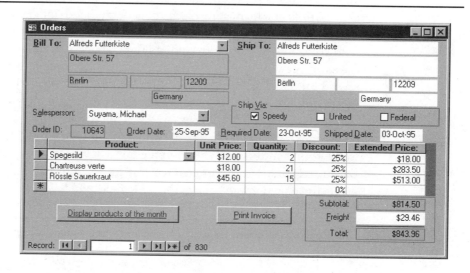

AutoLookup is a valuable technique when you are designing a form for data entry into a table and you want to automatically look up information from another table.

# Communication between Controls and Fields

When you use an AutoLookup query as the record source for a form, the control that is bound to the join field plays a special role: when you change the value in this control, Access automatically changes the values displayed in the controls bound to the Lookup fields. There is communication between the join control and the Lookup controls. However, when the form is not based on an AutoLookup query and all of the controls on a form are bound to table fields from the form's recordset, there is no communication among the controls. For example, each control in the Employees form in Northwind is bound to a field in the Employees table. If you change the value in any one control, such as the FirstName control, no other control is affected.

Binding a control to a table field creates a two-way communication path between the control and the field. When you first display a record in a form, each bound control displays the data stored in its table field. When you enter or change data in a form control, the new or changed data is placed in a control buffer in memory. The control displays the edited value in the buffer, but the table field continues to store the unedited data. When you move to another control of the same record, Access updates the control buffer placing the edited data in a record buffer in memory. While you are editing a record, the form control display the edits while the table continues to store the original record. It is only when you save the record that Access updates the record buffer and saves the new or changed data to the table record. After saving the record, the data displayed in the form controls and stored in the table fields is identical. The table field sends the stored value to the form control and, in the other direction, the form control sends the edited value back to the table field when you save the record.

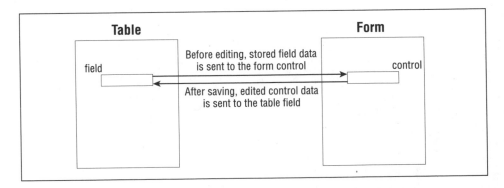

When a control is bound to a table field, you can enter new data or change existing data by typing a value into the control. Each control that is bound to a table field is independent of the other controls on the form.

There are two ways you can arrange for the controls on a form to pass information to each other: by using calculated fields in the form's record source or by using a calculated control on the form.

## Using Calculated Query Fields

A *calculated field* is a query field that displays the result of a calculation instead of displaying a data value stored in a database table. You can create a calculated field by typing an expression in an empty Field cell in the query design grid. You name the calculated field by typing in a name followed by a colon to the left of the expression. (If you don't name the field, Access uses the default name ExprN where N is an integer that Access increments for each calculated field in the query.) The expression can include operators, functions, references to other fields in the query, and references to values that can be returned by other objects, such as values in controls on open forms. For example, suppose you wanted to display the full name of an employee in a single control in a form based on the Employees table.

1. Create a query based on the Employees table and include all of the table fields in the query.

2. Add a calculated query field by entering the expression:

   **FullName: LastName & ", " & FirstName**

   in a new Field cell in the query design grid. Save the query as qryEmployeeField. Figure 4.9a shows the Design view of the query.

3. Use the AutoForm Wizard to create a new form based on the query. Figure 4.9b shows the form (with the controls rearranged).

4. Confirm that you can't change the value in the FullName control.

5. Change the value in the FirstName control and tab to the next control. When you tab out of the changed control, the change is communicated to the FullName control automatically.

6. Close the form and save it as frmEmployeeField.

**FIGURE 4.9:**

Using a calculated field in a query (a) to concatenate two field values. The control bound to the calculated field updates automatically when the field values are changed (b).

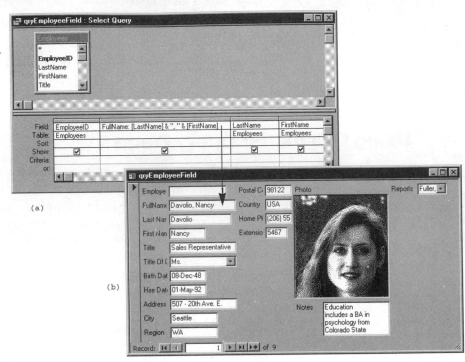

(a)

(b)

# Using Calculated Form Controls

As an alternative to using a calculated query field you can use a calculated form control. A *calculated control* is a control that displays the result of an expression. You enter the expression preceded by an equal sign (=) in the control's ControlSource property. The expression can include operators, functions, references to other controls on the form, references to fields in the form's data source, and references to values that can be returned by other objects, such as values in controls on other open forms. You set the control's Name property to a name that is different from the name of any other control on the form.

1.  Using the AutoForm Wizard, create a new form based on the Employees table.

2.  Place an unbound control on the form named FullName and set the ControlSource property to the expression

    = LastName & ", " & FirstName

3. Confirm that you cannot change the value in the calculated control.

4. Change the value in the FirstName control and tab to the next control. When you tab out of the changed control, the FullName control shows the changed value automatically.

5. Close the form and save it as frmEmployeesControl.

An unbound, calculated control has a one-way communication path to the data in its ControlSource expression. You set the ControlSource property to an expression that "pulls" data into the control. You can use the ControlSource expression to pull in data from three sources:

- from the same form

- from another open form

- from another data source using the DLookup() function

The path is one way because changes you make in the data source are communicated to the calculated control but you can't make changes directly to the calculated control (so the calculated control can't send any changes back to the data source).

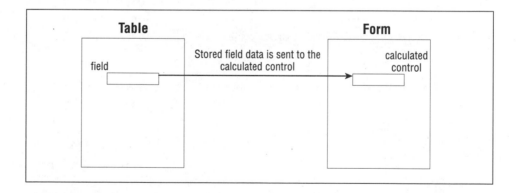

## Pulling Data from the Same Form

You can pull data into an unbound control from other controls on the same form, or from fields in the form's data source, by setting the control's ControlSource property to an expression that refers to these controls or fields. You use the short syntax (the unqualified reference) when you refer to a field or control. When you use the short syntax and refer to a field or control by its name, Access assumes a field in the form's data source or a control on the same form. Table 4.1, which is on the CD under Tables\Chapter4.pdf, lists examples of expressions for calculated controls that pull data from the same form.

**NOTE**    When you use an aggregate function such as Sum(), Avg(), or Count() in an expression for a calculated control, the function can refer only to fields in the form's data source. You must use a field name and not a control name to refer to the field and you can not refer to a calculated control. If you refer to a control that is bound to a field but has a name that is different from the field name, the control displays #Name? to indicate the error. For example, to calculate the sum of values in a control named GrandTotal that is bound to a table field named Amount, refer to the table field using the expression =Sum(Amount) instead of the expression =Sum(GrandTotal). Or, if you refer to a calculated control in an aggregate function, the control displays #Name? to indicate the error.

**Using the Screen Object**    You can use the properties of the Screen object in the ControlSource expression of an unbound control. For example, you can display the number of the current record in an unbound control by setting the control's ControlSource property to

=Screen.ActiveForm.CurrentRecord

When you navigate to a different record, Access automatically recalculates the new values in the unbound controls on the form.

Explore the Screen object as follows:

1.  Place two unbound text boxes on the frmEmployeesControl form with Name and ControlSource properties as follows:

    | Name | ControlSource |
    | --- | --- |
    | txtPrevious | =Screen.PreviousControl |
    | txtActive | =Screen.ActiveControl |

2. When you switch to Form view, the txtActive control displays EmployeeID as the value in the active control. The txtPrevious control displays #Error because there is no control that previously had the focus when you first open the form (see Figure 4.10a).

3. Tab to the next control without making any changes. Neither txtActive nor txtPrevious updates automatically.

4. Force the unbound controls to update by selecting the Refresh command in the Records menu or by pressing the F9 function key (see Figure 4.10b).

5. Edit the LastName control and then tab to the next control. The FullName and the txtPrevious calculated controls update automatically.

**FIGURE 4.10:**

Using properties of the Screen object in calculated controls to pull data from the same form. When you first display the form there is no "previous control" (a). When you tab to another control, you have to force the update of the calculated controls (b).

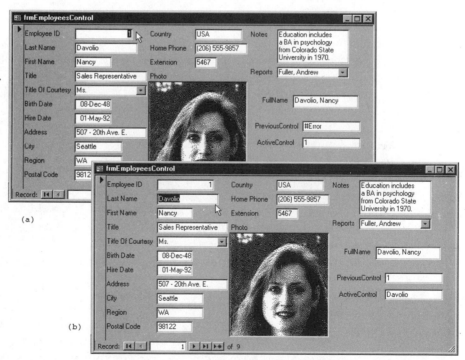

(a)

(b)

**Displaying Current Data**   In this example, the unbound controls don't update automatically unless you edit a control on the form. If you are working interactively, you can force the update of calculated controls by pressing the F9 function key. It takes programming to achieve consistent automatic update behavior. Specifically, you can write a program to refresh the record when you move to a second control whether or not you edited the first control. The trick in creating an updating program is deciding which event should trigger the program. When you move to a different control on the same form, the control you move out of recognizes the Exit and LostFocus events and the control you move to recognizes the Enter and the GotFocus events. You can use any of these events to trigger the program, as long as you are moving among controls on the same form. If you are moving back and forth between controls on two separate forms or on a main form and a subform, the choice of an event is more subtle because the controls may not recognize all of these events. (See Chapter 2 "Getting Started with Objects and Events" for information on when these events are triggered.)

## Displaying Current Data

The data displayed in the active window may not be current for a number of reasons. Here are a few examples:

- When you have two windows open or when you are viewing data in a multi-user environment changes made in one window may not be reflected automatically in the other window.

- The values in calculated controls on a form may not be recalculated automatically until you move to a different record.

- Data in the list box or combo box of a Lookup field from another table is not updated automatically when changes are made to the other table.

There are three ways to update the display: refresh, recalculate, and requery.

**Refresh** updates data in the existing record. To refresh the active window, choose the Refresh command on the Records menu or press the F9 function key. Refresh does not reorder the records, display added records, remove deleted records (a deleted record is indicated with the value #Deleted in each field of the record), or remove records that no longer satisfy specified filter or query criteria. To update the window

*(continued)*

to display added records, remove deleted records, and display only records that meet specified filter or query criteria, you must requery the form.

**Recalculate** calculated controls by pressing the F9 function key.

**Requery** reruns the query on which the object is based or, if the object is based on a table, requery "reruns" the table and displays only the current table records. You can requery the form interactively by pressing Shift+F9.

Note that if the form contains a combo box or a list box that displays rows from a data source other than the form's data source, requerying the data source of the form doesn't requery the data source of the combo box or list box control. You can observe this behavior with the Products and Categories forms in Northwind. The data source of the Products form is the Products table and the data source of the form's Category combo box is an SQL statement based on the Categories table. Open both forms in Form view, add a new category in the Categories form, and save the new record. When you display the Category combo list in Products, the new category is not displayed. Pressing Shift+F9 requeries the data source of the form, but does not requery the data source of the combo box. Pressing F9 refreshes the form and requeries the combo box but does not requery the form. Updating the Products form interactively is a two-step process: press F9 and then press Shift+F9. (Another interactive method for requerying both the form and its combo box and list box controls is to close and reopen the form.)

You can automate the refresh, requery, and recalculate operations with macros and VBA procedures.

## Pulling Data from Another Open Form or an Open Report

You can pull data into an unbound control from controls on another open form or from fields in another form's data source by setting the control's ControlSource property to an expression that refers to these controls or fields. In this case, you use the fully qualified reference because you are referring to controls or fields on another open form. For example, with the Orders and Employees forms in Northwind both open, you can display the employee's full name on the Orders form by placing an unbound control on the Orders form and setting the ControlSource property to

=Forms! Employees!LastName & ", " & Forms! Employees!FirstName

Table 4.2 lists examples of ControlSource expressions that pull data from another open form. In these examples, the unbound control is on the Orders form or its subform and refers to controls on the Customer Orders form in Northwind.

**TABLE 4.2:** ControlSource expressions for referring to another open form

| ControlSource Expression | Description |
|---|---|
| =Forms![Customer Orders]!CustomerID | Displays the value of the CustomerID field in the data source of the Customer Orders form. |
| =Forms![Customer Orders]![Customer Orders Subform1]!OrderDate | Displays the value of the OrderDate control of the current record in the Customer Orders Subform1 subform of the Customer Orders form. |
| =[Orders Subform]!UnitPrice | Displays the value of the UnitPrice control of the current record in the Orders Subform of the active form. The calculated control is located on the main form. |
| =Parent!OrderID | Displays the value of the OrderID control on the parent form of the current subform. The calculated control is located on the subform. |

You can combine references to two open forms in an expression. For example, with the Customers and Employees forms open:

1. Place an unbound control named txtBoth on the Customers form that displays the current record numbers of the two open forms by setting the ControlSource property to

   ="The Customers current record is " &
       Screen.ActiveForm.CurrentRecord & " and the Employees current
       record is " & Forms!Employees.CurrentRecord

2. Browse through the records on the Customers form. Note that the control updates automatically to display the record number of the current form (see Figure 4.11).

FIGURE 4.11:

The calculated control
updates automatically
when you browse the
records of the
Customers form (a) but
not when you browse the
records of the
Employees form (b).

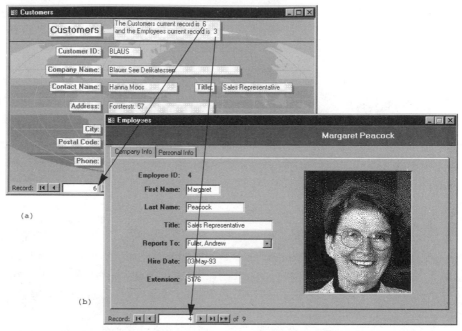

(a)

(b)

3.  Browse through the records on the Employees form and then click back
    into the Customers form. Note that the txtBoth control does not update
    automatically.

4.  Force the recalculation of the controls on the Customers form by moving to
    another record, choosing Refresh from the Records menu, or by pressing F9.

With programming, you can automate the update. You can create a macro or VBA
procedure to update the Customers form when you click into it. When you click
into a form, it recognizes the Activate event, so you could use the Activate event
to trigger the program.

## Pulling Data from Another Data Source Using the DLookup() Function

Sometimes you want a form to look up information that is stored in a table or
query that is not the form's underlying record source. In this case, you can use
the DLookup() function in the ControlSource property of a calculated control to
display data from the other table or query. For example, when you enter a new
product in the Products form, you may want the form to look up and display the

category description from the Categories table. You can create an unbound control on the Products form and set the control's ControlSource property to a DLookup() function that looks up the description directly from the Categories table.

## Domain Aggregate Functions

The DLookup function is an example of a *domain aggregate function*—a built-in Access function that you can use to perform calculations based on the values in a field of a table or query. You can specify criteria to select the set of records in the table or query that you want to use for the calculation. The selection criteria are optional; if you don't specify additional criteria then all of the records in the table or query are used. The table or query is called the *domain*. You must also specify the field that you want the function to work with (instead of specifying a field, you can specify an expression that performs a calculation on values in a field). Once the domain and criteria are specified and the particular field is selected, the function performs a calculation on the values in the field and returns the result of the calculation. The domain aggregate functions are:

**DLookup()**    Returns the value in the specified field.

**DMin(), DMax()**    Return the minimum or maximum value in the specified field.

**DFirst(), DLast()**    Return the value in the specified field from the first or last physical record.

**DAvg()**    Returns the arithmetical average of the values in the specified field.

**DSum()**    Returns the sum of the values in the specified field.

**DStDev(), DStDevP()**    Return the standard deviation or population standard deviation for the specified field.

**DVar(), DVarP()**    Returns the variance or population variance for the specified field.

**DCount()**    Returns the number of records with non-null values in the specified field.

**The Syntax for the DLookup() Function**    You use the DLookup() function to retrieve the value in a particular field in a table or query. You can use the DLookup() function

**In a query**    In a calculated field expression in a Field cell, to specify criteria in a Criteria cell, or in an expression in the Update To cell in an update query.

**In a macro**    In a condition or an action argument.

**In a VBA procedure**    In a condition or method argument.

**In a form or report**    In a calculated control.

The table or query that the function searches is called the *domain*. The DLookup() function takes three arguments. In the simplest case, the first argument is the name of the field in the table or query that holds the data you want to look up, the second argument is the name of the table or query (the domain), and the third argument is the search condition you are using to select the record. The syntax is:

DLookup(*"fieldname"*, *"tablename"* or *"queryname"*, *"search condition"*)

All three arguments must be expressed as strings. If the search condition returns more than one record, the DLookup() function returns the value of the field in the first record that satisfies the condition. If you don't specify a search condition at all, the DLookup() function returns the field value from a random record in the domain.

To see how the DLookup() function works:

1. Place an unbound text box named txtDescription on the Products form and set the ControlSource property to the expression

   =DLookup("Description","Categories","CategoryID = Forms!
       Products!CategoryID")

In this expression, the search condition tells Access to select the record whose CategoryID field matches the value in the form's CategoryID control. The syntax for the search condition is

*fieldname* = Forms!*formname*!*controlname*

where the left side of the search condition is the name of the field in the table or query you are searching and the right side is the fully qualified reference to the form control with the value you are searching for.

2. Browse through the records in the Products form. Note that the Description text box updates automatically (see Figure 4.12).

3. Select a different category from the category combo box. Note that the unbound control does not update automatically.

4. Update the control interactively by choosing the Refresh command from the Records menu or by pressing F9.

**FIGURE 4.12:**

The Category Description control uses the DLookup function to look up the description in the Categories table

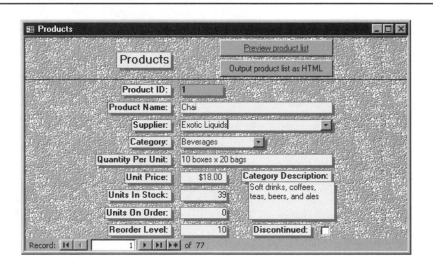

**Using the Domain Aggregate Functions**    You can use any of the domain aggregate functions in the ControlSource expression; for example, use the DSum() function to return the sum of a set of values. All of the domain aggregate functions use the same syntax. In the most general case, the first argument can be either a field name for one of the fields in the domain or an expression based on at least one of the fields. The second argument is the set of records in the table or query (the domain). The third argument is the search condition that restricts the set to a smaller group (the restricted domain). The third argument is optional; if you don't specify a search condition, the function uses the larger set of records (the domain). If no record satisfies the search condition, or if the domain contains no records, the domain aggregate function returns a Null. The syntax is

> DFunction("*fieldname*" or "*expression*", "*tablename*" or "*queryname*", "*search condition*")

or, when there is no search condition to restrict the domain,

> DFunction("*fieldname*" or "*expression*", "*tablename*" or "*queryname*")

Table 4.3 (on the CD under Tables\Chapter4.pdf) gives examples of pulling data from other data sources into an unbound control.

> **NOTE** The domain aggregate functions are actually SQL statements in a different format. You can think of a domain aggregate function as a query that returns a single value. The search condition is equivalent to an SQL WHERE clause without the word WHERE. Every time you use one of these functions, you run a query as an SQL statement. Before running an SQL statement, the Jet engine must analyze the statement to determine the optimal way to execute it. As a result, the domain aggregate functions may be slower than other alternatives for looking up information.

## Using an Unbound Control as a Variable

In programming terminology, a *variable* is a temporary storage location in memory that is used to hold a value. You can think of an unbound form control as a type of variable. The value displayed in an unbound control is not stored anywhere in the database and exists only as long as the form is open; this means that the lifetime of the unbound control variable is the time interval when the form is open. An unbound control is a *global variable* because its value is available to all other queries, forms, and reports in the database.

In Part III we'll see that in VBA programming there are ways to create variables without using form controls as temporary storage containers. However, there are no other ways to create variables in macro programming.

## Pulling and Pushing Data into an Unbound Control

There are two ways to set a value in an unbound control. We've seen that you can use the ControlSource property of an unbound control to "pull" data into the control. You can pull data from controls on other forms or reports, from fields in the form's underlying record source, and from fields in another table or query (using DLookup or another domain aggregate function).

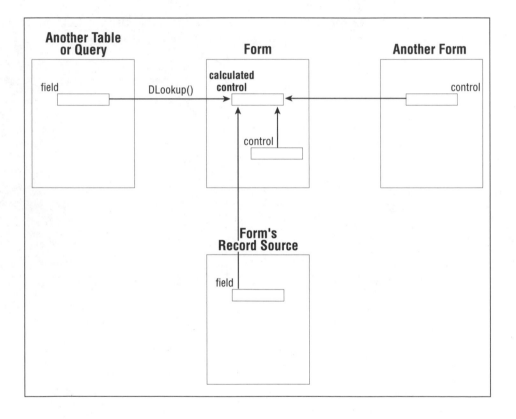

You can also place an unbound control with a blank ControlSource on a form; to set a value in such a control you must perform an action. The action you perform "pushes" data into the unbound control. You can push a value into an unbound control with a blank ControlSource property by typing the value directly from the keyboard, or you can push the value with a macro or VBA procedure.

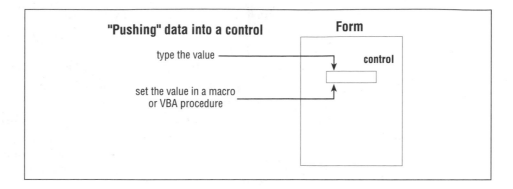

For example, the lookup combo box we placed on the Expense Reports by Employee form in Chapter 1 is an unbound control with a blank ControlSource property; this variable holds the value of the EmployeeID for the customer we want to look up. Choosing a value from the combo list pushes the value into the control. After you choose the value, a VBA procedure synchronizes the form to the value in the combo box variable.

## Using a Global Variables Form

Depending on what you are trying to do, you can place unbound controls as variables directly on the task forms in your application or you can create a separate global variables form to hold some of your global variables. If you need some of the values to be available the next time you start up the application, create a table to store the values that you want to be permanent, or *persistent*. In general, a global variables form may have both unbound controls for transient variables and bound controls for persistent variables. The form must be open whenever the application is open so that the values will be available to other forms and queries. If the user needs to type values directly into some of the controls, the form must be visible, but if the values are pulled into calculated controls or query expressions or are pushed into the controls with macros or VBA procedures, the form can be hidden.

# Saving a Calculated Result to the Database

Sometimes you use an expression to perform a calculation on a form and you want to save the result to the database. For example, suppose you calculate the total revenue for all orders for each customer and you want to save the total in the Customers table. (One of the guidelines of database design is that you don't store calculated values but that you recalculate them each time you need them. However, for summary values it is often convenient and faster to bend this rule and store the values.) When you use a calculated control for the calculation, you use the ControlSource property to hold the expression so you can't also use the ControlSource property to bind the control to a table field. The solution to the problem is to do the calculation in a macro or VBA procedure, instead of using the ControlSource property, and then push the result of the calculation into a bound control using another macro or VBA procedure. We'll see how to push values into bound and unbound controls in Parts II and III.

# Controls with Two Data Sources

In Access a form can have only one table, query, or SQL statement as its record source. The previous sections of the chapter explained techniques for getting around the one data source per form limitation. To summarize: you can look up values in another open form or report and you can use the DLookup function to look up values in any table or query. The result of these techniques is a single value that you can either pull into an unbound control using the ControlSource property or push into either a bound control or an unbound control that has a blank ControlSource property. These techniques are useful when you want to display a single value based on another data source but are less helpful when you want to display several values at the same time. The combo box and list box controls provide an efficient way to look up and display entire rows of values from a second data source.

## Using a Combo Box to Look Up Information

A combo box or a list box has a RowSource property, which you can use to specify a data source for the control that can be different from the data source of the form. This means that you can display records from the table, query, or SQL statement in the RowSource property as rows of a *mini-datasheet*. The RowSource property pulls entire rows of data from a data source into the combo box list.

When you display the combo list, you display the mini-datasheet of the second data source. The combo box also has a ControlSource property and a BoundColumn property. You can use the BoundColumn property of the combo box or list box to specify which column in the mini-datasheet to use for the value of the control. Finally, you can use the ControlSource property to bind the control to a field in the form's data source.

To explore these concepts we'll modify the SupplierID combo box on the Products form to display additional fields from the Suppliers table.

1. Open the Products form in Design view and click the SupplierID combo box. Figure 4.13a shows the properties of the combo box. The ControlSource property setting indicates that the combo box is bound to the SupplierID field in the Products table. The RowSource property setting is an SQL statement that retrieves rows with SupplierID and CompanyName from the Suppliers table. The BoundColumn property setting indicates that the value in the first column of the selected row is held in the combo box. The ColumnWidths property indicates that the SupplierID is hidden and the CompanyName values are displayed in the combo list. In the next step you add columns to the list.

2. Click the Build button at the right of the RowSource property box to display the Query Builder. Drag the ContactName and Phone fields to the design grid (see Figure 4.13b). Close the Query Builder and save the changes.

3. Change the combo box properties to display the additional fields as rows of a mini-datasheet as shown below.

| | |
|---|---|
| ColumnCount | 4 |
| ColumnWidths | 0"; 1.2"; 1"; 0.5" |
| ListWidth | 3.2" |

4. Save the form, switch to Form view, and drop the Supplier combo list (see Figure 4.14). The combo list displays three columns from the Suppliers table as a mini-datasheet.

FIGURE 4.13:

The properties of the
SupplierID combo box
indicate that the first
column is held in the
control and the second
column is displayed in
the combo box list (a).
Add the ContactName
and Phone columns to
the combo box row
source (b)

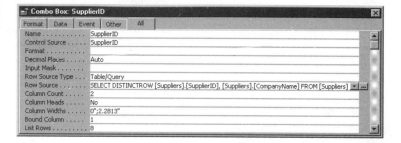

(a)

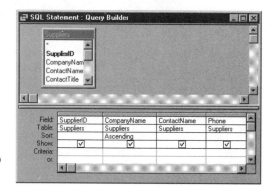

(b)

FIGURE 4.14:

The Products form is
based on the Products
table and the Suppliers
combo box list displays a
mini-datasheet based on
the Suppliers table.

## Using the Column Property to Pull Data from a Combo Box List into an Unbound Control

You can display the value from any column of a combo box (or list box) in another control on a form in one of two ways: you can pull the value in a calculated control using the ControlSource property or you can push the value into a bound or unbound control using a macro or a VBA procedure to set the value of the control. In either case, you use the Column property of the combo box or list box to refer to a specific column or to a specific column and row.

To demonstrate the pulling technique, we'll pull the contact name and phone information into unbound controls on the Products form using the ControlSource property.

1.  Place two unbound text box controls on the Products form with the properties shown below (when you enter the ControlSource expressions, Access encloses each word in square brackets). The Column property is zero-based; this means that Column(0) refers to the first column and so on.

    | Name | ControlSource |
    | --- | --- |
    | txtContactName | =SupplierID.Column(2) |
    | txtPhone | =SupplierID.Column(3) |

2.  Browse through the records. The unbound controls automatically update to display the information passed using the combo box (see Figure 4.15). Any time the value in the combo box changes, the unbound controls on the form that refer to the columns in the combo box pull their values from the combo box. As always, calculated controls are read-only, so you can't modify the pulled values.

You can also refer to the values in one or more columns in an expression. For example, you can concatenate the information in two columns of the mini-datasheet and display the result in a single unbound text box by setting its ControlSource property.

1.  Delete the txtContactName and txtPhone text boxes and place a single unbound text box on the form with the following properties:

    | Name | ControlSource |
    | --- | --- |
    | txtContactInf | =SupplierID.Column(2) & ": " & SupplierID.Column(3) |

2. Switch to Form view and browse the records.

By default, the values you display in the columns of a combo box have the Text data type. Before you can use a value in calculations, you may need to convert the data type from Text to another data type. For example, to use the value as a number you can use one of the five numeric conversion formulas in Table 4.4 (on the CD under Tables\Chapter4.pdf).

**FIGURE 4.15:**

Using unbound controls to pull data from columns displayed in a combo box list

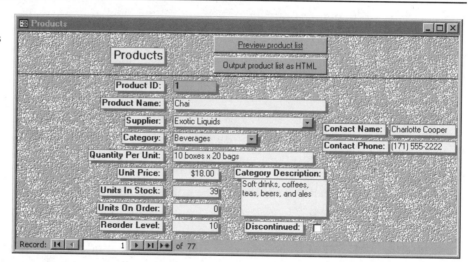

## Pushing Data from a Combo Box List into Bound Controls

Because it is the expression in a control's ControlSource property that pulls the value from a combo box column into the control, the pull method only works for unbound controls. A bound control necessarily has its ControlSource property set to the field it is bound to, so the ControlSource property is not available for pulling values. When you want to fill a bound control with a value from a column in the mini-datasheet of a combo box or list box, you have to create either a macro or VBA procedure to *push* the data into the control. For example, the Bill To combo box on the Orders form in Northwind uses a VBA procedure to push the CustomerName selected in the combo box into the ShipName text box and the address data into the shipping address controls. In Parts II and III, you'll learn how to push data from a combo box list column into a control.

# Relations among Forms

This section focuses on the communication between the controls on two open forms. When two forms with different data sources are open, the forms are related if there is a relationship between their underlying tables or queries. For example, the Customers form and the Orders form are related because their underlying tables, the Customers table and Orders table, have a one-to-many relationship.

## Synchronizing Two Forms

When you open the two related forms, each form displays the first record in its own recordset and the forms are not synchronized. Synchronizing two related forms means displaying related records in both forms. Either form can regulate the synchronization. For example, if the Customers form regulates the synchronization, then synchronizing the forms means filtering the Orders form to display only the orders corresponding to the customer currently displayed in the Customers form. Keeping the forms synchronized means keeping the filter updated so that when you browse to another customer in the Customers form, the Orders form changes automatically to display only the corresponding records. On the other hand, if the Orders form regulates the synchronization, then synchronizing the forms means looking up the customer record corresponding to the order displayed in the Orders form. Keeping the forms synchronized means updating the customer lookup procedure so that when you browse to a different order, the Customers form always displays the related customer.

When two forms are displayed in separate windows, synchronizing the forms and keeping them synchronized is best handled with programming. In Parts II and III you learn synchronization techniques in macro and VBA programming. For now, we'll use the powerful Form Wizard to synchronize two forms.

The Form Wizard uses two different techniques for synchronizing related forms depending on whether the forms are displayed in separate windows or in a single window. When you want to display the forms in two separate windows, the Form Wizard uses VBA procedures to synchronize and resynchronize two related forms. When you display the forms in a separate window as a main form/subform combination, Access handles the synchronization internally and all you (or the Wizard) have to do is set linking properties. The next sections explain the two techniques.

## Using the Form Wizard to Synchronize Two Forms

You can use the Form Wizard to create separate forms for two related data sources and to write the procedures that keep the forms synchronized. To see how the wizard works, we'll use it to create synchronized forms for the Customers table and the Orders table in the Northwind_Ch4 database.

1. Start the Form Wizard by clicking the New button in the Forms pane of the Database window, select the Form Wizard, and click OK.

2. In the first screen you select the fields from the tables or queries that you want on the two forms (see Figure 4.16a). Select a few fields from the Customers table and then select a few fields from the Orders table.

3. The next screen gives you the opportunity to specify which form regulates the synchronization and to specify whether the result is a form with a subform or linked forms in separate windows (see Figure 4.16b). Select the second option, Linked forms.

4. The next screen provides a choice of styles for the forms. Select the Standard style.

**FIGURE 4.16:**

Use the Form Wizard to create and synchronize related forms.

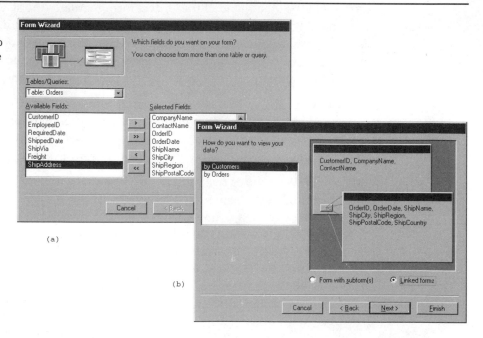

(a)

(b)

5. You use the final screen to specify titles for the linked forms. Enter **CustomersLinked** and **OrdersLinked** for the titles and then click the Finish button.

The Wizard creates the forms and displays the CustomersLinked form shown in Figure 4.17a. The CustomersLinked form regulates the synchronization. When you click the toggle button on the controlling form, the OrdersLinked form opens displaying the corresponding records; the lower left of the form indicates that a filter is being used to select the records (see Figure 4.17b). When you browse to another record on the CustomersLinked form, the filter in the OrdersLinked form is automatically changed and reapplied to keep the records synchronized.

**FIGURE 4.17:**

The Form Wizard creates a toggle button on the form that regulates the synchronization (a). Clicking the button opens the second form and filters its records (b).

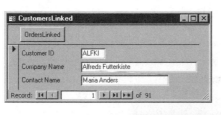

(a)

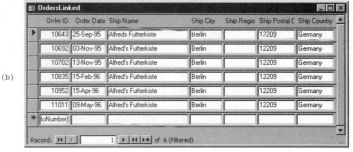

(b)

As long as the OrdersLinked form is open, the toggle button on the Customers-Linked form remains pushed in. When you click the pushed-in toggle button, the OrdersLinked form closes and the toggle button returns to an unpushed state. The Wizard uses at least two events to trigger each program:

**Click event of the toggle button**   When the toggle button is clicked, the OrdersLinked form is either opened or closed depending on the form's state when you click the button. If the OrdersLinked form is already open, clicking the button closes it; if the OrdersLinked form is already closed, clicking the button opens it and also creates and applies a filter to select the related records.

**Current event of the CustomersLinked form**    When you browse to another customer, the form recognizes the Current event. If the OrdersLinked form is closed, nothing happens; but if the OrdersLinked form is open, a new filter is created and applied to the OrdersLinked form to select the correct records.

Figure 4.18 shows the event procedures for the toggle button's Click event and the form's Current event. The Wizard also creates four other procedures that these two event procedures use (a procedure that is used by another procedure is called a *support procedure*). The four procedures are stored in the General section of the form module (see Figure 4.19).

After you work with the two forms, you realize that there are additional events triggering programs. Because the two forms are separate, you can open and close each form independently of the other. You can open the OrdersLinked form by clicking the toggle button on the CustomersLinked form, or you can open it directly from the Database window. Once open, the OrdersLinked form can be closed by clicking the toggle button on the CustomersLinked form, or it can be closed by clicking its default Close button. Whatever the sequence, notice that the toggle button automatically changes in its appearance to reflect the state of the OrdersLinked form. Suppose the CustomersLinked form is open. No matter how you open the OrdersLinked form, the toggle button is pushed in. No matter how you close the OrdersLinked form, the toggle button is pushed out. The behavior of the toggle button means that the wizard must be using events to trigger programs that change the state of the toggle button. The two additional events are the Load and Unload events recognized by the OrdersLinked form. Figure 4.20 shows the event procedures for each of these events, and Figure 4.21 shows the support procedure they use.

Don't be concerned with trying to understand the programs now. In Part III you learn how to write programs like these.

**FIGURE 4.18:**

The Form Wizard creates event procedures for the toggle button's Click event (a) and the controlling form's Current event (b).

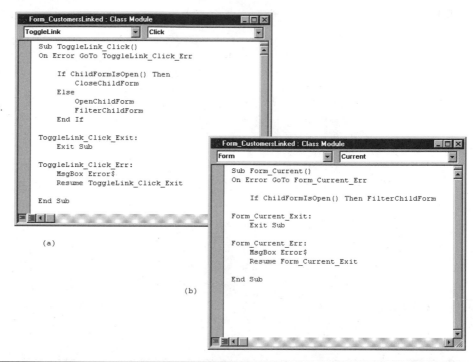

```
Form_CustomersLinked : Class Module
ToggleLink                    Click

Sub ToggleLink_Click()
On Error GoTo ToggleLink_Click_Err

    If ChildFormIsOpen() Then
        CloseChildForm
    Else
        OpenChildForm
        FilterChildForm
    End If

ToggleLink_Click_Exit:
    Exit Sub

ToggleLink_Click_Err:
    MsgBox Error$
    Resume ToggleLink_Click_Exit

End Sub
```

(a)

```
Form_CustomersLinked : Class Module
Form                          Current

Sub Form_Current()
On Error GoTo Form_Current_Err

    If ChildFormIsOpen() Then FilterChildForm

Form_Current_Exit:
    Exit Sub

Form_Current_Err:
    MsgBox Error$
    Resume Form_Current_Exit

End Sub
```

(b)

**FIGURE 4.19:**

The Form Wizard creates four support procedures that are used by the two event procedures.

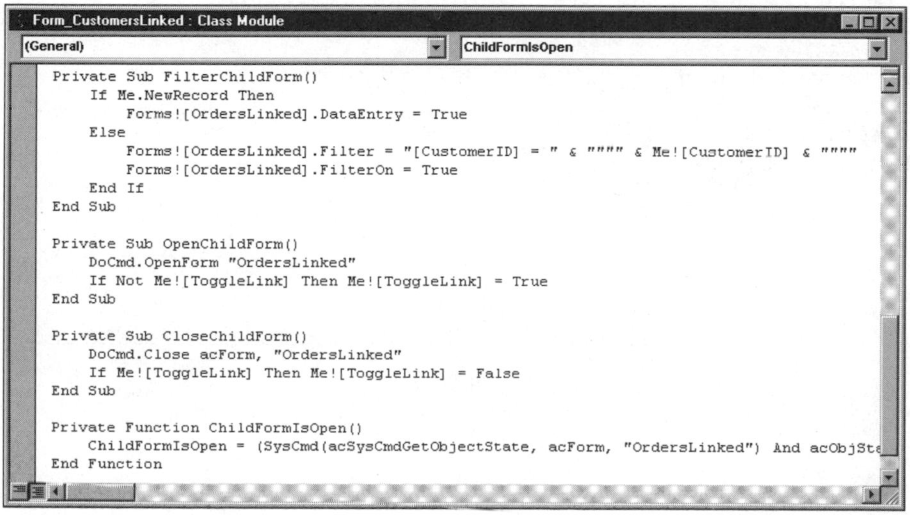

```
Form_CustomersLinked : Class Module
(General)                     ChildFormIsOpen

Private Sub FilterChildForm()
    If Me.NewRecord Then
        Forms![OrdersLinked].DataEntry = True
    Else
        Forms![OrdersLinked].Filter = "[CustomerID] = " & """" & Me![CustomerID] & """"
        Forms![OrdersLinked].FilterOn = True
    End If
End Sub

Private Sub OpenChildForm()
    DoCmd.OpenForm "OrdersLinked"
    If Not Me![ToggleLink] Then Me![ToggleLink] = True
End Sub

Private Sub CloseChildForm()
    DoCmd.Close acForm, "OrdersLinked"
    If Me![ToggleLink] Then Me![ToggleLink] = False
End Sub

Private Function ChildFormIsOpen()
    ChildFormIsOpen = (SysCmd(acSysCmdGetObjectState, acForm, "OrdersLinked") And acObjSta
End Function
```

**FIGURE 4.20:**

The wizard creates event procedures for the Load event (a) and the Unload event (b).

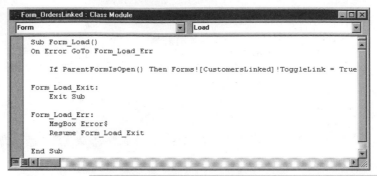

```
Form_OrdersLinked : Class Module
Form                              Load
Sub Form_Load()
On Error GoTo Form_Load_Err

    If ParentFormIsOpen() Then Forms![CustomersLinked]!ToggleLink = True

Form_Load_Exit:
    Exit Sub

Form_Load_Err:
    MsgBox Error$
    Resume Form_Load_Exit

End Sub
```

(a)

(b)

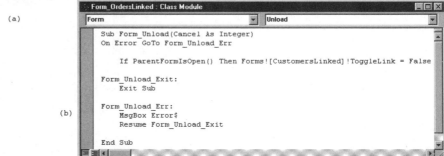

```
Form_OrdersLinked : Class Module
Form                              Unload
Sub Form_Unload(Cancel As Integer)
On Error GoTo Form_Unload_Err

    If ParentFormIsOpen() Then Forms![CustomersLinked]!ToggleLink = False

Form_Unload_Exit:
    Exit Sub

Form_Unload_Err:
    MsgBox Error$
    Resume Form_Unload_Exit

End Sub
```

**FIGURE 4.21:**

The wizard creates a support procedure used by both event procedures that keep the toggle button in synch.

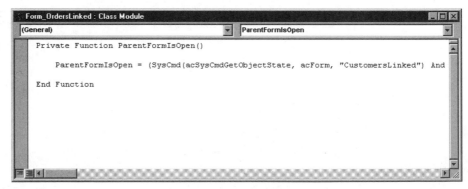

```
Form_OrdersLinked : Class Module
(General)                         ParentFormIsOpen
Private Function ParentFormIsOpen()

    ParentFormIsOpen = (SysCmd(acSysCmdGetObjectState, acForm, "CustomersLinked") And

End Function
```

# Using the Form/Subform Technique to Synchronize Two Forms

You can use the built-in form/subform technique to display two forms in a single window. When you use the built-in form/subform technique to display information in related forms, Access handles the synchronization and resynchronization for you. This section describes how the form/subform technique works to give you greater insight into the subform/subreport control and its role in the synchronization process.

## Properties of the Subform Control

Access provides the subform/subreport control as a way to synchronize two forms (or two reports or a report and a form) and keep their records synchronized. One of the forms becomes the main form when you place a subform control on it. The three crucial properties of the subform control are the SourceObject, LinkChildFields, and LinkMasterFields. You connect the second form to the first when you set the SourceObject property of the subform control to the name of the second form; the second form then becomes a subform. When you open the main form in Form view, the subform control displays the second form. If you leave blank the two record-linking properties, LinkChildFields and LinkMasterFields, the forms are connected but their records aren't linked and you can browse their records independently. In fact, the underlying tables or queries for the two forms do not have to be related in order to display the forms in the single window of the form/subform arrangement.

If the data sources of the two forms are related, you can link the records by setting the subform control's two record-linking properties to the matching fields. If the forms are related on multiple fields, enter the field names separated by semicolons into the property boxes; make sure you enter matching fields in corresponding order. You can use the Subform/Subreport Linker to help in setting the record-linking properties. To start the Linker, open the main form in Design view, display the property sheet for the subform control, and then click the Build button to the right of either of the record-linking properties. Figure 4.22 shows the Subform Field Linker dialog where you specify the linking fields. The record-linking fields do not have to be included as controls on either the main form or the subform. After you set the two record-linking properties, the records are linked (synchronized) and remain synchronized. As you browse through the records of the main form, Access displays the synchronized records in the second form.

**FIGURE 4.22:**

Use the Subform/Subreport Linker to set record-linking properties.

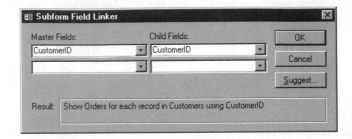

In the form/subform technique, all you need to do is set the subform control properties and Access automatically keeps the forms synchronized. Under certain conditions, Access even sets the subform control properties for you. If you create the subform or subreport by dragging a form or report from the Database window onto another form or report, Access automatically displays the dragged object within a subform/subreport control and sets the record-linking properties if the following two conditions are met:

- The main form or report is based on a table with a primary key. Access sets the LinkMasterFields property to the primary key field(s).

- The subform or subreport is based on a query or a table that contains a field (or fields) with the same name and the same or a compatible data type as the primary key of the table underlying the main form. Access sets the LinkChildFields property to the identically named fields from the subform's or subreport's data source.

You can use the form/subform technique to display a one-to-many relationship by basing the main form on the one side and the subform on the many side. For example, the Customers and Orders tables have a one-to-many relationship. With the main form based on the Customers table and a subform based on the Orders table, the form/subform displays all of the orders for a customer. Figure 4.23 shows the CustomerswithOrders form/subform that the Form Wizard creates.

## Using the Form Wizard to Synchronize Two Subforms

The Form Wizard is capable of creating both a simple form/subform combination such as the form shown in Figure 4.23 and a complex combination of a main form with a synchronized subform and a second subform synchronized to the

**FIGURE 4.23:**

You can use the form/subform to display a one-to-many relationship.

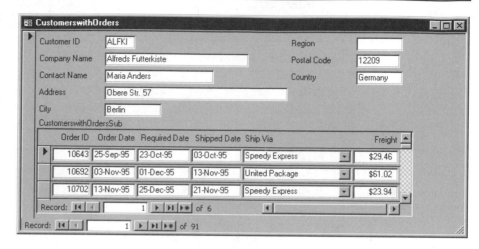

first subform. The Customer Orders form in Northwind demonstrates the wizard's power. Figure 4.24 shows the Customer Orders form with two synchronized subforms; the arrangement is called a one-to-many-to-many form.

**FIGURE 4.24:**

The one-to-many-to-many form

| Customer Orders |
|---|

Company Name **Alfreds Futterkiste**     Country **Germany**

Click an order...

| Order ID | Order Date | Required Date | Shipped Date |
|---|---|---|---|
| 10643 | 25-Sep-95 | 23-Oct-95 | 03-Oct-95 |
| 10692 | 03-Nov-95 | 01-Dec-95 | 13-Nov-95 |
| 10702 | 13-Nov-95 | 25-Dec-95 | 21-Nov-95 |
| 10835 | 15-Feb-96 | 14-Mar-96 | 21-Feb-96 |

...to see order details.

| Product Name | Unit Price | Quantity | Discount | Extended Price |
|---|---|---|---|---|
| Spegesild | $12.00 | 2 | 25% | $18.00 |
| Chartreuse verte | $18.00 | 21 | 25% | $283.50 |
| Rössle Sauerkraut | $45.60 | 15 | 25% | $513.00 |

Record: 1 of 91

The main form displays a customer record and the first subform displays the orders for the customer. This much is ordinary and uses the record-linking properties of the subform control to synchronize the records in the Customers table and the Orders table. Things get interesting when we look at the second subform. The second subform displays the details of an order. The second subform is based on the Order Details Extended query. Each record in this query corresponds to a product purchased in an order. The second subform is linked to the first subform using the OrderID as the matching field in both recordsets. Figure 4.25 shows the linking property settings set in the subform control for the second subform; these settings match the OrderID in the second subform to the OrderID in the first subform.

**FIGURE 4.25:**

The linking properties in the second subform control synchronize the second subform to the first subform.

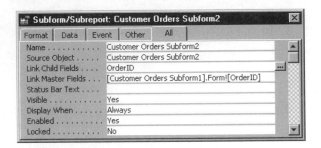

Note that the identifier for the LinkMasterFields property (shown below) uses the Form property of the subform control to refer to the form displayed inside the subform control. (The OrderID field in the second subform is not displayed in a control but you can still use the values in the field for linking.) When you select an order in the first subform, the second subform is synchronized to display the products purchased in the order.

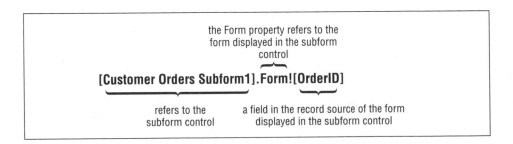

If you try to create this form without using the Form Wizard, you find that the second subform doesn't update automatically. When you select a different order, the second subform continues to display the records for the previous order. You can update the second subform interactively, by selecting an order in the second subform, clicking into a control on the main form, and then pressing F9. Note that selecting the Refresh command in the Records menu does not force the update of the second subform.

If you use the Form Wizard to create the form, the wizard handles updating for you. To observe how the wizard automates the synchronization

1.  Open the Customer Orders form in Design view. The main form regulates the synchronization with the first subform. The property sheet for the first subform control indicates the record linking based on the CustomerID values between the main form and the Customer Orders Subform1 form (see Figure 4.26a). The property sheet for the second subform control shown in Figure 4.26b indicates the record linking between the two subforms based on the OrderID values.

2.  Open the first subform in Design view. The property sheet for this form indicates that the Form Wizard has created an event procedure that is triggered by the form's Current event. (A form recognizes the Current event after the focus leaves one record and before the focus moves to another. A form also recognizes the Current event when the form is first opened and before the first record is displayed and whenever you requery the form.)

3.  To view the VBA procedure, click the Build button at the right of the OnCurrent property box (see Figure 4.27). In Part III you'll learn the meaning of each line in the procedure; for now, note the line that includes Requery is the instruction to requery the second subform. Whenever you click a different record in the first subform, this procedure runs and requeries the second subform.

**FIGURE 4.26:**

The record-linking properties for the linking between the main form and the first subform (a) and between the first and the second subforms (b)

(a)

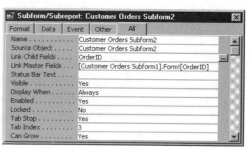

(b)

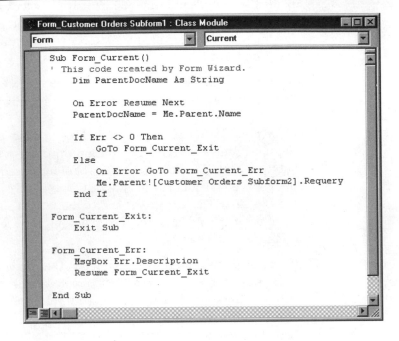

**FIGURE 4.27:**

The Form Wizard creates an event procedure for the Current event of the second subform that keeps the second subform in synch with the first subform.

```
Form_Customer Orders Subform1 : Class Module
Form                              Current

Sub Form_Current()
' This code created by Form Wizard.
    Dim ParentDocName As String

    On Error Resume Next
    ParentDocName = Me.Parent.Name

    If Err <> 0 Then
        GoTo Form_Current_Exit
    Else
        On Error GoTo Form_Current_Err
        Me.Parent![Customer Orders Subform2].Requery
    End If

Form_Current_Exit:
    Exit Sub

Form_Current_Err:
    MsgBox Err.Description
    Resume Form_Current_Exit

End Sub
```

# Summary

In most automated Access applications, the interface consists entirely of forms and reports. In automating a database, you write macros or VBA procedures that depend on understanding the connection between forms and the data in the tables and how forms can communicate information to each other.

- The setting of the RecordSource property of a form or report indicates whether the form or report is connected to a table or query. If the RecordSource property is blank, the form or report is unbound; otherwise the setting may be the name of a table or stored query or an SQL statement and the form or report is bound to the underlying data source.

- If the form has an AutoLookup query based on two tables in a one-to-many relationship as its record source, you can use the form to automatically look up information from the "one" table when you enter a value in a join field.

- A form or report has a single record source, but there are several ways that the form can obtain information from other data sources:

  **Calculated controls**   You can use calculated controls to look up information in another open form or report. You can use the DLookup function in a ControlSource expression of a calculated control to look up information in any table or query. ControlSource property expressions pull data into the control.

  **Programming**   You can use programming to look up or calculate a value and then push the value into an unbound control (if the control has a blank ControlSource property) of a bound control.

  **Combo box or list box control**   A combo box or list box control can be connected to two different tables or queries: the control can be bound to a field in the form's underlying record source and the control can display records from another data source. You can use these controls to pass values from another table or query into the form.

- When the form doesn't update automatically to display the most current data, programming is necessary to automate the update.

- When forms are based on related tables or queries, you can use the built-in linking properties of subform control to keep the forms synchronized in a main form/subform arrangement.

- Programming is required to synchronize related forms when the forms are displayed in separate windows. The Form Wizard uses VBA programming for the synchronization.

This chapter completes the preliminary topics essential for both macro and VBA programming. You are now ready to learn how to write the programs you have been observing in these chapters. If you haven't programmed before and you want to learn the fastest way to start automating a database, proceed on with macro programming in Part II. If you have some experience in another programming language, have already studied Access macros, or just want to move directly to Access VBA, you can skip Part II for now and start in on Part III.

# PART II

# Macro Programming

# Macro Basics

- Working in the macro Design window

- Using macro actions to duplicate your interactive steps

- Running a macro

- Using macros for simple forms navigation

- Making decisions by testing conditions

- Repeating actions in a macro loop

**A** *macro* is an instruction or a sequence of instructions that is carried out as a unit. In Access, these instructions are called *actions.* In this chapter, you learn to use specialized cells in a macro Design window, called *macrosheets*, to enter each component of the macro. Typically a macrosheet cell displays a list of the acceptable choices for the cell. This feature makes it easier to create macros by saving you the chore of memorizing or looking up the choices. Between the combo boxes and the structured design of the macrosheet, most of the details of macro programming syntax are taken care of. After creating a macro, you'll need to test it and arrange for Access to run the macro.

The fundamental goal of macro programming is to write programs that duplicate the steps you take when you work interactively with a database. You can design most macros by observing the interactive steps that you take to accomplish a task and then translating the steps into macro instructions. In this chapter, you learn how to control which sets of instructions are executed or skipped, how to design a macro that can make a choice between two alternatives, and how to design a macro that repeats actions.

The purpose of this chapter is to provide basic macro programming tools. Here, you will create only a few simple macros. In the remaining chapters of Part II, you learn how to use the basic tools to write macros that display custom error messages, that automate navigation among forms, records, and controls, that maintain data, and that work with groups of records.

# The Macro Window

Macros are created in a specially designed Macro window. You can open a new Macro window from the Macro tab of the Database window by clicking the New button or by clicking the down arrow of the New Object button on the toolbar and then choosing Macro. Access displays the macrosheet, shown in Figure 5.1.

In its default settings, Access displays only two of the four columns in the upper pane of the Macro window. You can change the default to display all four columns by checking the Names Column and the Conditions Column check boxes in the View pane of the Options dialog, as shown in Figure 5.2. (To see the Options dialog, select Tools ➤ Options.) If you change the defaults, new macrosheets display the four columns shown in Figure 5.3.

**FIGURE 5.1:**

The Macro window, showing Action and Comment columns

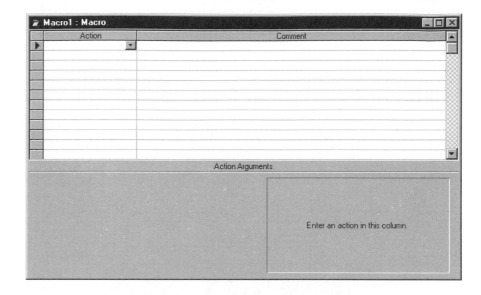

**FIGURE 5.2:**

Changing the Macro window defaults in the Options dialog box

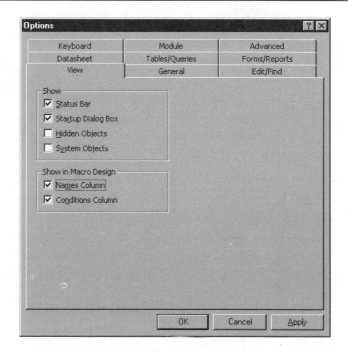

**FIGURE 5.3:**

The Macro window, showing Macro Name, Condition, Action, and Comments columns

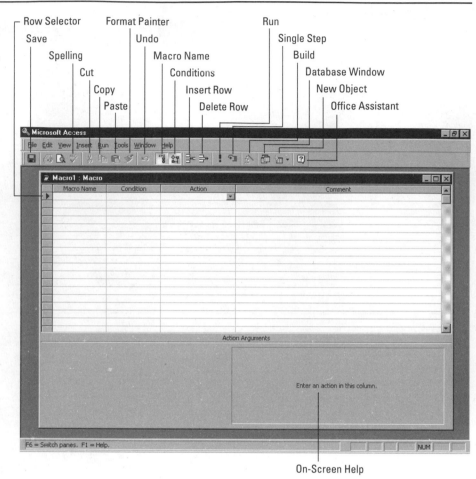

The upper pane of the Macro window contains specialized cells in four columns. Typically, you store several macros in a macrosheet and enter the names of individual macros in the Macro Name column. The Condition column is where you enter test conditions to control whether a part of the macro runs. The Action column is where you select macro actions by choosing from the combo box list displayed when you click the drop-down arrow. The Comments column is for recording the purpose or reason for the action and additional helpful comments (Access ignores the Comments column). The Comments column is a good place to describe what the macro accomplishes and when the macro should be run.

# The Macro Toolbar

The Macro toolbar, shown below, contains familiar editing tools for creating and editing macros, including the Save, Cut, Copy, Paste, Undo, Insert Row, and Delete Row buttons. Additionally, the toolbar contains buttons to show or hide the Macro Names and Condition columns, a Run button to run the first macro listed in the macrosheet, a Single Step button to help in troubleshooting macros, and a Build button to help in creating expressions. At the right end of the toolbar are buttons to display the Database window, to create a new object, and to obtain help from the Office Assistant.

The Run command in the Run menu and the Run button on the Macro Design toolbar run only the first macro listed in the macrosheet. Because a macrosheet normally holds several macros, you'll want convenient ways to select and run any macro in a macrosheet. While you are creating and testing new macros, it is often convenient to run them when the Database window or a Form is the active window as well as when the Macro window is the active window. You can customize the command bars for any view by adding a Run Macro command that allows you to run any macro stored in the macrosheet. We'll add a Run Macro button to the Macro Design, Form view, and the Database toolbars.

1. Right-click the Macro Design menu bar or toolbar and select the Customize command from the shortcut menu. In the Toolbars tab, click the Database and Form View check boxes (see Figure 5.4).

2. Click the Commands tab in the Customize dialog. With File selected in the Categories list box on the left, scroll down the Commands list box on the right to display the Run Macro command. Click the Run Macro command, drag the command to each of the menu bars and drop it just to the left of the Office Assistant toolbar button (see Figure 5.5).

3. Click the Toolbars tab in the Customize dialog, clear the Form View and Database toolbar checkboxes to hide the toolbars, and then click Close to close the dialog.

### FIGURE 5.4:

Customizing the
Database, Form
View, and Macro
Design toolbars

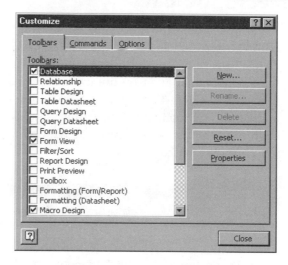

### FIGURE 5.5:

Adding the Run Macro
command to the toolbars

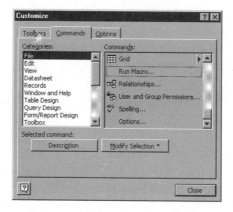

4. Click the new Run Macro button in the toolbar. The Run Macro dialog is
displayed (see Figure 5.6). Type the name of any macro you want to run, or
select it from the drop-down list.

### FIGURE 5.6:

You can type or select
the name of any macro
in the Run Macro dialog.

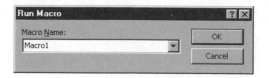

# Macro Actions

In macro programming, you create a macro as a set of instructions. Each instruction is a row in the macrosheet. For each instruction you select the action you want to perform from a list of 49 possible *macro actions*. Most of the macro actions duplicate the steps you take when you work interactively with Access by choosing a menu command, using the mouse to select and manipulate objects, or entering keystrokes as shortcut commands. Many of the macro actions are exactly equivalent to choosing menu commands such as the ApplyFilter, Close, and Save actions. There is a RunCommand action that you can use to run almost any built-in command. Many of the actions mimic manual user interactions, such as the SelectObject action to select a specified database window object and the Open-Form action to open a specified form. The SendKeys action sends keystrokes as if you had typed them in. There are other actions that provide capabilities not available interactively, such as the Beep action to beep and the Echo action to turn off screen updating while the macro runs. Table 5.1 (on the CD under Tables\Chapter5.pdf) shows the macro actions grouped by the kinds of tasks they perform.

## Macro Arguments

Most macro actions require additional information before Access can carry them out. Each piece of additional information, called an *action argument*, varies with the action and may include, for example, the name of the object you take the action on, or the criteria for selecting records to take action on.

Before you can decide on the appropriate macro action, you need to be familiar with the capabilities of the macro actions. Table A.1 in Appendix A provides an alphabetical listing of the macro actions together with their arguments and guidance on selecting the appropriate action. (Appendix A is on the CD under Appendixes\AppendixA.pdf.) Online Help provides in-depth information about macro actions and arguments. To get help on a particular macro action, choose the Microsoft Access Help Topics command from the Help menu, click the Index tab, and then enter the macro action (see Figure 5.7).

You can also get both on-screen and context-sensitive Help while you are creating macros. When you select a macro action from the combo list in the Action column, the on-screen help box in the lower pane displays information about the action. To get additional help, press F1 or click the Office Assistant button in the

**FIGURE 5.7:**

Getting help for the
MsgBox action using
Microsoft Access Help

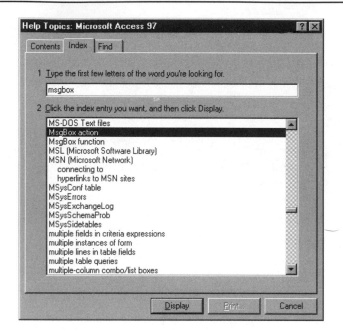

toolbar. Online Help displays detailed information about the action and its arguments; for example, Figure 5.8 shows help for the OpenForm action.

The action arguments for the OpenForm action are:

- Form Name to specify the name of the form to be opened

- View to specify whether to open the form in Form, Design, Print Preview, or Datasheet view

- Filter Name or the Where Condition to specify whether you want to restrict the records that the form displays

- Data Mode to specify whether you want to allow adding new records without the ability to edit existing records, editing existing and new records, or viewing only

- Window Mode to specify whether the form is hidden, minimized, behaves like a dialog box, or has the mode set in its property sheet

FIGURE 5.8:

Online Help for the
OpenForm action

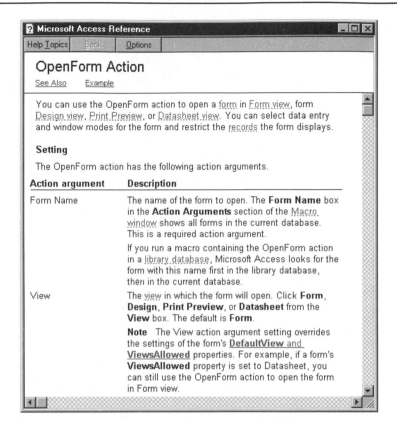

**FIGURE 5.8:**

Online Help for the
OpenForm action

After you enter a macro action in an Action cell by typing or selecting the name from the list, the lower pane of the macrosheet changes to display the action arguments for the selected macro action. When you click an argument box, the on-screen help box changes to display information for the selected argument. In many cases you can set the value for an argument by selecting from a combo box list. When an argument can be set to an expression, such as the Where Condition action argument for the OpenForm action, a Build button appears to the right of the argument box; clicking the Build button displays the Expression Builder. Access automatically fills in default values for some of the required action arguments; when a default value is not entered for an argument, the on-screen help box indicates whether the argument is required.

To explore these concepts,

1.  Display a new macrosheet and select the OpenForm action in the first Action cell. Figure 5.9 shows the action arguments for the OpenForm action. Note that the View, Data Mode, and Window Mode arguments are required and have default values.

2.  Click the View, Data Mode, and Window Mode arguments and note the choices in the combo lists. The Form Name argument is also a required argument although a default value is not displayed.

3.  Click the Form Name argument. Click the down-arrow to display the list of all of the existing forms in the database. You can select a form from the list or enter the name of a new form you haven't created yet. If you enter the name of a new form, you must create and save the form before running the macro action.

4.  Click the Where Condition argument. The Build button appears at the right of the argument box. Clicking the Build button displays the Expression Builder.

**FIGURE 5.9:**

Action arguments for the OpenForm action

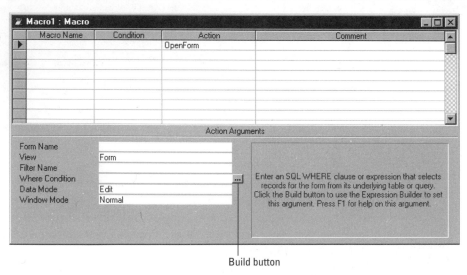

Build button

The rest of this section describes a few of the macro actions that are particularly important, including

- SetValue action for performing calculations and for setting values and properties on forms and reports
- RunCommand action for running a built-in command
- MsgBox action for displaying a custom message box
- SendKeys action for sending keystrokes
- RepaintObject and Requery actions for displaying current data

## Setting Values

A common task in macro programming is to change a value for a form or report. You may want to change

- a data value in the underlying record source of the form or report,
- a property setting for a form or report or one of its controls or sections, or
- a value that you want to calculate and store in an unbound control on a form (but not a calculated control).

You use the SetValue macro action to make these changes. The SetValue action has two arguments: Item (what you set) and Expression (what you set it to).

**NOTE** In macro programming, there are two ways you can change data stored in a table field: you can use the SetValue action to change a single data value, or you can use the OpenQuery or RunSQL macro actions to run an update query. The SetValue action applies only to forms and reports; you can't use the SetValue action to set the value of a field in a table or query directly. To change the value in a table field using the SetValue action, you must include the field in the record source for a form or report and run the action on the form or report.

## The Item Argument

The Item argument is the reference to the field, control, or property that you want to set. The form or report must be open. Normally you use the fully qualified reference for the item you want to set. Here are some examples:

| Item | Description |
| --- | --- |
| Forms!Categories.Caption | Sets or changes the Caption property of the Categories form. |
| Forms!Categories!Description | Sets or changes the data in the Description control on the form or the data in the Description field in the form's record source when there is no control bound to the field. |
| Reports!Invoice.Section(3).Visible | Sets or changes the Visible property of the page header section— Section(3) refers to a page header section—of the Invoice report. |
| Forms!Customers!LastYearPurchases | Sets the value of an unbound control on the Customers form that is not a calculated control; that is, the control has a blank ControlSource property setting. |

**NOTE** When you type the reference in the Item argument, you don't need to enclose the object or property name in square brackets if the name includes no spaces or reserved symbols. When you tab out of the argument box, Access automatically encloses each part of the reference in square brackets. For example, Access changes Forms!Categories .Caption to [Forms]![Categories].[Caption].

If the macro containing the SetValue action runs from the form or report with the field, control, or property you want to set, you can use the short, or unqualified reference. If the field, control, or property is on the form or report that is active when Access executes the SetValue action, you can use the properties of the Screen object to refer to the item. Here are some examples:

| Item | Description |
|---|---|
| Description | Sets or changes the value of the Description control or field when the macro runs from the Categories form. |
| Caption | Sets or changes the Caption property of the Categories form when the macro runs from the Categories form. |
| Screen.ActiveControl | Sets or changes the value of the active control. |
| Screen.ActiveReport.Caption | Sets or changes the caption of the active report. |

**NOTE**  A macro *runs from a form or report* when the macro is assigned to an event recognized by the form , a form control or section, or the report, or a report section on the report.

**Setting Data Values on a Form**   You can use the SetValue action for a form to set the value of a bound control or the value of an unbound control that is not a calculated control. When you set the value of a control using the SetValue action, Access doesn't test the control's ValidationRule property. However, if the control is bound to a table field, Access does test the ValidationRules properties for the field and the table. Also, Access doesn't test the InputMask property you may have set for the field or the control. You can also set the value of a field in an underlying table, even if there is no control bound to the field; use the Forms!*formname*!*fieldname* syntax to refer to the field directly.

When you are working interactively with a form and you change data values or add new values or records, the controls and the form recognize the data events described in Chapter 2, "Getting Started with Objects and Events." Most of the data events that occur when you work interactively do not occur when you use the SetValue macro action to change data values or add new values. For example, when you use the SetValue macro action, the control does not recognize the

BeforeUpdate, AfterUpdate, or the Change events; however, when you save the record, the form does recognize its BeforeUpdate and AfterUpdate events. When you use the SetValue action to set the values of a new record, the form does not recognize the BeforeInsert and AfterInsert events.

**Setting Data Values on a Report**    When you use the SetValue action for a report, the rules are a little different. You can use the SetValue action for a report to set the value of a control only if the ControlSource property is blank; that is, if the control is an unbound control that is not a calculated control.

## The Expression Argument

The Expression argument is the expression that Access uses to calculate a value and then set the item to the result. The expression can include operators, constants, functions, and references to fields, controls and properties on open forms and reports.

If the expression is a string value, enclose the string in double quotation marks. For example, for setting the LastName to Novalis, the Expression action argument is "Novalis". If the expression is a date value, enclose the date in number signs. For example, for setting the HireDate to 5/2/92, the Expression action argument is #5/2/92#. If the expression is a number value, no special symbols are required; for example, to set the UnitsInStock to 100, the Expression action argument is 100.

When you enter the Expression argument, note that Access assumes the value you enter is an expression (so you don't need an equal sign). For example, to set the HireDate to the current date, you set the Expression argument to Now(). If you do include an equal sign, Access evaluates the expression first and uses the result as the argument. Using an equal sign when it is not needed can cause the macro to fail. For example, if you want to set the value of a text box to "John Smith" and you type ="John Smith" in the Expression argument box, Access evaluates the expression and treats the result as the name of a control; when Access can't find the [John Smith] control, the SetValue action fails.

The expression may include references to fields, control, and properties on open forms and reports. You can refer to a field in the record source of a form whether or not the form has a control bound to the field, but you can reference the value of a field in the record source for a report only if the report has a control that is bound to the field or has a calculated control that refers to the field in the calculation. Normally, you use the fully qualified reference. However, if the macro containing the SetValue action runs from the form or report with the field, control, or property you want to refer to, you can use the short, or unqualified reference. If the field, control, or property you want to refer to is on the active form or report, you can use the properties of the Screen object. Here are some examples:

| Expression | Description |
| --- | --- |
| Forms!Employees!LastName | Sets the item to the value in the LastName control or field on the Employees form. |
| LastName & ", " & FirstName | Sets an item to the concatenation of values in the LastName and FirstName controls or fields on the Employees form when the macro runs from the Employees form. |
| Screen.ActiveControl | Sets the item to the value in the active control. |
| Reports!Invoice!CompanyName | Sets the item to the value in the CompanyName control on the Invoice report. |

When you want to use an aggregate function in the Expression argument to do calculations for a group of records, you must use the domain aggregate functions and not the SQL aggregate functions. For example, to calculate the sum of order subtotals, use DSum() instead of Sum().

**NOTE**  To perform a calculation on a group of records in a macro argument or in the Condition cell for a conditional macro, you must use the domain aggregate functions and not the SQL aggregate functions.

## Using the SetValue Action to Hold Temporary Values on Forms

One difference between macro programming and VBA programming is that each handles temporary values differently. In VBA programming, you can create and name a variable as a specific location in memory that holds the value. In macro programming you can't create a variable this way, but you can simulate a variable by storing a value temporarily in an unbound control on a form. To use a control as a variable, place an unbound control on a form and leave its ControlSource property blank. Often, you hide the control holding the variable by setting its Visible property to No. You use the SetValue action to store the value temporarily on the form. The value is available as long as the form is open; when the form closes, the value ceases to exist. Later in this chapter, we use an unbound control to hold the value of a counter that keeps track of repetitions of a macro loop; in Chapter 6 we use an unbound control to hold the primary key of a record so we can return to the record.

## Using the SetValue Action to Push Values into Controls

As explained in Chapter 4, "Communicating with Forms," there are two ways you can use a control on a form to hold the result of a calculation:

**Calculated controls**   You can enter the expression for the calculation as the ControlSource property of an unbound control; the expression "pulls" the result into the control. The calculated value is not stored and exists only while the form is open.

**Programming**   You can calculate a value as a programming instruction and "push" the result into either a bound or unbound control (but not into a calculated control). In macro programming, you use the SetValue macro action to calculate a value and push the calculated value into either a bound or unbound control. When the control is bound, the calculated value is stored permanently in the table field. When the control is unbound, the control simulates a variable holding its value only as long as the form is open.

Table 5.2 (on the CD under Tables\Chapter5.pdf) gives examples of using the SetValue action.

# Duplicating Built-in Commands

Access provides a large set of built-in commands. You run one of the built-in commands each time you choose a menu command from a built-in menu bar or a shortcut menu or click a button on a built-in toolbar. In Access 97, menu bars, shortcut menus, and toolbars are handled in similar ways and are called command bars.

When you work interactively with the default command bars, you can observe that each view that you work with has a specific set of commands arranged in its command bars. For example, if a form in Form view is the active window, the Form view menu and the Form view toolbar are displayed; right-clicking in the form, in a form control, in a subform, or in a control on a subform displays the Form view shortcut menus. Figure 5.10 shows the default Form view menu bar, the default toolbar, and the default shortcut menu displayed when you right-click in a subform. The default command bars for a view include the built-in commands that are appropriate for the view.

**FIGURE 5.10:**

The default Form view menu bar and toolbar with the shortcut menu for a subform displayed

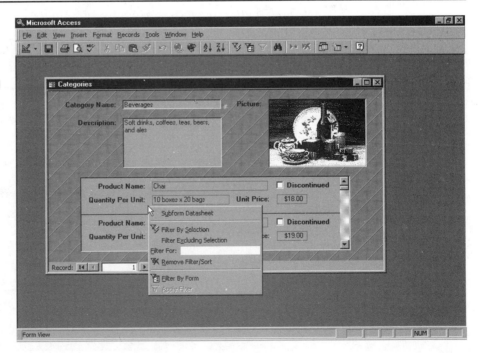

A specified built-in command may not be available for one of two reasons: The command may be appropriate for the view but may not be available at all times or the command may be inappropriate to the view.

**Appropriate but unavailable** Even if a command is included in a default command bar, the command may not always be available and may appear to be grayed out at different times as you work with the object. For example, in the Form view menu bar, the availability of the Undo commands in the Edit menu changes as you work with the form. When you first open a form in Form view, the command Edit ➤ Can't Undo is grayed out and unavailable. When you click a control and type a character, the command Edit ➤ Undo Typing is available. When you tab out of the control, the command Edit ➤ Undo Current Field/Record is available. When you save the record, the command Edit ➤ Undo Saved Record is available until you begin editing another record. When you begin editing another record, the cycle begins again and Edit ➤ Undo Typing is available.

**Inappropriate** Access 97 lets you modify the default command bars or create your own command bars for any view. In the customization process you can add any built-in command to the command bars for a view, but the resulting command may not be appropriate for the view. For example, you can add the MacroNames command (to display the MacroNames column in the macrosheet) to the Form view toolbar, but when a form is active and you click the new Macro Names button, Access displays the error message shown in Figure 5.11 because the MacroNames command is inappropriate to Form view.

**FIGURE 5.11:**

The error message that appears when you try to run an inappropriate command

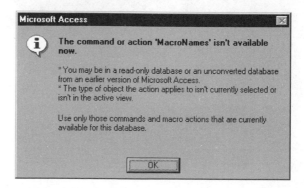

When you use the RunCommand macro action, you can specify any built-in command. Be careful to select only commands that are both appropriate to the view and available under the conditions that will be current when the macro runs. If you specify a menu command that isn't appropriate or available when the macro runs, Access can't execute the RunCommand action. For example, if you try to run a macro with the RunCommand action for the Undo command when you first open a form, Access can't execute the action; Access displays the error message (see Figure 5.12a) and then the Action Failed dialog (see Figure 5.12b). Figure 5.12 shows the error message displayed when you try to run an unavailable menu command.

**FIGURE 5.12:**

The error message (a) and the Action Failed dialog (b)

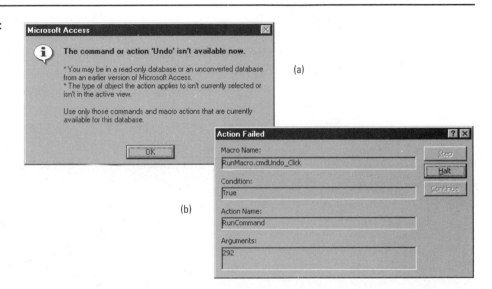

I always thought the best way to avoid failure is to become very familiar with hard work, honesty, and good friends. The best way to avoid failure is to become very familiar with the commands that are appropriate for the Form and Print Preview views. It can be difficult to know if a particular command that may be appropriate for a view will also be available at the instant you plan to run the macro; testing your macros and seeing when they fail is the best way to learn.

## Sending Messages

To display a message, use the MsgBox action. The result of the action is a *message box* that displays a custom message, a title, and the icon that you specify using the MsgBox arguments. The message box has a single OK button that the user must press to close the message box and continue. Figure 5.13 shows a typical message box.

**FIGURE 5.13:**

Use the MsgBox action to display a custom message.

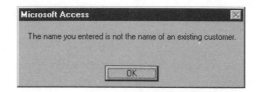

The arguments of the MsgBox action are as follows:

| MsgBox Argument | Description |
| --- | --- |
| Message | You can enter up to 255 characters as the message. The message can be either a set of characters that you enter as the text message or can be the result of an expression that you enter as the Message argument preceded by an equal (=) sign. |
| Beep | You can sound a beep by setting the Beep argument to Yes. |
| Type | You can specify whether the message box displays no icon or an icon for the following types of messages: Critical, Warning?, Warning!, or Information. |
| Title | You can specify text to be displayed in the title bar of the message box. |

**NOTE**
You can also use built-in formatting to format the message in three sections. The first section is displayed in bold starting on the first line; the second section is displayed in plain text below the first section; and the third section is displayed in plain text beginning on the next line. Separate the three sections with the @ symbol.

Table 5.3 gives examples of custom messages.

**TABLE 5.3:** Examples of Message arguments for the MsgBox action

| Message Argument | Description |
|---|---|
| The name you entered is not an existing customer | The text message is displayed in the message box. |
| ="The name "&[LastName]&"is not the name of an existing customer" | Displays a message containing the value in the LastName control on the active form (see Figure 5.14a). |
| Unrecognized name@ The name you entered is not an existing customer.@ Press the New button to enter a new customer. | Displays the formatted message shown in Figure 5.14b. |

**FIGURE 5.14:**

Using an expression in the Message argument to display a specific value (a) and to display a formatted error message (b)

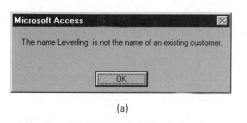

(a)

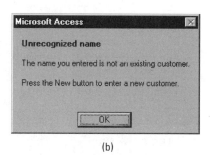

(b)

The MsgBox macro action displays only a single OK button. However, sometimes you need a message box that gives the user a choice. The Msgbox() function is a built-in function that displays a message box with a custom message and title and a set of buttons that the user can choose. The value returned by the function depends on which button was chosen. See the section "Using the MsgBox Function as a Condition," later in the chapter for more information.

## Sending Keystrokes

Use the SendKeys macro action to send keystrokes to Access or to another active Windows application.

| SendKeys Arguments | Description |
| --- | --- |
| Keystrokes | Enter the characters (up to 255) that you want to send. If a key represents a character that is displayed when you press the key, then enter the character (for example, to send v, enter **v** as the Keystrokes argument). If a key represents a character that isn't displayed when you press the key, such as Tab, Enter, or a function key, you must enter a code in the Keystrokes argument. |
| Wait | Enter Yes to pause the macro until the keystrokes have been processed; otherwise, enter No. |

Table 5.4 (on the CD under Tables\Chapter5.pdf) shows the keystrokes you can send and their codes.

You can use the SendKeys action together with the RunCommand action to automate a menu command that requires you to enter additional information before the command can be carried out. For example, the Save As command requires you to enter a new name if you are saving the object in the same database (see Figure 5.15).

**FIGURE 5.15:**

The Save As command displays the Save As dialog. Type in a name and press Enter.

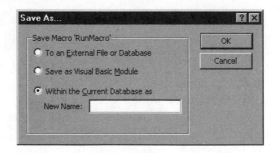

When a command requires additional information (such as a new name), Access displays a dialog and suspends execution of the command until you enter the information and close the dialog. When you use the RunCommand macro action to run the command, Access suspends execution of the macro action until you enter the information and close the dialog. Because Access suspends execution when the dialog is displayed, the macro must send the information before displaying the dialog. You can duplicate the interactive steps as follows:

1.  Use the SendKeys macro action to send keystrokes containing the information to the dialog.

2.  Use the SendKeys macro action a second time to send the characters {enter} or the ~ code for pressing the Enter key. Send the information and the keystroke to close the dialog before running the command that displays the dialog. Set the Wait argument of both SendKeys actions to No so that Access stores the keystrokes in a buffer and sends them to the dialog when the RunCommand action runs. When the RunCommand displays the dialog, Access inserts the information and carries out the command.

3.  Use the RunCommand macro action to execute the command that displays the dialog.

As an example, suppose you want to use a macro to save a new form with the name frmExpenses. The mcrSaveAs macro, shown in Table 5.5, automates the procedure.

**TABLE 5.5:** A macro to automate saving a form with a new name

| Action | Action Arguments |
| --- | --- |
| SendKeys | Keystrokes: frmExpenses |
| | Wait: No |
| SendKeys | Keystrokes: {enter} |
| | Wait: No |
| RunCommand | Command: SaveAs |

To test the macro:

1.  Enter the macro shown in Table 5.5 in a new macrosheet and save the macrosheet as mcrSaveAs.

2.  Open a new form in Design view.

3. With the form as the active window, choose the Macro command in the Tools menu and then choose the Run Macro command in the fly-out menu (or click the Run Macro button you added earlier to the toolbar). Select the mcrSaveAs macro in the Run Macro dialog and click OK. The macro runs and saves the form under the new name.

## Displaying Current Data

There are several situations where controls on the active form do not display the most current data. Chapter 4 shows several examples where it is necessary to force recalculation of calculated controls by choosing the Refresh command from the Records menu or by pressing F9. Another situation requiring you to update controls yourself occurs when two open forms display data from the same table. If you *change* data in one form, the second form updates automatically; however, if you *add* a new record to one form, the second form does not update automatically to show the new record. Explore the updating problem as follows:

1. Open the Customers and Customer Orders forms in Form view and arrange them side by side. The Customers and Customer Orders forms are based on data in the Customers table.

2. Modify the company name of the first record in the Customers form and press Shift+Enter to save the change. When you change a record in the Customers, the Customer Orders form refreshes automatically. That is, the changes are displayed immediately in the Customer Orders form (see Figure 5.16).

FIGURE 5.16:

When you change a record in one form, the second form updates automatically.

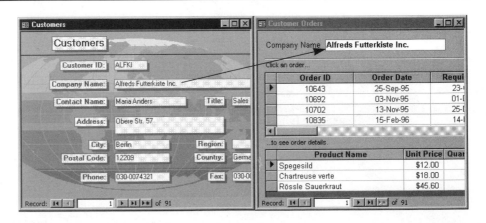

3. Add a new customer using the Customers form and save the new record. Note that the Customer Orders form does not include the new record (see Figure 5.17). When you add a new record in one form, the second form does not display the new record. To force the second form to display the current records you must requery this form.

**FIGURE 5.17:**

When you add a record using one form, the second form does not update automatically.

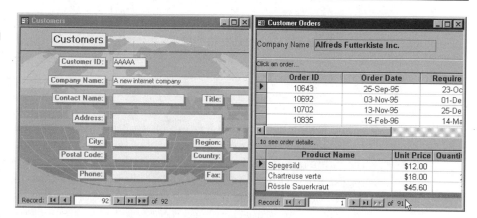

4. Click the CompanyName control on the Customer Orders form and press Shift+F9. Access retrieves the current records. (If the record you added has the AAAAA CustomerID, the new record becomes the first record in the Customers table and is displayed in the Customer Orders form.)

5. Click the Customers form and choose the Delete Record command from the Edit menu. The Customer Orders form displays the word #Deleted in each control for the deleted record (see Figure 5.18). To display the current records, you must requery the form.

6. Click the CompanyName control on the Customer Orders form and press Shift+F9. Access requeries the form and displays the current records.

You can use macros to automate these updates. You can use the RunCommand action to automate the Refresh command and the SendKeys action to send the F9 keystroke to recalculate calculated controls and the Shift+F9 keystrokes to requery the form's data source. You can also use the RepaintObject and the Requery actions.

**FIGURE 5.18:**

When you delete a record using one form, the second form does not update automatically.

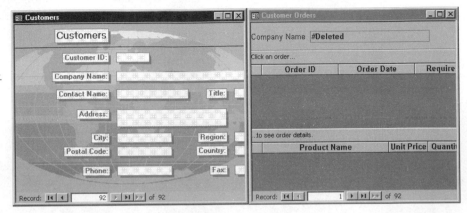

The RepaintObject action completes any pending screen updates and pending recalculations of controls. For example, if you use the SetValue action to change the value in a control and a second calculated control depends on the value in the first control, you can use the RepaintObject action to update the second control. The RepaintObject action does not requery the object's data source and does not update the currently displayed records to reflect changes made to the data in the underlying tables.

The Requery action can be used for a control on the active object or for any database object. The Requery action either reruns the query on which the control or object is based, or rereads the table on which the control or object is based. The Requery action displays the new or changed records or removes the deleted records.

**Requery action for a control on the active form**　To apply the action to a control, specify the name of the control as the Control Name argument using the short syntax. The Requery action updates the data in the specified control on the active object by requerying the source of the control. If the control is not based on a query or table, the Requery action recalculates the control.

**Requery action for the active database window object**　To apply the action to the active object, leave the Control Name argument blank. The Requery action has the same effect as selecting the database object and pressing Shift+F9. That is, the action requeries the underlying data source for the object that has the focus.

When a form contains controls that have separate data sources such as combo boxes, list boxes, controls with aggregate functions, subform controls, and OLE controls, use separate Requery actions for the form and for each control that has a different data source.

You can use the Requery action only for an active database window object or a control on the active form. If the object you want to requery is not active, you must include a macro action that selects the object before you use the Requery action.

# Creating Macros

Before you create a macro, you must decide which tasks you want Access to perform and when you want them performed. In Chapter 2, "Getting Started with Objects and Events," you learned that programming in Access is *event-driven*: an object recognizes special changes in its state that Access makes available to you as programming opportunities; Access automatically runs a program assigned to an event when the event occurs. Most of the macros you write are event macros. An *event macro* is a macro that runs in response to an event. You must decide which event is going to trigger the macro.

Because most macro actions duplicate interactive steps, often the best way to design a macro is to step through the task interactively and note the sequence of your actions. Normally there is a macro action corresponding to each step, so to create the macro, you simply translate your steps into macro actions. For more complicated tasks, it is often helpful to use a macro flow diagram to "record" your interactions.

## Using Macro Flow Diagrams

A *macro flow diagram* is a diagram that represents the macro actions you want to run. The first operation box indicates the operation that causes the event and the small solid triangle attached to the operation box represents the event (see Figure 5.19).

**FIGURE 5.19:**

Diagramming an operation that causes an event

Your action can directly or indirectly cause an event. For example, when you click a command button, your action directly causes the button to recognize the Click event. When you open a form you cause a series of events: the form recognizes the Open, Load, Resize, and Activate events, the first record recognizes the Current event, and the first control recognizes the Enter and GotFocus events. While you directly cause the Open event, you cause the subsequent events only indirectly. When direct user action causes the event, we'll use an operation box with a shadow (see Figure 5.20). Search order of events in online Help for more information on events.

**FIGURE 5.20:**

Diagramming a user operation that directly causes an event

Each subsequent operation box represents a macro action; each box includes an English phrase describing the action and the name of the macro action in italics. After the last macro action, you can include a termination box to indicate the end of execution; however, it is not necessary to include a macro action to terminate the macro. (A macro ends when it runs out of macro actions.)

Macro flow diagrams can be very useful for designing complex macros. Describing complex sequences of operations is easier through diagrams than text; a diagram is a precise and clear way to design and document your macros. Once you have drawn the macro flow diagram, you can generate the macro almost automatically. In this book, we'll use macro flow diagrams when the macro requires more than a few macro actions or when the sequence is complex.

## Storing Macros in Macro Groups

There are two ways to store macros:

- Use a macrosheet to create a single macro with one or more macro actions and save the macro as a macro object that appears in the list of macros in the Database window.

- Use a macrosheet to define several individual macros. In this case, the set of macros stored in the macrosheet is called a *macro group*. Only the name of the macro group is displayed as a macro object in the Database window (not the names of the individual macros in the group).

When you automate a database, you create tens if not hundreds of individual macros. Rather than creating macro objects for individual macros, it is more efficient to organize the various macros you create for a form or report into a single macro group called a *form macro group* or a *report macro group* and name the macro group to reflect the form or report as follows:

m[*formname*]      for a form macro group

m[*reportname*]      for a report macro group

As an example, you can store all of the macros for a switchboard form named frmSwitchboard in a form macro group named mfrmSwitchboard.

## Naming Individual Macros

You use an individual macro to trap an event recognized by an object. You can name the event macro by combining the object name and the event name separated by an underscore, as follows:

*objectname_eventname*

As examples, the individual macro named

cmdCategories_Click

contains the actions you want to carry out when you click the command button named cmdCategories. The macro named

Form_Activate

contains the actions you want to take when the form becomes the active window.

## Referring to a Macro in a Macro Group

To refer to an individual macro in a macro group, use the name of the macro group followed by a dot (.) followed by the name of the macro:

*macrogroupname.macroname*

This reference is called the *full identifier* for the macro. As an example,

mfrmSwitchboard.cmdCategories_Click

is the full identifier for the macro in the group mfrmSwitchboard assigned to the Click event of the cmdCategories button.

## Editing in the Macrosheet

Editing in the macrosheet is similar to editing in a datasheet. You can navigate around the macrosheet using the mouse or the normal Windows editing keys.

The rules for editing individual cells follow the normal Windows and Access editing rules. Tab into a cell to select its entire contents; when you tab to a cell you are in *navigating mode* and you can press F2 to switch to *editing mode* and then edit directly in the cell. For entering or editing longer expressions, press Shift+F2 to open the Zoom Box and display the entire contents in a separate edit window. The ← and → keys allow you to move the insertion point; the Delete key lets you delete the character to the right of the insertion point and the Backspace key lets you delete the character to the left of the insertion point.

You can copy individual characters or the entire contents of the cell to the clipboard by selecting what you want to copy, then pressing Ctrl+C, choosing Edit ➤ Copy, or clicking the Copy button on the toolbar. To paste the selection into another cell, click the paste cell (place the insertion point where you want the contents to be pasted), then press Ctrl+V, choose Edit ➤ Paste, or click the Paste button on the toolbar. When you copy the contents of a macro action cell, only the action (not the action arguments) is copied to the clipboard.

You can change the height of rows and the widths of columns just as you do in a datasheet, but the rules for editing rows and columns in the macrosheet are somewhat different because you can select a row but not a column. You can select a row by clicking into the row selector; you can select several contiguous rows by clicking into the first row selector and dragging to the last row or by pressing the Shift key and clicking into the last row selector (you cannot select noncontiguous rows). After selecting one or more rows, you can delete the selection by pressing the Delete key, or insert the same number of rows above the selection by pressing the Insert key, or copy the selection to the clipboard. When you copy a row the entire macro action is copied, including the action arguments you set.

Additionally, you can move rows by first selecting the rows to move, then pressing the left mouse button while clicking the selection and dragging to the rows where you want to insert the selection; a bold horizontal line indicates the new boundary of the selection (the new upper boundary if you are moving the selection up and the new lower boundary if you are moving the selection down).

You can copy a macro to another macrosheet by copying the rows of the macro to the clipboard and then pasting the selection to a new location in the other macrosheet. You can use the clipboard to paste a macro into another Access database, but since you have to close the current database and open the other one in order to paste, it is usually more convenient to export the macrosheet to another database or import it from another database using the usual Access methods (File ➤ Save As/Export, or File ➤ Get External Data).

## The Flow of Macro Execution

Access starts the execution of a simple macro with the first row containing the macro name, executes the action in this row if there is one, and ignores any comments in the row. Then Access looks for the next row that is not blank and moves to it. If there is an entry in the Macro Name cell, Access interprets this row as the beginning of another macro and stops execution. If the Macro Name cell is blank, Access moves to the Action cell to the right. If there is an entry in the Action cell, Access executes the action, ignores the comment, and moves to the next row that is not blank. If the Action cell is blank, Access moves to the next row that is not blank. Access continues to move down the rows of the macrosheet examining one row at a time, until it finds a row with an entry in the Macro Name cell, or until there are no more non-blank rows. In either case, the macro ends. You don't have to end a macro with a specific end action. Since Access ignores blank rows, you can insert them between the macro actions of an individual macro and between the individual macros in a macro group to make them easier to read.

This execution pattern is called a *sequential* flow pattern: macro actions are executed sequentially as listed in the macrosheet. The section "Controlling Macro Program Execution," later in the chapter, describes two other flow patterns for conditional and repetitive execution.

**TIP** When you create a macro, place only the macro name and a general comment in the first row and enter the first macro action in the second row. This macro design makes it easier to modify a macro later if you want to insert a new first action or copy the actions of the macro to another macro.

# Running Macros

There are many ways to run a macro in addition to using an event to trigger it. This section describes nine ways to run a macro.

## Running a Macro from the Macro Window

You can run the first macro in the active macrosheet by clicking the Run button in the toolbar or by choosing the Run command in the Run menu. You can run any macro in any macrosheet by clicking the Macro button in the (customized) toolbar or by choosing the Macro command in the (customized) Run menu to display the Run Macro dialog box. By default, the dialog box displays the name of the active macrosheet and you must select the full identifier for the macro you want to run. For example, to run a macro named cmdCategories_Click macro that you have stored in the mfrmSwitchboard macrosheet, you select mfrmSwitchboard .cmdCategories_Click in the Run Macro dialog (see Figure 5.21a). When you click OK, Access runs the macro.

## Running a Macro from Any Active Window

You can customize the menu bar and toolbar for any view to include the Macro command. With customized command bars you can run a macro from any active window by choosing the Macro command and entering the macro's full identifier in the Run Macro dialog. As an exception, the Macro command is unavailable when the Module window is the active window.

When the Database window is the active window, you can also run the first macro in a macro group by selecting the macro group in the Macro pane and clicking the Run button.

## Running a Macro from Another Macro

You can run a macro from a second macro using the RunMacro action. The second macro is referred to as the *calling macro* and the macro you run is referred to as the *called macro*. Use the RunMacro action in the calling macro and enter the full identifier of the macro you want to call in the Macro Name argument. You must enter the full identifier even if both macros are in the same macro group. Figure 5.21b shows a macro group with a calling macro and a called macro. When Access executes the RunMacro action, control is transferred to the called macro; when the called macro is finished running, control returns to the calling macro at the row following the row with the RunMacro action. When you leave

**FIGURE 5.21:**

Use the Run Macro dialog to run any macro in a macrosheet (a). Use the RunMacro macro action to run another macro. Enter the full identifier for the called macro in the Macro Name argument (b).

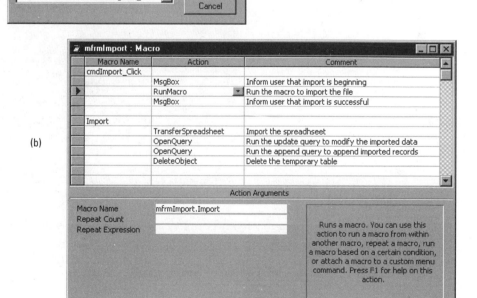

the two Repeat... arguments blank, Access runs the called macro once. You can use the Repeat... arguments to run the called macro in a repetitive loop. Macro loops are discussed later in this chapter.

## Running a Macro from a Command Bar

You can create a custom toolbar button that runs a macro and place the button on any command bar. For example, to place a custom button on a toolbar:

1. Right-click the toolbar and choose the Customize command from the short-cut menu.

2. Click the Commands tab and select the All Macros category in the list box on the left. The Commands list box on the right displays all of the macros in the database (see Figure 5.22).

**FIGURE 5.22:**

The All Macros category lists the macros in the database.

3. Select a macro and drag to the toolbar. Access displays a custom toolbar button. When you close the Customize dialog and move the pointer to the new button, a tooltip indicates the name of the macro that runs when you click the button. You can customize the button image, the tooltip, and the status bar text.

4. With the Customize dialog open, right-click on the new toolbar button and choose the Properties command on the shortcut menu. You can change the tooltip text in the Tooltip text box in the Macro Design Control Properties dialog (see Figure 5.23a). Click the Close button to close the dialog.

5. Right-click on the new toolbar button and choose the Change Button Image command to display the available button images (see Figure 5.23b).

**FIGURE 5.23:**

Customizing the tooltip text (a) and the button image (b) of a toolbar button

(a)

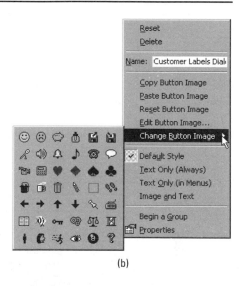

(b)

> **NOTE**
>
> When you add a custom command to run a macro to an application, the button appears in every database that you open. However, if you are in another database when you choose the command, the macro runs only if you have stored a copy of the macro in the current database.

## Running a Macro from a Shortcut Key

You can run a macro from a custom key combination. For example, you can assign the key combination Ctrl+Z to open the Zoom box (a more convenient key combination than the default Shift+F2). You can assign custom key combinations using a special macro group that must be named AutoKeys. To assign a macro to a key combination, enter a code for the key combination in the Macro Name column and then enter the actions for the macro or use the RunMacro action to call another macro. Not all key combinations are available for custom reassignment. Table 5.6 (on the CD under Tables\Chapter5.pdf) shows the available key combinations and the key codes.

The AutoKeys macro takes effect as soon as you save it. When you use an AutoKeys macro to reassign a key combination that Windows or Access normally uses, such as Ctrl+C for copy, your assignment takes precedence. To make your application easier to learn, do not reassign the common Windows and Access key combinations. Figure 5.24 shows an AutoKeys macro to open the Zoom box; this macro uses the SendKeys action to send the Shift+F2 key combination to Access.

**FIGURE 5.24:**

Using an AutoKeys macro to make custom key assignments

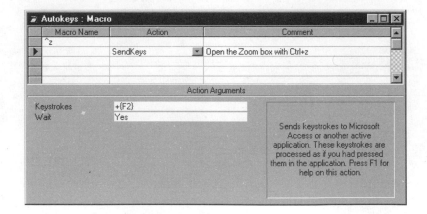

## Running a Macro at Startup

You can create a special macro and have Access run it automatically when you start up the database. You must create this macro in its own macrosheet and name the macrosheet AutoExec. (This is probably the only circumstance in which you must store a single macro in a macrosheet.) When you start up the database, Access uses the properties you set in the Startup dialog and then looks for an AutoExec macro. Access runs the AutoExec macro if there is one. While the Startup properties define most of the initial database settings, you can use an AutoExec macro for additional tasks you want to perform each time you start up the database; for example, you can open a hidden global variables form or arrange to download and to import new data automatically.

# Running a Macro from the Debug Window

You can run an individual macro action in the Debug window by typing DoCmd followed by a dot and the name of the macro action with the list of arguments. You must enclose all text arguments in quotation marks and use commas to separate multiple arguments. If you omit arguments, Access assumes the default values for the action; however, even if you omit an argument, you must still use a comma to hold the place of the omitted argument in the argument list unless you are omitting all arguments or you are omitting all arguments after the last one you want to specify.

> **NOTE**
>
> When you run a macro action this way, you are actually running the corresponding Visual Basic *method*. Nearly all macro actions have equivalent Visual Basic methods. You can get help on the corresponding method by searching online Help for the name of the action and choosing the corresponding method from the topics list.

For example,

1. Open the Debug window by pressing Ctrl+G. The lower pane of the Debug window, shown in Figure 5.25, is called the Immediate pane because statements you enter are evaluated immediately (see Chapter 6). Click the Immediate pane and type **DoCmd.** VBA displays a drop-down list of the macro actions you can run as VBA methods using the DoCmd (see Figure 5.25a). Choose the OpenForm action from the drop-down list and double-click to enter the action or type **OpenForm**.

2. Finish typing the expression **DoCmd. OpenForm "Categories"**. Notice that when you press the Spacebar following the OpenForm method, VBA displays the syntax for the OpenForm method in a small box below the line you are entering as shown in Figure 5.25b; ignore the box for now and finish typing.

3. Press Enter. When you press Enter, Access executes the statement you typed and opens the Categories form.

The OpenForm macro action has six arguments. However, to open the form with all default values, you can specify the name of the form and omit the remaining arguments. (The corresponding VBA OpenForm method has the same six arguments plus an additional argument called OpenArgs as shown in Figure 5.25b.)

You can run a macro in the Debug window by typing DoCmd. RunMacro followed by the full name of the macro enclosed in quotation marks. To run the macro once, use the following syntax:

DoCmd. RunMacro *"macrogroupname.macroname"*

**FIGURE 5.25:**

The Immediate pane of the Debug window displays the methods of the DoCmd object (a) and the syntax for the OpenForm method (b).

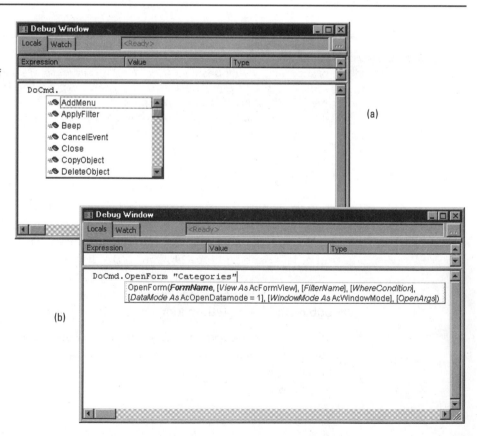

## Running a Macro from a VBA Procedure

You can run an individual macro action or a macro in a VBA procedure using the same syntax that you use to run the action or macro in the Debug window. (When you use the Debug window you are writing VBA statements.)

## Running a Macro by Trapping an Event on a Form or Report

Because Access uses the event-driven programming model discussed in Chapter 2, the most important way to run a macro is by assigning the macro to an event property of an object. When the object recognizes the event, Access automatically runs the macro that has been assigned; this procedure is also called *triggering* the macro. You can assign a macro to an event by entering the full identifier for the macro as the property setting for the event property, also called *trapping* an event. A macro that is assigned to an event is called an *event macro* or *event handler*. For example, Figure 5.26 shows an event macro assigned to the AfterUpdate event property of the Customers form.

**FIGURE 5.26:**

Assigning event macros in the object's property sheet

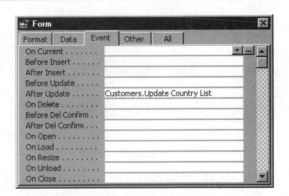

When you first start to program using macros, most of the macros you write are triggered by the Click event of command buttons. The user runs the macro explicitly by clicking the button. Before long, you are writing macros that are triggered by events that the user isn't aware of. For example, you can create a data validation macro to test a value when the user tabs out of a control, or a lookup macro that synchronizes a form to the value in a combo box when the user selects a value. When you use events other than the Click event to trigger macros, you minimize the need for the user to know when to run macros and you make your application easier to use.

## Interrupting Default Processing

When you set an event trap by assigning a macro to an event, you affect the default processing that Access would normally carry out following the occurrence of the event. For example, when you change the value in a text box and take an action to save the change, the text box recognizes the BeforeUpdate event. The subsequent default behavior is that Access updates the control and the control recognizes the AfterUpdate event. You can trap the BeforeUpdate event by assigning a macro for Access to determine if the edited value satisfies the validation rules for the control. The BeforeUpdate event is one of the events for which Access runs the macro before the default behavior takes place so the default behavior can be canceled. If the changed value in the text box fails to satisfy the validation rules you can cancel the default behavior with the CancelEvent action. If the changed value satisfies the validation rules, the macro finishes and then Access continues with the default behavior of updating the control.

### Steps in Creating Event Macros

Here is a list of basic guidelines:

1. Determine which object and event you want to trigger the macro execution.

2. Design the macro (use a macro flow diagram if necessary). Think through, or actually carry out, each step you take to accomplish the task. For more complex macros you should draw the macro flow diagram to document the macro, and to help with the design.

3. Determine the macro actions. If you are using a macro flow diagram, each operation box in the diagram translates into a separate macro action.

4. Create and save the macro. You must save a macro before you can run it.

5. Assign the macro to the corresponding event property.

*continued on next page*

## Steps for Assigning a Macro to an Event

Assign the macro to an event following these steps:

1. Open the form or report in Design view and select the object that recognizes the event.

2. Display the property sheet (by clicking the Properties button in the toolbar or choosing View ➤ Properties).

3. Click the Event tab in the property sheet and then click the event property for the event.

4. Enter the full identifier for the macro by typing or by clicking the arrow and selecting the macro from the list. Use the syntax *macrogroupname.macroname*.

5. Save the form or report.

### Testing the Macro

You should always test the macro in context by causing the triggering event to occur (for example, by clicking the command button). Testing a macro in context allows you to observe how the macro interacts with other macros. Often the interaction of two or more macros gives unexpected results, requiring you to either redesign a macro or choose a different event to trigger an interacting macro.

You can also test a macro without triggering the event by choosing the Macro command to run the individual macro and see if it accomplishes the intended task. Some macros require that specific forms and reports be open and that a specific object is active when you run the macro—make sure these conditions are satisfied before you run the macro.

# Documenting Macros

When you are working in a macrosheet, you can see the arguments for only one action at a time and you have to click the row that contains the action to see its argument settings. This limitation makes understanding how the macro works more difficult. You can compensate for this limitation, at least partially, by using comments for every action that has arguments and including the most important information from the action arguments in your comments. While the effort required to comment nearly every action is substantial, you will find the rewards equally substantial. In this regard, Visual Basic code has the advantage of displaying all the details of your program as text so that you can see the entire program at a glance. Figure 5.27 shows the macrosheet for a dialog form named fdlgSales.

With macros you can't see all the arguments for all the macros in a macrosheet on the screen, but you can print the macro's definition for reference. To print a macrosheet, choose File ➤ Print, and click OK on the Print Macro Definition dialog (see Figure 5.28). The printout shows all the conditions and arguments for all the macros in a macrosheet. Figure 5.29 shows a portion of the report for the macrosheet for the fdlgSales form.

Using flowcharts to document your macros is another way to document a macro and see its flow pattern at a glance.

**FIGURE 5.27:**

You can view the arguments for only one macro action at a time, so use comments to document macro actions.

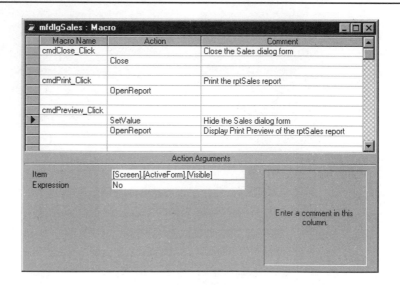

**FIGURE 5.28:**

You can print the macros in a macrosheet.

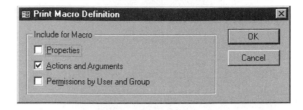

**FIGURE 5.29:**

Print Preview of a macrosheet

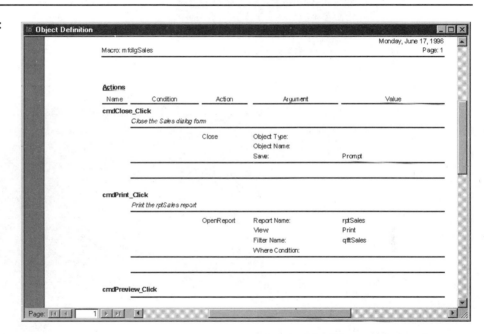

# Manipulating Objects with Macros

In this section, we look at some simple examples of creating and running macros. We construct macros to automate simple navigation among forms.

> **NOTE** In this chapter and the next few chapters, we'll be working with the Northwind database. Make a copy named NorthwindMacros.mdb of your original Northwind database.

*Let users see the basic organization of the application at a glance. Display a main menu form, or switchboard, with a list of the tasks they can carry out with the application.*

The Northwind database has a switchboard form called Main Switchboard that controls the navigation to the main tasks in the application (see Figure 5.30). There are command buttons to open the major task forms: Categories, Suppliers, Products, and Orders, a command button with the Print Sales Reports caption that opens the Sales Reports form as a secondary switchboard for selecting reports, a command button to close the Main Switchboard and display the Database window, and a command button to quit Access. The switchboard buttons are empowered with VBA procedures. For practice in creating macros we'll replace the VBA procedures with event macros.

**FIGURE 5.30:**

The Main Switchboard

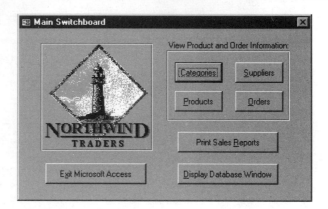

## Forms Navigation

We'll create macros to automate navigation between forms by opening, hiding, or closing them.

*A fundamental principle in forms navigation is that you allow users to work with only one form at a time.*

Usually this principle means displaying only one form at a time; but, if two forms are displayed, this means preventing users from changing data using both forms. By controlling how users work with your forms, you can avoid data integrity problems.

There are many ways to apply this fundamental principle. The simplest way is to hide the Main Switchboard when a task form is opened. You hide an object by setting its Visible property to No.

## Opening and Hiding Forms

For each of the five command buttons that opens a form, we create an event macro for the button's Click event that opens the form and hides the switchboard.

1. Open a new macrosheet and name it mMainSwitchboard. Resize and move the Macro window to display both the Database window and the Macro window.

2. Type **cmdCategories_Click** in the first Macro Name cell, click the Comment cell in the same row and enter the comment **Open the form and hide the Main Switchboard**. The next step shows another way to define a macro action that opens a form: the drag and drop technique.

3. In the Database window, click the Forms tab, then select Categories, drag the icon and drop it in the Action cell in the second row; enter the comment **Open Categories**. Access automatically sets the action to OpenForm and sets the Form Name argument to Categories.

4. Click the next cell and choose the SetValue action. Set the Item argument to refer to the Visible property of the Main Switchboard and set the Expression argument to No like this:

   Item:           Forms![Main Switchboard].Visible

   Expression:     No

   Note that Access adds square brackets around the words Forms and Visible after you tab out of the argument text box. Click the Comment cell and enter the comment **Hide the main Switchboard**

5. Save the macro. Table 5.7 shows the macro.

**NOTE**  When you drag a table, query, form, or report to the Macro window, Access inserts a row with an action to open the object and sets default arguments. When you drag a macro object, Access inserts a row with the RunMacro action.

**TABLE 5.7:** The macro to open a task form and hide the switchboard

| Macro Name | Action | Action Arguments |
|---|---|---|
| cmdCategories_Click | | |
| | OpenForm | Form Name: Categories |
| | SetValue | Item: Forms![Main Switchboard].Visible |
| | | Expression: No |

**NOTE** In this book, the comments and the default action arguments are not included explicitly in the tables that show the macros.

## Testing the Macro

The next step is to test the macro to be sure it runs properly. When you test an event macro, you need to duplicate the conditions under which the macro will run when it has been assigned to an event. In this case, make sure the Main Switchboard is open. (If the Main Switchboard isn't open, Access won't be able to carry out the SetValue action and the macro will fail.) Since there is only a single macro, run it by clicking the Run button in the toolbar. If the macro runs as intended, the Categories form is open and the switchboard form is still open but is hidden.

Before assigning the cmdCategories_Click macro, create macros similar to the cmdCategories macro in Table 5.7 for the command buttons that open the Suppliers, Products, Orders, and Sales Reports forms. Name the macro for opening the last form cmdSalesReports_Click. Since the SetValue action has identical arguments for all five macros, you can save time by copying the row with the SetValue action and pasting it to each macro. When you copy a row in the macrosheet, the argument settings are copied automatically. Save the macrosheet (see Figure 5.31a).

To assign the macros:

1. Unhide the switchboard by choosing the Unhide command from the Window menu and clicking the OK button in the Unhide Window dialog.

2. Switch to Design view and select the button with the Categories caption. Click the OnClick property in the property sheet. (The current property setting, =OpenForm("Categories"), is the VBA Function procedure.) A list of macro groups and the full identifiers of the individual macros is displayed.

3. Select mMainSwitchboard.cmdCategories_Click. The VBA Function procedure is now replaced by the macro (see Figure 5.31b).

4. Assign the other four macros to the OnClick property of their respective command buttons.

5. Save the form and switch to Form view.

**FIGURE 5.31:**

Replacing a VBA event procedure with an event macro

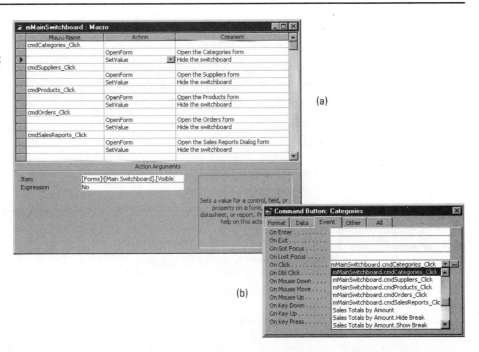

**NOTE**

If you double-click within the double-click time limit of your computer, the control recognizes both the DblClick and the Click events; otherwise it recognizes two Click events. You can change the double-click time limit on the Buttons tab of the Mouse option of the Windows Control Panel.

## Closing and Unhiding Forms

When you click one of the command buttons, a task form opens and the switch-board is hidden. After you are finished working with the task form, you need to close the form and unhide the switchboard.

**Creating Reusable Objects**    Each of the main task forms needs a command button to close the form and unhide the switchboard. Since several forms need exactly the same command button, you can avoid having to recreate the button and its macro for each form by creating the button and its macro just once and reusing them on other forms. Create the command button on the Categories form.

1. Click the Categories button in the Main Switchboard. The Categories form opens and the switchboard is hidden.

2. Switch to Design view. If the Control Wizards tool button is pushed in, click the button to deactivate the wizards and then select the Command Button tool.

3. Click the form and create a button; set the Name property to cmdReturn and set the Caption property to &Return

4. Save the form.

> **NOTE**    You can provide an *access key* that can be used in place of clicking a command button. Assign a keyboard combination Alt+*letter* where *letter* can be any letter in the button's Caption property. Specify your choice by typing the ampersand (&) immediately before the letter in the Caption property. For example, set the Caption property to &Return to have the button's caption displayed as Return and to have the keyboard shortcut be Alt+R.

**Creating a Global Macro**    We'll create the macro for the Return button in a global macrosheet taking care to avoid using names of specific objects that would prevent the macro from being reusable. A *global macrosheet* stores general macros that can be used on more than one form or report. Then, when you need the button, you can just copy it from the form to any other form.

1. Create a new macrosheet and save it as mcrGlobal. You can use this macrosheet to store global macros that can be assigned to objects on several forms and reports in your application.

2. Click the first cell of the Macro Name column and name the new macro cmdReturn_Click.

3. Click the Action cell of the next row and select the Close action. You can use the Close action to close a particular window by entering the type and name of the database object in the arguments; however, you can also use the action to close the active window by leaving the arguments blank. When you create a global macro, it should not refer to a specific form or report by name if the reference prevents the macro from being reusable.

4. Click the next action cell and select the SetValue action. Set the action arguments as shown below. Referring to the Main Switchboard form in this action doesn't prevent the macro from being reused in this application because you want to unhide the switchboard whenever you close a main task form.

    Item:            Forms![Main Switchboard].Visible

    Expression:    Yes

5. Save the macrosheet. Table 5.8 shows the macro.

**TABLE 5.8:**    The macro to close a form and unhide the switchboard

| Macro Name | Action | Action Arguments |
| --- | --- | --- |
| cmdReturn_Click | | |
| | Close | |
| | SetValue | Item: Forms![Main Switchboard].Visible |
| | | Expression: Yes |

**Pasting a Reusable Control**    After you assign the global macro to the Return button, the button is reusable. You can copy and paste the cmdReturn button to other forms in your database. When you paste a control, you paste its properties, too; this means that macros assigned to the control's event properties are also pasted.

1. Click the Categories form and select the Return button.

2. Click the OnClick event property and select the macro mcrGlobal.cmd Return_Click. The macro is assigned to the command button.

3. Select the cmdReturn button and copy to the clipboard. We'll paste this button and its macro to the other task forms.

4. Save the form, switch to Form view, and click the Return button. The Categories closes and the switchboard is displayed.

5. One by one, click the other command buttons on the switchboard that open the Suppliers, Orders, and Products forms, switch to Design view, paste the cmdReturn button into the form, move the button to the lower right corner, save the form, switch back to Form view, and click the form's new Return button.

6. Click the Print Sales Reports button, switch to Design view, and click the Cancel button. There is an event procedure assigned to the Click event that closes the form but does not unhide the switchboard. Click the OnClick property and select the mcrGlobal.cmdReturn_Click macro.

## Display the Database Window

When you click the command button with the Display Database Window caption on the Main Switchboard form, a VBA event procedure closes the switchboard and displays the Database window with the Categories table selected. Table 5.9 shows the equivalent macro that performs these operations. The macro closes the switchboard and uses the SelectObject action with the In Database Window argument set to Yes to select the table from the Tables pane in the Database window. The SelectObject action unhides the object if it is hidden and gives the object the focus. This means that if the Database window is hidden when you take the action, Access must unhide the Database window to display the object.

1. Enter the macro in Table 5.9 in the mMainSwitchboard macrosheet.

2. Click into the switchboard and switch to Design view. Select the DisplayDatabaseWindow button, click the OnClick property, and select the macro mMainSwitchboard.cmdDisplayDatabaseWindow_Click.

3. Save the form, switch to Form view, and click the button. The switchboard closes and the Categories table is selected in the Database window.

**TABLE 5.9:** A macro to select an object in the Database Window

| Macro Name | Action | Action Arguments |
|---|---|---|
| cmdDisplayDatabaseWindow_Click | | |
| | Close | |
| | SelectObject | Object Type: Table |
| | | Object Name: Categories |
| | | In Database Window: Yes |

> **NOTE**
>
> Normally, you use the SelectObject macro action with the In Database Window argument set to No to duplicate the user action of clicking in a window to select it. As in the interactive situation, the object must be open before you can select it, but you can also use the SelectObject macro action to select and unhide an object.

## Closing the Database

When you click the Exit Microsoft Access button on the Main Switchboard form, the VBA event procedure quits Microsoft Access. However, if you intend to work on another database, it is preferable to close a database without quitting Access. When you work interactively, you close the database by clicking the Close button on the Database window, or by choosing the Close command on the File menu when the Database window is the active object. We'll create a macro to automate the process. We can use the SelectObject action to activate the Database window (and select the Categories table) and then use the Close action to close the database. Table 5.10 shows the macro.

1. Enter the macro shown in Table 5.10 and save the macrosheet.

2. Click the switchboard and switch to Design view; select the Exit Microsoft Access button, change the Name property to cmdExitDatabase, the Caption property to Exit Database, and the ControlTipText to Close the Northwind database.

3. Click the OnClick property and assign the nMainSwitchboard.cmdExitDatabase_Click macro.

4. Save the form, switch to Form view and click the button. The NorthwindMacros database closes.

**TABLE 5.10:** A macro to close the database

| Macro Name | Action | Action Arguments |
|---|---|---|
| cmdExitDatabase_Click | | |
| | SelectObject | Object Type: Table |
| | | Object Name: Categories |
| | | In Database Window: Yes |
| | Close | |

## Discarding the Form's Module

We have replaced all of the form's VBA procedures with macros and the form no longer needs the form module stored with it. Whenever you load a form or report with a form or report module, Access must also take time to load the module. A new feature of Access 97 allows you to delete a form's module. A form without a form module is called a *lightweight form*.

1. Open the NorthwindMacros database.

2. Open the Main Switchboard in Design view and set the form's HasModule property to No. Click Yes in the confirmation dialog to confirm the deletion of the form's module.

# Controlling Macro Program Execution

When you create a program, you can control the order in which Access executes the actions, also called the *flow of execution*. There are three basic flow patterns.

**Sequential**   In a sequential pattern, Access executes the program by running the macro actions one after another.

**Conditional**   In a conditional pattern, Access makes a decision by testing the value of a condition and carries out one set of actions if the condition is true and another set of actions if the condition is false.

**Looping**   In a looping pattern, Access repeats a set of actions either a specified number of times or until a condition is met.

A *condition* is a logical expression that is either true or false. Here are some examples of conditions:

UnitsInStock > 0

UnitsInStock < = ReorderLevel

Date() < 12/31/96

Category = "Beverages"

Suppose a customer wants to purchase an item. Before you can fill the order, you need to determine if the item is in stock. If the item is in stock, you can sell the item, but if the item is not in stock, you can't make an immediate sale and must place a backorder instead. A macro to automate the ordering process would test the value of the condition UnitsInStock > 0 and then run different sets of actions to process the request.

## Conditional Macros

A *conditional macro* provides a way to test the value of a condition and take different actions depending on the value. A conditional macro contains a condition and two alternative sets of macro actions: one set of actions is carried out only when the condition is true; another set, only when the condition is false. In a macro flow diagram the condition is represented as a diamond-shaped decision box with two alternative paths, as shown in Figure 5.32.

If there isn't a separate set of actions that is carried out only when the condition is false, the conditional macro has one alternative (as shown in Figure 5.33).

**FIGURE 5.32:**

The flow diagram for a conditional macro with two alternatives

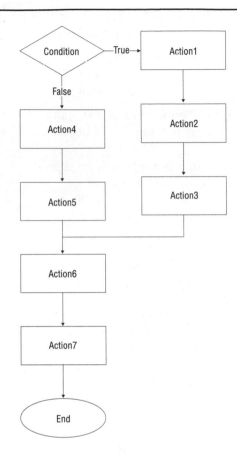

## Controlling the Flow of a Macro with Conditions

Enter the condition you want to test in a Condition cell in the macrosheet. If the condition is true, Access executes the macro action that is in the same row and then moves to the next row. If the condition is false, Access skips the macro action that is in the same row and moves directly to the next row. If the next row has a condition, the testing procedure is repeated; if the next row doesn't have a condition, Access takes the action in that row.

**FIGURE 5.33:**

The flow digram for a
conditional macro with
one alternative

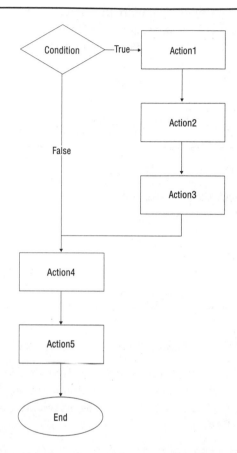

If you want to execute several consecutive actions when the condition is true, you can repeat the condition, or simply enter an ellipsis (…) in the Condition cell for each of the subsequent actions you want executed. The ellipsis acts like a ditto mark. When a consecutive subsequent row has an ellipsis in the Condition cell, Access executes the action if the condition is true, skips the action if the condition is false, and then moves to the next row.

## The Conditional Macro with One Alternative

By design, the macrosheet easily handles a conditional macro that has only one alternative. Enter the condition you want to test into a Condition cell, and enter the action you want to take if the condition is true in the same row. If there is more than one action you want to take if the condition is true, enter the actions in consecutive rows, with an ellipsis in each Condition cell. Then enter the actions you want to take regardless of the value of the condition. Table 5.11 shows a conditional macro with one alternative. If the condition is true, Access runs all five actions one after another; if the condition is false, Access runs only the last two.

**TABLE 5.11:** A conditional macro with one alternative in the macrosheet. If the condition is true, all actions are run; if the condition is false, only Actions 4 and 5 are run.

| Condition | Action |
| --- | --- |
| Condition | Action1 |
| ... | Action2 |
| ... | Action3 |
|  | Action4 |
|  | Action5 |

## The Conditional Macro with Two Alternatives

When a conditional macro has two alternatives (as shown in Figure 5.32), you can convert the macro into an equivalent macro with a pair of one-alternative conditions, as shown in Figure 5.34, in which the second condition is the opposite of the first.

Here are some examples of conditions and their opposites:

| Condition | Opposite Condition |
| --- | --- |
| [Amount] <=9 | [Amount] > 9 |
| [Name] = "Jones" | [Name] <> "Jones" |
| [EmployeeID] Is Null | [EmployeeID] Is Not Null |
| [Counter] < 4 | Not [Counter] < 4 |
| [Price] Between $.30 And $.50 | Not [Price] Between $.30 And $.50 |

The flow diagram for a macro with a pair of one-alternative conditions that is equivalent to a macro with a single two-alternative condition

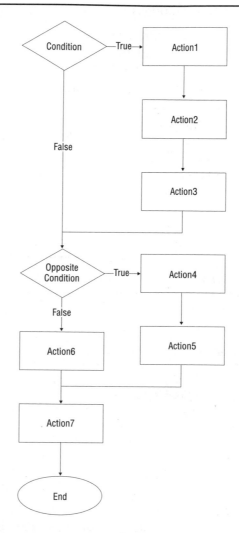

## The Opposite Condition

To create the *opposite condition* of a condition, you can either change the operator in the condition or just place the *Not* operator to the left of the condition as in the last two examples. You can use the Not operator to test the opposite of a condition as follows:

If *condition* is true then *Not condition* is false.

If *condition* is false then *Not condition* is true.

When a condition is false, its opposite condition is true.

In the macrosheet, you enter the condition in a Condition cell and enter the set of actions you want to take if the condition is true in consecutive rows, with an ellipsis in the Condition cell of each subsequent row. In the next row, you enter the opposite condition and then enter the set of actions you want to take if the opposite condition is true in consecutive rows, with an ellipsis in the Condition cell of each subsequent row. Finally, enter the actions you want to take regardless of the value of the condition. Table 5.12 shows a conditional macro with two alternatives (in a macrosheet layout). If the condition is true, Action1, Action2, Action3, Action6, and Action7 are run; if the condition is false, Action4, Action5, Action6, and Action7 are run.

**TABLE 5.12:** In the macrosheet, a pair of one-alternative conditions is equivalent to a single two-alternative condition.

| Condition | Action |
| --- | --- |
| Condition | Action1 |
| ... | Action2 |
| ... | Action3 |
| Opposite Condition | Action4 |
| ... | Action5 |
| | Action6 |
| | Action7 |

For example, suppose you are automating a catalog order business. When a customer calls to place an order for an item, the macro determines if the item is in stock. If UnitsInStock>0 the macro creates an invoice and decreases the inventory. If UnitsInStock<=0 the macro places a back order for the item. In either case, the macro places the customer on the mailing list.

If the conditional macro has two alternative sets of actions but no additional actions that you want to run regardless of the condition, you can use the StopMacro action to end the first alternative set. Table 5.13 shows a conditional macro: If the condition is true, Action1 and Action2 are run and the macro terminates with the StopMacro action. If the condition is false, Action3 and Action4 are run.

**TABLE 5.13:** You can use the StopMacro action to end the macro after the actions for the true alternative.

| Condition | Action |
|-----------|-----------|
| Condition | Action1 |
| ... | Action2 |
| ... | StopMacro |
| | Action3 |
| | Action4 |

Suppose you are automating a retail store that doesn't use a customer mailing list. In this case there are no instructions to carry out regardless of the stock level. The macro determines if the item is in stock. If UnitsInStock>0 the macro creates the sales slip, decreases the inventory, and quits using the StopMacro action. Otherwise, the macro places a back order and quits.

## Using the MsgBox() Function as a Condition

You can also ask the user to decide which set of actions to execute by using the MsgBox() function in the condition. The Msgbox() function displays a message box and a set of buttons that the user can choose. When the user clicks a button, the message box closes and the function returns a value corresponding to the chosen button. When you use the Msgbox() function in the Condition cell of a macro, Access displays the message box and pauses execution until the user selects a button. When the user clicks a button, the function returns the corresponding value; Access closes the message box, evaluates the condition using the returned value, and then continues to execute the macro.

As a simple example,

1. Open a new unbound form named frmMessage and create a command button named cmdMessage.

2. Click the OnClick property, click the Build button, select Macro Builder in the Choose Builder dialog (see Figure 5.35), and click OK. Save the macrosheet as mfrmMessage. By default, Access sets the event property to the name of the new macrosheet so you'll have to reassign the event property after you create an individual macro in the macrosheet.

**FIGURE 5.35:**

Click the Build button to the right of an event property to open the macrosheet containing the macro assigned to the event. If there is no macro assigned, a new macrosheet is displayed.

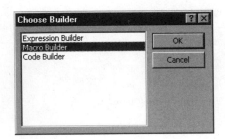

3. Enter the macro shown in Table 5.14 and save the macrosheet. The condition

   Msgbox("Do you want to continue?", 4, "Msgbox Function and Macro Action") = 6

   is true if you choose the Yes button and false if you choose the No button. The first argument is the message, the second argument specifies the buttons, and the third argument specifies the title of the message box.

4. Click the OnClick property and assign the mfrmMessage.cmdMessage_Click macro.

**TABLE 5.14:** Macro to use the Msgbox() function in a condition

| Macro Name | Condition | Action | Action Arguments |
|---|---|---|---|
| cmdMessage_Click | Msgbox("Do you want to continue?", 4) = 6 | MsgBox | Message: You clicked the Yes button |
| | ... | StopMacro | |
| | | MsgBox | Message: You clicked the No button |

5. Save the form, switch to Form view, and test the command button (see Figure 5.36).

**FIGURE 5.36:**

You can use the Msgbox() function as a macro condition to give the user a choice.

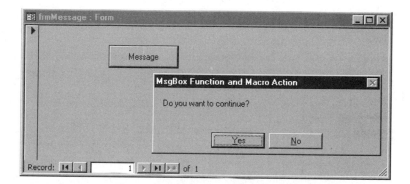

## Using the Message Box Function to Collect User Input

The MsgBox()function is a built-in function that displays a dialog box containing a custom message and title and a set of buttons from which you can choose. You can display any of the following sets of buttons:

| Button Sets | | | Button Set Type | VBA Constant |
|---|---|---|---|---|
| OK | | | 0 | vbOKOnly |
| OK | Cancel | | 1 | vbOKCancel |
| Abort | Retry | Ignore | 2 | vbAbortRetryIgnore |
| Yes | No | Cancel | 3 | vbYesNoCancel |
| Yes | No | | 4 | vbYesNo |
| Retry | Cancel | | 5 | vbRetryCancel |

Indicate the button set type by specifying the Button Set Type number or the built-in constant. When you use the MsgBox() function in macro programming,

*continued on next page*

you must use the numbers and not the built-in constants. The MsgBox() function returns a value depending on which button the user selects, as follows:

| MsgBox()<br>Function Value | Button Chosen | VBA Constant |
|---|---|---|
| 1 | OK | vbOK |
| 2 | Cancel | vbCancel |
| 3 | Abort | vbAbort |
| 4 | Retry | vbRetry |
| 5 | Ignore | vbIgnore |
| 6 | Yes | vbYes |
| 7 | No | vbNo |

The MsgBox() function has five arguments. The first three arguments are:

**Prompt**   This is the string expression you want displayed as a message in the dialog box.

**Buttons**   This is a numerical expression that allows you to customize the design of the dialog box by specifying four numerical codes as follows:

- The type and number of buttons you want to display (including one or more of the following: OK, Cancel, Yes, No, Abort, and Retry) by specifying the Button Set Type number

- The icon you want to display, if any (by specifying an Icon Type number

  - Which button is to be the default button if you display more than one (by specifying a Default Type number)

  - The mode of the message box (by specifying a Modal Type number)

  The Buttons argument is the sum of the four codes which can be expressed using numbers or built-in constants:

Buttons = Button Set Type + Icon Type + Default Type + Modal Type

*continued on next page*

The Buttons argument is optional: if you omit this argument, an OK button is displayed and there is no icon.

**Title**　This is the string expression you want displayed in the title bar of the dialog box. This argument is optional; if you omit this argument, the default title Microsoft Access is displayed. The fourth and fifth arguments allow you to identify context-sensitive help for the message box.

For reference, the Icon Type settings and their built-in constants are

| Icon Displayed | Icon Type | VBA Constant |
|---|---|---|
| Critical Message | 16 | vbCritical |
| Warning Query | 32 | vbQuestion |
| Warning Message | 48 | vbExclamation |
| Information | 64 | vbInformation |

The Default Type settings and their built-in constants are

| Default Button | Default Type | VBA Constant |
|---|---|---|
| First button | 0 | vbDefaultButton1 |
| Second button | 256 | vbDefaultButton2 |
| Third button | 512 | vbDefaultButton3 |
| Fourth button | 768 | vbDefaultButton4 |

And the Modal Type settings and built-in constants are

| Mode | Modal Type | VBA Constant |
|---|---|---|
| Respond before continuing work in Microsoft Access | 0 | vbApplicationModal |
| Respond before continuing in any application | 4096 | vbSystemModal |

# The Built-in Decision Functions

Another way to make decisions is to use a *decision function*. Access provides three built-in decision functions you can use to make decisions: IIf() (the Immediate If function), Choose(), and Switch(). A decision function returns different values depending on the value of an expression. The first argument is the expression and the remaining arguments are the possible values that the function can return. The three functions are closely related. Nevertheless, they allow you to make different kinds of decisions.

## The Immediate If Function

The IIf() function lets you make decisions by testing a condition and returning one of two different values depending on whether the condition is true or false. The function has three arguments: the first is the condition, the second is the result you want if the condition is true, and the third is the result you want if the condition is false.

> IIf(*condition,true,false*)

You can visualize the Immediate If function by using a diamond-shaped decision box to represent the condition and rectangular result boxes to represent the two possible results (see Figure 5.37).

---

**FIGURE 5.37:**

A flow diagram for the IIf() function

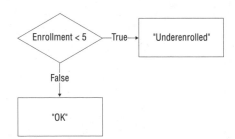

## The Choose() Function

The Choose() function creates a lookup table that returns a value from a list depending on the position of the value in the list. The Choose() function takes several arguments. The first argument, called *indexnumber*, takes an integer value of 1 or greater. The remaining arguments make up the list of values the function can return.

*Choose(indexnumber, value1, value2,…)*

If indexnumber = 1, value1 is returned, If indexnumber = 2, value 2 is returned, and so on.

The returned value must be a number, date, or string, or a function that returns a number, date, or string. There can be at most 13 values in the list. You can visualize the Choose() function as a set of decision diamonds for testing the value of the index number, as shown in Figure 5.38.

**FIGURE 5.38:**

A flow diagram for the Choose() function

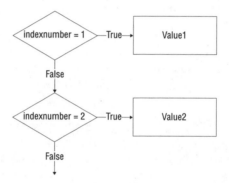

## The Switch() Function

The Switch() function takes pairs of expressions as its arguments:

*Switch(condition1, value1, condition2, value2,…)*

The first member of each pair of arguments is a condition that evaluates to true or false, and the second member of the pair is the value that is returned if the first member is true. The Switch() function evaluates the conditions, and for the first condition that is true, the Switch() function returns the corresponding value. If none of the conditions is true, the Switch() function returns a null value. You can visualize the Switch() function as a set of decision diamonds, as shown in Figure 5.39.

FIGURE 5.39:

A flow diagram for the
Switch() function.

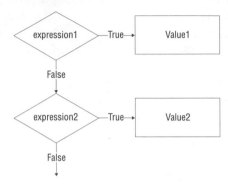

Table 5.15 (on the CD under Tables\Chapter5.pdf) shows examples of the decision functions.

You can use the decision functions in calculated controls on forms and reports and in queries to create calculated fields, to define query criteria, and to create query update expressions. You can also use decision functions in macros to define action arguments and condition expressions and in VBA procedures.

**NOTE**    Access carries out the decision functions in different ways. When you use the IIf( ) function on a form or on a report, Access evaluates the condition and then evaluates either the true or the false expression but not both. The Choose() and the Switch() functions work differently. The Choose() function evaluates every value in the list, even though it returns only one value. Likewise, the Switch() function evaluates every condition and every value, even though it returns only one value. Because Access is evaluating all of the expressions, these functions may be slow. Also, since all expressions are being evaluated, there can be undesirable results. For example, if one of the expressions that is not being returned results in a Division By Zero error, Access reports the error anyway.

## Macro Loops

Using conditions in macros gives you a way to define different results depending on the value of an expression—this is referred to as a *decision structure*. A decision structure allows you to control which actions Access executes. Access provides another way to control the flow by providing the ability to run a macro repeatedly; the macro actions that are repeated are called a *loop*. The RunMacro action provides two ways to repeat actions:

- By running another macro for a specified number of times (a *counted loop*)
- By running another macro until a given condition becomes true or false (a *tested loop*)

You use the first action argument, Macro Name, to specify the name of the macro to be run and use either of the remaining arguments to repeat the macro. You use the second argument, Repeat Count, to enter the specific number of times you want the macro to run, and the third argument, Repeat Expression, to enter an expression that evaluates to true or false as a repetition condition. If you leave both repeat arguments blank, the macro runs only once.

Using either of the Repeat arguments to run a macro repeatedly is an example of a *loop structure*. A loop structure requires two macros: one macro (the *calling macro*) to call for the loop and another macro (the *called macro*) containing the actions you want to repeat. We'll look at a simple example of each kind of loop.

## Create a Simple Loop to Run a Specific Number of Times

As an example of a counted loop, create a macro that calls another macro four times using the Repeat Count argument. The called macro displays a message box.

1. Open a new blank form in Design view. Save the form as frmLoop and set the Caption property to Loop Examples.

2. Place a command button on the form; set the Name property to cmdLoopCount and set the Caption property to Loop&Count.

3. Open a new macrosheet and save it as mfrmLoop.

4. Enter the macros shown in Table 5.16 and then save the macrosheet.

**TABLE 5.16:** Macros for a counted loop.

| Macro Name | Action | Action Argument |
|---|---|---|
| cmdLoopCount_Click | | |
| | RunMacro | Macro Name: mfrmLoop.LoopCount |
| | | Repeat Count: 4 |
| LoopCount | | |
| | MsgBox | Message: ="Loop" |

5. Assign the cmdLoopCount_Click macro to the OnClick property of the cmdLookCount button, save the form, and switch to Form view.

6. Click the button. A message box with the message Loop is displayed (see Figure 5.40).

7. Click OK. The message box is displayed again. Each time you click OK, the message box is displayed until it has been displayed four times.

**FIGURE 5.40:**

The message displayed by the called macro

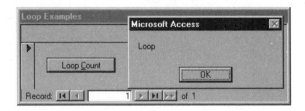

When you enter a number in the Repeat Count argument, Access automatically sets up an *implicit counter* to keep track of the number of passes through the loop, and stops execution after completing the specified number of passes. You can represent these macros with the macro flow diagram shown in Figure 5.41.

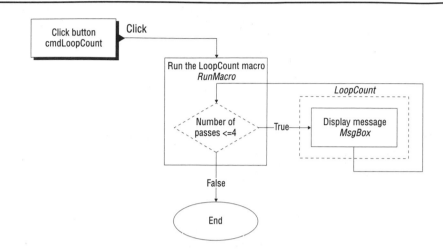

**FIGURE 5.41:**

The macro flow diagram for a loop to display a message four times. When you specify a number in the Repeat Count argument, Access sets up an implicit counter to keep track of the loops.

In the flow diagram, the operation box for the RunMacro action contains a dotted condition diamond to represent the testing of the implicit counter. Unless you keep track of how many message boxes have been displayed, you can't tell which pass Access is executing. You can have Access tell you which pass it is executing by defining an *explicit counter* and displaying the value of the counter as each pass is executed. Set the counter to 1 in the calling macro before the RunMacro action and modify the message to display the value of the counter. At the end of each pass you increase the counter by 1 before returning to the calling macro. Hold the value of the counter in an unbound text box on the form. You can use either loop structure to specify that the macro is to run 4 times: by using a counted loop (with the Repeat Count argument set to 4), or by using a tested loop with the Repeat Expression argument set to the expression

Counter <= 4

The result is the same: the macro runs for 4 circuits and displays identical sets of message boxes. Figure 5.42 shows the flow diagram for the tested loop.

**FIGURE 5.42:**

The macro flow diagram for a tested loop. The macro uses an explicit counter to keep track of the loops.

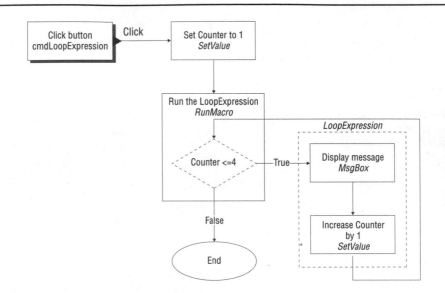

## Creating a Tested Loop with a Counter

Create an unbound text box to hold the value of the counter and a macro that uses the counter to keep track of how many times the loop is run.

1.  Place a second command button on the frmLoop form; set the Name property to cmdLoopExpression, the Caption property to Loop&Expression, and the OnClick property to mfrmLoop.cmdLoopExpression_Click.

2.  Select the Text Box tool, then click the form and place an unbound text box above the new command button. Next, set the Name property to Counter and set the Enabled property to No (but leave the Visible property setting as Yes so you can see the value of the counter variable). Select and delete the text box label.

3.  Click the macrosheet and enter the macros shown in Table 5.17. cmdLoopExpression_Click is the calling macro and LoopExpression is the called macro for the tested loop. The SetValue action in the LoopExpression macro increases the counter by 1 at the end of each circuit. Save the macrosheet.

**TABLE 5.17:** Macros for a tested loop with a counter

| Macro Name | Action | Action Arguments |
|---|---|---|
| cmdLoopExpression_Click | | |
| | SetValue | Item: Counter |
| | | Expression: 1 |
| | RunMacro | Macro Name: mfrmLoop.LoopExpression |
| | | Repeat Expression: Counter <= 4 |
| LoopExpression | | |
| | MsgBox | Message: ="Loop Counter ="&[Counter] |
| | SetValue | Item: Counter |
| | | Expression: Counter + 1 |

## Run the Loop

1. Click the form and switch to Form view.

2. Click the button. A message box displaying Counter = 1 appears, and the value in the text box control is 1 (see Figure 5.43).

**FIGURE 5.43:**

The message displayed by the tested loop with a counter

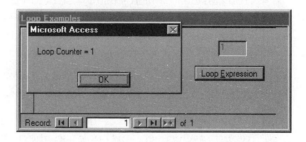

When you click OK on the Loop Counter message box, the called macro increments the counter and the first circuit is finished. Access returns to the calling macro, evaluates the Repeat Expression argument with the current value of the counter (Counter = 2), determines that the expression Counter <= 4 is true, and executes the next circuit. After two more repetitions, the message box displays the message Loop Counter = 4. When you click OK, the called macro increments the counter to 5 and the fourth circuit is now finished. Access returns to the calling macro, evaluates the Repeat Expression with the current value of the counter, determines that the expression Counter <= 4 is false, and terminates the calling macro.

3. Click OK four times. The value in the Counter text box is 5 and the loop terminates because the Repeat Expression is false.

4. Close frmLoop and mfrmLoop.

In this example you used an explicit counter in the RepeatExpression argument to control the loop. However, the expression that you use for the argument can be based on a value in a control, a property of a control, or the value returned from a function.

# Summary

The Access macro programming language is powerful yet surprisingly easy to learn. This chapter has introduced you to the basic components of the language. The main concepts are

- You can create macros using a structured macrosheet with specialized cells and combo lists of choices. The macrosheet design minimizes the need to learn programming syntax. Each instruction corresponds to a macro action with arguments to specify how the action is to be carried out.

- The macro actions duplicate the actions you take when you work interactively. In addition, there are macro actions that provide new capabilities.

- Typically, you store all of the macros for a form or a report in a form or report macrosheet. This book uses the naming standard *mformname*, or *mreportname* to document the association of the macrosheet with the form or report.

- Most macros are event macros that you assign to an event property of an object. Access runs the assigned macro automatically when the object recognizes the event. This book uses the naming standard *objectname_eventname* to document the association of the macro with the object and the event.

- Especially important macro actions include:

  **The SetValue macro action** is used to change values when you are working with a form or report. The SetValue action can change the value in the field in the underlying table or query or the value of a control, form, or report property.

  **The RunCommand action** is used to run any built-in command that is appropriate for the view that is active and for the existing conditions when you run the action.

  **The MsgBox action** is used to display a custom message box and provides one-way communication with the user. You can also use the MsgBox function to provide a choice of buttons.

  **The SendKeys action** is used to send key strokes as if you typed them using the keyboard.

- A goal in creating macros is to make them reusable. Normally, a reusable macro doesn't contain names of specific objects. A control with a reusable macro assigned to an event property can be copied and pasted to other forms.

- You can use unbound controls on forms to create variables that hold the temporary values that you need to refer to.

- Macro programming has three execution patterns: sequential, conditional, and looping. In a sequential macro, each macro action executes in the order listed in the macrosheet. In a conditional macro, you can provide alternative sets of instructions that you want carried out depending on the value of a condition. In a looping macro, the called macro executes repeatedly a specified number of times or until a condition is met.

In any kind of programming, the results aren't always what you intend. Mistakes may prevent a macro from running at all. If a macro does run to completion, you may get the wrong results. The next chapter describes the kinds of errors that will inevitably occur, how you can troubleshoot errors, and how you can prevent some errors from occurring.

# CHAPTER

## SIX

**6**

# Dealing with
# Errors in Macros

- Recognizing the three kinds of errors

- Using troubleshooting tools for macro programming

- Using the Immediate pane of the Debug window

- Understanding error codes

- Creating a simple VBA Error Handler

- Designing to avoid macro errors

In a broad sense, an *error* is anything that deviates from what you want in your application. Errors occur at every stage of application development, from the initial paper and pencil design of the database structure, to the creation of database objects and expressions, to the creation of macros and Visual Basic procedures that automate tasks and transform your interactive database into an application, to entering data and printing reports, and so on. There is a good chance of error at each step. Errors can be large and obvious or small and subtle. You deal with the obvious errors right away. It's the subtle ones that cause the real headaches—the hidden errors that you aren't aware of until they spring out at unexpected moments. The best way to deal with errors is to avoid them in the first place. Learning about the kinds of errors that can—and will—occur is the best way to begin.

This chapter describes the troubleshooting tools available in macro programming. Macro programming provides very limited ability to deal with errors that occur when a macro is running—because you can't deal with an error that has already occurred, the best strategy is to design macros that avoid run-time errors. VBA programming, by contrast, allows you to deal with errors that have already occurred. This chapter shows you how to create a simple VBA error handler that you can use in an application that is automated with macros.

# Kinds of Macro Errors

There are three kinds of macro errors:

- *Syntax errors* occur when you violate the rules of Access syntax as you are creating macros.

- *Run-time errors* occur when macros try to execute actions that are impossible to execute.

- *Logic errors* occur when your macros are free of syntax errors, execute all of their actions, and yet fail to produce the results you had intended.

## Syntax Errors

Syntax errors occur while you are creating a macro in the macrosheet. These errors occur when you violate the rules of Access *syntax*, which is the set of rules governing the spelling of certain words and the arrangement of words, symbols, and operators that you enter into the blanks in the macrosheet. If you spell a macro action incorrectly, a syntax error occurs, and Access provides you with the error message

The text you entered isn't an item in the list.

If you omit a parenthesis in an action argument or a condition, you generate a syntax error and Access displays the error message

Microsoft Access can't parse the expression: 'IsNull(Country'.

Access *parses* an expression when it separates the expression into its parts and recognizes the parts as known items that are correctly related according to a set of Access rules.

Access checks your syntax automatically and displays a default error message when it detects a syntax error. But some syntax errors aren't found until you run the macro. In this case, you may have entered an expression that Access can parse but used the wrong syntax for the situation. For example, if you use the wrong syntax to refer to a control in the GoToControl action, or if you forget to use an equal sign in the Find What argument of the FindRecord action, the macro won't run correctly.

## Run-Time Errors

Run-time errors occur when some circumstance makes it impossible to execute your macro. For example, if you misspell the name of a control in a macro condition or action argument, syntax checking won't find the error—the error lurks until you try to run the macro. For example, if you have a control named grpTitle and you misspell it as grpTitl in a macro argument, when you try to run the macro Access generates a run-time error and displays the error message

There is no field named 'grpTitl' in the current record.

to let you know that an expression in your macro refers to a field that doesn't exist.

One way to avoid identifier errors like this one is to use the Expression Builder when you create expressions. With the Expression Builder you create expressions by selecting object names from lists instead of typing the names, thus avoiding all misspellings. The Expression Builder is discussed in Chapter 4, "Communicating with Forms."

Here are some examples of situations that result in run-time errors in macros:

- Referring to a control on a form that isn't open

- Executing a built-in command that isn't available

- Moving the focus to a control using the control's full name instead of its short name

When it is not possible to execute a macro action, Access displays a default error message and stops the macro. For example, if you use the OpenForm action and misspell the form's name, Access displays the default error message shown in Figure 6.1.

**FIGURE 6.1:**

A typical default error message

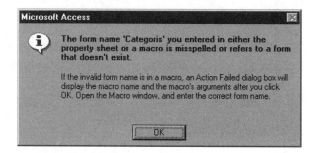

After you acknowledge the error message by clicking the OK button, Access displays the Action Failed dialog (see Figure 6.2).

**FIGURE 6.2:**

The Action Failed dialog indicates the name of the macro and action that Access cannot execute.

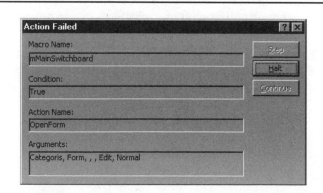

## The Action Failed Dialog

The Action Failed dialog tells you exactly where the error occurred by providing the name of the macro, the action that caused the error, and the action's arguments. If there is a condition for the action, the dialog displays the condition and whether the condition has the value True or False.

After you click the Halt button you must determine what caused the error. (Often the default error message alerts you to the cause immediately and troubleshooting isn't necessary.) Take whatever steps are required to eliminate the problem. For example, for a simple misspelling error, you need to correct the spelling error in the macro argument.

# Logic Errors

Logic errors occur when the macro action's arguments and conditions are correct and the macro executes without generating a run-time error, but the macro doesn't give you the result you intended. These errors are often the most difficult to understand and correct. Logic errors occur for a variety of reasons, such as:

- The macro actions are in the wrong sequence.

- Two macros are executed in the wrong order.

- An action has been omitted inadvertently.

- You misunderstood what a particular macro action does (for example, you used the RepaintObject action when the correct action is Requery).

- You specified the wrong field or control.

- You used the wrong operator (for example, you used < when you should have used <=).

- You attached the macro to the wrong event.

Because Access doesn't help you out by displaying a default error message or an Action Failed dialog when a logic error occurs, you have to develop a set of troubleshooting tools you can use to isolate the cause of the error.

# Troubleshooting

There are several troubleshooting tools available to help you to analyze run-time and logic errors. To troubleshoot successfully, you must thoroughly understand two things: how your macro is supposed to work and how your macro actually does work.

## Single Stepping Macros

You can use the Single Step feature to step through a macro one action at a time. Turn on the Single Step feature by choosing the Single Step command from the Run menu or clicking the Single Step button in the toolbar.

> **TIP**  Add the Single Step button to the Form view toolbar so you can turn the feature on and off when you are in Form view.

With Single Step turned on, the Single Step dialog appears when you start to run a macro (see Figure 6.3).

**FIGURE 6.3:**

Use the Single Step dialog to troubleshoot a macro.

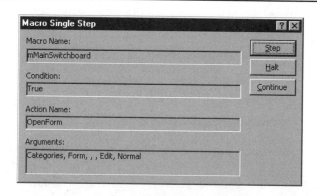

The dialog displays information about the action that is going to be executed next, including the name of the macro, the current value of the condition, the name of the action, and the settings of the action arguments. The Single Step dialog is similar to the Action Failed dialog, except that the Step and Continue buttons are available. You click the Step button to "step into" and execute the action displayed if the value of the condition is True. If the value of the condition is False, the action shown in the dialog is not executed; instead, Access steps into the next action and displays its Single Step dialog. Click the Continue button to step into the action and turn off the Single Step feature. If you don't click the Continue button, the Single Step feature remains on for the rest of the current macro and for all subsequent macros, until you turn it off. In between running macros, you can turn off the Single Step feature by clicking the Single Step button or by choosing (and unchecking) the Single Step command from the Run menu.

You can use the Single Step feature to watch the execution of each action that precedes an error; this information may help you to determine the error's cause. The Single Step feature can help you to observe the interaction of two macros that may have worked as intended when you ran them separately but don't work correctly when they interact. Such observation can be useful in deciding that one or the other macro traps the wrong event.

## Using Breakpoints

You can use a breakpoint when you want to stop a macro at a certain step and check the current values of controls and properties. You create a breakpoint by entering a dummy name, such as Break, in the Macro Name cell of the row where you want to stop.

You can use the Debug window (discussed below) to actually check current values.

> **NOTE**
>
> You can prevent execution of a specific action in a macro by entering **False** (or by entering **0**, which means the same thing) in the Condition cell in the same row. Use this technique when you want to run a macro without a particular action.

## Printing Macros

You can use the Database Documenter to print out your macros; reviewing an entire macro in print is an excellent way to understand how the macro works.

1. Choose the Analyze command from the Tools menu and then choose the Documenter command from the fly-out menu to start the Documenter. The Documenter dialog has a tab for each object type and displays a list of your database objects for the selected tab (see Figure 6.4).

2. Click the Macros tab and then click the Options button. You can choose to include information about macro properties, actions, arguments, and security (see Figure 6.5).

3. Select the macro objects you want to document, then click OK. Access produces an Object Definition report, which you can print. Figure 6.6 shows a portion of the report for the mfrmSwitchboard macro group.

**FIGURE 6.4:**

The Database Documenter

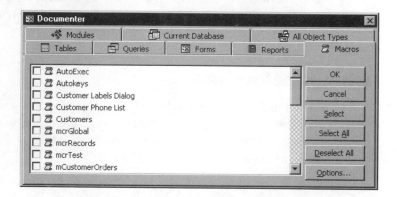

**FIGURE 6.5:**

The Documenter options

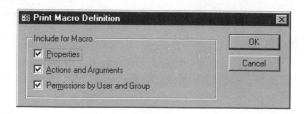

The Object Definition
report for a macro

## Using the MsgBox Action to Troubleshoot

Use the MsgBox action at critical points in a macro to tell yourself what the macro is doing. You can use a simple message, like "Got to this point," or you can display the current value of a control or a property. When you want to display a message, enter it into the Message argument as either the message itself

Got to here

or as the text expression

= "Got to here"

When you want to display the value of a control or property you can enter an expression that concatenates the text message and the control or property name, for example:

= "The value in the Address control is" & Forms!Customers!Address

A message box displaying this expression is shown in Figure 6.7.

**FIGURE 6.7:**

Using the MsgBox action
to display a value

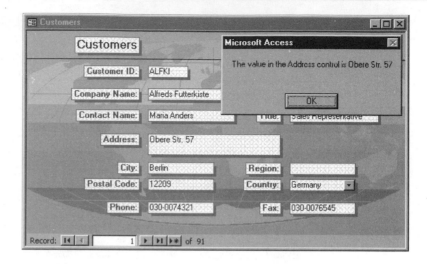

## Using the Debug Window to Troubleshoot

Another troubleshooting tool is the Debug window (see Figure 6.8). You can use the lower pane of the Debug window, called the *Immediate pane*, to display the value of a field, control, or property on a form or report, or to evaluate any valid expression. This information can help you to diagnose the error. You can also use the Immediate pane to assign values to controls and properties. In this way you can change the values and run the macro again to see the result. You can even use the Immediate pane to run a macro action, a macro, or Visual Basic code. (See Chapter 15 for information on how to use the upper pane of the Debug window.)

**NOTE**  There is a toolbar button for the Debug window, displayed by default on the Visual Basic toolbar. For troubleshooting purposes, you can add this button to the Macro and Form view toolbars. You can also open the Debug window by pressing Ctrl+G.

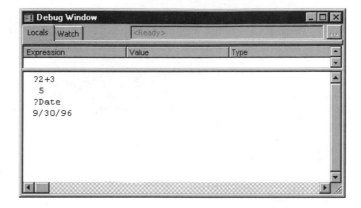

**FIGURE 6.8:**

The Debug window

## Using the Debug Window to Evaluate Expressions

You can display a value in the Debug window by typing a question mark followed by the expression you want Access to evaluate and then pressing Enter.

1. Press Ctrl+G.

2. Enter **?2+3** and press Enter. The value of the expression is displayed in the next line.

3. Enter **?Date()**. The next line displays the current date (see Figure 6.8).

4. Choose the Select All command in the Edit menu to select all of the text you entered and then press Delete to delete the text.

## Using the Debug Window to Display Values from Forms and Reports

You can display a value in the Debug window by typing a question mark followed by the name of the field, control, or property of a form or report. The form or report must be open and you must use the fully qualified reference to the object or property. For example, with the Customers form open, do as follows:

1. Type **?Forms!Customers!CompanyName** and press Enter. The next line of the Debug window displays the value in the CompanyName control for the current record.

2. Type **?Forms!Customers.RecordSource** and press Enter. The Debug window displays Customers as the name of the table that provides the records to the Customers form (see Figure 6.9).

**FIGURE 6.9:**

Displaying the value in a control and a property setting

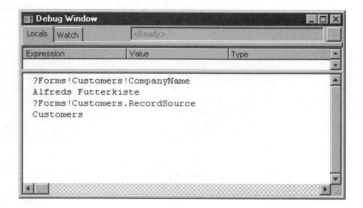

## Using the Debug Window to Run a Macro Action or a Macro

You can run a macro action by typing **DoCmd** followed by a dot and the name of the macro action with the list of arguments. Enclose all text arguments in quotation marks and use commas to separate multiple arguments. If you omit arguments, Access assumes the default values for the action; you must still use commas to hold the place of the omitted arguments in the argument list unless you are either omitting all arguments or omitting all arguments after the last one you want to specify.

**NOTE**

When you run a macro action this way, you are actually running the corresponding Visual Basic *method* of the DoCmd object. Nearly all macro actions have equivalent Visual Basic methods. You can get help on the corresponding method by searching online Help for the name of the action and choosing the corresponding method from the topics list.

• Type **DoCmd. OpenForm "Employees"** and press Enter. When you type DoCmd., a drop-down list appears displaying the methods of the DoCmd object (see Figure 6.10a). You can double-click an item from the list to enter the item in the statement or type the item yourself. When you press the space bar after entering the OpenForm method, Access displays a little window with the correct syntax for the method. (See Figure 6.10b). When you complete the statement and press Enter, Access opens the form. The OpenForm macro action has six arguments, and the corresponding Visual Basic OpenForm method has the same six plus an additional argument. To open the form with all default values, you can omit all arguments and specify only the name of the form.

**FIGURE 6.10:**

Access helps you to create statements in the Immediate pane by displaying a list of choices (a) and syntax (b).

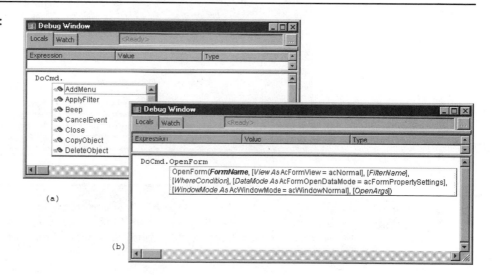

You can run a macro in the Debug window by typing **DoCmd. RunMacro** followed by the full name of the macro enclosed in quotation marks. For example, with the Main Switchboard open, enter **DoCmd. RunMacro "mMainSwitchboard.cmdCategories_Click"** and press Enter to run the macro you created in Chapter 5.

## Using the Debug Window to Assign Values to Forms and Reports

You can assign a value using the Debug window by typing the full identifier reference of the object followed by an equal sign followed by the value. If the value is a text expression, you must enclose the expression in quotation marks. For example, with the Customers form open enter the expression

**Forms!Customers.Caption = "Hi there!"** and press Enter. Access immediately changes the Caption property of Customers form to the expression you entered (see Figure 6.11).

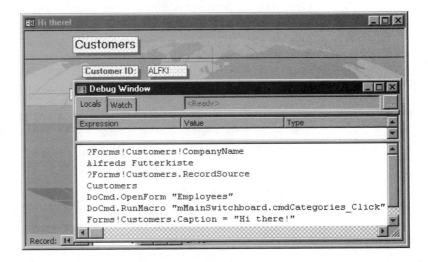

---

**NOTE**   If the Customers form is in Form view when you assign the value, the changed caption is temporary, but if the Customers form is in Design view the change is made in the form's property sheet and you can save the changed value.

# Handling Run-Time Errors: Macros versus Visual Basic

The result of successful troubleshooting is that you eliminate detectable run-time macro errors and you correct logic errors. But even with the most thorough macro testing procedures, the application you develop will probably still have some run-time errors. As examples, standard unavoidable run-time errors occur in the following situations:

- If you enter a name in a combo box that is not in the list and the LimitToList property has been set to Yes.

- If you enter a number that would result in an attempt to divide by zero.

- If you create or modify a record so that a required field is empty. (In this case, Access displays the default error message shown in Figure 6.12.)

---

**FIGURE 6.12:**

A default error message that appears when you leave a required field empty

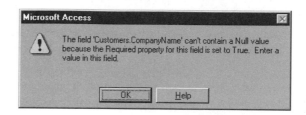

## The Error Code for an Error

Each run-time error has an integer value, called an *error code*, that uniquely identifies it. Table 6.1, which is on the CD under Tables\Chapter6.pdf, lists codes for some of the default error messages you may have seen.

When a run-time error occurs, Access displays the default error message and responds with default behavior. For example, when you try to save a new record without entering a value for the primary key, the run-time error with error code 3058 occurs, and Access displays the default error message and responds by canceling the save operation.

You can handle a run-time error by interrupting the default response, replacing the default message with a custom error message, and specifying the actions you want Access to take instead of the default behavior. Continuing with the same example, you can handle a 3058 error by displaying a custom message, moving the focus to the primary key control, suppressing the default message, and canceling the save operation. In order to handle a run-time error that has occurred, you must identify the error by its error code.

**WARNING**
A key difference between macros and Visual Basic is that you can't determine the error code with a macro—this means that you can't handle a run-time error that has already occurred using macro programming.

## Using Macro Programming

You can't use a macro to determine the error code after a run-time error has occurred, so you can't prevent Access from executing its default response. When you can't prevent a particular run-time error from occurring, you may be able to create a macro to display a custom message when the error does occur. For example, you can't prevent someone from entering a name that isn't in a combo list, so you can't prevent the run-time error (error code 2237) from occurring, but you can create a macro to display a custom message and trigger the macro with the NotInList event when such a name is entered (the custom message this macro displays in response to the NotInList event is in addition to the default error message that Access displays in response to the 2237 error).

If a run-time error causes a macro to fail, you can't stop Access from terminating the macro and displaying the Action Failed dialog. For example, if you run a macro to delete a record and a run-time error occurs because referential integrity prevents you from deleting the record (error code 3200), Access displays the default error message and the action to delete the record fails. In Chapter 8, "Data Maintenance with Macros," you'll learn how to modify this macro to prevent the 3200 error from occurring.

## Using Visual Basic Programming

An advantage of using Visual Basic programming is that you can create *error handling code* to determine the error code when a run-time error occurs and then interrupt and modify the default response to the error. You can handle a run-time error in one of two ways, depending on which part of Access generated the error.

- If the run-time error is generated by the interface or the database engine, the run-time error triggers the Error event for the active form or report; you can handle the error by creating a Visual Basic event procedure for the Error event.

- If the run-time error is generated by a Visual Basic procedure, you can handle the error by adding error handling code to the procedure itself.

Chapter 14, "Dealing with Errors in VBA," discusses the general techniques for writing error-handling code. Here we'll look at a simple error handler that you can use with your macro-automated application.

# A Simple Visual Basic Error Handler for the Error Event

A form or report recognizes the Error event whenever the interface or the database engine generates a run-time error. You can use the Error event to set traps for specific run-time errors that may occur and tell Access what to do if one of them does. Create an event procedure for the Error event in the form or report module that is stored with the form or report.

## The Form Module

As an example, we'll create an error handler for the Customers form.

1. Open the Customers form in Design view. Select the Country combo box and set the LimitToList property to Yes.

2. Click the form's OnError property, click the Build button to the right of the property box, select Code Builder, and click OK. The form module opens displaying a *code template* or *stub* for the Error event consisting of the first and last lines for the procedure (see Figure 6.13).

FIGURE 6.13:

The code template for a form's error-handler procedure

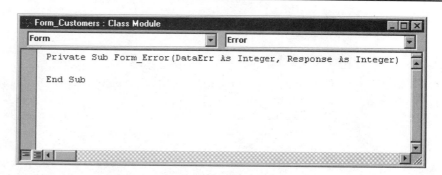

```
Form_Customers : Class Module

Form                                    Error

        Private Sub Form_Error(DataErr As Integer, Response As Integer)

        End Sub
```

Words that Visual Basic uses as part of its language are called *keywords*. In the first line of the code template, the Private keyword indicates that the procedure applies only to the form or report with which it is stored and the Sub keyword indicates the procedure doesn't return a value (only Function procedures return values). The End Sub keyword in the last line indicates the end of the procedure. Access names an event procedure for a form using the syntax

    Form_eventname

so the error handler for a form is Form_Error.

The Form_Error procedure has two arguments:

- DataErr is the error code of the run-time error that occurred. Access passes the value of the error code to the Form_Error procedure.

- Response is a response code that represents the way you want Access to respond to the run-time error. You set the value of this argument as one of the statements in the procedure. You can use built-in constants to specify the response. That is, to suppress the default error message you set Response to the constant acDataErrContinue and to display the default error message you set Response to the constant acDataErrDisplay.

You can enter Visual Basic code statements between the two lines of the code template. As an example, you can write a simple Visual Basic error handler that traps for two errors types:

- The error that occurs when you try to save a record without entering a value in a required field (error code 3314)

- The error that occurs when you enter a value in a combo box that isn't in the list and the LimitToList property has been set to Yes (error code 2237)

Listing 6.1 shows the code that traps for these errors:

## Listing 6.1

```
Private Sub Form_Error (DataErr As Integer, Response As Integer)
If DataErr = 3314 Then
    MsgBox "You must enter a CustomerID, please enter it now."
    Response = acDataErrContinue
ElseIf DataErr = 2237 Then
    MsgBox "The country you entered isn't on the list"
    Response = acDataErrContinue
Else
    Response = acDataErrDisplay
    MsgBox DataErr
End If
End Sub
```

When the form recognizes the Error event, Access runs the Form_Error procedure and sets the DataErr argument to the error code of the error that occurred. The procedure compares DataErr to specific error codes as follows:

- The If clause compares DataErr to 3058. If there is a match, the procedure displays the custom message using the MsgBox function and sets the Response argument to acDataErrContinue to suppress display of the default error message. The procedure jumps to the End Sub statement and terminates.

- If there is no match, the procedure jumps to the ElseIf statement which compares DataErr to 2237. If there is a match, the procedure displays the custom message and jumps to the End Sub statement.

- If there is no match for the If or ElseIf clause, Visual Basic executes the Else clause, which sets the Response argument to acDataErrDisplay to display the default error message for the error that did occur, displays the error code, and then terminates.

## Enter the Visual Basic Code

The title bar of the module in Figure 6.11 indicates that the module has been automatically named Form_Customers. Access automatically creates a form module to store the *event procedures* triggered by events recognized by the form and its controls. Form modules are analogous to the form macro groups we've been creating.

1. Type in the code in Listing 6.1.

2. Choose Run ➤ Compile Loaded Modules. When you *compile* a module, Access checks for errors and converts your code into a format that will execute faster. If there is an error in your code, Access stops compiling, displays a message, and highlights the line with the error.

3. Close the module. Notice that the OnError property displays the expression [Event Procedure] to indicate that a procedure has been assigned.

4. Save the form.

5. In the Database window, click the Modules tab. The Modules tab contains only the Startup and the Utility Functions modules because the form module you just created is stored with the form and is not a separate database object.

### Test the Visual Basic Error Handler

1. Click the New button in the toolbar (or at the bottom of the form).

2. Tab out of the CustomerID, enter a CompanyName, and press Shift+Enter to try to save the record. Your custom message appears.

3. Click OK. The default error message has been suppressed.

4. Click in Country combo box, type **Israel**, and press Enter. Your custom message appears and the list of countries drops down.

5. Press Escape twice to undo the record; close the form.

# Designing to Avoid Macro Errors

Because you can't use macros to identify error codes after run-time errors have occurred, the best strategy for dealing with run-time errors that cause macros to fail is to avoid them whenever possible. Following is a list of ways to help you to create error-free macros.

**Test preconditions in your macros.** Run-time errors occur when circumstances make your macro impossible to execute. Often you can avoid errors by creating and testing preconditions. A *precondition* is a condition for an action that you use to test whether running the action would cause a run-time error. For example:

- If a macro action refers to a control on another form, test to see if that form is open first.

- If a macro action requires the value of a control in a calculation, test to see if the value is null first.

- If a macro action tries to undo a change, test to see if the current record has been changed. (If you try to undo a record that hasn't been changed, the RunCommand action fails.)

- If a macro action saves a record, test to see if the primary key value is not null and is unique.

**Test for errors and fix them as they appear.** When you create a macro, try to anticipate the different ways the user will try to interact with your application. Test your application by trying out different sequences of interactions. For example, click command buttons in different sequences to see if you can deliberately trigger an error.

**Use macro flow diagrams.** A macro flow diagram is a valuable aid in understanding exactly what went wrong with your macro—for example, whether you are using the wrong event, the wrong macro action, or the wrong sequence of actions.

**Use comments.** When you troubleshoot a macro, you must understand the purpose of each of its actions. Comments in the macrosheet are essential for seeing the purpose of a macro action at a glance without having to select the row to view the action arguments.

**Use a consistent naming convention.** When you use a naming convention such as the one used in this book, your objects are self-documenting: the object name includes information about the type of the object and its purpose. This information can help you to understand your macros more easily.

**Create shorter macros.** Long macros are difficult to understand. It is often best to break a long macro into a set of short macros, each with a defined purpose. You can troubleshoot each short macro separately and isolate errors more quickly. This approach also helps you to create easily reusable macros.

# Exceptional Macro Actions

When you issue an instruction as a macro action and Access is unable to carry out the action, the normal behavior is that a macro run-time error is generated, a default error message is displayed, the macro is terminated, and the Action Failed dialog is displayed. However, there are several macro actions with exceptional behavior that you need to know about. Figure 6.14 shows the different kinds of behavior.

**Case 1** The macro action can't be executed, yet a run-time error is not generated and the macro doesn't terminate; examples are shown in Table 6.2, which is on the CD under Tables\Chapter6.pdf.

**Case 2** This is the normal behavior: a run-time error is generated, a default error message is displayed, the macro terminates and the Action Failed dialog is displayed. A few examples of macro actions with normal behavior are shown in Table 6.3, which is on the CD under Tables\Chapter6.pdf.

**FIGURE 6.14:**

The different behaviors that can occur when a macro action can't be executed

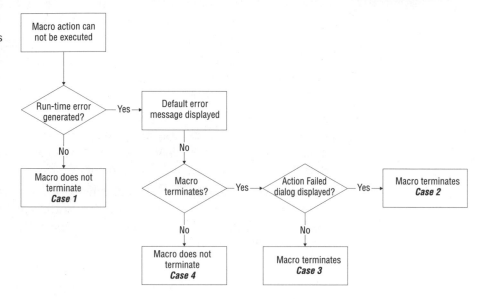

**Case 3** A run-time error is generated, a default error message is displayed, the macro terminates, but the Action Failed dialog is not displayed. As an example, the DoMenuItem with the Save Record or Refresh command generates the run-time error (with code 3314) when you try to run the action and a required field has a null value. The macro terminates but the Action Failed dialog is not displayed.

**Case 4** A run-time error is generated, a default error message is displayed, but the macro does not terminate. Examples of case 4 are shown in Table 6.4, which is on the CD under Tables\Chapter6.pdf.

Whenever a run-time error is generated, you can create a Visual Basic Form_Error event procedure that traps for specific errors. You can use the event procedure to display an informative custom message, suppress the default error message, and take additional actions within the procedure, but you can't prevent a macro action from failing. When the event procedure ends, the subsequent behavior depends on the macro action and the specific error generated; in the normal case, the Action Failed dialog is displayed and the macro terminates. In the exceptional Case 3, the macro terminates but the Action Failed dialog is not displayed, while in Case 4 the macro continues with the next action.

# Summary

This chapter has introduced you to dealing with errors in macro programming. The important points are:

- There are three kinds of errors: syntax errors, run-time errors, and logic errors.

- Access automatically provides syntax checking as you create the macro and displays an error message to indicate the error.

- When Access can't carry out a macro action (and a run-time error occurs), the Action Failed dialog is displayed indicating the action that couldn't be executed.

- Access provides troubleshooting tools that you can use to analyze errors. These tools include executing a single macro action at a time, stopping a macro at a certain step, using the Immediate pane of the Debug window to evaluate expressions when the macro is stopped, and using the MsgBox action to display values without stopping the macro.

- Two fundamental differences between macro and VBA programming are that with macros you cannot determine the error code of an error that has occurred, and that you can't prevent Access from terminating a macro. With VBA programming, you can determine the error code and write error handling code that replaces the default error handling.

- You can use a simple VBA error handler to handle errors that occur when you are working in the Access interface.

- The best way to deal with macro errors is to avoid them in the design phase. A useful technique is to test for preconditions, running the macro action only if the precondition is met.

With troubleshooting tools in hand, you are ready to learn how to automate your Access database using macros. The next three chapters take you through the major automation techniques.

# CHAPTER

## SEVEN

# Navigation
# with Macros

- Automating mouse and keystroke actions for going to a control

- Navigating using physical and logical techniques

- Finding a specific record and undoing the search

- Creating reusable controls and macros for logical navigation

- Synchronizing forms and keeping them synchronized

- Creating a startup macro

In Chapter 5, "Macro Basics," you learned how to automate one type of navigation: basic form navigation. You learned how to open a form displaying all of its records, how to hide and unhide a form, and how to close a form when you are finished. There are other ways that you travel around in a database. When you work interactively, you use keystrokes, menu commands, default navigation buttons, and the mouse to move among controls, between records, and from one Database window object to another. You can make your application easier to use by using macros to automate all types of navigation including

- moving the focus to a specified control on a form or a subform,

- moving to a specified record using custom navigation buttons,

- finding a record that satisfies criteria and returning to a previous record,

- and synchronizing two forms to display related records and keeping them synchronized.

This chapter shows you macro techniques for automating these navigational methods. The chapter ends with discussing a special macro, called the AutoExec macro, that you can use to run actions automatically at startup.

**NOTE**  In this chapter I assume you have customized the Form view, Macro Design and Database menu bars and toolbars to include the Macro command that displays the Run Macro dialog. If you haven't customized the command bars you can do so now using the instructions found in Chapter 1. In this chapter I will also assume that you've created the NorthwindMacros database as a copy of the Northwind database; if you didn't, create a copy now.

# Navigation through Controls

You can create macros for moving to specific controls on forms and subforms and within records. This section shows you how to use macros to move

- to a specific control on the active form,

- to a specific control on a subform of the active form,

- to a specific control on another open form,

- to a specific control on a subform of another open form,

- from one control to another control in the same record.

## Moving to a Specific Control on the Active Form

When working interactively, you move to a specific control on the active form by using the mouse to click the control; you can use the GoToControl macro action to automate this mouse action.

Use the GoToControl action to move the focus to a control on the active form or to a field in the active table or query. By design, you can use the GoToControl action only when the datasheet or form already has the focus. In the Control Name argument, enter the name of the control or field (using the short syntax).

**NOTE**  You must use the short syntax in the Control Name argument to refer to the field or control for the GoToControl action. If you use the full identifier syntax, Access displays an error message (see Figure 7.1) and the action fails.

**FIGURE 7.1:**

Using the full identifier in the Control Name argument of the GoToControl action leads to an error message.

Create a macro to move the focus to a control on a form.

1. Open the Orders form in the NorthwindMacros database.

2. Open a new macrosheet and save it as mcrTest. You'll use this macrosheet to store the example macros.

3. Enter the first macro in Table 7.1, named ToControl, and save the macrosheet.

4. Click in the Orders form, then click the Run Macro button on the toolbar (added in Chapter 5); select mcrTest.ToControl, and then click OK. The focus moves to the specified control.

**TABLE 7.1:** Macros to move among controls

| Macro Name | Action | Action Arguments |
| --- | --- | --- |
| ToControl | | |
| | GoToControl | Control Name: EmployeeID |
| ToControlOnSubform | | |
| | GoToControl | Control Name: [Orders Subform] |
| | GoToControl | Control Name: Discount |
| ToOtherFormControl | | |
| | SelectObject | Object Type: Form |
| | | Object Name: Orders |
| | GoToControl | Control Name: EmployeeID |
| ToOtherFormControlOnSubform | | |
| | SelectObject | Object Type: Form |
| | | Object Name: Orders |
| | GoToControl | Control Name: [Orders Subform] |
| | GoToControl | Control Name: Discount |
| ToNextControl | | |
| | SendKeys | Keystrokes: {tab} |
| | | Wait: Yes |

## Moving to a Specific Control on a Subform of the Active Form

When working interactively, you move the focus to a specific control on a subform by clicking the control. Automating this single mouse action requires two macro actions: first, you must move the focus to the subform control (using a GoToControl action), and then you move the focus to the control (using a second GoToControl action).

1. Enter the second macro of Table 7.1, named ToControlOnSubform, and then save the macrosheet.

2. Click in the Orders form, click the Run Macro button on the toolbar, select mcrTest.ToControlOnSubform, and click OK. The focus moves to the specified control in the first record of the subform.

You can test the effect of trying to move to the control without moving to the subform control first:

1. Type **False** in the Condition cell of the first GoToControl action. When you enter the value **False** in a Condition cell, Access skips the macro action in the row and moves to the next row.

2. Click in a control on the main form and run the ToControlOnSubform macro. Access displays the error message and the macro fails (see Figure 7.2). The macro fails because the focus is in a control on the main form, so Access looks for the control on the main form.

3. Delete the False condition and save the macrosheet.

FIGURE 7.2:

The error message (a) when you try to move to a control on a subform without first moving to the subform control, and the GoToControl macro action failure message (b)

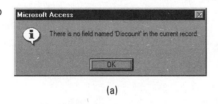

(a)

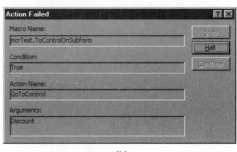

(b)

# Moving to a Specific Control on Another Open Form

When working interactively, you can move to a specific control on an open form that isn't active in one step by clicking in the control. To automate this process, you must use two macro actions: First, use the SelectObject action to activate the open form. Then, use the GoToControl action to move to the control.

1. Enter the third macro of Table 7.1, named ToOtherFormControl, and then save the macrosheet.

2. Click in the Main Switchboard form, click the Run Macro button on the toolbar, select mcrTest.ToOtherFormControl, and click OK. The focus moves from the switchboard to the form, then to the specified control.

## Moving to a Control on a Subform of Another Form

Moving to a specific control on a subform that's on another open form requires three actions: the SelectObject action to activate the form, the GoToControl action to move to the subform control, and the GoToControl action to move to the control.

1. Enter the fourth macro of Table 7.1, ToOtherFormControlOnSubform, and then save the macrosheet.

2. Click in the switchboard and click the Run Macro button on the toolbar. Select mcrTest.ToOtherFormControlOnSubform, and click OK. The focus moves from the switchboard, to the form, and then to the specified control in the first record of the subform.

# Moving within a Record

When you work interactively you can use the keyboard instead of the mouse to move the focus among the controls of the active form. The keystrokes for moving between controls are shown in Table 7.2 (which is on the CD under Tables\Chapter7.pdf).

You can use the SendKeys action to duplicate the keystrokes to move the focus among the controls of the active form. Set the Wait argument to Yes to pause the macro until the keystrokes are processed.

1. Enter the fifth macro of Table 7.1, named ToNextControl, and save the macrosheet.

2. Click the Orders form, click a control on the main form, and click the Run Macro button on the toolbar. Select mcrTest.ToOtherFormSubformControl and click OK. The focus moves from the next control in the tab order.

3. Click in a control on the subform and click the Run Macro button on the toolbar. Select mcrTest.ToOtherFormSubformControl and click OK. The focus moves to the next control in the subform's tab order.

# Physical Navigation among Records

When you work interactively, you can navigate among records according to their physical location within the recordset; this is called *physical navigation*. The record you navigate to becomes the current record. The *current record* is the record you modify with subsequent mouse or keyboard actions.

You can use keystroke combinations, the default navigation buttons (in the lower left corner of datasheets, forms, and reports), or the Go To command in the Edit menu to move to the first, previous, next, or last record in a set. Each of these physical navigation methods can be automated with macros.

## Automating Keystroke Navigation

When you work interactively, you can use keystrokes for navigation among controls, provided you are in navigation mode and not editing mode. When you first open a form, you are in navigation mode. You can toggle between editing mode and navigation mode by pressing F2. You can duplicate the keystroke combinations for physical navigation among records by using the SendKeys action in a macro; Table 7.3 (on the CD under Tables\Chapter7.pdf) shows examples of the corresponding Keystrokes arguments.

## Moving to the Last Record in a Subform

As an example, create a new macrosheet named mcrRecord to hold macros to move among the records of the Orders form. The first macro in Table 7.4 moves the focus to the last control of the last record of the active form.

1. Enter the first macro of Table 7.4 named ToLastControlLastRecord and save the macrosheet.

2. Click the main form of the Orders form. In navigation mode, click the Run Macro toolbar button, and select the mcrRecord.ToLastControlLastRecord macro and click OK. The focus moves to the last control of the last record.

3. Click the subform. In navigation mode, run the same macro as in the last step. The focus moves to the last control of the last record in the subform.

**TABLE 7.4:**    Macros to navigate among records

| Macro Name | Action | Action Arguments |
|---|---|---|
| ToLastControlLastRecord | | |
| | SendKeys | Keystrokes: ^{end} |
| | | Wait: Yes |
| ToLastRecord | | |
| | GoToRecord | Record: Last |
| ToNextRecord | | |
| | GoToRecord | Record: Next |
| ToLastSubformRecord | | |
| | GoToControl | Control Name: [Orders Subform] |
| | GoToRecord | Record: Last |

TABLE 7.4:    Macros to navigate among records (continued)

| Macro Name | Action | Action Arguments |
|---|---|---|
| ToHiddenRecord | | |
| | GoToRecord | Object Type: Form |
| | | Object Name: Orders |
| | | Record: First |
| | SetValue | Item: Forms!Orders!ShipName |
| | | Expression: "hiddenname" |

# Automating the Default Navigation Buttons and Menu Commands

You can use the GoToRecord action to duplicate the effect of clicking a default navigation button in the lower left corner of a form or choosing a subcommand in the fly-out menu of the Go To command on the Edit menu.

## Move to a Record on the Active Form

If the active form has a subform, there are two sets of records you can move among: the records for the main form and the records for the subform. The result of the GoToRecord action depends on whether the focus is in the main form or in the subform control when you initiate the action.

1.   Enter the Table 7.4 macros named ToLastRecord and ToNextRecord and save the macrosheet. When you leave the Object Type argument blank, the GoToRecord action makes the specified record in the active object the current record. If you want to make a record in another open object the current record, you can specify the Object Type and Object Name arguments as well.

2.   Click in the Orders form and click in a control on the main form. Click the Run Macro button in the toolbar, select the mcrRecords.ToLastRecord macro, and click OK. The last record in the set of records underlying the main form becomes the current record.

3. Click the Run Macro button, select the mcrRecords.ToNextRecord macro, and click OK. Access displays a blank record at the end of any recordset to which you can add new records. When you run this macro again there is no record to move to. Let's see what happens if we run the macro again.

4. Click the Run Macro button, select the mcrRecords.ToNextRecord macro, and click OK. The message box shown in Figure 7.3a is displayed followed by the Action Failed dialog shown in Figure 7.3b.

**FIGURE 7.3:**

The error message (a) and macro action failure (b) that appear when you try to move beyond the new record at the end of the recordset

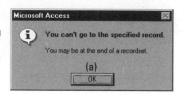

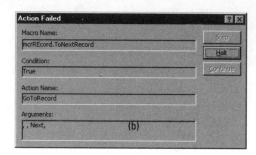

The ToNextRecord macro fails because there is no next record to move to when the blank record at the end of the recordset is the current record. You could prevent the failure by testing the form's NewRecord property. The NewRecord property has the value True if the current record is the new record and False otherwise.

1. Type **Not Screen.ActiveForm.NewRecord** in the Condition cell to the left of the GoToRecord action. If the current record is not the new record, this condition is true and the GoToRecord action runs; otherwise the action doesn't run.

2. Save the macrosheet.

3. Click the Run Macro button, select the mcrRecords.ToNextRecord macro, and click OK. Because the current record is the new record, Access takes no action and the error has been avoided.

Unfortunately, testing the value of the NewRecord property doesn't always work. The Not Screen.ActiveForm.NewRecord condition is successful in detecting the end of the recordset only if you can add new records to the recordset. If you set the form's Allow Additions property to No, there is no blank record at the end of the recordset. In this situation, the ToNextRecord macro fails when the last record is the current record and there is no other property you can test to avoid the failure. A similar situation arises when you use macros to move backwards through a recordset. If the current record is the first record and you try to use the GoToRecord action to move to the previous record, the action fails because there is no record to move to. At the beginning of the recordset, there is no property you can test using macros to determine if the current record is the first record.

The default navigation buttons and the built-in commands have internal code that detects the limits of a recordset. This code either disables the Next button and the Go To Next menu command automatically when the current record is the last record, or it disables the Previous button and the Go To Previous menu command when the current record is the first record. In VBA programming, you can test the EOF (End Of File) and BOF (Beginning Of File) properties to determine whether the current record is the end or beginning of a recordset so you can create event procedures for physical navigation through a recordset. You can use the VBA procedures to create custom navigation buttons for a form. Unfortunately, the EOF and BOF properties are not available in macro programming.

## Moving to a Record on a Subform of the Active Form

If the focus is in the subform, you can move to a specified record on the subform using the GoToRecord action. However, if the focus is in the main form of the active form and you want to move to a record on the subform, you must move the focus to the subform control first using the GoToControl action and then move to the record using the GoToRecord action. Note that you can't move to a record on the subform by setting the Object Type and Name arguments of the GoToRecord action.

1. Enter the second macro from Table 7.4, named ToLastSubformRecord, and save the macrosheet.

2. Click the Orders form and click a control on the main form. Click the Macro button in the toolbar, select the mcrRecords.ToLastSubformRecord macro, and click OK. The last subform record becomes the current record.

## Moving to a Record on Another Open Form

Use the GoToRecord action to select a record on a different open form. Use the Object Type and Object Name arguments to specify the database object that contains the record that you want to select. The GoToRecord action does not activate the database object—you can even select a record on a hidden form as the current record.

As an example, let's hide a form, move to a record on the hidden form, and edit the record.

1. Enter the third macro, named ToHiddenRecord, of Table 7.4 and save the macrosheet.

2. Click in Orders form, then choose the Hide command in the Window menu.

3. Click the Run Macro toolbar button, select mcrRecords.ToHiddenRecord, and click OK.

4. Choose the Unhide command in the Window menu, select Orders, and click OK. Access displays the first record with the value hiddenname entered in the ShipName control.

5. Press Escape to undo the change.

## Tabbing to the Next Record

By default, when you tab out of the last control of a record, you move to the first control of the next record. You can change the default behavior using the Cycle property. The Cycle property has three settings:

**CurrentRecord**   Use the CurrentRecord setting to prevent tabbing out of the record; then, if the focus is in the last control of the form's tab order when you press Tab, the focus moves to the first control in the same record.

**CurrentPage**   Use the CurrentPage setting to repeatedly cycle through the controls in a page for the same record.

**AllRecords**   Use the default AllRecords setting to allow tabbing to the next record or to the next page of the same record.

# Logical Navigation among Records

Working interactively, you can move to a specific record (if you happen to know its position number in the recordset) by entering its number in the record number box at the bottom of the window and pressing Enter. Normally, you don't know the record's position number. This number changes each time you use a different sort order and may also change when you add a record to the recordset.

An easier way to navigate to a specific record is to use the data in the record instead of its physical location within a recordset. This approach is called *logical navigation*. You can find a specific record interactively by choosing the Find command in the Edit menu or by clicking the Find button on the toolbar, entering search criteria in the Find dialog box, and navigating directly to the first record that matches the criteria. If you want to search for a matching value in a particular control, click the control before displaying the Find dialog box.

## Finding a Specific Record

Let's review the steps for finding a specific record interactively and then automate the process.

### Finding a Specific Record Interactively

As an example, we'll search for a specific customer in the Customers form in the NorthwindMacros application. The steps to find a specific customer are as follows:

1. Open the Customers form in Form view and click the CustomerID control. For the fastest search, select the search control and specify that you want to confine the search to the selected control.

2. Choose the Find command from the Edit menu or click the Find button on the toolbar. The Find in Field dialog is displayed (see Figure 7.4). Enter the search value in the Find What text box and set the various find options. (In this example, we'll find the record for the customer with company name Frankenversand with CustomerID FRANK.)

**FIGURE 7.4:**

Using the Find in Field dialog to search for a specific record

3. Enter **frank** in the Find What text box, select Whole Field from the Match combo list, and check the Search Only Current Field check box.

4. Click the Find First button. Access locates and displays the record.

## Automating the Search Process

You can automate the search process by placing a lookup combo box on the form to display the CustomerID and CompanyName. Access uses the primary key to find the record, but the user normally prefers to specify a search value using other data such as the CompanyName. Create a macro to find and display the record that corresponds to the CustomerID value you selected in the combo list. The macro synchronizes the form to the combo box.

**Creating the Combo Box** The two purposes of the combo box are to display a list of customers and to hold the search value that the user selects from the list. The combo box acts like a variable by temporarily holding the search value on the form.

1. Switch to Design view and create an unbound combo box in the form header. You can use the Combo Box Wizard to set some of the properties, or you can set all of the properties manually. Make sure the properties have the following values:

| Property | Setting | Property | Setting |
|---|---|---|---|
| Name | cboFind | ColumnWidths | 0.5; 1.75 |
| ControlSource | | BoundColumn | 1 |
| RowSource Type | Table/Query | ListWidth | 2.5 |
| RowSource | Customers | LimitToList | Yes |
| ColumnCount | 2 | Width | .75 |

2. Set the label's Caption property to Lookup.

3. Switch to Form view and click the arrow of the combo box, or place the cursor in the combo box control and press F4 or Alt+↓ to open the pick list (see Figure 7.5). When you select a value in the list, the value of the CustomerID is displayed in the combo box. The search value is held in the combo box.

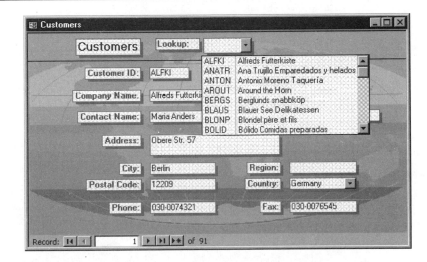

The important design features of the lookup combo box in this example are:

- When you search for a specific record, the search value is the primary key. To use the primary key as the value of the control, set the BoundColumn property to the primary key field. (This technique requires that the primary key be a single field.)

- The combo box must be unbound. The combo box control acts like a variable to hold the search value.

- The search can be successful only when the search value corresponds to the primary key of a record in the recordset. You should therefore set the LimitToList property to Yes.

- In creating the lookup combo box, you can use the Control Wizard or create the control manually. The final result is the same except that the Wizard creates an SQL statement for the RowSource property. You may see a slight performance gain by replacing the SQL statement with a stored query or a table.

## Creating a Macro to Find a Record

You create a macro to find the record that matches the search value in the combo box. You'll want the macro to run when you select a different value for the combo box and the combo box recognizes the AfterUpdate event.

**Using the FindRecord Action**   The simplest approach is to mimic the interactive steps:

1. Use the GoToControl action to move the focus to the control that you want to search (in this case the CustomerID control) and to limit the search to the values in that control. If you don't move the focus to a specific control, Access will search any of the controls on the form looking for the value you picked; when Access finds the value in the cboFind combo box itself, the search ends without finding the matching record.

2. Use the FindRecord action to find the first record that has a value in the CustomerID field that matches the value in the combo box.

3. Use the GoToControl action to return the focus to the combo box because that is where it was when you began the search and where you expect it to be after the search.

Table 7.5 shows the macro. This macro follows the *selection-centric approach* by selecting the control and then taking action on it.

**TABLE 7.5:**   The macro to find a specific record using the FindRecord action

| Macro Name | Action | Action Arguments |
| --- | --- | --- |
| cboFind_AfterUpdate | | |
| | GoToControl | Control Name: CustomerID |
| | FindRecord | Find What: = cboFind |
| | GoToControl | Control Name: cboFind |

**NOTE**

The Find What argument of the FindRecord action can be text, a number, a date, or an expression. When you use an expression, you must precede the expression by an equal sign (=). You can also use wildcard characters; for example, to find a record with a control value starting with the letter M, set the Find What argument to M*.

**Using the ApplyFilter Action**    A more efficient approach is to use a query to select the record directly from the form's recordset. The ApplyFilter macro action lets you apply a query to a table, form, or report to restrict or sort the records in the table or in the underlying recordset of the form or report. The ApplyFilter action has two arguments:

| Action Argument | Description |
| --- | --- |
| Filter Name | the name of a query or a filter saved as a query that restricts or sorts the records |
| Where Condition | an expression that restricts the records in the form of a valid SQL WHERE clause without the word WHERE (maximum length is 256 characters) |

You can apply the query directly as the Filter Name argument or you can enter the query's SQL WHERE clause (without the word WHERE) in the Where Condition argument. You must specify at least one of these arguments; whichever argument you specify for the query, the query's SQL WHERE clause must satisfy the maximum length requirement of 256 characters. If you specify both arguments, Access first applies the query and then applies the Where Condition to the result of the query.

**NOTE**

If you specify the name of a query whose SQL WHERE clause exceeds 256 characters as the Filter Name argument, the ApplyFilter action doesn't select the specified records—the entire recordset is displayed instead. The action does not fail and there is no default error message to indicate a problem.

The Where Condition argument for synchronizing the form to the value in the combo box is as follows:

[*fieldname*]=Forms![*formname*]![*controlname*]

In this expression, [*fieldname*] refers to the field in the underlying table or query of the form, and [*controlname*] refers to the control on the form that contains the value you want to match. For example, to synchronize the Customers form to the value displayed in the cboFind combo box, use the expression

[CustomerID]=Forms![Customers]![cboFind]

or use the Screen object to refer to the active form as follows:

[CustomerID]=Screen.ActiveForm.cboFind

Notice that the full syntax is required on the right side of the expression, even though Orders is the active form when the macro executes the OpenForm action—this is an example of a case where you must use the full syntax to refer to a control on the active object. Notice also that the short syntax is required on the left-hand side of the expression.

Table 7.6 shows the macro. This macro follows the object-centric approach by taking action directly on the form's recordset. The macro performs better because Access doesn't have to take time to move the focus back and forth.

**TABLE 7.6:**    A macro to find a record using the ApplyFilter action

| Macro Name | Action | Action Arguments |
| --- | --- | --- |
| cboFind_AfterUpdate | | |
| | ApplyFilter | Where Condition: CustomerID=Screen.ActiveForm.cboFind |

1. Create a new macrosheet named mCustomers, enter the macro in Table 7.2, and save the macrosheet.

2. Assign the mCustomers.cboFind_AfterUpdate macro to the AfterUpdate event of the cboFind combo box.

3. Save the form and switch to Form view.

4. Pick a customer from the combo list. Access selects and displays the record with the matching CustomerID. The message to the right of the default navigation buttons indicates that a filter has been applied (see Figure 7.6).

5. Click in the combo box and type **frank**; then select and delete the entire expression in the combo box and press Enter. Access displays a blank record.

**FIGURE 7.6:**

Synchronizing a form to a lookup combo box using the ApplyFilter action

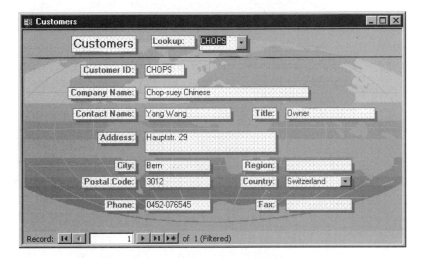

6. Click in the combo box, type **zzz**, and press Enter. Access displays an error message. If you created the custom VBA error handler described in Chapter 6, the custom error message shown in Figure 7.7a is displayed—the message was intended for the Country combo box and the VBA procedure we wrote in Chapter 6 isn't set up to distinguish between the two combo boxes. If you didn't create the VBA error handler, Access displays the default error message shown in Figure 7.7b.

**FIGURE 7.7:**

The custom VBA error message that is displayed when you enter a value not in the combo list (a), and default error message (b)

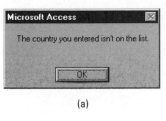

(a)

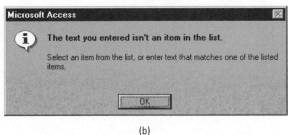

(b)

## When the Value Is Not in the Combo List

There is another way to handle the case when the typed value is not in the combo list that lets you display the typed value in a custom message box. When you type a value in the text box part of the combo list, the value is entered into a temporary control buffer. When the LimitToList property is set to Yes, Access compares the value in the buffer to the combo list. If the value is not in the list, the NotInList event occurs and the run-time error is generated because Access cannot update the control. The typed value is in the buffer and is not available for you to display in a custom message box.

Instead of relying on Access to handle this situation, you can handle it yourself with macro programming. First, set the LimitToList property to No because you are going to create your own test. You can find out if the entered value is in the list by using the DCount() function to determine if there is another record in the combo box row source having a primary key value that matches the entered value. Use the syntax

> DCount("*","[*tablename*]","[*fieldname*]=
> Forms![*formname*]![*controlname*]")

Use the asterisk in the first argument to count all of the records. The second argument is the name of the table or query that provides the combo box rows. The third argument is the search condition for finding a combo box row matching the typed combo box value. In the search condition, the fieldname is the name of the matching field in the combo box row source and controlname is the name of the control on the open form that displays the value you want to match. Enclose each argument of the DCount() function in quotation marks. In this example, the condition

> DCount("*","Customers","CustomerID=Screen.ActiveForm.cboFind") = 0

is true if there are no records in the Customers table whose CustomerID field has the same value as that displayed in the cboFind combo box on the active form. If the condition is true, the modified macro displays a custom message, sets the value in the combo box to null, and terminates. If the condition is false, the typed value is in the list and the macro continues as before. Table 7.7 shows the modified version of the macro.

**TABLE 7.7:** The modified search macro determines if the entered value is in the list before trying to find the record. (The LimitToList property must be set to No.)

| Macro Name | Condition | Action | Action Arguments |
|---|---|---|---|
| cboFind_AfterUpdate | | | |
| | DCount("*","Customers", "CustomerID=Screen. ActiveForm.cboFind") = 0 | MsgBox | Message: ="The value you entered, " &[cboFind]& ", is not in the list of existing CustomerID's." |
| | ... | SetValue | Item: cboFind |
| | | | Expression: Null |
| | ... | StopMacro | |
| | | ApplyFilter | Where Condition: CustomerID=Screen. ActiveForm.cboFind |

# Returning to the Previous Record

After finding a particular record, you may want to undo the search and return to the previously displayed record. In order to undo the search, you need to know which record was displayed last. You can keep track of the previous record by holding the value of its primary key in a new unbound, hidden text box (named PreviousID) in the form's header. Modify the cboFind_AfterUpdate macro to set the value of the PreviousID text box to the value of the primary key of the current record before running the ApplyFilter action (see Table 7.8).

**TABLE 7.8:** The modified cboFind_AfterUpdate macro stores the value of the primary key of the current record.

| Macro Name | Condition | Action | Action Arguments |
|---|---|---|---|
| cboFind_AfterUpdate | | | |
| | DCount("*","Customers", "CustomerID=Screen. ActiveForm.cboFind") = 0 | MsgBox | Message: ="The value you entered, " &[cboFind]& ", is not in the list of existing CustomerID's." |

**TABLE 7.8:** The modified cboFind_AfterUpdate macro stores the value of the primary key of the current record. (continued)

| Macro Name | Condition | Action | Action Arguments |
|---|---|---|---|
| ... | SetValue | Item: cboFind | |
| | | | Expression: Null |
| | ... | StopMacro | |
| | | SetValue | Item: PreviousID |
| | | | Expression: CustomerID |
| | | ApplyFilter | Where Condition: CustomerID=Screen .ActiveForm.cboFind |

To return to the previous record, we'll place a command button (named cmdPrevious) in the form's header, and create a macro which uses the value held in the PreviousID text box to find and display the previous record (see Table 7.9). After displaying the previous record, the macro sets the value in the combo box to match the current record.

**TABLE 7.9:** The macro to return to the previous record

| Macro Name | Action | Action Arguments |
|---|---|---|
| cmdPrevious_Click | | |
| | ApplyFilter | Where Condition: CustomerID=Screen.ActiveForm.PreviousID |
| | SetValue | Item: cboFind |
| | | Expression: PreviousID |

Here are the steps for undoing the search and returning to the previous record:

1. Click in the mCustomers macrosheet and modify the cboFind_AfterUpdate macro as shown in Table 7.8.

2. Enter the macro shown in Table 7.9 and save the macrosheet.

3. Click in the Customers form and switch to Design view. Place an unbound text box in the header section; set the Name property to PreviousID and the Visible property to No; delete the label.

4. Place a command button in the header section and set the Name property to cmdPrevious and the Caption property to Pre&vious (see Figure 7.8). Set the button's OnClick property to mCustomers.cmdPrevious_Click.

5. Save the form and switch to Form view.

**FIGURE 7.8:**

Using a hidden unbound text box as a variable to hold the primary key value of the previous record

PreviousID hidden text box

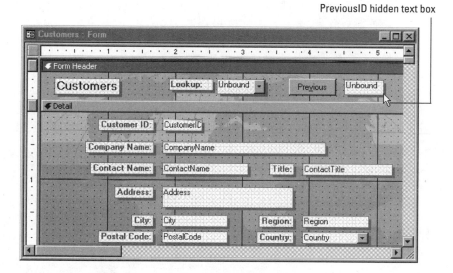

Let's test the new logical navigation controls:

1. Use the combo box to select a customer. Note the customer you selected.

2. Use the combo box to select another customer and then click Previous. The previous customer is displayed.

3. Close the Customers form, then reopen the form in Form view. When you first open the Customers form, there is no value held in the PreviousID text box.

4. Without selecting a course, click Previous. Access displays a blank record. When you click Previous and there is no value held in the PreviousID text box, Access displays the blank record at the end of the recordset.

# Remove Navigation Buttons from a Form with Logical Navigation

The default navigation buttons at the bottom of the form allow you to move back and forth through the records and display a new record. Normally, in data entry operations, you don't need physical navigation; instead, you need to navigate in a logical manner: you locate and edit an existing record, locate and display another existing record, perhaps return to the previous record you just edited, and display a new blank record for data entry. Once you've provided for the logical navigation between records, the default navigation buttons for physical navigation are no longer necessary. (In Chapter 8, "Data Maintenance with Macros," you'll place a command button on the form to display a blank record.)

1. Switch to Design view, select the form, and set the NavigationButtons property to No.

2. Save the form and switch to Form view (see Figure 7.9).

**FIGURE 7.9:**

The Customers form with logical navigation controls. The default navigation buttons have been removed.

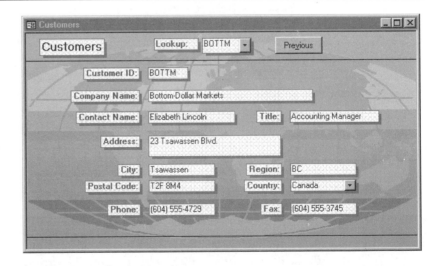

> **NOTE**
>
> If you want to provide physical navigation as well as logical navigation, you have to create a custom set of command buttons that update the value held in the PreviousID text box so clicking the Previous command button displays the previous record regardless of whether that record was selected logically or physically. The default navigation buttons do not update the PreviousID text box, so leaving them on a form with logical navigation gives inconsistent behavior.

## Adding Logical Navigation to Another Form

The techniques for finding a record and then undoing the search depend on four controls and two macros:

| Logical Navigation Controls | Macros |
|---|---|
| cboFind combo box | cboFind_AfterUpdate |
| combo box label | cmdPrevious_Click |
| cmdPrevious command button | |
| PreviousID text box | |

We wrote the macros shown in Tables 7.8 and 7.9 to find customers by selecting a value for the CustomerID field of the Customers table. We can add logical navigation to any form that has the Customers table as an underlying table and find customer's records just by pasting these controls.

As examples, we'll add logical navigation to the Customer Phone List, Customer Orders, and Orders forms in the NorthwindMacros application. The record source for the first two forms is the Customers table while the record source for the Orders form is an SQL statement that includes the Customers table as one of its tables. None of these forms has a control bound to the CustomerID field; nevertheless, the macros work just fine because if a field is not bound to a control on a form then the fully qualified identifier, Forms!*formname*!*fieldname*, and the short syntax, *fieldname*, refer directly to the field in the underlying table.

1. Switch to Design view, select the four logical navigation controls, and copy them to the clipboard.

2. Open the Customer Phone List form in Design view, increase the height of the header section, and paste the logical navigation controls in the header.

3. Save the form, switch to Form view, and select a customer from the list (see Figure 7.10a).

4. Open the Customer Orders form in Design view, choose Form Header/Footer from the View menu to display a header section, and paste the logical navigation controls in the header. Set the form's AllowEdits property to Yes—with the No value you can't change the value in the combo box and the search technique doesn't work.

5. Save the form, switch to Form view, and select a customer from the list (see Figure 7.10b).

6. Open the form in Design view, choose Form Header/Footer from the View menu to display a header section, and paste the logical navigation controls in the header.

**FIGURE 7.10:**

You can paste the logical navigation controls to any form that has Customers as an underlying table including the Customer Phone List form (a) and the Customer Orders form (b).

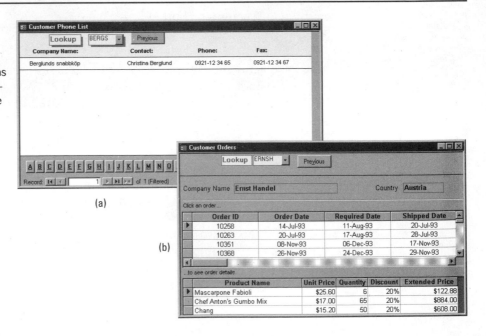

7. Save the form, switch to Form view, and select a customer from the list (see Figure 7.11). When you select a customer, the macro selects all of the orders for the customer and you can use the default physical navigation controls to browse through the selected records.

**FIGURE 7.11:**

Use the logical naviga-
tion controls to select a
customer in the Orders
form and then use the
default physical naviga-
tion controls to browse
the customer's orders.

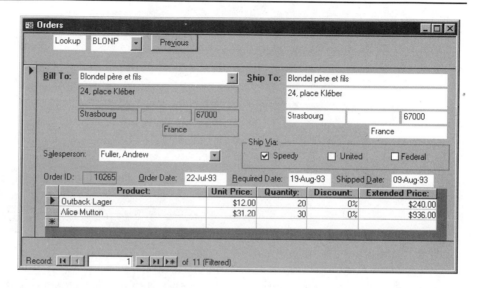

Adding logical navigation to select records based on another field in another table isn't this easy. You have to redesign the combo box with a new row source to display the new list, making sure to set the BoundColumn property to the column you are using for the search. You also have to modify the two macros to refer to the new search field and the new table.

# Synchronizing Two Forms

Often when you are using a particular form for a task, you need to refer to information on another form. For example, while placing an order with the Orders form you may need to edit the customer information using the Customers form (see Figure 7.12).

**FIGURE 7.12:**

While taking an order using the Orders form (a), you may need to edit the information in the Customers form (b).

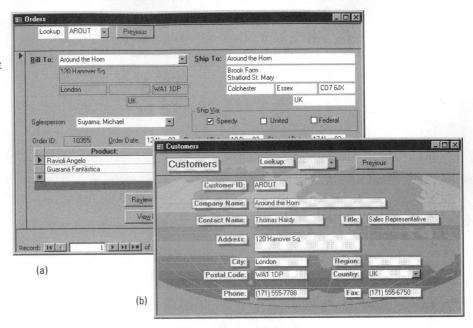

(a)

(b)

The Orders form in Northwind is designed for placing orders. The customer address information in the upper part of the main form is locked and disabled, so you can't edit customer information with this form.

> **TIP**
>
> One way to avoid data integrity problems in two tables that have a one-to-many relationship is to use separate forms for data entry into the tables. In the current example, Customers is the one table and Order Details is the many table. The data entry form for the table on the many side (Orders) displays information from the table on the one side (Customers) in controls that are locked in order to impose a sequence for data entry. By requiring records for new customers to be entered and saved using a separate form, you easily avoid the problem of trying to place an order for a non-existent (as far as Access is concerned) customer.

When you work interactively, in order to edit the customer's information, you open the Customers form and find the corresponding customer record (as shown in Figure 7.12b). In Chapter 4 "Communicating with Forms," you learned how to use the Form Wizard to create a pair of related forms. The Form Wizard creates VBA procedures to synchronize and resynchronize related forms. In this section you learn how to create macros to do the synchronizations.

To automate this operation, we'll place a command button on the Orders form and create a macro that opens the Customers form and displays the relevant record. This procedure is called *synchronizing the forms*.

In addition to opening a form, the OpenForm macro action also lets you apply a query to restrict or sort the records displayed when the form opens. You can apply the query directly as the Filter Name argument or you can enter the query's SQL WHERE clause (without the word WHERE) in the Where Condition argument of the OpenForm action as follows:

| Action Argument | Description |
| --- | --- |
| Filter Name | The name of a query or a filter saved as a query that restricts or sorts the records. The query must include all of the fields in the form you are opening (or have the OutputAllFields query property set to Yes). |
| Where Condition | An expression that restricts the records in the form of a valid SQL WHERE clause without the word WHERE (maximum length is 256 characters). |

You can specify either of the arguments. Whichever argument you use, the query's SQL WHERE clause must satisfy the maximum length requirement of 256 characters. If you specify both arguments, Access first applies the query and then applies the Where Condition to the result of the query.

**NOTE** If you specify the name of a query whose SQL WHERE clause exceeds 256 characters as the Filter Name argument, the OpenForm action doesn't select the specified records—the entire recordset is displayed instead. The action does not fail and there is no default error message to indicate a problem.

Table 7.10 shows the macro that uses the Where Condition argument of the OpenForm action to synchronize the form being opened as follows:

[*fieldname*]=Forms![*formname*]![*controlname*]

In this expression, *fieldname* refers to the field in the underlying table or query of the form you want to open, and *controlname* refers to the control on the other form that contains the value you want to match. For example, to open the Customers form displaying a record synchronized to the record in the Orders form, use the expression

[CustomerID]=Forms![Orders]![CustomerID]

or use the Screen object to refer to the active form as follows:

[CustomerID]=Screen.ActiveForm.CustomerID

Notice that the full syntax is required on the right side of the expression, even though Orders is the active form when the macro executes the OpenForm action—this is an example of a case where you must use the full syntax to refer to a control on the active object. Notice also that the short syntax is required on the left-hand side of the expression.

**TABLE 7.10:** A macro to open and synchronize a form to another form

| Macro Name | Action | Action Arguments |
| --- | --- | --- |
| cmdReviewCustomer_Click | | |
| | OpenForm | Form Name: Customers |
| | | Where Condition: CustomerID= Screen.ActiveForm.CustomerID |

To control which form the user can work with, you can require that the user work only with the Customers form and close the form before returning to work with the Orders form by setting the Modal and PopUp properties to Yes.

Here are the steps for automating the process:

1. Create a new macrosheet named mOrders, enter the macro shown in Table 7.10, and save the macrosheet.

2. Place a command button named cmdReviewCustomer on the Orders form and set the Caption property to Review &Customer. Click in the button's OnClick property and select the mOrders.cmdReviewCustomer_Click macro.

3. Save the form and switch to Form view.

4. Set the following form properties of the Customers form:

   | | |
   |---|---|
   | PopUp | Yes |
   | Modal | Yes |

5. Save and close the Customers form.

With these settings, when you click the Review Customers button on the Orders form, the synchronized Customers form opens as a dialog box. After you edit the customer information and close the Customers form, the Orders form immediately refreshes and displays the updated information.

**NOTE** A form with the Modal property set to Yes retains the focus until you close the form. You can't click in another window while the modal form is open; but you can click in menu commands and toolbar buttons. To prevent clicking in the menu commands and toolbars, set the PopUp property to Yes. A pop-up form stays on top of other open forms. A dialog is an example of a form with Modal and PopUp properties set to Yes.

# Adding the Review Button to Another Form

An advantage of using the Screen object to refer to the active form is that the cmdReviewCustomer button and its macro can be copied from the Orders form to any other form that has the Customers table as one of its underlying tables such as the Customer Phone List or the Customer Orders form without modification. As an example, we'll paste the button to the Customer Orders form.

1. Open the Orders form in Design view, select the cmdReviewCustomer button, and copy to the clipboard.

2. Open the Customer Orders form in Design view and paste the button in the form header.

3. Save the Customer Orders form and switch to Form view (see Figure 7.13).

4. Verify that the button works.

## Keeping the Forms Synchronized

Sometimes you'll want to leave a related form open so you can view its information while you return to work in a different form. Each time you move to another record in the form, the related form should stay "in sync" by locating and displaying the correct related record. Suppose you want to view product information when you are taking an order using the Orders form. We'll place a command button on the Orders form and create a macro that opens and synchronizes a form displaying product information for the product currently selected in the Orders subform: As you click a different record in the Orders subform, the product information form needs to remain synchronized.

**FIGURE 7.13:**

The Review Customer button and its macro can be pasted to the Customer Orders form (a) without modifying the macro because the macro uses the Screen object to refer to the active form. Clicking the button opens and synchronizes the Customers form (b).

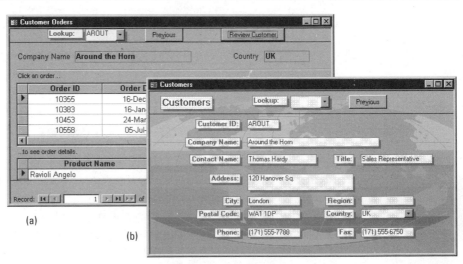

(a)

(b)

To avoid updating problems, we'll create a view-only copy of the Product List called frmViewProduct.

1. In the Database window, select the Product List form. Press Ctrl+C to copy the form, press Ctrl+V to paste it as a new form, and enter frmViewProduct as the name of the new form.

2. Open the frmViewProduct form in Design view and set the form properties as shown below. Set the form's PopUp property to Yes so the form remains on top but leave the Modal property set to No so the user can edit the Orders form while the frmViewProduct form is open.

| | |
|---|---|
| Caption | View Product |
| DefaultView | Single Form |
| PopUp | Yes |

3. Select the ProductName, QuantityPerUnit, Discontinued, and UnitPrice controls and set their Enabled property to No and their Locked property to Yes. We lock the data controls on the frmViewProduct form because the form is intended as a view only form.

4. Save and close the form.

5. Open the mOrders macrosheet and enter the macro shown in Table 7.11. Save the macrosheet.

**TABLE 7.11:** A macro to open and synchronize a form to another form

| Macro Name | Action | Action Arguments |
|---|---|---|
| cmdProduct_Click | | |
| | OpenForm | Form Name: frmViewProduct |
| | | Where Condition: [ProductID] = [Forms]![Orders]![Orders Subform]![ProductID] |

6. Open the Orders form in Design view. Place a command button named cmdProduct near the bottom of the form and set the Caption property to Vie&w Product. Click the OnClick property and select the mOrders.cmdProduct_Click macro.

7. Save the form and switch to Form view.

8. Click a record in the subform and then click the View Product button. The View Product form opens and displays information for the selected product (see Figure 7.14).

9. Click the Orders form and select a different record in the subform. The View Product form continues to display the first product.

**FIGURE 7.14:**

The View Product form is a PopUp form synchronized to a record in the Orders subform.

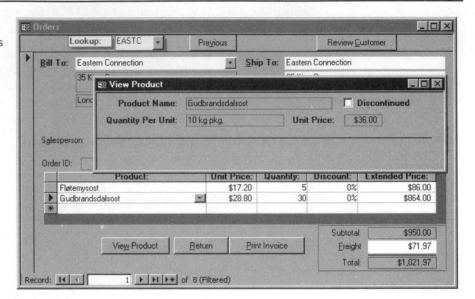

## Create a Macro to Keep the Forms Synchronized

When you move to a different record in the Orders subform, it becomes the current record and the Orders Subform form recognizes the Current event. If frmViewProduct is open when you move to a different record, you can resynchronize frmViewProduct with a macro that uses the same OpenForm action. Because the form is already open, the OpenForm action just recalculates the Where Condition. If frmViewProduct isn't open when you move to a different order, don't take any action. Figure 7.15 shows the macro flow diagram.

Resynchronizing a form
using the Current event

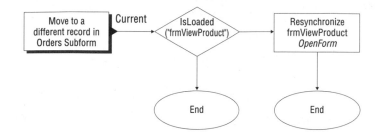

You can use the IsLoaded() function in the UtilityFunctions module in NorthwindMacros to determine if a form is open. Enter the name of the form enclosed in quotation marks as the argument of the IsLoaded() function. The IsLoaded() function returns the True value if the form is open and displays records and returns the False value otherwise.

1.  Open a new macrosheet named mOrdersSubform, enter the macro shown in Table 7.12, and save and close the macrosheet.

**TABLE 7.12:**  A macro to resynchronize another form

| Macro Name | Condition | Action | Action Arguments |
|---|---|---|---|
| Form_Current | | | |
| | IsLoaded("frmViewProduct") | OpenForm | Form Name: frmViewProduct |
| | | | Where Condition:[ProductID]= [Forms]![Orders]![Orders Subform]![ProductID] |

2.  Open the Orders Subform in Design view, click the form's OnCurrent property, and select the macro mOrdersSubform.From_Current.

3.  Save and close the subform.

4.  Click a row on the Orders subform and then click the View Product button on the Orders form. The View Product form opens synchronized to the selected product.

5. Click another row in the subform for the same order. The View Product form resynchronizes.

6. Close the View Product form. Click another row of the subform. The View Product form does not reopen.

## Create a Macro to Close the Related Form

When you close the Orders form, the View Product form should close also (if it is open). Create a new macro and run it when the Orders form closes and recognizes the Close event. This macro, called Form_Close, closes frmViewProduct if the form is open. Table 7.13 shows the macro.

**TABLE 7.13:** A macro to close another form

| Macro Name | Action | Action Arguments |
| --- | --- | --- |
| Form_Close | | |
| | Close | Object Type: Form |
| | | Object Type: frmViewProduct |

**NOTE**   The Close action does not fail and a run-time error does not occur if you specify the name of an object that isn't open or that doesn't exist. This means that it is not necessary to test to determine if a form is open before running the Close action.

1. Click the mOrders macrosheet, enter the macro shown in Table 7.13, and save the macrosheet.

2. Click the Orders form and switch to Design view. Click the form's OnClose property and select the mOrders.Form_Close macro.

3. Save the form and switch to Form view.

4. Click the View Product button. The View Product form opens.

5. Click the Close button on the Orders form. Both forms close.

6. Open the Orders form in Form view. Click the Close button on the form. The form closes.

## Synchronizing a Report to a Form

When you are finished taking the order, you can print out an invoice for the order. By default the Northwind application uses a VBA procedure to synchronize the Invoice report to the Orders form. We'll replace the procedure with a macro that uses the Filter Name argument to synchronize the report.

The record source for the Invoice report is the Invoices query. The Northwind database also has a query named Invoices Filter based on the Invoices query that you can use to select an invoice for an order. Figure 7.16 shows the Invoices Filter query in Design view. The Criteria cell below the OrderID Field cell indicates that the query selects the records corresponding to the order displayed in the Orders form (the query uses Query By Form to get criteria from a open form).

**FIGURE 7.16:**

The filter query uses Query By Form to select a record.

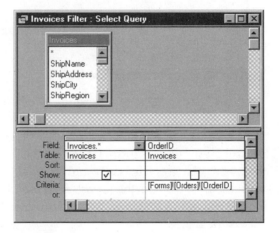

To see how the query works

1. Open the Orders form and select an order.

2. Select the Invoices Filter query in the Database window and double-click to run the query. The query produces a record for each product in the selected order (see Figure 7.17).

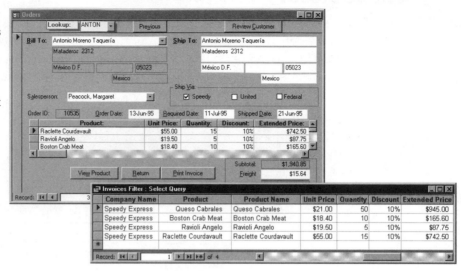

**FIGURE 7.17:**

The filter query produces a record for each product in an order. You can run the filter query when the Invoice report opens to synchronize the report to the Orders form.

## Testing for Report Data

We'll design the macro to determine if there really is an order before preparing the invoice. If an order contains no products, we don't want to print the report. A simple way to determine if there are products is by testing the value in the Total control on the Orders form. If this value is zero, nothing has been ordered, and the macro displays a message and stops. If this value is a number greater than zero, the macro opens the report, runs the filter query to select the invoice record for the order, and displays the synchronized Invoice in Print Preview. Table 7.14 shows the macro.

1. Click the mOrders macrosheet, enter the macro shown in Table 7.14, and save the macrosheet.

2. Click the Orders form and switch to Design view.

3. Select the PrintInvoice command button, click the OnClick property, and replace the VBA event procedure with the mOrders.PrintInvoice_Click macro.

4. Save the form and switch to Form view.

5. Select an order and click the Print Invoice button. The synchronized Invoice report is displayed.

**TABLE 7.14:** A macro to synchronize a report to a form by applying a filter query

| Macro Name | Condition | Action | Action Arguments |
|---|---|---|---|
| PrintInvoice_Click | | | |
| | [Total] <= 0 | MsgBox | Message: No products have been ordered. An Invoice won't be printed. |
| | ... | StopMacro | |
| | | OpenReport | Report Name: Invoice |
| | | | View: Print Preview |
| | | | Filter Name: Invoices Filter |

# Creating a Startup Macro

The Startup dialog allows you to customize the way your application starts. As an example:

1. Choose the Startup command from the Tools menu.

2. Enter the settings in Figure 7.18 to start the NorthwindMacros application by hiding the Database window, displaying the Main Switchboard, and replacing the default application title with Northwind Powered By Macros.

3. Click OK. The application title bar changes immediately.

**FIGURE 7.18:**

Setting startup properties using the Startup dialog

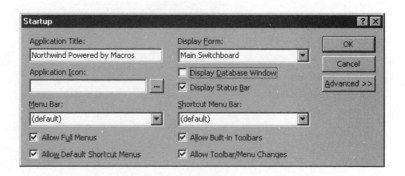

You can set additional startup conditions by creating a macro in a separate macrosheet and saving the macrosheet under the special name, AutoExec. When the database starts up Access first uses the startup properties in the Startup dialog and then runs the AutoExec macro (if there is one). As an example, we'll create a simple AutoExec macro that uses the MsgBox() function as a condition to ask if the user wants to import data. The second argument of the function specifies that the message box has Yes and No buttons and displays a question mark as an icon. Table 7.15 shows the macro.

**TABLE 7.15:** An AutoExec macro

| Condition | Action | Action Arguments |
| --- | --- | --- |
| MsgBox("Do you want to import data now? (Under construction)", 4+32,"Startup import") = 6 | MsgBox | Message: Starting the Import process. |
|  | ... | StopMacro |
|  | MsgBox | Message: Import will not take place now. |

1. Open a new macrosheet and save it with the name AutoExec. Enter the macro shown in Table 7.15 and save the macrosheet.

2. Test the macro by choosing the Run command from the Run menu.

3. Close the database and reopen. Access opens the database using the startup properties set in Figure 7.18 and displays the custom message box (see Figure 7.19). Because the import process hasn't been developed, either choice leads to closing the message box(s) and returning to the Main Switchboard form.

**FIGURE 7.19:**

Use an AutoExec macro to run macro actions on startup.

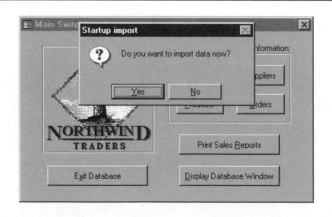

> **NOTE** Bypass the Startup properties and the AutoExec macro by holding down the Shift key when you open the database.

# Summary

This chapter has introduced you to using macro programming to automate navigation between controls, records, and forms. The important techniques are:

- You can use the GoToControl macro action to move the focus to a specified control on an active form or datasheet. Moving to a control may require other actions to select the form or datasheet first.

- You can automate navigation among records according to their physical location (physical navigation) by duplicating keyboard combinations using the SendKeys macro action or by using the GoToRecord macro action.

- In macro programming there is no way to test whether the current record is the first record in a recordset and only a limited way to test whether the current record is the last record in a recordset.

- You can automate navigation to a specific record using data in the record (logical navigation) in two ways: you can duplicate the interactive search technique using the FindRecord macro action, and you can use the ApplyFilter action to apply a query to select the record. This second technique is normally more efficient.

- You can undo a search by creating macros that store the primary key of a record in a hidden text box and use the stored value to return to the record.

- In many cases you can create reusable macros by using properties of the Screen object to refer to the active form or control and avoid including the name of the object in the macro.

- You can use arguments of the OpenForm macro action to synchronize a second form to the first form. You can keep the second form synchronized as you browse records of the first form by using the form's Current event to repeat the OpenForm action each time you move to a different record.

- You can create a macro named AutoExec that Access runs automatically immediately after setting the startup conditions you specified in the Startup dialog.

# Data Maintenance with Macros

- Changing the timing of validation testing

- Using preconditions to avoid macro errors

- Using the DCount() function

- Using the MsgBox() function

- Carrying values forward to a new record

- Entering data in two open forms

- Refreshing versus requerying

In this chapter you learn how to automate data entry operations. For several of these tasks, you can create reusable controls, linked to reusable macros, that you can paste directly to other data entry forms. In order for the data entry macros to be reusable, the primary key control must have the same Name property on all data entry forms; that way the macro can always use the same reference for this control. You'll change the primary key control's Name property on each data entry form.

> **NOTE**
>
> Changing the Name property of a bound control does not affect the field name in the underlying table. You can refer to the field using either Forms!*formname*!*controlname* to refer to the control or Forms!*formname*!*fieldname* to refer to the field.

In addition, whether the automated operation is reusable or not, we use the properties of the Screen object to avoid referring to specific forms and controls (in order to minimize changes when you use the operation on another form).

In this chapter you'll learn to automate operations that add new records; edit, enter, and validate data; reverse changes made during editing; save records; delete records; and work with two open data entry forms. When two data entry forms are based on the same underlying data, you can use macro programming to automate the update of records to ensure that both forms display the most current data.

> **NOTE**
>
> This chapter assumes you have customized the Form view, Macro Design and Database menu bars and toolbars to include the Macro command that displays the Run Macro dialog. If you haven't customized the command bars you can do so now, as described in Chapter 5. This chapter also assumes that you've created the NorthwindMacros database as a copy of the Northwind database. Create a copy now, if necessary.

# Using Macros to Validate Data

Typically, a data entry form is designed with combo boxes, list boxes, option groups, and check boxes to aid in fast and accurate data entry. In addition to using these special controls to improve accuracy, you can protect your data with validation rules that specify requirements for the data you enter.

## Using ValidationRule Properties

Access provides opportunities to validate data by setting ValidationRule properties and to display custom messages when the validation rules are not satisfied by setting the ValidationText properties. You can create validation rules and messages when you set field and table properties in table design and when you set control properties in form design, as follows:

- For an individual field, set the ValidationRule property in the field properties list in the table's Design view. Access tests a field's ValidationRule property when you try to tab out of the field. A field validation rule cannot contain references to other fields. If the validation rule is satisfied, Access updates the field to the record buffer; otherwise, Access doesn't update the field, but displays the message you set in the ValidationText property (or a default message if you didn't set one) and prevents you from tabbing out of the field until you either undo the entry or enter a value that satisfies the rule (refer to Chapter 2 for more information on the update process).

- For a record in a table, set the ValidationRule property in the table's property sheet in table Design view. A record validation rule can refer to other fields in the same record. Access tests the ValidationRule property for the record when you try to save the record. Access also tests the referential integrity options you've elected when you try to save the record. If the validation rule for the record is satisfied, Access updates the record to the table. Otherwise, Access doesn't update the record, but displays your custom message (or a default message) and prevents you from saving the record until you either undo the record or enter values that satisfy the validation rule. Figure 8.1 shows the ValidationRule property in the field properties list and in the table properties sheet.

**FIGURE 8.1:**

The ValidationRule property in the field properties list and in the Table Properties sheet

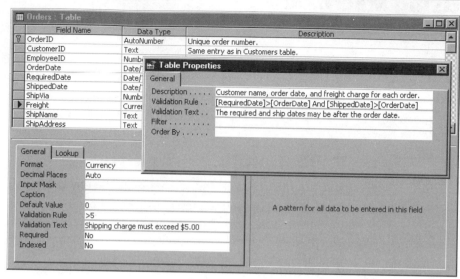

- For an individual control displayed in a form, set the ValidationRule property in the control's property sheet in form Design view. A control's validation rule can refer to other fields in the table, to fields and controls in other forms, or to the results of calculations with domain aggregate functions. Access tests the control's validation rule when you try to tab out of the control. If the control's validation rule is satisfied, Access updates the control to the record buffer. Otherwise, Access doesn't update the control, but displays your custom message (or a default message) and prevents you from tabbing out of the control until you undo the value or enter valid data. Figure 8.2 shows the ValidationRule property in a control's property sheet.

When you set validation rules in a form as well as in its underlying table, Access enforces both sets of rules. A validation rule that you set for a control at the form level overrides any validation rules you may have set at the table level. Validation rules for controls and fields are enforced in the following order:

1. The control's ValidationRule property as set in the control's property sheet

2. The field's ValidationRule property as set in the field's property sheet

3. The record's ValidationRule property as set in the table's property sheet

**FIGURE 8.2:**

The ValidationRule property in a control's property sheet

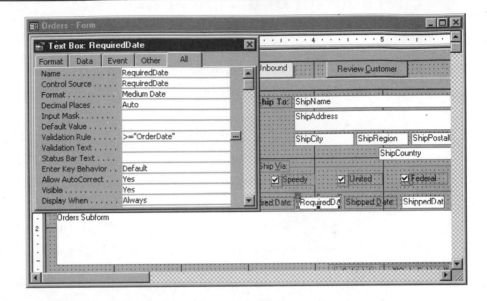

You can use macros and VBA procedures to set more complicated validation rules. For example, you can use programming when you want to

- display different messages depending on the value entered,

- ask the user for input on whether to use a validation rule,

- use more than one validation rule to validate a record,

- or change the timing of the validation.

The order of validation depends on which event triggers the validation macro or procedure. For example, a macro triggered by the BeforeUpdate event of a control is executed before the control's ValidationRule property is enforced.

**NOTE**  This chapter assumes the primary key for a table is a single field unless the table is a linking table. You'll have to modify the techniques when the primary key is more than one field.

# Checking for Duplicate Primary Key Values

In this section, you'll use a macro to change the timing of the test for uniqueness of the primary key value. By default, Access tests for uniqueness when you try to save the record—you'll create a macro to perform the test as soon as you enter a value in the primary key control instead.

When you design a data table, you specify how the primary key is entered. You can

- automatically assign sequential numbers by using an AutoNumber field as the primary key,

- create your own expressions to assign unique values automatically,

- or permit the primary key to be entered as part of data entry.

No matter how the value is entered, Access checks for duplicate values when you try to save the record. Often, it is more convenient to test for uniqueness as soon as you leave the primary key control instead of waiting until you enter values in all of the data controls and try to save the record. You can create a macro to handle the uniqueness test yourself and run the macro as soon as you try to update the changed control.

## Using DCount() to Test for Uniqueness

You can check for uniqueness by using the DCount() function to determine if there is another record in the table having a primary key value that matches the value entered in the control. Use the syntax

DCount("*", "[*tablename*]", "[*fieldname*]=Forms![*formname*]![*controlname*]")

The first argument is the name of the field you are using to count the records; you can use either the primary key field or the asterisk to count all of the records that satisfy the search condition. The second argument is the name of the table. The third argument is the search condition for including table records where field-name is the name of the matching field in the table and controlname is the name of the control on the open form that displays the value you want to match. Enclose each argument of the DCount() function in quotation marks.

As an example, we'll create a macro to validate the CustomerID for the Customers form in NorthwindMacros. In this case, the expression

DCount("*","Customers","CourseID=Screen.ActiveForm.PrimaryID")

counts the number of records in the Customers table whose CourseID field has the same value as that displayed in the PrimaryID control on the active form. If there is another record with the same primary key value, the DCount() function has the value 1; in this case, the macro displays a custom message and cancels the updating. If there isn't another record, the DCount() function has the value 0, the macro terminates, and Access updates the control. You run the macro after Access acknowledges that the data in the control has changed but before you update the control. That is, you run the macro when the control recognizes the BeforeUpdate event. Table 8.1 shows the macro. The macro uses the CancelEvent action to cancel the updating of the control. (Refer to Chapter 2, "Getting Started with Objects and Events," for more information on canceling the default behavior following an event.)

**TABLE 8.1:** A macro to validate the uniqueness of the primary key value when you try to update the primary key control

| Macro Name | Condition | Action | Action Arguments |
| --- | --- | --- | --- |
| PrimaryID_BeforeUpdate | | | |
| | DCount("*","Customers", "CustomerID=Screen .ActiveForm.PrimaryID")>0 | MsgBox | Message: There is another record with this ID. You must enter a unique ID or press the Esc key to undo the record. |
| | ... | CancelEvent | |

1. Open the mCustomers macrosheet, enter the macro in Table 8.1 and save the macrosheet.

2. Open the Customers form in Design view and select the PrimaryID control. (If you haven't changed the name of the CustomerID control to PrimaryID, you can do so now.)

3. Click in the BeforeUpdate property and select the macro mCustomers .PrimaryID_BeforeUpdate. (Replace the Customer.ValidateID macro.)

4. Save the form and switch to Form view.

5. Choose the Go To command and then the New Record subcommand from the Edit menu. Enter ALFKI for the CustomerID and press Tab. Access displays the custom message (see Figure 8.3).

**FIGURE 8.3:**

Displaying a custom message before canceling the update

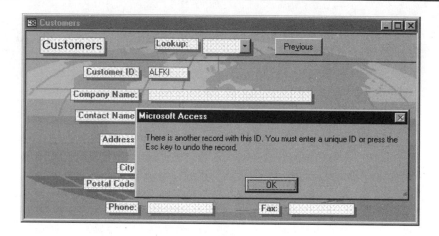

# Display a Primary Key Violation Form instead of a Message

Instead of displaying a message that there is another record with the same primary key value entered previously in the table, it is often more helpful to display the previous record itself. With the previous record displayed, you can determine whether the record you are trying to enter duplicates a record already in the table or that the record only needs a different primary key value before it can be saved.

## Create a Primary Key Violation Form

Create a copy of the Customers form to display the record with the duplicate primary key as follows:

1. Close the Customers form, select the form in the Database window, then copy the form and paste it as frmViewCustomer. We modify the new form in the new steps.

2. Open the new frmViewCustomer form in Design view, uncheck the Form Header/Footer command from the View menu to delete the header and footer sections. Click Yes in the confirmation dialog to delete the header and the header controls.

3. Select all of the data controls and set their Enabled property to No and their Locked property to Yes; rearrange the controls to minimize the size of the form.

4. Select the form and set the following form properties:

    Caption          Primary Key Violation

    BorderStyle      Dialog

    PopUp            Yes

    Picture

5. Save and close the form. (Figure 8.4 shows the form.)

---

**FIGURE 8.4:**

You can display the record that has the duplicate primary key instead of a message. Avoid data inconsistencies by displaying a form with locked controls.

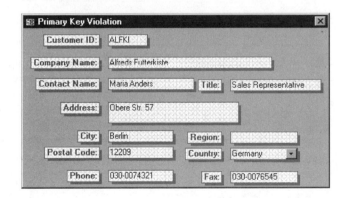

## Modify the Macro

Modify the macro to open frmViewCustomer and display the synchronized record as shown in Table 8.2.

**TABLE 8.2:** A macro to validate the uniqueness of the primary key and display a primary key violation form

| Macro Name | Condition | Action | Action Arguments |
|---|---|---|---|
| PrimaryID_BeforeUpdate | | | |
| | DCount("*","Customers", "CustomerID=Screen .ActiveForm.PrimaryID")>0 | OpenForm | Form Name: frmViewCustomer |
| | | | Where Condition: CustomerID = Screen.ActiveForm. PrimaryID |
| | ... | CancelEvent | |

1. Click in mCustomers macrosheet, modify the macro as shown in Table 8.2, and save the macrosheet.

2. Open the Customers form in Form view.

3. Choose the Go To command and then the New Record subcommand from the Edit menu. Enter ALFKI for the CustomerID and press Tab. Access displays the Primary Key Violation form for the CustomerID.

4. Close the Primary Key Violation form; press Escape twice to undo first the control and then the record. (See Chapter 2 for information on the two-buffer system that Access uses for updating fields and records.)

# Adding New Records

You can automate a set of standard operations that all simple data entry forms need. You begin with operations for adding a new record, undoing changes, and saving a record.

In each case, you analyze the interactive process, create a command button, and then design a macro to automate the process. In designing the macro you'll anticipate macro errors and standard run-time errors, and you'll include tests of preconditions in order to avoid those errors. By avoiding names of specific forms, you can make the control and macros reusable so you can copy them to other forms with little or no modification.

## Creating Command Buttons for Data Entry Operations

Create a set of three command buttons for the data entry operations for the Customers form.

1. Open the Customers form in Design view.

2. With the Control Wizards tool deselected, place three command buttons in the header section (rearrange the controls to make room as in Figure 8.5), and set a Name and Caption property for each as follows:

| Name | Caption |
|------|---------|
| cmdNew | &New |
| cmdUndo | &Undo |
| cmdSave | &Save |

**FIGURE 8.5:**

Place command buttons for adding a new record, undoing changes, and saving the record in the header section.

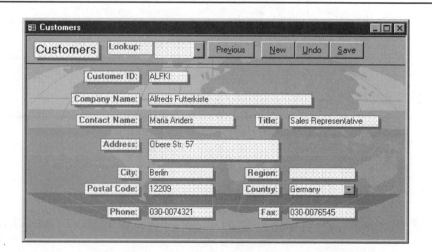

# Analyze and Automate the Process

When you work interactively, you can add a new record by selecting the Go To command from the Edit menu and the New Record command from the fly-out menu, or by clicking the New button (either on the toolbar or grouped with the default navigation buttons on the form).

1.  Select the Edit ➤ Go To ➤ New Record command. A new blank record is displayed.

2.  Select the Edit ➤ Go To ➤ New Record command again. Because a new record is the current record, the New Record command is grayed out and unavailable.

You can use the GoToRecord macro action to move to a new record, duplicating the effect of the built-in command.

## Create the Macro

You can create a macro that uses the GoToRecord action to go to a new record (see Table 8.3).

**TABLE 8.3:**  A macro to display a new record

| Macro Name | Action | Action Arguments |
| --- | --- | --- |
| cmdNew_Click | | |
| | GoToRecord | Record: New |

1.  Open the mcrGlobal macrosheet, enter the macro in Table 8.3, and save the macrosheet. We are creating reusable macros for the data entry operations, so we'll store them in the global macrosheet instead of the form's macrosheet.

2.  Select the New button in the form, click the OnClick property, and select mcrGlobal.cmdNew_Click.

3.  Save the form and switch to Form view.

4.  Switch to Form view and click the form's New button. A new record is displayed.

5. Click the New button again. There is no response to additional clicks of the New button because the GoToRecord action doesn't fail when the current record is the new record.

# Undoing Changes

After you make changes to a control, you can undo the changes interactively either by selecting the Edit ➤ Undo Typing command (if the focus has not left the control) or by selecting the Edit ➤ Undo Current Field/Record command (if the focus has left the control but you have not moved to another record). If you have not made any changes to the record, neither Undo command is available.

Take a look at how the Undo commands respond to changes in focus:

1. With the new record displayed, click the Edit menu. The Can't Undo command is grayed out and unavailable.

2. Using the Lookup combo box (or the default navigation buttons if you haven't hidden them), move to another record and click the Edit menu. The Can't Undo command is still grayed out.

3. Click in the Address control, change the address, then click the Edit menu. The Undo Typing command is available.

4. Tab to the next control and click the Edit menu. The UndoCurrentField command is available.

## Design a Macro to Test the Dirty Property

You can create a macro with a RunCommand macro action to issue an Undo command. You must design the macro to run the Undo command only when the command is available, otherwise the macro action will fail. Because one of the Undo commands is available only when you have actually made a change to the record, you need a way to test whether the current record has been changed before issuing the command. To do so, you can use the form's Dirty property. (Yes, it is actually called the Dirty property.) The Dirty property has the value True if the current record has been modified since it was last saved, and it has the value False otherwise. The Dirty property is not listed in the form's property sheet because you can't set this property. Access controls the value of the Dirty property; you can only observe the value.

If the Dirty property is True, the record has been changed and your macro reverses the change. If the Dirty property is False, the macro terminates. Table 8.4 shows the macro. This macro uses the Form property to refer to the active form.

**TABLE 8.4:** A macro to undo a change. This macro determines if the record has been changed before issuing the command.

| Macro Name | Condition | Action | Action Arguments |
|---|---|---|---|
| cmdUndo_Click | | | |
| | Screen.ActiveForm.Dirty | RunCommand | Command: Undo |

1. Click in mcrGlobal, enter the macro shown in Table 8.4, and save the macrosheet.

2. Click in the form and switch to Design view. Click the Undo button, click in the OnClick property, and then select the mcrGlobal.cmdUndo_Click macro.

3. Switch to Form view. Use the lookup combo box to select a customer, then click in the Address control and make a change.

4. Click the Undo button. The change is reversed.

5. Click in the Address control, make a change, and tab to the next control.

6. Click the Undo button. The change is reversed.

7. Select another existing record and click the Undo button. There is no response. The record has not been changed; the macro tests the precondition and terminates before trying to run the Undo command.

8. Click the New button and then click the Undo button. There is no response.

# Saving Changes

When you work interactively with a form, there are several ways you can save changes to a record, including choosing Records ➤ Save Record to save changes without moving the focus, choosing File ➤ Close to close the active form, pressing Shift+Enter to save changes without moving the focus, pressing Ctrl+F4 to close the active form, and moving the focus to a different or new record.

You can also initiate saving a record by using the custom controls you've placed on the form, including clicking the Return button on the form, clicking the New button on the form, and selecting another record using the lookup combo box.

## Create the Macro

You can create a macro with a RunCommand macro action to issue the Save Record command (see Table 8.5).

**TABLE 8.5:**   A macro to save a record

| Macro Name | Action | Action Arguments |
| --- | --- | --- |
| cmdSave_Click | | |
| | RunCommand | Command: SaveRecord |

1. Click in mcrGlobal, enter the macro shown in Table 8.5, and save the macrosheet.

2. Click in Customers, select the Save button, click the OnClick property, and select the mcrGlobal.cmdSave_Click macro.

3. Save the form and switch to Form view.

4. Edit a record and click the form's Save button.

## Date-Stamp a Changed Record

You can create a macro that saves the current date when you edit a record. Include a DateModified field with a Date/Time data type in each data table to keep track of the last edit date. It isn't necessary to place a control on the data entry form: you can use a macro to set the value of a field whether or not the form has a control bound to the field. Use the fully qualified identifier

Forms!*formname*!*fieldname*

or the short syntax when the macro runs from the active form

*fieldname*

to refer directly to a field in the underlying table or query. If you do place a DateModified control on a data entry form, set its Enabled property to No and its Locked property to Yes, set the TabStop property to No, and set the visual cues to indicate the control can't be changed.

## Add a DateModified Field and Control

As an example, let's add a DateModified field to the Customers table and a control to the Customers form.

1. Close the Customers form and open the Customers table in Design view.

2. Add a DateModified field, set the data type to Date/Time, and then save and close the table.

3. Open the Customers form in Design view. Drag the DateModified field from the field list to the upper right corner of detail section of the form.

4. Set the control's properties as follows:

| Property | Setting |
|---|---|
| BackStyle | Transparent |
| Special Effect | Flat |
| BorderStyle | Transparent |
| Enabled | No |
| Locked | Yes |

5. Click the Format Painter button in the toolbar and click the label for the DateModified control.

You can create a macro that uses the built-in Now() function to set the value of the DateModified control to the current date and time (see Table 8.6). Run the macro after Access acknowledges that the record has been changed, but before the changes are updated to the table. (That is, run the macro when the form recognizes the BeforeUpdate event.)

**TABLE 8.6:** A macro to date-stamp a record

| Macro Name | Action | Action Arguments |
|---|---|---|
| Form_BeforeUpdate | | |
| | SetValue | Item: DateModified |
| | | Expression: Now() |

1. Click mcrGlobal, enter the macro shown in Table 8.6, and save the macrosheet.

2. Click the Customers form, click the form's BeforeUpdate event property, and select the mcrGlobal.Form_BeforeUpdate macro.

3. Save the form and switch to Form view.

4. Make a change in a control and click the form's Save button. The DateModified control displays the current date and time (see Figure 8.6).

**FIGURE 8.6:**

Date-stamping a record

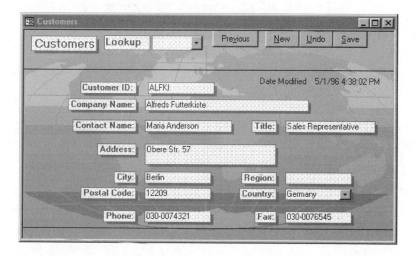

# Saving a New Record

When you save a new record on a data entry form that has a lookup combo box, Access doesn't automatically run the query that provides the records for the combo box list. To illustrate this, we'll add a new customer using the Customers form.

1. Open the Customers form in Form view, click the New button, and add a new customer as follows:

   | | |
   |---|---|
   | CustomerID | ARCHP |
   | CompanyName | Archipelago Mercantile |

2. Click the Save button.

3. Click the down arrow of the Lookup combo box. The new record does not appear in the lookup combo list.

4. Update the combo box by choosing Records ➤ Refresh or by pressing the F9 key. Click the down arrow of the Lookup combo box. The new record is in the list.

You can automate the update by creating a macro that requeries the combo box using the Requery action and running the macro just after the new record is saved (that is, when the form recognizes the AfterInsert event). Table 8.7 shows the macro.

**TABLE 8.7:** A macro to requery the Lookup combo box

| Macro Name | Action | Action Arguments |
|---|---|---|
| Form_AfterInsert | | |
| | Requery | Control Name: cboFind |

1. Open the mcrGlobal macrosheet, enter the macro shown in Table 8.7, and save the macrosheet.

2. Click Customers and switch to Design view.

3. Click the form's AfterInsert property and select the mCustomers.Form_AfterInsert macro.

4. Save the form and switch to Form view.

5. Click the form's New button and enter the new customer:

CustomerID          BOULD

CompanyName    Boulder Steamers

6. Click the form's Save button and then click the arrow of the combo box. The new customer appears in the list.

# Carrying Values Forward to a New Record

When you are creating a new record and the new record has fields with the same values as the previous record, you can speed data entry by having the fields in the new record filled in automatically. One way to carry values forward from the current record to the new record is to use the DefaultValue property. When you display the blank data entry record, Access automatically fills in any default values that you have set. This means that if you set the DefaultValue property of a control to the value it has in the current record then when you move to the new record Access will carry the value to the new record.

You can create a macro to set the DefaultValue property for each control whose value you want to carry forward and run the macro when you take some action to save the changes in the current record. Use the form's BeforeUpdate event to trigger the macro so that the DefaultValue property settings that the macro makes are saved along with the data changes.

## Setting the DefaultValue Property

The macro that we create to carry the values forward uses the SetValue action to set the DefaultValue property of a control; the only tricky part is the Expression argument.

If the control has a numeric value, you can use the control name as the Expression argument setting, as follows:

| Action | Action Arguments |
|--------|------------------|
| SetValue | Item: numcontrol.DefaultValue |
| | Expression: numcontrol |

For example, the SupplierID is a number in the Northwind database so you can set the DefaultValue of the SupplierID control as follows:

| Action | Action Arguments |
|--------|------------------|
| SetValue | Item: SupplierID.DefaultValue |
| | Expression: SupplierID |

However, if the control has a string value, special handling of the Expression argument is required. For example, to set the DefaultValue property for a LastName control to a *specific* string value such as Peacock, you must enclose the string in quotation marks as follows:

| Action | Action Arguments |
|--------|------------------|
| SetValue | Item:LastName.DefaultValue |
| | Expression: "Peacock" |

But we want to set the property to a string *variable*, not to a specific value. To set a property to a string variable, Access needs to evaluate the variable and concatenate the result into a string. The final setting for the Expression argument is a string within a string. Access uses special syntax for indicating a string within a string. For example, to set the DefaultValue property for the LastName control to the current value in the LastName control, you can use the following syntax:

| Action | Action Arguments |
|--------|------------------|
| SetValue | Item:LastName.DefaultValue |
| | Expression: """"&LastName&"""" |

This syntax encloses the inner string "&LastName&" with pairs of double quotation marks. The pairs of double quotation marks simply mark the beginning and the end of the inner string. The result is the value in the LastName control which must then be enclosed with double quotation marks because the result is a string. (The final result includes four sets of double quotation marks.)

## Strings within Strings

Use string delimiters to identify a string within a string. *A string delimiter* is a character or group of characters that marks the beginning or end of a string. You can use either single or double quotation marks to delimit the inner string. There are three ways to identify a string within a string:

**Single quotation marks**   Identify the inner string using single quotation marks as follows:

' "& *controlname* &" '

then enclose the inner string in double quotation marks for the final result:

" ' "& *controlname* &" ' "

Because the single quotation mark is an apostrophe, this syntax does not work properly if the value of the string variable also contains an apostrophe. In this case Access can't distinguish between ' used as an apostrophe and ' used as a string delimiter, and so Access generates a run-time error.

**Double quotation marks**   Identify the inner string using pairs of double quotation marks as follows:

"" "& *controlname* &" ""

then enclose the inner string in double quotation marks for the final result:

" "" "& *controlname* &" "" "

Use this syntax to avoid the run-time error generated if a value of the string variable contains an apostrophe.

**VBA**   In VBA there is a third way to identify a string within a string. You can use the ANSI representation for the double quotation marks Chr$(34) or a string variable to represent the double quotation marks, such as strDouble. In this case, indicate the inner string by

```
strDouble & controlname & strDouble
```

then enclose the inner string in double quotation marks for the final result:

```
"strDouble & controlname & strDouble"
```

For example, when the Northwind company starts working with a new supplier, data entry for new products is required. During the data entry session for the supplier's products using the Products form, each new record has the same supplier name and, perhaps, the same category and even the same quantity per unit (see Figure 8.7a). In the Products form, the supplier and category controls are displayed as lookup fields. However the values in these controls are the numerical values of the SupplierID and CategoryID. The QuantityPerUnit control contains text values. The macro shown in Table 8.8 uses the double quotation syntax to delimit a string within a string for the QuantityPerUnit control.

**TABLE 8.8:** A macro to carry values to a new record by setting the DefaultValue property.

| Macro Name | Action | Action Arguments |
|---|---|---|
| Form_BeforeUpdate | | |
| | SetValue: | Item: SupplierID.DefaultValue |
| | | Expression: SupplierID |
| | SetValue: | Item: CategoryID.DefaultValue |
| | | Expression: CategoryID |
| | SetValue | Item: QuantityPerUnit.DefaultValue |
| | | Expression: """" & QuantityPerUnit & """" |

1. Create a new macrosheet named mProducts, enter the macro shown in Table 8.8, and save the macrosheet.

2. Assign the mProducts.Form_BeforeUpdate macro to the BeforeUpdate event of the Products form, save the form, and switch to Form view.

3. Change the value of the Units in Stock control and click the New button in the toolbar. The new record displays the values carried from the record you just edited (see Figure 8.7b).

FIGURE 8.7:

Use a macro to set the DefaultValue property for controls whose values you want to carry to a new record.

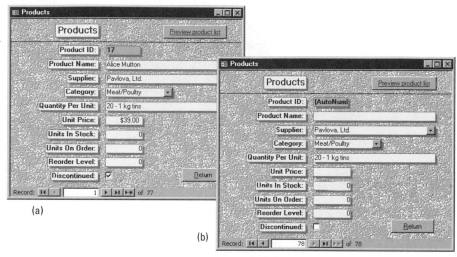

(a)

(b)

# To Delete or Not to Delete?

When working interactively, you can delete a record by choosing Edit ➤ Delete Record or by selecting the record and pressing Delete. In designing the application you can decide whether you want to allow record deletions from a particular table.

**WARNING** Once someone deletes a record, the information is gone. As you design your application, think carefully about whether or not to permit deletions. In many cases the database must provide a complete audit trail for all entries, and in that case you shouldn't permit any record deletions.

## Not to Delete

In many applications the choice is to prevent all deletions in order to maintain an audit trail of all transactions. To prevent deletions you can use the form's AllowDeletions property. When you set the AllowDeletions property to No, the Delete Record command in the Edit menu is grayed out; if you select the record and press Delete, the system beeps and the record is not deleted. You can prevent deletions of customers for the Customers form in NorthwindMacros as follows:

1. Open the Customers form in Design view and set the AllowDeletions property to No.

2. Save the form and switch to Form view.

When you try to choose the Delete Record command in the Edit menu, the command is grayed out and unavailable.

## To Delete

If you want to allow record deletion, you can automate the interactive process by creating a command button named cmdDelete and a macro that runs the RunCommand action to issue the DeleteRecord command. Table 8.9 shows the macro.

**TABLE 8.9:** A macro to delete a record

| Macro Name | Action | Action Arguments |
| --- | --- | --- |
| cmdDelete_Click | | |
| | RunCommand | Command: DeleteRecord |

As an example, we'll allow deletions of a supplier using the Suppliers form.

1. Create a new macrosheet named mSuppliers, enter the macro shown in Table 8.9, and save the macrosheet.

2. Open the Suppliers form in Design view and place a command button in the upper right corner of the detail section; set the Name property to cmdDelete and the Caption property to &Delete

3. Click in the OnClick property and choose the mSuppliers.cmdDelete_Click macro.

4. Save the form and switch to Form view.

5. Click the Delete button. Access displays the default error message shown in Figure 8.8. Click OK. Access displays the Action Failed dialog box. The macro action fails because Access is unable to delete the record.

---

The default error message displayed when you try to delete a record that has related records in another table and the Cascade Delete Related Records option is not checked.

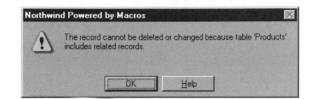

---

Access recognizes that the Suppliers table has related records in other tables. The Relationships layout, available by choosing the Relationships command from the Tools menu, shows that the Suppliers table is the `one' table in a one-to-many relationship with the Products table. Double-clicking the join line displays the Relationships dialog shown in Figure 8.9.

---

The Relationships dialog indicates that the Cascade Delete Related Records is not checked so you can delete a supplier only if the supplier isn't providing any products.

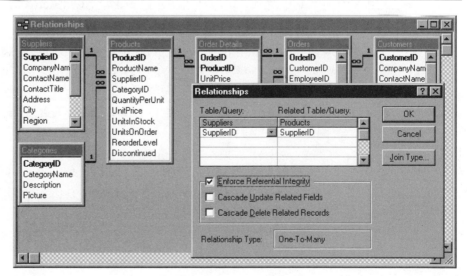

The Relationships dialog indicates that the Cascade Delete Related Records option is not selected; therefore you can delete a supplier only if the supplier isn't providing you with products. (Access permits you to delete a record from the `one' table only if there are no related records.) The default error message indicates that the supplier, Exotic Liquids is providing Northwind with at least one product.

## Handling the Macro Error When There Are Related Records

You can avoid macro failure by testing to determine if there are related records and running the action to delete only if there are no related records. You can use the DCount() function to count the number of related records. The syntax is:

DCount("*","*tblRelated*", "*fieldname*=Forms!*formname*!*controlname*")

where *tblRelated* is the name of the related table, *fieldname* is the name of the matching field in the related table, and *controlname* is the name of the control on the open form that displays the value you want to match. In this example, you use the DCount() function to create the test condition:

DCount("*","Products","SupplierID=Screen.ActiveForm.SupplierID")=0

If the condition is true, the supplier is providing no products and the macro deletes the supplier. If the condition is false, the supplier must be providing at least one product, so the macro displays a message and terminates. We'll include the count of the products in the message. Table 8.10 shows the modified macro.

1. Click in mSuppliers, modify the cmdDelete_Click macro as shown in Table 8.10, and save the macrosheet.

2. Click in the Suppliers form and click the Delete button. Your custom message is displayed and the macro error is avoided (see Figure 8.10).

3. Add a new supplier with company name Golden Horizons. Save the record and then click the Delete button. The default confirmation message is displayed (see Figure 8.11). Click No.

**TABLE 8.10:** A macro to delete a record if there are related records

| Macro Name | Condition | Action | Action Arguments |
|---|---|---|---|
| cmdDelete_Click | | | |
| | DCount("*","Products", "SupplierID=Screen.Active Form.SupplierID")=0 | RunCommand | Command: DeleteRecord |
| | ... | StopMacro | |
| | | MsgBox | Message: ="You can't delete this supplier because the supplier is providing "&DCount("*","Products","Sup-plierID=Screen.ActiveForm .SupplierID")&" products." |

**FIGURE 8.10:**

The custom message displayed when you can't delete the record

**FIGURE 8.11:**

The default confirmation message that appears when Access is about to delete a record

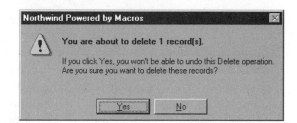

### Modify the Macro to Suppress the Confirmation Box and Screen Updates

You can choose to suppress the default confirmation box by starting the macro with the SetWarnings action. You can also include the Echo action to suppress screen updates while the macro runs.

1. Click in the macrosheet and insert two rows just after the row containing the macro name cmdDelete_Click.

2. In the first inserted row, select the Echo action and set the Echo On argument to No.

3. In the second inserted row, select the SetWarnings action.

4. Save the macro.

5. Click in the Suppliers form and click the Delete button on the form. The record is deleted without the confirmation box.

## Cascading a Delete

Sometimes you want to allow a record that has related records to be deleted. If you elect the Cascade Delete Related Records option, then when you try to delete the record, Access displays the message shown in Figure 8.12. You see this message in NorthwindMacros if you try to delete an order using the Orders form.

**FIGURE 8.12:**

The default message displayed when you try to delete a record that has related records and the Cascade Delete Related Records option is checked

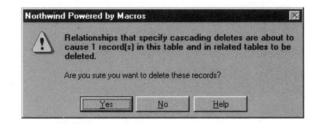

The problem with the default message is that it doesn't give you very much information. You don't know how many records will be deleted if you continue. You also don't know how many tables are involved. You can replace this message with a custom message box that indicates the number of related records that will be deleted and the tables that will be affected if the operation continues. You can use the DCount() function to count the number of related records and the built-in MsgBox()function to create a message box with several buttons to provide a choice.

As an example, in the Northwind application the Orders and Order Details tables are related (each record in the Order Details table corresponds to a product sold in an order). You can verify that the Cascade Delete Related Records options is checked for the relationship. We'll place a command button named cmdDelete on the Orders form and create a macro that allows the deletion of records that have related records. Use the DCount() function to determine the number of Order Details records that would be deleted, as follows:

DCount("*","[Order Details]", "OrderID=Screen.ActiveForm.OrderID")

If there are no Order Details records for an order, the macro runs the menu command to delete the order. If there are Order Details records, the macro displays a custom message box to indicate the number of records that will be deleted and asks for confirmation; if the user confirms, the macro deletes the order and the related Order Details records; otherwise, the macro terminates. Figure 8.13 shows the macro flow diagram for the macro and Table 8.11 shows the macro.

1. Open the mOrders macrosheet, enter the macro in Table 8.11, and save the macrosheet.

2. Place a command button in the header section of the Orders form, set the Name property to cmdDelete and the Caption property to &Delete.

3. Assign the mOrders.cmdDelete_Click macro to the OnClick property of the command button.

4. Save the form and switch to Form view.

5. Select an order and click the Delete button. Figure 8.14 shows the custom message box. Click No and close the form.

**TABLE 8.11:** A macro to delete a record when the Cascade Delete Related Records option is selected

| Macro Name | Condition | Action | Action Arguments |
|---|---|---|---|
| cmdDelete_Click | DCount("*","[Order Details]", "OrderID=Screen.ActiveForm. OrderID")=0 | RunCommand | Command: DeleteRecord |
| | ... | StopMacro | |
| | MsgBox("There are "&DCount("*", "[Order Details]", "OrderID=Screen .ActiveForm.OrderID")&" Order Details records related to this order. Do you want to delete all?",4+64)=6 | RunCommand | Command: DeleteRecord |

FIGURE 8.13:

Macro flow diagram to determine the number of related records and allow the choice to delete

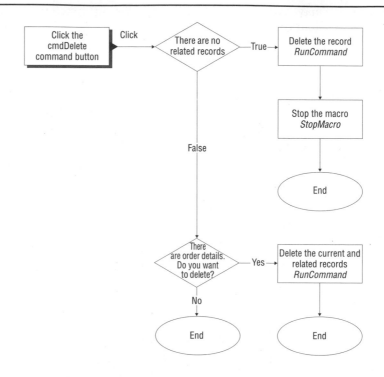

FIGURE 8.14:

The custom message box to display the number of records in the related table that would be deleted

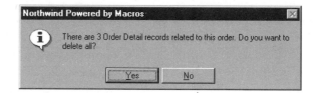

## Other Ways to Delete a Record

The techniques we've created for deleting a record automate deletion using a custom command button. If you are working with a record that has related records in another table and you try to delete your record by choosing the Delete Record command in the Edit menu or by selecting the record and pressing Delete, Access displays either of the default error messages shown in Figure 8.8 and

Figure 8.12. You can prevent the default error messages by eliminating the alternate ways to delete a record:

- You can customize the command bars to eliminate the Delete Record command. (See Chapter 1 "Automating a Database Without Programming," for information on customizing command bars.)
- You can disable the Delete key by adding a key assignment to the AutoKeys macro group (see Chapter 5). Table 8.12 shows the macro for reassigning the Delete key. To disable the key assignment, you can stop the macro without taking any other action.

**NOTE**　When you reassign a key using an AutoKeys macro, the reassignment is effective throughout the database, even when you are working in edit mode.

**TABLE 8.12 :** A macro in the AutoKeys macro group to disable the Delete key

| Macro Name | Action |
| --- | --- |
| {Del} | StopMacro |

# Working with Data in Two Open Forms

There are times when you want to allow two data entry forms to be open at the same time. When two data entry forms are open, you need to make sure that both forms display the most current information. In Chapter 4 you learned that while Access automatically updates the second form if you make changes to a record in the first form, it doesn't update the second form when you add a new record or delete a record in the first form. In this next section you'll learn how to use macro programming to update open forms.

# Edit an Existing Record

While reviewing orders using the Customer Orders form, you may need to edit information in the customer's record; if the customer is new, you may also need to add a new customer record. In either case, you need to open the Customers form as a second open form.

### Observing the Automatic Update of Edited Data

When you open the Customers form and edit an existing record, Access refreshes (automatically updates) the data in the active window. To observe the automatic refresh:

1. Open the Customer Orders form, select an existing customer using the lookup combo list, and click the Review Customer button.

2. Change the spelling of the company name and click the Save button on the Customer form. Notice that the changed spelling is displayed automatically in the Customer Orders form.

3. Locate the same customer in the combo box list. Notice that the changed spelling is also displayed in the combo box list.

When you change data using the Customers form, Access updates the data displayed in Customer Orders form as soon as the Customer Orders form becomes the active form.

# Add a New Record

When a new customer calls, you need to display a new data entry record for the Customers form. We'll automate the process by placing a command button named cmdNewCustomer on the Customer Orders form and creating a macro to open the Customers form displaying a new blank record ready for data entry. Table 8.13 shows the macro.

**TABLE 8.13:** A macro to open a new data entry record

| Macro Name | Action | Action Arguments |
|---|---|---|
| cmdNewCustomer_Click | | |
| | OpenForm | FormName: Customers |
| | | Data Mode: Add |

1. Create a new macrosheet named mCustomerOrders, enter the macro in Table 8.13, and save the macrosheet.

2. Click in the Customer Orders form and switch to Design view.

3. Place a command button in the header section and set the Name property to cmdNewCustomer and the Caption property to &New Customer

4. Click in the button's OnClick property and select mCustomerOrders.cmdNew_Click.

5. Save the form and switch to Form view.

6. Click the New Customer button. Access opens a new record in the Customers form.

7. Enter a new customer:

   CustomerID: CAMDE

   CompanyName: Cameron Designs

8. Close the Customers form. The new customer is saved.

9. Click the arrow on the lookup combo box in the Customer Orders form. The new customer does not appear in the pick list.

**Refresh Does Not Display New Records**  When you edit an existing record, Access automatically refreshes (updates), but does not display *new* records. In order to display new records, you must requery the controls and the form. When working interactively, requery a control by pressing F9 and requery the form by pressing Shift+F9; separate actions are needed because Access can requery only one object at a time.

**Requery the Combo Box and the Form Interactively**   Let's go through the requery process interactively and then create a macro to automate it.

1.   With the Customer Orders form active, press F9.

2.   Click the arrow of the combo box. The new customer appears in the combo list.

3.   Select the new customer from the list. The new customer's record is not displayed.

4.   Press Shift+F9 and select the new customer again using the combo box. The new customer's record is displayed.

## Creating a Macro to Requery a Form and Its Controls

You can create a macro that requeries the Customer Orders form and its cboFind combo box just after the new record is saved (that is, when the Customers form recognizes the AfterInsert event). If you display the property sheet for Customers, you can see that the form's AfterInsert event is already triggering the mCustomers.Form_AfterInsert macro, which requeries the lookup combo box on Customers as part of the logical navigation technique added in Chapter 7, "Navigation with Macros." You can modify this macro to requery the Customer Orders form and its combo box.

Of course, you only want to requery if the Customer Orders form is open. During the order review process, the Customer Orders form is open; however, if you've opened Customers directly to enter or edit customer information, the Customer Orders form isn't open. You can determine if Customer Orders is open by using the IsLoaded() function. If Customer Orders is not open, the macro terminates. If the Customer Orders form is open, the macro uses the SelectObject action to select the form before requerying (because the Requery action applies only to an active object) and then applies the Requery action to the combo box and then to the form itself. Figure 8.15 shows the macro flow diagram and Table 8.14 shows the macro.

FIGURE 8.15:

This is the macro flow diagram for the Form_AfterInsert macro. The macro determines if another form is open before taking action on it.

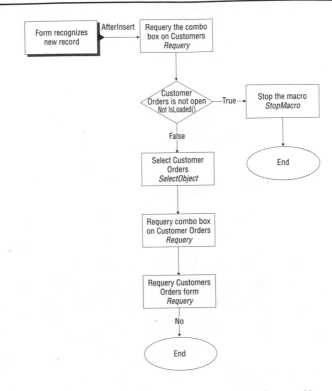

TABLE 8.14: A macro to select another form and requery the form and its control

| Macro Name | Condition | Action | Action Arguments |
|---|---|---|---|
| Form_AfterInsert | | | |
| | | Requery | Control Name: cboFind |
| | Not IsLoaded("Customer Orders") | StopMacro | |
| | | SelectObject | Object Type: Form |
| | | | Object Name: Customer Orders |
| | | Requery | Control Name: cboFind |
| | | Requery | |

1. Open the mCustomers macrosheet, enter the macro shown in Table 8.14 and save the macrosheet. The macro requeries the cboFind combo box on Customers and then takes action on Customer Orders. Leave the Control Name argument blank in the third Requery action; when no control is specified, Access requeries the active object.

2. Open the Customers form in Design view, click the AfterInsert property and replace the mcrGlobal.Form_AfterInsert macro with the mCustomers.Form_AfterInsert macro.

3. Save and close the form.

4. Click Customer Orders.

5. Click the New button and enter a new customer:

   CustomerID: GREER

   CompanyName: Greer Gourmet

6. Click the Return button. Observe that when Customer Orders form is requeried, the form displays the first record in the default sort order.

7. Select the new customer's name from the lookup combo box. The new customer's record is displayed.

8. Close the Customer Orders form.

# Summary

This chapter has introduced macro techniques for automating routine data entry operation. The important techniques are:

- You can use macros to set complex rules for validating data. For example, you can change the timing of the validation test.

- You can create reusable macros for command buttons to add a new record, undo changes, and save a record.

- Because the Undo command is not always available, you should design the macro to test the Dirty property to determine if the command is available before running it.

- You can date stamp a record by using the form's BeforeUpdate event to run a macro that sets the current date.

- You can create a macro to set a control's DefaultValue property to carry values forward to a new record. Special syntax is required when the control contains string values.

- You can create macros to delete records, test for related records, and offer the choice to delete a record and its related records (if the Cascade Delete Related Records option is set for the relationship).

- Because Access does not update a form automatically when you add or delete records in another form, you can create macros to update the open forms.

# CHAPTER

## NINE

# Working with Groups of Records Using Macros

- Using the OrderBy and OrderByOn properties

- Creating filter queries

- Using Query By Form

- Using a union query to add a null row

- Using Multiple criteria to select records

- Synchronizing two combo boxes

- Using a custom dialog to collect input

- Using action queries to modify records

In the previous two chapters you've learned techniques for working with a single record, including navigating among controls, records, and forms, finding a specific record, and automating data entry operations.

This chapter focuses on working with groups of records. You learn how to automate two standard database operations: sorting and selecting groups of records. You learn how to sort records by using a macro to set a form's sorting properties. You learn how to use a form to collect your selection criteria, pass the values to a filter query (called Query By Form), and then use the filter query to retrieve the specific records. We'll also use the Query By Form technique to synchronize two combo boxes on a form.

The chapter also shows you how to create a custom dialog to collect user input and pass the collected values to a filter query that selects records from a report's record source. The last section shows you a technique for carrying values in a data entry form forwarding to the next data entry session. This technique uses a data entry table to hold the new record and action queries to append the new record to the data storage table and update the data entry table to hold only the values you want to carry forward.

**NOTE**  This chapter assumes you have customized the Form view, Macro Design and Database menu bars and toolbars to include the Macro command that displays the Run Macro dialog. If you haven't customized the command bars you can do so now. This chapter also assumes that you've created the NorthwindMacros database as a copy of the Northwind database. Create a copy now if necessary.

We begin by creating a new form for the NorthwindMacros database that we'll use to illustrate the macros. You can create the new form, named frmOrderStatus, using the Form Wizard and then modify the results. Figure 9.1 shows the new frmOrderStatus form. Here are the steps:

1. Use the Form Wizard to create a new tabular form. Select OrderID, OrderDate, RequiredDate, ShippedDate from the Orders table, CompanyName from the Shippers table, CompanyName from the Customers table, and LastName from the Employees table. Name the form frmOrderStatus.

2. Set the form's Caption property to Order Status and set the AllowAdditions property to No. The Order Status form is a review form and is not intended for data entry; setting the AllowAdditions property to No hides the blank record at the end of the recordset.

3. Select all of the data controls, set their Locked property to Yes, and set their formatting properties as shown below. Because the form is not intended for data entry, lock the control to prevent inadvertent changes.

| | |
|---|---|
| BackColor | gray |
| SpecialEffect | Flat |
| BorderStyle | Transparent |

**NOTE** The reason you set the Locked property to individual controls rather than setting the form's AllowEdits property is as follows: if you set the form's AllowEdits property to No, you can't use a combo box on the form to choose records because you can't change (edit) the search value in the combo box.

4. Rearrange the controls, change the Caption properties for the labels as shown in Figure 9.1, and set the FontWeight property for the labels to Bold.

5. Choose the Save As/Export command from the File menu and save a copy of the form with the new name frmOrderStatusClean in the current database. We'll use this copy of the form in Chapter 18.

# Sorting Records

When working interactively, you can easily sort a group of records displayed in a form by the values in a single field. To sort by the values in a single field in ascending or descending order, right-click in the control and select the Sort Ascending or Sort Descending command in the shortcut menu. To remove the sort, right-click in a control and select Remove Filter/Sort in the shortcut menu.

FIGURE 9.1:

Create an Order Status
form for sorting and
selecting.

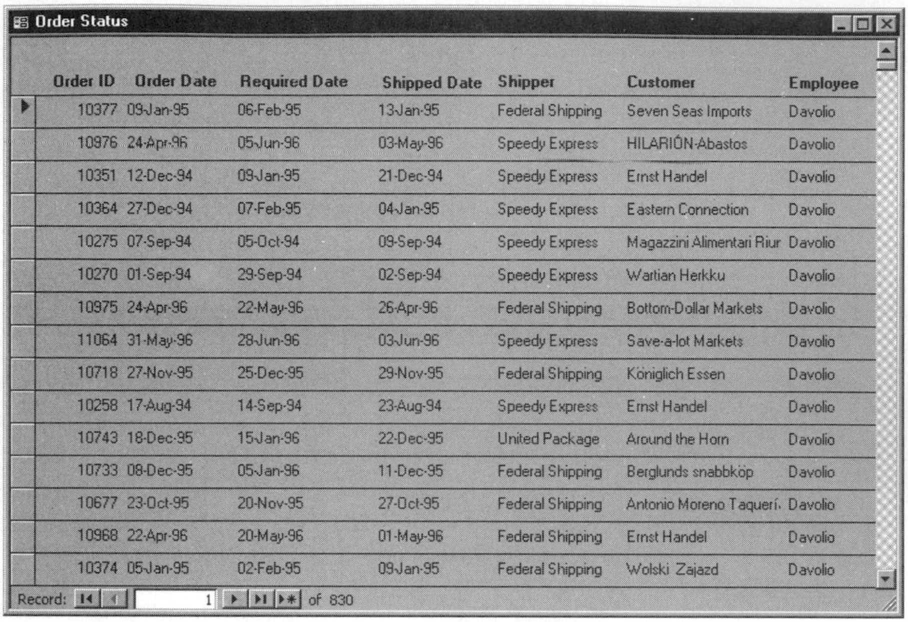

| Order ID | Order Date | Required Date | Shipped Date | Shipper | Customer | Employee |
|----------|-----------|---------------|--------------|---------|----------|----------|
| 10377 | 09-Jan-95 | 06-Feb-95 | 13-Jan-95 | Federal Shipping | Seven Seas Imports | Davolio |
| 10976 | 24-Apr-96 | 05-Jun-96 | 03-May-96 | Speedy Express | HILARIÓN-Abastos | Davolio |
| 10351 | 12-Dec-94 | 09-Jan-95 | 21-Dec-94 | Speedy Express | Ernst Handel | Davolio |
| 10364 | 27-Dec-94 | 07-Feb-95 | 04-Jan-95 | Speedy Express | Eastern Connection | Davolio |
| 10275 | 07-Sep-94 | 05-Oct-94 | 09-Sep-94 | Speedy Express | Magazzini Alimentari Riur | Davolio |
| 10270 | 01-Sep-94 | 29-Sep-94 | 02-Sep-94 | Speedy Express | Wartian Herkku | Davolio |
| 10975 | 24-Apr-96 | 22-May-96 | 26-Apr-96 | Federal Shipping | Bottom-Dollar Markets | Davolio |
| 11064 | 31-May-96 | 28-Jun-96 | 03-Jun-96 | Speedy Express | Save-a-lot Markets | Davolio |
| 10718 | 27-Nov-95 | 25-Dec-95 | 29-Nov-95 | Federal Shipping | Königlich Essen | Davolio |
| 10258 | 17-Aug-94 | 14-Sep-94 | 23-Aug-94 | Speedy Express | Ernst Handel | Davolio |
| 10743 | 18-Dec-95 | 15-Jan-96 | 22-Dec-95 | United Package | Around the Horn | Davolio |
| 10733 | 08-Dec-95 | 05-Jan-96 | 11-Dec-95 | Federal Shipping | Berglunds snabbköp | Davolio |
| 10677 | 23-Oct-95 | 20-Nov-95 | 27-Oct-95 | Federal Shipping | Antonio Moreno Taquerí. | Davolio |
| 10968 | 22-Apr-96 | 20-May-96 | 01-May-96 | Federal Shipping | Ernst Handel | Davolio |
| 10374 | 05-Jan-95 | 02-Feb-95 | 09-Jan-95 | Federal Shipping | Wolski Zajazd | Davolio |

Record: 1 of 830

# Sorting Interactively

For practice, sort the frmOrderStatus form by any one of its columns:

1. Click a control in the Customer column and then click the Sort Descending
   button. The records are sorted in descending order by the values in the
   column.

2. Switch to Design view and observe that the form's OrderBy property is set
   to Customer.CompanyName DESC.

3. Right-click in a control and choose the Remove Filter/Sort command in the
   shortcut menu. The sort is removed and the records are displayed in their
   original order. If you switch to Design view, you will see that the OrderBy
   property is still set to Customer.CompanyName DESC.

4. Choose the Apply Filter/Sort command in the Records menu. The sort is
   applied.

5. Save, close, and reopen the form. Access applies the OrderBy setting.

6.   Remove the sort, then save, close, and reopen the form. Access does not apply the OrderBy setting.

## The OrderBy Property

You can use a form's OrderBy property to sort by a single field, or you can create a complex sort by several fields with some fields in ascending and others in descending order. The OrderBy property is a string expression that consists of the name of the field or fields you want to sort, arranged in the order of the sort and separated by commas; to sort a field in descending order, you type DESC after the name of the field. For example, to sort by customer and then by order date in descending order, you set the OrderBy property to

Customers.CompanyName, OrderDate DESC

You can set the OrderBy property in the form's property sheet; the setting is saved when you close the form. Interactively, you apply and remove the OrderBy setting using the ApplyFilter/Sort and RemoveFilter/Sort menu commands.

# Automate the Sort Process

You can automate sort process using the OrderBy and OrderByOn properties.

## Using the OrderByOn Property

You use the OrderByOn property to apply or remove the sort specified in the OrderBy property by setting the OrderByOn property to Yes or No (or True or False in VBA). For a form you can set the OrderBy property in the form's property sheet in a macro or VBA procedure and then use a macro or VBA procedure to apply and remove the sort using the OrderByOn property. For a report you can also set the OrderByOn property in the report's property sheet.

## Using a Triple-State Toggle Button

As an example, we'll create a button and a macro to sort the Order Status records by customer. We are going to use a toggle button instead of a command button because a toggle button has a value that can be used by the macro. Normally a toggle button has two values ,True and False; setting the TripleState property to Yes gives a third value, Null.

- When the toggle button has the value False, it looks like a command button.

- Clicking the button changes it to the Null state in which the button flattens but still appears raised.

- Clicking the button again changes it to the True state in which the flattened button appears sunken.

We'll create a macro to test the button's state and remove the sort if the button is in the False state, apply an ascending sort if the button is in the Null state, and apply a descending sort if the button is in the True state (see Table 9.1). Figure 9.2 shows the three states of the toggle button and the resulting sorts by customer.

**TABLE 9.1:**  A macro for three sort orders for the triple state toggle button

| Macro Name | Condition | Action | Action Arguments |
|---|---|---|---|
| tglCustomer_Click | | | |
| | Not Screen.ActiveControl | SetValue | Item:  Screen.ActiveForm.OrderByOn |
| | | | Expression: True |
| | IsNull (Screen.ActiveControl) | SetValue | Item: Screen.ActiveForm.OrderBy |
| | | | Expression: "Customers.CompanyName" |
| | Screen.ActiveControl | SetValue | Item: Screen.ActiveForm.OrderBy |
| | | | Expression: "Customers.CompanyName DESC" |

FIGURE 9.2:

Use a triple-state toggle button to remove a sort when the toggle button is False (a), apply an ascending sort when the button is Null (b), and apply a descending sort when the button is True (c).

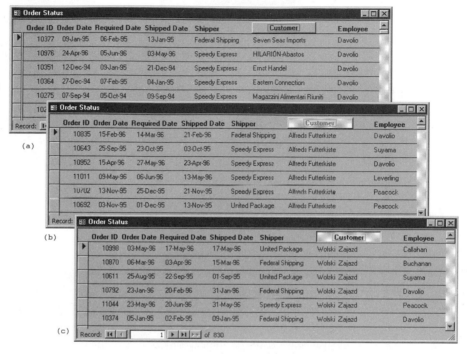

1. Switch to Design view; select all of the controls in the detail section and set their Enabled properties to No, and then switch back to Form view. The controls don't need to be enabled when you use the OrderBy property for the sort.

2. Create a new macrosheet named mfrmOrderStatus, enter the macro shown in Table 9.1, and save the macrosheet. The macro uses Screen.ActiveControl to refer to the toggle button's value. When the toggle button has the value False, the Not Screen.ActiveControl is True and the macro sets the OrderBy property to "" (that is, the zero-length string) which is equivalent to removing the sort.

3. Delete the Customer label in the header section, replace it with a toggle button, and set the properties as follows:

| | |
|---|---|
| Name | tglCustomer |
| Caption | Customer |

| | |
|---|---|
| TripleState property | Yes |
| Default Value | False |
| ControlTip Text | Click to toggle ascending, descending, and no sort |

4.  Assign the mfrmOrderStatus.tglCustomer_Click macro to the OnClick property of the toggle button.

5.  Save the form, switch to Form view, and click the toggle button (see Figure 9.3). As you cycle through the states, the records are sorted by customer name in ascending order and then in descending order, and then the sort is removed.

   Although Access saves the OrderBy and OrderByOn settings that are in effect when you close the form, it does not save the state of the toggle button. As a result, the property settings and the toggle button can get out of synch with one another when you first open the form. We'll use the macro shown in Table 9.2 to initialize the OrderBy and OrderByOn settings when the form opens. You have to refer to the form explicitly in this macro and can't use the Screen object because the form is not the active object when the Open event occurs. (A form's Activate event occurs after the form's Open, Load, and Resize events. See Chapter 2, "Getting Started with Objects and Events," for information on the order of events.)

**TABLE 9.2:**   A macro to initialize the sort settings

| Macro name | Action | Action Arguments |
|---|---|---|
| Form_Open | | |
| | SetValue | Item: Forms!frmOrderStatus.OrderByOn |
| | | Expression: True |
| | SetValue | Item: Forms!frmOrderStatus.OrderBy |
| | | Expression: "" |

1.  Click the mfrmOrderStatus macrosheet, enter the macro in Table 9.2, and save the macrosheet.

2. Assign the macro to the OnOpen event property of the form.

3. Save and close the form.

4. Open the form. The two sort property settings are initialized and in synch with the toggle button.

## Sort by Any Column

When records are displayed in a tabular form, you can automate sorting the records by specific columns: replace the label of each column you want to sort by with a triple state toggle button and create a macro to sort the records by a field in the column such as the one in Table 9.1. Using this technique, each of the sorts is independent, and the last button clicked determines the sort. This means that if you toggle the Customers button to sort ascending by customer and then toggle the Employees button to sort ascending by employee, the result is that the records are sorted in ascending order by employee. Figure 9.3 shows the result; notice that the state of the Customers toggle button is out of synch because the toggle button is in the flattened raised state (to indicate an ascending sort by customer) while the records are sorted by employee.

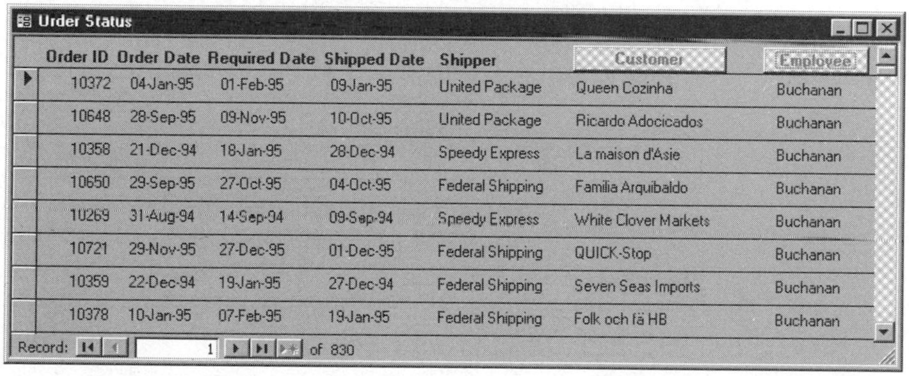

**FIGURE 9.3:**

The state of the Customer toggle button is out of synch: the button indicates an ascending sort by customer but the records do not reflect the customer sort.

| | Order ID | Order Date | Required Date | Shipped Date | Shipper | Customer | Employee |
|---|---|---|---|---|---|---|---|
| ▶ | 10372 | 04-Jan-95 | 01-Feb-95 | 09-Jan-95 | United Package | Queen Cozinha | Buchanan |
| | 10648 | 28-Sep-95 | 09-Nov-95 | 10-Oct-95 | United Package | Ricardo Adocicados | Buchanan |
| | 10358 | 21-Dec-94 | 18-Jan-95 | 28-Dec-94 | Speedy Express | La maison d'Asie | Buchanan |
| | 10650 | 29-Sep-95 | 27-Oct-95 | 04-Oct-95 | Federal Shipping | Familia Arquibaldo | Buchanan |
| | 10269 | 31-Aug-94 | 14-Sep-94 | 09-Sep-94 | Speedy Express | White Clover Markets | Buchanan |
| | 10721 | 29-Nov-95 | 27-Dec-95 | 01-Dec-95 | Federal Shipping | QUICK-Stop | Buchanan |
| | 10359 | 22-Dec-94 | 19-Jan-95 | 27-Dec-94 | Federal Shipping | Seven Seas Imports | Buchanan |
| | 10378 | 10-Jan-95 | 07-Feb-95 | 19-Jan-95 | Federal Shipping | Folk och fä HB | Buchanan |

Record: |◀| |◀| 1 |▶| |▶|| |▶*| of 830

## Macros for a Complex Sort

It is possible to write macros to keep the toggle buttons in synch with the current sort. Keeping the toggle buttons in synch with the current sort involves the same kind of macro programming that is required for a complex sort. In a complex sort each subsequent sort on any field takes previous sorts into account. For example, in a complex sort, toggling a sort by customer and then a sort by employee would produce records sorted by customer and then the records for each customer would be sorted by employee.

We'll do a complex sort for the Customer and Employee triple state toggle buttons. When you click the Customer toggle button, the macro sets the sort depending on the current state of the Employee button. For example, if your click changes the Customer toggle button to Null (to sort ascending by customer), the macro determines the state of the Employee button and sets the form's OrderBy property as follows:

| If the State of the Employee Button Is | The Macro Sets the OrderBy Property To |
| --- | --- |
| False (no sort by employee) | "Customers.CompanyName" |
| Null (ascending sort by employee) | "LastName, Customers.CompanyName" |
| True (descending sort by employee) | "LastName DESC, Customers.CompanyName" |

Similarly, when you click the Customer Toggle button and change it to True (to sort descending by customer), there are three alternative sets of actions, and when you toggle the Customer button to False (for no sort by customer), there are three more alternatives. The macro for the Customer toggle button has the nine alternatives shown in Table 9.3.

**TABLE 9.3:** The macro for the Customer toggle button has three alternatives depending on the current state of the Employee button for each of the three states for the Customer button.

| Macro Name | Condition | Action | Action Arguments |
| --- | --- | --- | --- |
| tglCustomer_Click | | | |
| | Not tglEmployee And Not Screen.ActiveControl | SetValue | Item: Screen.ActiveForm.OrderBy<br><br>Expression: "" |
| | IsNull(tglEmployee) And Not Screen.ActiveControl | SetValue | Item: Screen.ActiveForm.OrderBy<br><br>Expression: "LastName" |

**TABLE 9.3:** The macro for the Customer toggle button has three alternatives depending on the current state of the Employee button for each of the three states for the Customer button. (continued)

| Macro Name | Condition | Action | Action Arguments |
|---|---|---|---|
| | tglEmployee And Not Screen.ActiveControl | SetValue | Item: Screen.ActiveForm.OrderBy<br><br>Expression: "LastName DESC" |
| | IsNull(tglEmployee) And IsNull(Screen.ActiveControl) | SetValue | Item: Screen.ActiveForm.OrderBy<br><br>Expression: "LastName, Customers.CompanyName" |
| | (tglEmployee) And IsNull(Screen.ActiveControl) | SetValue | Item: Screen.ActiveForm.OrderBy<br><br>Expression: "LastName DESC, Customers.CompanyName" |
| | Not (tglEmployee) And IsNull(Screen.ActiveControl) | SetValue | Item: Screen.ActiveForm.OrderBy<br><br>Expression: "Customers.CompanyName" |
| | IsNull(tglEmployee) And (Screen.ActiveControl) | SetValue | Item: Screen.ActiveForm.OrderBy<br><br>Expression: "LastName, Customers.CompanyName DESC" |
| | (tglEmployee) And (Screen.ActiveControl) | SetValue | Item: Screen.ActiveForm.OrderBy<br><br>Expression: "LastName DESC, Customers.CompanyName DESC" |
| | Not (tglEmployee) And (Screen.ActiveControl) | SetValue | Item: Screen.ActiveForm.OrderBy<br><br>Expression: "Customers.CompanyName DESC" |

1. Open the frmOrderStatus form in Design view.

2. Following the steps for the Customer toggle button, replace the Employee label with an Employee toggle button named tglEmployee and set the properties as described for the Customer toggle button.

3. In the mfrmOrderStatus macrosheet, create the tglEmployee_Click macro modifying the macro in Table 9.1 to replace Customers.CompanyName with LastName. Save the macrosheet and assign the tglEmployee_Click macro to the OnClick property of the tglEmployee toggle button.

4. Click the mfrmOrderStatus macrosheet and modify the tglCustomer_Click macro as shown in Table 9.3. Save the macrosheet.

5. Save the form and switch to Form view.

6. Click the Employee toggle button. The records are now sorted by Employee (see Figure 9.4a).

7. Click the Customer toggle button. The records are now sorted first by Employee and then by Customer (see Figure 9.4b).

**FIGURE 9.4:**

The records are sorted by employee (a), and then the records for each employee are sorted by customer (b).

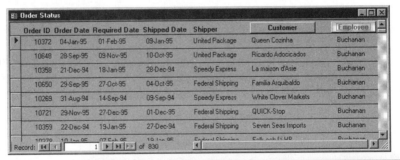

(a)

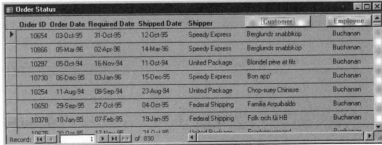

(b)

At this point the macro for the Customer toggle button is able to detect the state of the Employee button before setting the sort order; however, to complete the complex sort, we would need to modify the macro for the Employee button to detect the state of the Customer button. The tglEmployee_Click button can be modified to include nine alternatives similar to those given in the macro in Table 9.3.

If there are three toggle buttons, there are three alternative states that need to be considered for each button or a total twenty seven ($3 \times 3 \times 3 = 3^3$) for each button. While it is possible to use macro programming for three or more toggle buttons, a much better solution is to create on-the-fly the sort order that includes the sort fields in the order the user selects them. This solution can be programmed much more efficiently using VBA so we won't continue with the macro solution (see Chapter 17 "Working with Groups of Records Using Access VBA," for more information).

# Using Query By Form to Find a Group of Records

An important database operation is selecting a group of records that meet one or more selection criteria. For example, in the Order Status form you may want to display a list of orders for a particular customer, shipper, or employee; you may want to review all orders taken by an employee after a specific date; or you may want to see all orders to be shipped by a specific shipper before a certain required date.

When working interactively, you can select a specific group of records by creating and applying a filter. Microsoft Access provides several ways to create filters interactively, including Filter By Form and Filter By Selection. These techniques give the user powerful ad hoc querying abilities. You can also customize these techniques with programming. This section describes another technique called Query By Form that you can use to provide a simple interface for selecting a group of records.

## Selecting a Group of Records Interactively

In this section, you'll select the orders for a specific customer. First, modify the record source to include the CustomerID from the Orders table so the primary key can be used to select records.

1. Open the frmOrderStatus form in Design view. Click the form's RecordSource property and click the Build button at the right of the property box. The Query Builder opens (see Figure 9.5).

FIGURE 9.5:

The record source for the frmOrderStatus form

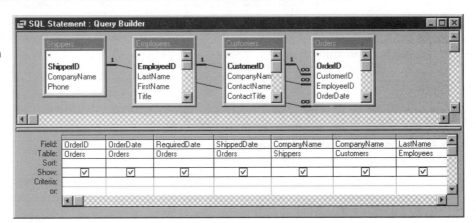

2. Select CustomerID, EmployeeID and ShipVia from the Orders table and drag them to the grid. You'll be ready to sort by employee or shipper later by including their primary key fields now.

3. Choose File ➤ Save As/Export and save the query as qryOrderStatus. Close the Query Builder window, click Yes to save the query, and click Yes in the next dialog to update the form's RecordSource property.

4. Choose Records ➤ Filter ➤ Advanced Filter/Sort. The Filter design window opens.

5. From the field list, drag the CustomerID field to the first Field cell in the filter grid and type **alfki** in the Criteria cell (see Figure 9.6).

6. Click the Apply Filter button on the toolbar. The filter window closes and the selected records are displayed. Access indicates the number of filtered records in the lower left corner of the form (see Figure 9.7).

7. Click the Remove Filter button on the toolbar to remove the filter.

**FIGURE 9.6:**

Using the Filter design window to create a filter

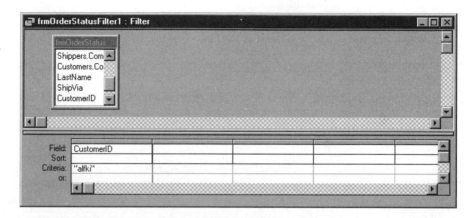

**FIGURE 9.7:**

The filtered records

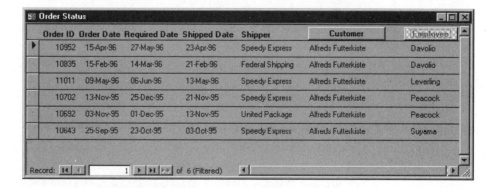

## Creating a Filter Query

A filter is temporary and is destroyed when you close the form. Rather than use a filter, you can create a query and use it to select records. A *filter query* must be based on the same query that the form is based on and must include all the same fields.

1. In the Database window, select the qryOrderStatus query, then copy and paste the query as qfltOrderStatus.

2. Open the qfltOrderStatus query in Design view, right-click the upper pane, and choose the Properties command in the shortcut menu. Set the Output All Fields property to Yes. With this property setting you can delete all fields from the query design grid except the fields you are using to select or sort records.

3. Delete all columns in the query design grid except the CustomerID column. In the next section you enter selection criteria for the CustomerID field.

4. Save and close the query.

## Automate the Selection Process

To automate the selection process, we'll use a search technique similar to the technique we used to find a single record in Chapter 7, "Navigation with Macros." The search technique uses a combo box variable to hold the search value and a macro triggered by the control's AfterUpdate event to apply a filter and select the records. Specifically, we'll

- place a combo box named cboCustomer that displays a list of customer IDs and company names in the header of the form,

- modify the qfltOrderStatus query to use the value selected in the combo box as the criteria for the CustomerID field, and

- create a macro that uses the ApplyFilter action to run the filter query and display the filtered records when the combo box recognizes the AfterUpdate event.

### Placing a Selection Combo Box on the Form

Creating the combo box is easy because the CustomerID field in the Orders table is a lookup field. When you drag a lookup field created as a combo box (or list box) to a form, its lookup properties are copied; the field is displayed as a combo box (or a list box) on the form. Although we do not want the search combo box to be a bound control, we can save the work of creating a combo box by dragging the lookup field to the form and changing the control's properties.

1. Switch to Design view and increase the height of the header section. Select all the labels and drag them down to the bottom of the header section. Select CustomerID from the field list and drag to the header section above the Customer toggle button. The field is displayed as a combo box.

2. Change the combo box Name property to cboCustomer and delete the setting for the ControlSource property. The ControlSource must be blank so that the combo box can be used to hold the search value as a variable. Note that the BoundColumn property is set to 1 so the combo box holds the value of the CustomerID for the combo box row that you select.

3. Change the label's Caption property to Select Customer and move the label above the combo box.

4. Save the form and switch to Form view (see Figure 9.8).

**FIGURE 9.8:**

Create the lookup combo box by dragging the lookup field and deleting the ControlSource property. The lookup combo box must be unbound in order to set a variable.

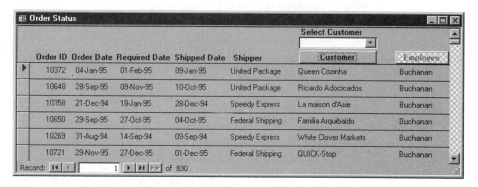

## Setting the Filter Query Criteria

Modify the filter query to use the value selected in the combo box as the criteria for the query's prefix field.

1. Open the qfltOrderStatus query in Design view.

2. Click the Criteria cell below CustomerID. We enter an expression in the Criteria cell so that the cell gets its value from the combo box on the form. When you design a parameter query to take its criteria values from a form, you are using *Query By Form* (also called *QBF*).

3.  Click Shift+F2 (or Ctrl+Z , the custom key combination created in Chapter 5, "Macro Basics") to open the Zoom box and enter the full identifier of the combo box shown below (or click the toolbar Build button and use the Expression Builder to construct the expression). You don't have to type the square brackets yourself when the names don't include spaces or symbols; Access supplies the square brackets for you.

    **[Forms]![frmOrderStatus]![cboCustomer]**

4.  Save the query. If you select a customer in the combo box and then click into the query and run it, the query selects the orders for the customer you chose.

## Creating a Macro to Apply the Filter

Use the ApplyFilter action to restrict or sort the records in a table or in the record source of a form or report. Chapter 5 looked at examples of using the Filter Name and the Where Condition arguments to specify the filter. Here we use the ApplyFilter action to apply the qfltOrderStatus filter saved as a query. Table 9.4 shows the macro.

**TABLE 9.4:**   A macro to filter the records

| Macro name | Action | Action Arguments |
| --- | --- | --- |
| cboCustomer_AfterUpdate | | |
| | ApplyFilter | Filter Name: qfltOrderStatus |

1.  Click the mfrmOrderStatus macrosheet, enter the macro in Table 9.4, and save the macrosheet.

2.  Assign the mfrmOrderStatus.cboCustomer_AfterUpdate macro to the AfterUpdate event property of the combo box.

3.  Save the form and switch to Form view.

4.  Select a customer from the combo box. The records are filtered and displayed; Access displays the number of filtered records in the lower left corner of the form (see Figure 9.9).

5.  Click the Employee toggle button. The selection is sorted in ascending order by employee.

6. Choose the Remove Filter/Sort command in the Records menu or right-click on the form title bar and select Remove Filter/Sort from the context menu. The filter and the sort are removed and all records are displayed.

**FIGURE 9.9:**

After you select a customer, the macro applies the filter query that uses the combo box value to select records (Query By Form).

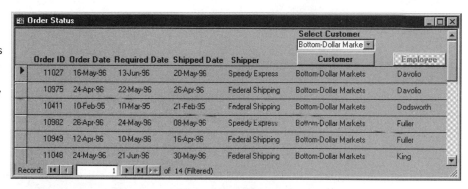

## Automate the Removal of the Filter

You can automate the removal of the filter by placing a command button in the form header and creating a macro to remove the filter.

1. Switch to Design view, place a command button in the header section, and set the Name property to cmdShowAll and the Caption property to &Show All.

2. Click in mfrmOrderStatus, then click in a new row and name the new macro cmdShowAll_Click.

3. Click in the next row and select the ShowAllRecords action. The ShowAllRecords action removes the filter and sort and requeries the records.

4. Save the macro.

5. Assign the mfrmOrderStatus.cmdShowAll_Click macro to the command button.

6. Save the form and switch to Form view (see Figure 9.10).

7. Click the Show All button. The filter and sort are removed, but the combo box continues to display the value selected.

FIGURE 9.10:

The macro for the Show All button removes the filter and displays all of the records.

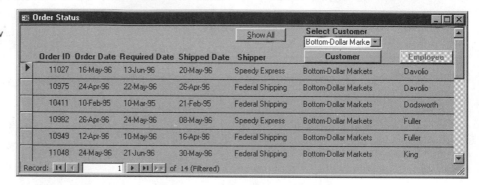

After you click the Show All button to remove the filter, the combo box should be null to indicate all records are displayed. Modify the macro that removes the filter so that it also sets the value of the combo box to Null. Table 9.5 shows the new macro.

TABLE 9.5: A macro to remove the filter and sort and initialize the combo box

| Macro Name | Action | Action Arguments |
|---|---|---|
| cmdShowAll_Click | | |
| | ShowAllRecords | |
| | SetValue | Item: cboCustomer |
| | | Expression: Null |

1. Click the mfrmOrderStatus macrosheet, modify the cmdShowAll_Click macro as shown in Table 9.5, and save the macrosheet.

2. Click frmOrderStatus and click the Show All button. The combo box is null and all the records are displayed.

# Using Multiple Criteria to Select a Group of Records

Often you want to use more than one criterion for selecting records. For example, you may want to find all orders that are handled by a specific employee for a certain customer. You can place a selection combo box in the form header for each field you want to use in selecting records, modify the filter query to include the additional criteria, create a macro to apply the filter for each new combo box, and, finally, modify the macro that removes the filter so that it also sets the combo boxes to null.

## Creating a Second Selection Combo Box

As an example, let's create a second process to select records for an employee.

1.  Switch to Design view, and drag the EmployeeID lookup field to the header section above the Employee toggle button.

2.  Change the Name property to cboEmployee and delete the setting for the ControlSource property.

3.  Change the label's Caption property to Select Employee and move the label above the combo box. The next step is to modify the filter query to include the value in the cboEmployee combo box as a selection criterion.

4.  Click qfltOrderStatus, drag EmployeeID to the second Field cell, click the Criteria cell, and enter the expression **Forms!frmOrderStatus!cboEmployee** (or click the Build button on the toolbar to use the Expression Builder).

5.  Save and close the query. The next step is to create the macro to apply the filter after the user selects an employee using the new combo box.

6.  Click the mfrmOrderStatus macrosheet, select and copy the cboCustomer_AfterUpdate macro, and then click in a new row and paste the copied rows.

7.  Change the name of the pasted macro to cboEmployee_AfterUpdate. The next step is to modify the macro that removes the filter and clears the combo boxes.

8. Click in the empty row below the last row of the macro cmdShowAll_Click, then select the SetValue action and set its arguments as follows:

    Item:              cboEmployee

    Expression:   Null

9. Save the macrosheet. The final step is to assign the new cboEmployee_AfterUpdate macro.

10. Assign the new cboEmployee_AfterUpdate macro to the cboEmployee combo box; save and close the form.

## Testing the Multi-Criteria Selection Process

Let's test the process:

1. Open the frmOrderStatus form.

2. Click the Customer combo box and select Alfreds Futterkiste. Surprisingly, no records are displayed.

3. Click the Employee combo box and select the employee, Margaret Peacock. The two orders handled by Ms. Peacock are displayed.

## Modify the Query Criteria to Return Records for All Values of an Empty Combo Box

As currently designed, the filter query requires that you make selections for both combo boxes (see Figure 9.11).

If the combo box for a field is null, the filter query looks for records with a null value in that field; finding no such records, the query displays none. Instead, the query returns records for all values in a field with a null combo box value. You can return all records for a combo box whose value is Null by changing the criteria to include a test for Null. For example, for the Customer combo box, use the expression:

    Forms!frmOrderStatus!cboCustomer Or
    Forms!frmOrderStatus!cboCustomer Is Null

If the value in cboCustomer is Null, this expression evaluates to True and the query returns records with all values of CustomerID.

**FIGURE 9.11:**

A filter query that returns records only when both combo boxes have a non-null value

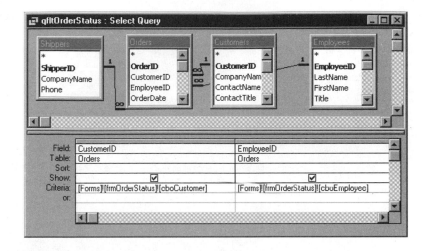

1. Click in the qfltOrderStatus query. In the Criteria cell for the CustomerID field, replace the criteria with the expression

   **Forms!frmOrderStatus!cboCustomer Or**
   **Forms!frmOrderStatus!cboCustomer Is Null**

2. In the Criteria cell for the EmployeeID field, replace the criteria with the expression

   **Forms!frmOrderStatus!cboEmployee Or**
   **Forms!frmOrderStatus!cboEmployee Is Null**

3. Save and close the query.

Retest the multi-criteria selection process as follows:

1. Click the Show All button. All records are displayed and all combo boxes are blank.

2. Select Alfreds Futterkiste from the Customer combo box. The six orders for the customer are displayed (see Figure 9.12a).

3. Select Peacock, Margaret from the Employee combo box. The two orders for the customer that are handled by this employee are displayed (see Figure 9.12b).

**FIGURE 9.12:**

You can select records using one combo box (a) and then narrow the selection with the second combo box (b).

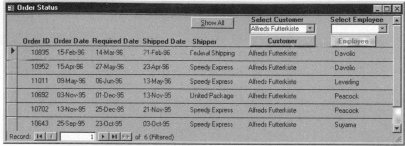

(a)

(b)

## Adding a Null Row to a Selection Combo List

The multiple criteria selection process works, but there is an additional refinement you may want to make. After you select a value for one of the combo boxes, you should be able to reset the value of this combo box to null and remove part of the filter. For example, after you select orders for a specific customer and employee, you should be able either to view all of the orders for the customer by simply selecting a null row in the Employee combo box or to view all the orders handled by an employee by selecting a null row in the Customer combo box.

### Adding a Null Row by Using a Union Query

Displaying a null row in a combo box list is more difficult than you might expect. One solution is to create a second query consisting of rows with all null values and to then combine the two queries using a special query called a *union query.* You can use a union query to combine two select queries into a single recordset that contains the rows of both the first query and the second query and eliminates duplicate rows. A union query is an SQL specific query and must therefore be created in SQL view. In this example, we'll create each of the two select queries in query design view, paste their equivalent SQL statements together, and modify the result into a union query.

## Union Queries

Use a union query when you want to create a single query that contains rows from two select queries. The two select queries must have the same number of fields, and the fields must be in the same order. Corresponding fields don't need to have the same names, but they must have compatible data types.

You can create a union query in SQL view by using the UNION operator to combine the SQL statements for each select query. The operator uses the field names from the first SELECT statement.

The UNION operator eliminates duplicate rows; use the UNION ALL operator if you want to return duplicate records. If you want to sort the rows, use a single ORDER BY at the end of the last SELECT statement; the field names that you use in the sort must come from the first SELECT statement.

You can learn more about creating SQL statements by searching for SQL in the online Help.

Here are the steps for adding a null row to the cboCustomers combo list:

1. Switch to Design view, select the cboCustomer combo box, click into its RowSource property, and click the Build button at the right of the property box. Figure 9.13a shows the query in Design view and Figure 9.13b shows the equivalent SQL statement.

2. Select the entire SQL statement and copy it to the clipboard. You'll need this statement later when you combine the two SQL statements.

3. Modify the SQL expression by removing the reference to the table name and the ORDER BY clause as shown below. The modified SQL statement displays two null fields in each row (see Figure 9.14).

    SELECT Null AS CustomerID, Null AS CompanyName FROM Customers;

FIGURE 9.13:

The row source for the customers combo box in Design view (a) and in SQL view (b)

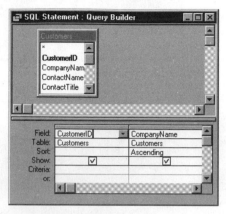

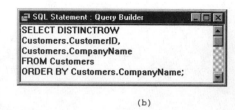

(b)

(a)

4.   Switch to Form view and click the arrow for the Customer combo box. An empty list is displayed (see Figure 9.15); if you select a row in the empty list, all class prefixes are returned.

You now have two SQL statements: the first SQL statement (currently saved on the clipboard) produces a list with values in the CustomerID and CompanyName fields, while the second SQL statement produces a list with null values in these fields. You can combine the two lists into a single list and eliminate the duplicate null rows so that the combined list has a single null row followed by the values.

FIGURE 9.14

The Design view for a query that returns null rows

**FIGURE 9.15:**

Using null values to display an empty list

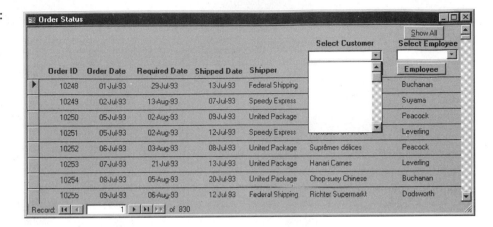

## Creating the Combined List as a Union Query

You construct a union query by entering the expression for the SQL statement (without the final semicolon) that you want first in the combined list, then the UNION operator, then the expression for the SQL statement that you want second in the combined list. The final statement must end with a semicolon.

1. Switch to Design view, select the Customer combo box, click in the RowSource property, and click the Build button. To display the null row first in the list, use the displayed expression as the first SQL statement.

2. Delete the semicolon, type **UNION**, and paste the SQL statement that you copied earlier. Delete the ORDER BY clause because it is unnecessary. The final expression for the RowSource property is shown in Figure 9.16a. The Datasheet view for this union query is shown in Figure 9.16b.

3. Switch back to Form view and click the drop-down arrow for the Customer combo box. The first row is the null row.

## Adding a Null Row to Another Combo List

Use the same procedure to modify the SQL statement for the row source for the Employees combo box. This time the ORDER BY clause is needed to insure that the final list is in ascending order by name. Figure 9.17 shows the final result.

**FIGURE 9.16:**

The SQL statement for the union query to start the customer list with a null row (a) and the Datasheet view for the union query (b)

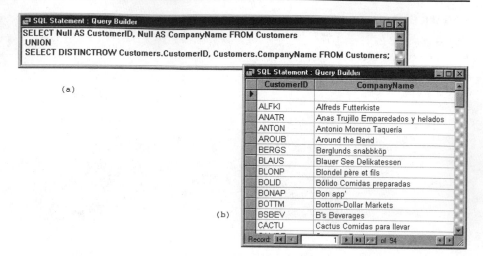

**FIGURE 9.17:**

The SQL statement for the union query to start the employee list with a null row

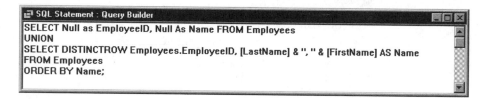

## Testing the Modification

With each combo box displaying a null row, the multiple criteria selection process is much more powerful.

1. Select a customer from the Customer combo list. All orders for the customer are displayed.

2. Select an employee from the Employee combo list. Only orders for the customer that are handled by this employee are displayed.

3. Select the null row in the Customer combo list. All orders handled by the selected employee are displayed.

4. Select the null row in the Employee combo list. All orders are displayed.

You can continue to modify the frmOrderStatus form with combo boxes for each of the other fields you want to use to select records.

# Synchronizing Two Combo Boxes

When the list displayed in a combo box is long, you can use two combo boxes instead of one, and you can design the pair so that the contents displayed by the second combo box depend on the value you select in the first—that is, *the second combo box is synchronized to the first*. For example, in an orders database, the list of customers is typically several hundred or thousand in length, so you can use one combo box to select the first letter (or pair of letters) and a second combo box to display the customers whose names begin with the letter (or combination). Figure 9.18 shows our goal for this section: the Customers form with a pair of synchronized combo boxes.

**FIGURE 9.18:**

Using a pair of synchronized combo boxes; you select the first letter in the combo box on the left, and the combo box on the right displays the customers whose company name begins with the selected letter.

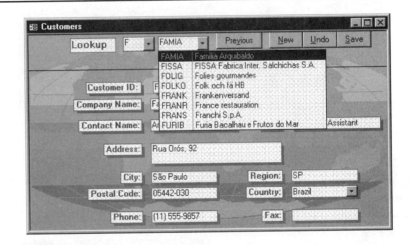

## Creating a Combo Box to Display the First Letter

The first combo box must display a list of the first letter of the CustomerID. We could just construct a table with a record for each letter in the alphabet. While this would be easier, you would miss out on some interesting techniques that you might want to modify and use in your applications. Instead of the table, we'll create a query named qryFirst as the row source for the first combo box named cboFirst.

1. Create a new query named qryFirst based on the Customers table and use the Left() function to select the first letter (or two) from the CustomerID. The Left() function takes two arguments: the first argument is the string expression and the second argument is the number of characters you want to select starting from the left end of the string. Figure 9.19a shows the query.

2. Set the UniqueValues property to Yes so that the datasheet displays each letter only once (see Figure 9.19b).

**FIGURE 9.19:**

The query uses the Left function to select the first letter of the CustomerID (a) and the UniqueValues property setting to avoid duplicate rows (b).

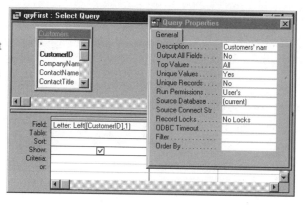
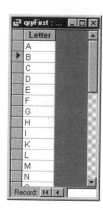

(a)                                            (b)

3. Modify the SQL statement to display a null row. Figure 9.20 shows the modified SQL statement.

**FIGURE 9.20:**

The modified union query displays a null row.

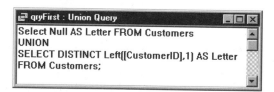

4. Place a new unbound combo box named cboFirst in the header of the Customers form just to the left of the cboFind combo box (move the label to the left to make room). Set the RowSource property to qryFirst and delete the label.

5. Save the form and switch to Form view. Click the down arrow of the new combo box. The list displays a null row followed by the first letter of each CustomerID in the Customers table.

## Synchronizing the Second Combo Box Using Query By Form

You design the interaction of the two combo boxes such that the second combo box, cboFind, displays customers with names beginning with the letter selected in the cboFirst combo box. If you haven't selected a value in the cboFirst combo box, the cboFind combo list displays all of the customers names. You modify the RowSource property of the cboFind combo box to select only the rows that have a CustomerID value beginning with the letter selected in the cboFirst combo box.

1. Switch to Design view, select the cboCustomer combo box, click in its RowSource property, and click the Build button.

2. Drag the CustomerID and CompanyName fields to the design grid.

This query must select records that have a CustomerID beginning with the letter displayed in the first combo box. For example, if we wanted to select records beginning with the letter D, the search criteria for CustomerID would be

Like "D*"

In our case the letter is given by the value in the first combo box, a value we refer to as Screen.ActiveForm.cboFirst. To use this reference with the Like operator, you must specify that the reference is to be evaluated before the wildcard search takes place; so you enclose the reference between vertical bars ( | | )to indicate the order of operations as follows:

Like" | Screen.ActiveForm.cboFirst | *"

Finally, if the user doesn't select a letter in the cboFirst combo box, the value in the cboFirst combo box is Null and the cboFind combo list must display all of the names. You modify the criteria expression to evaluate to True if the value in cboFirst is Null as follows:

Like" | Screen.ActiveForm.cboFirst | *" OR Screen.ActiveForm.cboFirst Is Null

3. Enter this expression in the Criteria cell below the CustomerID Field cell.

4. Save the result as qrySecond; verify that the RowSource property is set to qrySecond. The RowSource property now uses Query By Form to select rows for the cboFind combo box.

5. Save and close the Customers form.

6. Open the Customers form, select a value from the first combo box, and then select a value from the synchronized list in the second combo list.

7. Select a different value in the first combo box; drop the second combo list. The second combo list doesn't remain synchronized.

## Creating a Macro to Keep the Second Combo Box Synchronized

When you select a different value in the cboFirst combo box, the cboFind combo box doesn't update automatically, so you need to rerun the query for the cboFind combo box. We'll create a macro that requeries the cboFind combo box, sets its value to Null, and then moves the focus to the cboFind combo box, ready for you to select a customer. You run the macro when the value in the cboFirst combo box is changed and the combo box recognizes the AfterUpdate event. Table 9.6 shows the macro.

TABLE 9.6: A macro to keep the second combo box synchronized

| Macro Name | Action | Action Arguments |
|---|---|---|
| cboFirst_AfterUpdate | | |
| | Requery | Control Name: cboFind |
| | SetValue | Item: cboFind |
| | | Expression: Null |
| | GoToControl | ControlName: cboFind |

1. Click in the mCustomers macrogroup, enter the macro shown in Table 9.6, and save the macrosheet.

2. Assign the mCustomers.cboFirst_AfterUpdate macro to the AfterUpdate event property of the cboFirst combo box.

3. Save the form and switch to Form view.

4. Without selecting a letter, drop the cboFind combo list. All of the customers' names are displayed.

5. Select a customer from the cboFind combo box. The customer's record is displayed in the form.

6. Select a letter from the cboFirst combo box and click the drop-down arrow of the cboFind combo list. Only the names beginning with the selected letter are displayed.

7. Select a name from the cboFind combo box. The customer's record is displayed.

8. Click the Previous command button. The previously selected record is displayed.

# Finding Records to Print

The written reports you generate are important products of your application. In an order entry database, for example, you need to print invoices for individual orders, and the shipping department needs a printed order status for review.

This section shows you how to automate the selection of records for reports and the printing of reports. In Chapter 7, "Navigation with Macros," you learned how to generate a report for a single record. Now you'll learn how to generate a report for a group of records using two different methods to select the records:

- Select and display the records on a form and print a report synchronized to the form.

- Use a custom dialog to collect selection criteria from the user when the report isn't based on records displayed in a form.

# Printing a Group of Records Based on the Current Form

After reviewing the status of orders using the frmOrderStatus form and selecting orders using the selection combo boxes, you can print out a report for the selected orders. First, create a simple tabular report, named rptOrderStatus, using the Report Wizard. We'll base the report on the same query that the frmOrderStatus form is based on so we can use the same filter query for both the form and the report.

1. In the first screen of the Report Wizard, choose the qryOrderStatus query. Select the OrderID, OrderDate, RequiredDate, ShippedDate, CompanyName, CompanyName, and LastName fields. Click Next to accept the defaults in the next four wizard screens, and then choose the Formal style. In the last screen, set the report title to rptOrderStatus, select the Modify the report's design option button, and click Finish.

2. Set the Caption property of both the report and the label in the report header to Order Status

3. Rearrange the controls and change the Caption properties for the labels as shown in Figure 9.21.

4. Save and close the report.

Even though the frmOrderStatus form and the Order Status report have the same record source, when you open each object, Access creates a separate record-set for each.

1. Open the frmOrderStatus form in Form view and select orders using the selection combo boxes.

2. In the Database window, double-click the rptOrderStatus report to open it in Print Preview. The report displays all of the orders, not just those selected using frmOrderStatus. (The form and the report have the save RecordSource property setting, but each object opens with its own independent recordset.)

**FIGURE 9.21:**

An Order Status report created using the Report Wizard

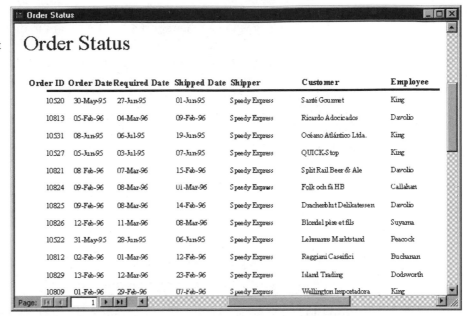

## Design the Macro to Synchronize the Report to the Form

Because the frmOrderStatus form and the rptOrderStatus report are based on the same record source, you can synchronize the report to the form by applying the same filter query to the report that you used to select records for the form, qfltOrderStatus. You can automate the process by placing a command button named cmdPrint in the form header and creating a macro that applies the filter when the report is opened (see Table 9.7).

**TABLE 9.7:**    A macro to open and synchronize a report

| Macro Name | Action | Action Arguments |
| --- | --- | --- |
| cmdPrint_Click | | |
| | OpenReport | Report Name: rptOrderStatus |
| | | View: Print Preview |
| | | Filter Name: qfltOrderStatus |

Before printing a report however, we want to determine if there are any records to print. There are a few ways to determine whether there are any records in the selection. One way is to use the report's NoData event to determine if there are any orders for the customer handled by the specified employee. The NoData event occurs when Access recognizes that the record source for the report has no records. If the recordset is empty, the report recognizes the NoData event immediately following its Open event and before its Activate event. You'll use the NoData event to trigger another macro, one that displays a message and then executes the CancelEvent action to cancel the subsequent steps that Access would take to format and print the report with no records. The macro determines whether one or both combo boxes have null values and displays different messages depending on which combo box combination you've selected:

both a customer and an employee

a customer but not an employee

an employee but not a customer

neither a customer nor an employee

You can create messages that refer to the selected customer and employee by concatenating the combo box values with message text.

The flow diagram for the cmdPrint_Click macro (which runs when you click the Print button) and the Report_NoData macro (which is triggered when the recordset is empty) is shown in Figure 9.22. Table 9.8 shows the Report_NoData macro. The combo boxes on the frmOrderStatus form hold the values of the CustomerID and the EmployeeID and display the values of the CompanyName and the employee's name. We want the macro's messages to use the values displayed by the combo boxes. The displayed values are in the second column of each combo list, so we use the column property to specify the second column. Because the column property is zero-based we use Column(1) to specify the second column.

**FIGURE 9.22:**

A flow diagram for two macros: a macro that selects records for a report by applying a filter and a macro that stops the print process and displays separate messages when there are no orders for the selected customer or employee

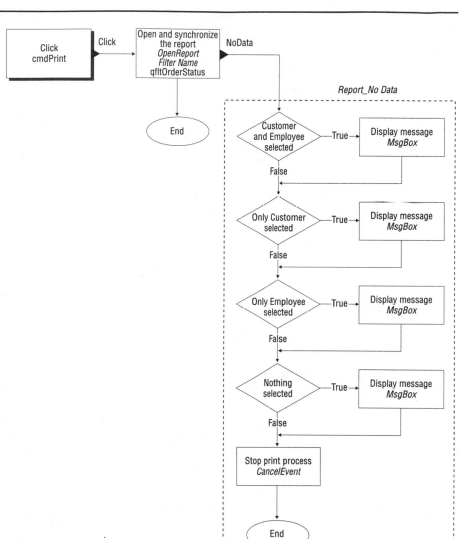

**TABLE 9.8:** The macro triggered by the report's NoData event displays a message box and cancels the printing process.

| Macro Name | Condition | Action | Action Arguments |
|---|---|---|---|
| Report_NoData | | | |
| | Not IsNull(Forms!frmOrderStatus! cboCustomer) And Not IsNull(Forms!frmOrderStatus! cboEmployee) | MsgBox | Message: ="There are no orders for the customer named " & Forms!frmOrderStatus! cboCustomer.Column(1) & " handled by the employee named " & Forms! frmOrderStatus! cboEmployee.Column(1) |
| | Not IsNull(Forms!frmOrderStatus! cboCustomer) And IsNull(Forms!frmOrderStatus! cboEmployee) | MsgBox | Message: ="There are no orders for the customer named " & Forms!frmOrderStatus! cboCustomer.Column(1) |
| | IsNull(Forms!frmOrderStatus! cboCustomer) And Not IsNull(Forms!frmOrderStatus! cboEmployee) | MsgBox | Message: ="There are no orders handled by the employee named " & Forms!frmOrderStatus! cboEmployee.Column(1) |
| | IsNull(Forms!frmOrderStatus! cboCustomer) And IsNull(Forms!frmOrderStatus! cboEmployee) | MsgBox | Message: There are no orders. |
| | | CancelEvent | |

Place a Print button on frmOrderStatus and then create a macro to open and synchronize the Order Status report to the form by applying the form's filter to the report.

1.  Click the mfrmOrderStatus macrosheet, enter the macro in Table 9.7, and save the macrosheet. Next, you'll create the macro from Table 9.8 that displays a message and then cancels the printing operation when there are no records.

2. Open a new macrosheet named mrptOrderStatus, enter the macro shown in Table 9.8, and save the macrosheet.

3. Open the frmOrderStatus form in Design view. Place a command button in the form's header section; set the Name property to cmdPrint and the Caption property to &Print.

4. Assign the cmdPrint_Click macro to the OnClick event property of the command button. Save the form and switch to Form view.

5. Select the first customer and the employee named Margaret Peacock, then click the Print button. The report for these orders is displayed.

6. Switch to Design view of the report, click in the NoData event, and then select the mrptOrderStatus.Report_NoData macro.

7. Save and close the report.

8. Select the customer named Bottom Dollar Market and the employee named Laura Callahan, then click the Print button. Access displays a message telling the user that there are no orders (see Figure 9.23). Click OK and make several other selections to display the messages.

9. Close the rptOrderStatus report.

10. Close the frmOrderStatus form.

**FIGURE 9.23:**

The message displayed when there are no orders for the selected customers handled by the selected employee

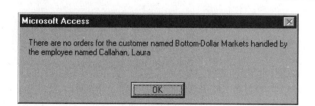

# Using a Custom Dialog to Select Records

Instead of using a form to select and display the records that you want to print, you can create a custom dialog to collect selection criteria from the user and use these values as criteria for a filter query that selects the records for the report.

**TIP**

The custom dialog technique is useful for routine reports when there is no need to view the records in a form before printing the reports; the performance of your application improves because using the custom dialog eliminates the time used to display the form.

**TIP**

The Customer Labels Dialog form lets you select customer labels for all countries or for one specific country (see Figure 9.24a). The form is powered by macros in the Customer Labels Dialog macrosheet. These macros use the Where Condition argument of the OpenReport action to select records. The Customer Labels report can be opened independently to list labels for all customers.

The NorthwindMacros application uses customer dialog forms to collect user input as follows:

- The Sales by Year Dialog lets you specify a date range and whether the report should be a detail or summary report (see Figure 9.24b). The Sales by Year report is based on the Sales by Year query which uses Query By Form to obtain its criteria from the Sales by Year Dialog form; this means that you can't run the Sales by Year report independently and must specify a date range using the Sales by Year Dialog. (The report is powered by VBA procedures which format the report depending on whether you checked the Show Details check box on the dialog form.)

- The Sales Reports Dialog lets you specify any of three reports (see Figure 9.24c): the Employee Sales by Country report is based on a parameter query and displays default input boxes to collect user input for the date interval for the report, the Sales Totals by Amount report requires no user input, and the Sales by Category report uses the Where Condition argument of the OpenReport method to select records.

**FIGURE 9.24:**

The NorthwindMacros database uses custom dialogs to select customer labels (a), to specify a date range for a sales report (b), and to specify one of three sales reports (c).

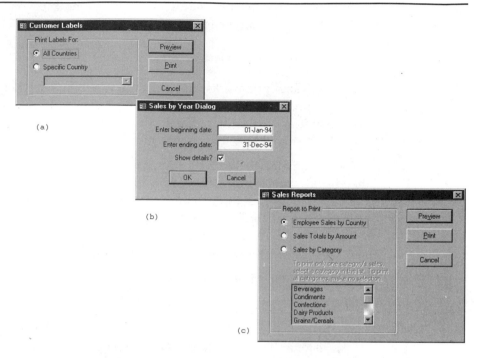

(a)

(b)

(c)

These custom dialog forms use two basic techniques to select records:

**Parameter query as the record source** In this technique the report's record source is a parameter query that requires input either from a default dialog or custom dialog. In this technique the report cannot be run without entering input into the dialog.

**OpenReport macro action** In this technique the OpenReport macro action (or the OpenReport VBA method) uses the Where Condition argument to select records based on user input in the custom dialog. In this technique, the report can be run independently without displaying a dialog because the report's underlying record source is not used to specify selection criteria.

The second technique is more flexible because it allows the report to be used either with or without a custom dialog. Recall that there are two action arguments for the OpenReport action that you can use to restrict records: the Where

Condition and the Filter Name argument. When the selection criterion is based on a single expression such as

Country = Screen.ActiveForm.[Select Country]

the Where Condition works well; however, when the selection criteria become more complicated, it is easier to create a filter query and use the Filter Name argument to apply the filter instead. The filter query obtains its selection criteria from the custom dialog form using Query By Form.

As an example, we'll create a custom dialog to select records for a new report that displays sales information by customer and by employee. The dialog provides choices for the customer and employee and then prints only the orders corresponding to the selection. In this section, you'll create a custom dialog to select orders for all customers and a specific employee, one customer and all employees, one customer and one employee, all customers and all employees.

Create the new report as follows:

1.  Open the Sales by Category query in Design view and drag the CustomerID and EmployeeID fields from the Orders table to the design grid. CustomerID and EmployeeID are lookup fields; when included in the report, the CustomerID field looks up and displays the CompanyName and the EmployeeID field looks up and displays the employee's LastName.

2.  Save the new query as qrySales.

3.  Use the AutoReport: Tabular Wizard to create a new report based on the qrySales query and save the report as rptSales. Switch to Design view. Delete the CategoryID control and its label. Change the report's Caption property and the Caption property of the title label in the report header to Sales by Customer and Employee. Rearrange the controls as shown in Figure 9.25.

## Create a Filter Query for the Report

When you are working with a form, you can create a filter while the form is in Form view, because the filter commands (Advanced Filter/Sort, Apply Filter/Sort, and Remove Filter/Sort) are available. However, the filter commands are not available for a report, so you work with the report's underlying record source to create the filter.

FIGURE 9.25:

The rptSales report

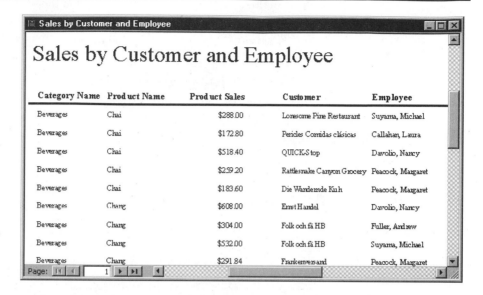

A filter query must include all of the tables that contain fields in the report or form that you are applying the filter to and all of the fields in the report or form. When you create the filter query, either drag all of the fields in the report's (or form's) field list to the design grid, or set the query's OutputAllFields property to Yes to show all of the fields in the query's data source. With the OutputAll-Fields property set to Yes, the only fields that must be shown in the filter query's design grid are the ones you are using to sort by or specify criteria for. (When you save a filter as a query, the OutputAllFields is automatically set to Yes.)

## Create a Filter Query Based on the Report's Record Source

After determining the report's record source, you create a filter query to specify criteria for the Customer and Employee fields.

1. In the Database window, select the query qrySales, click the arrow on the New Object button in the toolbar, and then select the Query button and click OK. The query design window opens with the field list for qrySales in the upper pane.

2. Choose the Properties command in the View menu (or right-click in the upper pane and select the Properties command); click in the

OutputAllFields property and choose Yes. With the OutputAllFields property set to Yes, the datasheet includes all of the query fields (regardless of which fields are displayed in the design grid). In this example, you'll use the Customer and Employee fields to collect the user's choices.

3. Select the CustomerID and EmployeeID fields and drag them to the design grid. The selection criteria for these fields will come from the custom dialog that you create next.

4. Save the query as qfltSales (see Figure 9.26).

FIGURE 9.26:

When you create a filter query, set the OutputAllFields property to display all the query fields.

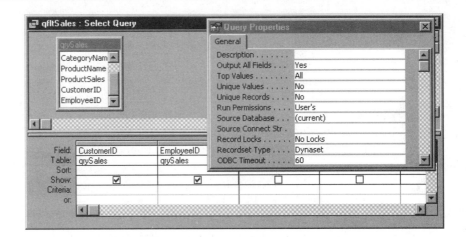

## Creating a Custom Dialog

We'll create a custom dialog and set the form properties so that the form has the look and feel of a standard Windows dialog, with one exception: while you are developing the application, let the PopUp property remain at the default No value so you can switch between Design and Form view and use the menus and toolbars. When you are finished with the development stage, you can set the PopUp property to Yes to prevent access to the menus and toolbars.

1. Create a new blank form named fdlgSales and set the Caption property to Select Sales by Customer or Employee.

2. Set the following custom dialog form properties:

| Property | Setting | Property | Setting |
| --- | --- | --- | --- |
| Default View | Single Form | Border Style | Dialog |
| Views Allowed | Form | Modal | Yes |
| Scroll Bars | Neither | Control Box | No |
| Record Selectors | No | Min MaxButtons | None |
| Navigation Buttons | No | Close Button | No |
| Auto Center | Yes | Shortcut Menu | No |

You'll want to place unbound list boxes for customer and employee selection on the dialog. Design both list boxes to display an empty first row using the techniques you learned earlier, in the section, "Using Multiple Criteria to Select a Group of Records." When you choose the null value for a list box, the filter query returns records with all values for that list box. In fact, we can reuse the combo boxes for the frmOrderStatus form; we'll paste them to the dialog, change them from combo boxes to list boxes, and delete the macros that are pasted along with the combo boxes. (If you didn't create the combo boxes earlier, you can create them now.)

1. Open the frmOrderStatus form in Design view, select the Customer and Employee combo boxes and their labels, and copy them to the clipboard. Close the form.

2. Click into the dialog form and paste the clipboard contents.

3. Select the Customer combo box and choose Format ➤ Change To ➤ List Box. Change the Name property to lstCustomer and delete the AfterUpdate event property setting.

4. Similarly change the Employee combo box to a list box, change the Name property to lstEmployee, and delete the AfterUpdate event property setting.

## Placing Command Buttons on the Dialog

Place command buttons to display the report in Print Preview, print the report directly, and close the dialog.

1. Place three command buttons on the fdlgSales form and set the following properties for the two buttons:

    | Name | Caption |
    | --- | --- |
    | cmdPreview | Print Pre&view |
    | cmdPrint | &Print |
    | cmdClose | &Close |

2. Switch to Form view, Window ➤ Size to Fit, and then choose File ➤ Save (see Figure 9.27).

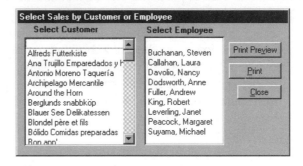

## Setting Criteria for the Filter Query

The selection criteria expressions for the qfltSales filter query are based on the values you select in the list boxes. If you don't select a customer, or if you select the null value, the filter query returns sales for all customers. If you don't select an employee, or if you select the null value, the filter query returns sales for all employees. The criteria expressions are similar to those you created earlier to select records for the frmOrderStatus form depending on the values in two combo boxes.

1. Click the qfltSales query, click the Criteria cell below Customer, and type the expression

    **Forms!fdlgSales!lstCustomer Or Forms!fdlgSales!lstCustomer Is Null**

2. Click in the Criteria cell below Employee and type the expression

**Forms!fdlgSales!lstEmployee Or Forms!fdlgSales!lstEmployee Is Null**

3. Save the query.

## Creating the Macros for the Buttons on the Dialog

The fdlgSales dialog collects criteria for selecting one set of sales records to print. When you click the Print Preview button, a macro hides the dialog, opens the rptSales report, and applies the filter query to the report's underlying query. Because the dialog must remain open in order to provide the selection criteria to the filter query, you hide rather than close it. When you close the report window, another macro triggered by the report's Close event unhides the dialog. Table 9.9 shows the macro for the Print Preview button and the macro to unhide the dialog.

**TABLE 9.9:** The macro for the Print Preview button opens the report and hides the dialog. The macro for the report unhides the dialog.

| Macro Name | Action | Action Arguments |
| --- | --- | --- |
| cmdPreview_Click | | |
| | SetValue | Item: Screen.ActiveForm.Visible |
| | | Expression: No |
| | OpenReport: | Report Name: rptSales |
| | | View: Print Preview |
| | | Filter Name: qfltSales |
| Report_Close | | |
| | SetValue | Item: Forms!fdlgSales.Visible |
| | | Expression: Yes |

The macro for the Print button doesn't display the report, so the macro opens the rptSales report without hiding the dialog and then applies the filter query to the report's underlying query. The macro for the Close button uses the Close action to close the form. Table 9.10 shows the macros for the the Print and Close buttons.

**TABLE 9.10:** The macro to print the report without displaying it

| Macro Name | Action | Action Arguments |
|---|---|---|
| cmdPrint_Click | | |
| | OpenReport: | Report Name: rptSales |
| | | View: Print |
| | | Filter Name: qfltSales |
| cmdClose_Click | | |
| | Close | |

1. Open a new macrosheet and save it as mrptSales. You store the macro triggered by the report's Close event in this macrosheet.

2. Enter the Report_Close macro from Table 9.9 and save the macrosheet.

3. Save and close the macrosheet.

4. Open a new macrosheet and save it as mfdlgSales. You store the macros for the cmdPreview and cmdPrint buttons in this macrosheet.

5. Enter the cmdPreview_Click macro from Table 9.9 and both macros from Table 9.10 and save the macrosheet.

6. Assign the cmdPreview_Click, cmdPrint_Click, and cmdClose_Click macros to the OnClick event property of the cmdPreview, cmdPrint, and cmdClose command buttons respectively.

7. Save the dialog form and switch to Form view.

## Attach and Test the Macros

1. Select a Customer from the first list box and click the Print Preview button. The report opens in Print Preview with the selected sales information.

2. Switch to Design view and set the report's OnClose property to mrptSales.Report_Close.

3. Save the report and switch to Report Preview.

4. Close the report. The fdlgSales dialog is unhidden.

5. Click the Print Preview button without making any list box selections. The report opens in Print Preview with all sales.

6. Close the report.

7. Select the Alfreds Futterkiste customer and the employee named Fuller, and then click the Print Preview button. There no sales for this combination, and so a report with no data is generated.

## Creating a Macro for the NoData Event

You can use the NoData event, recognized by the rptSales report when there are no sales records, to trigger a macro that displays a message and cancels the printing process (see Table 9.11).

**TABLE 9.11:** A macro to cancel the opening of the report when there are no records

| Macro Name | Action | Action Arguments |
| --- | --- | --- |
| Report_NoData | | |
| | MsgBox | Message: There are no sales records for this customer handled by the selected employee. |
| | CancelEvent | |

1. Open the mrptSales macrosheet, enter the macro in Table 9.11, close and save the macrosheet.

2. Click the rptSales report and switch to Design view. Click the NoData event and select the mrptSales.Report_NoData macro.

3. Save and close the report.

4. Select the Alfreds Futterkiste customer and the employee named Fuller, and then click the Print Preview button. Access displays the message (see Figure 9.28), cancels the printing process, and unhides the dialog.

**FIGURE 9.28:**

The message displayed when the report has no data

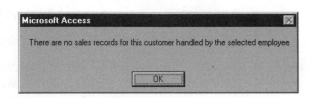

# Modifying a Group of Records

You can automate the modification of groups of records in two ways:

**Action Queries**   You can create an action query to add, delete, or update groups of records; and you can then use the OpenQuery macro action to run the query.

**SQL Statements**   You can create an SQL statement to change a group of records, and you can use the RunSQL macro action to run the SQL statement.

Normally you get better performance by creating the action query in query Design view storing the result as a saved action query and then using the OpenQuery macro action to run the query. When you save a query, Jet analyzes the query and saves an optimized execution plan along with the query; Jet can later use the execution plan to run the saved query. By contrast, when you use the RunSQL macro action to run an SQL statement, Jet must optimize the SQL statement on-the-fly each time you run the SQL statement.

## Using the OpenQuery Action to Run an Action Query

When you are creating a new record and the new record has fields with the same values as the previous records, you can speed data entry by having the fields in the new record filled in automatically. In Chapter 8 "Data Maintenance with Macros," you used a macro to set the DefaultValue property for controls whose values you want to carry to the new record. Those settings are temporary and cease to exist when you close the form. Sometimes you want the most recent values entered in a data entry session to be saved when you close the form or the database and then displayed in the data entry form the next time you open the form. In this case the values that you want to carry to the new record must be stored in a table so they can be stored when you close the database.

## Carrying Values Forward to the Next Data Entry Session

This section describes a technique for saving values between data entry sessions and carrying the values to the new record in the next data entry session. The technique is based on using a table that we'll call the *new record table* to hold the data values that you want to carry forward and using a macro to run action queries

Enter the new record into the new record table; when you save the new record, the macro runs an append query to add the record to the data table and runs an update query to save only the values in the new record table that you want to carry forward and to set to null those fields that you don't want to carry forward.

As an example, we'll set up the technique for new products in Northwind-Macros. We'll plan to carry forward to the next data entry session only the values in the SupplierID, CategoryID and QuantityPerUnit fields. We'll create a new form for data entry. (You could modify the Products form but it is easier to create a new form.)

### Creating the New Record Table

1. In the Database window, copy the Products table and paste it (structure only) as tblNewProduct. The new record table is designed to contain only a single record: either the new record you have entered but not yet saved, or a record with values you are carrying forward.

2. Open the table in Design view. Remove the primary key index for the ProductID field. Click the ProductName field and set the Required property to No. Save the table.

The tblNewProduct table stores only a single record and doesn't need a primary key. Because we don't want to carry the ProductName forward to the new record, the ProductName field in tblNewProduct will be null after the macro runs. This means that we must change the Required property to No so we can save the record to tblNewProduct table. We can make sure that the record that we save to the Products table has a non-null value for the ProductName field by validating the field using a macro instead of validating the field using the Required property.

**Creating the Data Entry Form**     We create a new form for entering data into the tblNewProduct table.

1.  In the Database window, copy the Products form and paste it as frmNewProduct. Open this new form in Design view, delete the BeforeUpdate property setting you added in Chapter 8, and set the following properties:

    | | |
    |---|---|
    | RecordSource | tblNewProduct |
    | Caption | NewProduct |
    | NavigationButtons | No |

2.  Place a command button in the header of frmNewProduct; set the Name property to cmdSave and the Caption property to &Save

3.  Select and delete the ProductID control and its label. The macro takes care of setting the value of the ProductID control, so this control doesn't need to appear on the data entry form.

4.  Save the form and switch to Form view (see Figure 9.29).

**Creating the Action Queries**     You create two queries: an append query to append the new data record to the Products table and an update query that sets to null those data fields that you don't want to carry forward.

1.  Create a new query based on tblNewProduct; use the asterisk method to select and drag all the fields to the first Field cell of the query. Click the Query type button in the toolbar and choose Append; enter Products as the name of the table to append the data to. Save the query as qappProduct (see Figure 9.30a).

**FIGURE 9.29:**

The new data entry form for products has the temporary table for its record source.

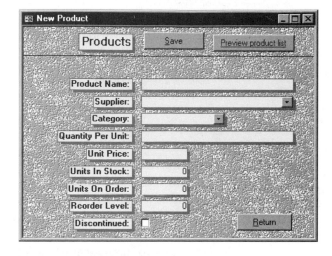

**FIGURE 9.30:**

The append query appends data to the Products table (a), and the update query sets to Null the fields whose values are not carried forward (b).

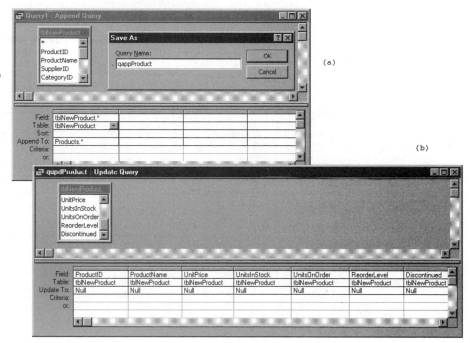

(a)

(b)

2. Create a second query based on tblNewProduct. Drag all fields except SupplierID, CategoryID, and QuantityPerUnit to the design grid. (You should drag to the design grid all of the fields for which you are not carrying values to the new record.)

3. Click the Query type button in the toolbar and choose Update. Enter Null in the Update To cell of each field. Save the query as qupdProduct (see Figure 9.30b).

**Creating the Macro**     You create a macro for the cmdSave button on the frmNewProduct form. The macro validates the data, sets the primary key value, saves the record to the tblNewProduct table, and then runs the action queries (see Table 9.12). The macro validates the data by testing for an entry in the ProductName field. If the field is null, the macro displays a message, places the insertion point in the ProductName control, and terminates. If the field is not null, the macro sets the ProductID value to a number that is one greater than the largest ProductID value in the Products table. (The SetValue action uses the DMax() domain aggregate function to determine the largest value in the table). The macro uses the SetWarnings action to turn off the default confirmation messages that Access displays before running an action query and then runs the queries.

**TABLE 9.12:** A macro to automatically fill a new record with data from a previous record stored in a table

| Macro Name | Condition | Action | Action Arguments |
|---|---|---|---|
| cmdSave_Click | | | |
| | IsNull(ProductName) | MsgBox | Message: You must enter a product name before saving the record. |
| | ... | GoToControl | ProductName |
| | ... | StopMacro | |
| | | SetValue | Item:ProductID |
| | | | Expression: DMax("ProductID","Products") + 1 |
| | | SetWarnings | Warnings On: No |

**TABLE 9.12 :** A macro to automatically fill a new record with data from a previous record stored in a table (continued)

| Macro Name | Condition | Action | Action Arguments |
|------------|-----------|--------|------------------|
| | | RunCommand | Command: SaveRecord |
| | | OpenQuery | Query Name: qappProduct |
| | | OpenQuery | Query name: qupdProduct |

1. Open a new macrosheet named mfrmNewProduct and create the macro shown in Table 9.12.

2. Assign the macro to the Click event of the cmdSave button, save the frmNewProduct form, and switch to Form view.

**Testing the Technique**   To test the technique:

1. Open the frmNewProduct form, enter data for a new product (see Figure 9.31a), and click the Save button. If you entered a value in the ProductName control, the record is saved to the Products table, and frmNewProduct displays a new record with the specified fields filled in with values from the previous record (see Figure 9.31b). If you didn't enter a value in the ProductName control, the custom message is displayed and the macro terminates (see Figure 9.32).

2. Open the Products table and verify that the new record has been added.

3. Open the tblNewProduct table and observe the single record storing the values that we want to carry forward.

**FIGURE 9.31:**

Use the new data entry form to enter a new record into the temporary table (a). After you save the new record the three values are carried forward (b).

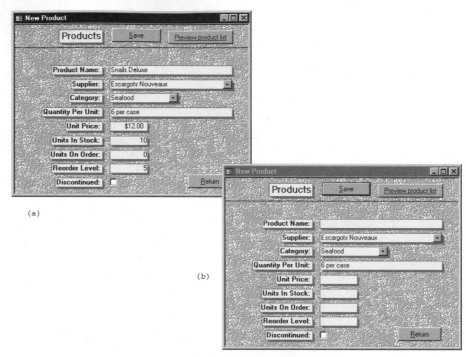

**FIGURE 9.32:**

The message that appears if you don't enter a required value

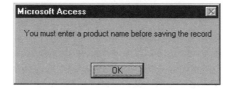

## Summary

This chapter has introduced you to macro techniques for working with groups of records. The important techniques covered include:

- You can automate simple and complex sorts using macros to set the OrderBy and OrderByOn properties of a form.

- A simple way to find a group of records that satisfy a set of criteria is to use Query By Form. Use combo boxes or list boxes to provide choices and hold the selected values. Macros assigned to the AfterUpdate event property run a filter query that uses the values in the combo boxes or list boxes to select records.

- You can use a union query to display an empty row in a combo box or list box.

- When a combo box list is long, you can use synchronized combo boxes. The row source for the second combo box uses Query By Form to select rows based on the value in the first combo box.

- You can use a form to select a group of records and base a report on the selected records; in the simplest method, the report has the same record source as the form.

- You can create a custom dialog form for collecting selection criteria for a report. A macro uses the input to filter the record source for the report. In this method, the report's record source is not modified.

- You can carry data values forward to another data entry session using a technique that enters data into a new record table and uses a macro to append the new data to the data table. The new record table stores the values until the next time you open the data entry form.

You have now completed the chapters that cover macro programming. The chapters of Part II have covered the most important macro techniques and have demonstrated the fundamental approach to macro programming:

> *You can design most macros by observing the interactive steps you take to accomplish a task and then translate your steps to macro instructions.*

You now have the skills to modify the techniques presented in this book and to create your own techniques. If you are new to programming, you should spend several weeks or months using macros to automate your databases. When you are thoroughly comfortable with macros and have a good understanding of the events that objects recognize, you'll be ready to continue on with VBA programming in Part III.

# PART III

# Access VBA
# Programming

# CHAPTER
## TEN

**10**

# The Access Object Model Revisited

- Using assignment statements to set and get property values

- Manipulating an object by calling one of its methods

- Running a method of the DoCmd object

- VBA-only features of forms and reports

- Referring to objects in VBA

- Properties and methods available only in VBA

This chapter revisits several concepts that were introduced in Parts I and II. Part I introduced you to the basic concepts of the Access programming model:

- Access defines a set of entities that you can manipulate and calls them *objects*.

- Access defines a set of changes in state that an object recognizes and calls them *events*.

- You manipulate an object by writing a program and telling Access to run the program when an object recognizes an event.

Part II introduced you to macro programming as a simplified version of programming in Access. As we move on to Visual Basic programming, we need to reexamine some concepts, including:

**Variables**   In VBA programming, a variable is a temporary storage location in memory that you name and use to hold a value or to refer to an object. In macro programming, the only way to define a variable is to use an unbound control on a form to hold the temporary value. In VBA programming, we still use controls in this way, but we generalize the concept of a variable in two ways: we remove the variable's physical representation as a control on a form, and we allow a variable to either hold a value or refer to an object. In VBA, a variable lives in memory without a physical representation in the user interface.

**Objects**   In Part macro programming, we've used the word "object" freely and informally to refer to physical entities in the Database window that have properties and events. Now, we'll use the word "entity" to describe those things, and we'll formalize the definition of "object" as a fundamentally different concept.

**Recordsets**   We'll look again at how a form is related to the records it displays. In VBA programming, there is a fundamentally new way to work with forms in which you can manipulate a copy of a form's recordset in memory without affecting the records displayed by the form.

This chapter takes a deeper look at the Access object model. The first half of the chapter focuses on the features that are available only in VBA programming, including manipulating an object by running one of the object's methods, creating an independent current record pointer so that you can work with a form's recordset without disturbing the record displayed on the screen, and saving your place in a recordset so that you can return quickly to a record. You'll learn about the additional objects and properties that are available in VBA programming and the additional ways you can refer to objects in VBA programs, including using the Me property to refer to a form or a report in a VBA procedure stored in the form's or report's module. The second half of the chapter, a continuation of Chapter 3's description of the Access application object model, is an in-depth reference to Access objects, properties, and methods (including features not covered in Chapter 3).

**NOTE**　　The examples in Chapters 10 and 11 use the Northwind sample application. Make a fresh copy of Northwind.mdb named Northwind_Ch10,11.

# Objects, Properties, and Methods

VBA programming views the Access world as objects that have

**properties** that describe an object's characteristics,

**methods** that describe the operations an object can perform on itself, and

**events** that you can use to run programs (procedures).

A fundamental difference between a macro object and a VBA object is that a VBA object knows how to perform operations. You can think of a *method* as a small program or a script for one of the operations the element can perform on itself. Here are some examples of methods: Delete, Close, Edit, Quit, Move, Requery, Save, Update, and Undo. In all, there are more than 100 methods in Access VBA. In one sense, methods and macro actions are similar in that they are both prewritten, built-in scripts for actions; some of the names are even the same. Methods and macro actions are different in that macro actions are perceived as separate from the entities they manipulate, and methods are perceived as an integral part of the objects.

In a macro, you execute macro actions to read and change properties of entities (using the SetValue action) and to manipulate the entity. Figure 10.1 depicts the entity in macro programming; the methods are shown dotted because they are not available.

In VBA, we perceive the object as a package of its properties and methods. In a VBA procedure, you read and change properties directly (using an assignment statement), and you ask an object to use one of its methods to manipulate itself. Figure 10.2 depicts the object in VBA programming.

**FIGURE 10.1:**

In a macro, you execute a macro action to set or read properties or to manipulate an entity.

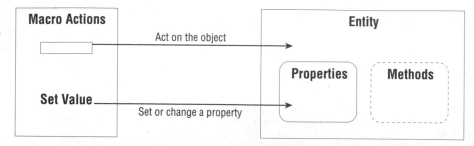

**FIGURE 10.2:**

In a VBA procedure, you set or read a property, or you ask the object to use one of its methods to manipulate itself.

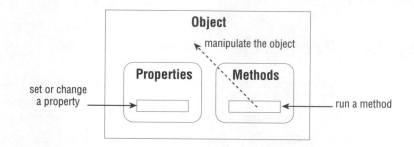

## Encapsulation

In VBA, we perceive an object as a package of its properties and methods. The packaging together of properties and methods with the object is called *encapsulation*. Encapsulation is one of the basic elements of the object-oriented model. We can't say that VBA is an object-oriented programming language, because it lacks one of the other basic elements (called inheritance). We can say, however, that VBA is *object-enabled* and that Access is an object-enabled database management system because VBA does use the model that properties and methods are stored together as a unit inside the capsule. In this model, the capsule is a barrier to the outside world; anyone who wants to manipulate the object calls one of the object's methods to do the work.

*(continued)*

Although we *perceive* an object as a package of its properties and methods, in reality, it doesn't work quite this way. Actually storing the scripts for each object's methods together with the object would lead to enormous redundancy. True encapsulation would mean, for example, that each form in the database would have its own copy of the scripts for every one of the Form object methods. In reality, an object's methods are stored only once with the object's class. Nevertheless, it is useful to think of an object as a *virtual* package of its properties and its methods.

## Using the Debug Window

One of the most useful tools for working with Visual Basic is the Debug window. We'll use the Debug Window frequently to test expressions and values, run procedures, and troubleshoot errors. Open the Debug window when any window is active by pressing Ctrl+G. The Access application object called Debug represents the Debug window. The Debug object has no properties but has a single method, called the Print method, that prints text in the Immediate pane of the Debug window. Here is the syntax:

```
Debug.Print outputlist
```

where *outputlist* is a numeric or string expression or a list of numeric or string expressions separated by either spaces or semicolons. If you omit the *outputlist* argument, a blank line is printed. When you are working in the Debug window, you don't have to refer to the Debug object explicitly and can use the syntax

```
Print outputlist
```

or use the question mark (?) as the shortcut abbreviation for Print as follows

```
? outputlist
```

We'll use the Debug window throughout the chapter to get hands-on experience with the Application objects, properties, and methods.

**NOTE**   You can specify how you want the output formatted in the Debug window; see Print Method in online Help.

# Setting Properties

When you work with properties in VBA, you can take two actions:

You can change the value of a property, that is, *set* a property, and

you can read the value of a property, that is, *get* a property setting.

In either case, you refer to the object's property by using the dot operator to separate the reference to the object from the name of the property. When you *set* a property, you assign a value to the property. To set a property, you use the equals (=) sign as an *assignment operator* as follows:

```
object.propertyname = value
```

where *object* is a reference to the object, *propertyname* is the name of the property you want to set, and *value* is what you are changing the property setting to. For example:

```
Forms!Employees.Caption = "Hi there!"
```

changes the Caption property of the Employees form to Hi there! Because the Caption property value is a string, you must enclose the text in quotation marks. You can think of the assignment operator as a left-pointing arrow that takes whatever is on the right side of the equals sign, sends it to the left side, and stores it in whatever is on the left side:

```
object.propertyname < value
```

## Setting Properties in the Debug Window

You can use the Immediate pane of the Debug window to set property values. Use the full identifier reference for the object. As an example, we'll change the Caption property of a form. Follow these steps:

1. Open the Employees form in Form view.

2. Press Ctrl+G to open the Debug window. Type the expression **Forms!Employees.Caption = "Hi there!"** and press Enter. The form's title bar displays Hi there! (see Figure 10.3). The changed property setting exists as long as the form is open; when you close the form, the changed value is discarded.

3. Click in the form and switch to Design view. The form's Caption property is not changed in the property sheet.

4. Click in the Debug window, place the insertion point anywhere in the line you entered in step 2, and press Enter. Click in the form. VB executes the line again and changes the Caption property in the property sheet. You can save or discard the change.

5. Close the Employees form without saving the changes.

---

**FIGURE 10.3:**

If the form is in Form view when you set the Caption property in the Debug window, the property setting lasts until you close the form.

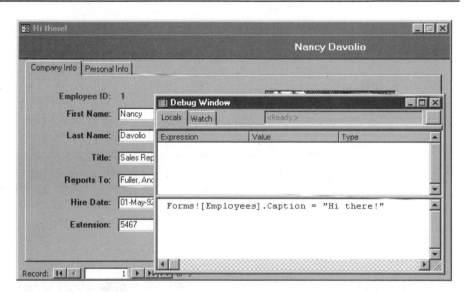

> **NOTE**
> If a form is in Form view when you set a property value programmatically (in a macro, in a VBA procedure, or in the Debug window), the setting is temporary and is discarded when you close the form. If you want to change a property such as the Caption property permanently, you have to change the setting in Design view (either interactively or programmatically) and save the change. In Chapter 12, "Mechanics of Procedures: Basics," we examine the lifetime for settings.

## Getting Properties

When you get a property setting, you are reading the current setting of the property, and you need to hold the result somewhere. You usually use a variable for this purpose. When a property setting is a text value, you can hold the result by assigning the value to a variable using the equals (=) sign as an assignment operator as follows:

```
Let variable = object.propertyname
```

where the Let keyword indicates that the value on the right of the equals sign is assigned to the variable on the left. The Let keyword is optional, and you'll find that most programmers prefer the simpler assignment statement:

```
variable = object.propertyname
```

For example, if strSource is the name of a string variable (using the str tag of Hungarian naming style), then

```
strSource = Forms!Employees.RecordSource
```

assigns the value of the RecordSource property of the Employees form to the strSource variable. Once you assign the value to a variable in a VBA procedure, you can use the variable when you want to work with the property; for example, you can use strSource in the procedure instead of having to type the reference Forms!Employees.RecordSource each time you need to refer to the property. A mundane, but practical, reason for using variables in VBA programming is to reduce the number of characters you have to type by using short names.

In macro and VBA programming, you can also work with properties that represent objects; for example, the ActiveForm property of the Screen object represents the active form. When a property setting refers to an object, you assign the result to an *object variable* using the statement

```
Set variable = object.propertyname
```

where the Set keyword indicates that the object on the right is assigned to the object variable on the left. The Set keyword is not optional. For example

```
Set frm = Screen.ActiveForm
```

assigns the active form to the frm object variable.

## Getting Property Settings in the Debug Window

When a property setting is a text value, you can display the value in the Immediate pane by entering a question mark (?) followed by the reference to the property. The Immediate pane can only print text; so if the property setting refers to an object, using the syntax ? object.property causes an error (see Figure 10.4).

**FIGURE 10.4:**

The error generated
when you try to display
a property setting for a
property that refers to
an object

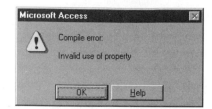

To explore these ideas, follow these steps:

1. Open the Employees form in Form view, and type **?Forms!Employees .RecordSource**. Press Enter. The value is displayed on the next line. You can create a variable to hold a text value and assign a value to the variable in the Debug window. One way to create a variable in the Debug window is to simply type the name.

2. Open the Product List form and type **strVar= Forms![Product List] .RecordSource** and press Enter. Visual Basic creates the strVar variable and assigns the value to it.

3. Type **? strVar** and press Enter (see Figure 10.5).

**FIGURE 10.5:**

You can use the Immedi-
ate pane of the Debug
window to set and get
properties.

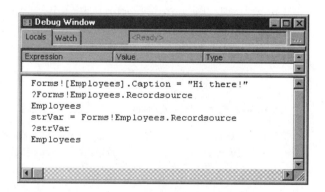

**NOTE**  Creating a new variable by just using it is called *implicit declaration*. Although we'll use implicit declaration of variables for the explorative work we are doing in Chapters 10 and 11, we'll use *explicit declaration* when we start writing VBA procedures in Chapter 12. When you allow variables to be created just by using them, you can't protect your work from typos. For example, if you create a variable by typing **varname** and later want to refer to this variable but mistakenly type **vername**, Visual Basic sets up a new variable for vername and doesn't recognize that you have make a typing error; Visual Basic is unable to associate *vername* with *varname*. When you use explicit declaration, you specify the words that you will be using as variable names; later, when you enter a word that you intend as a variable, the computer compares the entry with the list of declared variables and displays an error message if the entry isn't found on the list.

## Calling Methods

When you want to ask an object to run one of its methods, you *call* the method by using a reference for the object and the name of the method, separating the two with the dot operator. The syntax for calling a method is:

```
object.method
```

For example, the Form object has a Requery method. The Requery method updates the data in a form's data source; so to ask a form to requery itself, you call its Requery method as follows:

```
Forms!formname.Requery
```

### Passing Arguments to Methods

Most methods have additional information, called *arguments*, that you use to specify how the method is carried out. Specifying arguments is called *passing arguments* to the method. The syntax for arguments depends on whether the method returns a result. When a method doesn't return a result, you pass arguments to it by listing the arguments immediately after the name of the method, separating multiple arguments with commas as follows:

```
object.methodname argument1, argument2, . . [.,argumentN]
```

You enclose optional arguments in square brackets: in the expression above , the last argument is optional. Arguments that are not enclosed in square brackets are required. When a method returns a value, you enclose the argument list in parentheses as follows:

```
object.methodname (argument1, argument2, . . [.,argumentN])
```

For example, the GoToPage method of the Form object moves the focus to the first control on a specified page in the active form and does not return a result. The GoToPage method takes three arguments; the syntax is:

```
form.GoToPage pagenumber[.right, down]
```

where *form* is a reference to the form, *pagenumber* is a numeric expression that is a valid page number for the active form, and *right* and *down* are numeric expressions for horizontal and vertical offsets from the upper left corner of the window. For example, if Employees (page break) is the active form, the following statement:

```
Forms![Employees (page break)].GoToPage 2
```

moves the focus to the first control on the second page.

An example of a method that returns a result is the GetOption method of the Application object, which returns the current value of an option in the Options dialog (choose Tools ➤ Options to display the dialog). If you want to find out if the status bar is displayed, use the statement:

```
Application.GetOption ("Show Status Bar")
```

If the Status Bar checkbox is checked, the GetOption method returns True; otherwise, the GetOption method returns False.

**Passing Arguments by Order and by Name**    You can pass arguments to a method in two ways: by order and by name.

> **By order**    When you pass arguments by order, you list the values of the arguments in the order specified in the method's syntax. You can leave an optional argument blank in the middle of the argument list, but you must include the argument's comma. If you leave one or more trailing arguments blank, don't use a comma following the last argument that you do specify.
>
> **By name**    When you pass arguments by name, you specify the name of the argument followed by the colon equals (:=) assignment operator, followed by the value for the argument. You can list named arguments in any order, and the need for placeholders for omitted arguments is eliminated.

For example, to move the focus to the second page with a vertical offset of 600 twips, you can pass the arguments by order:

```
Forms![Employees (page break)].GoToPage 2, ,600
```

where the second comma is a placeholder for the blank right argument. To leave both trailing arguments blank, you can use:

```
Forms![Employees (page break)].GoToPage 2
```

Instead, you can pass named arguments in any order as follows:

```
Forms![Employees (page break)].GoToPage down:= 600, pagenumber:=2
Forms![Employees (page break)].GoToPage pagenumber:=2
```

## Assigning the Result of a Method

Most methods do not return a result, but there are methods that return text values, and other methods that return objects. When the method returns something, you can assign the result to a variable. If the method returns a text value, you can use a Let assignment statement to assign the value to a variable as follows:

```
Let variable = object.method
```

or, since the Let keyword is optional,

```
variable = object.method
```

For example, when you determine if the status bar is displayed, you can assign the result using:

```
blnStatus = Application.GetOption ("Show Status Bar")
```

When the method returns an object, you use the Set assignment statement to assign the result to an object variable:

```
Set variable = object.method
```

## Calling Methods in the Debug Window

You can call a method in the Immediate pane by entering the reference to the object and the method name, separating the two with the dot operator. Enter the list of arguments following the method name and enclose the arguments with parentheses if the method returns a result. You can pass arguments to the methods either by order or by name. When the method returns a value, you can display the value in the Debug window or assign the value to a variable. When the method returns an object, you can assign the object to an object variable. Here are some examples:

1. Type **Forms![Employees (page break)].GoToPage 2** and press Enter. The form displays its second page.

2. Type **?Application.GetOption ("Show Status Bar")** and press Enter. As you type, the Debug window offers assistance: After you type the dot, the Debug window displays a list of the properties and methods of the Application object (see Figure 10.6a); and when you type the first parenthesis, the Debug window displays the syntax for the GetOption method as a guide (see Figure 10.6b). If your status bar is turned on, −1 (True) is returned; otherwise 0 (False) is returned.

3. Type **blnStatus = Application.GetOption ("Show Status Bar")** and press Enter. The blnStatus variable is created, and the value of the property is assigned to it. To test the value of the variable, type **?blnStatus** and press Enter.

**FIGURE 10.6:**

The Debug window may display a list of the properties and methods of the object (a) and the syntax for the selected method (b)

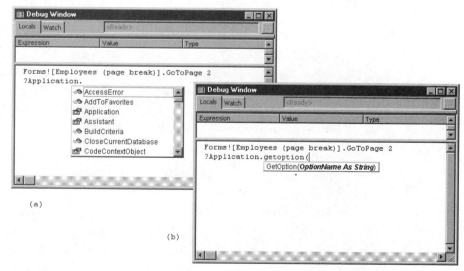

(a)

(b)

# Manipulating the Access Application Objects

Calling one of an object's methods is one way to manipulate an object. For the Access application objects, you can operate on objects in two additional ways: using the methods of the DoCmd object and using built-in functions and statements.

## Using the Methods of the DoCmd Object

Most of the operations you can take on the Application objects duplicate the steps you take when working interactively in Access. These operations are defined as the macro actions discussed in Chapter 5, "Macro Basics". Most of the macro actions are available in VBA as methods of the DoCmd object. (Table 10.21 later in the chapter lists the macro actions that don't have corresponding DoCmd methods.)

### The DoCmd Object and Automation

When Microsoft evolved VBA as the common language for the Office applications and settled on Automation (called OLE automation in previous versions) as the way for one application to work with the objects in another application, it was necessary to retain a way for external applications to run the macro actions. The solution Microsoft decided on is the DoCmd object.

In order for external applications, such as Excel or the stand-alone Visual Basic application, to be able to use Automation to work fully with Access, there had to be a way for these external applications to execute macro actions. In the Automation model, an application such as Access makes its objects available to other applications. Through programming, the external application can ask an Access object to use its methods. To make a macro action available to an external application in Automation,

*(continued on next page)*

the macro action had to be the method of some object. The simple solution was to create an artificial object that could have the macro actions as its methods—the DoCmd object was born. The external application can execute a macro action through Automation, by asking the DoCmd object to use the method that corresponds to the macro action. Most of the macro actions are available in VBA as methods of the DoCmd object.

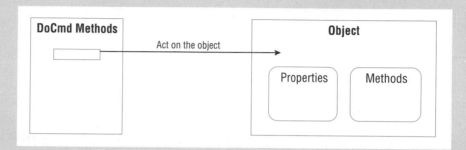

With the requirements of Automation taken care of, Microsoft had to decide how Access VBA should deal with the operations that macro actions carry out. Many of these macro actions could have been defined as methods for each of the other Access objects to which they apply. For example, the MoveSize macro action that you use to move and resize the active window might have been defined as a method of the Form and Report object instead of as a method of the DoCmd object. Decisions regarding the macro actions are not consistent: Although the 41 macro actions have corresponding methods for the DoCmd object, several of the macro actions have also been defined as methods of specific objects. For example, Requery is defined as a method of the Form object and the Control object as well as a method of the DoCmd object; Repaint is defined as a method of the Form object, and RepaintObject is a method of the DoCmd object; on the other hand, Close is only a method of the DoCmd object and is not also defined as a method of the object that is closed.

When a macro action has a corresponding DoCmd object method, typically, the method carries out the exact equivalent of the macro action. The macro action arguments are listed as method arguments in the same order as the action arguments appear in the macro Design window. The methods of the DoCmd object do not return values or objects, so the syntax for a method is:

```
DoCmd.method argument1, argument2, ..., argumentN
```

For example, the GoToControl macro action with the Control Name argument has an exactly equivalent GoToControl method with the syntax

```
DoCmd.GoToControl controlname
```

where *controlname* is a string expression that is the name of a control on the active form or datasheet.

Method arguments use intrinsic constants in place of the built-in macro action argument lists. For example, the intrinsic constants acTable, acQuery, acForm, acReport, acMacro, and acModule are used in place of a list of the Database objects. In addition, method arguments use the Boolean values, True(–1) and False(0), in place of the macro action argument Yes and No values. (Table 10.22 on the CD under Tables\Chapter10.pdf lists those DoCmd object methods in which the method and the corresponding macro action are slightly different.)

A fundamental difference between a macro action and its corresponding method is that whenever an argument for a macro action specifies the name of an object, the argument for the method is a string expression that is the name of the object. For example, the Form Name argument of the OpenForm macro action must be the name of a specific form, but the formname argument of the OpenForm method is an expression. The expression can be a variable as shown in the second example below.

There are two types of DoCmd methods for working on an Access application object. In one type, you must specify the object as an argument for the method. In the second type, the DoCmd method applies to the active object, so you don't specify the object as an argument. In the first two examples below, the OpenReport and OpenForm methods open objects that you must specify as arguments; in the last three examples, the methods operate on the active object.

| Statements | Description |
|---|---|
| DoCmd.OpenReport "Customer Labels", acPreview | When you use the OpenReport method, you specify the report as an argument of the method. |
| strname = "Customers"<br>DoCmd.OpenForm strname | The first statement creates strname as a variable and assigns the value "Customers". The second statement opens the Customers form. |
| DoCmd.GoToRecord , , acNext | Moves the focus to the next record in the active form or datasheet. |
| DoCmd.GoToControl "Country" | Moves the focus to the control named Country on the active form. |
| DoCmd.Close | Closes the active window. |

**NOTE** When an argument of a method is a string expression that is the name of an object and the name contains spaces, do not enclose the name in square brackets. For example, using "[Customer Labels]" as the report-name argument generates an error; use "Customer Labels" instead.

## Using Functions and Statements

You can use a few special built-in functions and statements to carry out operations. For example, to create new Form, Report, or Control objects, you use Create... functions. To delete a control, you use a DeleteControl statement. These functions and statements are discussed in the section "Creating New Application Objects" later in the chapter.

# VBA-Only Form and Report Features

In this section we look at some features of forms and reports that are available only in VBA programmng.

## Record Sources and Recordsets

When you open a table or run a query or an SQL statement, a set of records is returned and displayed in a datasheet. You can think of the set of returned records as an object: the Recordset object represents the set of records in a table or returned by a query or an SQL statement. (Recordset objects are data access objects and are managed by the Jet database engine. We'll look at the the the Recordset object and its properties and methods in Chapter 11, "The Data Access Objects.")

When you specify the RecordSource property of a form, you are assigning a specific recordset object to the form. When you open the form, Jet automatically creates the form's recordset object and Access displays the records in the form. Two forms may have the same RecordSource property, but each form has its own recordset that Jet creates in memory. When you first open two forms with the same RecordSource property, they may display the same record; however, because each form has its own recordset, you can navigate among the records in each form independently. For example, create a copy of the Customers form named frmMyCustomers in Northwind. Figure 10.7 shows the Customers form with record number 1 as its current record and frmMyCustomers with record number 5 as its current record. As long as the forms have different current records, you can edit records in each form independently.

---

**FIGURE 10.7:**

Two forms with the same RecordSource property setting have different form recordsets in memory.

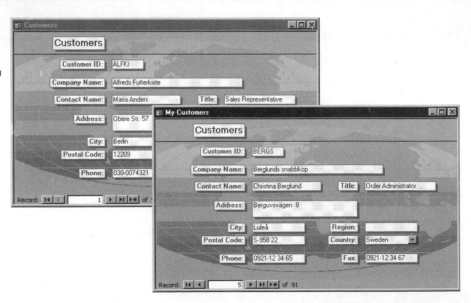

---

# Record Locking

When the forms have the same current record, the record-locking procedure in effect determines the access. By default, the records are not locked, and you can edit the data in the same record with both forms at the same time. If you save edits made in one form and then try to save the edits made in the second form, a message is displayed, giving you the option to overwrite the changes made in the first form, copy the record in the second form to the Clipboard, or discard the changes in the second form.

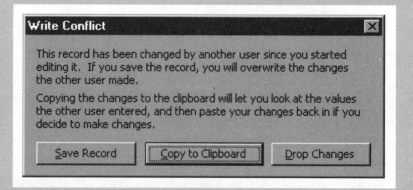

**Write Conflict**

This record has been changed by another user since you started editing it. If you save the record, you will overwrite the changes the other user made.

Copying the changes to the clipboard will let you look at the values the other user entered, and then paste your changes back in if you decide to make changes.

| Save Record | Copy to Clipboard | Drop Changes |

You can change the record-locking options in the Advanced pane of the Options dialog (choose Tools ➤ Options to display the dialog).

## Creating a Second Current Record Pointer for a Form

When you open a form that is bound to a table or a query, Jet creates a recordset object in memory. The form may display one or several records, depending on whether you are in Single Form, Continuous Forms, or Datasheet view, but the record selector points to a single record called the *current record*. As you browse to another record using the form's default navigation buttons, the record selector points to the record to which you moved. In VBA, you can create another, separate current record pointer that you can use to browse through the records in memory independent of the records displayed by the form. You create the new pointer using the form's RecordsetClone property. Figure 10.8 depicts a form, the form's recordset, and the independent current record pointer that you create using the RecordsetClone property.

**FIGURE 10.8:**

The relationship among a form, the form's record-set, and the form's recordset clone.

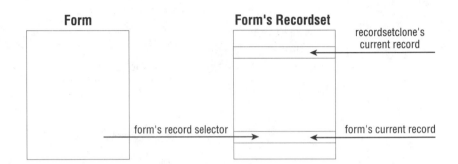

The form's RecordsetClone property is one of the properties that refers to another object; the RecordsetClone property refers to the form's recordset but with a separate current record pointer; this object is called the recordsetclone. For example, you can create a recordsetclone for the Customers form using the syntax:

```
Set clone = Forms!Customers.RecordsetClone
```

In Chapter 11, you'll learn about the properties and methods of the Recordset object as one of the data access objects. One reason to create a recordsetclone for a form is that using a recordsetclone gives you access to most of the properties and methods of the Recordset object. For example, suppose you want to determine programmatically the number of records displayed by a form. The Form object has no properties for determining the number, but the Recordset object does. The Recordset object has a RecordCount property that you can use to determine the number of records in a recordset. You can use the RecordCount property to determine the number of records in the form's recordset as follows:

1. Type **?Forms!Customers.RecordsetClone.RecordCount** in the Debug window and press Enter. The number of records in the recordset is returned.

2. You can refer to the value of a field such as the CustomerID field. Type **?Forms!Customers.RecordsetClone!CustomerID** and press Enter. The value in the CustomerID field for the current record is returned.

**NOTE**    When you create a clone of the form's recordset using the Recordset-Clone property, you can't use all the properties and methods of the Recordset object. For example, although the Recordset object has Sort and Filter properties that you can use to sort or select the records in the recordset, you can't use these properties with the clone because the clone doesn't have a Filter or Sort property.

The main purpose of the recordsetclone concept is to provide a way to let you navigate or manipulate records without affecting the records displayed in the form; you navigate and manipulate records using the clone's independent current record pointer. You can use the Debug window to observe the two current record pointers. To do so, follow these steps:

1.  Open the Customers form and test the following references in the Debug window:

    **?Forms!Customers!CustomerID**

    **?Forms!Customers.RecordsetClone!CustomerID**

    Both return the CustomerID of the first record.

2.  Browse to a different record and test the references again; the form's record-set points to the new current record, and the recordsetclone continues to point to the first record (see Figure 10.9a).

You can navigate in the form's recordset without affecting the recordsetclone using the navigation buttons on the form. You can also navigate through the recordsetclone without affecting the form. In Chapter 11, you'll learn about the Move methods that you use to navigate through the records of a Recordset object.

You can use the same Move methods to move the clone's current record pointer from one record to another in the recordset. Table 10.1 describes the Move methods of recordset objects.

**FIGURE 10.9:**

You can navigate in the form's recordset without affecting the recordset clone (a). You can use the Move methods to navigate in the clone without affecting the form's recordset (b).

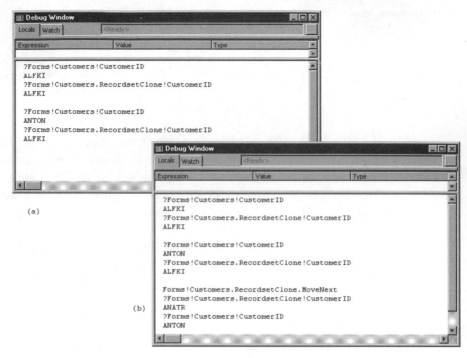

(a)

(b)

**TABLE 10.1:** The Move methods of the Recordset object

| Method | Description |
| --- | --- |
| MoveFirst | Move to the first record and make it the current record. |
| MoveLast | Move to the last record and make it the current record. |
| MoveNext | Move to the next record and make it the current record. |
| MovePrev | Move to the previous record and make it the current record. |

Follow these steps:

1. Call the MoveNext method for the clone in the Debug window by typing **Forms!Customers.RecordsetClone.MoveNext** and pressing Enter.

2. Type **?Forms!Customers.RecordsetClone.CustomerID** and press Enter. The clone now points to the second record and the form is not affected (see Figure 10.9b).

You can use the RecordsetClone property whenever you want to work with two current record pointers for a form's recordset. In Chapter 1, we used the Combo Box Wizard to create a lookup combo box. The Wizard wrote a VBA procedure that uses the RecordsetClone property to find a record. We'll use this technique for finding a specific record in Chapter 14, "Navigation with Access VBA."

## Using Bookmarks

To track records in a recordset, Access creates bookmarks. A *bookmark* is a unique binary string that Access creates for each record in a form's recordset each time you open a form. The value of a record's bookmark is not the same as the record number displayed in the lower left of the form. The exact value of a record's bookmark is not important; you can't display the value or use the value in any way. Nevertheless, you can refer to the value of a record's bookmark using the form's Bookmark property. The value of the form's Bookmark property is the value of the bookmark of the current record. You can perform two operations with bookmarks:

**You can store the bookmark**   You can store the value of the current record's bookmark by assigning the value of the Bookmark property to a string variable. In other words, you can save your place in a recordset by storing a bookmark.

**You can set the form's Bookmark to a previously stored value**   You can set the value of the form's Bookmark property to the value of the variable. The result is that the form displays the original record.

Bookmarks provide the fastest way to return to a record. Here is how the bookmark technique works. If you know that you want to return to the current record, store the current record's bookmark in a string variable. For example, if strMark is a string variable, store the bookmark for the current record in the frmCustomers form using:

```
strMark = Forms!Customers.Bookmark
```

To quickly return to the original record after you have moved to a different record, set the form's Bookmark property to the value of that variable. For example, you can return to the record that was current when you set the bookmark using:

```
Forms!Customers.Bookmark = strMark
```

You can try out bookmarks in the Debug window as follows:

1. Type the assignment statement **strMark = Forms!Customers.Bookmark** and press Enter. This statement creates the strMark variable and sets the variable to the bookmark for the current record in the Customers form. Note the record number.

2. Navigate to a different record. You can return to the original record by setting the bookmark to the value stored in the variable.

3. Type the assignment statement **Forms!Customers.Bookmark = strMark** and press Enter. The form displays the original record.

You can save additional bookmarks for other records in the recordset by making a record the current record and assigning its bookmark to a different variable.

Bookmarks are not saved with the records; when you close the form, the recordset and the bookmarks cease to exist. Access creates a new unique set of bookmarks every time you open the form.

### Bookmarks for the Recordset Clone

As a general rule, bookmarks from different recordsets can't be used interchangeably because each recordset has its own set of bookmarks. When you create a recordsetclone, however, you are creating an independent current record pointer to the form's recordset. You can, therefore, store a bookmark for a record in the clone as follows:

```
strMark = Forms!formname.RecordsetClone.Bookmark
```

and then display the record in the form by setting the form's Bookmark property to the stored value as follows:

```
Forms!formname.Bookmark = strMark
```

You can see how this works using the Debug window. Open the Customers form. We'll move the current record pointer in the recordset clone and save our place with a bookmark. We'll then move the form's current record pointer to the place we saved in the recordset clone. Here are the steps:

1. Type **Forms!Customers.RecordsetClone.Move 10** and press Enter. This statement creates the clone, moves 10 records forward, and makes the record you moved to the current record in the clone. Confirm by testing the value of **?Forms.Customers.RecordsetClone!CustomerID**

2. Type **strMark = Forms!Customers.RecordsetClone.Bookmark** and press Enter.

3. Move the form to the saved place by typing **Forms!Customers.Bookmark = strMark** and pressing Enter. Confirm by clicking into the form and noting that the CustomerID matches the value of the clone.

## Using Me to Refer to a Form or Report

Another VBA-only object property that returns an object is the Me property. Me is a property of both the Form and the Report objects. You use the Me property to refer to the form or report in a VBA procedure that is stored in the form's or report's module.

For example, in procedures stored in the form module of the frmEmployees form you can set the form's Caption property with the statement:

```
Me.Caption = "Hi there!"
```

You can get the form's RecordSource property and store it in the strDataSource variable using the statement:

```
strDataSource= Me.RecordSource
```

You can update the form's data source by calling its Requery method as follows:

```
Me.Requery
```

> **NOTE** You can't use test statements that include the Me property in the Debug window. You can use the Me property only in a procedure stored in a form or a report module.

**The Screen Object and Me**  Often, when you are running a procedure stored in a form or a report module, the form or report is also the active object; in this case, you could use either the Me property or the ActiveForm or ActiveReport property of the Screen object to refer to the form or report. However, the form or report in which the procedure is running may not be the active object. Because the Me property always refers to the form or report housing the procedure, you should use the Me property instead of the ActiveForm or ActiveReport property when you need to refer to the form or report.

Both the Screen object and Me are useful in referring to a form or report without using its name. The differences between the Screen object properties and Me are the following:

- Me has to do with where you are when you are referring to a form or report. Me can only be used in a procedure that is stored in the form's or report's module, and Me only refers to the form or report with which the module is stored. Me has nothing to do with whether the form or report has the focus.

- The Screen object has to do with whether the object you are referring to has the focus. You can be anywhere when you use the Screen object to refer to the active form or report—in a macro, in a procedure, in a ControlSource property expression for an unbound control, or in an expression for a query.

# Referring to Objects in Collections

When you want to manipulate an object in a program, you must first refer to it. In Part I we focused on referring to an object explicitly by its name; we used the exclamation point operator syntax for referring to an object in a collection. For example, Forms!Employees!LastName refers to the LastName control in the Controls collection of the Employees form in the Forms collection. You use the exclamation point syntax whenever you need to refer to an object explicitly by its name; this syntax is required in query expressions and SQL statements, in macro conditions and arguments, and in ControlSource expressions for unbound controls.

Access VBA provides three additional ways to refer to objects in collections; each uses a syntax with parentheses to point to, or *index*, the object. In Access VBA, you can use parenthetical syntax to refer to an object explicitly by its name, by the variable you are using to refer to the object, and by a number. Table 10.2, which is on the CD under Tables\Chapter10.pdf, lists the four types of references.

Each syntax has advantages. We'll look at some examples using the Debug window.

**Index by name**   You can use the index by name reference to refer to the object using a string expression that evaluates to the object's name. Type **?Forms("Customers").Caption** and press Enter. The Customers form's Caption property setting is displayed. Note that you can use any string expression that evaluates to the name of the object, such as Forms("Cus" & "tomers")

**Index by variable**    Often in a VBA procedure, you create a variable to represent a value. Type **strName = "Customers"** and press Enter to create strName as a variable and assign the string expression to it. You can use the index by variable reference to refer to the object using the variable. Type **?Forms(strName).RecordSource** and press Enter. The form's RecordSource property setting is displayed.

**Index by position**    When you know the position number of an object in its collection, you can refer to the object using just the number. If Customers is the first form you opened, you can refer to it using Forms(0) (an index number of zero corresponds to the first open form). Type **?Forms(0).Caption** and press Enter. The Caption property of the first form in your Forms collection is displayed.

# Indexing a Collection by Number

Access and Jet organize the objects in a collection in a list and automatically assign each member an index number. Both Access VBA and Jet assign index numbers beginning with zero instead of one, so their collection indexes are called *zerobased*. Members can be added to or deleted from collections, and the positions of individual members can change when the collection changes. A new set of index numbers is assigned to the objects the first time you refer to the collection. When an object is added to or removed from the collection, the positions of the other objects in the list may be affected because Access and Jet automatically update the index numbers when the collection changes. For example, for the Forms collection, Access assigns index numbers according to the order in which forms are loaded and changes the index numbers when forms are unloaded. If Employees is the first open form, its index number is 0, and Forms(0) refers to it. If you open Customers next, its index number is 1, and Forms(1) refers to Customers. If you close Employees, the index number of Customers changes to 0, and Forms(0) refers to it.

As another example, the second control in the Detail section of the Customers form is the CustomerID control (the first control is the label control). You can use any of the following references for the CustomerID control:

```
Forms!Customers!CustomerID
Forms!Customers("CustomerID")
Forms!Customers(1)
```

You can use the Debug window to test these references. If a VBA procedure is stored in the Customers form module, you can use the following references to the CustomerID control in the procedure:

```
Me!CustomerID
Me("CustomerID")
Me(1)
```

When you want to operate on each member of a collection, for example, to change the locked property of all the controls on a form, it is most efficient to refer to the controls by index number and loop through the collection (you learn how to loop through a collection in Chapter 14, "Mechanics of Procedures III: Contolling Execution").

# The Access Application Object Hierarchy

In Chapter 3, "Introducing the Access Object Model," we looked at the Access Application objects and those properties that are particularly useful in both macro and VBA programming. Here we look at additional objects and properties that either are available only in VBA programming or are useful when you are combining both macros and VBA procedures to automate tasks. In addition, we look at the methods for the Access Application objects. This section gives an overview of most of the available properties and methods so that you'll have a sense of the range of possibilities you can include in your programs. Before using a property or a method in your code, search online Help for information on using the property, for the method's syntax, and for code examples.

## Application Object

Chapter 3 described the properties available in both macro and VBA programming. Additional properties available only in VBA are listed in Table 10.3. Table 10.4 lists the methods of the Application object. Access 97 includes methods for working with the Internet, including the AddToFavorites and FollowHyperlink methods. (Tables 10.3 and 10.4 can be found on the CD under Tables\Chapter10.pdf.)

# Requery Methods

You use the Requery methods to ensure that a form or a control displays the most recent data. In VBA, there are two Requery methods: the Requery method for a form or control object, and the Requery method for the DoCmd object. The DoCmd Requery method is the equivalent of the Requery macro action; both update data only on the active object. The DoCmd Requery method and the Requery method of a form or report vary in two key ways:

- You can use the Requery method of a form or control to update data when the form is not the active object. The DoCmd Requery method updates data only on the active object.

- When you use the DoCmd Requery method (or the Requery macro action), Access closes the query or table and reloads it from the database. When you use the Requery method of a form or control, Access reruns the query or table without closing and reloading it. As a result, the Requery method of a form or control is faster.

The Requery method of a form or control does one of the following:

- Reruns the query or SQL statement that is the data source for the form or control

- Updates a table data source for a form or control by displaying new or changed records and removing deleted records

- Updates records displayed in a form based on changes to the form's Filter property

When the control is based on a table or query—which is often the case when the control is a list box, a combo box, a subform control, or an ActiveX control or when the control is a calculated control with a ControlSource expression based on an aggregate function—the Requery method requeries the data source; otherwise, the Requery method refreshes the control's data.

# The Collections

The Forms, Reports, Modules, and Controls collection objects have the two properties listed in Table 10.5 (on the CD under Tables\Chapter10.pdf).

The Forms, Reports, Modules, and Controls collection objects have no methods. Access manages these collections for you. For example, when you open a form or create a new form using the CreateForm function in a VBA procedure, Access automatically adds the form to the Forms collection and assigns it the next consecutive index number. When you close a form, Access automatically removes it from the Forms collection and adjusts the index numbers of the other open forms.

## Form

The Form object refers to a specific open form. Form objects are members of the Forms collection. You can't add or delete a Form object from the Forms collection (except by opening or closing a form). There are more than 100 Form object properties for changing a form's appear-ance and its behavior; you can set about 75 of the properties in the form's prop-erty sheet. The property sheet also includes the 29 event properties that a form recognizes. Chapter 3 lists the properties of the Form object that are useful in both macro and VBA programming. Here we'll look at additional properties, most of which are read-only, that are particularly useful in VBA programming. Table 10.6 lists the additional properties, and Table 10.7 lists the methods of the Form object; both tables can be found on the CD under Tables\Chapter10.pdf.

## Report

Chapter 3 lists many of the properties of the Report object useful both in macro and VBA programming. Table 10.8 lists additional properties of the Report object. Table 10.9 lists the methods of the Report object. Both tables can be found on the CD under Tables\Chapter10.pdf

## The Module Object

The Module object refers to a specific open module. The two kinds of Module objects are standard and class.

- A standard module is listed in the Modules pane of the Database window. You use it to store procedures that you want to make available to other procedures and to store function procedures that you want to use as event handlers in one or more forms or reports.

- A class module contains the definition of new objects; you create the object by creating a new instance of the class defined by the module. The two kinds of class modules are form and report modules and independent class modules. Form and report modules are stored as part of forms and reports, and independent class modules are stored as separate objects in the Modules pane of the Database window. When you open a form or report interactively or by using the OpenForm or OpenReport macro action or method, you are creating the form or report as the default instance of the form or report module. You use VBA procedures to create nondefault instances of form and report modules and to create all instances of independent class modules (see Chapter 19, "Creating and Modifying Database Objects," for more information on creating nondefault instances of a class module).

Normally, you create modules interactively by typing in the Module window; however, at times you might want to create or change a module programmatically. The purpose of defining a Module object is to allow you to create and modify modules directly from other VBA procedures. You use the properties and methods of the Module object to create new procedures in standard and class modules; to create new event procedures in form and report modules; and to insert, replace, and delete lines of code in a module.

## Independent Class Modules

Independent class modules are a new feature in Access 97. In Access 95, class modules exist only as form and report modules. Independent class modules allow you to define new objects that are not associated with a form or report.

Access itself uses independent classes for defining its objects. For example, a built-in class defines each control in the toolbox; when you place a control on a form or a report, you are creating a new instance of the control's class.

*(continued on next page)*

You can use an independent class module to define your own objects. For example, you can create an Orders class with the properties typically stored in an Orders table and with methods for calculating sales tax, for checking inventory levels, and for printing an invoice. Each order is an instance of the class. By creating an Orders class module, you package (encapsulate) all the information for the class into a single module and make it easier to modify the class later. Ease of modification is one reason for using class modules, but the main reason is that you can create class modules that are reusable in other Access databases and even in non-Access applications. With a set of reusable objects on hand, development time can be reduced.

Access 97 provides two new events that class modules recognize. A class module recognizes the Initialize event when you create a new instance of the class module in a VBA procedure, and it recognizes the Terminate event when the instance is removed from memory.

The addition of independent class modules gives Access VBA the new object-oriented features necessary for creating the reusable objects required for efficient database development.

**NOTE**     Code lines in a module are numbered beginning with zero.

Table 10.10 lists the properties of the Module object, and Table 10.11 lists the methods of the Module object. Both tables can be found on the CD under Tables\Chapter10.pdf.

## Control

Chapter 3 describes many of the properties of controls that are available in both macro and VBA programming. In addition, some properties are available only in VBA. This section describes many of the VBA-only properties and the methods of the Control objects. This section also describes new objects associated with controls, including the new Hyperlink object associated with the Command button, Image and Label controls, and the new Page object and Pages collection associated with the new Tab control. Tables 10.12 and 10.13 (on the CD under Tables\Chapter10.pdf) describe a few properties and methods shared by general categories of controls.

You can use the Debug window to test these methods. For example, with the Customers form open in Form view, follow these steps:

1. Type **Forms!Customers!Country.SetFocus** and press Enter. The Country control has the focus; confirm by clicking into the Customers form and observing that Country is the active control.

2. Type **Forms!Customers!Country.Requery** and press Enter. The Country control is updated by requerying the SQL statement that is the row source for the combo box.

3. Type **Forms!Customers.Requery** and press Enter. The record source of the Customers form is requeried.

## Combo Box and List Box Controls

Combo boxes and list boxes have several properties and methods that are particularly useful in VBA programming. Table 10.14 lists examples of these properties, and Table 10.15 lists the methods; these tables are on the CD under Tables\Chapter10.pdf. (Chapter 3 lists examples of properties of combo and list boxes available in both macro and VBA programming.)

You can use the Debug window to test these properties and methods. For example, with Customers as an open form, follow these steps:

1. Type **Set cbo = Forms!Customers!Country** and press Enter. This statement creates cbo as an object variable to represent the combo box. We'll use the variable as an abbreviation for the full reference.

2. Type **?cbo.ListCount** and press Enter. The list contains 22 countries.

3. Type **?cbo.ListIndex** and press Enter. The index number for the country in the current row is displayed.

4. Type **?cbo.ItemData(3)** and press Enter. The Debug window displays the data in the fourth row. Although you use the ItemData method to return the data in a specific column (the bound column), you can use the Column property to display the data in any column. The Column property has two

arguments that you use to specify the index for the column and row. Both index numbers are zero based; the first argument is the column that contains the data, and the second argument is the row. If you omit the second argument, the data for the current row is returned.

5. Type **?cbo.Column(0)** and press Enter. The Debug window displays the data in the first column of the current row. To display the data in any row, use the second parameter of the Column property. For example, type **?cbo.Column(0,2)** and press Enter to display the data in the third row.

**Using the ItemsSelected Collection of a List Box Control**     The standard list box allows you to select a single item from the list; however, you can use the MultiSelect property to choose more than one item. A dotted rectangle encloses the current row in a list box. The MultiSelect property has the following values:

**None** for a single selection. You select an item by clicking on the row or by using the arrow keys to move the current record pointer up or down a row and select the new current record. When you select a new record, the previous record is deselected automatically. After you select a row, the only way to deselect it is to select another row.

**Simple** to select multiple items by choosing each item separately. You select an item by clicking on the row. After you select a row, you can deselect it by clicking on it a second time.

**Extended** to extend the selection of multiple items. After you select an item, you can extend the selection in three ways. You can hold down the left mouse button and drag to another row. You can press the Shift key and click another row. You can press the Shift key and then press an arrow key. In each case, you extend the selection from the previously selected item to the current item. After you have made an extended selection, you can select or deselect any item by pressing the Ctrl key and then clicking the item.

When you select multiple items in the list, Access creates a collection called the ItemsSelected collection. Each member of the ItemsSelected collection is an integer that refers to a selected row in the list box or combo box. Even though the members of the ItemsSelected collection are integers, their data type is Variant by default. The ItemsSelected collection has no methods and has the single Count property that returns the number of items selected. See Chapter 18, "Working with Groups of Records Using Access VBA," for more information about the multi-select list box.

## Hyperlink Object

A new feature in Access 97 is direct access to the Internet. Access VBA provides a new Hyperlink object that is associated with the Command button, Image control, and Label control. You use the Hyperlink object to manipulate the hyperlink in VBA procedures. The Command button, Image control, and Label control have a new Hyperlink property that refers to the Hyperlink object and gives you access to the properties and methods of the Hyperlink object. Although you can set the HyperlinkAddress and HyperlinkSubAddress properties in the control's property sheet, you can also specify the address in VBA using the Address and SubAddress properties of the Hyperlink object. The Hyperlink object also has the methods shown in Table 10.16. (Table 10.16 is on the CD under Tables\Chapter10.pdf.) The syntax for these methods is

```
object.Hyperlink.methodname
```

where *object* is a reference to the Control object that contains the hyperlink. Search the methodname in online Help for the syntax of the method's arguments and code examples.

## The Tab Control

The Tab control is a new Form control in Access 97. A Tab control has one or more pages, each with its own tab. You can place other Form controls on each page. When the user clicks on a tab, the corresponding page becomes active. In previous versions of Access, you could achieve a similar effect by creating a form with several pages with Command buttons to display other pages, (or you could have used the Tab or TabStrip custom control provided with the Access Developers Toolkit); in Access 97, the built-in Tab control makes the multipage aspect of a form more obvious and easier to use. Northwind contains both kinds of forms. The Employees (page break) form uses the Page Break control to define separate pages (see Figure 10.10a), and the Employees form uses the new Tab control (see Figure 10.10b).

**The Page Object and the Pages Collection**  Normally, you create the Tab control and its pages in form Design view; however, you can also create, move, or delete pages programmatically using VBA. A page is represented by a Page object, and the Tab control has a Pages collection containing all the Page objects. The Pages collection is zero-based and has a Count property that you can use to determine the number of pages in the Tab control. Table 10.17 (on the CD under Tables\Chapter10.pdf) lists the methods of the Pages collection.

**FIGURE 10.10:**

You can display several pages in a single form by using the Page Break control (a) or using the new Tab control (b).

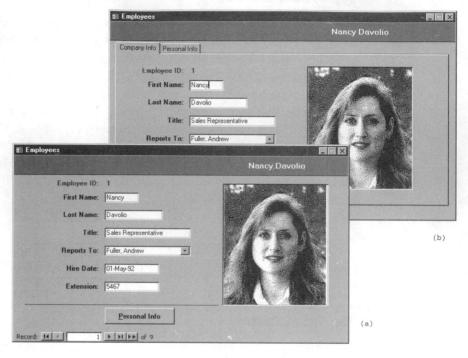

Each page has a unique name and is represented by a Page object. You can refer to a specific page using any of the syntax types listed in Table 10.2. For example, in the Employees form, the name of the Tab control is Tabctl0, and you can refer to the Company Info page using the fully qualified reference:

```
Forms!Customers!Tabctl0.Pages!CompanyInfo
```

You can refer to a control on the page by referring to the page's Controls collection and then to the control; for example, to refer to the LastName control on the CompanyInfo page, use the reference:

```
Forms!Customers!Tabctl0.Pages!CompanyInfo.Controls!LastName
```

Table 10.18 lists properties of the Page object, and Table 10.19 lists methods. Both tables are on the CD under Tables\Chapter10.pdf.

# Screen

The Screen object refers to the particular form, report, or control that currently has the focus or to the control that previously had the focus. By using the Screen object in a macro or in a VBA procedure, you can refer to the active object without knowing the object's name. Referring to the Screen object does not make the form, report, or control the active object, however. Chapter 3 described the properties of the Screen object. All these properties return objects. When you use the Screen object in a VBA procedure, you normally create an object variable to refer to the returned object, for example:

```
Set frmvar = Screen.ActiveForm
```

Table 10.20 (on the CD under Tables\Chapter10.pdf) shows an additional VBA-only property of the Screen object. The Screen object has no methods.

In VBA, the role of the Screen object is often taken over by the Me object. For example, when you want to refer to a form in a VBA procedure that is stored in the form's module, it is preferable to use the Me object in order to avoid errors if, for some unexpected reason, an object other than the form is active.

# DoCmd

The DoCmd object is an extraordinary object available only in Visual Basic. The DoCmd object doesn't represent a physical entity with properties and behaviors. Instead, it represents an important connection between macro and VBA programming—you use the DoCmd object when you run macro actions from Visual Basic. You can use the DoCmd object to run 41 of the 49 macro actions as corresponding VBA methods. Table 10.21 (on the CD under Tables\Chapter10.pdf) lists the eight macro actions that do not have corresponding DoCmd methods and describes how these operations are handled in Access VBA.

For the 41 macro actions that do have corresponding DoCmd methods, typically the method carries out the equivalent of the corresponding macro action with the action arguments listed as method arguments in the same order as the action arguments appear in the macro Design window. You use intrinsic constants to specify many arguments for a method, and you use the True and False values instead of Yes and No.

> **NOTE**   There is a fundamental difference between a macro action and the corresponding method of the DoCmd object: When an argument for a macro action requires the name of a specific form, a control, or other object as a literal, the argument for the method can be a string expression or a variable. Because you can use variables as arguments for methods, it is usually possible to design a procedure to be reusable.

Table 10.22 (on the CD under Tables\Chapter10.pdf) lists those DoCmd object methods that differ from the corresponding macro action.

In some cases, even though a DoCmd method may correspond to a macro action, there may be a preferred way to carry out the operation. Table 10.23 lists DoCmd methods for which there is a preferred VBA technique.

## Properties Collection

Every Access Application object contains a Properties collection with a set of built-in Property objects that we normally just call properties. In Chapter 19, "Creating and Modifying Database Objects," you learn how to create custom properties for forms and reports; however, the custom properties you create for forms and reports are not added to the Properties collections, which is reserved for built-in properties only. (In Chapter 19, you learn that the data access objects model uses the Properties collection for custom as well as built-in properties.)

The Properties collection has properties shown in Table 10.24 and has no documented methods. (Table 10.24 is on the CD under Tables\Chapter10.pdf.)

With the Customers form open, follow these steps:

1. Type **? Forms!Customers.Properties.Count in the Debug window** and press Enter. The number of built-in form properties, 122, is displayed in the Debug window.

2. Type **? Forms!Customers!Country.Properties.Count** and press Enter. The number of built-in properties for the combo box control, 80, is displayed in the Debug window.

# Property

Each built-in property of an Access object has a corresponding Property object. For example, the Visible property of a control has a corresponding Property object. A Property object has properties of its own, including the properties listed in Table 10.25. (Table 10.25 is on the CD under Tables\Chapter10.pdf.) The Access Property object has no methods.

With the Customers form open, type **? Forms!Customers!Country.Properties! Visible.Value** and press Enter. The Debug window displays True. Because Properties is the default collection for a control and Value is the default property, you can type **? Forms!Customers!Country.Visible** and press Enter.

# The References Collection

When you create an Access application that uses VBA to manipulate objects in other Access databases or in other applications such as Microsoft Excel or Microsoft Word, you provide information about the objects in the other application by creating a reference to the other application's type library. Normally, you create and remove references interactively using the References dialog (choose Tools ➤ References) when a module window is the active window; however, a new feature of Access 97 is that you can also add and remove references programmatically using VBA.

**FIGURE 10.11:**

Use the References dialog to create a reference to the type library of another Access database or to another application.

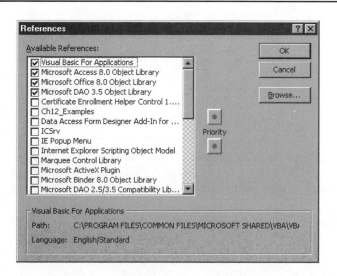

Each reference is represented by a Reference object, and the References collection of the Application object contains the Reference objects currently set for the database. The References collection has a Count property that you can use to determine the number of references currently set, and it has the methods listed in Table 10.26. (Table 10.26 is on the CD under Tables\Chapter10.pdf.) Access 97 introduces two new events that the References collection recognizes. When you add a reference programmatically, the References collection recognizes the ItemAdded event. When you remove a reference programmatically, the References collection recognizes the ItemRemoved event.

## The Reference Object

The Reference object represents a specific reference currently set to the type library of another application or another Access database. You can refer to a Reference object using the normal syntax for a member of a collection; for example, to refer to the Access type library, use the syntax References!Access. The Reference object has the properties listed in Table 10.27 (which is on the CD under Tables\Chapter10.pdf) and has no methods.

## The Access Visual Basic Objects

Access Visual Basic has three objects: Err, Debug, and Collection.

### Err

The Err object holds information about an error in a VBA procedure that occurs while the procedure is running (called a *VBA run-time error*). The properties of the Err object are filled by the generator of the error with information that uniquely identifies the error. (A VBA run-time error can be generated by an object, by VBA, or by you as the VBA programmer.) Because there is only one Err object, you work with a single VBA run-time error at a time. The Err object's properties are cleared (reset to zero or the zero-length string) automatically after any Resume statement, after any On Error statement, or after an Exit Sub, Exit Function, or Exit Property statement. Table 10.28 lists the properties for the Err object, and Table 10.29 lists the methods for the Err object. (Both tables are on the CD under Tables\Chapter10.pdf.)

### Debug

The Debug object has no properties and has a single method, Print. The Print method prints text in the Immediate pane of the Debug window. The syntax is Debug.Print *[outputlist]*. When you are working in the Debug window, you can use the question mark (?) as an abbreviation that follows ? *[outputlist]*, but when you want to print to the Debug window from a VBA procedure, you must use the full syntax to refer to the Debug object. We have been using the Immediate pane of the Debug window to evaluate expressions, to set and get property values, and to call methods. In Chapter 15, "Dealing with Errors in VBA," you learn how to use the other two panes: the Locals pane and the Watch pane.

### Collection

The Collection object refers to a set of items of the same kind. The purpose of the Collection object is to allow you to create your own collections. You use the Collection object in Chapter 19 when you create multiple form objects, that is, multiple instances of a form module.

When you add members to the Collection object, they are automatically indexed. Note that the index for a user-defined collection begins with one and not with zero. The Collection object has the properties listed in Table 10.30 and the methods listed in Table 10.31. (Both tables are on the CD under Tables\Chapter10.pdf.)

## The Microsoft Office Shared Objects

Microsoft Office 97 introduces a set of shared features, including Command Bars for customizing menu bars, shortcut menus, and toolbars; the Office Assistant for providing a new type of online help; and FileSearch for providing enhanced file-search capabilities. Normally, you work with these features interactively; however, Office 97 provides object models so that you can control and customize these features programmatically with VBA. A discussion of these object models is beyond the scope of this book. The Developer's Solutions sample application includes examples that demonstrate programming the Command Bars and the Office Assistant.

# Using the Object Browser

Using the Object Browser is a good way to learn more about the Access Application objects as well as the data access objects and the objects that other applications make available through Automation. The Object Browser displays information in the application's type library, which is the file that includes information about the application's objects, properties, and methods as well as the intrinsic constants that the application uses.

The Object Browser is available only when the Module window is the active window. To explore the Object Browser, follow these steps:

1. Select the Module tab in the Database window, choose Startup, and click on Design to display the module window.

2. Click on the Object Browser button in the toolbar or choose View ➤ Object Browser to open the Object Browser (see Figure 10.12). The first combo box lists the currently open database and a set of libraries about which the current database is aware. (See Chapter 20 for more information on libraries and the Object Browser.)

The Project/Library selection combo box at the top of the window contains a list of the type libraries that the current database knows about. The default choice <All Libraries> indicates that items from all these type libraries are included. Select the type library you want to work with.

You use the Search Text combo box to search in the selected library for an item; enter the text string you want to search for, and click the Search button. Figure 10.13 shows the result of finding the text string "line". Click on the Show Search Results button with the double-arrow to hide or display the results of the search.

The Classes list box on the left contains a list of the contents of the selected library, including constants and objects. The <globals> item is the top-level item for the selected type library. The list box is called Classes for the following reason. The definition of each type of object is called its class; when you create a new object such as a form, you use the form class module as the definition or blueprint to create the form as an *instance* of the class.

**FIGURE 10.12:**

The Object Browser

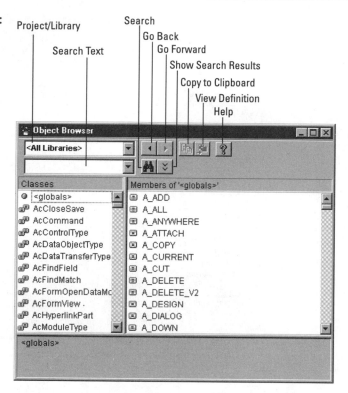

Project/Library

Search Text

Search

Go Back

Go Forward

Show Search Results

Copy to Clipboard

View Definition

Help

When you select an item in the Classes list box, the Members list box on the right changes to display the information for the item, such as constants, properties, methods, and events. When you select an item in the Members list box, the rectangle at the bottom of the Object Browser displays information such as the syntax for a selected method. Click on the Help button to display online Help for the selected item. Use the Go Back and Go Forward buttons to browse between selected items.

If the item you selected in the Classes list box is a standard or class module, click on the View Definition button to open and display the module. If you select a procedure in the module and then click on the View Definition button, the module opens with the insertion point in the selected procedure. To paste code into a module, choose an item in the Members list box, click on the Copy to Clipboard button, click in the module where you want to paste the item, and press Ctrl+V to paste the selection.

**FIGURE 10.13:**

You can search for a text string in a selected type library.

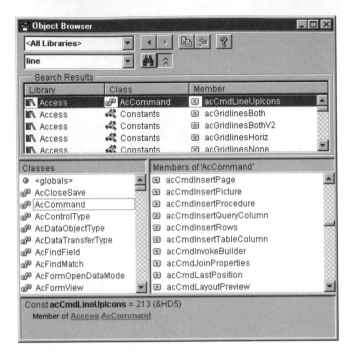

Explore the Access type library as follows:

1. Select Access from the combo list. The Classes list box on the left includes a list of the Access Application objects and categories of intrinsic constants.

2. Select the Form object class in the Classes list box, and select GoToPage in the Members list box. The Members list box displays the properties, methods, and events for the Form object class using different icons for each kind of member. The rectangle in the lower part of the Object Browser displays the syntax for the method (see Figure 10.14a).

3. Click on the Object Browser's Help button to display online help for the selected member.

4. Click on the Copy to Clipboard button in the Object Browser to copy the member's code template. You can switch to the module window and paste the code template into the module.

5. Select Constants in the Classes list box. The Members list box displays the intrinsic constants that Access and Visual Basic provide. When you select a constant, the numeric value of the constant is displayed in the lower rectangle (see Figure 10.14b).

**FIGURE 10.14:**

The Object Browser uses different icons for the members of the Form class, including the properties, methods, and events, and displays the syntax for the selected member (a). Choose Constants to display the Access application and Visual Basic constants (b).

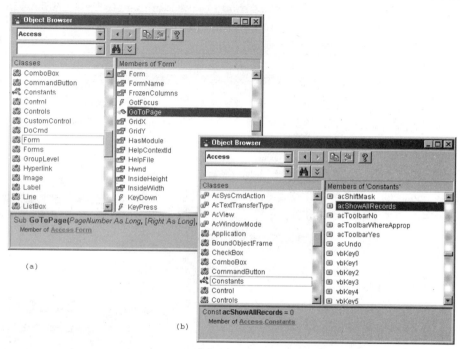

(a)

(b)

Explore the Object Browser for an Access project as follows:

1. In the Project/Libraries combo box, choose the Northwind project. By default, the project name doesn't change when you create a new copy of a database, so the current database is listed by its project name. (You may see either Northwind or Nwind.mdb as the project name for the database.) When you select an Access project, the Classes list box lists in bold font all the standard and class modules you have created. When you select a module in the Classes list box, the Members list box on the right changes to display information relevant to that module.

2.  Select the Form_Main Switchboard form module in the Classes list box. The Members list box includes the form's built-in properties, events, and methods and displays in bold the names of procedures stored in the module using different icons for each type of member(see Figure 10.15a).

3.  Choose the Startup standard module. When you choose a standard or independent class module, the Members list box displays in bold the names of the procedures stored in the module (see Figure 10.15b).

**FIGURE 10.15:**

Use the Object Browser to explore an Access project. You can view the class module for a form or a report (a) or the procedures in a standard or independent class module (b).

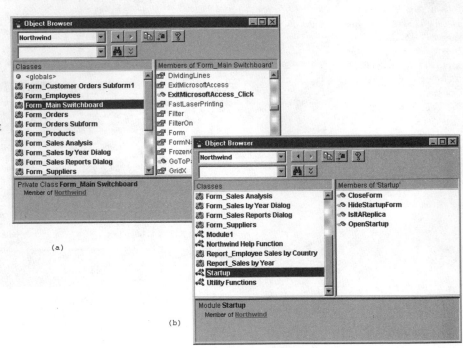

(a)

(b)

# Summary

This chapter has expanded the tour of the Access Application object model to cover the most important features in VBA programming. The important points are:

- An object is an element with an identity described with a set of properties that define the object's characteristics and with a set of methods that define the actions an object can take on itself. The objects in the Access application model have properties and methods that are available only in VBA programming. Some objects in the Access application model are available only in VBA programming, including the Module object and Modules collection and the Reference object and the References collection.

- You can set a property to a text value using an assignment statement as follows: *object.propertyname = value*. You can read, or get, a text value for a property and assign the value to a variable using an assignment statement as follows: *variable = object.propertyname*. If the property returns an object, you get the reference to the object and assign the reference to an object variable using an assignment statement as follows: Set *objectvariable = object.propertyname*.

- You run, or call, a method using the syntax *object.method*. Most methods return nothing, but a method can return either a text value or an object. Most methods have additional information that you must specify as method arguments before you run the method.

- You manipulate an object by setting a property, by running one of the object's methods, by running a method of the DoCmd object, or by running a built-in Access function or statement. You use the DoCmd object to run methods equivalent to most of the macro actions.

- You can use a form's RecordsetClone property to create an independent current record pointer in the form's recordset. You can use the clone's current record pointer to walk through the recordset without affecting the record displayed in the form.

- You can use a form's Bookmark property to store the bookmark for the current record in a variable and return to the marked record later.

- You can use the Me property of a form or report to refer to the form or report in a procedure that is stored in the form's or report's module. Using the Me reference is the fastest way to refer to the form or report.

# CHAPTER

## ELEVEN

# The Data Access Objects

- Referring to a data access object

- Understanding the types of objects and properties

- Creating new data access objects

- Using the Recordset object

- Navigating in a recordset

- Finding a record in a recordset

- Adding, editing, and deleting records

- Using clones and recordsetclones

This chapter introduces the Jet database engine component of Microsoft Access. Because VBA gives you the ability to write programs for Jet, the chapter also introduces the Jet objects that your programs will manipulate: the data access objects. There are 31 data access objects, and each has its own properties and methods. All the details of programming with Jet are more than I could teach you in this book. The goals of this chapter are to give you the following:

- Hands-on experience with those data access objects, properties, and methods that you'll be needing as you learn to use VBA to automate an Access database

- Casual familiarity with the rest

We'll use the Immediate pane of the Debug Window throughout this chapter to learn how to refer to specific data access objects, how to determine their property settings, and what happens when you execute some of their methods.

> **NOTE**　　The examples in Chapters 10 and 11 use the Northwind sample application. In Chapter 10 you created a copy named Northwind_Ch10,11. If you didn't make a copy, do so now.

The Jet database engine is the database management system for Access. When you work interactively with Access or when you create macros to automate your database, you don't need to be aware of the differing functions and capabilities of the two major components of Access: the Application layer and the Jet engine. The Access interface takes care of all of the negotiations with Jet for you because Microsoft Access has all the necessary instructions to Jet built into its internal code. Here are some examples of the database management services that Jet provides to Access:

- When you design a table or a query, the Application layer uses its built-in, hard-coded routines to arrange for Jet to create and store the object you designed in table or query Design view.

- When you elect referential integrity options in the Relationships window, (choose Tools ➤ Relationships) Jet enforces the options you select.

- When you link to an external table by choosing File ➤ Get External Data, the interface arranges for Jet to create and manage the connection.

- When you run a query, the interface sends the equivalent SQL statement to Jet for processing; Jet creates the appropriate recordset and passes it back for Access to display in some interface object.

- When you set up security using one of the Security dialogs (choose Tools ➤ Security), the interface arranges for Jet to create and store the security information.

- When two or more users attempt to edit the same record or when one user attempts to work with two versions of the same record, the Access Application arranges with Jet to handle the conflicts.

An advantage of VBA programming is that you can create procedures that arrange with Jet for these same database services. Within your VBA application, you can write procedures to create new tables and queries; you can even create your own custom objects. You can modify built-in objects by creating custom properties and methods for them. You can create procedures that link the database to external tables and that update the links automatically when a table is moved. You can create procedures to enforce referential integrity, monitor security, and modify record locking.

When you work interactively or use only macro programming, you can open only one database at a time. When you work with VBA programming, you can open multiple databases simultaneously. You can even create separate workspaces with each workspace guarded by its own security permissions, and you can open multiple databases within each workspace. Exploring all the power that Jet gives you would take us far beyond the bounds of this book; however, in Chapter 16, "Navigation with Access VBA," we'll look at an interesting problem that requires opening a second database.

With Visual Basic, you can control when and how the Application interacts with Jet, because Jet gives you access to the objects you need to specify the interaction. The objects that Jet makes available are the data access objects.

# The Jet Database Engine and Automation

The Jet database engine is a database management engine that provides a set of database management services to any application that knows how to communicate with it. Jet is application-independent. Jet simply makes its data access objects with their properties and methods available to other applications that want to use its services. The Jet database engine is an OLE Automation server. *OLE* originally referred to object linking and embedding and was a set of rules that applications could follow if they wanted to share one another's documents. OLE, now called ActiveX, has evolved to a much broader technology that now includes specifications for additional features, including Automation.

Automation is a technology that allows applications, called *Automation servers*, to make the blueprints, called class definitions, for certain of their objects public so that other applications, called *Automation controllers*, can create objects in the server application according to the blueprints. The objects created are called *Automation objects*. You create programs in the Automation controller to carry out the standard two operations for objects: The Automation controller can get and set an Automation object's properties and can call the object's methods. Microsoft Excel, Microsoft Project, and Microsoft Access are examples of Automation controllers that can use Automation to take advantage of the Jet database engine. These three applications are also Automation servers and make their own objects available to other applications.

Excel, Project, and Access are all executables (.exe). An *executable* is a program that the operating system can run to carry out a particular set of functions. An executable runs in a *process*. Each executable that you start up runs in a separate process. If the Automation server is an executable, the Automation controller must call out of its own process into the Automation server process. An AutomationE server that is an executable is called an *out-of-process Automation server*. For example, you can use Automation in Access to create a spreadsheet object in Excel and then manipulate the spreadsheet. Excel is an out-of-process

Automation server. Access must, therefore, call out of its own process into Excel's process to create and manipulate the spreadsheet. You can also use Automation in Access to manipulate another instance of Access that is acting as an out-of-process Automation server. (When you start up another instance of an executable, the second instance runs in its own process; you can observe the icon for each instance in the Windows 95 task bar.)

Most of Jet's components are dynamic-link libraries (DLLs) instead of executables. In particular, Jet's Automation capability is based on a special set of OLE DLLs. Unlike an executable, a DLL runs in the same process as the application that called it. An Automation server that runs as an OLE DLL is called an *in-process Automation server*. Because the OLE DLL runs in the same process as the client application, calling an in-process server is much faster than calling an out-of-process server. Jet is an in-process Automation server.

When applications such as Excel or Project use Jet as an Automation server, they use VBA code to call the dynamic link library (DAO DLL) containing the files that provide access to the data access objects. Access, on the other hand, has calls to Jet written into its internal code. When you work with Access interactively or when you run macros, Access calls Jet directly using internal code. When you use Access VBA code to work with Jet, however, your code calls the DAO DLL instead.

## The Data Access Object Hierarchy

Chapter 3 describes the hierarchy of collections and objects that make up the Jet object model. Figure 11.1 shows the hierarchy of 29 of the 31 data access objects arranged in 7 levels. The objects not shown in the figure are the Properties collection and the Property objects. At the top of the hierarchy is the DBEngine that you use to refer to the Jet database engine in a VBA procedure. The remaining data access objects are either collections or members of collections. In addition, each object except the Errors collection and Error objects has its own Properties collection containing separate Property objects for each built-in property (not shown).

**FIGURE 11.1:**

The Jet object model for Microsoft Jet Workspaces. In addition to the 29 different objects shown, each object except the Errors collection and Error objects has a Properties collection containing Property objects for each built-in property.

Data Access Object Model for Microsoft Jet Workspaces

See Also    Specifics

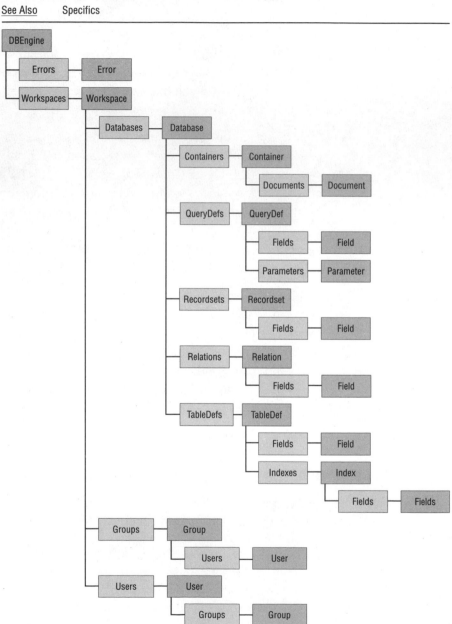

## Referring to a Data Access Object

When you want to refer to a data access object in a VBA procedure, you start by referring to the DBEngine, and then you traverse along the hierarchical path to the object, recording references to the objects and collection objects that you encounter along the way. You use the dot operator (.) when stepping from an object to one of its collections. When you are stepping from a collection to one of its members, you can use any of the four references:

- Use the exclamation point (!) operator to refer to a member explicitly by name.

- Use the parenthetical syntax to refer to a member by name.

- Use the parenthetical syntax to refer to a member by a variable.

- Use the parenthetical syntax to refer to a member by its position in the collection.

The collections in Jet are all zero-based. Normally, you use a mixture of syntax types. For example, when you start Access, Jet starts automatically and opens a default workspace that we'll refer to by position using Workspace(0). You can refer to the database you open by name, but since it is the first database open, you can also refer to it by position, using Databases(0):

```
DBEngine.Workspaces(0).Databases(0)
```

Suppose you want to refer to the ValidationRule property of the CustomerID field in the Customers table in the current database. You continue traversing the path as follows:

```
DBEngine.Workspaces(0).Databases(0).TableDefs!Customers.Fields!Cu
stomerID.Properties!ValidationRule
```

## Using Default Collections

Fortunately, almost all data access objects have default collections, so you can usually abbreviate references by omitting the names of the default collections. The TableDefs collection is the default collection for the Database object, the Fields collection is the default collection for the TableDef object, and the Properties collection is the default collection for an object when referring to a built-in property. (When you refer to a custom property, however, you have to include a reference to the Properties collection as follows: *object.Properties!customproperty*.) You separate an object reference and a built-in property with the dot operator:

```
object.property
```

Taking advantage of these default collections, you can abbreviate the reference to the current database as:

```
DBEngine(0)(0)
```

and use the following syntax for the reference to the ValidationRule property:

```
DBEngine(0)(0)!tblCustomers!CustomerID.ValidationRule
```

Table 11.1 (on the CD under Tables\Chapter11.pdf) lists the additional default collections for the data access objects.

If you are using another application, such as Excel, to work with an Access database using Automation, the most abbreviated syntax for referring to the database is DBEngine(0)(0). When you are using Access to work with the database, there is an alternate way to refer to the current database. Access provides a special function called the CurrentDb function to refer to the current database. If you are working in Access, you can use either Jet's syntax, DBEngine(0)(0), or Access's syntax, CurrentDb, to refer to the current database. With the latter choice, the syntax for the example becomes:

```
CurrentDb!Customers!CustomerID.ValidationRule
```

**NOTE**  Although they refer to the same database, Jet's DBEngine(0)(0) and Access's CurrentDb are not exactly the same. Every time you use CurrentDb, you are requiring Access to create a new object that refers to the current database. On the other hand, Jet uses only the single reference to the current database, DBEngine(0)(0), so it isn't necessary to create a new object. Creating a new reference with CurrentDb is slower that using DBEngine(0)(0). To balance this, however, CurrentDb is always in synch with the user interface. For example, new tables you create appear immediately in the Database window. When you use DBEngine(0)(0), you have to execute the RefreshDatabaseWindow method of the Application object to update the Database window. The net result is that using CurrentDb may be faster.

## The Data Access Objects

The DAO object model hierarchy exists separately from the Access Application hierarchy or separately from the object hierarchy of whatever external application you are using with Jet. Table 11.2 (on the CD under Tables\Chapter 11.pdf) gives a brief description of the data access objects.

# Types of DAO Objects

You can separate the DAO objects into two categories: those that are saved in some file (persistent) and those that are not (nonpersistent).

## Persistent Objects

Persistent objects are saved in the database file (.mdb) or in the workgroup information database file (.mdw). Persistent objects include the Database, TableDef, Index, QueryDef, Parameter, Relation, User, Group, and Field objects for the TableDef and QueryDef objects. The Property objects of a persistent object are persistent as well. The collection objects that contain these objects are not persistent objects. Collection objects are created anew each time you open the database; they are dynamic and change each time a member is added to or deleted from the collection. The Container and Document objects are not persistent objects even though they contain administrative information about persistent objects. The Container and Document objects include information for the DAO objects representing the database, tables, queries, and relationships as well as information for the objects created in Access representing the forms, reports, macros, and modules.

## Nonpersistent Objects

Nonpersistent objects are not saved in files. Nonpersistent objects include the DBEngine, Error, Workspace, Container, Document, Recordset, and Field objects for the Recordset object. The Property objects of a nonpersistent object are nonpersistent. All collection objects are nonpersistent.

You must create a nonpersistent object that is a member of a collection before you can refer to the object. For example, you create a new Recordset object using the OpenRecordset of the Database object before you can work with the recordset.

# Types of DAO Properties

Jet has two kinds of properties: built-in properties and user-defined properties.

## Built-in Properties

Built-in properties are those that Jet automatically creates and maintains. When you create a new data access object through DAO, such as a new QueryDef, Jet automatically creates a set of properties for the new query. Jet includes only the built-in properties in the new object's Properties collection. The built-in properties define the basic characterstics of an object.

## User-Defined Properties

User-defined properties are those you create and add to an object. You add a user-defined property by appending it to the object's Properties collection. For example, if you want to describe the purpose of a new query, you can use a VBA procedure to create a user-defined property called Purpose and append it to the query's Properties collection. See Chapter 19, "Creating and Modifying Database Objects," for examples of procedures that create custom properties.

The two kinds of user-defined properties for the data access objects are properties that you create from scratch yourself and properties that an application such as Access creates. The next section describes the user-defined properties that Access creates.

## Application-Defined Properties

When you use Access to create a Jet object, Access typically adds several properties called *application-defined properties*. For example, when you create a new query in the query Design window, most of the query properties listed in the query property sheet are application-defined properties and are not built-in DAO properties, including the Description and OutputAllFields properties. As far as Jet is concerned, the application-defined properties do not exist until you actually type values for them in the appropriate property sheet or write procedures to add the application-defined properties to the object's Properties collection. If you enter a description in the Description property box in the query property sheet for the new query, the Description property is added to that query's Properties collection. But, if you haven't set the value of a property in the interface and you want to set the property in a VBA procedure, you must first create the property and append it to the Properties collection of the object in a procedure.

> **NOTE**
> You need to remember that each object has its own Properties collection; adding a Description property for one query does not automatically add a Description property to any other query. If you try to retrieve the Description property for a query for which you haven't typed a description, Jet generates an error. Chapter 18, "Creating and Modifying Database Objects," describes how to create and append user-defined properties, and Chapter 14, "Dealing with Errors in VBA," discusses how to handle Jet errors.

**Startup Properties**  The Startup properties are an interesting example of application-defined properties. Startup properties are properties of the Database object that Access defines. Thirteen of the 14 startup properties can be set in the Startup dialog (choose Tools ➤ Startup). Only those Startup properties that you set in the Startup dialog are added to the Properties collection of the Database object. To use a VBA procedure to set a startup property that you haven't previously set in the Startup dialog, you must first create the property and append it to the Properties collection in a VBA procedure.

The Startup property that isn't available in the Startup dialog is the crucially important AllowBypassKey property. You use the AllowBypassKey property to specify whether the Shift key is enabled for bypassing the Startup properties and the AutoExec macro. Because you can set several Startup properties to protect an application—for example, by hiding the Database window—disabling the Shift key as a startup bypass key is an important technique for protecting a database. Chapter 19 shows you how to disable the Shift key to prevent bypassing the Startup properties and the AutoExec macro.

# Using Data Access Objects

In a VBA procedure, you work with the data access objects using two fundamental operations: you read and change properties and you ask an object to use one of its methods to manipulate itself. Before you can carry out either operation, you must refer to the object.

## Referring to Existing Data Access Objects

When you start Access, Jet starts automatically and creates, in memory, a new DBEngine object to represent itself. The DBEngine object is a temporary object that exists only while Access is open; when you quit Access, the DBEngine object ceases to exist. Jet automatically creates, in memory, a default Workspace object as a temporary object (for simplicity, we'll look only at the case in which security is not enabled). When you open an existing database, Jet creates, again in memory, a Database object to represent the database you opened. You can use either Jet's DBEngine(0)(0) or Access's CurrentDb function to refer to the database object. To refer to an existing data access object, you need only traverse the hierarchy to the object using any of the four ways shown below to refer to an object in a collection:

| | |
|---|---|
| Exclamation point reference | CurrentDb!QueryDefs!Invoices |
| Index by name | CurrentDb.QueryDefs("Invoices") |
| Index using a variable | strName = Invoices |
| | CurrentDb.QueryDefs(strName) |
| Index by number | CurrentDb.QueryDefs(0) |

Open Northwind_Ch10,11 and display the Debug Window by pressing Ctrl+G. Test the following references:

1. Type **?CurrentDb.Name** in the Immediate pane and press Enter. The path to your open database is returned.

2. Type **?CurrentDb!Employees!Title.Required** and press Enter. False is returned.

3. Type **CurrentDb!Employees!Title.Required = True** and press Enter. To test the property setting, open the Employees table and try to save a new record without entering a value in the Title field.

## Opening Two Databases Simultaneously

A limitation of working interactively with Access or using only macro programming is that you can have only one database open at a time; to open another database, you must start a second instance of Access. VBA programming removes this limitation, at least partially. You can use the OpenDatabase method of the Workspace object to open a specified database. Opening a second database, however, is not like opening a second workbook in Excel or a second document in Word because you can't see the second database: Jet opens the second database in memory; there is no visual representation. With VBA programming, however, you can work with the second invisible database almost as though it were visible in the Access interface.

The OpenDatabase method returns the opened database as a Database object. When you use a method that returns something, you can assign the result to a variable. Because the OpenDatabase method returns an object, you assign the result to an *object variable*. The assignment statement for an object variable is as follows:

```
Set objectvariable = object
```

where the Set keyword indicates the assignment of the object to an object variable. Chapter 13, "Mechanics of Procedures II: Using Variables," gives a detailed treatment of object variables.

The syntax for the OpenDatabase method is:

```
Set objectvariable = workspace.OpenDatabase(dbname,options,read-
only, connect)
```

where:

> *workspace* is an optional reference to the Workspace object that will contain the database. To use the default Workspace object, omit the reference.
>
> *dbname* is a string expression that is the name of an existing database file that you want to open. Required.
>
> *options* sets various options for the database such as whether you are opening the database for exclusive or shared access. Optional.
>
> *read-only* is True if the database is to be opened for read-only access and False if the database is to be opened for read/write access; the default is False. Optional.
>
> *connect* is an optional string expression for specifying connection information such as passwords.

When you call the OpenDatabase method, Jet opens the database and adds the database automatically to the Databases collection.

If you haven't opened two databases before, try to do so in the Debug Window. We'll open another sample Access database, Orders.mdb, as follows:

1. Type **Set mydb= DBEngine(0).OpenDatabase("c:\Program Files\Microsoft Office\Office\Samples\orders.mdb")** and press Enter. (This is the path to the Orders.mdb file for a default installation of Microsoft Access. You may need to enter a different path.) Jet opens the Orders.mdb database immediately; the *mydb* variable refers to, or *points to*, the database object. How can you confirm that the database is open? The object variable *mydb* points to

the open database; you can confirm that the database is open by retrieving the value of the Name property for the database, that is, by retrieving mydb.Name.

2. Type **?mydb.Name** and press Enter. The Immediate pane of the Debug window displays the full path name for the Orders.mdb database. Having confirmed that the second database is open, close it using the Close method of the Database object. When you use the Close method, the open database is closed and removed from the Databases collection.

3. Type **mydb.Close** and press Enter. Jet closes the Orders.mdb database. To confirm the closure, take the next step.

4. Type **?mydb.Name** and press Enter. The error message in Figure 11.2 tells you that the mydb object variable is invalid or not set, because the database that the mydb variable was pointing to no longer exists in memory.

**FIGURE 11.2:**

When you point an object variable to an object and then close the object, the object no longer exists in memory

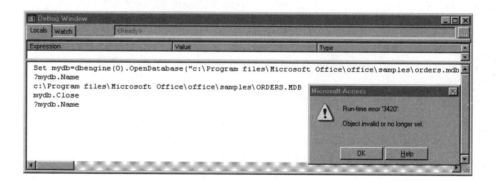

## Creating New Data Access Objects

If a data access object doesn't exist when you want to refer to it in a VBA procedure, you'll need to create it. In general, creating a new data access object is a three-step process:

1. Create the object using the Create... method of the parent object.

2. Define the new object's characteristics by setting its properties. Many of an object's properties can be set only when you create the new object, and they become read-only after the object is saved to the database. In some cases, you also have to create child objects for the new object; for example, when

you create a new table, you must also create at least one field before you can save the table.

3. Append the object to its collection using the Append method of the collection.

In general, the object that is created in memory is saved to the database only when you append it to its collection. Here are some exceptions:

**Workspace object**   When you create a new Workspace object using the CreateWorkspace method of the DBEngine object, you don't have to append it before you can use it. Workspace objects are temporary and can't be saved to disk. If you need to refer to the new Workspace through the Workspaces collection, however, you'll have to append it to the collection.

**Database object**   When you create a new Database object using the CreateDatabase method of the Workspace object, the new database is automatically appended to the Databases collection and saved to disk.

**QueryDef object**   When you create a new QueryDef object using the CreateQueryDef method of the Database object, the new query is automatically appended to the QueryDefs collection and saved to disk.

**Recordset object**   When you create a new Recordset object using the OpenRecordset method of any of the objects including the Database, TableDef, QueryDef or Recordset objects, the new Recordset object is automatically added to the Recordsets collection. (The name OpenRecordset is a misnomer because you are creating a new Recordset object and not opening an existing Recordset object.)

A Create... method returns the object being created. The syntax for each Create... method includes the Set keyword to assign the result of the method to an object variable. The syntax for the CreateDatabase method is:

```
Set database = workspace.CreateDatabase(name, locale,options)
```

where:

*workspace* is a reference to the existing Workspace object that will contain the database. To use the default Workspace, omit the reference.

*databasename* is a string expression that can have a maximum of 255 characters and is the name of the database file you are creating. You can specify a path and a filename. You can only create an .mdb file with this method.

*locale* is a required string expression that specifies the language to be used for the sort order for text values. Use dbLangGeneral to specify English, German, French, Portuguese, Italian, and Modern Spanish.

*options* is an optional integer that specifies the Jet database engine file format and determines whether to encrypt the database.

As an example, we'll create a new empty database using the CreateDatabase method of the Workspace object and using newdb as the object variable. Type **Set newdb = DBEngine.Workspaces(0).CreateDatabase("c:\mynew.mdb", dbLangGeneral)** and press Enter. A new empty database is created and saved on disk. To test, choose File ➤ Open Database and select Mynew.mdb; the new empty database opens.

Often the object you want to create has required child objects; for example, you can't create a table without at least one field. Other examples are the Index and Relation objects, which also require at least one field. In these cases, creating the parent requires additional steps. As a model, here are the steps for creating a new TableDef named myShipping with a single field named ShipperID. You can create the sample table using the Immediate pane of the Debug window; for each step, type the statement in the Immediate pane and press Enter.

1.  Create a new TableDef object using the CreateTableDef method of the Database object. Type:

    **Set tdfShip = CurrentDB.CreateTableDef("myShipping")**

2.  Create at least one Field object using the CreateField method of the TableDef object. Type:

    **Set fldID = tdfShip.CreateField("ShipperName", dbText, 40)**

3.  Append the Field objects to the Fields collection. Type:

    **tdfShip.Fields.Append fldID**

4.  Append the new TableDef object to the TableDefs collection. Type:

    **CurrentDB.TableDefs.Append tdfShip**

5.  Update the database window. Type:

    **RefreshDatabaseWindow**

## Creating New QueryDefs

Frequently you need to create new queries in a VBA procedure. You create a new query as a QueryDef object. The syntax for the CreateQueryDef method of the Database object is:

```
Set qdf = database.CreateQueryDef(name,sqltext)
```

where:

> *qdf* is an object variable for the new QueryDef object.
>
> *database* is a reference to the open Database object that will contain the new QueryDef. (In an ODBCDirect Workspace, use a reference to the open Connection object instead.)
>
> *name* is an optional string expression that names the new QueryDef object.
>
> *sqltext* is an optional valid SQL statement as a string expression that defines the QueryDef.

If you don't specify the name and sqltext arguments of the CreateQueryDef method, you can use assignment statements to specify the Name and SQLText properties of the new QueryDef object.

Creating new queries in VBA requires that you know how to write SQL statements. In truth, if you don't know SQL, you can avoid learning it a little longer by creating a sample of the new query in query Design view, switching to SQL view, and pasting the equivalent SQL statement into the sqltext argument. As an example, we'll create a new query that displays the records in the Employees table and sorts the records by LastName. Here are the steps:

1. In query Design view, create a new query based on the Employees table. Use the Asterisk (*) method to include all the fields. Drag the LastName field to the grid, click on the Show checkbox to hide the field, and enter Ascending in the Sort cell.

2. Switch to SQL view and copy the following SQL statement to the Clipboard:

    SELECT Employees.* FROM Employees ORDER BY
        Employees.LastName;

3. Type the following in the Immediate pane, pasting the SQL statement from the Clipboard, and enclosing the statement in double quotation marks:

**Set myquery = CurrentDB.CreateQueryDef("EmployeeSort", "SELECT Employees.\* FROM Employees ORDER BY Employees.LastName;")**

Type the entire statement on one line. When you press Enter, the query is created and saved to disk.

4. Type **RefreshDatabaseWindow and** press Enter. The Database window updates to display the new query.

If the query you want to create is an SQL-specific query that can't be created in query Design view, you'll have to create the SQL statement directly. See the *Access 97 Developer's Handbook* by Paul Litwin, Ken Getz, and Mike Gilbert (Sybex, 1997) for guidance on creating SQL statements.

## Creating Recordsets

The most common type of data access object you create in VBA procedures is the Recordset. You'll notice in Table 11.2 (on the CD under Tables\Chapter11.pdf) that neither the TableDef nor the QueryDef objects represent the data stored in the database tables. Browsing further down the table reveals that the data values are available only as the Value property setting of the Field object of the Recordset object. Thus, if you are going to manipulate data in VBA using the data access objects, you'll be working with Recordset objects.

In Chapter 4, "Communicating with Forms," we worked with recordsets as data sources for forms. By definition, a recordset is the set of records in a table or the set of records produced by running a query or an SQL statement that produces records. The Recordset data access object represents a recordset. The Recordset object has more than 20 properties and more than 20 methods for working with data. All the power of Jet's data access objects to sort, search, update, add, and delete data resides in the Recordset object.

---

**NOTE**    However, the data access object technique for manipulating data discussed in this chapter isn't the only way, or even the best way, to work with the data. Using Structured Query Language (SQL) provides an entirely different appproach to working with data and typically gives better performance. Chapters 16 and 18 discuss techniques involving both methods.

**Types of Recordsets** Four types of Recordset objects are available (a fifth type is available in ODBCDirect workspaces). The four types differ in significant ways and are used for different purposes. Each offers advantages and disadvantages. Table 11.3 (on the CD under Tables\Chapter11.pdf) explains the features and differences.

**Creating a Recordset Object** You can manipulate data in a VBA procedure in two ways:

- You can open a form that is bound to the data and use the Application objects to manipulate the data.

- You can create a Recordset object in memory to represent the data and use the data access objects to manipulate the data.

Using the Application objects involves writing less code because the Application does so much of the work for you (see Chapter 17, "Data Maintenance with Access VBA," for examples of procedures for both approaches). Using the data access objects does mean writing more code, but it gives you more opportunity to specify how and when you want Jet to carry out each step of an operation. This chapter focuses on using data access objects.

You use the OpenRecordset method of the Database object to create a new Recordset object on an existing table or query or on an SQL statement that returns records. The OpenRecordset method automatically appends the new Recordset object to the Recordsets collection. The syntax is:

```
Set rst = database.OpenRecordset (source,type,options,lockedits)
```

where:

> *rst* is the object variable for the object.
>
> *database* is a reference to an existing Database object you want to use.
>
> *source* is a string specifying the name of a table, the name of a query, or an SQL SELECT statement that returns records. For table-type Recordset objects, the source must be a table name in the database.
>
> *type* is an optional Integer, or intrinsic constant, representing the type as follows:
>
> - dbOpenTable to create a table-type Recordset object
>
> - dbOpenDynamic to create a dynamic-type Recordset object (ODBC-Direct workspaces only)

- dbOpenDynaset to create a dynaset-type Recordset object
- dbOpenSnapshot to create a snapshot-type Recordset object
- dbOpenForwardOnly to create a forward-only-type Recordset object

The default type depends on the source you specified. If you specified a table in the current database, the default is table-type; if you specified an attached table, a query, or an SQL statement, the default is dynaset-type.

*options* is an optional combination of constants specifying the characteristics of the new object.

*lockedits* is an optional constant that determines the locking for the recordset.

You can also create a new Recordset object based on an existing TableDef or QueryDef object. You can even create a new Recordset object based on an existing Recordset object. These objects have their own OpenRecordset methods with the following syntax:

```
Set rst = object.OpenRecordset (type,options,lockedits)
```

where *object* is an existing TableDef, QueryDef, or Recordset object, and the other parts are the same as in the first syntax.

You can use the Immediate pane to create the following recordsets:

1. Type **Set rstEmployees = CurrentDB.OpenRecordset("Employees", dbOpenDynaset)** and press Enter to create a dynaset-type Recordset object on the Employees table.

2. Type **Set rstCategories = CurrentDB.OpenRecordset("Categories")** and press Enter to create a table-type Recordset object on the Categories table.

3. Type **Set rstSuppliers = CurrentDB.OpenRecordset("SELECT * FROM Suppliers ORDER BY [CompanyName]", dbOpenSnapshot)** and press Enter to create a snapshot-type Recordset object on the SQL statement.

4. Type **Set rstCustomers = CurrentDB! Customers.OpenRecordset** and press Enter to create a table-type Recordset object on the Customers table.

5. Type **Set rstSales = CurrentDB.QueryDefs("Sales by Category"). OpenRecordset** and press Enter to create a dynaset-type recordset on the Sales by Category query.

**NOTE**
If you open a recordset on a table in the database (in a Microsoft Jet workspace) and don't specify a type, Jet creates a table-type Recordset. If you open a query or a linked table and don't specify a type, Jet creates a dynaset-type Recordset.

**Closing a Recordset** Every Recordset object that you create in a VBA procedure exists only while that procedure is running; when the procedure is finished, the Recordset object ceases to exist. If you need to close a Recordset object during the procedure, use the Close method. Using the Close method closes an open Recordset object and removes it from the Recordsets collection. For example, to close rstSales, type **rstSales.Close** in the Immediate pane and press Enter.

**TIP**
Although it isn't necessary to explicitly close Recordset objects before the procedure ends, you make your code easier to understand if you explicitly close them.

## Manipulating Data in a Recordset Object

When you create a Recordset object, you are placing rows of data in a memory buffer; the rows are not displayed on the screen. You are pointing to one row at a time; the row you are pointing to is called the *current record*. The current record is the only record that you can modify or retrieve data from. When you refer to fields in a Recordset object, you get values from the current record. Only one record in the recordset can be the current record at any one time. When you first create a Recordset object using the OpenRecordset method, the first record is the current record if there are any records. At times, a Recordset object doesn't have a current record; for example, if the recordset has no records, the Recordset object doesn't have a current record.

With only a single record available at one time, you'll need ways to navigate from one record to another record, making the record you navigate to the current record so that you can work with it. The two basic kinds of navigation among records are *physical navigation* and *logical navigation*. In interactive Access, you are using physical navigation when you click on the navigation buttons in the lower left corner of a form or datasheet to move from one record to another according to their physical location within the recordset. When you use the Find dialog (choose Edit ➤ Find) and enter search criteria in the Find What text box, you are using logical navigation to move directly to the first record that matches the criteria. The Recordset object has methods and properties for both kinds of navigation.

## Physical Navigation

You can move from one record to another according to physical location in two ways. You can use the Move... methods to duplicate the effect of the navigation buttons of interactive Access, or you can save your place in a recordset by setting a bookmark and then returning later to the same record.

**Using the Move... Methods**   You can move from one record to another record according to the record's physical location in the recordset using the Move... methods of a Recordset object. The MoveFirst, MoveLast, MoveNext, or MovePrevious methods move the current record position to the first, last, next, or previous record of a specified Recordset object. The syntax of the Move... methods is:

```
rst.{MoveFirst | MoveLast | MoveNext | MovePrevious}
```

where *rst* refers to an open Recordset object. In a forward-only-type recordset, you can use only the MoveNext method because you can only move the current record pointer forward toward the last record of the recordset.

For example, when you created rstEmployees in the last section, the first record was the current record. You can use the Debug Window to test the Move methods as follows:

1. Type **?rstEmployees.EmployeeID** and press Enter. The number 1 is displayed. Now let's move to the next record.

2. Type **rstEmployees.MoveNext** and press Enter. Then type **?rstEmployees.EmployeeID** and press Enter. The number 2 is displayed. Let's move to the last record and see what happens if we try to use the MoveNext method.

3. Type **rstEmployees.MoveLast** and press Enter. The last record in the recordset is now the current record.

4. Type **rstEmployees.MoveNext** and press Enter. You have now moved beyond the last record of the recordset. Type **?rstEmployees.EmployeeID** and press Enter. The error message indicates there is no current record (see Figure 11.3).

## FIGURE 11.3:

The error message that is displayed when you move beyond the limits of a recordset

**BOF, EOF Properties** You use the BOF (Beginning of File) and EOF (End of File) properties of the Recordset object to determine whether you've gone beyond the limits of the recordset. Both properties have the value False as long as you are pointing to a record in the recordset, that is, as long as there is a current record. If you move after the last record, there is no current record, and the EOF property is set to True; if you move before the first record, there is no current record, and the BOF property is set to True. If the recordset has no records at all, both the BOF and EOF properties are True.

To confirm this, type **?rstEmployees.EOF** in the Debug Window and press Enter. The value True is returned.

> **NOTE**  A standard VBA procedure for working with a set of records is to create a Recordset object and use the MoveNext method to loop through the records one by one. To determine when you are finished, you test the value of the EOF property at the beginning of each pass through the loop. As long as EOF is False, you take another pass, but as soon as EOF is True, you have moved beyond the last record of the recordset and the loop is finished. Chapter 14, "Mechanics of Procedures III: Controlling Execution," shows you how to create procedures for looping through a recordset.

**Using Bookmarks** In Chapter 10 you learned that Access tracks records in a form's recordset by creating a bookmark as a unique binary string for each record as soon as you open the form. Jet also creates bookmarks. When you create a Recordset object, Jet automatically assigns a set of unique bookmarks. If you are pointing to a record that you want to return to later, you can save your place by saving the record's bookmark to a variable; to return to the record later, you set the Bookmark property to the saved value. Test the technique in the Debug window as follows:

1. Type **rstEmployees.MoveFirst** and press Enter. Then, type **rstEmployees.MoveNext** and press Enter. The current record is the second record (EmployeeID = 2). You save your place in the next step.

2. Type **strMark = rstEmployees.Bookmark** and press Enter. The strMark variable stores the bookmark.

3. Use the Move... methods to move to some other record. Now return to the saved place.

4. Type **rstEmployees.Bookmark = strMark** and press Enter. Confirm by entering **?rstEmployees.EmployeeID** and press Enter. You have returned.

**Using the Move Method**    You can use the Move method to move the current record position forward (toward the last record) or backward (toward the first row) a specified number of rows. You can even specify that you want to start moving from a particular record. The syntax of the Move method is:

```
rst.Move row,start
```
where:

> *rst* is the reference to the Recordset object.
>
> *rows* is a signed Long integer indicating the number of rows. If rows is positive, you move forward; otherwise, you move backward.
>
> *start* is an optional string variable that identifies a bookmark.

For a forward-only-type Recordset object, *rows* must be a positive integer.

You can test the Move method in the Immediate pane of the Debug window. Type **rstEmployees.Move 4** and press Enter. Confirm that you are now at the record with EmployeeID = 6.

## Logical Navigation

When you want to locate a record that satisfies a search condition, the technique you use depends on the type of Recordset you've created. If you are working with a table-type Recordset, you can take advantage of indexes and use the Seek method. If you are working with a dynaset- or snapshot-type Recordset, indexes are not appropriate, and you use the Find... methods instead. If either search technique succeeds in finding a record that matches the search condition, the found record becomes the current record. If no record is located, there is no current record after you run the method. To determine if the search is successful, you check the NoMatch property of the Recordset object. If the search is successful, a match has been found, and NoMatch is False; if the search fails, there is no match, and the NoMatch property is True.

**Using the Seek Method**    The Seek method uses indexes to locate records in the fastest way possible. You can use the Seek method only for a Table-type Recordset because the search condition is based on values in an index. Before you can use the Seek method, the table you are working with must have at least one index, and you must set the Index property of the Recordset object to the particular index you want to use in the search. For example, the Customers table has the indexes shown in Figure 11.4.

You can use any of the existing indexes, or you can create a new Index object (see Chapter 19). The value of the Index property is called the *current index*.

The syntax for the Seek method is:

```
tablerecordset.Seek comparison, key1, key2... key13
```

**FIGURE 11.4:**

The indexes defined for the Customers table

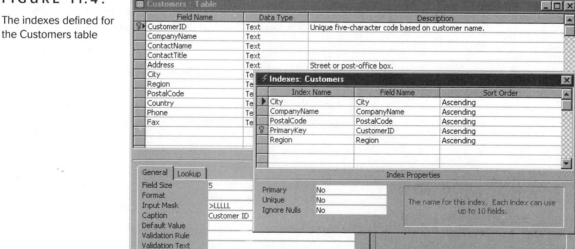

where:

> *tablerecordset* is a reference to the existing table-type Recordset object that has a current index specified by the Recordset object's Index property.
>
> *comparison* is a string expression that includes one of the following comparison operators: <, <=, =, >=, or >. You must follow the operator with a comma.
>
> *key1, key2... key13* are one to thirteen values of fields in the current index.

For example, to search for customers from a particular city, follow these steps:

1.  To set the current index to City, type **rstCustomers.Index = "City"** and press Enter.

2.  To locate the first customer from London, type **rstCustomers.Seek "=", "London"** and press Enter.

3.  To determine if the search was successful, type **?rstCustomers.NoMatch** and press Enter. The search is successful, and False is returned.

4.  Type **?rstCustomers.CompanyName** and press Enter. The name of the first customer is returned as Around the Horn.

**Using the Find... Methods**   The Seek method works only with table-type Recordsets. When your Recordset object is the dynaset-type or snapshot-type, you use the Find... methods instead. The Find... methods do not apply to table-type Recordsets.

You can duplicate the effect of the Find command of interactive Access with the Find... methods of the Recordset object. The FindFirst, FindLast, FindNext, or FindPrevious method locates the first, last, next, or previous record that satisfies specified criteria and makes that record the current record. The syntax for the Find... method is:

```
rst.{FindFirst | FindLast | FindNext | FindPrevious} criteria
```

where:

> *rst* is a reference to an existing dynaset- or snapshot-type Recordset.
>
> *criteria* is a string expression for locating the record. (The expression is the WHERE clause of an SQL statement but without the WHERE word.)

For example, find the first supplier from Berlin as follows:

1. Type **rstSuppliers.FindFirst "City = 'Berlin'"** in the Debug Window and press Enter.

2. To determine the name of the supplier, type **?rstSuppliers.Companyname** and press Enter.

## Adding, Editing, and Deleting Records

What experienced programmers find so satisfying about the data access objects is that they *are able* to control every operation; what inexperienced programmers find so overwhelming is that they *must* control every operation. To understand which methods you must include in procedures that modify data using the data access objects, you need to be aware that Jet does not automatically carry out the steps that are automatically carried out when you write procedures to modify data with a form using the Application object.

**Edit and Update**  When you want to modify the data in a record, you must first make that record the current record. You can use the Move... methods or the Find... or Seek methods to move the current record pointer to the record you want to change. The crux of editing data is that the changes are not made directly to the record; instead, the record is copied into a location in memory called the *copy buffer* that Jet creates for editing. Your VBA code has to deal with moving content in and out of the copy buffer. You can work along in the Debug Window to change the data in the rstCustomers Recordset object; you'll change the company name from Around the Horn to Around the Cape in the record you found earlier using the Seek method. Follow these steps:

1. To copy the current record to the copy buffer for editing using the Edit method, type **rstCustomers.Edit** and press Enter.

2. To assign the new values to the fields you want to change, type **rstCustomers.CompanyName = "Around the Cape"** and press Enter. The new value is now in the copy buffer; to copy the contents of the copy buffer back to the Recordset object, you must use the Update method. If you perform any operation that moves to another record, ends the VBA procedure, or closes the Recordset object without first using the Update method, your changes are not saved, and the contents of the copy buffer are discarded without warning.

3. To save the changes to the current record using the Update method, type **rstCustomers.Update** and press Enter.

4. To confirm that the change was saved, type **?rstCustomers.CustomerName** and press Enter. The Immediate pane displays the new value.

Editing a record provides an example of the fundamental differences between modifying data using the Access interface and using the data access objects: When you work interactively, you locate the record you want to change in a form and type your changes into a control. The moment you type the first character, the edit pencil in the record selector indicates that you are entering the new values into the copy buffer (effectively, the Application has called the Edit method for you). When you are finished making changes, you can save the changes in a variety of ways, such as clicking into another record, pressing Shift+Enter, or closing the form. When you take any of these operations, effectively, the Application calls the Update method for you.

If you decide not to save the changes to the record, use the CancelUpdate method to flush out the copy buffer.

**NOTE** The Edit method does not apply to snapshot-type or forward-only-type Recordset objects because both of these are static copies of records.

**Add and Update** The crux of adding a new record is that you are not adding a record directly to the recordset; instead, the new record is added to the copy buffer in memory. Your VBA code uses the AddNew method to add the contents of the copy buffer to the recordset.

Where the new record gets inserted depends on the type of recordset. The new record is added to the end of a dynaset-type recordset. It is placed in its proper sort order in a table-type recordset if the Index property has been set; otherwise, it is placed at the end of the recordset. When you add the new record, Jet creates a bookmark for it and stores the bookmark in the LastModified property. All this takes place without affecting the current record; the current record continues to be the record that was current before you added a record. If you want the new record to be the current record, you have to move the current record pointer to it.

You can work along in the Debug Window to add a new record to the rstCustomers Recordset object. Follow these steps:

1.  To create a new record in the buffer using the AddNew method of the Recordset object, type **rstCustomers.AddNew** and press Enter.

2.  To assign new values to fields in the buffer, type the following assignment statements in the Debug Window and press Enter after each:

    **rstCustomers.CustomerID = "ROUND"**

    **rstCustomers.CompanyName = "Round the Bend"**

    **rstCustomers.City = "London"**

3.  To add the contents to the recordset, type **rstCustomers.Update** and press Enter. Because rstCustomers is a table-type recordset and there is a current index (earlier, you set the Index property to London), the new record is placed with the other London customers. The current record is still the record with company name Around the Cape.

4.  To confirm, type **?rstCustomers.CompanyName** and press Enter.

5.  To move to the new record, set the Bookmark property to the new record's bookmark stored as the LastModified property setting. Type **rstCustomers.Bookmark = rstCustomers.LastModified** and press Enter.

6.  To confirm, type **?rstCustomers.CompanyName** and press Enter.

If you decide not to add the new record, you can use the CancelUpdate method to flush out the buffer.

**Delete**  The crux of deleting a record is that you are not deleting the record directly from the recordset; instead, the record is placed in a location in memory, which we'll call the *delete buffer*, that Jet creates for deletions. Interestingly, the record continues to be the current record even though you can't edit or use it; referring to the deleted record produces a run-time error. Notice that there is no CancelDelete method to undo the operation; effectively, the record is simply gone without warning. (If you want to display a delete confirmation message, you can create a set of statements called a transaction to undo the deletion if the user decides not to delete the record. See Chapter 18 for information on creating transactions.)

You can work along in the Debug Window to delete the record that you just added to the rstCustomers Recordset object. Follow these steps:

1. To place the record in the delete buffer using the Delete method, type **rstCustomers.Delete** and press Enter. Confirm by typing **?rstCustomers .CompanyName**. An error message indicates the record is unavailable.

2. Move to another record to make it the current record. Type **rstCustomers.MoveNext** and press Enter. Confirm by typing **?rstCustomers.CompanyName** and pressing Enter.

## Using Clones

In Chapters 15, 16, and 17, you learn that at times it is convenient to have more than one current record pointer for a Recordset object. You use the Clone method to create a new Recordset object that duplicates an existing Recordset object. The syntax is:

```
Set rstclone] = original.Clone
```

where:

> *rstclone* is the new object variable for the Recordset object.
>
> *original* is the reference to the Recordset object.

When you create a clone, the clone object and the original Recordset object each have their own current records, and you can navigate in the Recordset object independently. An important feature of the Clone method is that the duplicate Recordset has the same bookmarks as the original Recordset; thus, you can set a bookmark with the clone and retrieve the bookmark with the original and vice versa. The original and the clone are not exactly identical, however. For example, if the recordset is a table-type recordset with a current index, the clone does not inherit the value of the Index property. And, if the original is a dynaset- or snapshot-type recordset, the clone does not inherit the values of the Filter and Sort properties.

Because both the original and the clone Recordsets refer to the same stored table or query, you can modify data, add new records, or delete records using either the original or the duplicate. You can use the Close method for either the original or the clone object without closing the other object.

**RecordsetClone**   Chapter 10, "The Access Object Model Revisited," introduced the RecordsetClone property of the Form object. We can now look at the RecordsetClone property from the perspective of the data access objects. When you open a bound form, Jet creates a Recordset object based on the table, query, or SQL statement specified in the form's RecordSource property. When you use the form's RecordsetClone property, you are creating a new current record pointer for the form's Recordset object but you are not creating a new Recordset object.

The benefit of using the RecordsetClone property in your VBA code is that you don't have to walk the Jet object hierarchy to get to the Recordset object. With the RecordsetClone property, you create a reference to a data access object without having to go through the DAO red tape; that is, you are making an end-run around the DAO hierarchy. Having created the RecordsetClone, you can use the methods of the Recordset object for the clone.

> **NOTE**   Don't be confused by the similar terminology. The RecordsetClone property only creates an independent current record pointer for the form's recordset and does not create a separate Recordset object. By contrast, the Clone method creates a separate Recordset object that is the duplicate of the original Recordset object and has the same bookmarks as the original.

# The Data Access Object Model

The remainder of this chapter is a reference to the data access objects. For the DBEngine object and for each object in a collection, a description of the important features is followed by tables of the object's documented properties and methods. No events are defined for the data access objects. The properties and methods of each object are described briefly. Before using a property or a method for the first time, refer to the complete description available in online Help in Microsoft Access.

> **NOTE** A new feature of Access 97 and the Microsoft DAO 3.5 object model is that you can use the Jet database engine to access data or you can use the new ODBCDirect technology to work with ODBC servers such as Microsoft SQL server without loading Jet. This section of the chapter mentions several of the new properties associated with ODBCDirect. See the *Access 97 Developer's Handbook*, by Paul Litwin, Ken Getz, and Mike Gilbert (Sybex, 1997) for more information on using ODBCDirect.

## DBEngine

You use the DBEngine object to maintain database files, to examine error details, and to create new sessions. (A *session* begins when you log on and ends when you log off. If you don't have security implemented, Access logs on or off automatically when you start or exit Access.) Think of a session as a workspace guarded by the security permissions you have set. Tables 11.4 and 11.5 (both of which are on the CD under Tables\Chapter11.pdf) list properties and methods of the DBEngine object.

> **NOTE** A new feature in Access 97 is that you can run the CompactDatabase and RepairDatabase commands on an open database (choose Tools ➤ Database Utilities).

## The Collection Objects

The 15 data access collection objects have the Count property that returns the number of objects in a collection and as many as three methods as follows:

| Method | Abbreviation | Description |
| --- | --- | --- |
| Append | A | Adds a new data access object to a collection. |
| Delete | D | Deletes a saved data access object from a collection. |
| Refresh | R | Updates the objects in a collection to reflect the true inventory of members in the collection. |

Table 11.6 (on the CD under Tables\Chapter11.pdf) lists the collections and their methods using the A, D, and R abbreviations, together with comments.

> **NOTE**
>
> Normally, as you add new objects to a collection or delete objects from a collection, the Jet engine keeps an accurate inventory. Jet may, however, get out of synch with the true inventory when you are working in a multiuser environment. This can occur if you use SQL statements that add or delete objects or if you add or delete objects in the Access user interface. In these cases, you can be sure you are viewing the most up-to-date version by using the Refresh method to update the collection. Refresh a collection only when necessary, however, because the Refresh method is a time-consuming operation.

## Workspace Object

The Workspace object defines a session. A *session* begins when you log on and ends when you log off. All operations that take place during the session are subject to the permissions governed by your username and password. During a session, you can create new databases, open multiple databases, manage transactions, and create new security users and groups. A *transaction* is a series of changes made as a single unit. In a transaction, the database engine treats the series of operations as an all-or-nothing proposition. A transaction affects all the databases in the session and is not limited to one database.

When you start Access, you start Jet as well. Jet automatically creates a new Workspace object. If you haven't enabled security, Jet opens the default Workspace object named #Default Workspace# with admin as the default user name and the zero-length string as the default password. You can confirm this in the Debug Window by typing **?DBEngine.Workspaces(0).Name** or, using the default collection, **?DBEngine(0).Name** and pressing Enter.

Tables 11.7 and 11.8 (both of which are on the CD under Tables\Chapter11.pdf) list properties and methods of the Workspace object.

## Database Object

The Database object represents an open database. Several databases can be open simultaneously in a workspace. You open an existing database in a VBA procedure using the OpenDatabase method of the Workspace object. When several databases are open, you normally refer to each by name; for example:

```
DBEngine(0)![Northwind.mdb]
DBEngine(0).Databases("Northwind.mdb")
```

517

To refer to the current database, you can also use the Access CurrentDB() function.

Tables 11.9 and 11.10 (on the CD under Tables\Chapter11.pdf) list properties and methods of the Database object.

## TableDef

The TableDef object represents the stored definition of a table. The table can be in a Jet database (called a *local table* or a *base table*) or in another database and linked to a Jet database (called a *linked table*). The TableDef object does not represent the data stored in the table. The only data access objects that represent data stored in a table are the Field objects in the Fields collection of a Recordset.

Tables 11.11 and 11.12 (on the CD under Tables\Chapter11.pdf) list properties and methods of the TableDef object.

## Field

The Field object represents a column of data that has a common set of properties and a common data type.

The TableDef, QueryDef, Index, and Relation objects all have Fields collections containing Field objects. In these cases, the Field object properties include the specifications for the field, but do not contain data. These field objects do not have a Value property. You can use the Debug Window to evaluate the Field properties. To do so, follow these steps:

1. Type **?CurrentDB!Customers!CustomerID.AllowZeroLength** and press Enter to view the property setting.

2. Type **?CurrentDB!Customers!CustomerID.Value** and press Enter. Access displays the error message in Figure 11.5 because the Field object for a TableDef contains no data and, therefore, does not have a Value property.

So, where is the data? The data is in the fields of the recordset that Jet creates when you open a table or run a query or an SQL statement that returns records. The Recordset object has a Fields collection containing Field objects. In this case, the Fields collection contains fields that represent a single row of the actual data, the data in the current record. You use the Field objects in a Recordset to inspect or change the data in the current record. The Value property of a Field

**FIGURE 11.5:**

Access displays the error
message when you try to
determine the data value
in a table field, because
the Value property is
valid only for fields in a
recordset.

object returns the value of the data in a field in the current record. You can use the Debug window to evaluate the properties of the Field object. To do so, follow these steps:

1. Type **?rstCustomers.CustomerID.AllowZeroLength** and press Enter to view the property setting.

2. Type **?rstCustomers.CustomerID.Value** and press Enter to view the value of the field. Or, because Value is the default property in this case, you can view the value of the data in the field by typing **?rstCustomers.CustomerID** and pressing Enter.

Tables 11.13 and 11.14 (on the CD under Tables\Chapter11.pdf) list properties and methods of the Field object. The properties and methods for a Field object depend on its parent object. The parent object is the object that contains the Fields collection to which the Field object is appended. The tables use the following abbreviations:

| Parent Object | Abbreviation |
| --- | --- |
| Index | I |
| QueryDef | Q |
| Recordset | Rec |
| Relation | Rel |
| TableDef | T |

## Index

The Index object represents an index for a database table. You use an index for two purposes: to specify the order for records returned in a table-type Recordset object based on a stored table and to specify whether records can have duplicate values in the fields that make up the index. You don't have to create an index for a stored table, but you normally do. Because Jet is able to locate records and create joins more efficiently using indexes, you normally create several indexes for each table. Jet maintains all indexes for the tables in the database, updating indexes automatically whenever you modify, add, or delete records in the table.

In one situation, creating an index is required. If you want to create a relationship between two tables, you must define a primary key for the table on the one side of the one-to-many relationship; the matching field(s) in the table on the many side of the relationship are the foreign key. Jet automatically defines the *primary index* for the "one" table to be its primary key. If, in addition, the relationship enforces referential integrity, Jet automatically creates another index for the "one" table with the Foreign property set to the foreign key of the "many" table.

## What Is an Index?

The records in a database table are stored in pages. When you want to find records with a particular value, such as all customers from Argentina, Access searches through all the pages for the Customers table to find the records. An *index* is a lookup table (stored separately in its own set of pages) that relates the value of a field in the lookup table to the location of the page that holds a record with the field value.

In an index, the values are arranged in ascending order. When you use an index for a search, Access reads the pages of the index, finds the indexed value, and looks up the data page or pages that hold the corresponding record or records. Because the values in an index are in order and the index is small (including only the index fields and not the other fields in the table), Access can find the search value quickly.

When you create an index in the Access interface, Access takes care of the details automatically, but when you create an index in VBA, you have to explicitly step through each operation in the sequence. For example, in Northwind, you can create an index for the Employees table consisting of the LastName and

FirstName fields. Here are the steps you take in VBA when you create this index (see Chapter 19 for a VBA procedure that creates an index):

1. Create and name the index by specifying the index's Name property, for example, FullName.

2. Create each field for the index and set the field's Name property to the name of the field. In this case, you create two index fields—LastName and FirstName.

3. Add each field to the index's Fields collection.

4. Add the index to the table's Indexes collection.

Tables 11.15 and 11.16 (on the CD under Tables\Chapter11.pdf) list properties and methods of the Index object.

## Relation

The Relation object represents a relationship between fields in tables or queries. You use the Relation object in a VBA procedure to create a new relationship or to modify or examine the characteristics of an existing relationhip. A relationship links a single row in one table or query, called the *primary table* or *primary query*, with any number of rows in the second table or query, called the *foreign table* or *foreign query*. You can create a relationship between two tables, between a table and a query, or between two queries; the tables may be local tables in the current database or linked tables. Although queries and linked tables can be members of a relationship, Jet cannot enforce referential integrity for the relationship unless the members are local tables.

You create the relationship by specifying a matching field or fields in each member; the matching field or fields in the primary table or primary query must be a primary key that uniquely specifies a row. The matching field or fields in the foreign table or foreign query is called the *foreign key*. To create the relation, you add each primary key field to the relation's Fields collection and specify the name of the corresponding matching field in the foreign key using the ForeignName property.

When you create a relation in the Access interface, Access takes care of the details automatically; but when you create a relation in VBA, you have to explicitly step through each operation in the sequence. For example, in Northwind you can create a relation between the Customers table as a primary table with CustomerID as its primary key field and the Orders table as a foreign table with

CustomerID as its foreign key field. Here are the steps you take in VBA when you create this relationship (see Chapter 19 for a VBA procedure that creates a similar relationship):

1. Create and name the relationship by specifying the relation's Name property (for example, CustomersOrdersRelation), the Table property as the name of the primary table or query, and the ForeignTable property as the name of the foreign table or query.

2. Create each field for the relation by specifying the primary key field. In this case, you create a single field for the relation and set the field's Name property to the name of the single primary key field, CustomerID.

3. For each field in the relation, specify the ForeignName as the name of the corresponding foreign key field. In this case, you set the ForeignName property to CustomerID. (In this example, the primary key and the foreign key fields have the same name, but the names can be different.)

4. Add the field to the relation's Fields collection.

5. Add the relation to the database's Relations collection.

You use the Attributes property to specify whether the relationship is one-to-one or one-to-many and whether the relationship between fields is left join or right join.

You also use the Attributes property to specify whether you want Jet to enforce referential integrity and cascade options for a relationship. Jet can enforce referential integrity only for a relationship between tables in the current database. Before you can enforce referential integrity, a unique index must already exist for the matching field in the table on the one side of the relationship; when you enforce referential integrity, Jet automatically creates an index for the matching field in the table on the many side of the relationship.

Tables 11.17 and 11.18 (on the CD under Tables\Chapter11.pdf) list properties and methods of the Relation object.

## Recordset

The Recordset object represents the set of records in a table in the database or the set of records that result from running a query or an SQL statement. In a Recordset object that has at least one record, you point to one record at a time as the current record. The Fields collection of the Recordset object contains Field objects that represent the fields in the current record; in particular, the Value property setting of each of the Field objects is the value of the data stored in the field in the table. Earlier sections of the chapter describe the types of Recordset objects and the techniques for navigating through a recordset and for manipulating data.

Tables 11.19 and 11.20 (on the CD under Tables\Chapter 11.pdf) list properties and methods of the Recordset object. These tables use the following abbreviations:

| Recordset Type | Abbreviations |
|---|---|
| Table-type Recordset | T |
| Dynaset-type Recordset | D |
| Snapshot-type Recordset | S |
| Forward-type-only Recordset | F |

If a type is not indicated, the property or method applies to all four types of Recordsets.

> **NOTE** ODBCDirect workspaces provide a fifth kind of Recordset object called the dynamic-type Recordset. Recordsets in ODBC workspaces have additional properties and methods that are not available in a Jet workspace. See the *Access 97 Developer's Handbook* by Paul Litwin, Ken Getz, and Mike Gilbert (Sybex, 1997) for more information.

## QueryDef

The QueryDef object represents the stored definition of a query. The QueryDef object does not represent the data stored in the tables. The only data access objects that represent data stored in tables are the Field objects in the Fields collection of a Recordset.

Tables 11.21 and 11.22 (on the CD under Tables\Chapter 11.pdf) list properties and methods of the QueryDef object.

## Parameter

The Parameter object represents a query parameter in a parameter query. You don't create Parameter objects and append them to the Parameters collection.

Instead, you create query parameters as part of the definition of the parameter query. After creating the parameter query, you use the Parameter object to refer to an existing query parameter. Table 11.23 (on the CD under Tables\Chapter11.pdf) lists properties of the Parameter object. The Parameter object has no methods.

# Error

Tables 11.24 (on the CD under Tables\Chapter11.pdf) lists properties of the Error object. The Error object has no methods.

# Property

The Property object represents a built-in property or a user defined property of a data access object. Every data access object except the Error object (and the Connection object in ODBCDirect) has a Properties collection containing Property objects.

Table 11.25 (on the CD under Tables\Chapter11.pdf) lists the properties of the Property object. The Property object has no methods.

# Container

The Jet database engine is application-independent. In addition to Access, several other applications use Jet to manage their data including Excel, Visual Basic, and Visual C++. When you work with one of these applications as an Automation client that uses Jet as an Automation server, you create application-specific objects. For example, you use the Access Application to create Access objects such as forms, reports, macros, and modules, and you use Excel to create Excel objects such as worksheets, charts, and modules. Usually the Automation client application stores its own objects in its own file; for example, Excel stores its objects in its .xls files. Access, however, stores its own objects in the .mdb database file managed by Jet. Jet tracks the Access objects using a Containers collection that has a separate Container object for each kind of Access object.

Table 11.26 (on the CD under Tables\Chapter11.pdf) lists the properties of the Container object. The Container object has no methods.

# Document

A Document object contains information about a specific instance of an object, that is, a specific table, relationship, form, or report.

Table 11.27 lists the properties of the Document object. Table 11.28 lists the single method of the Document object. (Both tables are on the CD under Tables\Chapter11.pdf.)

## User

A User object represents a specific user that has been given permission to use the objects in the database when security has been implemented for the workspace. You identify a *user account* with a user name and a personal identifier. When security has been implemented, each user logs on using a user name and password and has the access privileges that you have set up as permissions for specific users and groups.

Tables 11.29 and 11.30 (on the CD under Tables\Chapter11.pdf) list properties and methods of the User object.

## Group

A Group object represents a set of user accounts for which you have set common access permissions.

Tables 11.31 and 11.32 (on the CD under Tables\Chapter11.pdf) list properties and methods of the Group object.

# Using the Object Browser

You can use the Object Browser to learn more about the data access objects. The Object Browser is available only when the Module window is the active window. See Chapter 10 for more information.

Follow these steps:

1. Open any module.

2. Click the Object Browser button in the Module toolbar or choose View ➤ Object Browser.

3. In the Object Browser, select DAO in the Project/Libraries combo box. By default, when you install Access, a reference to the type library of the Jet database engine is installed automatically.

4. Choose the object you want to learn about in the Classes list box, and choose the property or method in the Members list box. Figure 11.6 shows the Object Browser with the FindFirst method of the Recordset object selected.

**FIGURE 11.6:**

Use the Object Browser to learn about the properties and methods of the data access objects.

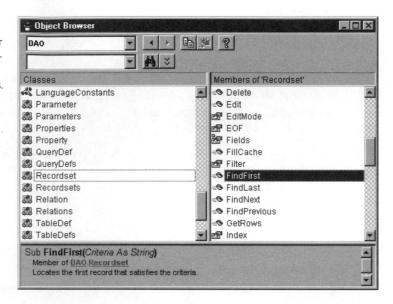

5. Click the Help button in the Object Browser to display online Help for the selected member. The lower pane of the Object Browser also displays information about the member. When you select a method, the lower pane displays the syntax for the method. You can copy the syntax to the clipboard by clicking the Copy to Clipboard button in the Object Browser. To paste the method's syntax into a module, click the module window and press Ctrl+V.

# Summary

This chapter has introduced you to the data access objects that represent those elements of the Jet database engine that you can manipulate in VBA procedures. The important points are:

- When you are referring to a data access object in a VBA procedure, you start at the top of the data access object hierarchy and traverse to the object.

- A data access object has built-in properties created by Jet. The object may also have properties that the host application creates and properties that you create yourself. Each property is represented by a Property object contained in the object's Properties collection.

- You can create new data access objects. Each object has specific creation and destruction rules: Some objects require that child objects be created before saving, some objects must be appended to their collection before saving, and some objects are created anew and destroyed automatically when the procedure ends or when the database closes.

- You use the Recordset object to work with the data in the database. There are four types of Recordset objects.

- When you create a new recordset, you can work with only one record (called the current record) at a time.

- You can navigate among the records of a Recordset using the Move... methods. You can use the EOF and BOF properties to determine if you have moved beyond the limits of the recordset.

- You can locate a specific record satisfying search criteria using the Seek method for Table-type Recordsets and the Find... methods for Dynaset-type and Snapshot-type Recordsets. You can use the NoMatch property to determine if the search was successful.

- You can use the data access objects in VBA procedures to add new records, modify existing records, and delete records.

- You can use the Clone method to duplicate a Recordset object. The duplicate Recordset object has the same bookmarks as the original.

Chapters 10 and 11 have provided you with tours of the two object models that contain the objects that you can manipulate in VBA programs. As you learn to write programs in the remainder of the book, you'll be returning to these chapters as reference to determine whether an object has a property or method that your program needs. Before using a property or method for the first time, search the item in the Object Browser or online Help to understand the item's capability and limitations.

In the next three chapters, you learn how to write programs using the Visual Basic for Applications language.

# CHAPTER
## TWELVE

**12**

# Mechanics of Procedures I:
# The Basics

- ■ **Understanding the Access VBA data types**

- ■ **Understanding  procedures and modules**

- ■ **The Access VBA programming environment**

- ■ **Running function procedures**

- ■ **Running sub procedures**

**A**s a programming *language*, Visual Basic for Applications has the fundamental features shared by all languages: it has a grammar that is concerned with the form and structure of words and their arrangement in phrases and statements (syntax). As a particular form of expression for human-computer interaction, it has a special set of symbols, letters, words, and rules that you use to communicate instructions to the computer. Chapters 10 and 11 have dealt with the basic parts of speech: you can think of objects as nouns, properties as adjectives, and methods as verbs. You've met the objects in both the Access application and the Jet database engine and you've gotten plenty of hands-on experience setting and getting their properties and calling their methods in the Immediate pane of the Debug window. You've actually been writing Access VBA statements in the Immediate pane and executing them one at a time each time you press the Enter key.

A *statement* is a combination of keywords, constants, variables, operator symbols, objects, properties, and methods that expresses a single definition, declaration, or operation. These elements must be combined correctly according to the syntax rules of the Access VBA interpreter before the statement can be executed. In the Debug window, you use a single line for each statement. Here is an inventory of the statements you learned in Chapters 10 and 11:

| Description | Syntax |
| --- | --- |
| Printing a value | ? *value*<br>Debug.Print *value* or Print *value* |
| Assigning a value to a property | *object.property = value* |
| Assigning a property value to a variable | Let *var = object.property*<br>*var = object.property* |
| Assigning an object returned by a property to an object variable | Set *obj = object.property* |
| Calling a method with nothing returned | *object.method argumentlist* |
| Calling a method with a value returned | Let *var = object.method* (*argumentlist*)<br>*var = object.method* (*argumentlist*) |
| Calling a method with an object returned | Set *obj = object.method* (*argumentlist*) |

The Debug window has been a terrific tool for running individual VBA statements. VBA programming involves packaging one or more statements together into a unit called a *procedure* and asking the computer to run the procedure.

This is the first of three chapters that describe all of the basic features of the Visual Basic for Applications programming language as it is used in Microsoft Access. In this chapter, you learn the basics of writing procedures. The chapter begins with a discussion of the data types and object data types in Access VBA and then introduces the mechanics of writing procedures: the kinds of procedures you can write, where you store them in the database file, and how to run them. In Chapter 13, you will learn about using variables and constants in procedures: the reasons for using variables, how to share variables and constants among procedures, and the mechanics of writing procedures with variables. In Chapter 14, you will learn about controlling execution: how to control whether a set of statements is executed and how many times to repeat a set of statements. You will also learn about many of the useful statements and functions that are built into Access.

# Data Types

The types of values that variables can hold are referred to as *data types*. When you work interactively with Access, you specify data types when you create table fields, but otherwise you don't need to pay too much attention to them. In VBA programming, data type is an important concept. When you create a variable to hold a value or refer to an object, you can let VBA handle the data type for you. VBA has an all-purpose data type, called the *Variant* data type, that it uses unless you specify another one. The problems with this approach are that variables with the Variant data type take a lot of memory and VBA procedures that use them run more slowly. So, to create programs that use less memory and run as fast as possible, you'll have to learn something about data types.

**NOTE** The topic of data types is complicated by the fact that there are four systems of data types that you'll be dealing with: the field data types you specify when you create tables interactively, the VBA and DAO data types you'll learn about in this chapter, and the SQL data types.

# Fundamental Data Types

You are already familiar with the field data types you assign to table fields when you create Access tables. Access VBA has its own set of VBA data types, most of which match the familiar field data types. Table 12.1 (on the CD under Tables\ Chapter12.pdf) lists the VBA data types, commonly used name tags, compatible field data types, and a brief description of each data type.

> **NOTE**   Some programmers prefer to use a *type-declaration character* appended to a variable name to indicate the variable's data type. The data types that have such characters and their type-declaration characters are Integer (%), Long (&), Single (!), Double (#), Currency (@), and String ($).

## Literals

When you assign literal values to a variable with one of the fundamental data types, you must follow these rules:

**String**   Enclose a literal string in double quotation marks; for example, strName = "Betsy Evart".

**Date**   Enclose a literal date in number signs; for example, dtmOrderDate = #5/10/96#.

**Currency**   Omit the dollar sign and commas; for example, curAmount = 3200.

There are two VBA data types that have no counterpart in the field data types: Variant and Object. You'll learn about these data types in the next two sections.

# Variant Data Type

The Variant data type is a chameleon data type: it can store any other fundamental data type except the fixed-length String data type. The purpose of the Variant data type is to let you manipulate values with different data types without having to convert their data types yourself. The Variant data type is the default data type in Access VBA: if you don't explicitly specify the data type for a variable, VBA assigns the Variant data type. When you work in the Debug window, you can't explicitly specify a data type using the data type declaration statements that you'll learn about in the next chapter. You can specify a variable's data type in the Debug window using the type-declaration characters for those data types that have them. If you don't use type-declaration characters, the variables that you create in the Debug window have the Variant data type.

## Automatic Conversion of Data Type

VBA automatically attempts to convert between data types when necessary for a calculation. Of course, the conversion isn't always possible and there are restrictions on the operations that you can perform with Variant data types. For example, to perform arithmetic calculations on Variant variables, the variables must contain valid numbers; otherwise, a run-time error is generated. You can use the built-in IsNumeric function to determine if the value of a Variant variable is a valid number before doing the arithmetic calculation. Similarly, performing date arithmetic on Variant variables requires that the variables contain valid date/time values. You can use the built-in IsDate function to determine if a Variant variable contains a value that can be converted to a date before doing date arithmetic.

**The + and & Operators**    The result of using the + operator with two Variant variables depends on the values of the Variant variables. If both Variant variables contain strings, the + operator concatenates the strings. If both Variant variables contain numbers, the + operator adds the numbers. If one of the values is a number and the other is a string, VBA attempts to convert the string to a number; if the conversion is successful, VBA adds the two numbers; otherwise, VBA generates an error. You can avoid ambiguity by using the ampersand operator (&) when you want to concatenate two strings; leave a space between the variable names and the & operator.

To explore these concepts, open the Debug window and enter each of the following expressions:

| When You Enter | The Result Is |
| --- | --- |
| varone = 4 | The Variant variable named varone is created and holds the integer 4. |
| ? IsNumeric(varone) | The value True is displayed. |

| When You Enter | The Result Is |
|---|---|
| vartwo = "3" | The Variant variable named vartwo is created and holds the string "3". |
| ? IsNumeric(vartwo) | The value True is displayed. |
| ?varone+vartwo | The value 7 is displayed. |
| ?Varone & vartwo | The value 43 is displayed as the result because VBA converts varone to a string and concatenates the two results. |

While the Variant data type offers the advantage of handling the conversion of data type automatically, the disadvantages are that the Variant type takes more memory and VBA code is slower when you use Variant data types, for the following reasons: When you use the Variant data type, VBA has to take time to determine if a conversion is necessary and then take additional time to do the conversion. Also, when you use the Variant data type for an object variable, VBA has to take time to determine if the properties and methods you are using in the statement are appropriate to the object.

**Data Conversion Functions**   Access provides the set of data conversion functions shown in Table 12.2 (on the CD under Tables\Chapter12.pdf) that you can use to force, or coerce, a string or numeric expression to a specific data type.

## The Null and Empty Values

The Variant data type has two special values: Null and Empty.

**Null**   The purpose of the Null value is to indicate missing, unknown, or inapplicable data. The special Null value is not a real value like "Peacock" or $12.45 but is an indicator that data is missing, unknown, or doesn't apply. The data in a table or query field or in a form or report control has the Variant data type by default. When you leave a field or control blank, a Null is stored automatically. You are familiar with ways to determine if a field or control contains a Null value. As examples, you can use a query to search for records with a Null value in a field by setting the Criteria cell for the field to Is Null, and you can determine if a control contains a Null value using the IsNull function.

The Null value requires special handling for the following reasons:

- If any part of an expression evaluates to the Null value, the entire expression also has the Null value. This is called *propagation of Null values*. In addition, if an argument of a built-in or custom function evaluates to Null, the function usually returns a Null value. For example, if you use an SQL or domain aggregate function to calculate a summary value of field for a group of records, records with Null values in the field won't be included. To explore, open the Northwind database, press Ctrl+G to display the Debug window, and enter each of the following expressions in the Immediate pane:

| When You Enter | The Result Is |
|---|---|
| varone = 4 | The Variant variable holds the integer 4. |
| vartwo = null | The Variant variable holds the Null value. |
| ?varone + vartwo | Null is displayed as the result because the Null value in vartwo has been propagated to the sum. |
| ?DCount("Fax", "Suppliers") | The value 13 is displayed as the number of suppliers with a value entered as a Fax number. |

- When you join tables in a query, records with Null values in the join field are not included in the query result. For example, if you create a query based on the Orders and Employees tables in Northwind, only records for employees who handled orders and records for orders handled by specific employees are included; the query result does not contain records for employees who didn't handle orders or for orders not assigned to an employee.

- When you create a relationship and enforce referential integrity, you can still create orphan records in the child table by leaving the join field blank in the child table. In the Northwind database, you can add new orphan orders just by leaving the EmployeeID or the CustomerID fields blank.

In VBA, only Variant variables can contain Null values. You can determine if a Variant variable contains the Null value using the IsNull function. You can set a Variant variable to the Null value using an assignment statement as follows:

    varname = Null

**Empty**    The purpose of the Empty value is to be a place holder when you have not assigned a value to a variable with the Variant data type. When you first create a Variant variable, it has the Empty value until it is assigned a value; the Empty value is replaced when you assign a value to the variable. You can use the

IsEmpty function to determine if a Variant variable has the Empty value. After assigning a value to a Variant variable, you can set the Variant variable back to the Empty value using the following assignment statement:

    varname = Empty

The Empty value is not the same as zero, the zero-length string (""), or the Null value. However, because VBA automatically converts Variant variables to the data type needed in a manipulation, when you use a Variant variable with the Empty value in expressions, VBA automatically converts the value to a zero if the expression requires a numeric value or to the zero-length string ("") if the expression requires a string value.

To get hands-on experience with these concepts, enter the following in the Debug window:

| When You Enter | The Result Is |
| --- | --- |
| varthree = "test" | The Variant variable varthree is created and assigned the string value test. |
| ?IsEmpty(varthree) | The value False is displayed because the variable holds a value. |
| varthree = Empty | The variable now holds the Empty value. |
| ?IsEmpty(varthree) | The value True is displayed because the variable holds the Empty value. |
| varthree = Null | The variable now holds the Null value. |
| ?IsNull(varthree) | True, because the variable holds the Null value. |
| ?IsEmpty(varthree) | The value False is displayed because the variable holds the Null and not the Empty value. |

## Using the VarType Function

Since a Variant variable can hold different data types and the data type can change each time you assign a value to the variable, you need a way to determine what type of data the variable is currently holding. You can use the VarType function for this purpose. The VarType function returns an integer value corresponding to the current data type of the variable; Table 12.3 (on the CD under Tables\Chapter12.pdf) shows some of the integer values and corresponding intrinsic constants that the VarType function returns.

You can test the Vartype function in the Debug window by entering the following expressions:

| When You Enter | The Result Is |
|---|---|
| varone = Empty | The Variant variable now holds the Empty value. |
| ?vartype(varone) | 0 |
| varone = "test" | The Variant variable now holds a string value. |
| ?vartype(varone) | 8 |
| varone = #3/15/96# | The Variant variable now holds a date value. |
| ?vartype(varone) | 7 |
| varone = False | The Variant variable now holds a Boolean value. |
| ?vartype(varone) | 11 |

## Advantages and Disadvantages of Variant Variables

The main advantages of using Variant variables are:

- It is easier to create code because you don't have to know about data types and you don't have to worry about whether the data types of your variables are compatible.

- The Variant data type is the only one that can have the Null value. If you want to assign a variable to fields in a table that may have the Null value, using a Variant variable avoids having to write code to handle the Null data values.

The main disadvantages of using the Variant variables are:

- They take the most memory—the more memory tied up in storing variables, the less is available to run your application.

- Procedures that use Variant variables are slower. Each time code refers to a Variant variable, VBA must take the time to convert the data type and for an object variable to determine if the properties and methods referred to in your code are appropriate to the object.

# The Object Data Type

You use an object variable to refer, or point, to an object. You can use the Object data type as the data type for the pointer to an object. (The pointer, or reference, is the 4-byte memory address of the object.) The Object data type listed in Table 12.1 (on the CD under Tables\Chapter12.pdf) is generic and can be used for any object, however there are specific *object data types* that you can use instead. Table 12.4 (on the CD under Tables\Chapter12.pdf) lists examples of object data types, name tags commonly used in Hungarian naming styles, and corresponding database objects. Using specific object data types results in faster execution because VBA knows which properties and methods are appropriate to an object with a specified object data type and doesn't have to take time during execution to determine whether a property or method used in your code is appropriate.

You can use the IsObject function to determine whether a variable refers to an object. The IsObject Function returns True if the variable refers to an object and False otherwise.

## Nothing

The Object data type has a special value called the Nothing value. The purpose of the Nothing value is to act as a placeholder when you have not assigned an object to a variable with the Object data type. The Nothing value is analogous to the Empty value for the Variant data type. When you first create an object variable, it has the Nothing value until you assign an object to it. After assigning an object to an Object variable, you can set the variable back to Nothing so that it no longer refers to the object using an assignment statement:

```
Set objMyObject = Nothing
```

You can explore these concepts in the Debug window. When you work with objects in the Debug window, a variable you create to refer to an object has the Variant data type with the object subtype. Open the Employees form in Form view and type the following in the Immediate pane:

| When You Enter | The Result Is |
| --- | --- |
| Set frm = Forms!Employees | The Variant variable named frm is created, and points to the Employees form |
| ?VarType(frm) | The value 9 is displayed because the variable points to an object. |

| When You Enter | The Result Is |
|---|---|
| ?IsObject(frm) | The value True is displayed because the variable points to an object. |
| Set frm = Nothing | The variable no longer points to any object. |
| ?IsObject(frm) | The value True is displayed because the variable once referred to an object. |
| Set frm = Empty | A Type mismatch error is generated because you can't set an object variable to empty. |
| Set frm = Null | A Type mismatch error is generated because you can't set an object variable to Null. |

# Procedures and Modules

A procedure is a sequence of statements that is executed as a unit. Procedures are the basic building blocks of Visual Basic. A procedure performs a specific task; the task may be a single operation such as opening a form or running a query to select and display a group of records, or a complex set of multiple operations such as importing and manipulating data. A procedure can accept additional information as *arguments* that determine how the procedure operates.

## Kinds of Procedures

There are three kinds of procedures in VBA: *function, sub,* and *property* procedures. Each has a different purpose and its own pair of special statements to indicate its beginning and end:

- A function procedure performs a task and may return a single value. The returned value is computed in the procedure and assigned to the function name as one of the procedure's statements. You use function procedures to create your own custom functions and use them in expressions in the same way you use the built-in functions. You begin a function procedure with a Function statement and end it with an End Function statement. The basic syntax for a function procedure is

```
Function functionname [(argumentlist)]
    [statements]
    [functionname = expression]
End Function
```

Figure 12.1 shows the IsLoaded function procedure in Northwind. The IsLoaded function takes the name of a form as an argument, determines if the form is open, and sets the function name to True if the form is open.

**FIGURE 12.1:**

The IsLoaded function determines whether a form is open in Form or Datasheet view.

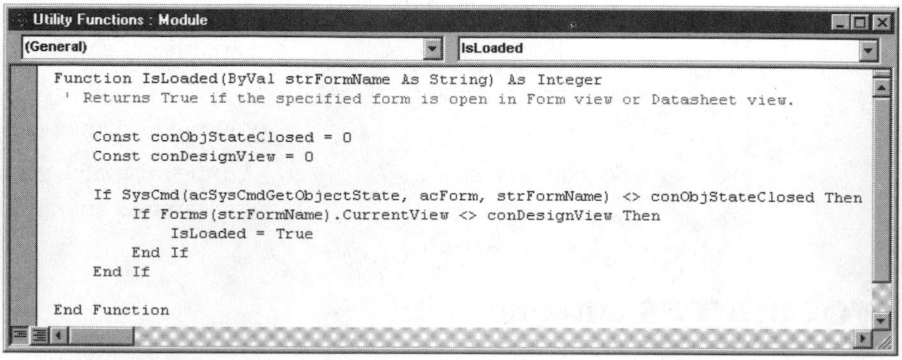

```
Utility Functions : Module
(General)                                              IsLoaded

Function IsLoaded(ByVal strFormName As String) As Integer
    ' Returns True if the specified form is open in Form view or Datasheet view.

    Const conObjStateClosed = 0
    Const conDesignView = 0

    If SysCmd(acSysCmdGetObjectState, acForm, strFormName) <> conObjStateClosed Then
        If Forms(strFormName).CurrentView <> conDesignView Then
            IsLoaded = True
        End If
    End If

End Function
```

You can also use a function procedure to respond to an event; Access runs the procedure automatically when the event occurs and discards the function's returned value if there is one. Figure 12.2 shows the OpenForms function used to open a specified form by clicking a command button on the Main Switchboard form in Northwind. The OpenForms function takes the name of a form as an argument, opens the form, and ends without returning a value.

- A sub procedure performs a task but does not return a value. Primarily, you use sub procedures to respond to events. You begin a sub procedure with a Sub statement and end it with an End Sub statement. The basic syntax for a sub procedure is

```
Sub subname [(argumentlist)]
    [statements]
End Sub
```

When you use a sub procedure to respond to an event, it is called an *event procedure*. An event procedure must follow specific rules, such as naming rules. An event procedure for an event recognized by a form or report is named as follows: Form_*eventname* or Report_*eventname* where eventname is the name of the event. An event procedure recognized by a section or a control on a form or report is named as follows: *sectionname_eventname* or *controlname_eventname*. In addition, for each event, the argument list for an event

**FIGURE 12.2:**

The OpenForms function procedure is assigned to the Click event of the Categories command button on the Main Switchboard.

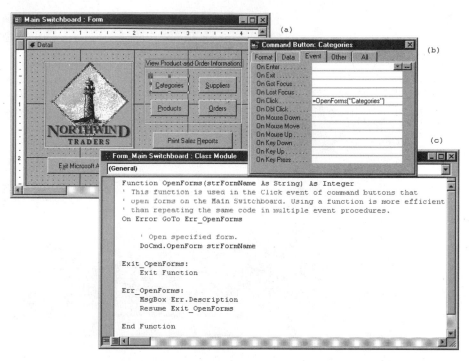

procedure is predefined; for example, an event procedure for the click event has no arguments. Figure 12.3 shows the DisplayDatabaseWindow_Click event procedure. This event procedure closes the Main Switchboard form, displays the Database window, and ends.

- A property procedure performs the task of creating a custom property for an object. Normally, you create a custom property with a pair of property procedures using one kind to set the property and another to return the setting. You begin a property procedure to set the property with either a Property Let statement when you are assigning a value or a Property Set statement when you are assigning a reference to an object. Property Let and Set procedures do not return values. You begin a property procedure to return the setting with a Property Get statement. You end a property procedure with an End Property statement. We'll discuss property procedures in Chapter 19.

**FIGURE 12.3:**

The DisplayDatabase-Window_Click sub procedure (c) is assigned to the Click event of the DisplayDatabaseWindow command button (b) in the Main Switchboard form (a).

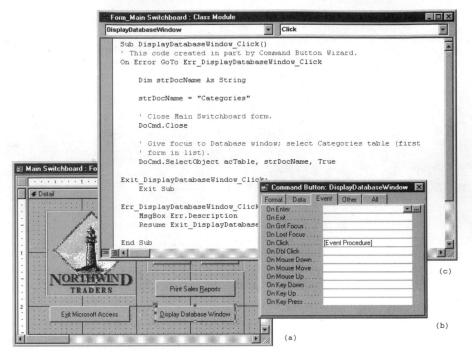

## Calling a Procedure

When you request that Access execute a procedure, you are *calling* the procedure. You can classify procedures according to how you call them as follows:

**In expressions and as property settings**    Because Function procedures return values, you can call them directly in expressions and property settings in the same way you call the built-in functions. You can use function procedures as settings in the property sheets of tables, queries, forms, and reports, in the condition cells and argument settings in macros, and in the field cells and criteria cells in queries.

**As event-handling procedures**    You can use both Sub and Function procedures to respond to events. A procedure that you assign to an event is called an *event-handling procedure*. Microsoft reserves the term *event procedure* for a Sub procedure that is assigned to an event.

**As support or general procedures** You call a procedure indirectly when you include it in a statement of a another procedure. A procedure that you call from another procedure is referred to as a *support procedure* or a *general procedure*. You use support procedures to divide a complicated task with several operations into a set of simpler procedures and to create general purpose procedures that can be called from several other procedures. You can use both Function and Sub procedures as support procedures, using a Function procedure when you need to pass a value from one procedure to another, and a Sub procedure otherwise. For example, the event procedures for the Print Preview and Print buttons on the Sales Report Dialog form in Northwind call the PrintReports sub procedure (see Figure 12.4). When a procedure calls a support procedure, Access interrupts execution of the calling procedure, executes the support procedure, and then returns to continue executing the calling procedure.

**FIGURE 12.4:**

The Preview_Click and Print_Click event procedures call the Print-Reports sub procedure.

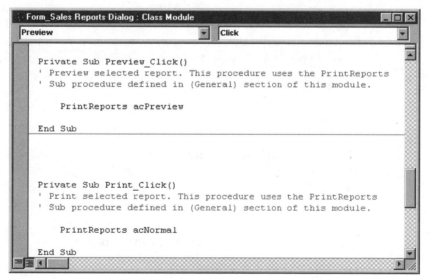

```
Private Sub Preview_Click()
' Preview selected report. This procedure uses the PrintReports
' Sub procedure defined in (General) section of this module.

    PrintReports acPreview

End Sub




Private Sub Print_Click()
' Print selected report. This procedure uses the PrintReports
' Sub procedure defined in (General) section of this module.

    PrintReports acNormal

End Sub
```

## Modules

A *module* is the object you use to create and store procedures. A module is a code listing of one or more procedures, declarations, and statements that you store together as a unit. There are two kinds of modules that you use to organize your procedures: *class modules* and *standard modules*.

**Class Modules**    A class module contains the procedures that you can use to create the definition for a new object. The procedures in the module include the properties and methods for the new object. There are two kinds of class modules: those associated with forms and reports, and those that exist independently of forms and reports. (Independent class modules are a new feature of Access 97 and are an advanced topic not covered in depth in this book.)

You create a form or report module by opening the form or report in Design view and choosing View ➤ Code or clicking the Code button in the toolbar. The module window opens and displays a module that will be stored as part of the form or report when you save the form or report. Access automatically sets the form's or report's HasModule property to Yes and names the built-in form or report module using the form's or report's name as follows: Form_*formname* or Report_*reportname*. These built-in modules are stored with the form or report and are not listed separately in the Database window. The primary purpose of a form or report module is to store all of the event procedures for the events recognized by the form or report and its controls and sections; however, the form or report module can also store general function and sub procedures. Form and report modules are very convenient ways to store the procedures associated with a form; if you copy the form or report, you also copy the form or report module. When you delete a form or report you delete the form or report module also. You can delete the form or report module without deleting the form or report by setting the form's or report's HasModule property to No. Figures 12.2c and 12.3c show two panes of the Form_Main Switchboard form module.

**Standard Modules**    Each standard module is listed as a separate object in the Modules pane of the database window. Naming rules for a standard module are the same as the rules for any database window object. Usually, you use standard modules to hold the custom functions and support procedures that you want to call from anywhere in the application. Figure 12.5 shows a pane of the RefreshTableLinks standard module in the orders.mdb sample application.

**The Layout of a Module**    All modules have the same layout. A module begins with a Declarations section that contains option settings and declarations that apply to every procedure in the module. You use the Declarations section to define custom data types and to declare those constants and variables that you want to share among the procedures in the module and among procedures in other modules and even in other databases. In addition, if you are using procedures that are stored externally in a separate file called a dynamic link library, you provide information about the name of the procedure and the library in the Declarations section. Code that you enter in the Declarations section is called *module-level code*. Figure 12.5 shows the first part of the Declarations section for the RefreshTableLinks standard module in the Orders.mdb application including the two option settings, the declaration of two functions stored in the comdlg32.dll dynamic link library (see Chapter 20 for information on dynamic link libraries), and the first several statements that define a custom data type named MSA_OPENFILENAME.

**FIGURE 12.5:**

The Declarations section of a module includes declaration statements for custom data types, procedures stored in external files (dynamic link libraries), and declaration statements for module-level constants and variables.

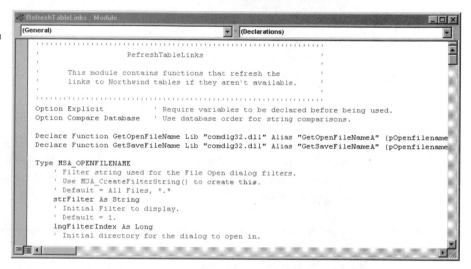

Following the Declarations section is the Procedures section, where you store the module's procedures. Procedures in a module must have unique names; however, procedures in different modules can have the same name.

## Referring to Procedures

The syntax for referring to a procedure in a module is:

```
modulename.procedurename
```

This syntax is the *fully qualified reference* for the procedure. As examples,

```
[Utility Function].IsLoaded
[Form_Main Switchboard].OpenForms
```

refer to procedures in Northwind; in both examples the module names must be enclosed in square bracket because the module names contain spaces. Often you can omit the module name and just refer to a procedure by its name. The basic rules are as follows:

- When you are referring to a procedure from within the same module, you can usually omit the reference to the module name because VBA assumes you are referring to the same module when you omit the module name. As an exception, if the procedure has the same name as the module, you must include the module name.

- When you are on a form or report you can usually refer to a procedure in the form's or report's module just by its name because VBA assumes you are referring to the form's module when you omit the module name. As an exception, if the form or report has a control with the same name as the procedure, you must include the module name.

- When you are referring to a procedure in a form or report module from outside the module, you must include the module name.

- When you are referring to a procedure that has the same name in two or more other modules, you must include the module name in the reference so that VBA knows which procedure you are referring to.

## Names in Visual Basic

The names of modules, procedures, variables, and constants must begin with a letter, cannot contain embedded periods or type-declaration characters, and cannot be restricted keywords that Visual Basic uses as part of its language. Examples of restricted keywords are If, Then, End, While, Loop, and Sub.

The name of a module must not conflict with the naming convention that Access uses for form and report modules; don't preface a module name with Form_ or Report_

A procedure can have the same name as a module. In this case, you must use the fully qualified reference to the procedure.

**NOTE**

You can refer to a public procedure in a form module of a subform when the form is open in Form view as a method of the form displayed in the subform control. Use the reference Forms!*formname*!*subformcontrolname*.Form.*procedurename*

## Sharing Procedures: Public versus Private Procedures

When you create a procedure, you can specify whether the procedure is *public* or *private*. A public procedure can be run by procedures in other modules, while a private procedure can only be run by procedures in the same module. You can use the Public and Private keywords to specify the procedure's availability to other procedures, called its *visibility* or *scope*. By default, procedures with neither keyword in their declaration statements are public and can be called by any procedure in the application. You don't have to use the Public keyword, but your code is easier to understand if you use the Public keyword in a public procedure's declaration statement; for example, Public Function FirstFunction explicitly specifies the FirstFunction procedure as public.

When you use the built-in code-building tools for an event procedure, Access includes the Private keyword in the code stub by default because, normally, event procedures are used only in the form or report in which they are stored. However, you can delete the Private keyword to make an event procedure public.

**TIP**

Make it a rule to use either the Public or Private keyword when creating procedures. You'll learn more quickly about scope, which is one of the subtler and more difficult VBA programming concepts.

**NOTE**

The public procedures stored in standard modules are also available to other databases by default. You can restrict the public procedures in a standard module for use in the current database only by including Option Private with the other option settings in the module's Declarations section. By contrast, the public procedures stored in form and report modules are available only to the current database.

**NOTE**   To use the public procedures in a standard module that is stored in another database, you must first add a reference to the other database. See Chapter 20 for information on adding a reference.

## Simple Examples of Procedures

Let's explore some of these ideas by creating and calling a few simple Sub and Function procedures. The procedures that we create now do little more than display custom messages using the MsgBox function to indicate that they are being executed. After we get the mechanics down in this chapter and the next two by creating simple examples, we'll turn our skills to creating the more complicated procedures necessary to automate a database. Also, in the next section of this chapter, we'll do a thorough study of the module Design window, so don't worry about the details for now.

1. Create a new database and name it Ch12_Examples.

2. Create a new form named frm1; place a command button on the form and set the Name property to cmdButton1 and the Caption property to Call an Event Procedure.

**Creating an Event Procedure**   We'll create the first procedure as an event procedure that runs when the command button is clicked. Event procedures are the most common procedures in an Access application. We'll use the special event procedure code building tools that Access provides.

1. Click in the button's OnClick event property, click the Build button at the right of the property box, select Code Builder in the Choose Builder dialog (see Figure 12.6a), and click OK. The module window for built-in form module opens (see Figure 12.6b). The module begins with the Declararations section. The Declarations section displays the two option statements that VBA includes by default: Option Compare Database and the Option Explicit statements. You use the Option Compare Database statement to specify that you want Access to compare string expressions according to the database sort order that has been set for the database (we'll look at other options in the next section). You use the Option Explicit statement to require that all variables be declared explicitly in a declarations statement before you can use them in procedures in

the module. The line below the two option statements, called a procedure separator, separates the Declarations section from the first procedure. Following the Declarations section, VBA displays two lines of code called a *stub* or *code template* and places the insertion point between them ready for you to enter the code for the procedure.

**FIGURE 12.6:**

Clicking the Build button for an event property displays the Choose Builder dialog(a). Choosing the Code Builder displays the form's module with the event procedure for the event (b)

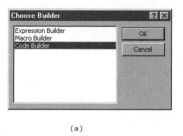

(a)

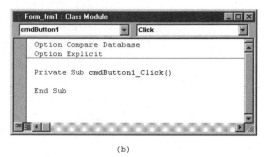

(b)

2. Create the event procedure by typing the two lines of code between the code template lines as shown below. The first line you type uses an assignment statement to set the form's Caption property to the current date using the built-in Date function, and the second line uses the built-in MsgBox function to display a custom message box. As you type in the lines, note that VBA checks your entries and makes suggestions and corrections. For example, if you enter the parentheses after the Date function, Date(), VBA automatically removes the parentheses. When you use the Date function in a property setting, query expression, or in a macro, you must include parentheses after the function; Date(); however, the parentheses are not used in Visual Basic, and VBA removes them. As another example, after you type Msgbox, VBA displays a box with the syntax for the function as a guide to the function's required and optional arguments and the function's returned value (seeFigure 12.7).

```
Private Sub cmdButton1_Click()
    Forms!frm1.Caption = "Today is " & Date
    MsgBox "This is cmdButton1_Click in module Form_frm1"
End Sub
```

3. Click in the form. The OnClick property for the command button displays the setting [Event Procedure] to indicate that an event procedure has been assigned automatically to the button's Click event.

**FIGURE 12.7:**

When you type a built-in function, VBA displays a syntax box as a guide to the function's arguments and returned value.

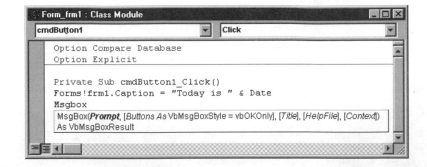

4. Switch to Form view and click the command button. The procedure sets the form's caption to the current date and displays the message box (see Figure 12.8). Click OK to close the message box.

**FIGURE 12.8:**

The event procedure changes the form's caption and displays a message box.

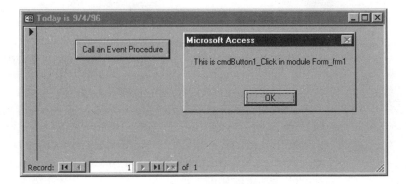

# Event Procedure Syntax and Code Building Tools

Because event procedures are so common in an Access application, Access provides special event procedure code building tools. Here are the steps to create an event procedure using the built-in tools:

1. In Design view, select the object that recognizes the event and click in the event property in the property sheet.

2. Click the Build button at the right of the property box, select Code Builder, and click OK (see Figure 12.6).

The module window for the built-in form or report module is displayed. VBA automatically displays two lines of code called a *stub* or *code template*; the stub blocks out space in the module for the new procedure. VBA places the insertion point on a blank line between these two statements, ready for you to enter code.

The first line of the stub signals the beginning of the event procedure and depends on the event you selected. Access automatically names event procedures and specifies the arguments. If you selected an event recognized by the form or report, the first line is either

```
Private Sub Form_eventname(eventargumentlist)
```

or

```
Private Sub Report_eventname(eventargumentlist)
```

If you selected an event recognized by a control or section, the first line is

```
Private Sub objectname_eventname(eventargumentlist)
```

The second line signals the end of the procedure and is the same for all Sub procedures.

**Creating a Function Procedure** We'll create the next procedure as a function procedure and call the function in an expression for the ControlSource property of a calculated control.

1. Switch to Design view and click the Code button or choose View ➤ Code. Choose Insert ➤ Procedure, enter Function1 in the Name text box of the Insert Procedure dialog (see Figure 12.9), and click OK. VBA inserts a procedure separator line below the previous procedure and displays the stub for the function.

2. Enter the Function1 procedure below. This function procedure has an argument named A which must be supplied when you run the procedure. The

You use the Insert Procedure dialog to name the new procedure and to specify its type and scope.

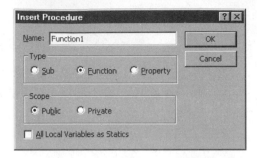

first line of code adds one to the argument and assigns the sum as the function's return value. The second line displays a message.

```
Function Function1(A)
    Function1 = A + 1
    MsgBox "This is Function1 in module Form_frm1"
End Function
```

3. We'll display the value returned by the function in a text box on the form. Switch to Design view and place a text box on the form. Set the Name property to txtCalculated and type the following expression in the ControlSource property

   **= "The value calculated by Function1 in module Form_frm1 is " & Function1(2)**

   When you display the form in Form view, VBA evaluates the ControlSource expression as follows: the function procedure runs with its argument set to 2, the function returns the value 3, then VBA uses the returned value in the ControlSource expression and displays the result in the text box.

4. Switch to Form view and click OK when the message box is displayed. The text box displays the result (see Figure 12.10).

The expression for the ControlSource property includes the custom function.

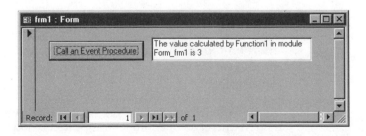

**Running Another Procedure in the Module**    In VBA, you can call a procedure from another procedure. This means that you can divide a complicated programming task into a set of simpler tasks and create separate procedures for each task. You get two important benefits from this division of labor. First, shorter procedures for simple tasks are easier to write and debug. Second, when there is a task you need to use again in another part of your application or in another application, you can often write a procedure so that you can reuse it without modification. The second reason is so important that you should adopt it as a fundamental programming guideline:

*Create reusable procedures whenever possible.*

We'll create a command button that calls the Function1 procedure.

1.  Switch to Design view, place a command button on the form, and set its Name property to cmdButton2 and Caption property to Call a procedure in the form's module.

2.  Click the button's OnClick event property, click the Build button at the right of the property box, select Code Builder in the Choose Builder dialog, and click OK. The module window opens and displays the code template for the new event procedure.

3.  Type the event procedure below. The first line of code calls the Function1 procedure with the argument 3. The procedure that is called is referred to as a *called procedure* or a *nested procedure*. The second line displays a message.

```
Private.Sub cmdButton2_Click ()
    Call Function1(3)
    MsgBox " This is cmdButton2_Click in Form_frm1"
End Sub
```

4.  Switch to Form view. The expression in the text box's ControlSource property calls Function1 with argument 2 as before. Click the OK button so that VBA can continue evaluating the ControlSource expression.

5.  Click the new command button with the caption Call a procedure in another module. The event procedure calls Function1 with 3 as the argument. The Function1 procedure adds one to the argument and returns 4 as value of the function. However, when you use the Call statement to call a function, VBA ignores the function's returned value. Function1 displays its message. When you click OK, the cmdButton2_Click event procedure displays its message.

**Running a Procedure in Another Module**    You can also run a procedure that is stored in another module. In most databases, you create one or more standard modules and use them to store general procedures that you use in several forms or reports. We'll create a standard module and use it to store a new function procedure that we'll run from a third button on the form.

1. Click the New Object button in the toolbar, choose Module, and save the standard module as bas1. The module window opens, displaying the Declarations section of the standard module. The Declarations section displays the two default option statements.

2. Create a new Function procedure by typing Public Function Function1(A) on a new line. You use the Public keyword to make the procedure available to procedures in other modules. When you press Enter, VBA automatically enters a procedure separator and displays the code template. Enter the procedure shown below. (We are deliberately using the same name for the new function.)

```
Public Function Function1(A)
    Function1 = A + 2
    MsgBox "This is Function1 in module bas1."
End Function
```

3. Click in the form and switch to Design view. Create a new command button and set its Name property to cmdButton3 and its Caption property to Call a procedure in another module. Create the event procedure below for the button's Click event. Because there are two Function1 procedures, VBA will have to make a choice.

```
Private Sub cmdButton3_Click()
    Call Function1(3)
    MsgBox "This is cmdButton3_Click in module Form_frm1."
End Sub
```

4. Switch to Form view. As before, the expression in the text box's Control-Source property calls Function1 with argument 2. Click the OK button.

5. Click the new button. The message box indicates the choice VBA makes: VBA runs the Function1 procedure in the form module. When a procedure calls a second procedure, VBA looks for the called procedure in the same module first; if the called procedure isn't in the module, VBA looks for the called procedure in other modules. In this case, VBA found a Function1 procedure in the form module and ran it. To call the Function1 procedure in the

standard module, you have to include a reference to the module name (the fully qualified reference for the procedure).

6. Click in the form module and modify the event procedure shown below.

```
Private Sub cmdButton3_Click()
    Call bas1.Function1(3)
    MsgBox "This is cmdButton3_Click in module Form_frm1."
End Sub
```

7. Click the new button. This time, VBA runs the Function1 procedure in the standard module.

**Hiding a Procedure**   When you use the built-in event procedure code building tools, the code template for the event procedure includes the Private keyword. In VBA, you can decide which procedures in your application can use a specified procedure. You can make a procedure available only to other procedures stored in the same module and hide the procedure from procedures stored in other modules by using the Private keyword in the first line of the procedure's declaration statement.

1. Click in the bas1 module and change Public to Private in the first line of the Function1 declaration statement. With this declaration, the procedure is available only to other procedures in the bas1 module.

2. Click in the form and then click the new button. Access is unable to run the procedure and displays the error message shown in Figure 12.11a. When you use the Private keyword to hide a procedure, the procedure is not visible to procedures in other modules. From the viewpoint of a procedure in the form module, the Function1 procedure in bas1 doesn't exist, so the run-time error is generated.

3. Click OK. The module window displays clues to the problem: VBA highlights the name of the procedure that failed, displays an arrow in the margin at the left, and changes the background color for the code statement that failed (see Figure 12.11b). You'll learn about the troubleshooting tools in Chapter 15.

4. Click the Close box of the module window. Click Yes to reset the code and stop running the procedure.

**FIGURE 12.11:**

The run-time error when
you call a Private proce-
dure from a procedure in
a different module (a).
When a procedure fails,
VBA highlights the name
of the procedure and
changes the background
color for the statement
that failed (b).

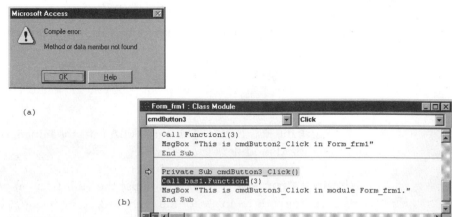

These simple examples demonstrate several important concepts, including:

- Calling a procedure as the result of an event

- Calling a function procedure in an expression

- Calling procedures from other procedures

- Calling another procedure in the same module and in a different module

- Using the fully qualified reference when procedures in two modules have the same name

- Hiding a procedure from procedures in other modules

These examples are especially simple because they don't use variables (except for the argument of the function procedure). The rest of this chapter explains more fully the mechanics of creating and running procedures.

# The Access VBA Programming Environment

We begin our study of the Access VBA programming environment with an investigation of the Module view and the mechanics of creating and editing code.

## Module View

You create code in a module window in the Module view. To display a module, do the the following:

**Standard module**   You open a new standard module by pressing the New button in the Modules pane of the Database window or by clicking the New Object button in the toolbar and choosing Module. If you are in Module view, you can open a new standard module by choosing Insert ➤ Module or by clicking the Insert Module button in the toolbar. You open an existing standard module by selecting the module in the Database window and double-clicking or by clicking the Design button.

**Form or Report module**   You open a form or report module by opening the form or report in Design view and choosing View ➤ Code from the menu or clicking the Code button on the toolbar. You can open a form or report and its module simultaneously by selecting the form or report in the Database window and clicking the Code button in the toolbar. (By default, a new form or report doesn't have a module and the form or report is called lightweight. Access creates the form's or report's module the first time you try to open the module.) A form or report module is saved along with the form or report and is not listed in the Modules pane of the Database window.

**Independent Class module**   You open a new independent class module by clicking the New Object button in the toolbar and choosing Class Module. If you are in module Design view, you can open a new independent class module by choosing the Insert ➤ Class Module command in the menu or by clicking the Class Module button in the toolbar. When you save an independent class module, it is listed within the Modules tab of the Database window along with the standard modules; VBA uses different icons for standard and independent modules (see Figure 12.12). You open an existing independent class module by selecting the module in the Database window and double-clicking or clicking the Design button.

In each case, the module window opens, displaying the Declarations section with the default options; the window's title bar indicates the name and type of the module (see Figure 12.13).

FIGURE 12.12:

Standard modules and independent class modules are listed with different icons in the Database window.

FIGURE 12.13:

The Module window for a standard module (a), a form module (b), and an independent class module (c). The title bar displays the module's name and type.

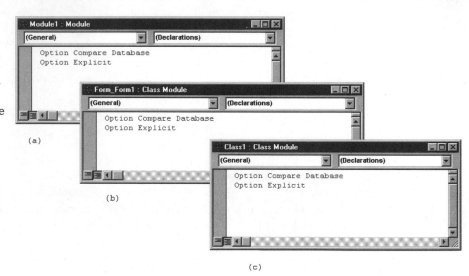

You use the two combo boxes below the Module window title bar to determine the contents of the module as follows:

**Standard module**   The combo box on the left displays (General) as its only item. The (General) item represents the module itself. The combo box on the right displays (Declarations) as the first item followed by the names of the general procedures in the module. Figure 12.14 displays the procedures stored in the UtilityFunctions standard module in the orders.mdb sample application. The (Declarations) item represents the declarations section of the

**FIGURE 12.14:**

The combo box on the right lists the procedures stored in the standard module.

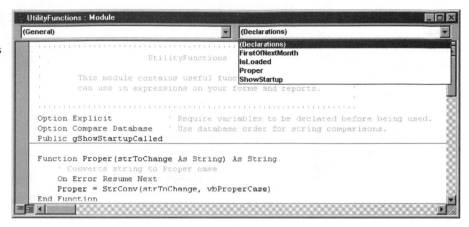

module. When you select a procedure name from the list, the code for the procedure is displayed.

**Form or Report module** The combo box on the left in Figure 12.15 lists (General) followed by a list of objects associated with the form or report, including the name of each control that recognizes events, the name of each section displayed, and the form or report itself indicated by Form or Report. Figure 12.15a shows the list of objects in the Orders form in the orders.mdb database. When you select the (General) item, the combo box on the right displays (Declarations) as the first item, followed by the names of the general procedures in the module; when you select a general procedure name from the list, the module window displays the code for the procedure. When you select an object from the combo box on the left, the combo box on the right displays a list of the events that the object recognizes. When the module contains an event procedure for an object's event, that event is shown in bold (see Figure 12.15b). When you select an event shown in bold, the corresponding event procedure is displayed. For example, Figure 12.15b shows the Form_AfterUpdate event procedure. When you select an event that is not listed in bold, VBA creates and displays a code template for the event procedure; once the code template for an event has been created, the list displays the event in bold even if you don't enter any code between the lines of the template. After you delete an event procedure or the code template for an event, the list displays the event in regular font.

FIGURE 12.15:

The combo boxes for a form or report module provide an inventory of the module. The Object combo box lists the objects in the form or report (a) and the Procedures combo box lists the events recognized by a selected object (b).

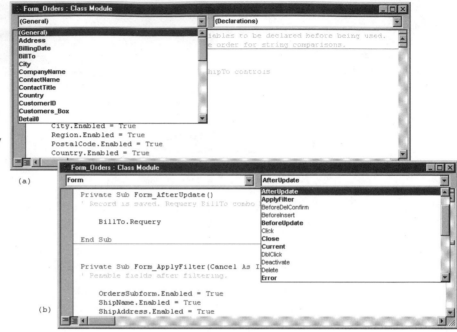

You can navigate through all the procedures in a module using shortcut keys: pressing Ctrl+Up Arrow or Ctrl+Down Arrow displays the previous or next procedure, respectively.

## Viewing an Event Procedure Directly

Another way to view a particular event procedure is to click into the event property in the object's property sheet. If an event procedure exists for an event, the event's property setting is [Event Procedure]; clicking the Build button at the right of the property box opens the form or report module and displays the event procedure. You can create a new event procedure for an event by clicking the Build button to the right of the event's property box and choosing Code Builder in the Choose Builder dialog box (see Figure 12.6a); when you click OK, the form or report module opens, displaying the stub for the event procedure. The next section describes a faster way to display an event procedure.

## Setting Options

This section explores the many options you can set when working in VBA. To set options, select Tools ➤ Options. The Options dialog will appear.

**String Comparisons**　By default, the first statement in the Declarations section of a module is the Option Compare Database statement, which indicates that VBA is using the same sort order for comparing string expressions in the module that Access is using to compare string expressions in the database. You can change the alphabet that is used for string comparisons in the General pane of the Options dialog box. The combo box list for the New Database Sort Order displays the available sort orders (see Figure 12.16).

**FIGURE 12.16:**

Use the General pane of the Options dialog to change the alphabet that Access uses to compare and sort strings.

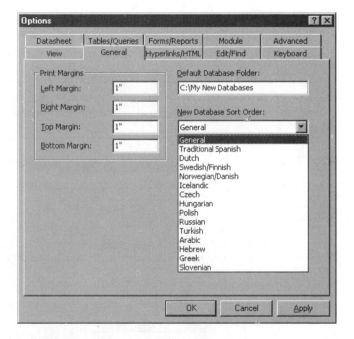

The default General value represents a case-insensitive sort order based on the English alphabet. If you change the setting, the sort order is changed only for new databases; existing databases, including the current database, are not affected.

The syntax for the Option Compare statement is

Option Compare {Binary | Text | Database}

Using Binary results in string comparisons made according to a case-sensitive sort order that is based on the ASCII code for the characters. Using Text results in case-insensitive string comparisons based on the ASCII code. Normally, you use the default; if you don't include an Option Compare statement, VBA uses Option Compare Binary.

> **TIP**
>
> You can change the default folder that Access displays when you choose the Open Database command in the File menu by entering the path of the folder in the Default Database Folder text box in the General Pane of the Options dialog.

**Module Options**   Click the Module tab to display the module options that you can change. There are three categories of options: code colors and font, coding options, and window settings (see Figure 12.17).

**Code Colors and Font**   You can set the font color and background for different types of code. The text area combo box lists the types of code, including, for example, normal text, comment text, and keyword text.

**FIGURE 12.17:**

The module options with the default settings

After you select the type of text, you select foreground and background colors using their combo boxes.

**Comment text**   It is very helpful to display comments in another color. You use the apostrophe (') to indicate comments; characters on the same line and to the right of an apostrophe are ignored by VBA. Comments can identify the purpose of your code and make it more readable. Comments can appear on a separate line or to the right of a VBA statement or declaration; Figure 12.14 shows both comment styles.

**Keyword text**   It is also helpful to display keywords in another color. Keywords are the words that VBA reserves for its own use. When you type a keyword correctly, VBA colors the word. If you have made a typographical error, the word is not colored. To avoid typographical errors, color keywords in another color.

You can change the font and font size for all of the text in your modules by choosing from the Font and Size combo lists.

**Coding Options**   Coding options help you to write VBA code more quickly. The coding options you can set are described in Table 12.5. (Table 12.5 is on the CD under Tables\Chapter12.pdf.) Access 97 introduces several new options to help in writing code, including Auto List Members, Auto Quick Info, and Auto Data Tips.

**Window Settings**   The window settings you can change are described in Table 12.6. (Table 12.6 is on the CD under Tables\Chapter12.pdf.)

Another way to change the way a module is displayed is to split the window into two panes by choosing Window ➤ Split Window. You can scroll the panes independently and work with two procedures in the same module (see Figure 12.18). With the window split into two panes, you can switch between the upper and lower panes by pressing the F6 function key.

**TIP**

You can make creating new event procedures more efficient by checking the Always Use Event Procedures option on the Forms/Reports tab (see Figure 12.19). Checking this option eliminates the Code Builder dialog. When you click the Build button to the right of an event property, the form or report module opens immediately and displays the code template for the new event procedure.

**FIGURE 12.18:**

You can split a module window into two panes and scroll each pane independently.

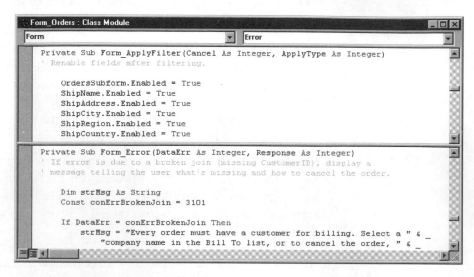

**FIGURE 12.19:**

Check the Always Use Event Procedures option to eliminate the Code Builder dialog for new event procedures.

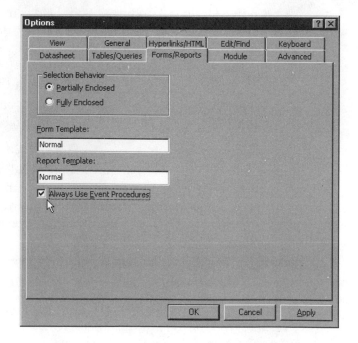

## Module Menu Commands and Toolbar

The menus in module Design view contain commands to help you create, edit, run, and troubleshoot procedures. The module toolbar includes toolbar buttons for most of the commands. Table 12.7 describes the Visual Basic toolbar buttons. Table 12.8 lists most of the additional menu commands specific to modules that aren't represented by default toolbar buttons. (Both tables are on the CD under Tables\Chapter12.pdf.) We'll discuss the tools for editing and running procedures in this chapter and discuss the debugging tools, including breakpoints and the watch commands, in Chapter 15.

Table 12.8 includes the new Access 97 commands in the Edit menu that you can use to display lists of properties, methods, constants, parameters, or syntax information for selected code in the Module window. For example, if you type DoCmd and choose the List Properties/Methods command, VBA displays a small list box in the module window with a list of the methods of the DoCmd object. Double-click a selected item to insert the item at the insertion point (see Figure 12.20a). If you type IsNull and choose the Quick Info command, VBA displays a small text box with the syntax for the built-in function (see Figure 12.20b).

## Setting Bookmarks in Code

Another new feature in Access 97 is the ability to save your place in a procedure by setting a bookmark. To set a bookmark, place the insertion point in the line of code you want to mark, choose Edit ➤ Bookmark, and then choose Bookmark from the fly-out menu. VBA displays a blue rectangle in the margin indicator bar to the left of the line of code (see Figure 12.20c). You can set as many bookmarks as you need in a module and browse the bookmarks using the Next Bookmark and Previous Bookmark commands in the Bookmark fly-out menu. You can remove all bookmarks in the active module by choosing the Clear All Bookmarks command in the fly-out menu.

Use menu commands to display a list of properties and methods (a); display the syntax for a variable, constant, or method (b); or set a bookmark to quickly return to a marked line of code (c).

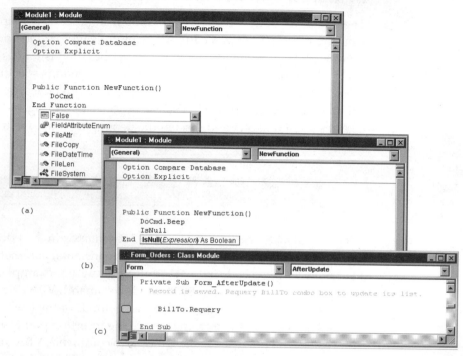

(a)

(b)

(c)

## Editing in the Module Window

Writing VBA code is similar to writing text. In fact, you can create procedures in any text editor, such as Notepad, and then paste them into VBA modules. The usual text editing tools are available in Module view. You can cut, copy, and paste text selections using menu commands or the usual keyboard short cuts Ctrl+X, Ctrl+C, and Ctrl+V. You can also clear a selection without placing a copy on the Clipboard by choosing Edit ➤ Clear. New to Access 97 is the drag-and-drop feature, which you can use to move selected text to another location.

You can use the familiar Find or Replace commands on the Edit menu to search for a specified text expression or search for a specified text expression and replace it with another expression; you can search for the specified string in the current procedure, the current module, or in all modules of the current database (see Figure 12.21).

**FIGURE 12.21:**

**FIGURE 12.21:**

Use the Find dialog to search in the current procedure, the current module, or all modules in the current database.

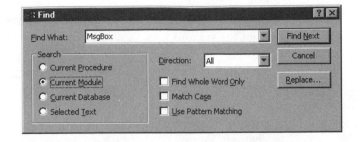

## Syntax Checking

To enable automatic syntax checking, select the Auto Syntax Check option in the Module pane of the Options dialog. As you type statements, VBA processes your entry, looking for grammatical errors. Figure 12.22 shows typical syntax error checking messages, including messages that a statement is missing a parenthesis (Figure 12.22a); that you have misspelled a keyword in a structure, such as "Thn" instead of "Then" in an "If...Then" structure (Figure 12.22b); and that you omitted a required part of a structure, such as typing Do Until without entering a condition (Figure 12.22c).

**FIGURE 12.22:**

Typical syntax error-checking messages

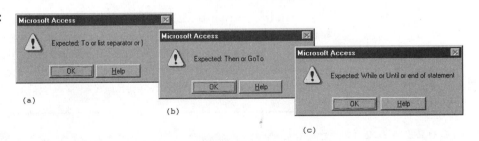

With Auto Syntax Check turned on, Access may reformat your statement by adding or removing spaces, may change the capitalization of keywords and variables to match the capitalization in the variable declaration statement, and may correct minor syntax errors such as adding a missing double-quotation mark.

# Programming Style

As you write code, consider the following recommendations for making your code easier to read and understand:

**Indent**. Normally a procedure has several sections. There may be a section for error-handling code, groups of code lines for repetitive operations, alternative groups of statements to be executed under some conditions but not under other conditions. Indenting lines is a useful way to identify code sections. Figure 12.23 shows the IsLoaded function procedure that determines if a particular form is loaded. Even before studying how to write code that makes decisions, you can easily observe the structure of the code because of the levels of indentation.

**Use comments**. As you are creating code, the purpose and logic of a procedure's statements may seem obvious. Days or weeks later, the logic may be elusive to you and downright opaque to someone else. You can save yourself and others time and effort by commenting your code. You should include comments at the beginning of a procedure to describe the procedure's purpose, the arguments, and the value returned by a function procedure. While it is unnecessary and probably excessive to comment every line of code, you should at least include a comment to explain the logic of each group of statements.

**Use naming conventions**. Chapter 2 discusses the importance of naming conventions for naming the objects you create in your application. With a properly chosen, consistently applied naming convention for procedures, objects, constants, and variables, your VBA code becomes more self-documenting and easier to understand.

**FIGURE 12.23:**

Indenting makes the structure of code easier to understand.

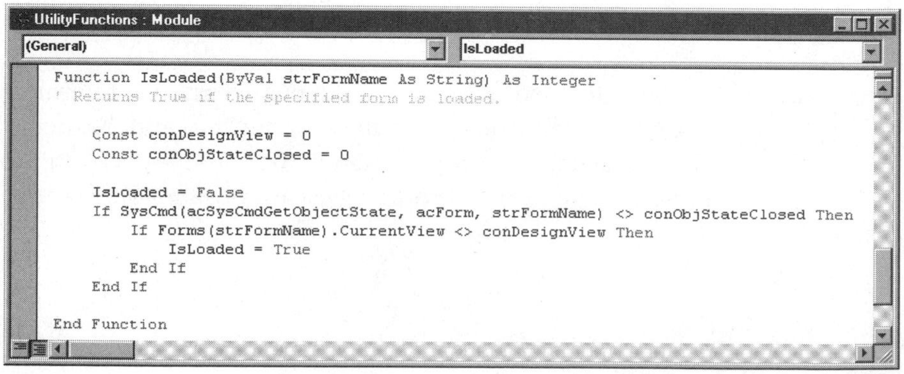

```
UtilityFunctions : Module
(General)                                    IsLoaded

Function IsLoaded(ByVal strFormName As String) As Integer
    ' Returns True if the specified form is loaded.

    Const conDesignView = 0
    Const conObjStateClosed = 0

    IsLoaded = False
    If SysCmd(acSysCmdGetObjectState, acForm, strFormName) <> conObjStateClosed Then
        If Forms(strFormName).CurrentView <> conDesignView Then
            IsLoaded = True
        End If
    End If

End Function
```

**Use separate lines for each statement**. While you can string together several statements separated by colons (:) on a single line, doing so may make your code difficult to read.

**Use the line continuation character**. The Module window does not have a word wrapping feature. If you enter a very long statement, you can "wrap" the statement yourself using the *line continuation character*. The line continuation character consists of a space followed by an underscore (_). If you don't break the line with the line continuation character, you will have to use the horizontal scroll bar to view parts of the statement. You can't use the line continuation character to wrap a string expression to another line; instead you can divide the string into smaller pieces and concatenate the pieces (see Chapter 18 for examples).

**Declare variables and constants at the beginning of a procedure**. By grouping all declaration statements at the beginning of a procedure, you can see the constants and variables at a glance and avoid having to hunt through procedure code to find them.

## The Access VBA Compiler

The statements that you enter into a module are called *source code*. Access doesn't run the statements as you enter them. Before you can run a procedure, Access must first compile it. Compiling is the process of converting the readable source code that you entered into a format called a *compiled state* that the computer can run. Compilation prepares your code for execution but doesn't execute it. During compiling, Access views the procedure as a whole and checks for errors that may involve more than one statement. Errors that Access detects during compiling are called *compile-time* errors. When Access discovers compile-time errors, an error message is displayed. Figure 12.24 shows typical compile-time errors. Access won't run the procedure until you eliminate the source of the error. See Chapter 15 for more information on the Access VBA compiler and dealing with errors.

**FIGURE 12.24:**

Typical compile-time error messages

## Saving a Database without Source Code

A new feature of Access 97 is that you can save a version of a database with Visual Basic code as a new type of file called an *mde file* that includes only the compiled version and has the source code removed. An mde file has the following features:

- The forms, reports and modules cannot be changed.

- Modules cannot be viewed. Your code is fully secured and cannot be read or used by others.

- The mde file is smaller than the original database file.

- Memory usage is optimized and performance may improve.

- Forms, reports, and modules cannot be imported or exported, however, tables, queries, and macros can be imported or exported to non-mde databases.

- You cannot change references to object libraries or databases.

- You cannot change the VBA project name for the database.

To create an mde file:

1. Close the database. If you are in a multi-user environment, all copies of the database must be closed.

2. Choose Tools ➤ Database Utilities and then the Make MDE File command in the fly-out menu. Select the database in the Database To Save As MDE dialog, and then click the Make MDE button (see Figure 12.25a).

3. Specify the name of the new file and select the folder for storing the file in the Save MDE As dialog and then click the Save button (see Figure 12.25b).

**WARNING** You should always save the original version of the database that you use to create an mde file. If you need to change the forms, reports, or modules, you must make the changes to the original database and then create a new mde file. In addition, you probably won't be able to run or convert an mde file in future versions of Access, but you will be able to convert the original database file.

**FIGURE 12.25:**

Creating an mde file with the VBA source code removed

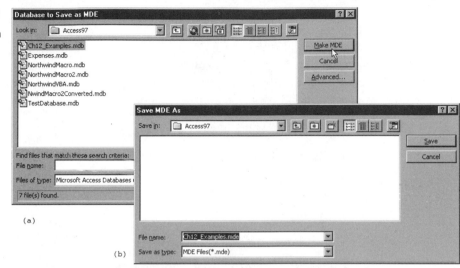

(a)

(b)

Creating an mde file is a simple way to secure the forms, reports, and modules in your database against changes without implementing user-level security. However, if you later make changes to the original file and prepare a new mde file for your users, you'll have to deal with the fact that users have probably changed the data in the mde file they have been using. To avoid data reconciliation problems between the two mde files, you can split the database application into a front-end database containing all the database objects except the data tables and a back-end database containing the data tables. Save only the front-end database as an mde file linked to the data tables in the back-end database. Later, you can make changes to the original front-end database (as long as you don't change the structure of the database that require changes to the back-end database), save the changes to a new mde file, and give the new mde file to your users to use with the back-end database.

There are some restrictions to saving a database as an mde file. For example, if the database refers to other databases or add-ins, that is, if you have set a reference to another database or an add-in in the References dialog, you must save all of the other databases and add-ins as mde files. For more information on the restrictions, search for mde files in online Help.

# Running Procedures

This section looks at calling procedures. (The terms call and run are used interchangeably.) Because a function procedure can return a value but a sub procedure cannot, you have more flexibility in calling function procedures; for example, you can call a function procedure but not a sub procedure in an expression.

## Running Function Procedures

The following is a list of the ways you can call a function procedure:

- Call in an expression
- Run in the Debug window
- Call from a procedure in the same module
- Call from a procedure in another module
- Trigger by an event
- Call from a macro
- Call from another application

> **NOTE** When you call a function procedure in an expression, VBA uses the function's return value in evaluating the expression. In all other ways of calling a function, VBA discards the return value.

### Call in an Expression

You can call a function procedure in an expression the same way you call a built-in function: you can include a function procedure in expressions for calculated fields or criteria cells in queries, in expressions for calculated controls on forms and reports, in macro conditions and action arguments, in property settings, and in expressions used in VBA statements and SQL statements. For example, the Concatenate function below is useful for concatenating a person's first and last names into the last name, first name format.

```
Public Function Concatenate (A,B)
    Concatenate = A & ", " & B
```

```
    MsgBox "This is the Concatenate procedure in bas2"
End Function
```

The function has the arguments A and B; when you pass values for the arguments, the function concatenates the values with the string ", " between them and returns the string. To see the function in action:

1.  Create a new standard module named bas2 in Ch12_Examples. Choose Insert ➤ Procedure and create a new procedure named Concatenate with the Function type and Public scope.

2.  Enter the two lines of code for the Concatenate function procedure.

3.  Import the Employees table from the Northwind database. Create a new query named qryEmployees based on the Employees table and enter the following expression in the first Field cell:

    FullName: Concatenate(LastName, FirstName)

4.  Run the query.

When you run the query, VBA executes the following sequence for each row in the query result: first, it calculates the return value of the function and holds the value in memory, then it displays the message, and then it creates and displays the calculated field in the query's datasheet (see Figure 12.26).

**FIGURE 12.26:**

The Field cell expression in the query calls the Concatenate function for each row in the query result.

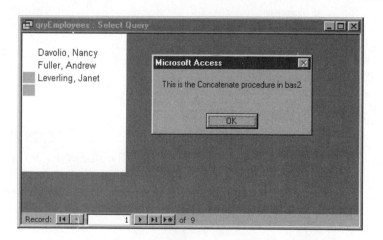

**NOTE**   We include the MsgBox function in most of the procedures in the chapter as a learning tool or as a troubleshooting tool to observe when a procedure runs. You can comment out, or delete, the statements with the MsgBox function when you use the procedures in an application.

## Run in the Debug Window

The Debug window is an extremely useful tool for running procedures. Because it is a debugging tool, the Debug window has the advantage of better eyesight: the Debug window sees and can run both public and private procedures if you use a fully qualified reference. The syntax you use to run a function procedure depends on whether it is stored in a standard module or a form or report module and whether you want to use the return value.

**Running a Function Procedure Stored in a Standard Module**    If the function is stored in a standard module, you can print the return value by typing **? functionname (argumentlist)** and pressing Enter. If you want to use the return value in another statement, you can create a variable in the Debug window to hold the function's return value as follows:

> **var = functionname (argumentlist)** if the function returns a value, or
>
> **Set objvar = functionname (argumentlist)** if the function returns an object.

 For example, open the Debug window by clicking the Debug window button in the toolbar.

1. Type **? Concatenate("Shaw","Cameron")** and press Enter. The function runs, the message is displayed, and the result is printed in the Debug window.

2. Type **var = Concatenate("Shaw","Cameron")** and press Enter. The message is displayed and the returned value is stored in the variable.

3. Type **?var** and press Enter. The stored result is printed in the Debug window.

If you don't need the return value of a function stored in a standard module, you can run the function in the Debug window using either of the following:

> Call *functionname* (*argumentlist*)
>
> *functionname argumentlist*

If you use the Call keyword to call a function procedure that requires arguments, you must enclose the argument list in parentheses. If the function doesn't require arguments, you can include or omit the parentheses. If you omit the Call keyword, you must also omit the parentheses enclosing the argument list. When you use either of these statements, VBA throws away the function's return value. For example, in the Debug window,

1. Type **Call Concatenate ("Shaw", "Cameron")** and press Enter. VBA runs the function, displays the message, and throws away the function's return value; the insertion point just moves to the next line without printing anything.

2. Type **Concatenate "Shaw", "Cameron"** and press Enter—you get the same result.

3. Type **Concatenate ("Shaw", "Cameron")** and press Enter. VBA generates an error and displays an error message (see Figure 12.27).

**FIGURE 12.27:**

The error message when you omit the Call keyword but enclose the arguments in parentheses

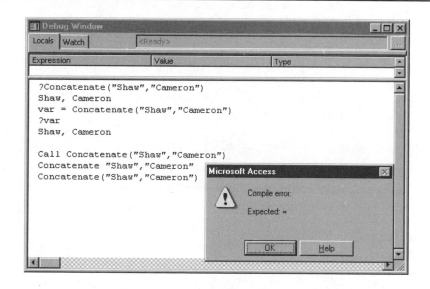

You can run both public and private function procedures in the Debug window. To run a private function in the Debug window, you must use the full identifier. For example:

1. Change Public to Private as the keyword in the declaration statement of the Concatenate function in the bas2 module.

2. Type **?bas2.Concatenate ("Shaw", "Cameron")** and press Enter. VBA runs the Concatenate procedure, displays the message, and displays the returned value.

3. Type **?Concatenate ("Shaw", "Cameron")** and press Enter. VBA generates a run-time error when you try to run a private function without including the module name in the reference.

4. Change Private back to Public as the keyword in the declaration statement of the Concatenate function.

**Running a Function Procedure Stored in a Form or Report Module**   If the function procedure is stored in a form or report module, you must use the full identifier of the function in these expressions. For example, if a function in a form module returns a value, you can print the value in the Debug window using the syntax

> ? Form_*formname.functionname* (*argumentlist*)

and you can run the function and discard its return value using the syntax

> Call Form_*formname.functionname* (*argumentlist*)

The form or report does not have to be open in order to run a procedure in its module. In the Debug window,

1. Type **? Form_frm1.Function1(3)** and press Enter. VBA runs the function, displays the message, and prints 4 (Function1 adds one to the argument and returns the sum). Make sure the frm1 form is closed when you call the function.

2. Type **?Function1(3)** and press Enter. When you try to run a function in a form or report module in the Debug window without including the reference to the module, a run-time error occurs (see Figure 12.28).

---

**FIGURE 12.28:**

The run-time error when you run a function in a form module in the Debug window without including the reference to the module

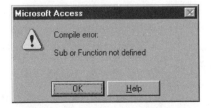

## Call from a Procedure in the Same Module

When you call a function procedure from another function or sub procedure, the syntax you use depends on whether you want to use the function's return value.

If you want to use the return value, you must use the function procedure in an expression in a VBA statement. For example,

1.  Create a new function procedure named GetReturnValue in the bas2 module as shown below. The GetReturnValue function calls the Concatenate function as an argument of the Msgbox function and displays the returned value in a message box.

```
Public Function GetReturnValue()
    Msgbox Concatenate ("Shaw", "Cameron")
End Sub
```

2.  Run the GetReturnValue function in the Debug window by typing **Call GetReturnValue()** and pressing Enter. You can also call the function by typing **GetReturnValue** and pressing Enter. Because the GetReturnValue function has no arguments, you can also call the function by typing **Call GetReturnValue** and pressing Enter. Notice that the GetReturnValue function does not have a return value.

If you don't need its return value, you can run the function procedure from another function or sub procedure using either of the following statements:

Call *functionname (argumentlist)*

*functionname argumentlist*

The syntax depends on whether you use the Call keyword. If you use the Call keyword to call a function procedure that requires arguments, you must enclose the argument list in parentheses. If the function doesn't require arguments, you can include or omit the parentheses. If you don't use the Call keyword, you must omit the parenthesis around the argument list. In either case, the function's return value is discarded. For example, the DiscardReturn function below runs the Concatenate function discarding the return value. The DiscardReturn function takes no arguments and doesn't return a value.

```
Public Function DiscardReturnValue()
    Call Concatenate ("Shaw", "Cameron")
End Sub
```

1. Enter the DiscardReturnValue function in bas2.

2. Run the function in the Debug window by typing **Call DiscardReturnValue** and pressing Enter. VBA runs the Concatenate function, displays the message, and discards the return value.

3. Modify the procedure by omitting both the Call keyword and the parentheses as follows:

```
Public Function DiscardReturnValue()
    Concatenate "Shaw", "Cameron"
End Sub
```

4. Run the function by typing **DiscardReturnValue** and pressing Enter.

## Call from a Procedure in Another Module

You can call a public, but not a private, function procedure from a procedure stored in another module. If you are calling a public function procedure in another module, you may need to include the module name in the reference. For example, the function procedure RunFormFunction shown below runs the public Function1 function in the form module of the frm1 form.

```
Public Function RunPublicFunction()
    MsgBox Form_frm1.Function1(3)
End Function
```

1. Enter the RunPublicFunction procedure in the bas2 module.

2. Type **Call RunPublicFunction** in the Debug window and press Enter. The Function1 procedure runs and displays its message boxes.

3. Enter the RunPrivateFunction procedure in the bas2 module as follows:

```
Public Function RunPrivateFunction()
    MsgBox bas1.Function1(3)
End Function
```

4. Type **Call RunPrivateFunction** in the Debug window and press Enter. VBA generates a run-time error because you can't run a private procedure stored in another module (see Figure 12.29). VBA highlights the name of the procedure, displays an arrow in the margin bar, and changes the background color of the statement that failed.

5. Click the Reset button in the toolbar to reset the code.

FIGURE 12.29:

The run-time error when you try to run a private procedure stored in another module

## Trigger by an Event

You can use an event to trigger a function. To run a function when an event occurs, use the following syntax in the event's property box:

= *functionname(argumentlist)*

The parentheses are required even if the function has no arguments. The function's return value, if there is one, is discarded. For example:

1. Select the frm1 form in the Database window and click the Code button in the toolbar. The form and its module open.

2. Click the Insert button in the toolbar and choose Procedure. Name the new procedure EventFunction and then choose the function type and public scope.

3. Enter the EventFunction below. This function takes no arguments and returns the value True.

```
Public Function EventFunction()
    EventFunction = True
    MsgBox "This is the EventFunction in the Form_frm1 module"
End Function
```

4. Click in the Detail section, click the OnClick event property box, and type **= EventFunction()** Save the form and switch to Form view.

5. When the Function1 function procedure finishes running, double-click in the form's detail section; VBA runs the EventFunction procedure, displays its message box, and discards the function's return value.

The syntax for the event property setting uses the function name without a qualifying module name; in fact, you cannot use the fully qualified reference for a procedure as the event property setting. This means that you can use an event to trigger a public function stored in a standard module, as long as the function's name is unique and doesn't require the fully qualified reference, but you can't trigger a public function stored in another form or report module because using a function in another form or report module requires the fully qualified reference. For example:

1. Switch to Design view, click in the txtCalculate text box, and then click in the OnClick property. We'll use the Click event of the txtCalculate text box to trigger the Concatenate function stored in the bas2 standard module.

2. Type = **Concatenate ("Shaw", "Cameron")** in the property box. Save the form and switch to Form view.

3. When the Function1 function finishes running, click the text box. VBA runs the Concatenate function, displays its message, and discards the returned value.

## Call from a Macro

To run a function procedure from a macro, use the RunCode macro action. Use the following syntax for the action's Function Name argument:

> *functionname* (*argumentlist*)

Include arguments in parenthesis and do not use an equal sign. The function's return value is discarded. The syntax for the Function Name argument requires an unqualified function name. This means that you can use the RunCode action to run a public function stored in a standard module if you don't have to qualify its name. In addition, if the macro action runs in response to an event on a form or report, Access looks for the function first in the form or report module before looking in standard modules, so in this case you can also run a function stored in a form or report module.

For an example of how to run a function in a standard module, we'll run the Concatenate function:

1. Open a new macrosheet named mcrRunCode. Select the RunCode action in the first action cell and set the Function Name argument to Concatenate ("Shaw", "Cameron"). Figure 12.30 shows the macrosheet.

2. Save the macrosheet. Click the Run button in the macro toolbar. Access runs the macro. The macro runs the Concatenate function, which displays its message, discards the function's return value, and then quits.

FIGURE 12.30:

You can run a function
procedure from a macro.

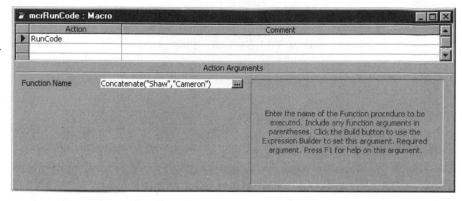

## Call from Another Application

You can use the Run method to run a function from another application through
Automation, using the syntax:

*Application.Run functionname[, argument1, argument2, ..., argumentN]*

Access ignores the function's return value.

# Running Sub Procedures

The following is a list of ways to call a Sub procedure:

- Trigger by an event
- Run in the Debug window
- Call from another procedure
- Call from another application

The main difference between a Sub and a Function procedure is that you can't call a
Sub by using its name in an expression. You also can't call a Sub procedure directly
from a macro.

**Trigger by an Event**   When you create an event procedure by clicking the
Build button at the right of an event property box and entering code between the

lines of the code template that Access provides, the sub procedure is automatically assigned to the event and runs when the event is recognized. Access automatically names the procedure using the syntax Form_*eventname* or Report_*eventname* for an event recognized by a form or a report and the syntax *objectname_eventname* for an event recognized by an object. Access also includes the predefined argument list for the event procedure. After naming the procedure, Access sets the event property to [Event Procedure]. If you want to create an event procedure from scratch, you must follow the same rules:

- You must use the same naming convention and the same argument list.

- You must store the procedure in the form's or report's module.

- You must set the event property to [Event Procedure].

As an example, we'll create an event procedure from scratch to close a form:

1. Open the frm1 form in Design view, place a command button on the form, and set the Name property to cmdClose and the Caption property to Close.

2. Click the Code button in the toolbar and place the insertion point in the line following the last statement in the module.

3. Enter the following procedure at the insertion point

```
Private Sub cmdclose_Click()
    DoCmd.Close
    Msgbox "This is cmdclose_Click in module Form_frm1"
End Sub
```

When you enter the first line, VBA automatically inserts a procedure separator and completes the code template. Access matches the event procedure name with the new button and automatically assigns the procedure to the button's Click event. Click in the property sheet of the command button to observe the assignment.

4. Save the form and switch to Form view. The Function1 procedure runs.

5. Click the Close button. Access closes the form and then displays the message for the cmdClose_Click event procedure.

**NOTE**

If you change the name of a control after assigning an event procedure to it, VBA won't be able to match the event procedure to the control. VBA moves the event procedure to the General section of the module. You must change the event procedure's name so that it matches the new name of the control. Select (General) from the Object combo box, select the event procedure from the Procedure combo box, change the event procedure's name, and save the form.

**TIP**

When you copy and paste a control with event procedures to another form, the event procedure is not copied to the form module of the new form. If you want to be able to copy and paste procedures along with controls, use event-handling function procedures instead of event procedures and store the functions in a standard module.

**Run in the Debug window**    You run a Sub procedure in the Debug window using the same syntax that you use to run a function when the return value is discarded. The syntax you use depends on whether the Sub procedure is stored in a standard module or a form or report module When the sub procedure is stored in a standard module, use either syntax below:

> Call *subroutinename* (*argumentlist*)
>
> *subroutinename argumentlist*

If the sub procedure is stored in a form or report module, you must use the fully qualified reference for the function in these expressions; for example:

> Form_*formname.subroutinename argumentlist*

You can run both public and private sub procedures in the Debug window. A form or report must be open in order to run a sub procedure in its module. By contrast, a form or report does not have to be open in order to run in the Debug window a function procedure stored in its module. For example, to call the event procedure for the cmdButton1 button on the frm1 form, open the frm1 form in Design or Form view, type **Call Form_frm1.cmdButton1_Click** in the Debug window, and press Enter. VBA runs the event procedure and displays its message.

**Call from Another Procedure**   You run a Sub procedure from another procedure using the same syntax that you use to run a function (when the return value is discarded). The syntax you use depends on whether you use the Call keyword. If you use the Call keyword to call a sub procedure that requires arguments, you must enclose the argument list in parenthesis. If the sub procedure doesn't require arguments, you can include or omit the parentheses.

Call *subroutinename* (*argumentlist*)

*subroutinename argumentlist*

**Cannot Call in an Expression**   Because a sub procedure doesn't return a value, you can't use a sub procedure in an expression. If you want to run a sub procedure as part of an expression, you can create a function that calls the subroutine and then use the function in an expression.

**Can't Call from a Macro Directly**   You can't call a sub procedure directly from a macro; however, you can create a function procedure that calls the sub procedure and run the function using the RunCode macro action.

**Call from Another Application**   You can use the Run method to run a sub procedure from another application through Automation using the syntax:

```
Application.Run subroutinename[, argument1, argument2, ...,
    argumentN]
```

# Summary

This chapter introduces you to some of the fundamentals of writing Access VBA code. The important points are:

- Access VBA has its own set of data types. While it is possible to avoid assigning data types yourself by letting VBA assign the Variant type for all variables, your code runs faster when you assign specific data types.

- Access VBA has an Object data type that you can use for object variables that refer to objects. In addition, there are subtypes for the Access and data access objects.

- There are two kinds of modules:

  **Standard modules** store procedures that are not associated with a specific object.

  **Class modules** store the definitions for new objects. There are two kinds of class modules: Independent class modules are not associated with a form or a report and are stored as separate objects in the database. Form or report modules are stored as part of a form or report.

- There are two kinds of procedures:

  **Function procedures** may return a value. Normally, you use function procedures in expressions, and VBA runs the procedure when the expression is evaluated. When you run a function procedure using any other calling technique, the function's return value is ignored.

  **Sub procedures** do not return a value. Normally, you store a sub procedure in a form's or report's module and run the procedure when an object on the form or report recognizes an event.

- The Access VBA programming environment includes a Module window in which you enter code statements and a set of built-in command bars with commands for creating, editing, and troubleshooting code. You can set module options, including changing the text colors, turning on syntax checking and code building tools, and changing the window display.

- You can save the database as an mde file in which the Visual Basic source code is removed and only the compiled version remains. The forms, reports, and modules in an mde file cannot be changed.

- You can run function procedures by calling them in expressions, calling them from other procedures, calling them from a macro or another application (using Automation), triggering them by events, and calling them in the Debug window.

- You can run sub procedures by calling them from other procedures, calling them from another application (using Automation), triggering them by events, and calling them in the Debug window.

The next chapter continues with the fundamentals of Access Visual Basic by introducing you to using variables and constants in procedures.

# THIRTEEN

# Mechanics of Procedures II: Using Variables

- Why use variables in procedures?

- Declaring variables and constants

- Understanding the lifetime and visibility of a variable

- Passing data to a procedure

- Understanding procedure-level and module-level variables and constants

- Using arrays

- Creating your own data types

In the last chapter you learned the basics of creating procedures and storing them in modules. This chapter continues to lay the foundation for creating VBA procedures by teaching you how to use variables in procedures. The use of variables is a fundamental difference between macro and VBA programming and is the key to creating reusable code. While the concept of a variable can be stated quite simply:

> A *variable* is a named location in memory that holds a value or refers to an object

the implementation of the concept in Access VBA is rather complicated because of the enormous flexibility that using variables provides. In this chapter we'll examine how to create a variable, how to share a variable with other procedures, how to pass variables when you call a procedure, and how to destroy a variable when you are finished with it. Because variables are kept in memory, we'll consider the effects that variables have on memory usage and performance. After discussing variables, the chapter covers creating custom constants and using arrays to work with several variables at the same time. In the last section of the chapter, you learn how to create your own data types.

**NOTE**  For hands-on experience with the concepts we'll explore in this chapter, create a copy of the Northwind database named Northwind_Ch13. Make sure that you have selected the Always Use Event Procedures option in the Forms/Reports tab in the Options dialog (available by choosing the Tools ➤ Options command).

# Using Variables in Procedures

All of the procedures you created in the the last chapter (in the Ch12_Examples.mdb database) are of the simplest variety:

- The code statements you wrote are trivial, because you were learning only how to create, store, and run procedures (we'll postpone more interesting and practical statements until later chapters).

- The use of variables was extremely limited because the procedures used variables only as arguments. When we ran procedures with arguments, we specified literal values for the arguments such as Concatenate( "Shaw", "Cameron") and Function1(3).

- We did not explicitly declare data types, so the arguments, the values we specified, and the function return values are all variants. As explained in the last chapter, the Variant data type uses more than twice as much memory as any other fundamental data type and causes slower performance than if we had declared a specific data type.

The purpose of this section is to learn how to use variables in procedures. Here are the two most important reasons for using variables:

- To create reusable code. If you can reuse procedures, you end up writing less code!

- To create faster code. Nobody wants slow code.

Two simple examples of how this works should remove any doubts you may have.

## Using Variables to Create Reusable Code

Suppose you are creating a switchboard form with command buttons to open other forms and hide the switchboard. The first approach is to place command buttons on the new switchboard and create event procedures to carry out the actions. To be specific, we'll go through the steps to open the Customers form in the Northwind application as follows:

1. Create a new form in Northwind_Ch13 named frmSwitchboard.

2. Place a command button on the form and set the Name property to cmdCustomers and the Caption property to Customers.

3. Click in the OnClick property and click the Build button to the right of the property box. Access creates and opens the form module and displays the code template for the event procedure.

4. Enter the event procedure shown below:

```
Private Sub cmdCustomers_Click()
    DoCmd.OpenForm "Customers"
    Forms!frmSwitchboard.Visible = False
End Sub
```

The cmdCustomers_Click procedure runs the OpenForm method of the DoCmd object to open the form. The procedure specifies the formname argument of the OpenForm method as the literal value "Customers". To hide the switchboard, the procedure sets the form's Visible property to False. With no more tasks to carry out, the procedure ends.

5. Save the form, switch to Form view, and click the button. The Customers form opens and the switchboard is hidden.

Now let's improve the procedure.

## Using the Me Property for Better Performance

In the cmdCustomers_Click procedure, in order to run the statement that hides the switchboard, Access has to deal with the hierarchical reference for the Visible property:

```
Forms!frmSwitchboard.Visible
```

Each level of the reference requires processing time. That is, each exclamation point and each dot represents execution time required to process the reference. You can avoid the hierarchy in this statement by using the special Me property. This property is one of the special optimization tools that Access provides when you are creating procedures in a form or report module. Using the Me property in a procedure in a form's or report's module is the fastest way to refer to the form or report because VBA doesn't have to take time to process a fully qualified reference. In this procedure, the first step towards improved performance is to replace Forms!frmSwitchboard with Me.

## Using an Argument Instead of a Literal

The switchboard form typically has several buttons to open different forms. Instead of creating a separate event procedure for each button, the goal is to create a single procedure that we can reuse. The first step in making an existing procedure reusable is to determine exactly what prevents it from being reusable. In the cmdCustomers_Click procedure, the problem is the presence of the literal "Customers" in the argument of the OpenForm method. We'll move the literal out of the procedure by replacing the literal in the OpenForm argument with a string variable that we'll name strFormname (using the str name tag because we are now concerning ourselves with data types) and then arrange to pass the literal back into the procedure as an argument of the procedure. You use the syntax

```
procedurename (argumentname [As datatype])
```

to declare the data type for an argument.

Using a "typed" argument, the procedure looks like this:

```
Private Sub cmdCustomers_Click(strFormname As String)
    DoCmd.OpenForm strFormname
    Me.Visible = False
End Sub
```

## Changing to a Function Procedure

The modified version of our procedure is no longer an event procedure, because, by definition, an event procedure for the Click event can't have any arguments. If you try to compile the procedure, VBA generates a compile error. There are two alternatives. We could change the name of this subprocedure so that it doesn't use the syntax reserved for an event procedure and call the subprocedure from a new event procedure. This isn't a very good solution, however, because we'd only be passing the problem of the literal to the new event procedure. If we rename the subprocedure to OpenAForm and call it from an event procedure, the literal is still part of the VBA code:

```
Private Sub cmdCustomers_Click()
    Call OpenAForm ("Customers")
End Sub
```

A literal value that is entered in the Module window is called a *hard-coded value* and usually prevents the code from being reusable.

A better solution is to change the procedure to a Function procedure named OpenAForm so that the literal can be entered in the property sheet instead of being hard-coded in the module. When you create a function procedure, VBA automatically sets aside a memory location for a return value, whether or not the function actually returns a result; if we don't specify a data type for this location, VBA assumes the Variant data type. To avoid the memory-hungry, performance-degrading Variant data type, we'll type the function's phantom return value as Integer. You specify the data type for a function procedure's return value in the function declaration statement using the following syntax:

```
[Public|Private] Function functionname [(argumentlist)] [As type]
```

The function procedure shown below

```
Public Function OpenAForm (strFormname As String) As Integer
DoCmd.OpenForm strFormname
Me.Visible = False
End Sub
```

can now be reused by other command buttons on the same form. You assign the function procedure to the Click event for a command button on the form using this syntax:

```
=OpenAForm("formname")
```

The next step is to make the function procedure reusable on any form. Because a fully reusable function procedure is not associated with a specific form, we'll store the function procedure in a standard module. A price of moving the procedure to a standard module is that you can no longer use the Me reference (you can use Me to refer to a form or report only in a procedure stored in the form's or report's module). To keep the procedure reusable, you can use the Screen object to refer to the form that holds the command button and hide the form before before opening the Customers form. (If you don't interchange the order of the statements, the procedure opens and then closes the specified form because the newly opened form becomes the active form.)

1. Create a new standard module named basNavigation and insert a new public function named OpenAForm. Enter the procedure shown here

   ```
   Public Function OpenAForm (strFormname As String) As Integer
       Screen.ActiveForm.Visible = False
       DoCmd.OpenForm strFormname
   End Sub
   ```

2. Click in the button's OnClick property and replace the [Event Procedure] with the event function procedure with a literal argument by typing **= OpenAForm("Customers")**.

3. Set the form's HasModule property to No. Save the form and switch to Form view.

4. Click the button. VBA runs the event function procedure to hide the frmSwitchboard form and open the Customers form. You'll copy and paste the button to open another form (see Figure 13.1a).

5. Open the frmSwitchboard form in Design view. Copy and paste the button. Select the pasted button, change the Name property to cmdEmployees and

the Caption property to Employees. Click in the OnClick property and change the argument of the event function to "Employees".

6. Save the form, switch to Form view (see Figure 13.1b),.and click the Employees button. Access runs the event function procedure (see Figure 13.1c).

The command buttons on the form (a) run the same event function procedure. Assign the function as an expression in the event property setting (b). Clicking the command button passes the name of the form you want to open to the function (c).

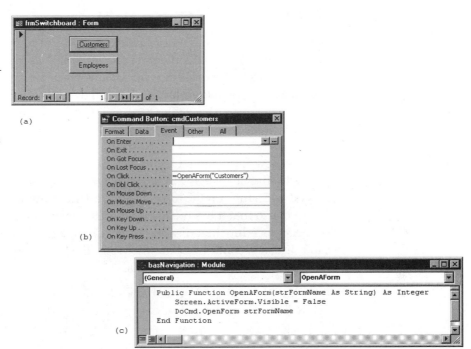

As a final step, the OpenAForm function procedure would be even more reusable if you used the form name as the command button's caption. In this case the procedure determines the Caption property of the command button and you don't have to pass the form name as an argument. The modified function is

```
Public Function OpenAForm () As Integer
    Dim strFormname as string
    strFormname = Screen.ActiveControl.Caption
    Screen.ActiveForm.Visible = False
    DoCmd.OpenForm strFormname
End Sub
```

and the OnClick property is OpenAForm()

## Using Variables for Faster Code

Suppose you have a form that you want to use both for review and for data entry. In the typical data entry mode, the data controls are enabled, unlocked, and have the standard white background, but for review mode you disable and lock each data control to prevent inadvertent changes to the data, and you change its back-color to match the form's backcolor as a visual cue that the data can't be changed. We'll look at a procedure to change the properties of one control.

1. Create a new form named frmDots. Place a command button with the Name property cmdChange, the Caption property Change, and a text box control named txtChange on the form. Make sure the command button is first in the Tab Order so that it has the focus when the form opens. In the next step we create a procedure that disables the txtChange text box and because you can't disable a control that has the focus, the txtChange control cannot have the focus when the procedure runs.

2. In the basNavigation standard module, insert the Change procedure shown below. The Change procedure changes the properties of the txtChange text box:

```
Public Function Change ()
    Forms!frmDots!txtChange.Enabled = False
    Forms!frmDots!txtChange.Locked = True
    Forms!frmDots!txtChange.BackColor = 12632256
End Sub
```

3. Click in the OnClick property of the command button and type = **Change()**. Save the form and switch to Form view (see Figure 13.2a).

4. Click the Change button. The properties of the text box control change.

Let's improve the procedure.

## Eliminating Points and Dots

As explained previously, each exclamation point and dot represents execution time spent processing the reference. The Change procedure has nine points and dots. Each point or dot that you eliminate results in faster code. For a single procedure the number of points and dots may not matter much, but think of the number of points and dots there can be in a fully automated application. So, the name of the game is to count and minimize the dots. How do you get rid of points and dots? With variables!

In the Change procedure, the object referred to is a text box control so you create a new object variable to represent the text box. To create a variable in a procedure you can use a statement with the syntax

```
Dim variablename [As type]
```

This statement is called a *variable declaration statement* and causes Access to set aside a memory location and assign it the name *variablename*. The amount of memory set aside is determined by the As *type* part of the statement; this part is optional and Access will assign the memory-hungry Variant data type unless you specify another data type. In our case the object is a text box control so we use the TextBox object data type:

```
Dim ctl As TextBox
```

This statement creates ctl as an object variable of the TextBox type. The memory location is set aside but contains nothing (the Nothing value, that is) until you assign an object with an assignment statement:

```
Set ctl = Screen.ActiveForm.txtChange
```

Here we use the Screen object to refer to the active form and eliminate the reference to a specific form. We can now replace the hierarchical reference to the control with the variable. The Change procedure is now:

```
Public Function Change ()
    Dim ctl As TextBox
    Set ctl = Screen.ActiveForm.txtChange
    ctl.Enabled = False
    ctl.Locked = True
    ctl.BackColor = 12632256
End Sub
```

Count the points and dots—now there are only five! The procedure should run much faster than when there were nine.

## Creating a Custom Constant

A final adjustment to the procedure is to deal with the number that Access uses for the color gray, by creating a custom constant. By defining a custom constant you can avoid having to type the number ever again. You can create a custom constant in a procedure using the following *constant declaration statement*:

```
Const constantname [As type] = value
```

Like a variable declaration statement, a constant declaration statement sets aside a memory location and names it with the specified name; you use the As *type* part of the statement to specify the constant's data type so that Access knows how much memory to allocate for the constant. A difference between a variable and a constant declaration statement is that you actually use the constant declaration statement to assign the unchanging value.

In our example, the number is an integer but exceeds the limits of the Integer data type so we declare it as Long as follows:

```
Const Gray As Long = 12632256
```

The improved procedure is shown below (and in Figure 13.2b). In Chapter 14 you'll learn about an additional technique (With...End With) for improving the performance of this procedure.

```
Public Sub Change ()
    Const Gray As Long = 12632256
    Dim ctl As TextBox
    Set ctl = Forms!frmDots!txtChange
    ctl.Enabled = False
    ctl.Locked = True
    ctl.BackColor = Gray
End Sub
```

**FIGURE 13.2:**

The Change button on the form (a) triggers an event function procedure (b)

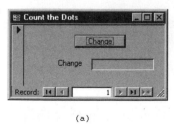

(a)

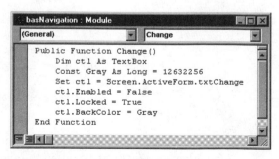

(b)

# How Procedures Use Variables

The two examples of the last section illustrate some of the ways procedures use variables and constants. A procedure can use variables and constants in these ways:

- It can create variables and constants for its own use. Variables and constants that are created within a procedure are available only to the procedure in which they are created and are not available to any other procedures, even to other procedures in the same module. Variables and constants created within a procedure are called *local* or *procedure-level*.

- It can use variables as arguments. A procedure may require additional information as arguments in order to specify how the procedure is to be carried out. The additional information in the form of variable arguments can be given to, or *passed to* the procedure when you call the procedure.

- It can use variables and constants created elsewhere. You can create public variables and constants in the Declarations section of a module and make them available to some or all of the procedures in the database. Variables and constants created in the Declarations section of a module are called *module-level*.

- It can execute statements that can change the values of the variables that the procedure has access to.

- It can return a variable. A Function procedure may return a variable.

The next sections describe the different ways to create and destroy variables and how to pass variables from one procedure to another.

# Declaring Variables

You can create both constants and variables just by using them in statements. The first time you use the name of a constant or variable VBA automatically creates a temporary storage location in memory with the name you selected; this is called *implicit declaration*. One problem with implicit declaration is that VBA doesn't recognize your typographical errors and simply creates a new variable if you misspell a name without associating the two names. You avoid this unnecessary error source by setting the Option Explicit statement in the Declarations section of every module to require that all variables and constants be explicitly created in declaration statements. Typical declaration statements are the two statements placed at the beginning of the Change procedure above:

```
Dim ctl as TextBox
Const Gray As Long = 12632256
```

**NOTE**  This chapter assumes that all variables and constants are explicitly declared and that the Option Explicit statement is used in the Declarations section of every module. You can have VBA enter the Option Explicit statement automatically by checking the Require Variable Declaration check box in the Options dialog, available by choosing the Options command in the Tools menu (the option is checked by default).

There are only two places you can create a variable:

- Place a declaration statement within a procedure or in the procedure's argument list to create a *local* or *procedure-level variable*.

- Place a declaration statement in the Declarations section of a module to create a *module-level variable*.

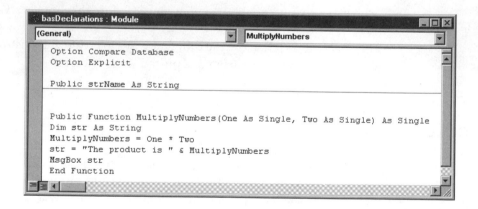

```
basDeclarations : Module
(General)                              MultiplyNumbers

    Option Compare Database
    Option Explicit

    Public strName As String


    Public Function MultiplyNumbers(One As Single, Two As Single) As Single
    Dim str As String
    MultiplyNumbers = One * Two
    str = "The product is " & MultiplyNumbers
    MsgBox str
    End Function
```

When you create a constant or variable, you specify the following four characteristics:

- The name.

- The data type of the constant or regular variable, or the object data type of an object variable.

- The *lifetime* of the variable. The lifetime is the execution time between the creation of the constant or variable and when it ceases to exist.

- The *scope* of the constant or variable: the scope defines which procedures can "see" and use the constant or variable.

## Naming Constants and Variables

You use declaration statements to specify the constant's or variable's name. VBA names are not case-sensitive; this means that VBA does not distinguish between frmcustomers and frmCustomers. However, after you explicitly create a variable, VBA automatically changes subsequent occurrences of the name to match the upper- and lowercase letters that you specify in the declaration statement.

Names of constants and variables must begin with a letter, contain only letters, numbers and the underscore character (_), contain no keywords, and contain not more than 255 characters. Chapter 2 discusses adopting a naming convention to help in making your VBA code more readable and easier to understand.

## Specifying a Data Type

You can use the As *type* phrase in the declaration statement to specify the data type for variables. While declaring the data type is optional, if you don't specify a data type, VBA assigns the Variant data type. As Table 12.1 (on the CD under Tables\Chapter12.pdf) indicates, the Variant data type uses more than twice the memory of any other fundamental data type. Because memory is always limited, the more memory that is tied up in variable storage, the less is available for Access and other applications you are running. With less memory, Access runs more slowly, so you should avoid using the Variant data type on the basis of memory management alone. However, there are additional performance reasons for avoiding the Variant data type:

- Each time a procedure assigns a value to a variable with the Variant data type, VBA must take execution time to determine what kind of data the value has and then change the data type of the variable to match the data; this process is called *coercing* the variant variable.

- When you use a coerced variant variable in a calculation, VBA may need to take additional execution time to convert the data type in order to do the calculation. If VBA can't convert the data type, a run-time error is generated.

- To avoid run-time errors you often have to include statements to check the variable's data type. For example, if you are doing a numeric calculation, you can avoid errors by using the IsNumeric function to determine whether a variable has a numeric data type before doing the calculation. Executing code to check the data type takes additional execution time. If you use a specific data type instead, VBA can do the data type compatibility checking for you when you compile your code.

Unless there is a specific reason to use the Variant data type, you should type variables explicitly. For regular variables, this means choosing the data type with the smallest memory requirement from the list of fundamental data types listed in Table 12.1 (on the CD under Tables\Chapter12.pdf). Similarly, for object variables, you should avoid using the generic Object data type. Using the Object data type for an object variable is like using the Variant data type for a regular variable in that each time a procedure assigns an object: VBA must take execution time to determine what kind of object has been assigned, and each time the procedure refers to a property or method, VBA must take execution time to determine if the property or method is valid for the object. If you use a specific object data type instead, VBA can do the property and method validity checking when you compile the code. For an object variable, using a specific object data type is called *hard typing*.

> **NOTE**    For the most efficient memory management and the fastest code, use the most specific data type for regular variables and the most specific object type for object variables.

# The Life Cycle of a Variable

When VBA reads the declaration statement for a variable, such as

```
Dim intX As Integer
Dim txt As TextBox
```

it creates and names the temporary memory location, allocates the amount of storage specified by the data type you specify, and sets the variable to a default value depending on that data type. A variable with any numeric data type is set to zero, a variable with the string data type is set to the zero-length string (""), a variable with the Variant data type is set to the special Empty value, and an object variable is set to the special Nothing value. The declaration statements above set the variable intX to zero and the object variable txt to Nothing. What happens next depends on whether the variable is a regular variable or an object variable.

## The Life Cycle of a Regular Variable

After a regular variable is created, you can manipulate the variable in statements. You start by using an assignment statement to assign a value to the variable name, such as

```
intX = 1
```

After the variable is assigned, you use the variable name in other statements to change the value, such as the statement

```
intX = intX + 1
```

that increases the value of intX by one and assigns the result to intX. You can also use an assignment statement to reinitialize a variable by setting the variable to its default value. For regular variables with a specific data type, initializing the variable simply means setting its value to either zero or the zero-length string. For example, the statement

```
intX = 0
```

reinitializes the intX variable. Finally, the variable itself is destroyed. Destroying a variable means destroying its temporary memory location and releasing the memory for reuse. How do you destroy a variable? Let's postpone the answer for a moment.

## The Life Cycle of an Object Variable

For an object variable, the story is more complicated because there are two items to keep track of: the object variable and the object itself. After an object variable is declared you use an assignment statement to point the object variable to an object, such as

```
Set txt = Forms!frmDots!txtChange
```

The object that the variable points to may already exist in memory, or the assignment statement may actually create the object in memory. For example, when you open a form interactively, such as when you open frmDots from the Database window, Access creates the form object in memory. When you declare an object variable, such as

```
Dim frm As Form
```

and point frm to the form with the assignment statement

```
Set frm = Forms!frmDots
```

you are pointing the object variable to an object that already exists in memory. By contrast, when you declare a recordset object variable, such as

```
Dim rst As Recordset
```

you are actually creating a new recordset object with the assignment statement

```
Set rst = CurrentDB.OpenRecordset("Customers")
```

Because there is both an object variable and an object, there are two memory requirements: the memory consumed by the object variable and the memory taken by the object. As Table 12.1 (on the CD under Tables\Chapter12.pdf) indicates, an object variable takes four bytes no matter what it is pointing to (the four bytes simply store an address which is usually a long integer), but the object being pointed at may take up hundreds or thousands of bytes of memory.

After the object variable is assigned, you use the object variable in other statements to change the object. When you change an object variable in a VBA statement, you are actually changing the object; for example, in the Change procedure, the three statements that change the properties of the txt object variable actually change the properties of the txtChange text box that sits on the form.

You can also use an assignment statement to reinitialize an object variable by setting the object variable to its default value: When you set an object variable to

Nothing, you are destroying the link between the object variable and the object itself. After you destroy the link, the object variable still exists (and still takes up its four bytes of memory) while the object may or may not continue to exist. For example, if frm is the object variable that was pointing to the frmDots form and you set

```
frm = Nothing
```

the form object continues to exist in memory as long as the form is open; setting frm to Nothing only severs the link between the object variable and the object. By contrast, if rst is the only object variable pointing to the recordset created with the assignment statement

```
Set rst = CurrentDB.OpenRecordset("Customers")
```

then setting rst to Nothing severs the link and destroys the object. In this case the object is destroyed because of the following rule:

*For an object to remain in existence in memory, it must either be assigned to an object variable or have an implicit reference created by Access.*

When you open a form, Access automatically creates an implicit reference to the form object that continues as long as the form is open. Your code cannot affect the implicit reference to the form as long as the form is open. By contrast, when you open a recordset, there is no implicit reference to the recordset object. As long as your code has at least one object variable pointing to a recordset object, the recordset object continues to exist in memory. When all references to the recordset object are severed, either by setting object variables to Nothing or by destroying the object variables, the recordset object itself is destroyed and its memory is released for other purposes.

You can destroy objects in memory by closing them. For example, you can close a form in a procedure using the Close method of the DoCmd object and you can close a recordset using its own Close method. If your code opens another database, you can close it using its Close method, but, as an exception, using the Close method on the current database (the database that is open in the Access window) does not close it. When you use one of the Close methods on an object, the object variable that pointed to the object is in a state of limbo: the object it pointed to may no longer exist but the variable itself still exists and can be assigned to another object.

## Destroying Variables

Because of the memory that variables take up, you'll want to destroy them as soon as you are finished with them. But, the question we haven't answered yet is how do you destroy a variable? Interestingly, Access does not provide a "destroy" statement, so there is no way you can explicitly destroy a variable. Instead, Access provides two alternatives:

- You can declare a variable within a procedure as a local or procedure-level variable and Access will destroy it automatically, by default, when the procedure finishes.

- You can declare a variable in the Declarations section of a module as a module-level variable and Access will destroy it when you close the database, but not before.

We'll see in the next section that there are valid reasons for using module-level variables, however, the general rule is obvious: because of the memory that variables consume, use local variables instead of module-level variables whenever you can.

# Procedure-Level Variables

There are two ways to declare a variable in a procedure: in a separate declaration statement within the procedure and in the argument list of a procedure called by another procedure.

## Declaring a Variable within the Procedure

A procedure-level variable can be created by placing a declaration statement within a procedure. The basic syntax is

```
Dim variablename [As type]
```

Examples are

```
Dim intCounter As Integer
Dim strLastName As String
Dim frmCustomers As Form
```

You can declare several variables with a single declaration statement, but you need to include the data type for each variable separately. The statement

```
Dim frm1 As Form, frm2 As Form
```

declares frm1 and frm2 as the Form object type, but the statement

```
Dim frm1, frm2 As Form
```

declares frm2 as the Form object type and frm1 as a Variant.

The declaration statement creates and names the variable, allocates the memory as specified in the As *type* phrase, and initializes the variable. The declaration statement does not assign a value; you need a separate assignment statement to assign the value. For example, in the following procedure

```
Public Sub SomeProcedure()
    Dim db As Database
    Set db = CurrentDB
    ...
End Sub
```

the declaration statement

```
Dim db As Database
```

creates db as an object variable of the Database object type, and the assignment statement

```
Set db = CurrentDB
```

points the object variable to the current database.

**NOTE**  There is another version of the declaration statement that you can use for an object variable. You can use the New keyword in declaring an object variable using the syntax Dim *objvar* As New *objecttype*. When you include the New keyword, VBA creates a new instance of the object automatically and you don't have to use the Set statement to assign the object variable. See Chapter 19 for more information on the New keyword.

## Declaring a Variable in the Argument List

When you place an argument in a procedure's argument list, you are also creating a procedure-level variable. You can use an As *type* phrase to specify each argument variable's type as follows:

```
argumentname As type
```

for example

```
Public Function Concatenate (A As String, B As String)
```

When you declare a variable in an argument list, VBA automatically allocates the memory specified in the As type phrase and initializes the variable. However, you don't need a separate assignment statement because VBA automatically assigns a value to the variable in an argument list when you call the procedure. For example, when VBA executes the statement

```
MsgBox Concatenate ("Shaw","Cameron")
```

VBA goes to the Concatenate function and automatically assigns the value "Shaw" to the variable A and "Cameron" to the variable B.

```
Public Sub CallingProcedure()
    MsgBox Concatenate ("Shaw","Cameron")
End Sub

Public Function Concatenate(Lname As String, FName As String)
    Concatenate = LnameA & ", " & Fname
End Sub
```

## Visibility of Procedure-Level Variables

A procedure-level variable created either in a declaration statement or in the argument list is visible only to the procedure in which it is created. Other procedures cannot see or use the variable. The only way another procedure can get access to a procedure-level variable is for the procedure that created the variable to call the other procedure and pass it the variable as an argument. A variable passed as an argument to a called procedure can, in turn, be passed if the called procedure calls yet another procedure. The subsequent chain of called procedures is referred to as the procedure's *call tree*.

Procedure-level variables created in a procedure may be passed as arguments to other procedures in its call tree.

Let's look at an example to clarify these ideas:

1.  Create a new module named basVariables. Insert a new public procedure named LocalVariable as shown below. The LocalVariable procedure declares strLocal as a local or procedure-level string variable.

```
Public Sub LocalVariable()
    Dim strLocal As String
    strLocal = "'Local variable in LocalVariable procedure'"
    MsgBox strLocal
End Sub
```

2.  Run the procedure in the Debug window by typing **Call LocalVariable** and pressing Enter. The only procedures that can use the strLocal variable are the LocalVariable procedure and the procedures that the LocalVariable procedure passes the variable to as an argument.

3.  Create the GetLocal procedure below in either the same module (or another module) and run it in the Debug window.

```
Public Sub GetLocal()
    MsgBox strLocal
End Sub
```

The procedure fails (see Figure 13.3) because the GetLocal procedure can't see the strLocal variable in the LocalVariable procedure. As far as the GetLocal procedure is concerned, the strLocal variable has not been defined.

---

**FIGURE 13.3:**

The error message when you try to call a local (procedure-level) variable from another procedure

4. Click the Reset button in the toolbar. In the next step, you modify the Local-Variable procedure to call the GetLocal procedure without passing the variable to it.

5. Insert a Call GetLocal statement after the MsgBox statement in the Local-Variable procedure and then run the LocalVariable procedure in the Debug window.

The GetVariable procedure fails with a "Variable not defined" error whether you call it independently or from LocalVariable because the GetVariable procedure cannot see the strLocal variable.

Just calling a procedure from a procedure that has a local variable does not make the local variable available to the called procedure; if you want the called procedure to use the variable you must pass the variable as an argument to the called procedure.

1. Modify both procedures as shown below. With these changes, the LocalVariable procedure calls GetLocal and passes strLocal as an argument, and the GetLocal procedure receives the variable as an argument.

```
Public Sub LocalVariable()
    Dim strLocal As String
    strLocal = "'Local variable in LocalVariable procedure'"
    MsgBox strLocal
    Call GetLocal(strLocal)
End Sub

Public Sub GetLocal(strA As String)
    MsgBox strA & " passed as an argument to GetLocal"
End Sub
```

2. In the Debug window type **Call LocalVariable** and press Enter. The LocalVariable procedure defines and displays the local variable in a message box (see Figure 13.4a) and then calls the GetLocal procedure passing the strLocal variable to it as an argument. The GetLocal procedure can use the passed variable and displays it in a message box (see Figure 13.4b).

**NOTE**  It is good programming practice to place declaration statements for all procedure-level variables at the beginning of the procedure.

**FIGURE 13.4:**

The procedure displays its local variable (a) and then passes the local variable to another procedure which displays the passed variable (b).

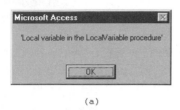

(a)

(b)

# Lifetime of Procedure-Level Variables

After you declare a procedure-level variable and assign it a value in a procedure, other statements may change its value; the variable retains the new value until the value is changed again or until the procedure terminates.

## Using the Static Keyword

By default, procedure-level variables cease to exist when the procedure ends; Access discards their values and releases their storage locations in memory for reuse. However, you can extend the lifetime of a procedure-level variable beyond the life of the procedure by using the Static keyword instead of the Dim keyword when you create the variable. Using the Static keyword extends the lifetime of a procedure's variable to the entire time VBA code is running in any module. When you create a static variable, VBA preserves its value when the procedure ends and sets the variable to the preserved value the next time the procedure runs.

As an example,

1. Insert the StaticVariable procedure below in the basVariables module.

```
Public Sub StaticVariable()
    Dim strNonStatic As String
    Static sstrStatic As String
    strNonStatic = strNonStatic & " nonstatic"
    sstrStatic = sstrStatic & " static"
    Debug.Print strNonStatic
    Debug.Print sstrStatic
End
```

The StaticVariable procedure creates the strNonStatic variable as a nonstatic variable and sstrStatic as a static variable and initializes both variables to the zero-length string. (You can use the s prefix to indicate a static variable.) The assignment statements concatenate the value of strNonStatic with the word *non-static* and the value of sstrStatic with the word *static*. The concatenated values are then printed in the Debug window.

2. Run the procedure in the Debug window by typing **Call StaticVariable** and pressing Enter. The first time you run the procedure both variables are initialized to the zero length string so Debug prints a single word on each line. When the procedure ends, Access destroys the strNonStatic variable but retains the sstrStatic variable and its value.

3. Run the procedure a second time.

The second time you run the procedure, the strNonStatic variable is recreated and reinitialized to the zero-length string and sstrStatic variable still has its retained value. The assignment statement for srtNonStatic produces the word nonstatic as before, but the assignment statement for sstrStatic appends the word *static* to the current string. Each time you run the procedure, the nonstatic variable is reinitialized and the assignment statement sets the variable to the word *nonstatic* but the value of the static variable is retained and the assignment statement appends the word *static* to the current value. Figure 13.5a shows the Debug window after running the procedure three times.

You can make all of the local variables in a procedure static by placing the Static keyword in the procedure's declaration statement. For example,

1. Select all of the statements of the StaticVariable procedure and press Ctrl+C to copy. Place the insertion point after the last procedure in the module and press Ctrl+V to paste. Change the procedure's declaration statement by inserting the Static keyword and changing the procedure's name as shown below:

```
Public Static Sub StaticProcedure()
    Dim strNonStatic As String
    Static sstrStatic As String
    strNonStatic = strNonStatic & " 'nonstatic'"
    sstrStatic = sstrStatic & " 'static'"
    Debug.Print strNonStatic
    Debug.Print sstrStatic
End
```

2. Click in the Debug window, choose the Select All command in the Edit menu, and press Del.

3. Run the StaticProcedure procedure in the Debug window three times. Observe that both variables are now static. Using the Static keyword in the procedure definition overrides the declaration using the Dim keyword inside the procedure (see Figure 13.5b)

4. Click in the basVariables module and press the Reset button in the toolbar. When you reset the module, you discard all variables declared in the module and release their storage space.

**FIGURE 13.5:**

A static variable retains its value between calls to the procedure and a non-static variable is reinitialized each time you call the procedure (a). Using the Static keyword in the procedure's declaration allocates storage space for all of the local variables and preserves their values the entire time the module runs, that is, until you restart or reset the module (b).

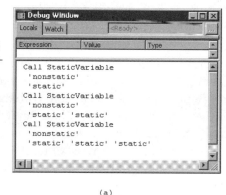

(a)

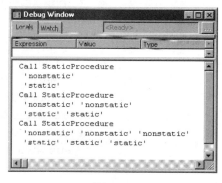

(b)

When you insert a new procedure you can make all of the local variables static by checking the All Local Variables as Statics in the Insert Procedure dialog (see Figure 13.6). With this option checked, VBA inserts the Static keyword in the procedure declaration for you.

**FIGURE 13.6:**

Select the All Local Variables As Static option in the Insert Procedure dialog to preserve the values of all local variables declared in the procedure.

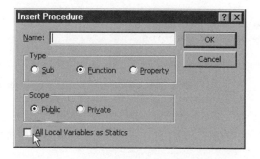

To summarize the features of a procedure-level variable:

- You create a procedure-level variable with a declaration statement placed inside a procedure using the syntax

    ```
    Dim [Static] variablename As type
    ```

or as an argument in the procedure's argument list using the syntax

    ```
    argumentname As type
    ```

- The procedure-level variable is not visible to any other procedure directly. The only way a procedure can make a procedure-level variable available to another procedure is to pass the local variable as an argument to the other procedure.

- When the procedure ends, Access destroys the procedure-level variables and releases their storage space, by default. You can override the default behavior by declaring a procedure-level variable with the Static keyword instead of the Dim keyword or by using the Static keyword in the procedure's declaration to make all of its local variables static. The value of a static variable is preserved until you restart or reset the module. You cannot extend the life of an argument declared in the procedure's argument list.

## Passing Data to a Procedure

The ability to call one procedure from another allows you to separate your code into smaller, simpler procedures. When you call one procedure from another, you can send data to the procedure being called. You can send literal data and you can send variables.

We look first at passing literal data to the called procedure.

1. In the basVariables module insert the PassingLiteral and GetData sub procedures below.

```
Public Sub PassingLiteral()
    MsgBox "Literal"
    Call GetData("'Literal'")
    MsgBox "Returning from the GetData procedure"
End Sub

Public Sub GetData (A As String)
```

```
    MsgBox A & " is passed to the GetData procedure as an
    ➥argument."
End Sub
```

The statement

```
Call GetData("'Literal'")
```

in the PassingLiteral procedure calls the GetData procedure and passes the literal value "Literal".

2. Run the PassingLiteral procedure in the Debug window.

The PassingLiteral procedure displays its message (see Figure 13.7a) and then calls the GetData procedure, passing it the literal value. VBA replaces the letter A everywhere it appears in the called procedure with the value passed in. The GetData procedure displays its message (see Figure 13.7b) and quits. VBA returns to the PassingLiteral procedure at the next statement, displays the message (see Figure 13.7c), and quits.

**FIGURE 13.7:**

The calling procedure displays the literal (a) and passes the literal to the called procedure (b). After the called procedure ends, control returns to the calling procedure (c).

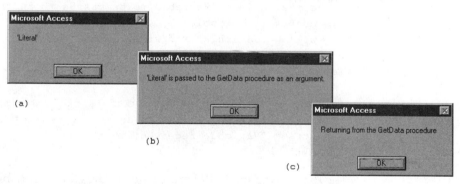

## Passing a Variable by Reference or by Value

Now let's pass a variable instead of a literal. Access provides two ways of sending variable data: you can send the variable itself or you can send a copy of the variable's value.

- When you send the variable itself, the called procedure can manipulate the variable and change its value. Sending the variable itself is called *passing the variable by reference* and is the default method of sending a variable.

- When you send a copy of the variable's value, VBA creates a copy in another temporary storage location in memory and sends the copy; the called procedure can use the copy and may even change its value but because the called procedure is working with a copy, the variable itself is not affected. Sending a copy of the variable is called *passing the variable by value.*

To specify which method you are using, you precede the argument name, in the argument list of the procedure being called, with either the keyword ByRef to pass the variable itself and ByVal to pass a copy as follows:

```
[ByRef|ByVal] argumentname [As type]
```

To explore, you'll create a pair of procedures that pass a variable first by reference and then by value:

1. In the basVariables module, create the PassingVariableByRef and GetVariableByRef procedures as shown below.

```
Public Sub PassingVariableByRef()
    Dim strVariable as String
    strVariable = "Variable to be passed to another procedure"
    MsgBox strVariable
    Call GetVariableByRef(strVariable)
    MsgBox strVariable
End Sub

Public Sub GetVariableByRef ByRef (strA As String)
    MsgBox strA & " is passed as an argument of the procedure."
    strA = "Variable received. Thank you"
End Sub
```

The PassingVariableByRef procedure declares the strVariable variable, assigns and then displays the string value (see Figure 13.8a). The procedure calls the GetVariableByRef procedure, passing it the variable. The GetVariableByRef procedure receives the variable itself, displays the variable (see Figure 13.8b), and changes its value. When the GetVariableByRef procedure ends, VBA returns to the next statement of the calling procedure, displays the changed variable (see Figure 13.8c), and ends.

**FIGURE 13.8:**

When you pass a variable (a) by reference, the called procedure receives the variable itself (b) and can change its value. The calling procedure uses the changed value (c).

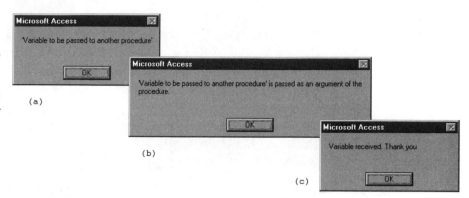

2. Run the PassingVariablesByRef procedure in the Debug window.

3. In the module window, copy all of the code for both procedures to the clipboard, place the insertion point below the last procedure and paste the contents of the clipboard. You'll use the Replace dialog to modify the procedures to pass the variable by value.

4. Select the pasted procedures, choose Replace from the Edit menu, type **ByRef** in the Find what text box and **ByVal** in the Replace with text box, make sure the Select text option is selected in the Search option group, and click Replace All (see Figure 13.9). Click OK to confirm the four replacements. Type **passed** in the Find what text box and **passed by value** in the Replace text box and click Replace All. Click OK to confirm the two replacements and close the Replace dialog.

5. Run the PassingVariableByVal procedure in the Debug window.

**FIGURE 13.9:**

Using the Replace dialog to modify procedures by replacing values

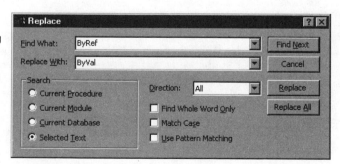

This time only a copy of the variable's value is passed to the called procedure. The calling procedure displays the variable (see Figure 13.10a). The called procedure receives a copy of the variable and displays its message (see Figure 13.10b) and then changes the value as before, but only the copy is changed. After finishing the called procedure, Access returns to the calling procedure and displays the last message box with the value of the unaltered variable (see Figure 13.10c).

**FIGURE 13.10:**

When you pass a variable (a) by value, the called procedure uses a copy of the variable (b). Although the called procedure may change the value of the copy, the original variable retains its value (c).

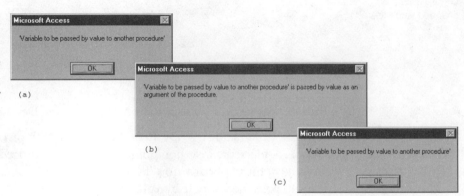

Although the terms are different, the two methods are analogous to the familiar methods of linking and embedding a document. When you pass an argument ByRef you are "linking" the procedure to the variable so that changes made in the procedure are made to the variable. When you pass an argument ByVal, you are "embedding" a copy of the variable and there is no link to the variable itself, so that changes made in the procedure are not made to the variable. Sending a variable by reference is faster because Access doesn't have to take the time to create a copy of the variable.

**NOTE**  Passing variables by reference blurs the distinction between a function procedure and a subprocedure. When you pass variables by reference, the function or subprocedure that receives the variables as arguments can change their values or the objects they refer to and then return the changed variables. This means that both function procedures and subprocedures can return values through the arguments that are passed by reference. Only a function procedure has the ability to return an additional value separate from the values returned by its arguments.

## Using Named Arguments

There are two ways to pass arguments to a procedure: by order and by name.

**By order**   When you pass arguments by order, you list the values of the arguments in the order specified in the procedure's syntax. If you omit an optional argument, you must include a comma as a placeholder for a missing argument in the argument list.

**By name**   When you pass arguments by name, you specify the name of the argument followed by the colon-equals (:=) assignment operator, followed by the value for the argument. You can list named arguments in any order and you can omit optional arguments.

As an example, the Concatenate procedure's declaration specifies its arguments as follows:

```
Public Function Concatenate(A,B)
```

Each of the following statements call the function:

```
Call Concatenate("Shaw", "Cameron")
Call Concatenate(A:="Cameron", B:="Shaw")
```

You created the Concatenate function in the last chapter so it is stored in another database. You can make the function available in the current database by setting a reference to the Ch12_Examples database.

1.  Choose the References command in the Tools menu. Click the Browse button in the References dialog.

2.  In the Add Reference dialog, choose Databases in the Files of type combo list, locate the Ch12_Examples.mdb database (see Figure 13.11a), and click OK. The reference to the database is added to the list (see Figure 13.11b).

3.  In the Debug window, type each of the following and press Enter.

    **? Concatenate("Shaw", "Cameron")**

    **? Concatenate(A:="Cameron", B:="Shaw")**

This example shows that when you pass arguments by name, you can list the arguments in any order.

**FIGURE 13.11:**

Adding a reference to another database

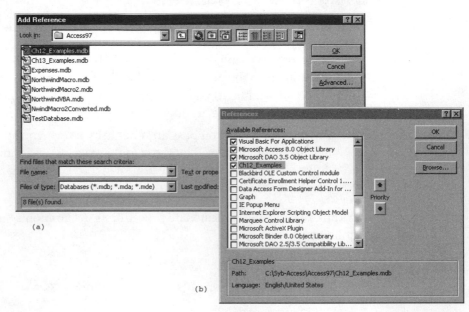

(a)

(b)

## Variant Arguments

You can create a procedure that accepts data with more than one data type by using variant arguments. For example, the Multiply function multiplies its arguments and returns the product.

```
Public Function Multiply (X,Y)
    Multiply = X*Y
End Function
```

You can call this function and pass it two values of any data type. If VBA is able to convert the data types to compatible types, the product can be calculated.

For example,

1. Enter the public function procedure Multiply and the public sub procedure CallMultiply in the basVariables module. The CallMultiply procedure declares variables of several data types and attempts to calculate the product by passing the variables to the Multiply function.

```
Public Sub CallMultiply
    Dim intX As Integer, sngY As Single
```

```
Dim dtmX As Date
Dim strX As String, strY As String
intX = 2
sngY = 3
dtmX = #5/12/96#
strX = "2"
strY = "Three"
MsgBox "Numbers of different data type " &
➥Multiply (intX, sngY)
MsgBox "Number and date " & Multiply (dtmX, sngY)
MsgBox "Number and convertible string " &
➥Multiply(strX, sngY)
MsgBox "Number and non-convertible string " &
➥Multiply(intX,strY)
End Sub
```

2.  Run the CallMultiply procedure in the Debug window.

When you pass two numbers of different numerical data types, VBA successfully converts the data types (see Figure 13.12a), when you pass a number and a date, VBA converts the date to its numerical equivalent and calculates the product (see Figure 13.12b), when you pass a number as a string, such as "2" VBA converts the string to a numerical data type and calculates the product (see Figure 13.12c), but when you pass a string, such as "Three", VBA can't convert the data type and displays a "Type mismatch" error message (see Figure 13.12d).

**FIGURE 13.12:**

The procedure successfully converts numbers of different data types (a), a date (b), and a convertible string (c), but fails when VBA can't convert an unconvertible string to a number (d).

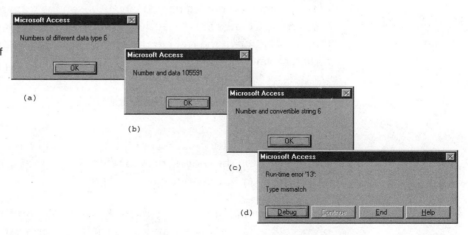

You can avoid run-time errors in procedures that have variant arguments by doing your own data type checking in the procedure before performing the calculations. You can use the built-in functions shown in Table 13.1 (on the CD under Tables\Chapter13.pdf) to examine the data. See Chapter 14 for examples of procedures that test data types before doing calculations.

## Passing Objects as Arguments

You can pass objects as arguments of procedures. As an example, we create a function procedure that changes the Caption property of an object and then we call the function passing it the object whose caption we want to change.

1. Create a new form named frmCaption. Place a label control on the form, type **Label** as the Caption property, and set the label's Name property to lblCaption.

2. Insert the ChangeCaption function as shown below in the basVariables standard module.

```
Public Function ChangeCaption(objectname As Object)
    objectname.Caption = "My Caption"
End Function
```

We use the Object data type for the argument so that we can pass any type of object that has a Caption property. We'll call this function from two command buttons on the form.

3. Place a command button named cmdLabel on the form and set its Caption property to Change Label Caption. Click in the OnClick property and click the Build button at the right of the property box. Enter the code below in the code template:

```
Private Sub cmdLabel_Click()
    Call ChangeCaption (lblCaption)
End Sub
```

This procedure calls the ChangeCaption function and passes the label control as an argument using the short syntax to refer to the control. When you click the button the label's caption changes to My Caption.

4. Place a command button named cmdForm on the form and set its Caption property to Change Form Caption. Click in the form's module and insert the

event procedure below (VBA automatically assigns the procedure to the button's OnClick property).

```
Private Sub cmdForm_Click()
Call ChangeCaption (Forms!frmCaption)
End Sub
```

This procedure calls the ChangeCaption function and passes the form as an argument using the exclamation point syntax to refer to the form by name. When you click the button the form's caption changes to My Caption.

5. Save the form and switch to Form view. Click the Change Label Caption button (see Figure 13.13a). Click the Change Form Caption button (see Figure 13.13b).

**FIGURE 13.13:**

Passing a label control (a) and the form object (b) as arguments to a procedure

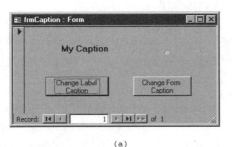

(a)                    (b)

**Passing Me as an Argument**   Let's explore other ways to pass the form as an argument. When you are running a procedure stored in a form's module and you want to call another procedure and pass a reference to the form, you can use the Me property to refer to the form. (When a procedure is running in a form's module, the Me property refers to the form.) For example,

1. Click in the frmCaption form and switch to Design view. Click in the form's module and change the cmdForm_Click() event procedure as shown below:

```
Private Sub cmdForm_Click()
    Call ChangeCaption(Me)
End Sub
```

2. Save the form, switch to Form view, and click the Change Form Caption button. The form's Caption changes as before.

**Passing Form as an Argument** You can also use the Form property to refer to the form. For example, change the cmdForm_Click event procedure as shown below and test the button.

```
Private Sub cmdForm_Click()
    Call ChangeCaption(Form)
End Sub
```

Using the Form property to pass the form as an argument is useful when you are using an event function procedure. For example, you can call the ChangeCaption function to change the form's caption when the form opens:

1. Switch to Design view, click in the Form's OnClick property and enter the following expression in the form's OnOpen event property

   **= ChangeCaption (Form)**

2. Save the form and switch to Form view. The function procedure runs and changes the form's Caption.

You can't use the Me property to refer to the form in an event property setting. Entering the expression **= ChangeCaption(Me)** in the form's OnOpen event property causes the error shown in Figure 13.14. (You can only use the Me property in a form's or report's module to refer to the form or report.)

---

**FIGURE 13.14:**

The error message displayed when you try to refer to the form as Me in an event property setting

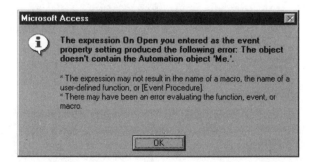

Microsoft Access

The expression On Open you entered as the event property setting produced the following error: The object doesn't contain the Automation object 'Me.'.

* The expression may not result in the name of a macro, the name of a user-defined function, or [Event Procedure].
* There may have been an error evaluating the function, event, or macro.

[ OK ]

## Using an Indefinite Number of Arguments

By default, the arguments in a procedure's argument list are required; a run-time error occurs if you fail to send values for all of the arguments. Sometimes it is convenient to create a procedure with an indefinite number of arguments. There are three ways to provide this flexibility:

- Specify that arguments are optional.
- Use arguments with user-defined data types.
- Use array arguments.

This section shows you how to specify optional arguments. See the sections "Creating Your Own Data Types" and "Using Arrays" later in this chapter for information on these two methods for creating procedures with an indefinite number of arguments.

## Optional Arguments

You can specify that some of the arguments in the argument list are optional by preceding the optional arguments with the Optional keyword. Optional arguments can have any data type. (This is a new feature in Access 97; previously Optional arguments were required to have the Variant data type.) The optional arguments must be at the end of the argument list; once you specify that an argument is optional, all subsequent arguments in the list must be specified as optional also.

To illustrate these concepts, suppose you want to create a function that calculates the product of two or three numbers. The Product function procedure below multiplies three numbers when three variables are passed but fails when the optional argument is not sent.

```
Public Function Product (X, Y, Optional Z)
    Product = X*Y
    Product = Product*Z
End Function
```

1. In the basVariables module, insert the Product procedure.

2. In the Debug window, call the function by typing each of the following and pressing Enter. The first product is calculated but the second entry causes an error.

    **?Product(2,3,4)**

    **?Product(2,3)**

When the code in a procedure would cause a run-time error if the argument is not passed, you can use the IsMissing function to determine whether an optional argument has been passed. The IsMissing(*argname*) function returns True if no value has been passed for the *argname* argument and False otherwise. In this example, you can modify the Product function to use the IsMissing function as shown below.

```
Public Function Product (X, Y, Optional Z)
    Product = X*Y
    If IsMissing(Z) Then Exit Function
    Product = Product*Z
End Function
```

The modified procedure determines whether the third argument has been passed to the function; if the third argument has not been passed, the procedure exits without executing the

```
Product = Product*Z
```

statement. See the section "Controlling the Flow of Execution" later in the chapter for information on making decisions in a procedure.

## Passing Data to an Event Procedure

Access specifies both the names and arguments of sub event procedures automatically. You can't change the argument list in any way (except as noted below). The purpose of the default argument list for an event is to provide a means of communication between your code and Access. As an example, the event procedure for the NotInList event recognized by a combo box has the syntax

```
Private Sub controlname_NotInList(NewData As String, Response As
Integer)
```

where

- NewData is a (read-only) string that Access uses to pass the text that the user entered into the text box part of the combo box; Access passes the text to the event procedure.

- Response is a constant that you use to specify whether to display or suppress the default message and to add the value in NewData to the combo box list; the event procedure passes the constant back to Access.

> **NOTE**
> The one change you can make to the argument list of an event proce-
> dure is that you can use the standard prefixes for VBA variables. For
> example, you can replace the arguments of the NotInList event proce-
> dure with strNewData and intREsponse.

Most of the events have no associated arguments; for example, the Click, Load, Activate, AfterUpdate, Initialize, and Terminate events have no arguments. An event for which you can cancel the default behavior following the event has an argument named Cancel with an Integer data type; for example, the DblClick, Unload, and BeforeUpdate events each have a Cancel As Integer argument. To cancel the default behavior following the event, you set the Cancel argument to True in an assignment statement in the event procedure. Table 13.2 (on the CD under Tables\Chapter13.pdf) lists the arguments for the event procedures, grouping the events by argument. You'll see examples of passing arguments to event procedures in the next chapters.

# Module-Level Variables

You create a module-level variable by placing a declaration statement in the Declarations section of a module using the syntax.

```
[Private|Public] variablename As type
```

The keyword you use in the declaration statement determines the scope of the variable, that is, which procedures can see and use the variable. Just as with procedures, module-level variables can be private or public. Use the Private keyword to create private module-level variables, which can be seen only by procedures within the module; use the Public keyword to create public module-level variables, which can be seen by all procedures in all modules of the project (a *project* is the set of all modules in the database).

To explore module-level variables:

1. Declare the module-level variables in the Declarations section of the basVariables module as shown below. A public module-level variable is

also called a *global variable* and you can use the prefix g to indicate a public module-level variable.

```
Private strPrivate As String
Public gstrPublic As String
```

2.  Insert the PublicScoping and SamePublic procedures shown below in the basVariables module. The PublicScoping procedure assigns the value 'Public' to the public module-level variable gstrPublic and calls the SamePublic procedure stored in the same module and the OtherPublic procedure stored in another module.

```
Public Sub PublicScoping()
    gstrPublic = "'Public'"
    Call SamePublic
    Call OtherPublic
End Sub

Public Sub SamePublic()
    MsgBox gstrPublic & " from the same module.", , "SamePublic"
End Sub
```

3.  Create a new module named basOther and insert the OtherPublic procedure as follows:

```
Public Sub OtherPublic()
    MsgBox gstrPublic & " from another module.", ,"OtherPublic"
End Sub
```

4.  Type **PublicScoping** in the Immediate pane of the Debug window and press Enter.

After assigning a value to the public variable, the PublicScoping() procedure calls another procedure in the same module, which displays the variable (see Figure 13.15a). It then calls another procedure, in another module which displays the variable (see Figure 13.15b). Both called procedures see the public module-level variable.

**FIGURE 13.15:**

A public module-level variable can be seen by procedures in the same module (a) and by procedures in any other module in the project (b).

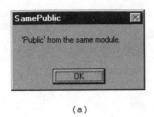

(a)

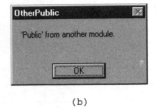

(b)

5. Insert the PrivateScoping and SamePrivate procedures below in the basVariables module. The PrivateScoping procedure assigns the value 'Private' to the private module-level variable strPrivate and calls procedures in the same module and in another module.

```
Public Sub PrivateScoping()
    strPrivate = "Private"
    Call SamePrivate
    Call OtherPrivate
End Sub

Public Sub SamePrivate()
    MsgBox strPrivate & " from the same module.", , "SamePrivate"
End Sub
```

6. Insert the OtherPrivate procedure in the basOther module as follows:

```
Public Sub OtherPrivate()
    MsgBox strPrivate & " from another module.", , "OtherPrivate"
End Sub
```

7. Type **PrivateScoping** in the Debug window and press Enter.

After assigning a value to the private variable, the PrivateScoping procedure calls another procedure in the same module, which displays the variable (see Figure 13.16a). The PrivateScoping procedure calls another procedure in another module. This time VBA generates a run-time error (see Figure 13.16b). Because the strPrivate variable is private to the procedures in the basVariables module, it is not visible to the OtherPrivate procedure stored in the basOther module.

8. Click the Reset button.

FIGURE 13.16:

A private module-level variable can be seen only by procedures in the same module (a) and not by procedures in other modules (b).

(a)                    (b)

> **NOTE**   To declare a private variable at the module level, you can also use the Dim keyword instead of Private, but using the Private keyword makes your code easier to understand.

> **NOTE**   Public module-level variables declared in a standard or an independent class module (but not in a form or report module) can also be used in any other databases that reference the database in which the public variables are declared. You can restrict public module-level variables to the current database by including the Option Private Module statement in the Declarations section of the standard or independent class module in which they are declared. Don't be confused by the use of the Private keyword: when used in the Option Private Module statement, the Private keyword means private to the database, but when used in a variable or procedure declaration statement, it means private to the module.

## Visibility of Module-Level Variables Created in a Form or Report Module

The visibility (scoping) rules differ between module-level variables created in standard modules and independent class modules and module-level variables created in form and report modules. The basic purpose of a form or report module is to store the constants, variables, and procedures that are needed by the form or report. In keeping with this purpose, the visibility of constants and variables declared in a form or report module is limited. In particular, you cannot create public constants at all, and only some variables can be made public. Here are the specific details for module-level variables in a form or report module:

- You cannot declare a public variable as a fixed-length string.

- You cannot declare a public array.

- Public variables created in form or report modules are available only to other modules in the current database and are not available to other databases.

> **NOTE** Procedures that are stored in dynamic link libraries (*DLL procedures*) and declared in the Declarations section of a module can be public or private. A DLL procedure declared with a Public Declare statement can be called by any procedure in any module, and a DLL procedure declared with a Private Declare statement can be called only by procedures in the module in which the procedure is defined. For a standard or independent class module, you can declare both public and private DLL procedures (if you don't use either keyword, the DLL procedure is public by default). By contrast, in a form or report module, you can declare only private DLL procedures.

## Lifetime of Module-Level Variables

When you first open an Access database, Access opens only the modules it needs to get started and then opens modules as the procedures in them are called. For example, if a form has a form module, that module is loaded into memory the first time you open the form. A standard or class module is loaded the first time you call a procedure stored in it. When a module is loaded into memory, VBA allocates storage space for all of the variables and constants declared in the Declarations section. Once a module is loaded into memory, it is not removed from memory while the computer is turned on. This is true even for form and report modules—closing the form or report does not remove its module from memory. A consequence is that module-level variables (and static procedure-level variables) consume memory and retain their values until you close the database. The obvious performance tip is to use module-level variables only when they are absolutely necessary.

To explore the lifetime of module-level variables:

1. Declare a public module-level variable in the Declarations section of the basVariables module as shown below. (The Public keyword also makes the variable available in the Debug window.)

```
Public strModule As String
```

2. Insert the LifetimeModule procedure shown below into the basVariables module:

```
Public Sub LifetimeModule()
    strModule = "'Module-level variable exists until you close
    ⮕the database.'"
    MsgBox strModule, , "LifetimeModule"
End Sub
```

The LifetimeModule procedure sets the value of the strModule variable, displays a message, and ends.

3. Type **LifetimeModule** in the Debug window and press Enter. The procedure assigns and displays the value (see Figure 13.17a).

The strModule variable retains the value set by this procedure until you change the value or close the database, or until you click the Reset button.

4. Insert the StillThere procedure shown below. The StillThere procedure displays the current value of the strModule variable.

```
Public Sub StillThere()
    MsgBox strModule, , "StillThere"
End Sub
```

5. Type **StillThere** in the Debug window and press Enter. The message box displays the current value (see Figure 13.17b).

6. Click the Reset button in the Module toolbar. VBA clears all public and private variables in the module and releases their storage space.

7. Run the StillThere procedure in the Debug window. The message box is blank because the variable has been reinitialized to the zero-length string (see Figure 13.17c).

**FIGURE 13.17:**

The LifetimeModule procedure assigns a value to a public module-level variable (a). The StillThere procedure displays the current value of the variable (b). After resetting the module, the variable is initialized (c).

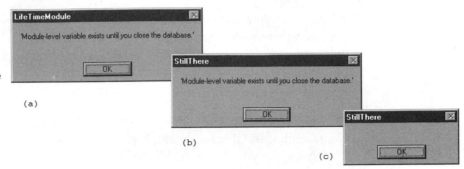

(a)

(b)

(c)

# Summary of Declarations and Data Typing

Table 13.3 (on the CD under Tables\Chapter13.pdf) summarizes the declaration statements for procedures and variables and the data typing of variables and function procedure return values.

# Using Constants

When you find that certain constant values appear over and over again in your code, you can make your code more readable by using *constants*. A constant is a meaningful name that takes the place of a number or string that does not change. Usually the operating system and the applications you are using supply sets of *intrinsic* constants but you can also create your own *user-defined* constants.

**TIP** Using constants makes your code run faster because VBA writes the value into the compiled version when you compile the code and doesn't have to look up the values during run time.

# Using Intrinsic Constants

In Access VBA, you can use the following system-defined constants and intrinsic constants. A *system-defined constant* is a constant provided by the operating system and an *instrinsic constant* is a meaningful name provided by an application to replace a number that doesn't change.

**System-defined constants**   Access has four system defined constants—Yes, No, On, and Off—that you can use in all database objects except in modules, and three additional system-defined constants—True, False, and Null—that you can use in all database objects including modules.

**Access instrinsic constants**   Access VBA has a set of instrinsic constants that you use to represent the arguments of various Access methods, functions, and properties. These constants have an ac prefix; examples are acCmdRefresh, acForm, acPrevious, and acPreview. A new feature in Access 97 is the grouping of intrinsic constants; when an argument for a method, function, or property requires an intrinsic constant, the set of constants for the argument, called the set of *enumerated constants* for the argument, is given a name. For example, the Record argument of the GoToRecord method has a set of intrinsic constants called AcRecord which includes the enumerated constants acFirst, asGoTo, asLast, acNewRec, acNext, acPrevious.

**VBA intrinsic constants**   VBA also has a set of instrinsic constants with the vb prefix that you use primarily to specify property settings and arguments of methods in VBA code. Examples are vbAbort, vbQuestion, and vbCancel that you use to specify the arguments for the MsgBox function. VBA groups intrinsic constants into categories including ColorConstants, Constants, KeyCodeConstants, SystemConstants. VBA also groups intrinsic constants into sets of enumerated constants including the prefix Vb in the group name. For example, VbDayOfWeek is the name of the set of enumerated constants vbFriday, vbMonday, vbSaturday, vbSunday, vbThursday, vbTuesday, vbUseSystemDayOfWeek, and vbWednesday.

**Jet intrinsic constants**   The Jet database engine has a set of intrinsic constants with the db prefix that you use primarily to specify property setting and arguments of methods of the data access objects. Examples are dbDenyRead, dbOpenTable, and dbOpenDynaset that you use to specify the OpenRecordset method. Jet also groups intrinsic constants into sets of enumerated constants and names each group using a descriptive name and the suffix Enum. For example, RecordsetTypeEnum is the set of enumerated constants representing the types of recordsets including dbOpenDynamic, dbOpenDynaset, dbOpenForwardOnly, dbOpenSnapshot, and dbOpenTable.

## Using the Object Browser

You can use the Object Browser to view the intrinsic constants for an application as follows:

1. In Module view, click the Object Browser button in the toolbar, press F2, or choose the Object Browser command in the View menu.

The Object Browser dialog is displayed (see Figure 13.18a). See Chapter 10 for an explanation of how to use the Object Browser dialog. The Project/Library combo list includes the current project and the reference we set earlier to the Ch12_Examples project. The combo list also includes references to the three object libraries that are created in the System directory in your Windows folder when you install Access: Access (Microsoft Access 97), DAO (Microsoft DAO 3.5 object library for Jet), and VBA (Visual Basic for Applications). These object libraries contain references to the constants provided by these applications in addition to other reference information on objects and commands.

2. Select Access as the object library. Select AcFormView in the Classes list box in the lower left of the dialog. The Members list box displays the set of enumerated constants (see Figure 13.18b). AcFormView is the name of the group of enumerated constants for the View argument of the OpenForm method. The Classes list box includes the names of all the sets of enumerated constants for the methods, functions, and properties using the prefix Ac to indicate a name. The enumerated constants in each set are displayed in the Members list box and have the prefix ac.

3. Select an object library and then select Constants from the Classes list box in the lower left of the dialog box. The Members list box on the right displays the instrinsic constants. Choose acPreview in the Members list box. The area below the list boxes displays the number that corresponds to the constant and additional information about the constant. Click the Help button, if it is enabled, to display online Help.

4. Select DAO as the object library. Select DataTypeEnum in the Classes list box. The Members list box displays the set of enumerated constants (see Figure 13.18c). The Classes list box includes the names of the sets of enumerated constants using a syntax that includes a descriptive name with

the suffix Enum. For example, DataTypeEnum is the set of intrinsic constants that represent the data types used by Jet.

5. Choose dbBoolean in the Members list box to view additional information for the constant.

**FIGURE 13.18:**

The Project/Library combo box lists the projects and object libraries for which the current database has references set (a). You can use the Object Browser to learn about the set of enumerated constants for an argument of a method, function or property in Access (b) or in DAO (c).

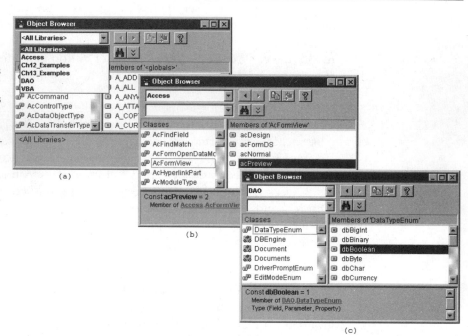

The numerical values represented by intrinsic constants may change in future versions of Access. Because of this, you should always use the intrinsic constants instead of their actual values in your code.

## Creating Your Own Constants

You can create your own constants using declaration statements. Creating constants is similar to creating variables: you can create both procedure-level and module-level constants. The difference is that the declaration statement for a constant also includes the assignment of the constant value as follows:

```
Const constantname As type = constantvalue
```

When VBA reads the declaration statement for a constant, it creates and names a temporary memory location, allocates the amount of storage specified by the data type you specify, and stores the value. The As *type* part is optional; if you don't specify a data type, VBA chooses the most efficient storage type for the value you entered.

## Procedure-Level Constants

You create a procedure-level constant and set its value using a declaration statement within a procedure as follows

```
Const constantname As type =constantvalue
```

For example,

```
Const intMax As Integer = 144
```

A procedure-level constant is not visible outside the procedure.

## Module-Level Constants

You create module-level constants by placing the declaration statement in the Declarations section of a module. For a standard module, you can create public and private module-level constants using the syntax

```
[Public|Private]Const constantname [As type] = constantvalue
```

If you omit the Public or Private keyword, the constant is private by default and available only to procedures in the module in which the constant is created. For example, these lines:

```
Public Const gsngInterestRate As Single = 7.75
Private Const sngTaxRate As Single = 32.5
```

create gsngInterestRate as a public constant that can be seen and used by any procedure in the project and sngTaxRate as a constant that can be seen and used only by the procedures in the module and is invisible to procedures in other modules.

For a form or report module, you can create only private constants. This means that entering a statement such as

```
Public Const intMyConstant As Integer = 2
```

in the Declarations section of a form or report module leads to an error (see Figure 13.19).

FIGURE 13.19:

The error message displayed when you try to declare a Public constant in a form or report module

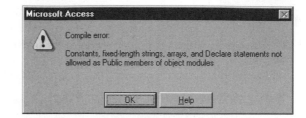

# Using Arrays

VBA provides *arrays* as a way to work efficiently with several variables that have the same data type; for example, you can create an array of the text box controls on a form, or an array of open forms in the database. An array is a series of variables that you refer to using the same name and using a number, called the *index*, to tell the variables apart. The variables in an array must have the same data type. However, if the array has the Variant data type, the individual elements of the array can contain different kinds of data such as numbers, strings, or objects. You can create an array with a fundamental data type, an object data type, or a user-defined data type. The collections of the Application objects and the data access objects discussed in Chapters 10 and 11 are object arrays; for examples, Forms is an array of the open forms and TableDefs is an array of the tables in the database.

The main purpose of arrays is to make your code simpler and more efficient. When you want to process a set of items in an array, you can easily loop through each item using the index number to keep track of the repetitions. Chapter 14 explains looping through an array.

You can create an array with a fixed number of elements. (A *fixed-size array* is also called an *ordinary array*.) You can also create an array without specifying the number of elements and then size the array while a procedure is running; an array declared without a specific number of elements is a *dynamic array*. Suppose you need to keep track of the values in the controls on a specific form. Because you know the number of controls on the form, you could use a fixed-size array to hold the values. However, if you want to use the procedure for any form, you could use a dynamic array because the number of controls may be different for each form. In either case, you can create local arrays within procedures and shared arrays in the Declarations sections of modules. By default, VBA uses zero as the first index number (the *lower bound*) for the array; in this case the highest index number (the *upper bound*) is one less than the number of elements. Arrays can be multidimensional and can have up to 60 dimensions. Table 13.4 (on the CD under Tables\Chapter13.pdf) lists the built-in array-handling functions.

> **NOTE** The basic memory requirement of an array of any data type is 20 bytes plus 4 bytes for each array dimension plus the number of bytes for the data itself. The memory for the data itself is the product of the number of data elements and the size of each element. A Variant variable containing an array requires 12 bytes in addition to the memory required by the array.

## Fixed-Size Arrays

You create a procedure-level fixed-size array using a Dim or Static statement within the procedure or in the argument list of the procedure. To declare the array, you follow the array name with the bounds for the index numbers in parenthesis, as in the following examples. (You can use the prefix "a" in the variable name to indicate an array if you are using a Hungarian style naming standard.)

| Declaration | Description |
| --- | --- |
| `Dim astrNames (20) As String` | Declares an array named astrNames of 21 elements with the String data type and with index numbers from 0 to 20. When the lower bound of an array is 0, you enclose the upper bound in parentheses in the declaration statement. |
| `Static asngTaxRates (1 To 10) As Single` | Declares a static array named asngTaxRates of 10 elements with the Single data type and with index numbers from 1 to 10. When the lower bound of an array is greater than 0, include both bounds and the To keyword in parentheses in the declaration statement. |
| `Public Function Addresses (astrNames(20) As String)` | Declares an array named astrNames of 21 elements with the String data type as an argument of the Addresses function. |

You can create a module-level, fixed-size array by declaring the array in the Declarations section of the module. Use the Public keyword to share the array among all procedures in all modules in the project or use the Private keyword to share the array only among the procedures in the module in which the array is created. As an exception, you cannot create a Public array in a form or report module. Here are some examples of shared array declarations:

| Declaration | Description |
|---|---|
| `Public aintMatrix (9,9) As Integer` | Declares a two-dimensional public array named aintMatrix of 100 elements with the Integer data type, having index number pairs from (0,0) to (9,9). |
| `Private atxtAmounts(1 To 6) As TextBox` | Declares a private array named atxtAmounts of 6 text box object elements with index numbers from 1 to 6. |

## Using the Erase Statement

You can use the Erase statement to reinitialize the elements of a fixed-size array.

To explore arrays, create a new module named basArrays to store the procedures we create in this section.

1. Create the CreateArray procedure as shown below:

```
Public Sub CreateArray()
    Dim astrArray(3) As String
    astrArray(0) = "Margaret"
    astrArray(1) = "Peacock"
    astrArray(2) = "Sales Representative"
    MsgBox astrArray(1) & ", " & astrArray(0) & " is a " & 
    ➥astrArray(2)
    Erase astrArray
    MsgBox astrArray(1) & ", " & astrArray(0) & " is a " & 
    ➥astrArray(2)
End Sub
```

2. Run the procedure in the Debug window.

The procedure creates a fixed-size string array with three elements, assigns the string values and displays the values in a message box (see Figure 13.20a). After you dismiss the message, the procedure uses the Erase statement to reinitialize the elements to zero-length strings and displays the initialized values in a message box (see Figure 13.20b).

**FIGURE 13.20:**

Creating a fixed-size array (a) and using the Erase statement to reinitialize the elements of the array (b)

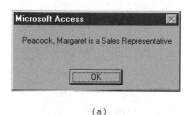

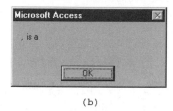

(a)

(b)

## Using the Array Function

You can use the Array function to create an array based on values in a list.

1.  Create the ArrayFunction procedure shown below in the basArrays module:

```
Public Sub ArrayFunction()
    Dim varData As Variant
    varData = Array("Margaret", "Peacock", #5/3/93#)
    MsgBox LBound(varData) & " to " & UBound(varData)
    MsgBox varData(0) & " " & varData(1) & " was hired on " &
    ➥varData(2)
End Sub
```

2.  Run the procedure in the Debug window.

The procedure creates a variant variable and uses the Array function to create an array of the three values in the list and assigns the result to the variant variable. (The varData variable must have the Variant data type in order to store values that have different data types.) A message box displays the lower and upper bounds of the array (see Figure 13.21a) and a second message box displays the values (see Figure 13.21b). In this procedure the varData variable contains an array.

**FIGURE 13.21:**

Use the UBound and LBound functions to determine the size of an array created using the Array function (a). The message displays the three values of the array (b).

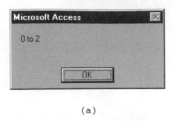

(a)

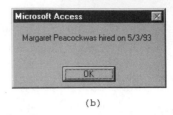

(b)

## Dynamic Arrays

You use a dynamic array instead of a fixed-size array when you don't know beforehand how many elements the array has. You create a dynamic array by using two statements: one statement to declare the array and a second statement to specify the size. You declare the array using the same syntax as for a fixed-size array without specifying the number of elements (leave a blank between the parentheses) and use the Redim statement in a procedure to specify the size and allocate the storage space required by the specified data type.

You can create a procedure-level dynamic array by including a declaration statement within the procedure using the syntax

```
(Dim|Static) arrayname() [As type]
```

and then including a Redim statement in the procedure to specify the size.

| Statement | Description |
| --- | --- |
| Dim astrNames( ) As String | Creates a local dynamic array. |
| ReDim astrNames (4) | Sets the number of elements to 5 with index numbers from 0 to 4. |

You can create a module-level dynamic array by placing a declaration statement in the Declarations section of a module using the syntax

```
[Public|Private] arrayname () [As type]
```

and then including a Redim statement in any procedure that refers to the array to specify its size.

| Statement | Description |
|---|---|
| `Public asngTaxRates () As Single` | Placed in the Declarations section of a module. Creates a module-level dynamic array. |
| `ReDim asngTaxRates (1 To 5)` | Placed within a procedure. Sets the number of elements to 5 with index nuumbers from 1 to 5. |

You can also set the bounds of a dynamic array using integer variables as in the following example:

```
ReDim asngTaxRates (intlower To intupper)
```

The ReDim statement specifies the size of the array and initializes its elements according to the array's data type. This means that Redim initializes each value to zero for a numeric array, to the zero-length string for a string array, to Empty for a Variant array, and to Nothing for an array of objects. You can use the ReDim statement to change the size of an array as often as you want; however, ReDim discards any values currently stored in the array elements when you run the statement unless you include the Preserve keyword.

You can use the Preserve keyword when you want to preserve the values in the array and also change the size of the array at the same time. You can only resize the last array dimension. If you decrease the size of the last array dimension, the data in the eliminated elements is discarded. When you use the Preserve keyword you cannot change the number of dimensions, only the size of the last array dimension.

To explore these ideas,

1. Create the DynamicArray procedure below in the basArrays module:

```
Public Sub DynamicArray()
    Dim avar() As Variant, str As String
    ReDim avar(2)
    avar(0) = 101
    avar(1) = 202
    MsgBox avar(0) & vbCrLf & avar(1), ,"Two element array"
    ReDim avar(3,2)
    avar(0,0) = "zero": avar(0,1) = 0
    avar(1,0) = "one": avar(1,1) = 1
    avar(2,0) = "two": avar(2,1) = 2
    str = avar(0,0) & "; " & avar(0,1) & vbCrLf
```

```
        str = str & avar(1,0) & "; " & avar(1,1) & vbCrLf
        str = str & avar(2,0) & "; " & avar(2,1)
        MsgBox str, , "Three rows and two columns"
        ReDim Preserve avar(3,1)
        str = avar(0,0) & vbCrLf & avar(1,0) & vbCrLf & avar(2,0)
        MsgBox str, ,"Discard the second column"
    End Sub
```

The procedure creates the avar array as a dynamic array of variants and uses a sequence of ReDim statements to size the array. The first ReDim statement sizes the array as a two-element array. The second ReDim statement discards the values assigned and resizes the array as a two-dimensional array with three rows and two columns. Each of the next three lines includes a pair of assignment statements using a colon to separate the statements. The third ReDim statement includes a Preserve keyword to save with values when the last dimension of the array is resized; the array is resized to a three-element array with three rows and one column and discards the data in the second column.

2. Run the procedure in the Debug window. The message boxes track the progress through the procedure (see Figure 13.22).

**FIGURE 13.22:**

The procedure uses a dynamic array and the ReDim statement to represent a two-element array (a) and a two dimensional array with three rows and two columns (b). The procedure uses the ReDim Preserve statement to discard the second column (c).

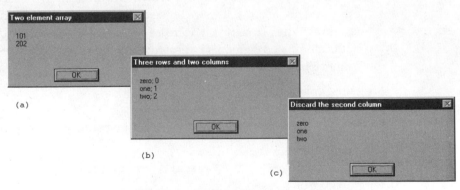

NOTE  The VBA instrinsic constant vbCrLf represents a carriage return followed by a line feed. Use the constant to begin a new line in the message box.

### Using the Erase Statement

The Erase statement works differently for fixed-size arrays and dynamic arrays. When you use the Erase statement for a dynamic array, the storage space that was used by the dynamic array is reclaimed and available for reuse. By contrast, when you use the Erase statement with a fixed-size array, the elements are reinitialized but the memory is not reclaimed.

> **TIP**
>
> If you only need to use an array part of the time, you can declare it as a dynamic array and reclaim the memory when you are finished using the Erase statement.

## Using Arrays as Arguments

If you don't want to specify the number of arguments that a called procedure can receive, you can use the ParamArray keyword to take an arbitrary number of arguments from the calling procedure and place them in an array of variants. The ParamArray argument must be the last argument in the argument list. For example, if you are creating a generic procedure to calculate the average of a set of numerical values, you can use the ParamArray keyword in the argument as follows

```
Public Function Average(ParamArray aArgs())
```

where aArgs is the name of the array. When you call the Average function you can send an arbitrary number of arguments as shown in the following calling statement

```
Call Average(2,5,46,23,1)
```

When you use the ParamArray keyword, the arguments are the Variant data type by default and you cannot specify another data type. You cannot include the ByRef, ByVal, or Optional keywords together with the ParamArray keyword.

## Creating Your Own Data Types

You can also create your own data type based on the fundamental data types listed in Table 12.1 in the last chapter. You can create a custom data type for a single variable that holds several elements of information with different data types.

For example, you can use a single variable to refer to a customer's name (String data type), the date of an order (Date data type) and the amount of the order (Currency data type). You can define a custom data type only in the Declarations section of a module. You create the custom data type using the Type and End Type statements. After defining a custom data type, you can declare a variable with the custom data type as a procedure-level or module-level variable. Once you have declared a variable with the custom data type, you can refer to an element of the variable using the syntax

```
variablename.elementname
```

and assign values to its elements using the normal assignment statements.

To explore these concepts,

1. Create the custom data type named OrderInfo in the Declarations section of basVariables as follows

```
Public Type OrderInfo
Customer As String
OrderDate As Date
Amount As Currency
End Type
```

2. Create the ViewOrder procedure shown below in the basVariables module:

```
Public Sub ViewOrder()
    Dim ord As OrderInfo
    ord.Customer = "Alfreds Futterkiste"
    ord.OrderDate = #5/10/96#
    ord.Amount = 3124.98
    MsgBox ord.Customer &" placed an order on "& ord.OrderDate &
    ➥" for $"& ord.Amount
End Sub
```

3. Run the ViewOrder procedure in the Debug window. The procedure declares a variable of the new OrderInfo data type and assigns values to each element. The message box displays the elements of the ord variable (see Figure 13.23).

**FIGURE 13.23:**

A single variable with a custom data type holds the customer's name, order date, and order amount.

User-defined data types can contain objects, fixed-size arrays, and dynamic arrays as shown in the following examples:

```
Private Type Orders
frmInput as Form
rptOutput as Report
dbOrders as Database
End Type

Public Type CustomerInfo
Customer As String
Address(2) As String   'A fixed-size array with two elements
Phone() As String   'A dynamic array
FirstOrder As Date
End Type
```

## Using Custom Data Types as Arguments

You can use a single custom data type to pass several arguments to a procedure using a single variable. For example, you can pass the four variables of the CustomerInfo data type to the CustomerDataEntry procedure as a single variable as follows:

```
Public Sub CustomerDataEntry(CurrentCustomer As CustomerInfo)
```

# Summary

This chapter has introduced you to using variables in procedures. The main reasons for using variables are that your code runs faster when you use variables and specify their data types and that you can create procedures that are reusable because you can use variables to replace the names of specific objects. The important points we covered are these:

- You can control which other procedures can use a variable and how long a variable "lives" by specifying a variable as a procedure-level or a module-level variable and using keywords in the declaration.

- You should declare variables with the most specific data types for faster code.

- You can declare procedure-level variables in two places:

    - In a separate declaration statement within the procedure

    - In the argument list of a procedure called by another procedure

- You can declare module-level variables in the Declarations section of the module.

- You can pass values and objects to a procedure as arguments in two ways:

    - By reference; the procedure receives the variable itself

    - By value; the procedure receives a copy of the variable

- Event procedures have predefined names and argument lists.

- You can create custom constants to make your code more readable.

- You can use arrays to handle several variables that have the same data type. If the array has the Variant data type, the elements may have different data types.

- You can create a custom data type for a variable that can hold several elements with different data types.

The next chapter completes the introduction to Access VBA by explaining the special statements you can use to control which instructions are executed and how many times a set of instructions is executed.

# CHAPTER

## FOURTEEN

**14**

# Mechanics of Procedures III: Controlling Execution

- Making decisions in a procedure

- Using loops to repeat operations

- Using the With...End With statements for faster code

- Using Not to toggle a property

- Understanding the Timer and DoEvents functions

- Understanding the SysCmd function

**U**nless you include specific directions to the contrary, VBA executes a procedure's statements consecutively: beginning with the first statement, VBA executes each statement from left to right and then moves down to the next consecutive statement; when VBA comes to the End... statement, the procedure terminates. This left-to-right, top-to-bottom execution pattern is called *sequential flow*. VBA provides several statements you can use to change the *flow of execution*: you can change the order in which statements are executed, whether a set of statements is executed at all, and whether a set of statements is repeated. To indicate that you want to change the order of execution for a set of statements, you use a keyword or a control statement to mark the beginning and another keyword or control statement to mark the end of the set; the control statements you use to control the flow are called *control structures*. Most of the power of VBA comes from two kinds of control structures:

**Decision structures**    You use decision structures to test conditions and perform different sets of statements depending on the outcome of the test.

**Loop structures**    You use loop structures to execute a set of statements repetitively.

In this chapter you'll learn about the different versions of both kinds of control structures that VBA provides. You'll use the structures to create several of the standard programming techniques that you'll want to include in your programming toolbox such as testing the data type of variables before doing calculations, efficient ways to loop through a collection, and walking a recordset. The second part of the chapter is a brief discussion of useful built-in statements and functions.

**NOTE**    For hands-on experience with the control structures described in this section, create a new copy of the Northwind database named Northwind_Ch14 and create a new module named basControlStructures. Create the example procedures in the basControlStructures module or in the form module specified in the example. Run the example procedures in the Debug window unless the example gives other calling directions.

# Making Decisions with Conditions

You use a decision structure to execute different sets of statements depending on the result of testing a condition. The condition can be any string or numeric expression that evaluates to True or False. The condition is usually a comparison, such as intCount > 0, but it can be any expression that evaluates to a numeric value, such as intCount. If the numeric value is zero, the condition is False; if the numeric value is nonzero, the condition is True.

## If...Then

Suppose you have a set of statements that you want to execute if a condition is True and that you want to skip otherwise. In this case you can use the If...Then decision structure. You use the If...Then structure to evaluate a test condition and perform a statement, or a set of statements, if the test condition evaluates to True. The test condition can be any expression that evaluates to True or False. There are two versions of the If...Then structure:

**Single-line syntax:**

```
If condition Then statements
```

If the test condition evaluates to True, the *statements* on the line are executed and VBA moves to the next statement in the procedure. If the test condition evaluates to False, the *statements* on the line are not executed and execution flows to the next statement in the procedure.

**Multiple-line syntax** (also called the *block syntax*):

```
If condition Then
    statements
End If
```

If the test condition evaluates to True, the *statements* are executed, VBA moves to the End If statement and exits the control structure. If the test condition evaluates to False, the *statements* are skipped, VBA moves to the End If statement and exits the control structure. Figure 14.1 depicts the If...Then decision structure.

**FIGURE 14.1:**

The If...Then decision
structure

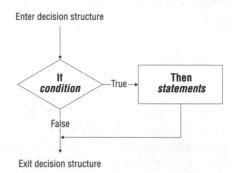

You can use the single-line syntax for multiple statements but the statements must be on one line and separated by colons (:). The single-line syntax is useful for simple tests, however, the multiple-line syntax is usually easier to read even when there is a single statement.

Here are examples of the If...Then structure:

1. Insert the NullToZero procedure in the basControlStructures module. This procedure tests the function's argument. If the value is Null, the procedure sets the value to Zero, otherwise the procedure does nothing.

```
Public Function NullToZero(X)
    If IsNull(X) Then NullToZero = 0
End Function
```

2. In the Debug window, type each of the following and press Enter. In the first case, the condition is false so the procedure ends without returning a value. In the second case, the condition is true, and the value of the function is set to zero. The Debug window displays the returned value.

   **?NullToZero(4)**

   **?NullToZero(Null)**

3. Open the Customers form in Design view, click in the form's OnUnload event property, and click the Build button. Enter the Form_Unload event procedure shown below.

```
Private Sub Form_Unload (Cancel As Integer)
    If MsgBox ("Close form? ", vbYesNo) = vbNo Then
```

```
        Cancel = True
    End If
End Sub
```

4. Save the form, switch to Form view, and click the form's Close box. The procedure displays a Yes/No message box. If you choose the No button, the condition is true and the procedure sets the Cancel argument to True (which informs Access to cancel the closing of the form). If you choose the Yes button, the condition is false, the procedure ends, and Access closes the form.

The If, Then, and End If keywords are required parts of these decision control structures. If you omit a required keyword in any control structure, VBA generates a compile error. Figure 14.2 shows the error message when you delete the End If statement.

**FIGURE 14.2:**

VBA generates an error when you omit a required End If statement in a decision structure

## If...Then...Else

Suppose you have two alternative sets and want to execute only one set depending on the value of a condition. In this case you can use the If...Then...Else decision structure. You use the If...Then...Else decision structure to evaluate a test condition and execute one set of statements if the test condition evaluates to True and another set of statements if the test condition evaluates to False. There are two versions of the If...Then...Else structure, the single-line syntax version and the multiple-line syntax version.

**Single-line Syntax**    The single-line syntax approach to If…Then…Else statements is written as follows:

```
If condition Then statements [Else elsestatements]
```

VBA evaluates the condition. If the condition evaluates to True, VBA executes the statements following Then and otherwise VBA executes the statements following Else. After executing either set of statements, VBA moves to the next statement in the procedure. You can use the single-line syntax for multiple statements, but the statements must be on one line and separated by colons (:). Normally, to make your code easier to read, you use the single-line syntax only when there is a single statement for each alternative.

**Multiple-line syntax**  The multiple line syntax can be used when there is one test condition and a pair of alternative sets of statements, as in the following example:

```
If condition Then
    [statements]
[Else
    elsestatements]
End If
```

The syntax can also be used when there is more than one test condition and several blocks of statements as possible blocks to be executed. You can use the If...Then...Else structure to determine which one of the several blocks of statements to perform as follows:

```
If condition1 Then
    [block1statements]
[ElseIf condition2 Then
    block2 statements]
...
[Else
    blockn statements]
End If
```

VBA evaluates the first condition. If *condition1* evaluates to True, VBA executes the *block1* statements and then jumps out of the decision structure to the next statement following the End If statement skipping the remaining statements in between. If *condition1* evaluates to False, VBA tests the next condition in the ElseIf statement and either carries out its statement block and jumps out of the decision structure if the condition is True, or moves to testing the next condition if it isn't. When it finds a True condition, VBA executes its statement block and jumps out. If none of the conditions evaluates to True, VBA can execute the optional Else statement block and then leave the decision structure. You can have any number of ElseIf clauses or none. The only required lines of the syntax are the If...Then and End If statements. Figure 14.3 depicts the If...Then...Else decision structure in the case of a single condition.

**FIGURE 14.3:**

The If...Then...Else decision structure

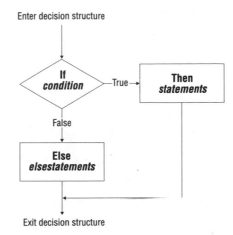

Here are some examples of the If...Then...Else structure:

1. Enter the Multiply3 function shown below in the basControlStructures module. The Multiply3 function determines if the optional argument has been passed and uses different formulas depending on the result.

```
Public Function Multiply3(X,Y,Optional Z)
    If IsMissing(Z) Then Multiply3 = X*Y Else Multiply3 = X*Y*Z
End Function
```

2. In the Debug window enter each of the following and press Enter. In the first example, the condition is true, so Access multiplies the two numbers and displays their product. In the second example, the condition is false, so Access multiplies the three numbers and displays their product.

    **? Multiply3(2,3)**

    **? Multiply3(2,3,4)**

3. Enter the MultiplyTest function in the basControlStructures module. The MultiplyTest function determines if the arguments have a numeric data type before performing the product.

```
Public Function MultiplyTest(X,Y)
    If IsNumeric(X) and IsNumeric(Y) Then
        MultiplyTest = X*Y
Else
```

```
        MsgBox "Non-numeric arguments"
    End If
End Function
```

4.  In the Debug window, enter each of the following and press Enter. In the first example, the condition is true, the numbers are multiplied and the product is displayed. In the second example, the condition is false and the message is printed.

    ? MultiplyTest(2,3)

    ? MultiplyTest("two",3)

## Using Typeof...Is to Determine an Object Type

Often when you are working with controls on forms, you need to be able to determine the control's type. For example, suppose you want to use a form for both review and editing; you need to toggle the controls' Locked property (and possibly the Enabled property) between the review and edit modes. The problem is that not all control types have a Locked property, so you need a way to determine if an arbitrary control has a specific control type before setting the property. You can use the expression

   TypeOf-*objectname* Is *objecttype*

as the test condition in order to determine whether an object has the specified object data type. To explore this concept, try the following:

1.  Insert the PreviousControlType function in the basControlStructures module. The PreviousControlType procedure determines if a control is a text box and displays a message if it is. This procedure is set up as a generic procedure that works with any form by using the PreviousControl property of the Screen object to refer to the control that previously had the focus.

```
Public Function PreviousControlType()
    If Typeof Screen.PreviousControl Is TextBox Then
        MsgBox "This is a text box", ,"Text Box Tester"
    End If
End Function
```

2.  Open the Customers form in Form view, create a command button named cmdControlType and with the caption Control Type on the Customers

form. Click the button's OnClick property and set the property to
= PreviousControlType(). By using an event-handling function stored in a
standard module instead of an event procedure, you can paste the button
to any form.

3. To test a control, click the control and then click the button. If you click a
text box, the message box is displayed (see Figure 14.4), otherwise there is
no response. If you click a label, the focus moves to the text box control
associated with the label and clicking the button displays the message.

**FIGURE 14.4:**

Using TypeOf...Is to
determine if a control is
a text box control

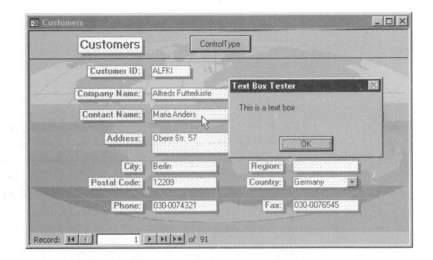

## Select Case

Suppose you have several sets of alternatives and you want to execute one set
depending on the value of an expression. In this case, you can use the Select
Case...End Select decision structure as an alternative to the If...Then...Else
structure. In the Select Case decision structure, you evaluate a test expression and
consider possible cases by comparing the value of the test expression to the
values appropriate to each case.

The Select Case decision structure has the syntax:

```
Select Case testexpression
    Case expressionlist1
        [block1 statements]
```

```
        Case expressionlist2
            [block2 statements]
    ...
        Case Else
            [blockn statements]
    End Select
```

Each *expressionlist* is a list of one or more values appropriate to the case and the corresponding statement block contains zero or more statements that are executed if the value of the test expression satisfies the expressionlist. An item in *expressionlist* can have any of the following three forms:

- *expression*   For example, Case 2, 4, 5, 7

- *expression*   To *expression* For example, Case 2 To 5. The expression that precedes To must be smaller than the expression that follows To.

- Is *operator expression*   For example Case Is >10. The operator can be any comparison operator except Is or Like.

After evaluating the *testexpression* in the Select Case statement, VBA tests the values in *expressionlist1*; if any value in *expressionlist1* matches the value of *testexpression*, VBA executes the *block1 statements* and then jumps out of the decision structure to the next statement following the End Select statement, skipping any blocks in between. If no value in *expressionlist1* matches the value of *testexpression*, VBA moves to the next Case statement and tests the values in its *expressionlist* and either carries out its statement block and jumps out if there is a match or moves to the next Case statement if there isn't a match. If there are no matching values in any *expressionlist*, VBA can execute the statements in the optional Case Else clause and then jump out of the decision structure. When the value of the *testexpression* matches a value in more than one Case, VBA executes the statements for the first matching Case clause. Figure 14.5 depicts the Select Case decision structure.

Here is an example of the Select Case structure:

1.   Enter the Numbergame procedure in the basControlStructures module. The procedure uses the InputBox function to collect an integer from the game player (see Figure 14.6); the number you enter is assigned to the intnumber variable. The Select Case decision structure tests the value of the number against the expressions in each Case and displays a message box for the matching Case.

```
Public Sub NumberGame()
    Dim intnumber as Integer
    intnumber = InputBox("Enter an integer from 1 to 20","Number
    ➥Game")
    Select Case intnumber
        Case 2, 4, 6, 8
            MsgBox "The number is even and less than 9"
        Case 9 To 20
            MsgBox "The number is from 9 to 20"
        Case Else
            MsgBox "The number is odd and less than 9"
    End Select
End Sub
```

2.  Run the Numbergame procedure in the Debug window. When you enter an integer between 1 and 20 in the input box, the procedure displays the correct message box depending on whether the number you entered is in the first case (2, 4, 6, or 8), the second case (9 to 20), or the else case (odd and less than 9). Note that the procedure does not test to determine if the value you entered in the input box is actually an integer between 1 and 20.

**FIGURE 14.5:**

The Select Case decision structure

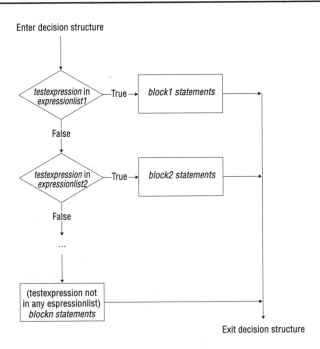

**FIGURE 14.6:**

The value you enter in the input box is assigned to a variable, which is tested using the Select Case decision structure

> **NOTE**
>
> You can't use the TypeOf *objectname* Is *objecttype* clause in the Select Case control structure.

> **NOTE**
>
> Another way to perform multiple branching is to use the On...GoSub and On...GoTo statements. These statements are a carryover from older versions of Basic in which line number and line labels are used to identify lines of code. The Select Case structure provides a more flexible way to do multiple branching and is the only method this book recommends.

# Loops for Repetitive Operations

There are times when you need to cycle through every element of an array or every member of a collection. For example, suppose you want to change a form from a data entry form to a review form. To protect the data controls on the form, you need to cycle through the controls on the form and lock each control that holds data. One approach is to write a separate statement for each specific control on the form that tests to determine if the control holds data and locks the control if it does. A more efficient solution is to write a single statement that tests and locks an arbitrary data control and then uses control statements to instruct VBA to loop through the controls on the form and execute the statement for each control. VBA provides several styles of loop structures that you can use to execute the same set of statements repeatedly either a specified number of times or until a condition is satisfied.

# For...Next

When you know how many times you want to execute the statements in the loop, you can use the For...Next structure. You use a *counter* variable to keep track of the repetitions and specify the counter's *start* and *end* values. The *start*, *end*, and *increment* arguments can be numeric values or expressions. The syntax for the For...Next loop structure is

```
For counter = start To end [Step increment]
    statements
Next [counter]
```

To understand how the loop works, let's assume the increment is positive or zero. When the loop begins, VBA sets the *counter* to the *start* value, tests the value of the counter, and takes one of the two alternatives:

- If *counter* is greater than the *end* value, VBA jumps out of the loop and executes the next statement following the Next statement.

- If *counter* is less than or equal to the *end* value, VBA executes the state-ments in the loop and increases the counter by the value of the *increment* argument. If you omit the Step clause, VBA increments the counter by one.

After executing the statements, VBA goes back to the For statement and repeats the process. The loop repeats until the *counter* is greater than the *end* value. When the increment is positive, the *end* value must be greater than the *start* value, otherwise the loop repeats endlessly. As an example of a positive increment, in the structure

```
For Count = 2 To 10 Step 2
    statements
Next Count
```

VBA begins the loop by setting Count to 2 and begins the first pass through the loop. VBA executes the statements, increases Count by 2, and returns to the For statement to compare the value of Count to 10. As long as the value of Count is less than or equal to 10, VBA takes another pass through the loop.

**TIP** While it is possible to set the increment to zero and change the value of the counter in the statements of the loop, you should avoid this practice because your code will be harder to debug than if you use a non-zero increment.

If the increment is a negative number, VBA begins as before by setting the counter to the start value, tests the value of the counter, and takes one of the two alternatives:

- If the counter is less than the end value, VBA jumps out of the loop and executes the next statement following the Next statement.

- If the counter is greater than or equal to the end value, VBA executes the statements in the loop and decreases the counter by the value of the *increment* argument.

After executing the statements, VBA goes back to the For statement and repeats the process. The loop repeats until the counter is less than the end value. The end value must be less than the start value. Here is an example of a negative step:

```
For Count = 7 to 3 Step −1
    statements
Next Count
```

**TIP**   You can omit the counter in the Next statement, but your code is easier to read if you include the counter.

Figure 14.7 depicts the For...Next loop structure.

**FIGURE 14.7:**

The For...Next loop structure

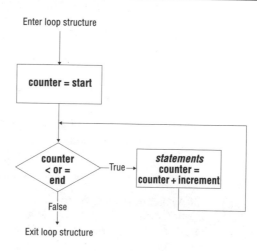

To explore the structure:

1. Insert the Counting procedure shown below in the basControlStructures module. The procedure defines iCount as the counter. The loop begins by setting the iCount variable to 1 and printing the value in the Debug window. VBA increments the counter by 2 and runs the loop again. VBA continues to increment the counter and runs the loop five times. When the counter has the value 11, VBA exits the loop.

```
Public Sub Counting()
    Dim iCount As Integer
    For iCount = 1 To 10 Step 2
        Debug.Print iCount
    Next iCount
End Sub
```

2. In the Debug window, type **Counting** and press Enter. VBA prints the odd integers from 1 through 9 in the Debug window.

## Using For...Next with a Collection

You can use the For...Next structure to loop through the elements of a collection. Every collection is an array and has a Count property that returns the number of elements in the array; use the syntax *collectionname*.Count to determine the number of elements in the collection. You can refer to an item in a collection by its position in the collection using its index number. Because object collections are zero-based in Access, the index number begins with 0 and ends with Count - 1. For example, Forms.Count is the number of forms that are currently open in a database, Forms(0) is the first open form, and Forms(Count - 1) is the form you last opened.

To use the For...Next structure to loop through the items in a collection, you can use the index number as the loop counter, starting the counter at 0 and ending at *collectionname*.Count - 1.

1. Insert the NameForms procedure shown below in the basControlStructures module. The NameForms procedure uses a For...Next loop structure with the collection's index number as the loop counter to list the name of each of the forms that are currently open.

```
Public Sub NameForms()
    Dim iCount As Integer
```

```
      For iCount = 0 To Forms.Count - 1
          Debug.Print Forms(iCount).Name
      Next iCount
End Sub
```

2. Open a few forms in either Form or Design view and then type **NameForms** in the Debug window and press Enter. VBA lists the name of each open form.

# For Each...Next

The For Each...Next loop is similar to the For...Next loop, but instead of repeating the statements a specified number of times, the For Each...Next loop repeats the statements once for each element of an array or each object in a collection. The For Each...Next loop is extremely powerful because it lets you loop through the array or collection without having to know how many elements there are. The syntax is

```
      For Each element In group
          statements
      Next [element]
```

where *group* is the name of a collection of objects or the name of an array. For a collection of objects, *element* is the variable representing an object in the collection and must have either the Variant data type or an object data type; for an array, *element* must have the Variant data type.

## Using For Each...Next with a Collection

You can use the For Each...Next structure to work with collections of Application objects and data access objects. When you work with collections of data access objects, you must use the full reference for the collection beginning at the top of the data access object hierarchy. If the collection is in the current database, you can use the CurrentDB function to refer to the current database. For example, CurrentDB.TableDefs refers to the collection of table definitions in the current database. You can use the For Each...Next loop structure to process each member of a collection. The following examples show how to use the For Each...Next structure to get or set the values of properties and to execute methods.

1. Insert the procedure shown below in the basControlStructures module. The NameEachTable procedure uses the For Each...Next structure to print the name of each table in the database, that is, the name of each TableDef in the TableDefs collection.

```
Public Sub NameEachTable()
    Dim tbl As TableDef
    For Each tbl in CurrentDB.TableDefs
        Debug.Print tbl.Name
    Next tbl
End Sub
```

2. In the Debug window, type NameEachTable and press Enter. VBA prints the name of each table in the database including the hidden system tables (see Figure 14.8).

**FIGURE 14.8:**

The NameEachTable procedure uses a For Each...Next loop structure to print the names of the tables in the Northwind database.

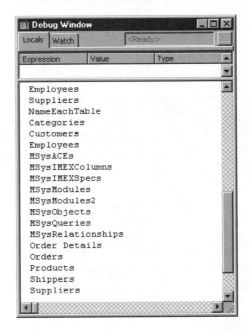

3. Insert the FontToRed function procedure in the basControlStructures module. The FontToRed procedure changes the font color of all the controls on a form to red. This procedure is designed as a generic function procedure that works with any form in which all controls have a ForeColor property. To allow the procedure to be reusable, the procedure uses the ActiveForm property of the Screen object to refer to the form and refers to the controls collection as Screen.ActiveForm.Controls. (Because Controls is the default collection of the

Form object, you can also refer to the collection as Screen.ActiveForm instead of Screen.ActiveForm.Controls.)

```
Public Function FontToRed()
    Const Red as Integer = 255
    Dim ctl As Control
    For Each ctl in Screen.ActiveForm.Controls
        ctl.ForeColor = Red
    Next ctl
End Function
```

4. Open the Customers form in Design view. On the Customers form, place a command button named cmdRed with the caption Change Font Color to Red. Click the button's OnClick property and set the property to =FontToRed()

5. Save the form, switch to Form view, and click the button. The font color of all of the controls changes to red.

> **NOTE**
>
> Using the For Each...Next structure to loop through a collection is faster than using the For...Next structure. The reason is that when you use the For...Next structure, VBA looks up the item using its index number. VBA must test the entire list until the matching item is found. By contrast, when you use the For Each...Next structure, VBA remembers its position in the list and simply moves forward by one item for each repetition of the loop. The only time you should use the For...Next structure for a collection is when you are using the loop to remove items from the collection. When you remove an item from the collection, the positions of the remaining items are affected and VBA may lose its place with unpredictable results if you use the For Each...Next structure.

## Do...Loop

The Do...Loop also lets you repeat statements an unspecified number of times. The Do...Loop structure uses a condition to decide when the loop is finished. The condition must be an expression that evaluates to True or False. There are four versions of the Do...Loop depending whether you want to evaluate the condition at the beginning or at the end of the loop and whether you want to continue the loop as long as the condition is True or as long as the condition is False.

## Do While...Loop

The syntax for the Do While...Loop structure is

```
Do While condition
    statements
Loop
```

VBA begins execution of the loop by testing the condition. If the condition evaluates to False, VBA immediately jumps out of the loop, skipping all of the loop statements, and executes the statement following the Loop statement. The loop statements are never executed if the condition is initially False. If the condition evaluates to True, VBA executes the statements and then returns to the Do While statement and tests the condition. The loop continues as long as the condition evaluates to True. Figure 14.9 depicts the Do While...Loop loop structure.

**FIGURE 14.9:**

The Do While...Loop loop structure

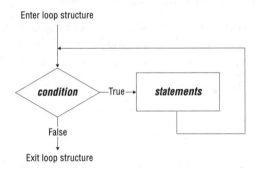

## Do...Loop While

When you place the While condition clause at the end of the structure, VBA is guaranteed to execute the statements within the loop at least once.

```
Do
    statements
Loop While condition
```

VBA executes the Do...Loop While structure by executing the loop statements first. After executing the statements, VBA moves to the Loop While statement and tests the condition; if the condition evaluates to False, VBA exits the loop and executes the next statement following the Loop While statement; otherwise, VBA goes to the beginning and executes the loop statements again. Figure 14.10 depicts the Do...Loop While loop structure.

**FIGURE 14.10:**

The Do...Loop While loop structure

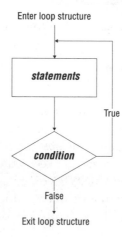

## Do Until...Loop and Do...Loop Until

When you replace the While keyword with the Until keyword, VBA continues repeated execution of the loop statements *until* the condition evaluates to True (which is the same as repeated execution *while* the condition evaluates to False).

The Do Until...Loop structure has the syntax

```
Do Until condition
    statements
Loop
```

If the condition is False, VBA executes the loop statements and returns to the Do statement. If the condition evaluates to True, VBA exits the loop and executes the next statement following the Loop statement. If the condition evaluates to True initially, the statements of the Do Until...Loop structure are not executed at all. Figure 14.11 depicts the Do Until...Loop loop structure.

The Do...Loop Until structure has the syntax

```
Do
    statements
Loop Until condition
```

VBA executes the statements and tests the condition. If the condition is False, VBA returns to the Do statement. If the condition is True, VBA exits the loop and continues with the next statement. If the condition evaluates to True initially, the statements of the Do...Loop Until structure are executed once. Figure 14.12 depicts the Do...Loop Until loop structure.

**FIGURE 14.11:**

The Do Until...Loop loop structure

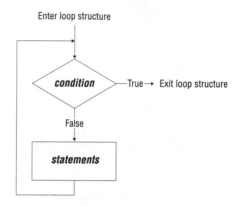

**FIGURE 14.12:**

The Do...Loop Until loop structure

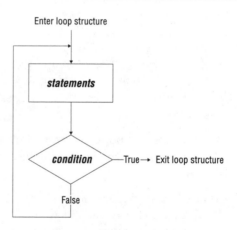

Here are examples of the four types of Do...Loop structures. Insert each of the procedures in the basControlStructures module.

1. Run the DoWhile procedure in the Debug window. The loop runs three times.

```
Public Sub DoWhile()
    Dim Counter As Integer
    Counter = 0
    Do While Counter < 3
        Debug.Print Counter
        Counter = Counter + 1
    Loop
End Sub
```

2.  Run in the DoLoopWhile procedure the Debug window. The loop runs three times.

```
Public Sub DoLoopWhile()
    Dim Counter As Integer
    Counter = 0
    Do
        Debug.Print Counter
        Counter = Counter +1
    Loop While Counter < 3
End Sub
```

3.  Run the DoUntil procedure in the Debug window. The loop is not executed at all because the condition is True initially.

```
Public Sub DoUntil()
    Dim Counter As Integer
    Counter = 0
    Do Until Counter < 3
        Debug.Print Counter
        Counter = Counter + 1
    Loop
End Sub
```

4.  Run the DoLoopUntil procedure in the Debug window. The loop runs once. At the end of the first loop, the condition evaluates to True so VBA exits the loop.

```
Public Sub DoLoopUntil()
    Dim Counter As Integer
    Counter = 0
    Do
        Debug.Print Counter
        Counter = Counter +
    Loop Until Counter < 3
End Sub
```

> **WARNING**
>
> You must be sure that at least one of the statements in the Do...Loop changes the value of the condition so that sooner or later the condition evaluates to False. Without such a statement, the structure is an *endless loop*. You can stop execution of most endless loops by pressing Ctrl+Break. It is possible, however, to create an endless loop called a *tight loop* that locks up the computer so that the only way to end the loop is to press Ctrl+Alt+Delete and exit from Access.

> **NOTE**
>
> Another way to perform looping is with the While...Wend structure. With the While...Wend structure you can specify the test condition only at the beginning of the loop and you can specify that the loop continues to execute until the test condition becomes True. The Do...Loop is more flexible because you can specify the test condition at the beginning or at the end of the loop and can specify whether the loop continues to execute until the test condition is True or until the text condition is False.

## Looping through a Recordset

A common operation in Access VBA is "walking a recordset." You can use a Do loop to walk through the every record of a recordset from beginning to end. Each pass through the loop points to a record (the current record) in the recordset, takes some action on the current record, and uses the MoveNext method to move the current record pointer to the next record. You use the recordset's EOF property to determine when the loop is finished. The EOF property is False as long as you are pointing to a record in the recordset and True if you move past the last record. When you are on the last record in the recordset, the MoveNext method moves the current record pointer beyond the recordset limits, the EOF property becomes True, and the loop terminates. Normally, you want the loop statements to execute only if a recordset actually has records, so you usually use a Do Until...Loop to walk the records; if the recordset has no records, the EOF property is True so the loop never executes. The structure for "walking a recordset" is shown in Listing 14.1

### Listing 14.1

```
Do Until rst.EOF
    statements acting on the current record
```

```
        rst.MoveNext
    Loop
```

where rst is an object variable representing a recordset object.

As an example, we'll use a Do Until...Loop to walk through the records of the Employees table as follows:

1. Enter the LoopRecordset procedure shown in Listing 14.2 in the basControl-Structures module. The procedure declares object variables to point to the current database and the open recordset and uses the reference DBEngine(0)(0) to refer to the current database. The procedure uses the OpenRecordset method of the Database object to open a table-type recordset on the Employees table.

### Listing 14.2

```
Public Sub LoopRecordset()
    Dim db As Database, rst As Recordset
    Set db = DBEngine(0)(0)
    Set rst = db.OpenRecordset("Employees", dbOpenTable)
    Do Until rst.EOF
        Debug.Print rst!LastName
        rst.MoveNext
    Loop
End Sub
```

2. Run the LoopRecordset procedure in the Debug window. Each pass through the Do loop prints the value in the LastName field of the current record and moves the current record pointer to the next record (see Figure 14.13). When the current record pointer has moved past the last record in the recordset, the EOF property is True and the loop ends.

# Nesting Control Structures

You can place control structures within other control structures; a control structure that is placed within another control structure is *nested*. As an example, suppose you want to lock all of the text boxes on a form. You can use a For Each...Next structure to loop through all of the controls on the form. For each control, you can use an If Typeof...Then...Else structure to determine whether the control is a text

**FIGURE 14.13:**

Walking a recordset
using a Do Until...Loop

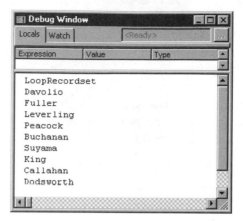

box and lock the control if it is a text box. We'll use the Screen object to refer to the active form so the locking procedure can be reused on any form.

1. Insert the LockControls procedure shown in Listing 14.3 in the basControl-Structures module. The If...Then decision structure is nested within the For Each...Next loop structure. The procedure uses Screen.ActiveForm.Controls to refer to the Controls collection of the active form.

### Listing 14.3

```
Public Function LockControls()
    Dim ctl As Control
    For Each ctl In Screen.ActiveForm.Controls
        If TypeOf ctl Is TextBox Then ctl.Locked = True
    Next ctl
End Function
```

2. Open the Customers form in Design view. Place a command button named cmdLockControls with the caption Lock the Text Boxes on the Customers form. Set the button's OnClick property to =LockControls().

3. Save the form, switch to Form view, and run the LockControls procedure by clicking the button. VBA locks all of the text box controls.

# Abbreviating Object References

There are times when you need to take several actions on an object. For example, suppose you want to disable the text boxes that are locked by the LockControls procedure in Listing 14.3. In addition, you want to provide visual cues to indicate that the form is in review mode instead of data entry mode. You can provide a visual cue by changing the background color of the text boxes. One solution for setting several properties for an object is to use a separate statement for each property as follows

```
object.property = value
```

For each statement, VBA has to look up the object; if the reference to the object includes traversing other objects in the hierarchy, looking up the object for each statement takes execution time. Instead, you can use the With...End With structure.

## With...End With

The With...End With block allows you to perform a set of statements on the same object without having to look up the object for each statement; instead, you use an abbreviated reference as follows:

```
With object
    [statements]
End With
```

where each statement may be one of the following simple types

```
.property = value
.method
```

that sets a property or runs a method. A statement may also contain an expression that refers to a property or a method.

When *object* is a simple object variable as in the example below, using the With structure may not save execution time but will save programming time because you have to enter the object variable only once. When the object is an expression that returns an object, such as Screen.ActiveControl, using the With structure saves execution time because VBA evaluates the expression just once. VBA evaluates the expression and assigns a reference to the object internally. VBA then places this hidden object variable in front of the dots in the statements inside the With structure.

As an example, the ReviewMode function procedure in Listing 14.4 uses the With...End With structure to set the Locked, Enabled, and Backcolor properties for a control. The procedure uses three levels of nested control structures to change any form from edit mode to review mode:

- The function procedure uses a For Each...Next structure to loop through the controls on the active form.

- For each control, the procedure nests an If TypeOf structure to determine if the control is a text box.

- If the control is a text box, the procedure uses a nested With...End With structure to change the control's properties.

Here are the steps:

1. Insert the ReviewMode procedure shown in Listing 14.4 in the basControl-Structures module. The procedure walks through the controls on the active form. (Controls is the default collection so the procedures uses Screen.Active-Form to refer to the collection.) For each control, the procedure determines if the control is a text box and if so, changes the control's properties, otherwise moves to the next control.

### Listing 14.4

```
Public Function ReviewMode()
    Const Red As Integer = 255
    Dim ctl As Control
    For Each ctl in Screen.ActiveForm
        If Typeof ctl Is TextBox Then
            With ctl
                .Locked = True
                .Enabled = False
                .ForeColor = Red
            End With
        End If
    Next
End Function
```

2. Open the Customers form in Design view. Place a command button named cmdReviewMode, with the caption Change to Review Mode, on the Customers form. Set the button's OnClick property to =ReviewMode().

3. Save the form, switch to Form view, and click the button to run the procedure. The procedure locks and disables the text boxes and sets their font color to red.

# Useful Statements and Functions

VBA provides an extensive set of built-in statements and functions that are useful in writing procedures. This section includes brief descriptions of a few of them. Online Help provides complete listings of the available statements and functions, see Figure 14.14. For example to find the statements reference, choose the Contents tab in Help, choose Microsoft Access and Visual Basic for Applications Reference, choose Statements, and then Statements Reference. The Statements Reference is a clickable list of available statements (see Figure 14.14).

---

**FIGURE 14.14:**

The statements reference is a clickable list of available statements.

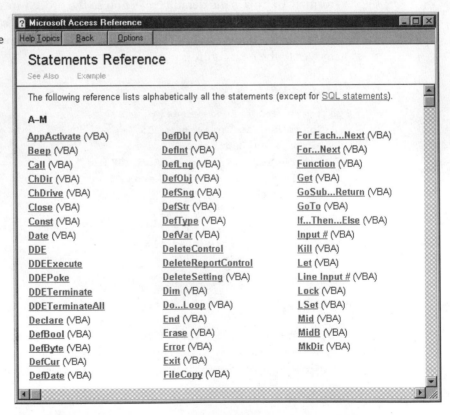

```
Microsoft Access Reference
Help Topics   Back   Options

Statements Reference
See Also    Example

The following reference lists alphabetically all the statements (except for SQL statements).

A-M
AppActivate (VBA)    DefDbl (VBA)           For Each...Next (VBA)
Beep (VBA)           DefInt (VBA)           For...Next (VBA)
Call (VBA)           DefLng (VBA)           Function (VBA)
ChDir (VBA)          DefObj (VBA)           Get (VBA)
ChDrive (VBA)        DefSng (VBA)           GoSub...Return (VBA)
Close (VBA)          DefStr (VBA)           GoTo (VBA)
Const (VBA)          DefType (VBA)          If...Then...Else (VBA)
Date (VBA)           DefVar (VBA)           Input # (VBA)
DDE                  DeleteControl          Kill (VBA)
DDEExecute           DeleteReportControl    Let (VBA)
DDEPoke              DeleteSetting (VBA)    Line Input # (VBA)
DDETerminate         Dim (VBA)              Lock (VBA)
DDETerminateAll      Do...Loop (VBA)        LSet (VBA)
Declare (VBA)        End (VBA)              Mid (VBA)
DefBool (VBA)        Erase (VBA)            MidB (VBA)
DefByte (VBA)        Error (VBA)            MkDir (VBA)
DefCur (VBA)         Exit (VBA)
DefDate (VBA)        FileCopy (VBA)
```

# Using Not to Toggle a Property

Many object properties have the value True or False. A toggle statement reverses the current value from True to False or from False to True. You can use an If...Then...Else structure as a toggle statement as follows:

```
If object.property Then object.property = False Else object.
property = True
```

VBA tests the *object.property* expression; if the expression evaluates to True, then VBA changes the value to False, otherwise, VBA changes the value to True.

A shorter toggle statement uses the Not operator as follows:

```
object.property = Not object.property
```

The Not operator reverses the expression on which it operates, so this statement assigns the value of *object.property* to its opposite value. For example, if a control is named ctl, the statement ctl.Locked = Not ctl.Locked toggles the control's Locked property.

As an example, the ToggleMode procedure toggles any form between review mode (with data controls locked and disabled) and edit mode (with data controls unlocked and enabled). The procedure toggles only the text box controls, but you can modify the procedure to test and toggle other types of controls.

1. Insert the ToggleMode procedure shown in Listing 14.5 in the basControlStructures module.

## Listing 14.5

```
Public Function ToggleMode()
    Dim ctl As Control
    For Each ctl in Screen.ActiveForm
        If Typeof ctl Is TextBox Then
            With ctl
                .Locked = Not .Locked
                .Enabled = Not .Enabled
            ............End With
        End If
    Next ctl
End Function
```

2. Open the Customers form in Design view. Create a command button named cmdToggleMode with the caption Toggle the Mode on the Customers form. Set the button's OnClick property to = ToggleMode().

3. Save the form, switch to Form view, and click the button a few times to run the ToggleMode procedure. The mode toggles back and forth between review and data entry mode (for the text box controls only).

## Exit Statements

VBA provides a set of Exit statements that you can use to exit a Function, Sub, Property procedure, or repetitive block of statements in a Do...Loop, For ...Next or a For Each...Next. Table 14.1 (which is on the CD under Tables\Chapter14.pdf) lists the Exit statements.

## Timer Function

You can use the built-in Timer function to time an operation in a procedure. The Timer function returns the number of seconds since midnight and provides the easiest way to approximate how long an operation takes. To use the Timer function as a timer, place the Timer function immediately before and after the operation you want to time and then calculate the difference.

For example, the QueryRunTime procedure tells you the number of seconds it takes to run a query.

1. Insert the QueryRunTime function procedure in basControlStructures. The procedure has the name of the query you want to time as a string argument. The procedure declares variables of the Single data type to hold the values of the Timer function at the beginning and at the end of the query execution.

```
Public Function QueryRunTime(strQueryName As String) As Single
    Dim sngBegin As Single, sngEnd As Single
    sngBegin = Timer
    DoCmd.OpenQuery strQueryName
    sngEnd = Timer
    QueryRunTime = sngEnd - sngBegin
    MsgBox strQueryName & " run time is " & QueryRunTime
End Sub
```

2. In the Debug window, type QueryRunTime("Invoices") and press Enter. The procedure runs the query, displays its datasheet, and displays the message box (see Figure 14.15).

---

**FIGURE 14.15:**

Using the Timer function to time the execution of the Invoices query

## DoEvents Function

There are two kinds of processes in Access: there are processes that send and receive Windows messages to and from the Access objects, and there are processes that do not send and receive Windows messages. For example, Access sends keyboard input and mouse clicks to Windows as messages, but VBA code that manipulates database objects does not send messages. When VBA is running a procedure, it uses processor time and Windows may not be able to process the messages it receives in a timely fashion. The unprocessed messages line up in a queue waiting to be processed. In addition, keystrokes line up in a SendKeys queue.

One solution to the problem of unprocessed messages and keys is to use the DoEvents function to pass control to Windows so that the waiting messages and keys can be processed. When you use the DoEvents function, control is not returned to Access until Windows has finished processing the messages in the queue. Normally, you include a DoEvents function in a loop that takes a long time and use the function to yield control only occasionally.

To illustrate the DoEvents function, the DoEventsLoop procedure shown below puts the computer to work calculating the square root of the loop index for values from 1 to 1 million.

1. Insert the DoEventsLoop procedure in the basControlStructures module. Run the procedure in the Debug window. (The million loops took 2.298828 seconds on my computer.)

```
Public Sub DoEventsLoop()
    Dim sngBegin As Single, sngEnd As Single, sngElapsed As Single
    Dim Counter as Long, Root As Double
```

```
      sngBegin = Timer
      For Counter = 1 To 1000000
          Root = Sqr(Counter)
      Next
      sngEnd = Timer
      sngElapsed = sngEnd - sngBegin
      MsgBox "Run time is " & sngElapsed
   End Sub
```

2. Modify the DoEventsLoop procedure so that is passes control to Windows once every 100,000 loops as follows. You can use the Mod operator to determine when control passes. The Mod operator has the syntax:

   *result = number1* Mod *number2*

   where *result* is the remainder after dividing the first number by the second number (for example 1 = 7 Mod 3). In the modified loop, the DoEvents function runs whenever the Counter is a multiple of 100,000. Run the modified procedure. (The million loops took 3.679688 seconds.)

```
Public Sub DoEventsLoop()
Dim sngBegin As Single, sngEnd As Single, sngElapsed As Single
Dim Counter As Long, Root As Double
sngBegin = Timer
For Counter = 1 To 1000000
    Root = Sqr(Counter)
    If Counter Mod 100000 = 0 Then DoEvents
Next
sngEnd = Timer
sngElapsed = sngEnd - sngBegin
MsgBox "Run time is " & sngElapsed
End Sub
```

# MsgBox and InputBox Functions

You use the MsgBox and InputBox functions to allow the user to communicate directly with your application. When you use the MsgBox function the user communicates by choosing from a set of buttons on a dialog box. When you use the InputBox function the user communicates by entering text in a text box on a dialog. You can create your own custom dialogs for direct communication that duplicate or improve on these two functions (see Chapter 9 for more information on creating a custom dialog); nevertheless, the MsgBox and InputBox functions provide fast and simple ways to display a default dialogs and collect a choice or text input from the user. See Chapter 8 for information on the MsgBox function.

The InputBox function has the syntax:

InputBox (*prompt, title, default, xpos, ypos, helpfile, context*)

where *prompt* is the required string expression that is displayed as the message, *title* is the optional string expression displayed as the title of the dialog, *default* is the optional string expression displayed in the text box as the default response, *xpos* and *ypos* are optional numerical expressions that specify the distance in twips from the upper-left corner of the dialog to the upper-left corner of the screen, *helpfile* is the optional string expression identifying the Help file you want to use and *context* is the optional numeric expression that is the Help context number for the Help file. (If you include the *helpfile* argument, you must also include *context* and vice versa.)

The dialog created by the InputBox function has a single text box for collecting a response and OK and Cancel buttons. When the user clicks one of the buttons or presses Enter, the value in the text box is returned to Access. Normally you store the returned value in a variable.

You can explore the InputBox function in the Debug window.

1. Type **var = InputBox ("Enter your name now.")** and press Enter. VBA displays the input dialog box and waits for your response. Figure 14.16 shows the input box.

2. Enter your name and click OK. VBA stores your input in the var variable. Type **? var** and press Enter to print the value of the variable.

**FIGURE 14.16:**

Using the InputBox function to collect a value

# SysCmd Function

The SysCmd function is actually three functions in one. You can use it as follows:

- To return the state of a Database window object
- To return Access system information
- To display a progress meter

## Returning the State of a Database Window Object

A common use of the SysCmd function is to determine the state of a database object: whether the object is open, whether the object is new, or whether the design of the object has been changed but not saved. The syntax for this version of the function is

```
returnvalue = SysCmd(acSysCmdGetObjectState ,objecttype,objectname)
```

where *objecttype* is one of the intrinsic constants for specifying one of the Database window objects (acTable, acQuery, acForm, acReport, acMacro, and acModule) and *objectname* is a string expression that is the valid name you have specified for the object. The function returns an integer that is a combination of the following values

| Numerical Value | Intrinsic Constant | State of the Object |
| --- | --- | --- |
| 0 | | not open or does not exist |
| 1 | acObjStateOpen | open |
| 2 | acObjStateDirty | changed but not saved |
| 4 | acObjStateNew | new |

You can explore this version of the SysCmd function in the Debug window.

1. With the Customers form closed, type **? SysCmd(acSysCmdGetObjectState, acForm, "Customers")** and press Enter. The Debug window prints 0 to indicate that the form is not open (we know it exists).

2. Open the Customers form in Design view and change the RecordSelectors property to Yes. Type **? SysCmd(acSysCmdGetObjectState, acForm, "Customers")** and press Enter. The Debug window prints 3 to indicate that the form is open and that the form has been changed but the change has not been saved.

## Returning Access System Information

You can use the SysCmd function to return information about Access such as version number, whether the version is a run-time version, the location of the Microsoft Access file, and the location of the workgroup file (System.mdw). In this case the syntax is

```
returnvalue = SysCmd(action)
```

where the return value is the information, usually returned as a string.

You can explore this version of the SysCmd function in the Debug window.

1. Type **?SysCmd(acSysCmdAccessVer)** and press Enter. The Debug window prints the version number of Access.

2. Type **?SysCmd(acSysCmdGetWorkgroupFile)** and press Enter. The Debug window prints the path to the workgroup file.

3. Type **?SysCmd(acSysCmdRuntime)** and press Enter. The Debug window prints True or False depending on whether you are running a run-time version of Access (the Access Developer's Toolkit allows you to create run-time versions of Access).

4. Type **?SysCmd(acSysCmdAccessDir)** and press Enter. The Debug window prints the name of the directory that contains Msaccess.exe.

5. Type **?SysCmd(acSysCmdProfile)** and press Enter. The Debug window prints the /profile setting specified when starting Access from the command line.

## Displaying a Progress Meter

You can use the SysCmd function to display a progress meter with text or to display a text message in the status bar to indicate the progress of an operation. In this version of the function the syntax is

```
returnvalue = SysCmd(action[,text][,value])
```

where *action* is an intrinsic constant that you use to specify the action to take including initializing, updating, or removing the progress meter and setting or resetting the status bar text. You use the optional *text* argument to identify the text that you want to display. You use the optional *value* argument to specify the maximum value of the meter when you use the function to initialize the meter and to specify the relative value of the meter when you use the function to update the meter.

To display a progress meter you must first use the function to display an initial meter specifying the action as the intrinsic constant acSysCmdInitMeter, the text as the text you want to display, and the value as the maximum value of the meter. To show the progress of an operation, use the function specifying the action as the intrinsic constant acSysCmdUpdateMeter and the value as the measure of progress. The SysCmd function calculates the percentage of progress to the maximum value and updates the meter.

To explore this version of the SysCmd function:

1.  Insert the Meter procedure in the basControlStructures module. The procedure uses a For...Next loop to calculate the square roots of the numbers between 1 and 1,000,000. Before starting the loop, the procedure displays the initial progress meter setting the maximum value to 1,000,000. Once every 100,000 loops, the procedure updates the progress meter using the value of the Counter variable. When the loop is finished, the procedure removes the progress meter.

```
Public Sub Meter()
Dim varReturn As Variant, str As String, Counter As Long
Dim Root As Double
str = "Calculating square roots..."
varReturn = SysCmd(acSysCmdInitMeter, str, 1000000)
For Counter = 1 To 1000000
    Root = Sqr(Counter)
    If Counter Mod 100000 = 0 Then
        varReturn = SysCmd(acSysCmdUpdateMeter, Counter)
    End If
Next Counter
varReturn = SysCmd(acSysCmdRemoveMeter)
End Sub
```

2.  Type Meter in the Immediate pane and press Enter. The progress meter displays the progress of the operation (see Figure 14.17)

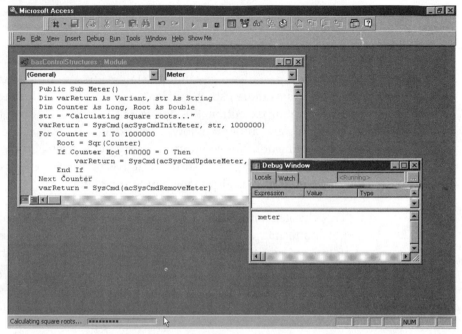

**FIGURE 14.17:**

Use the SysCmd function in three ways to display a progress meter: display an initial meter, update the meter, and then remove the meter.

```
Public Sub Meter()
Dim varReturn As Variant, str As String
Dim Counter As Long, Root As Double
str = "Calculating square roots..."
varReturn = SysCmd(acSysCmdInitMeter, str, 1000000)
For Counter = 1 To 1000000
    Root = Sqr(Counter)
    If Counter Mod 100000 = 0 Then
        varReturn = SysCmd(acSysCmdUpdateMeter,
    End If
Next Counter
varReturn = SysCmd(acSysCmdRemoveMeter)
```

# Summary

This chapter has introduced you to the keywords and statements that VBA provides for controlling the order in which statements are executed, whether statements are executed at all, and the number of times a set of statements is repeated.

- To control execution of a set of statements, use control statements at the beginning and end of the set to create a control structure.

- To make a decision you create one or more test conditions and use a decision control structure to test the conditions and execute different sets of statements depending on the value of the conditions. The decision control structures are If...Then, If...Then...Else, and Select Case.

- There are control structures that you can use to repeat a set of statements as follows: For...Next, For Each...Next, and Do...Loop.

- You can nest a control structure inside another control structure to create more complicated execution flow patterns.

- You can use the With...End With structure when you are setting several properties for the same object.

- Access provides many built-in statements and functions that make your programs more useful, efficient, and powerful including the Timer function for timing execution, the DoEvents function to interrupt execution of a procedure and allow Windows to respond to messages, the MsgBox and Input-Box functions for communicating with the user, and the SysCmd function for determining the state of a Database window object, gathering system information, or displaying a progress meter.

This chapter completes the introduction to Access VBA. You now have the concepts and techniques that are required to automate a database. However, before automating specific database operations, you should study the error-handling capabilities of Access VBA in the next chapter. The ability to handle errors is a fundamental difference between macro programming and Access VBA. Error handling is typically the first reason to start including VBA procedures in a database that you have begun to automate using macros.

# Dealing with Errors in VBA

- ■ Understanding the kinds of errors that will occur

- ■ Using the compiler to detect compile-time errors

- ■ Using the VBA troubleshooting tools to analyze errors

- ■ Planning to avoid errors

- ■ Writing error-handling code for interface and Jet errors

- ■ Writing error-handling code for VBA errors

In the broadest terms, an error is any deviation from correctness. An error occurs any time something happens that you didn't intend to happen. Depending on the type of error any of the following may occur:

- You may not be able to run a part of your application at all.

- The application may start to run, but when the error occurs Access uses its *default error handling* by displaying a default error message and, in some cases, by "crashing" your application and suspending further execution.

- The application runs but fails to carry out the operation you intended, even though Access gives no sign of a problem.

Access provides the following kinds of assistance to help you deal with errors:

- Access provides help by detecting some of the errors that can occur. VBA includes built-in syntax checking and compiling that detect an error that occurs when you violate the rules of VBA syntax. This type of error is called a *compile-time error*. When your syntax is correct and there are no compile-time errors, Access detects the error that occurs when you try run a procedure with a statement that VBA cannot execute; this type of error is called a *run-time error*. For both of these error types, Access displays either a compile-time or a run-time error message that provides information about the error.

- Access provides a set of troubleshooting tools that you can use to analyze an error. Once you understand why an error occurred, you can take the necessary steps to correct the problem. Sometimes you can correct the problem so that the error won't occur again. Other times the error is not one that you can eliminate, and you have to deal with the fact that it may occur again. Correcting this type of problem means writing a VBA procedure to provide instructions on how you want Access to handle the error the next time it occurs.

As you create custom applications, you *are* going to experience errors. The first step in dealing with errors is understanding how and why they occur. This chapter describes the different kinds of errors, how you can use the built-in syntax checking and the compiler to avoid some of them, how to use the troubleshooting tools to analyze an error, and how to replace the default error handling with your own error-handling code.

This chapter describes the Access VBA compiler, the troubleshooting tools that VBA provides to help you analyze errors, and a simple custom error handler. But first let's take a look at the kinds of errors that will occur.

# Avoidable and Unavoidable Errors

You will be faced with two fundamentally different kinds of errors: those you can avoid and those you can't.

## Avoidable Errors

Avoidable errors are the result of your own mistakes. Everyone makes mistakes! As your programming experience increases and if you are very careful, you'll make fewer mistakes, but you'll still make mistakes. Knowing the kinds of errors that can occur and knowing how to predict them is the best way to learn how to avoid them as you write your code. The three kinds of avoidable errors are

**Compile-time errors** that occur when you violate the rules of VBA syntax, such as when you misspell a word or forget the End If statement in an If...Then decision structure. You can eliminate these errors with VBA's built-in syntax checking and compiling. Enable the built-in syntax checking by checking the Auto Syntax Check option in the Module table of the Options dialog.

**Run-time errors** that occur when Access can't run a macro action or VBA statement because you made a mistake, such as when you specify the wrong data type or try to run the wrong method.

**Logic errors** that occur when your macros or VBA procedures execute without failing but you don't get the result you intended. For example, a logic error occurs when you assign a macro or an event procedure to the wrong event and two macros or procedures run in the wrong order as a result. (Logic errors are commonly called *bugs,* although bug is also used to refer to any error.)

You deal with avoidable errors by eliminating the source of the error (for example, correcting a typing error), using only valid properties and methods for an object, or triggering event procedures with the appropriate event. You can prevent many errors by writing your macro or VBA procedure to test the value of a precondition first and then execute a statement only if the precondition evaluates to True. For example, a statement to select a form fails if the form is not open, but you can avoid the error by using the IsLoaded function to determine if the form is open and running the statement to select the form only if the form is open.

Before you can correct a mistake you must realize that a mistake exists; then you can troubleshoot the error and take the steps necessary to correct the mistake. You know a mistake exists when an error message box appears, when your macro or VBA procedure won't even begin to run, or when you don't get the result you expected. When you know an error exists, you can use the VBA troubleshooting tools to analyze the error.

## Unavoidable Errors

Unavoidable errors are those that continue to occur even after you have eliminated all of your mistakes through careful design, testing, and troubleshooting. Here are some situations in which unavoidable errors occur:

- The user tries to save a new record without a primary key.
- The user enters a value in a combo box that isn't in the combo list.
- The power fails or the disk is full.
- The network disconnects unexpectedly.
- The user inserts the wrong floppy disk.

You can think of unavoidable errors as somebody else's fault: the user or the computer has done something that you have no control over. Nevertheless, it's your project, so your code still needs to deal with unavoidable errors.

## Fatal and Nonfatal Errors

Unavoidable errors come in two varieties: those that cause your macro or procedure to fail (fatal errors) and those that don't cause failure.

When a nonfatal error occurs, the default error handling is that Access or Jet displays a default error message and the macro or VBA procedure continues to run. As an example, if a procedure runs the ApplyFilter method with the name of a nonexistent query as the filtername argument, the procedure continues to run without displaying a run-time error message because the built-in method is designed so that a VBA run-time error is not generated.

Unfortunately, most errors are fatal! Fatal errors occur when a VBA statement can't execute and no built-in measures prevent a VBA run-time error from being generated. When a fatal error occurs, the *default error handling* is that DAO or VBA may display a default error message, Access displays the run-time error dialog box for the procedure, and Access suspends execution. For example, suppose you place a command button on a form and create an event procedure that runs the built-in Save Record command to save the record as follows:

```
Private Sub cmdSave_Click()
    DoCmd.RunCommand acCmdSaveRecord
End Sub
```

When you enter a new record but leave the primary key blank and try to save the record, the Jet engine won't be able to save the record, and Access displays the run-time error message shown in Figure 15.1 and suspends execution of the procedure at the DoCmd statement.

**FIGURE 15.1:**

The run-time error message for a fatal error

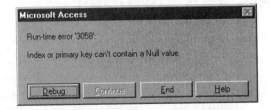

## Dealing with Unavoidable Errors

You deal with unavoidable errors by writing VBA code to replace the default error handling with your own custom error-handling code. Intercepting the default error handling when an error occurs is called *trapping the error*. You can write your own error handler that replaces the default error message with a custom message and that includes additional instructions for dealing with the error. Occasionally the instructions may require ending the procedure without accomplishing the intended task, but at least you can include instructions to end the procedure gracefully without displaying the failed procedure dialog that puts the procedure into the limbo state of suspended execution and the novice user into the panic state of suspended understanding.

As an illustration of custom error handling, the procedure to save a record shown in Listing 15.1 intercepts the default error handling that Access would carry out when the fatal error occurs because the primary key value is missing. The procedure includes statements to trap the error, replace the default message shown in Figure 15.1 with a custom message, and move the focus to the CustomerID control.

### Listing 15.1

```
Private Sub cmdSave_Click()
On Error GoTo Err_cmdSave_click
    DoCmd.RunCommand acCmdSaveRecord
Exit_cmdSave_Click:
    Exit Sub
Err_cmdSave_Click:
    MsgBox "You must enter a unique Customer ID before saving the
    ➥record."
    DoCmd.GoToControl "CustomerID"
    Resume Exit_cmdSave_Click
End Sub
```

# The Access VBA Compiler

Access VBA does not use a true compiler. A true compiler translates the code that you write in a programming language such as C++, Basic, or Pascal, called the *source code*, and generates a machine language version of the code called the *object code*. The advantages of using a true compiler are that the object code can run on a computer that doesn't have the compiler installed and that the object code runs much faster than noncompiled source code. By contrast, the Access VBA compiler translates the code into a state that is somewhere between source code and object code called *pseudocode*. You can't view or read the pseudocode, but it runs faster than source code (although not as fast as equivalent code that is compiled by a true compiler). Your computer must have Access installed in order to run the pseudocode.

> **NOTE**  In spite of the misnomers, this book follows the common practice of referring to the pseudocode generated by the Access VBA compiler as the *compiled state* and refers to the process of translating the source code into pseudocode as *compiling*.

Errors that Access detects during compiling are called compile-time errors. Typical compile errors occur when you use a variable that has not been declared or misspell a variable (but only if the module's Declarations section includes the Option Explicit statement), when you omit a required argument for a function or a method (Figure 15.2a), if you omit a required statement in a set such as the End If statement in an If...Then control structure (Figure 15.2b), and if your procedure calls another procedure that doesn't exist (Figure 15.2c).

**FIGURE 15.2:**

Typical compile-time error messages

**Automatic Compiling**

The first time you try to run a new or changed procedure, Access compiles the procedure automatically. By default, Access compiles only the code it must compile in order to run the procedure. Access compiles the procedure you want to run and also compiles any procedures that the current procedure calls, any procedures that the called procedures may call, and so on. The set of procedures that the current procedure may call forms the *current execution path* for the current procedure. In addition to compiling the current procedure and the procedures in its call tree, Access checks these procedures for errors in referring to variables to ensure that all the variables referred to are correctly declared (but only if the Option Explicit statement is included in the Declarations sections of all modules). In compiling a procedure, Access checks all references to the called procedures and also checks the variables that the procedure uses that are declared elsewhere (for example, in the Declarations section of a module).

During compilation, Access loads the modules containing all procedures in the current execution path and the modules declaring variables referred to in these procedures. If no compilation errors occur, Access compiles the procedures in the current execution path and creates a compiled version of the code. After compiling, when you call the procedure, Access runs the compiled version. Access also keeps track of the compilation state of a procedure; after compiling a procedure, Access doesn't compile the procedure again unless you make a change that causes the procedure to become decompiled. As an example, a procedure becomes decompiled if you make any changes to it.

> **NOTE** The editable version of a procedure displayed in the Module window is called source code. After compiling a procedure, Access creates the compiled version. You cannot view or edit the compiled version. A new feature in Access 97 is that you can save your application in an .mde file that has the source code removed. In an .mde file, your programming efforts are completely secure: No one can see or change your code. When you create an .mde file, be sure to keep a copy of the original database so that you'll be able to view and change your own code.

**The Compile on Demand Option**   You can set two levels of automatic compiling in the Module pane of the Options dialog. Display the dialog by choosing the Options command from the Tools menu (see Figure 15.3). With the Compile on Demand option checked (the default), Access compiles only the procedures in the current execution path of the procedure you are running. Other procedures in the current module or in the call tree of the procedure are not compiled. (The *call tree* of the procedure is the set of all modules that contain procedures that might be called by any procedure stored in the procedure's module.)

Although the Compile on Demand option makes writing and testing individual procedures faster, it doesn't find errors that may exist in your modules. When you uncheck this option, Access compiles all of the procedures in the call tree (whether they are called by the current procedure or not) and also compiles modules that declare variables referred to in the current and call tree procedures.

To explore the Compile on Demand option, make sure the option is checked in the Module pane of the Options dialog.

1.   Create a new database named Ch15_Examples.

2.   Create a module named basCompileNumber and create the following procedures:

```
Public Sub TestOne()
    Call TestA
End Sub
```

```
Public Sub TestTwo()
    Call TestB
End Sub
```

3. Create a second module named basCompileAlpha and create the next two procedures. The TestC procedure has a compile error because the TestD procedure does not exist. Note also that the TestTwo procedure in the basCompileNumber module has a similar compile error because the TestB procedure does not exist.

```
Public Sub TestA()
    MsgBox "This is TestA"
End Sub
```

```
Public Sub TestC()
    Call TestD
End Sub
```

4. Press Ctrl+G to display the Debug window. Type **Call TestOne** in the Immediate pane and press Enter. Access compiles TestOne and TestA and displays the message box. Access records the compilation state of the TestOne and TestA procedures and will not compile them again unless you

**FIGURE 15.3:**

With the Compile on Demand option checked, Access compiles only the procedures in the current execution path of the procedure you are running.

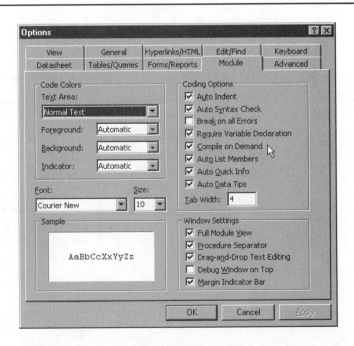

make a change. Because the Compile on Demand option is checked, VBA does not compile the TestTwo or the TestC procedures.

5.  Choose the Options command in the Tools menu, select the Modules pane, and clear the Compile on Demand check box.

6.  Change the TestOne procedure by adding a comment as shown below to force VBA to recompile the Test1 procedure. Run the procedure in the Debug window. This time VBA tries to compile all of the procedures in bas-CompileNumber and detects the compile error in the TestTwo procedure. VBA displays the compile error message box (Figure 15.4a) and highlights the problem statement in the TestTwo procedure (Figure 15.4b).

```
Sub TestOne()
    'call another procedure
    Call TestA
End Sub
```

7.  Change the highlighted statement to Call TestA and then run the TestOne procedure in the Debug window. This time the basCompileNumber module compiles successfully, but when Access tries to compile the basCompileAlpha module, a compile error is detected in the TestC procedure in the basCompile-Alpha module, even though this procedure isn't called by any of the current procedure or by any of the procedures in the basCompileNumber module.

8.  Choose the Options command in the Tools menu, select the Modules pane, and check the Compile on Demand checkbox.

---

**FIGURE 15.4:**

When you uncheck the Compile on Demand option, VBA attempts to compile all procedures in a call tree module, whether or not the procedures are called by the current procedure.

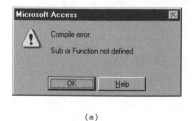

(a)

(b)

## Explicit Compiling

To compile a single procedure you can just run it. You can control when procedures are compiled by instructing Access to compile either all procedures in modules that are open or all procedures in the database.

 **Compile Loaded Modules**    To compile all procedures in modules that are open, choose the Compile Loaded Modules command in the Debug menu or click the Compile Loaded Modules button in the toolbar. In compiling the procedures in the open modules, Access loads the modules containing procedures that are called by the procedures in the open modules and then compiles all the procedures in the loaded modules.

**Compile All Modules**    To compile all procedures in all modules in the database, choose the Compile All Modules command in the Debug menu. After running this command, your database is in a compiled state with all procedures in all modules compiled and ready to run. Because compiling takes time, you should make sure that your database is in a compiled state after you finish making changes and are ready to run the completed database application.

**Compile and Save All Modules**    To compile all procedures in all modules in the database and save all code in both the source state and the compiled state, open any module and choose the Compile and Save All Modules command in the Debug menu.

## Decompilation

While you are in the process of creating an automated application, compiling all of the modules is probably a waste of time because many of the changes that you make to your database cause it to become decompiled. Any changes to code in a module decompiles the module. Changes to objects that have code assigned to them such as forms, reports, and controls also cause modules to become decompiled. Access stores the name of the database as part of the compilation state, so if you perform an operation that changes the name of the database such as compacting the database to a new name, the database becomes decompiled.

> **TIP**    You can avoid decompiling your application when you compact it by compacting the database to the same name.

## Conditional Compilation

You can instruct VBA to include or exclude statements from the compilation process by using conditional compilation. To use conditional compilation you can declare a *conditional compilation constant* in a module by preceding the constant declaration with the number symbol (#); then use the number symbol to mark a set of statements that you want to include or exclude from being compiled using an #If...#End If decision structure. (Decision structures are discussed in Chapter 14.) A statement preceded by the number sign is a special instruction for the compiler called a *compiler directive*.

As an example, suppose your code includes some debugging statements to print test values. When you are finished debugging, you could manually delete or comment out all the debugging statements. However, this solution would not be efficient because of the time required to locate each debugging statement. Furthermore, if you later make additional changes to your code, you may want to use the debugging statements again. A better solution is to declare conditional compilation variables in the Declarations section of each module in which you want to use conditional compilation and mark the debugging statements for conditional compilation. When you want to exclude the debugging statements you need only to change the values of the compilation constants. The syntax for defining a conditional compilation constant in a module is

```
#Const constantname = expression
```

where *constantname* is the name of the conditional compilation constant and *expression* can be a literal, another conditional compilation constant, or a combination of literals and conditional compilation constants that uses arithmetic or logical operators (except the Is operator). You usually set the value to True or False.

To explore conditional compilation:

1. Declare a compilation constant in the Declarations section of the basCompileNumber module as follows:

```
#Const CondCompile = True
```

2. Modify the TestOne procedure as shown next. If the value of the CondCompile constant is True, the Debug.Print statement is included when the procedure is compiled; otherwise, the statement is not included in the compiled version of the procedure.

```
Sub TestOne()
#If CondCompile Then
```

```
        Debug.Print "This is a debugging message"
    #End If
    Call TestA
    End Sub
```

3. Run the TestOne procedure in the Debug window. The Debug window prints the message.

4. Change the declaration statement for the compilation constant to False as shown below and run the TestOne procedure in the Debug window. The debug message is not printed or included in the compiled version of the code.

```
#Const CondCompile = False
```

> **NOTE** Constants declared with the #Const statement are private to the module in which they are declared.

Another way to declare conditional compilation constants is by setting the Conditional Compilation Arguments in the Advanced Tab of the Options dialog (see Figure 15.5). In this case, the conditional compilation constants can have only integer values. (False corresponds to 0, and True corresponds to –1.) You can define several constants by separating their definitions with colons. Here is the syntax:

```
compilerconstant1 = integer1: compilerconstant2 = integer2
```

# Troubleshooting Tools

VBA has tools that help you analyze both run-time errors that occur when VBA is unable to execute a statement while the code is running and logic errors that occur when VBA can execute your code but doesn't produce the result you expected. This section introduces most of the available troubleshooting tools.

VBA has two kinds of troubleshooting tools:

- Tools that let you observe what happens to data as code is running
- Tools that suspend execution of your code at a statement and let you use the Debug window to test and view data

FIGURE 15.5:

Defining a conditional
compilation constant in
the Advanced tab of the
Options dialog

## Using Help

Often the simplest way to analyze an error is to use the help that Access provides.
When a run-time error occurs, VBA displays an error message with the error code
and a very brief description of the reason for the error. Click the Help button on
the procedure error message dialog to display the online Help file for the error
that occurred. Often the Help file provides the clue you need to root out the bug.
As an example, Figure 15.6b shows the Jet Engine Error Message Reference for
the run-time error message in Figure 15.6a.

## Suspending Execution

Modules have three states (also called modes or times): design time when you
enter and edit code, run time when the code is running, and *break mode* when the
code is running but is suspended between executing statements. Most of the troubleshooting tools require the code to be in break mode. In break mode the
Module window displays the code that is running, and the variables and properties retain the values they had at the moment execution was suspended.

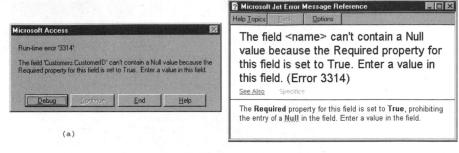

**FIGURE 15.6:**

Click the Help button on the run-time error message box to display online Help for the error.

## Entering and Leaving Break Mode

VBA enters break mode at a line of code in the following circumstances:

- A statement on a line generates a run-time error and no error trapping is in effect when the error occurs.

- You have set a breakpoint on a line. To enter break mode, you can set a breakpoint. A *breakpoint* is a statement at which VBA stops execution just before running the statement and puts the application in break mode. If you close the database and reopen, all breakpoints are cleared.

- A Stop statement occurs on the line. Stop temporarily halts execution, but you can continue running code by choosing Continue from the Run menu.

- You press Ctrl+Break when code is executing.

Using a breakpoint or Stop statement is useful when you know which statement caused the error or the general area of code in which the error occurred.

The procedure that is running when the execution is suspended and enters break mode is called the *current procedure*. VBA displays a yellow arrow in the margin bar to the left of the statement at which execution is paused and displays the text with a yellow background (see Figure 15.7). The marked statement is called the *current statement* and is the statement that will be run next.

**FIGURE 15.7:**

When a procedure is in break mode, VBA marks the current statement with an arrow and a colored background.

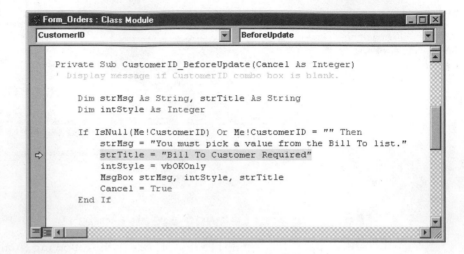

> **NOTE**  The difference between the Stop and End statements in a procedure is that the End statement terminates all execution and resets module-level variables and all static variables in all modules, while the Stop statement temporarily halts execution leaving the current values of all variables intact.

To leave break mode and reenter run time, you can either choose the Go/ Continue command from the Run menu or click the Continue button on the toolbar. To end code execution and reset all variables, click the End button on the toolbar or the End button in the run-time error dialog.

**The Run-Time Error Dialog**  When VBA enters break mode by generating an error and custom error handling is not in effect, Access displays the run-time error message. For example, if you try to change the Caption property of the Customers form using the assignment statement

```
Forms!Customers.Caption = "Customer Information"
```

but the Customers form isn't open when you run the statement, a run-time error is generated (see Figure 15.8a). Clicking the Debug button on the procedure error message dialog displays the current procedure in the Module window with the current statement marked by the arrow and a colored background (see Figure 15.8b).

**FIGURE 15.8:**

Clicking the Debug button in the error message (a) displays the current procedure with the current line marked by an arrow and a colored background (b).

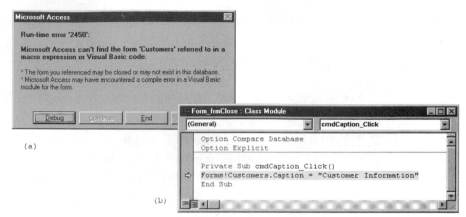

(a)

(b)

Sometimes you can fix the error immediately by changing the code. In this example, you can fix the error by including code to test whether the Customers form is open before running the statement. After you change the code, you may have to restart the procedure; in this case, VBA displays a message and gives you the option of accepting the change and resetting your code or continuing the procedure without the change (see Figure 15.9). If you don't have to restart, you can continue running the procedure by clicking the Continue button in the toolbar or by choosing the Continue command in the Run menu.

**FIGURE 15.9:**

After you change code, you may have to reset the current code.

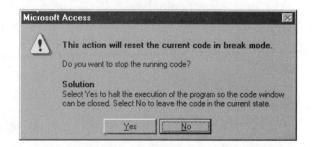

Clicking the End button in the run-time error message box ends code execution; when you click this button, module-level variables retain their values. (You have to click the Reset button to reset all variables.) Clicking the Help button displays online Help.

## Testing While in Break Mode

With execution suspended, you can examine what happened before the code halted by

- Switching to other windows and inspecting their state.

- Inspecting values of variables, controls, and properties to see if some statement set their values incorrectly.

- Making changes to your code and then continuing execution by choosing Continue from the Run menu. Some changes require code to be reinitialized; VBA displays a message when this is the case (refer to Figure 15.9).

## Reinitializing Code

You can reinitialize code when the program is running or is in break mode. Reinitializing sets all variables, including static and public variables, to their default initial values: numeric variables are set to zero, variable-length string variables are set to the zero-length string, fixed-length string variables are set to ANSI zero, variant variables are set to Empty, and object variables are set to Nothing. To reinitialize all variables, choose Reset from the Run menu.

## Setting and Removing Breakpoints

You set a breakpoint by clicking in the margin bar to the left of an executable statement, by placing the insertion point in an executable statement and clicking the Toggle Breakpoint button in the toolbar, by pressing F9, or by choosing the Toggle Breakpoint command in the Run menu. (Each of these actions is a *toggle*; by taking the action when the insertion point is in a breakpoint statement, you remove the breakpoint.) When you set a breakpoint, VBA displays a red circle in the margin bar and displays the line with white text on a red background by default (see Figure 15.10). (You can set the foreground and the background colors in the Module pane of the Options dialog, available by choosing the Options command in the Tools menu.) You can set more than one breakpoint in a procedure and you can set breakpoints in other procedures.

You can remove all breakpoints in all modules by choosing the Clear All Breakpoints command in the Run menu or by pressing Ctrl+Shift+F9. You can customize the module toolbar by adding a Clear All Breakpoints button. Figure 15.11 shows the Module Design category of toolbar buttons including the Clear All Breakpoints button and buttons for several other menu commands.

**FIGURE 15.10:**

VBA marks a breakpoint with a colored circle in the margin and white text on a colored background.

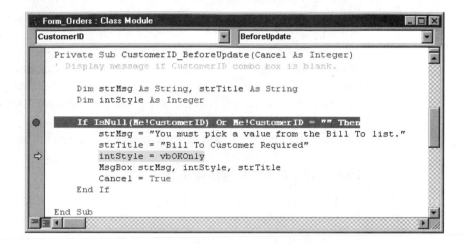

**FIGURE 15.11:**

Customize the Module Design toolbar by adding a Clear All Breakpoints button.

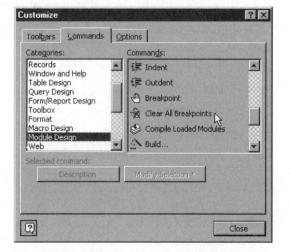

When you run a procedure with a breakpoint, VBA executes the statements before the breakpoint and then enters break mode by pausing before executing the breakpoint statement. With the procedure in break mode, you can single-step through your code, or you can leave break mode and return to normal execution mode by clicking the Go/Continue button in the toolbar, pressing F5, or choosing Continue in the Run menu.

You can use breakpoints to help to locate a bug. You start by setting a breakpoint at the statement you suspect is causing the problem and then running the procedure. When the breakpoint is reached and the procedure is paused, you can determine whether the error occurred before reaching the breakpoint. If the error has already occurred (in which case execution may terminate before you reach the breakpoint), you'll know that an earlier statement caused the error. You can examine the preceding statements and set an earlier breakpoint for further exploration. If the procedure reaches the breakpoint and the error has not occurred yet, you can step through the procedure statements line by line until the error occurs.

## Stepping through Code

VBA has three different ways to let you step through statements one at a time. (Stepping through statements is also called *tracing* statements.)

 **Step Into**   If you click the Step Into button in the toolbar, press F8, or choose the Step Into command in the Run menu, VBA switches into run time, executes the current statement, and then switches back to break mode. The F8 key is one of the most useful keys for troubleshooting a procedure. When a line has two or more statements (separated by a colon [:]), you can step one statement at a time. If the current statement is a call to another procedure, VBA proceeds to step into the statements of the called procedure one step at a time; when the called procedure finishes, VBA returns to the next statement in the current procedure.

 **Step Over**   Sometimes, you need to step through the statements in a procedure, but you don't need to step through the statements in a called procedure. When you use the Step Over command and the current statement is a call to another procedure, VBA executes the called procedure as a single step and then steps to the next statement of the current procedure. When you use the Step Over command, the Module window continues to display the current procedure while the called procedure is running. The Step Over command is available as a menu command in the Run menu, as a toolbar button, and as the Shift+F8 shortcut key.

 **Step Out**   When you use the Step Out command and the current procedure has been called by another procedure, VBA executes the rest of the current procedures and any nested procedures that it calls as a single step and then returns to the calling procedure and stops. If the current procedure was not called by another procedure, using the Step Out command is identical to using the Continue command.

You can alternate between the two types of stepping. When you want to stop running the procedure one statement at a time, press F5 to continue execution without interruption.

## Setting the Next Statement

If you are in break mode, you can skip lines or go back and repeat code by selecting the next statement that you want to execute. Move the insertion point to any line of code in the same procedure, right-click in the line, and choose the Set Next Statement command in the shortcut menu or choose the Set Next Statement command from the Run menu. VBA marks the selected statement as the current statement with the yellow arrow in the margin and the yellow background. After specifying the next statement to be executed, you can click the Go/Continue, Step Into, or Step Over buttons in the toolbar.

The Show Next Statement command in the Run menu lets you see the next statement that will execute in the procedure.

**TIP**    You can add toolbar buttons to the Module Design toolbar for the Set Next Statement and Show Next Statement commands.

## Executing a Group of Statements

When a procedure is in break mode, you can use the Run to Cursor command to run the program until the line you selected is run. Move the insertion point to any line of code in the same procedure and right-click in the line of code; then choose the Run to Cursor command in the shortcut menu, choose the Run to Cursor command in the Run menu, or press Ctrl+F8. VBA runs code beginning with the current statement to the line with the insertion point and then reenters break mode. Using Run to Cursor lets you avoid having to step through every statement in a procedure.

## Shortcut Keys for Troubleshooting

Table 15.1, which is on the CD under Tables\Chapter15.pdf, lists the shortcut keys that you can use in troubleshooting.

## Viewing Current Values in the Module Window

Access 97 provides a new feature that lets you view the current value of a variable or constant referred to in a procedure when the procedure is in break mode. Move the mouse pointer to the variable or constant that you want to inspect. VBA displays the current value as a Data Tip directly below the item (see Figure 15.12). You can turn off this feature by clearing the Auto Data Tip checkbox in the Module pane of the Options dialog.

**FIGURE 15.12:**

You can inspect the current value of a variable or constant referred to in a procedure that is in break mode.

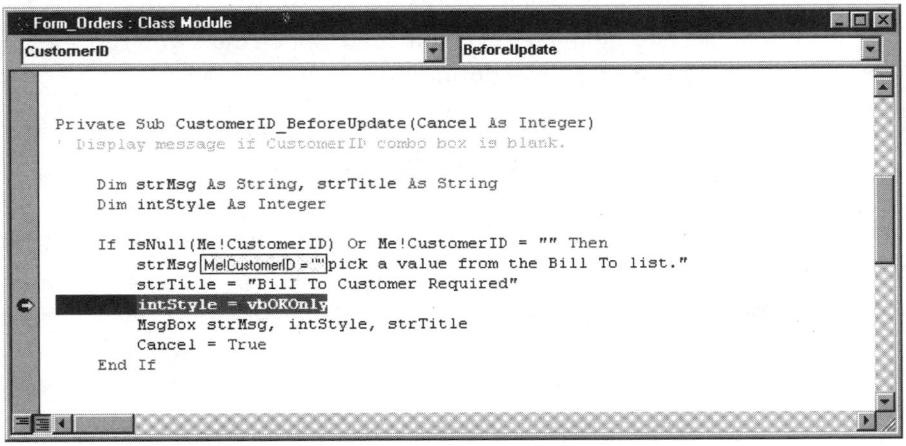

```
Form_Orders : Class Module

CustomerID                                    BeforeUpdate

Private Sub CustomerID_BeforeUpdate(Cancel As Integer)
' Display message if CustomerID combo box is blank.

    Dim strMsg As String, strTitle As String
    Dim intStyle As Integer

    If IsNull(Me!CustomerID) Or Me!CustomerID = "" Then
        strMsg  Me!CustomerID = ""  pick a value from the Bill To list."
        strTitle = "Bill To Customer Required"
        intStyle = vbOKOnly
        MsgBox strMsg, intStyle, strTitle
        Cancel = True
    End If
```

## Using the Debug Window for Debugging

You can also use the Immediate pane of the Debug window to print current values. The Immediate pane is available whether or not a module is in break mode. However, the values you can inspect depend on the mode as explained in the section, "Using the Immediate Pane." To print the current value of a variable or property, open the Debug window by pressing Ctrl+G and enter any of the following statements:

```
Debug.Print outputlist
Print outputlist
? outputlist
```

Press Enter to conclude.

**NOTE**  When entering statements in the Immediate window, the Debug object is the assumed object, so you don't have to refer to Debug explicitly. You can use Print without including Debug or the question mark (?) as a shortcut for the Print reserved word. When you want to include a statement in a procedure that prints to the Debug window however, you have to use the full reference Debug.Print *outputlist*.

## Navigation in the Immediate Window

Use the mouse or arrow keys to move around in the Immediate window. Press the Home and End keys to move to the beginning and end of the current line, the Page Up and Page Down keys to move forward and backward one page at a time, and the Ctrl+End combination to move to end of Immediate window.

## Execution in the Immediate Window

To execute a statement in the Immediate window, place the insertion point in the statement when the procedure is not in break mode and press Enter. You can execute the following:

- Any built-in function or statement

- A user-defined procedure (see Chapter 12 for the calling syntax)

- A control structure, but only if it can be expressed on one line, for example:

```
For I = 1 to 20: Print 2*I : Next I
```

- Any valid expression including expressions involving the values and properties for any open object

## Using the Debug Window in Break Mode

When VBA is in break mode, the Module window displays the currently running procedure with the current statement marked by a yellow arrow and background. Figure 15.13a shows the Debug window when a procedure is in break mode at the statement shown in Figure 15.13b.

The box below the title bar of the Debug window indicates the name of the procedure. The top half of the Debug window has tabs for two panes; click the Locals tab or the Watch tab to display one of the panes. The Locals pane displays the values

FIGURE 15.13:

The Debug window (a)
when a procedure is in
break mode (b)

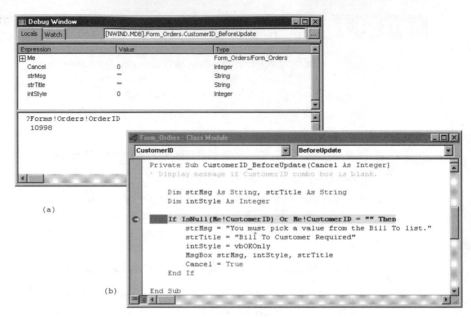

(a)

(b)

of all variables and information about all objects in the current procedure. The
Watch pane lets you view variables in any procedure and, in addition, lets you
examine the values of custom expressions that you create. The lower pane is the
Immediate pane that we have been using throughout the book.

**Using the Immediate Pane**   When you work in the Immediate pane while
VBA is in break mode, you are limited as to which variables you have access to
and which procedures you can run because code is actually running and
execution has been suspended *between* statements. Therefore, you can see only
the variables and call only the procedures that the currently running procedure
can see and call. You can see and modify only the values of the variables defined
in the current procedure or passed to the current procedure as arguments,
variables defined in the current module, or public variables defined in any module in the database. You can call any procedure in the current module and any
public procedure in any other module.

**Using the Locals Pane**   The Locals pane lists the variables and constants
referred to in the current procedure in the Expression column and their data types
in the Type column. The Value column displays the values of the variables and constants just before the current statement executes. As you step through statements,
the Locals pane updates to display the current values. For example, Figure15.13a

shows the values when the breakpoint is also the current statement, whereas Figure 15.14 shows the Locals pane after stepping into the next three statements.

You can also assign new values to variables in the Locals pane. To change a value, click the value in the Value column, type a new value, and press Enter.

**FIGURE 15.14:**

The Locals pane updates to display the current values of the variables in the procedure in break mode.

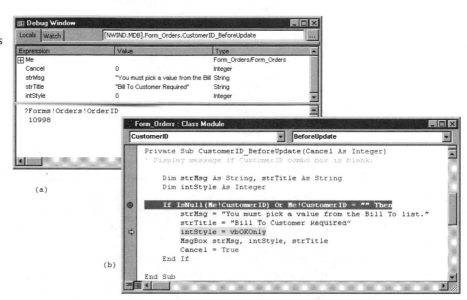

The Locals pane also displays information about objects. When the current procedure is an event procedure stored in a form or report module, the Locals pane includes information about the objects in the corresponding form or report. The form or report is referred to as Me. Click the plus sign to the left of an object in the Locals pane to expand the object and display all of its members. Figure 15.15 shows a partial expansion of the objects in a form.

**Using the Watch Pane**   You can define a particular expression or specify a variable whose value you want to observe as the code is running. You define such watch expressions in the Add Watch dialog box, available by choosing the Add Watch command in the Debug menu (see Figure 15.16a). Enter any variable, property, procedure call, or valid expression in the Expression box. You can specify the Context as the specific procedure or as a specific module that must be current before VBA evaluates the expression, or you can leave the range unrestricted and ask VBA to evaluate the expression for all modules. Use the Watch Type

FIGURE 15.15:

Click the plus sign to the left of an object to expand the object and display its properties and the objects it contains.

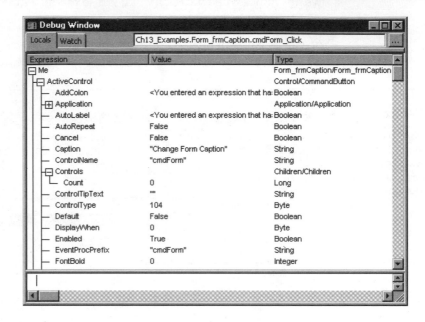

option to specify whether you want to view the value of the expression, use its value to suspend execution of code whenever the value of the expression is true, or whenever the value of the expression changes value.

After you define watch expressions, click the Watch tab in the Debug window to view the Watch pane listing the watch expressions, their current values, and the specified context. Figure 15.16b shows examples of the three different Watch Types with each type indicated by a different icon to the left of the expression.

To edit or delete a watch expression, use the Edit Watch dialog, available by choosing the Edit Watch command in the Debug menu.

## Using Quick Watch in Break Mode

When VBA is in break mode you can observe the value of a variable, property, or function call that you haven't defined as a watch expression. To view the value of an expression in the current procedure, select the expression in the procedure and click the Quick Watch button on the toolbar. The Quick Watch message box displays the expression and its current value (see Figure 15.17). Add the expression to the Watch pane as a watch expression by clicking the Add button.

**FIGURE 15.16:**

Create watch expressions in the Add Watch dialog (a) and view the values of the expressions in the Watch pane of the Debug window (b).

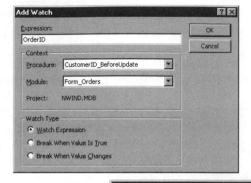

(a)

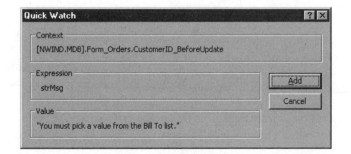

(b)

**FIGURE 15.17:**

Use the Quick Watch dialog to view the value of a variable, property, or function call in the current procedure in break mode.

## Using the Calls Box

When your code contains several layers of nested procedures, knowing whether the procedures have been called in the order you intended is helpful. You can use the Calls dialog to trace through the progress of nested procedures. The Calls dialog displays a list of the procedures that have started but have not completed execution; the first active procedure in the calling chain is at the bottom of

**715**

the list with subsequent procedures added to the top. You can display the Calls dialog when VBA is in break mode and either the Module window or the Debug window is open; click the Calls button on the toolbar (see Figure 15.18).

**FIGURE 15.18:**

The Call Stack dialog lists the procedures that have started but have not completed execution.

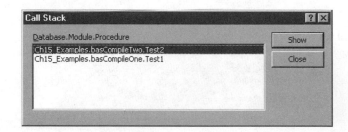

## Printing to the Debug Window from Code

To display values in the Immediate window from a procedure while the procedure is running, you must include an explicit reference to the Debug object in the statement and you can't use the question mark. Printing from code using

```
Debug.Print outputlist
```

is useful when you want to display the results of an while code is running. The *outputlist* argument is normally the numeric or string expression that you want to print with multiple expressions separated with a space, a semicolon, or a comma. You can also format the output in columns and specify where the insertion point is placed for the next character printed. (Search the Print method in online Help for the formatting syntax.) You must open the Debug window yourself; the window doesn't open automatically when your code comes across a Debug.Print statement.

Printing to the Debug window directly from code has two advantages: You don't have to halt execution to get feedback, and you can view changes in a separate area that doesn't interfere with what users will see. When you are trying to debug event procedures, monitoring values by printing them to the Debug window while the code runs may be the only way to analyze interacting event procedures. Using breakpoints in event procedures can affect the occurrence of events and prevent you from observing the interaction. For example, if you suspend execution in a MouseDown event procedure, the MouseUp event never occurs, so a MouseUp event procedure doesn't run.

# Avoiding Bugs

The best way to deal with errors is to avoid them in the first place if possible. Most errors are caused by changes. How many times have you been in the following situation? You decide to make a small change in an application that works just fine and then find that nothing works right after you make the change. Even the most minor modification can lead to several hours of debugging to remove all of the mistakes that the change introduces.

## Planning to Avoid Errors

As you plan your application, you may be able to plan for future changes and thus plan to avoid the errors that these changes would introduce. For example, when designing tables, think about additional fields that you may need in the future and include them in the beginning. Be sure to think very carefully about the relationships between your tables and whether a relationship should be one-to-many or many-to-many. Specifically, in an instructional application that tracks students, instructors, and classes, the usual relationship between instructors and classes is one-to-many because a class usually has a single instructor; however, if you ever expect to allow team teaching you should create a many-to-many relationship instead.

## Syntax Checking

You can have VBA check the syntax of your code as you type it in by checking the Auto Syntax Check option in the Modules pane of the Options dialog. (Choose Options from the Tools menu.) If you don't check this option, VBA checks the syntax only when you compile your code.

## Explicit Variable Declaration

A common source of errors is typographical errors in variable names. You can avoid these errors by including Option Explicit in the Declarations section of every module. Access includes the Option Explicit statement in all new modules if you check the Require Variable Declaration option in the Module pane of the Options dialog.

## Data Typing

You should explicitly specify a data type for all your variables. By defining variables with a specific data type instead of with the Variant or Object data types, you avoid the run-time errors that result when VBA is unable to convert the data type of a Variant variable in order to do a calculation or when VBA discovers that your code references a property or method that is inappropriate for the Object variable. By using the most specific data type, you force VBA to analyze the appropriateness of the references during compile time.

## Naming Conflicts

Naming conflicts can cause errors; for example, if two procedures use a variable with the same name as the module-level variable, one procedure could unintentionally overwrite a value set by another procedure. You can avoid most errors of this type by declaring variables with the narrowest scope possible. If a variable is used in a single procedure, then declare the variable within the procedure. If a variable is used only by the procedures in a single module, then declare the variable as a Private module-level variable. In particular, use Public module-level variables only when you need to make the variable available to several procedures in several modules. Naming conflicts can also arise with procedure names. Procedures in separate modules can have the same name. When you call such a procedure from another procedure in its own module there is no problem. However, when you call such a procedure from a procedure in another module, an error occurs if you don't include the module name in the procedure call because VBA is unable to determine which procedure to call.

## Using Comments

You need to strike a reasonable balance between writing comments for every statement and not including any comments in your code. A good rule is to include enough comments so that an intermediate-level VBA programmer can understand your code. You don't have to comment every statement or obvious structure, but you may want to include comments at the beginning of each module and procedure to describe its purpose and point out any variables defined in the module or procedure. Typically you should include comments describing the operation that each block of statements performs. Each comment takes a small fraction of a second. In lengthy code the fractions accumulate and can slow down your code, so you would be wise to avoid unnecessary or overly verbose comments.

## Testing Your Code

You can perform three kinds of tests to try out your code:

**Functional testing**   Does the application do what it is supposed to do? You need to test your application with a set of test data. For thorough testing, the test data must include examples of all of the possible variations and types of values that could be entered. Pay special attention to empty values. Do your forms look okay with null values? Do your procedures execute without error if input values are null, zero, or the zero-length string? For procedures that create recordsets, are the procedures error-free if a record-set has no records?

**Usability testing**   Is the application easy to use? Give your application to a novice user and observe how fast the user can learn to do productive work. Are there situations in which the user is stumped and can't figure out what to do next?

**Destructive testing**   Can your code be broken? What happens when you click the wrong button at the wrong time? Give your application to a user or another programmer with instructions to try to break your code.

# Error Handling

A goal of successful testing and troubleshooting is to detect as many errors as possible and analyze them to determine whether they can be corrected or avoided by changing your code. Even after eliminating your mistakes, the unavoidable errors remain; for example, the user neglects to enter a required piece of information, or the network disconnects unexpectedly. You deal with unavoidable errors by writing VBA code to replace the default error handling with your own custom error-handling code. In other words, even if you can't avoid an error you can anticipate it.

## Error Codes

Three parts of Access can generate errors:

- The Jet database engine manages the errors that occur when it can't carry out a task involving any of the data access objects.

- The Access interface manages macro errors and other interface-related errors.

- VBA manages run-time errors generated by VBA itself and your VBA code.

When an error occurs because some task cannot be carried out, the Access application, Jet, or VBA identifies the error from its predefined list of errors and assigns the numerical error code for the error. (See Table 6.1 in on the CD under Tables\Chapter6.pdf for common examples of error codes.) You can write your own error handling code only for errors that have been assigned an error code; the errors in the lists are called *trappable errors*. Jet and VBA have their own set of error codes and their own way of managing the information about the error. Jet stores error information in its Errors collection, while VBA uses its own Err object. In both cases, the object is rewritten each time a new error occurs. The information in the Errors collection describes the last Jet error, and the information in the Err object describes the last VBA error that occurred; when the next Jet or VBA error occurs, the Errors collection or Err object is cleared and replaced with information about the new error.

**NOTE**    When the interface or Jet is unable to carry out a task, there is the possibility of a single incident causing more than one error; for example, errors associated with ODBC databases often have a set of related errors with a different error for each level of the ODBC drivers. Jet stores each related error in a separate Error object; the set of errors generated by the single incident comprise the Errors collection. Thus the Errors collection stores the details about all of the related errors that are recognized when a single data access error occurs.

Online Help provides separate lists of trappable errors with error codes and messages for VBA and Jet. To obtain the list of VBA trappable errors, search trappable errors in online Help. To obtain the list of data access trappable errors, search Error object, select Error Object (DAO) from the list of Topics Found, and then click the See Also hot spot and choose Trappable Microsoft Jet and DAO Errors. Figures 15.19 and 15.20 show portions of the lists.

**FIGURE 15.19:**

Online Help provides a list of error codes and messages for VBA errors.

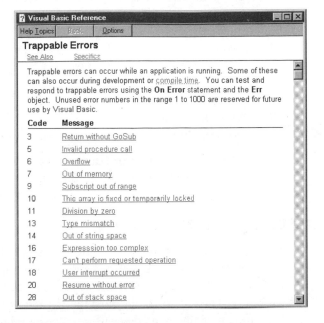

**FIGURE 15.20:**

Online Help provides a list of error codes and messages for data access and interface errors (b).

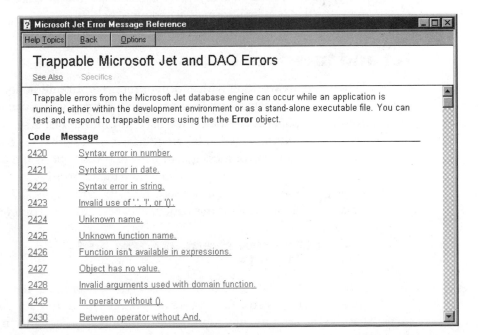

You can print your own copy of the table of the Access and Jet database engine errors as follows:

1. Search error codes in online Help. Access displays a function procedure for creating a table of the errors (see Figure 15.21a).

2. Copy the entire function procedure and paste in the basErrors module.

3. In the Immediate pane of the Debug window, type AccessAndJetErrorsTable and press Enter. Access creates the table and displays a message.

4. In the Database window, double-click the new AccessAndJetErrors to display the table (see Figure 15.21b).

# Custom Error Messages

You are familiar with the default error messages that occur when you work interactively with Access errors such as "Index or primary key can't contain a null value." or "Duplicate value in index, primary key or relationship. Changes were unsuccessful." and "The test you enter must match an entry in the list." Messages like these have little meaning to a novice user of your application. One of the reasons for handling the error yourself is to replace the default error message with a custom message that is more informative and more helpful.

# Jet and Interface Errors

When you are working with a form or report, your interactions can cause errors in the Access interface and Jet errors. For example, when you enter a value in a combo box that isn't in the combo list and Limit to List is set to Yes, Access cannot accept the value and generates an interface error with error code 2237; Access displays the default error message for this code and cancels the update of the combo box. When you try to save a record with a blank primary key, Jet cannot save the record and generates a data access error with error code 3058; Access displays the default error message for this code and cancels the save operation.

## Using the Error Event in Form and Report Modules

When either an interface or Jet engine error is generated, the form or report recognizes the Error event. You can create an event procedure for the Error event to handle the error by interrupting the default response, replacing the default error

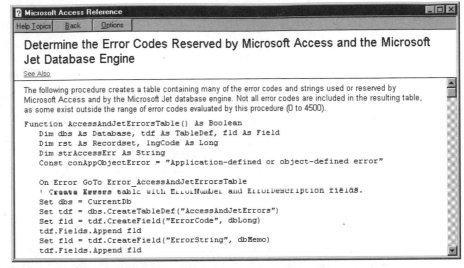

FIGURE 15.21:

Search error codes in online Help to display a function procedure for creating an errors table (a). The AccessAndJet-Errors table (b)

message with a custom error message, and specifying the actions you want Access to take instead of the default behavior. For example, you can handle a blank primary key error (error code = 3058) by displaying a custom message, suppressing the default error message, moving the focus to the primary key control, and canceling the save operation.

The event procedure code template for the Error event recognized by a form has the syntax:

```
Private Sub Form_Error(DataErr As Integer, Response As Integer)
```

You use the arguments to communicate with Access. The value of the DataErr argument is the error code of the interface or Jet engine error that occurred. When an interface or Jet error occurs, Access passes the error code as the value of DataErr to the form's or report's Error event procedure. You use the Response argument to tell Access whether to display or suppress the default error message. You use an intrinsic constant for the Response argument: set Response to acDataErrContinue to suppress the default error message and set Response to acDataErrDisplay to display it.

To explore these concepts, you'll create an error handler that handles specific errors for the Employees form in the Northwind database. The first step is to determine the error codes of the errors you want to handle; one way to do this is to create a simple event procedure to display the error code and then trigger the error.

1. Import the Employees form and the Employees table into the Ch15_Examples database from the Northwind sample database.

2. Open the Employees form in Design view. Click the OnError property, click the Build button, and enter the following event procedure. When the form recognizes the Error event, the MsgBox statement displays the error code; when you click OK to dismiss the message box, Access displays the default error message corresponding to the error code.

```
Private Sub Form_Error(DataErr As Integer, Response As Integer)
    MsgBox DataErr
End Sub
```

3. Save the form and switch to Form view. Display a new record, enter a last name without entering a first name, and press Shift + Enter to save the record. The message box displays the error code 3314 followed by the default error message (see Figure 15.22). The Jet engine generates this error because the FirstName field is a Required field.

---

**FIGURE 15.22:**

The Form_Error event procedure displays the error code (a) and Access displays a default error message for error generated by the Jet database engine (b).

(a)

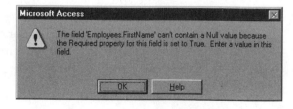

(b)

4. Enter a first name as well as a last name, tab to the Reports To combo box and enter **zzzz**. When you try to tab out of the combo box, the message box displays 2237 followed by the default error message (see Figure 15.23).

**FIGURE 15.23:**

The Form_Error event procedure displays the error code (a) for a default error message when you select an item not in the combo box list (b)

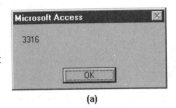

(a)

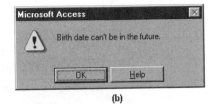

(b)

5. Select a name from the Reports To combo list. Press Shift+Enter to save the record. The message box displays the error code 3316 followed by the default error message (see Figure 15.24). You can now modify the event procedure to handle these three errors.

**FIGURE 15.24:**

The Form_Error event procedure displays the error code (a) when the validation rule for the BirthDate field is not met. The validation text is displayed as the error message (b)

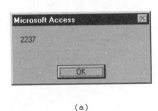

(a)

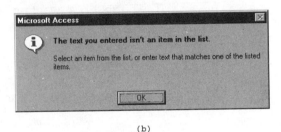

(b)

6. Press Esc to discard the current record. Modify the event procedure as shown below. You can use either the If...Then...Else or Select Case structures to set a trap for each specific error. The procedure tests the value of the error code and handles the three errors. If one of the errors occurs, the procedure displays a custom message and sets the Response to acDataErrContinue so that Access will not display the default error message. If no trapped error occurs, but another error occurs instead, the Case Else alternative is executed; setting the Response to acDataErrDisplay displays the default error message for the untrapped error. The purpose of the Case Else alternative is to specify what action to take if an unanticipated error occurs.

```
Private Sub Form_Error(DataErr As Integer, Response As Integer)
Select Case DataErr
    Case 2237
        MsgBox "You have made an invalid entry. Click the
        ➥list to display the valid choices."
        Response = acDataErrContinue
    Case 3314
        MsgBox "You must enter both first and last
        ➥names before you can save the record."
        Response = acDataErrContinue
    Case 3316
        MsgBox "You must enter a birth date earlier than
        ➥today's date."
Response = acDataErrContinue    Case Else
        Response = acDataErrDisplay
End Select
End Sub
```

7. Save the form and switch to Form view. Repeat steps 3 through 5.

The Form_Error event procedure is designed to deal only with interface and Jet errors that occur when the form has control; you cannot use this procedure to trap for VBA errors. If a VBA error occurs while the Form_Error event procedure is running, the VBA run-time error message is displayed. You must deal with VBA run-time errors by writing error handling code within the procedure. The next section describes how to handle VBA errors.

## VBA Errors

When a VBA error occurs while you are running a procedure, the default error handler is that VBA displays an error message and suspends execution of the code at the line that could not be executed. Listing 15.2 shows an event procedure created by the Command Button Wizard and provides a model for a simple VBA error handler. By current programming customs, VBA error handlers follow an older programming concept: procedures with error handling use *line labels* to identify lines of code and use statements to direct the flow of execution to the labeled lines. A line label must start in the first column, begin with a letter, and end with a colon(:).

## Listing 15.2

```
Private Sub cmdReturn_Click()
On Error GoTo Err_cmdReturn_Click

    DoCmd.Close

Exit_cmdReturn_Click:
Exit Sub

Err_cmdReturn_Click:
    MsgBox Err.Description
    Resume Exit_cmdReturn_Click
End Sub
```

Here are three basic steps for creating a simple VBA error handler such as this one:

**Enable the error handler.** You use the On Error statement to tell VBA that you are going to handle the error yourself. Place an On Error statement at the beginning of the procedure after the variable and constant declaration statements and before any executable statements. One form of the On Error statement has the syntax

```
On Error GoTo linelabel
```

By including the On Error statement you are *enabling* custom error handling and *setting an error trap*. The procedure's statements follow the On Error statement and an Exit Sub, Exit Function, or Exit Property statement follows the last statement of the procedure. Normally the error-handling code is placed after the procedure's statements, so you need the Exit state-ment to prevent the error-handling code from running when no error occurs. The On Error statement specifies where VBA goes if any error occurs in the state-ments that are listed after the On Error statement and before the Exit statement.

**Execute the error-handling code.** The line with the line label signals the beginning of the error handling code; this line must be in the same proce-dure as the On Error statement. If an error occurs, control moves to the error-handling code; an error handler that is in the process of handling an error is called an *active* error handler. VBA assigns the error code to the Number property of the Err object. The error-handling code can test the value of Err.Number and use either the If...Then...Else or Select Case struc-tures to provide alternative statements for each of the specific errors that the code is handling. A set of statements for an error number specifies the actions to take if an error with that number occurs. Write error-handling code for all the errors you anticipate and include error-handling code for unanticipated errors as well.

**Exit the error-handling code.** When the error handling code is finished, you need to specify what VBA should do next. Three common statements for exiting error handling code are

- **Resume** resumes program execution starting with the statement that caused the error.

- **Resume Next** resumes program execution starting at the statement immediately after the statement that caused the error. Use Resume Next when you want to continue running the procedure without retrying the statement that caused the error.

- **Resume** *line* resumes execution at the label specified by *line*. The line label must be in the same procedure as the error handler. Use the Resume *line* statement when you want to jump to a statement before the procedure's Exit statement (see Listing 15.2).

The simple error handlers that the Command Wizard creates use the following pattern:

```
'enable custom error-handling
On Error GoTo Err_procedurename
[statements]

'begin exit code
Exit_procedurename:
[statements]
Exit Sub

'begin error-handler
Err_procedurename:
[error-handling statements]
Resume Exit_procedurename

End Sub
```

## The On Error Statement

The On Error statement has three forms:

> **On Error GoTo** *linelabel* (described previously) specifies the location of an error handler within a procedure. When an error occurs, control goes to the error handler.
>
> **On Error Resume Next** tells Access to ignore the error and continue at the statement immediately following the statement that caused the error.
>
> **On Error GoTo 0** disables any enabled error handler in the procedure. This statement also resets the value of the Error object.

## The Err Object

When an error occurs while a VBA procedure is running, information about the error is stored as property settings of the VBA Err object. Chapter 10 describes the properties and methods of the Err object. The most commonly used properties are the Number property, which returns the error code as a Long integer, and Description, which returns a string as the error's description.

A common statement in error-handling code is to display a message box with the error code and description as follows:

```
MsgBox "Error number: " & Err.Number & " - " & Err.Description
```

When you have identified the error codes of the several errors that you want to trap in a procedure, use the Select Case structure in the error handler to provide alternative sets of statements for each error and use a Case Else structure to trap for unexpected or unknown errors as shown in the following example code:

```
Err_procedurename:
Select Case Err.Number
Case 3058
    [statements to handle the 3058 error]
Case 3022
    [statements to handle the 3022 error]
Case Else
    MsgBox "Error number: " & Err.Number & " - " &
Err.Description
End Select
Resume Exit_procedurename
```

## Creating a Generic Error Handler

For all but the simplest procedures, you should include at least a simple generic error handler that displays the error number and description for any trappable error that occurs. Listing 15.3 shows statements for a generic error handler that includes the Select Case structure to prepare for trapping specific errors.

### Listing 15.3

```
On Error GoTo Err_procedurename
[statements]

Exit_procedurename:
Exit Sub

Err_procedurename:
Select Case Err.Number
Case Else
    MsgBox "Error number: " & Err.Number & " - " &
Err.Description
End Select
Resume Exit_procedurename
```

As a simple example, we'll create a procedure to divide one number by another.

1.  Create a new module named basErrors in the Ch15_Examples database.

2.  Enter the Division procedure in Listing 15.4 in the basErrors module.

### Listing 15.4

```
Public Sub Division()
Dim dblnum As Double, dblden As Double, dblResult As Double
On Error GoTo Err_Division
dblnum = InputBox ("Enter the numerator.")
dblden = InputBox ("Enter the denominator")
dblResult = dblnum/dblden
MsgBox "The quotient is " & dblREsult

Exit_Division:
Exit Sub

Err_Division:
Select Case Err.Number
```

```
Case Else
    MsgBox "Error number: " & Err.Number & " - " &
Err.Description
End Select
Resume Exit_Division
End Sub
```

3. Run the Division procedure in the Debug window. The first time enter **24** and **12** in the text boxes (see Figure 15.25a). The procedure displays the quotient (see Figure 15.25b).

**FIGURE 15.25:**

The Division procedure collects two numbers and displays the quotient.

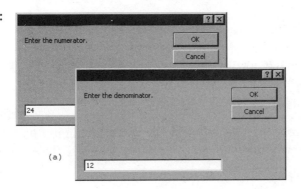

(a)

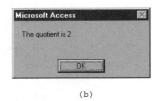

(b)

4. Run the procedure again. Enter **twenty** in the text box of the first input box (see Figure 15.26a). An error occurs because the procedure declares dblnum as a number of the Double data type and Access cannot set this variable to the string you entered. The error handler is active, and the custom error message indicates that the error has code 13 for a type mismatch error (see Figure 15.26b).

**FIGURE 15.26:**

When you enter a string instead of a number, VBA generates an error with code 13.

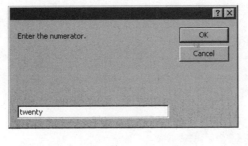

(a)

(b)

5.  Run the procedure again. This time enter **20** in the text box of the first input box and **0** (zero) in the text box of the second input box. Another error occurs because Access cannot divide a number by zero. The error handler is active and indicates that the error has code 11 for a division by zero error.

You can trap specifically for each of these errors by using a message box to inform the user that a number must be entered when the error with code 13 occurs and a separate message box to tell the user that the number entered for the denominator must not be 0. The procedure uses the MsgBox function to allow users to choose whether to try again or quit the procedure; we'll create the strAnswer variable to hold the user's selection.

6.  Modify the Division procedure as shown in Listing 15.5. When either error occurs and the user chooses to try again, the procedure uses the Resume statement to instruct Access to return to the statement that caused the error as follows:

```
If strAnswer = vbYes Then Resume
```

If the user chooses not to try again, control jumps down to the last statement of the error handler and control then jumps to the exit code:

```
Resume Exit_Division
```

The procedure continues to include the Case Else alternative to trap for unexpected errors.

## Listing 15.5

```
Public Sub Division()
Dim dblnum As Double, dblden As Double, dblResult As Double
Dim strAnswer As String
On Error GoTo Err_Division
dblnum = InputBox ("Enter the numerator.")
dblden = InputBox ("Enter the denominator")
dblResult = dblnum/dblden
MsgBox "The quotient is " & dblREsult
Exit_Division:
Exit Sub

Err_Division:
Select Case Err.Number
```

```
Case 13
    strAnswer = MsgBox ("You must enter a number. Do you want to
    ➡try again?", vbYesNo)
    If strAnswer = vbYes Then Resume
Case 11
    strAnswer = Msgbox ("You must enter a non-zero number. Do you
    ➡want to try again?", vbYesNo)
If strAnswer = vbYes Then Resume
Case Else
    MsgBox "Error number: " & Err.Number & " - " &
Err.Description
End Select
Resume Exit_Division
End Sub
```

7. Run the Division procedure in the Immediate pane. Type **twenty** in the text box of the first input box and click OK. This time the procedure traps the error and displays the message shown in Figure 15.27a. If you type a number in the text box of the first input box and **0** in the text box of the second, the procedure traps the error and displays the message shown in Figure 15.27b.

**FIGURE 15.27:**

Custom error-handling instructions display these message boxes so that the user can correct the error and try again.

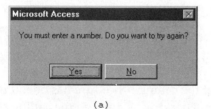
(a)

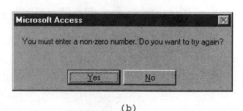
(b)

As an alternative to jumping from one part of the procedure to another, you can include Exit Sub statements any time you want to terminate a procedure. The result shown in Listing 15.6 may be easier to read; nevertheless, some programmers prefer to provide only a single exit point for a procedure.

**Listing 15.6**

```
Public Sub Division()
Dim dblnum As Double, dblden As Double, dblResult As Double
Dim strAnswer As String
On Error GoTo Err_Division
```

```
dblnum = InputBox ("Enter the numerator.")
dblden = InputBox ("Enter the denominator")
dblResult = dblnum/dblden
MsgBox "The quotient is " & dblResult

Err_Division:
Select Case Err.Number
Case 13
    strAnswer = MsgBox ("You must enter a number. Do you want to
    ➥try again?", vbYesNo)
    If strAnswer = vbYes Then Resume Else Exit Sub
Case 11
    strAnswer = Msgbox ("You must enter a non-zero number. Do you
    ➥want to try again?", vbYesNo)
If strAnswer = vbYes Then Resume Else Exit Sub
Case Else
    MsgBox "Error number: " & Err.Number & " - " &
Err.Description
End Select

End Sub
```

## Errors in Called Procedures

When an error occurs in a called procedure, VBA looks for an error handler first in the called procedure that is running when the error occurs. If it doesn't find an error handler in the called procedure, VBA returns to the calling procedure and executes its error handler if the calling procedure has one. If it encounters a chain of calling procedures, Access backtracks through the calling chain and executes the first error handler it finds. If it doesn't find any error handlers, Access executes the default error-handling routine; in this case Access displays the default error message first and then displays the run-time error dialog; then it terminates the procedure. For more information on dealing with errors in called procedures, see the *Access 97 Developer's Handbook* by Paul Litwin, Ken Getz, and Mike Gilbert (Sybex, 1997).

# Summary

This chapter introduces the complex subject of error handling. The important points covered in the chapter follow:

- Two kinds of errors occur in programs: avoidable and unavoidable. Careful design, testing, and troubleshooting can eliminate many avoidable errors. You can use custom error-handling code to specify the actions you want to take when an unavoidable error occurs.

- Access VBA provides built-in syntax checking and compiling routines for eliminating compile-time errors.

- Access provides two kinds of troubleshooting tools: those that do not interrupt execution and those that involve suspending execution and placing the procedure in break mode.

- With execution suspended you can execute a single statement at a time and test its effect. You can examine the values of variables and view an ordered list of calling procedures.

- Some techniques that can help you avoid errors when you design a procedure are to require explicit variable declaration, to use specific data typing, and to use comments.

- You can use the Error event of a form or report to trap for and write error-handling code for interface and Jet errors. The Error event is particularly useful for replacing default error messages with custom error messages.

- You can use the On Error statement in a procedure to enable error-handling code for VBA errors that occur when the procedure is running. The main purpose of custom error handling is to prevent the run-time error dialog and procedure failure.

- The error-handling code uses properties of the VBA Err object to determine the error code.

- All but the simplest VBA procedures should include a simple error handler that displays the error code and the default error message. The error handler can exit the procedure without executing the problem statement or include instructions for Access to follow if the error occurs.

# CHAPTER

## SIXTEEN

**16**

# Navigation with Access VBA

- Navigating among forms, records, and controls

- Using the Recordsetclone to access the form's recordset

- Creating custom navigation buttons

- Finding a specific record using a form

- Working directly with the data without opening a form

- Moving around in a recordset

- Finding specific records in a recordset

The first six chapters of Part III have laid the VBA foundation. In Chapters 10 and 11 you learned about the Access application objects and the Jet engine objects that you manipulate with VBA: how to discover and change their characteristics (properties) in a program and how to run an object's internal programs (methods). The subsequent three chapters covered the fundamentals of VBA: in Chapter 12 you learned the basic techniques for writing programs (procedures) to manipulate the objects, in Chapter 13 you learned how to use variables in procedures to make procedures reusable and run faster, and in Chapter 14 you learned how to control the execution of statements. In Chapter 15 you learned how to analyze and correct mistakes and anticipate unavoidable errors in your programs. These six chapters are the reference for the rest of the book. With the basic tools and skills in place, we are ready to put the concepts together and create procedures needed in a database application.

**NOTE**  Chapters 16, 17, and 18 are devoted to creating VBA procedures to automate the fundamental database operations: navigating among the forms, controls, and records of an application; maintaining the data by modifying or deleting existing data and adding new data; and selecting and changing groups of records. These chapters are the Access VBA approach to the same three topics treated using macro programming in Chapters 7, 8, and 9, respectively. Corresponding chapters treat some of the same examples and produce macros and VBA procedures that are similar. Each of these chapters also has separate examples not treated in the corresponding chapter, so you can benefit from reading all six chapters.

This chapter focuses on navigation. The first part deals with navigation using forms and introduces you to some of the real power of Access VBA. You learn about using the RecordsetClone property for navigation *in memory* through the form's records that is independent of the navigation *in the interface* provided by the form. You'll learn how to make applications easier to use by providing custom buttons on forms so that the user can easily travel between forms, controls, and records using the custom buttons as guides. You'll learn how to automate navigation to records in forms based on their physical location and how to automate the search for a record satisfying search criteria. The second part of the chapter shows you a new way to work with records: Using VBA you can open a

# Learning from the Wizards

A good way to get started with VBA is to use the Access wizards to create a first draft of a simple procedure and then modify the wizard's procedure. Access provides several code building wizards that create both simple and complex procedures including:

- The Command Button Wizard creates event procedures complete with simple error handling for basic database tasks including navigation and simple record, form, and report operations. These event procedures typically include only a few statements and are easy to modify.

- The Switchboard Manager creates a set of more complicated event procedures and support procedures to automate a switchboard. The Switchboard Manager uses more advanced programming techniques and creates procedures that are an excellent model of good programming design. Plan to spend a few hours understanding how these procedures work.

- The Form Wizard creates the code necessary to synchronize two forms including the event procedures and support procedures for both forms.

- The Database Wizard uses all of these wizards to help in creating a simple partially automated application complete with several automated switchboards and simple navigation to synchronized forms and reports.

One approach to learning how to use VBA is to create a draft for an application using the Database Wizard and then examine the kind of procedures the wizard uses to accomplish tasks. (See Chapter 1 "Automating a Database without Programming.") Typically, the code is very elegant. The word *elegant* as applied to programming means that the code is efficient because it uses the least amount of memory and the fewest number of statements to accomplish the task. Elegant code is optimized for the best performance because it uses the methods and control structures that accomplish the task in the shortest time.

recordset in memory without opening a form. Working with records in memory is much faster than working with records in forms because Access doesn't have to take the time to load a form into memory and create its visual representation on the screen.

> **NOTE** For hands-on experience with the techniques described in this chapter, create a new copy of the Northwind sample database named Northwind_Ch16 and work through the steps and examples.

# The Form and Its Recordset

When you open a bound form, Access opens the form's recordset in memory and displays records in the form using the form's record selector to indicate the form's current record. When you open a bound form, there are two objects you can manipulate in a VBA procedure: the form and the form's recordset. You can refer to the recordset directly by using the form's RecordsetClone property, which means that you can use the properties and methods of both the Form object (see Chapter 10) and the Recordset object (see Chapter 11) when you are writing procedures that manipulate the records in a form. When one of these objects lacks the property or method that you need, you can use the other object instead. For example, the Form object does not have a property or method to determine the number of records in a bound form; however, you can use the RecordCount property of the Recordset object. Learning how to use both the Form and Recordset objects in procedures is an important skill.

To work with a form's recordset in a procedure, you declare an object variable and point the object variable to the form's recordset using the form's RecordsetClone property. If *formname* is the name of the form, the statements are

```
Dim rst As Recordset, frm As Form
Set frm = Forms!formname
Set rst = frm.RecordsetClone
```

The second Set statement creates a special reference to the form's recordset object called the *recordsetclone*. The recordsetclone has its own current record pointer so it can point to a different record from the record that is displayed in the form.

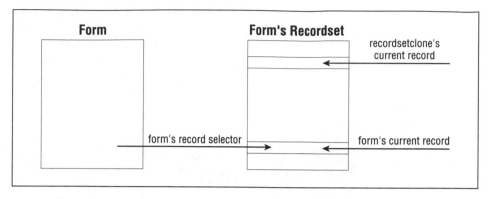

Consequently, you can use the recordsetclone to work with another record in a form's recordset while the form continues to display a specific record. When you first create the recordsetclone, its current record pointer is not defined; you can set the current record pointer in the procedure.

As an example of creating and using the recordsetclone, we'll create a procedure to print the last names of the employees in the Employees table.

1. Open the Employees form in Design view and place a command button named cmdRecordset and with the caption Print Last Names in the header section.

2. Click in the button's Onclick property and click the Build button to display the form's module. Create the cmdRecordset_Click() event procedure shown below. The procedure creates the recordsetclone, uses the MoveFirst method to set the recordsetclone's current record pointer to the first record, and then loops through the recordset. Each pass through the loop prints the last name in the recordsetclone's current record and uses the MoveNext method to move the current record pointer to the next record.

```
Private Sub cmdRecordset_Click()
    Dim rst As Recordset
    Set rst = Me.RecordsetClone
    rst.MoveFirst
    Do
        Debug.Print rst!LastName
        rst.MoveNext
    Loop Until rst.EOF
End Sub
```

3. Save the form and switch to Form view. Press Ctrl+G to open the Debug window and click the new command button. The Immediate pane prints the last names for all of the employees as evidence that the procedure has walked through all the records in the form's recordset while the form continues to display its first record (see Figure 16.1).

**FIGURE 16.1:**

The Print Last Names button runs a procedure that uses the RecordsetClone and walks through the form's recordset while the form displays its first record.

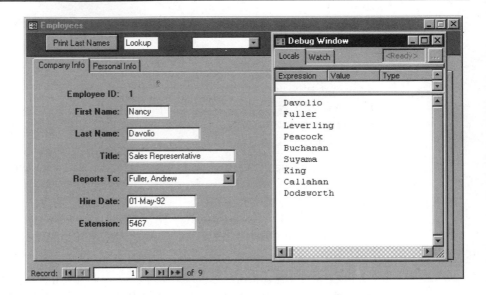

You can use Me to refer to the form because the event procedure is stored in the form's module. In the next example, we create a reusable function procedure that walks through the recordset of any form.

1. Create a new standard module named basNavigation. Insert the function procedure shown in Listing 16.1. This procedure creates the recordsetclone for the form passed as an argument to the function and prints the value in the first field of each record in the form's recordset. Because we want the function procedure to be reusable, we refer to the first field using the numerical index reference rst.Fields(0) or simply rst(0) (because Fields is the default collection for a recordset). You can run the FormRecordset function by passing the reference to any open form as the argument.

**Listing 16.1**

```
Public Function FormRecordset(frm As Form)
    Dim rst as Recordset
    Set rst = frm.RecordsetClone
    rst.MoveFirst
    Do
        Debug.Print rst(0)
        rst.MoveNext
    Loop Until rst.EOF
End Function
```

2. Open the Customers form and type **? FormRecordset(Forms!Customers)** in the Immediate window and press Enter. Note that you are passing the refer- ence to the form, not the name of the form. When you press enter, VBA prints the customer ID field to the Immediate pane. The next step shows how to run the function as an event function procedure.

3. Open the Categories form in Design view and assign the FormRecordset function as an event function procedure by typing **=FormRecordset(Form)** in the OnOpen event. Note that you are passing Form as the reference to the form. (You can also use the reference Forms!Categories, but you can't use the Me reference to refer to the form in a property sheet.)

4. Save the form and switch to Form view. When you switch to Form view, the form recognizes the Open event, so VBA runs the function procedure and prints the category ID field to the Immediate pane.

> **NOTE**  One of the fundamental advantages of VBA programming over macro programming is that you have access to the Recordset object in VBA and can work directly with records in memory.

# Interface Navigation

When you work interactively, you use keystrokes, menu commands, and the mouse to move between controls, between records, and from one Database win- dow object to another. The simplest approach to automating navigation in the interface is to place command buttons on forms and create procedures that run when you click the buttons. Access provides the methods of the DoCmd object for navigating through the interface; these methods duplicate the interactive instructions you give when you press a key, move the mouse and click a mouse button, or choose a menu command. We'll go through the steps of a very simple example in order to develop a set of guidelines for writing procedures that are reusable.

## Writing Reusable Procedures

Suppose you are working with a form and want to open another form; for example, when reviewing a customer using the Customers form, a user may want to open the Orders form. The simplest approach to automating this operation is to place a command button named cmdOrders on the Customers form and create an event procedure for the button's Click event. You use the OpenForm method of the DoCmd object to open the form. The OpenForm method has one required argument followed by six optional arguments. (Search OpenForm in online Help for information on the arguments.)

```
DoCmd.OpenForm formname[,view] [,filtername] [,wherecondition]
[,datamode] [,windowmode] [,openargs]
```

We'll accept the defaults for the optional arguments and use the *formname* argument to specify the name of the form to open. The *formname* argument is a string expression that is the valid name of any form in the current database.

The first draft for the procedure is

```
Private Sub cmdOrders_Click()
DoCmd.OpenForm "Orders"
End Sub
```

This event procedure works just fine—it opens the specified form. The problem with the procedure is that the OpenForm method uses the specific form name as an argument. Using specific names of objects as arguments of methods in a procedure causes unnecessary problems if you should want to reuse the procedure. To reuse a procedure that contains specific names for objects, you have to search through the statements to find the literal arguments and replace each one with the new name. We are going to make three modifications to the procedure to make it easier to reuse:

- Replace the method's literal argument with a variable.

- Move the declaration of the variable from the interior to the procedure's argument list.

- Move the procedure to a standard module.

The first improvement defines variables to hold the specific names and uses the variables as arguments of methods instead of the specific names. With this improvement, the procedure becomes

```
Private Sub cmdOrders_Click()
Dim strName As String
strName = "Orders"
DoCmd.OpenForm strName
End Sub
```

The cmdOrders_Click procedure is so simple that the significance of the modification may be obscured by the very simplicity. Imagine a procedure with dozens of statements having methods with arguments; by creating a set of variables to hold all the specific names and assigning the variables to the specific names at the beginning of the procedure, you can easily modify the procedure by looking in one place to change the names.

A second improvement takes the specific names out of the interior of the procedure by creating arguments for the procedure. With this improvement you pass the specific names as arguments when you call the procedure. If the procedure is an event procedure, you'll have to change the type of procedure as well because you can't create your own arguments for an event procedure. (An event procedure has a predefined syntax, including a naming convention, and predefined arguments for passing information back and forth between Access and the event procedure.) To create your own arguments for a procedure triggered by an event, you need to change to a function procedure.

**NOTE**    You can use an event to trigger a macro by setting the event property to the name of the macro using the syntax *macrogroupname.macroname*, to trigger an event procedure by setting the event property to [Event procedure] and creating the event procedure in the form's or report's module, or to trigger a function procedure by setting the event property using the syntax *=functionname(argumentlist)*. You cannot use an event to trigger a general sub procedure that doesn't follow the predefined syntax for an event procedure.

You can change the name of the command button and the event function to reflect its generic nature. In this example we'll change the name for both to cmdOpenForm. With this modification, the procedure becomes

```
Private Function cmdOpenForm(strName As String)
DoCmd.OpenForm strName
End Sub
```

With the variable declared in the argument list for the procedure, you no longer need a separate declaration statement in the procedure. The specific name of the form doesn't appear at all, so you can use the procedure to open any form. You supply the name of the form when you call the procedure. In this example, to call the procedure when the button is clicked, you assign the function to the event by entering = cmdOpenForm("Orders") in the button's property sheet. By specifying the arguments in the button's property sheet, you avoid having to work directly with the code in the module at all. If you want to open another form, you need only make the change in the button's property sheet.

The third improvement takes the procedure out of the form module and stores it as a public function in a standard module. With the function procedure stored in a standard module, the command button/function procedure combination is now fully reusable. When you copy the button, the assignment to the function procedure is copied also. With the button pasted to another form, you can specify the form to be opened in the button's property sheet; in addition, you don't have to open the module to change the procedure.

By placing an event function procedure assigned to a control in a standard module, you make the procedure *portable* and *independent* of a specific form in the application. Pasting the control pastes the assignment to the procedure also, and the control continues to work as long as the database contains the standard module. (The standard module could even be stored in another database, and the control would continue to work if you set a reference to the database that contains the standard module. See Chapter 20 for more information on setting references.)

The portable and independent command button/function procedure combination to open a form is

**Control:** command button named cmdOpenForm with OnClick property set to =OpenAForm(formname) where formname is the string expression that evaluates to the name of a form, such as "Orders"

**Event Function:** event function stored in the basNavigation standard module

```
Public Function OpenAForm(strName As String)
    DoCmd.OpenForm strName
End Sub
```

## Guidelines for Creating Reusable Procedures

To summarize, we'll use these guidelines in creating procedures in order to maximize their reusability. These suggestions are guidelines only, not rigid rules that must always be followed. For example, if an event procedure is unique to a specific form, you may not need to go beyond the first guideline.

- Do not use specific names or literal expressions as arguments of methods; declare variables and use variables as arguments instead.

- Define the variables in one of these ways:

    - In declaration statements within the procedure and assign them to the literal expressions.

    - As arguments of the procedure. Pass the literal expressions into the procedure. Change an event procedure to a function procedure in order to pass literal expressions as arguments.

- Store reusable procedures in standard modules instead of in form or report modules when you want to make the procedures independent of any form and easily portable to other forms. Change an event procedure to a function procedure in order to store it in a standard module.

**NOTE** When you store an event function procedure in a standard module, you can't use Me refer to the form. However, when the form is the active object, you can refer to the form using the ActiveForm property of the Screen object.

# Form Navigation

The simplest approach to automating navigation between forms is to place command buttons on the forms and create procedures that run when you click the buttons. Most forms navigation tasks are generic: opening a form from another form, opening and synchronizing a form or report to display specific records, closing or hiding forms, and performing other general tasks that you need to use several times in every application. For reusable, portable, and independent button procedures, we'll use event function procedures stored in a standard module.

For opening and closing forms, the simplest event functions are

- Opening a form

```
Public Function OpenAForm(strName As String)
    DoCmd.OpenForm strName
End Sub
```

- Closing a form

```
Public Function CloseAForm(strName As String)
    DoCmd.Close acForm, strName
End Sub
```

## Hiding and Unhiding a Form

When opening or closing a form, there may be additional tasks that the procedure needs to carry out. As an example, one of the application development guidelines that many developers follow to avoid data integrity problems is to allow users to change the data in only a single form at a time. One way to implement this guideline is to hide the first form when you open the second form and then when you close the second form. The procedure that closes the second form must know which form to unhide.

An interesting problem arises because typically the second form can be opened from several different forms depending on how you design the navigational paths. For example, you may design the navigation so that the user can open the Orders form from the Main Switchboard, the Customer Orders form, or the Customers form. The second form needs to remember which form opened it so that it knows which form to unhide when you close it. The Tag property is ideal for this purpose. We'll create a pair of procedures that use the Tag property of the form you are opening to store the name of the form that opened it. Listing 16.2 shows the OpenHide event function assigned to the command button on the first form. We'll call the first form the opener form and the second form the opened form.

### Listing 16.2

```
Public Function OpenHide (strName As String)
Dim strHide As String
    strHide = Screen.ActiveForm.Name
    Screen.ActiveForm.Visible = False
    DoCmd.OpenForm strName
    Screen.ActiveForm.Tag = strHide
End Function
```

The strHide variable holds the name of the opener form using the Screen object to refer to it. After storing the name of the opener form in the strHide variable, the procedure hides the opener form. The procedure opens the second form and sets the Tag property of the opened form to the name of the opener form.

When you close the second form by clicking a command button on it, you unhide the opener form using the CloseUnhide procedure shown in Listing 16.3.

### Listing 16.3

```
Public Function CloseUnhide()
Dim strUnhide As String
If IsNull(Screen.ActiveForm.Tag) Then
    DoCmd.Close
Else
    strUnhide = Screen.ActiveForm.Tag
    DoCmd.Close
    DoCmd.SelectObject acForm, strUnhide
End If
End Function
```

The CloseUnhide procedure first tests the opened form's Tag property. The Tag property either contains the name of the (hidden) opener form or the Tag property is null if the second form was opened in some other way that did not set its Tag property. If the Tag property is null, the Close method simply closes the form; otherwise, the procedure holds the name of the opener form in the strUnhide variable, closes the opened form using the Close method, and then unhides the opener form using the SelectObject method.

To test the procedures:

1. Insert the OpenHide and CloseHide function procedures in the basNavigation module.

2. Open the Products form in Design view. Place a command button named cmdOpenHide and with the caption Open Categories in the form's header. Set the button's Onclick property to = OpenHide("Categories"). Save the form and switch to Form view.

3. Open the Categories form in Design view. Place a command button named cmdCloseUnhide and with the caption Close Unhide on the form. Set the button's Onclick property to = CloseUnhide(). Save and close the form.

4. Click the Open Categories button on the Products form. The form is hidden and the Categories form opens. Click the Close Unhide button on the form. The Categories form closes, and the Products form is unhidden.

## Synchronizing Two Forms

Often when you use a procedure to open a form, you need to synchronize its records to the record displayed by the first form. For example, when opening the Customers form from the Orders form, you can use the filtername or wherecondition arguments of the OpenForm method to locate and display the customer record corresponding to the customer displayed in the Orders form. The filtername argument is a string expression that is the valid name of a query in the current database, and the wherecondition argument is a string expression that is a valid SQL WHERE clause without the word WHERE. You can use either argument to restrict records; if you specify both arguments, Access first applies the query and then applies the wherecondition to the result of the query.

We'll use the wherecondition argument to synchronize the form being opened to the current form as follows:

```
fieldname=Forms!formname!controlname
```

In this expression, *fieldname* refers to the field in the underlying table or query of the form you want to open, and *controlname* refers to the control on the form that contains the value you want to match. For example, to open the Customers form displaying a record synchronized to the record in the Orders form, use the expression

```
CustomerID=Forms!Orders!CustomerID
```

or use the Screen object to refer to the active form as follows:

```
CustomerID=Screen.ActiveForm.CustomerID
```

Notice that the full syntax is required on the right side of the expression, even though Orders is the active form when the procedure executes the OpenForm method—this example shows a case in which you must use the full syntax to refer to a control on the active object. Notice also that the short syntax is required on the left side of the expression. The wherecondition argument uses the syntax required by SQL to synchronize the records.

The event procedure shown in Listing 16.4 opens and synchronizes the Customers form to the Orders form.

### Listing 16.4

```
Private Sub cmdViewCustomer_Click()
Dim strForm As String
Dim strWhere As String
strForm = "Customers"
strWhere = "CustomerID = Forms!Orders!CustomerID"
    DoCmd.OpenForm formname:=strForm, wherecondition:=strWhere
End Sub
```

1.  Open the Orders form in Design view. Place a command button named cmdViewCustomer and with the caption View Customer on the form. Open the form's module and insert Listing 16.4.

2.  Save the form and switch to Form view. Use the default navigation buttons to select the order for a customer. Click the View Customer button. The Customers form opens, displaying the corresponding customer (see Figure 16.2).

3.  In the Orders form, select an order for a different customer. The Customers form does not remain synchronized.

## Keeping the Forms Synchronized

When you move to another record in the Orders form, the Customers form continues to display the previous customer and does not resynchronize automatically. We'll create an event procedure to resynchronize the Customers form when you move to a different record in the Orders form. When you move to a different record, the form recognizes the Current event. Listing 16.5 shows the Form_Current event procedure for the Orders form.

FIGURE 16.2:

**FIGURE 16.2:**

The View Customer button runs a procedure that opens and synchronizes the Customers form.

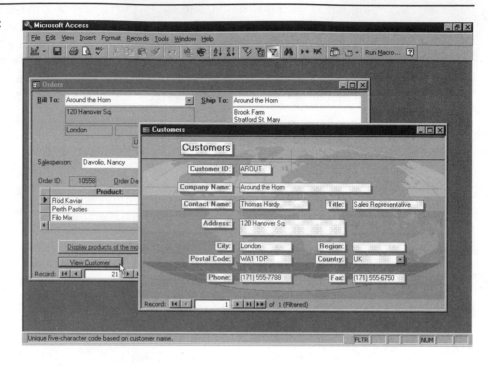

## Listing 16.5

```
Private Sub Form_Current()
Dim strForm As String
Dim strWhere As String
strForm = "Customers"
strWhere = "CustomerID = Forms!Orders!CustomerID"
If IsLoaded (strForm) Then
    DoCmd.OpenForm formname:=strForm, wherecondition:=strWhere
End If
End Sub
```

1. Click in the Orders form and switch to Design view. Open the form's module and insert the procedure in Listing 16.5. The procedure uses the custom IsLoaded function (stored in the Utility Function module) to determine if the Customers form is open. If the Customers form is open, the procedure uses the OpenForm method to resynchronize the form; otherwise, the procedure terminates.

2. Save the form and switch to Form view. Using the default navigation buttons, browse to the order of a different customer. The Customers form resynchronizes.

**Closing the Related Form**   When you close the Orders form, the Customers form should close also (if it is open). Listing 16.6 is an event procedure for the Close event of the Orders form that closes the Customers form if is it open.

### Listing 16.6

```
Private Sub Form_Close()
Dim strForm As String
strForm = "Customers"
DoCmd.Close acForm, strForm
End Sub
```

You won't need to determine if the Customers form is open before running the Close method to close it because of the exceptional nature of the Close method— the Close method does not fail if you specify the name of an object that isn't open or that doesn't exist.

1. Click in the Orders form and switch to Design view. Open the form's module and insert the procedure in Listing 16.6.

2. Save the form and switch to Form view. Click the default Close button on the form. Both the Orders and the Customers forms close.

# Navigation between Controls

When working interactively, you use keystrokes, menu commands, and the mouse to move through controls on forms. We'll create procedures to automate moving to specific controls on forms and subforms and to specific controls within records. For this exercise, we'll place command buttons on the Orders form and create event procedures for navigating between controls on the Orders form and the Quarterly Orders form.

## Moving to a Specific Control on the Active Form

You can move the focus to a specific control on the active form in two ways. You can use the GoToControl method of the DoCmd object, or you can use the control's SetFocus method.

**Using the GoToControl Method** The syntax for the GoToControl method is

```
DoCmd.GoToControl controlname
```

where *controlname* is a string expression that is the name of the control on the active form or datasheet. You must use only the name of the control; using the fully qualified reference causes a run-time error.

1. Open the Orders form in Design view. Create three command buttons on the Orders form empowered by the event procedures shown in Listings 16.7, 16.8 and 16.9. The procedure in Listing 16.7 moves the focus to a control on the Orders main form. Moving the focus to a specific control on a subform requires using the GoToControl method twice; you move the focus to the subform control with the first method and then to the control on the subform with the second method (see Listing 16.8). Moving the focus to a specific control on an open form that isn't active also takes two steps; the first step uses the SelectObject method of the DoCmd object to activate the open form and the second step uses the GoToControl method to move to the control (see Listing 16.9).

### Listing 16.7

```
Private Sub cmdToControl_Click()
Dim strControl As String
strControl = "EmployeeID"
    DoCmd.GoToControl strControl
End Sub
```

### Listing 16.8

```
Private Sub cmdToControlOnSubform_Click()
Dim strControl As String, strSubformControl As String
    strControl = "Discount" : strSubformControl = "Orders Subform"
    DoCmd.GoToControl strSubformControl
    DoCmd.GoToControl strControl
End Sub
```

### Listing 16.9

```
Private Sub cmdToOtherFormControl_Click()
Dim strControl As String, strForm As String
    strForm = "Quarterly Orders" : strControl = "Country"
```

```
        DoCmd.SelectObject acForm, strForm
        DoCmd.GoToControl strControl
    End Sub
```

2. Save the form and switch to Form view. Open the Quarterly Orders form. Test the three new command buttons on the Orders form. For example, clicking the To Control On Subform button moves the focus to the Discount control of the first record in the subform (see Figure 16.3).

**FIGURE 16.3:**

Click the To Control On Subform button to run a procedure that moves the focus first to the subform control and then to the Discount control of the first record in the subform.

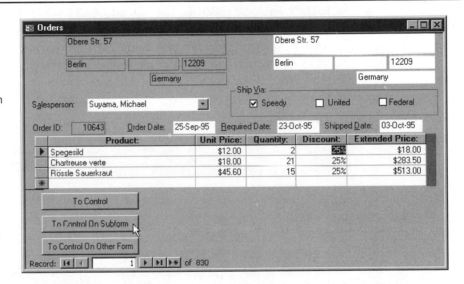

**Using the SetFocus Method**    The second method for moving the focus to a specific control on the active form uses the control's SetFocus method. The SetFocus method has the syntax

```
    object.SetFocus
```

where object is a Form or a Control object. The SetFocus method of the Control object moves the focus to the specified control on the active form or the specified field on the active datasheet. When the object is the Form object, the result depends on whether the form has any controls that can receive the focus; if the form has controls with the Enabled property set to True, the SetFocus method moves the focus to the last control on the form that had the focus; otherwise, the SetFocus method moves the focus to the form itself. When VBA executes an *object*.SetFocus statement, VBA is requesting that the object move the focus to itself.

1. With the Orders form in Design view, place three command buttons on the form and enter the event procedures in Listings 16.10, 16.11, and 16.12. Because SetFocus is a method of the Control object or the Form object, the procedures in Listings 16.10, 16.11, and 16.12 create object variables to refer to the objects and the Set keyword in the assignment statements that point the variables to specific objects. Use the fully qualified reference to refer to the forms and controls. The procedure in Listing 16.10 moves the focus to the combo box on the main form, the procedure in Listing 16.11 moves the focus first to the Subform object and then to the control on the subform, and the procedure in Listing 16.12 moves the focus first to the other form and then to a control on the form.

### Listing 16.10

```
Public Sub cmdSetControl_Click()
Dim cbo As ComboBox
Set cbo = Forms!Orders!EmployeeID
cbo.SetFocus
End Sub
```

### Listing 16.11

```
Public Sub cmdSetControlOnSubform_Click()
Dim sfr As Subform, txt As TextBox
Set sfr = Forms!Orders![Orders Subform]
Set txt = Forms!Orders![Orders Subform]!Discount
sfr.SetFocus
txt.SetFocus
End Sub
```

### Listing 16.12

```
Public Sub cmdSetOtherFormControl_Click()
Dim frm As Form, txt As TextBox
Set frm = Forms![Quarterly Orders]
Set txt = Forms![Quarterly Orders]!Country
frm.SetFocus
txt.SetFocus
End Sub
```

2. Save the form and switch to Form view. With the Quarterly Orders form open, test the three new buttons. For example, clicking the SetFocus To Control On Subform button moves the focus first to the subform control and then to the Discount control of the first record in the subform (see Figure 16.4).

**FIGURE 16.4:**

Click the SetFocus To Control On Subform button to run a procedure that uses the SetFocus method to move the focus first to the subform control and then to the Discount control of the first record in the subform.

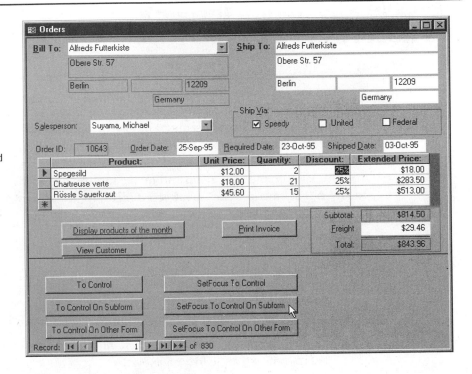

## Moving within a Record

When working interactively, you can use the keyboard to move the focus among the controls of the active form. Table 7.2 (on the CD under Tables\Chapter7.pdf) shows the keystrokes codes to move the focus. You can use the SendKeys statement to duplicate the keystrokes that move the focus. The syntax of the SendKeys statement is

```
SendKeys string, wait
```

where *string* is a string expression specifying the keystrokes you want to send and the optional *wait* argument is True if the keystrokes must be processed before the next statement executes and False if the next statement executes immediately after the keys are sent. For example, the statement that moves the focus to the first control in the current record and waits for the keystroke to be processed is

```
SendKeys "{home}", True
```

# Physical Navigation through the Records of a Form

When you work interactively, you navigate among records according to their physical location within the recordset. This process is called *physical navigation*. The record you move to becomes the current record—the *current record* is the record you modify with subsequent mouse or keyboard actions. You can use the GoToRecord method of the DoCmd object to duplicate the effect of clicking a default navigation button in the lower-left corner of a form (or of choosing the Go To command on the Edit menu and then choosing one of the subcommands on the fly-out submenu). The GoToRecord method has the syntax

```
DoCmd.GoToRecord [objecttype, objectname] [,record] [,offset]
```

where

> *objecttype* is one of the instrinic constants: acTable, acQuery, or acForm.
>
> *objectname* is an optional string expression that is the valid name of an object of the specified type.
>
> *record* is one of the intrinsic constants, acPrevious, acNext (the default), acFirst, acLast, acGoTo, or acNewRec.
>
> *offset* is a numeric expression that represents the number of records to move forward if you specify acNext, backward if you specify acPrevious, or a valid record number if you specify acGoTo.

All of the arguments are optional. If you omit the objecttype and objectname arguments, the active object is assumed. If you omit the record argument, the default constant is acNext.

# Creating Custom Navigation Buttons

We'll create a set of custom navigation buttons for a form. To make the buttons reusable on other forms, we automate the buttons with event function procedures stored in a new basNavigationButtons standard module.

1. Create a set of five command buttons in the footer section of the Products form named cmdFirst, cmdPrevious, cmdNext, cmdLast, and cmdNew (and with suitable captions) and assign the event function procedures shown in Listing 16.13. The function procedure for the New record button is named NewRec because NewRecord is the name of a form property and is not a valid name for a procedure.

### Listing 16.13

```
Public Function FirstRecord()
DoCmd.GoToRecord Record:= acFirst
End Function

Public Function PreviousRecord()
DoCmd.GoToRecord Record:= acPrevious
End Function

Public Function NextRecord()
DoCmd.GoToRecord Record:= acNext
End Function

Public Function LastRecord()
DoCmd.GoToRecord Record:= acLast
End Function

Public Function NewRec ()
DoCmd.GoToRecord Record:= acNewRec
End Function
```

2. Save the form and switch to Form view (see Figure 16.5). Test the new buttons.

FIGURE 16.5:

The custom navigation buttons

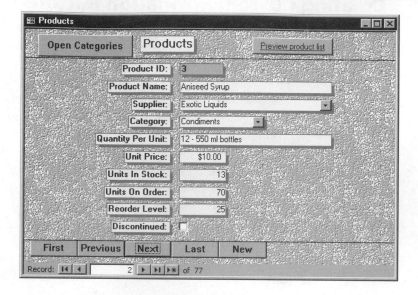

When you test the buttons you find that clicking the First button and then clicking the Previous button causes the PreviousRecord procedure to fail (see Figure 16.6a). The reason for the failure is that after you click the First button, the current record is the first record in the recordset; therefore, when you click the Previous button you are attempting to move beyond the limits of the recordset, and the procedure fails.

Clicking the Last button and then clicking the Next button twice causes the NextRec procedure to fail for a similar reason. After clicking the Last button and then clicking the Next button, the current record is the new record that follows the last record in the recordset. Therefore, when you click the Next button a second time, you are attempting to move beyond the limits of the recordset in the other direction.

Here are two methods for dealing with the run-time errors that occur when you try to move beyond the limits of a recordset:

- You can include error-handling code to avoid the run-time errors.

- You can create a set of smart navigation buttons that disable a button when clicking it would cause a run-time error.

## Adding Error-Handling Code to the Custom Navigation Buttons

As an example of using error handling to avoid a run-time error, we've added custom error handling to the PreviousRecord function procedure to terminate the procedure without failure when the error occurs. The modified PreviousRecord procedure that follows has an enabled error handler that displays the default error message when you try to move beyond the first record:

```
Public Function PreviousRecord()
On Error GoTo PreviousRecord_Err
    DoCmd.GoToRecord Record:=acPrevious


PreviousRecord_Exit:
Exit Function

PreviousRecord_Err:
    MsgBox Err.Description
    Resume PreviousRecord_Exit
End Function
```

After modifying the PreviousRecord procedure, clicking the First button and then clicking the Previous button still triggers the run-time error as before. However, this time the error trap is set and control moves to the error-handling code. The error handler displays the message shown in Figure 16.6b and exits the procedure without trying to execute the GoToRecord method. You can omit the MsgBox statement and simply have no response when you are at the first record and click the Previous button. You can write similar error handling code for the other navigation buttons.

**FIGURE 16.6:**

When you attempt to move beyond the limits of the recordset, the default error handling is that the procedure fails (a), but you can use custom error handling (b) to avoid failure.

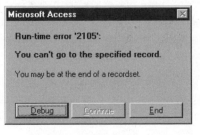

(a)

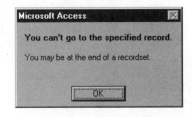

(b)

## Creating Smart Navigation Buttons

In the second approach to avoiding a run-time error, we create a procedure to disable a navigation button when clicking it would cause a run-time error and to enable it otherwise. Consequently, if the first record is the current record, the procedure disables the Previous button. We'll design the procedure to disable the First button also when the first record is the current record, even though the FirstRecord procedure doesn't fail when the First button is clicked repeatedly. In fact, the disabled First button is a visual cue that the first record is the current record. If the last record is the current record, the procedure disables the Last and Next buttons, and if the new record is the current record, the procedure disables the New, Last, and Next buttons.

In order to disable the appropriate buttons, you must know whether the current record is the first, last, or new record. Determining whether the current record is the new record is easy because a form has the NewRecord property that you can test. There is no FirstRecord or LastRecord property for a form, however, so we'll have to work harder to find out if the current record is the first or last record.

**Using the RecordSetClone**    Although a form has no properties that you can use to determine if the current record is the first or last record, the form's recordset does. A recordset has BOF and EOF properties that you can use to determine whether you have moved beyond the limits. If you've moved the current record position to before the first record, BOF is True; if you've moved the current record position to after the last record, EOF is True.

If we start moving around in the form's recordset, we'll disturb the screen display, so instead we'll use the form's RecordsetClone property to create a separate current record pointer, synchronize the recordsetclone so that it points to the current record that the form displays, and use the recordsetclone's pointer to move around in the recordset. For example, if we use the recordsetclone's MovePrevious method to move to the previous record in the recordset and find that BOF is True, the form must be displaying the first record.

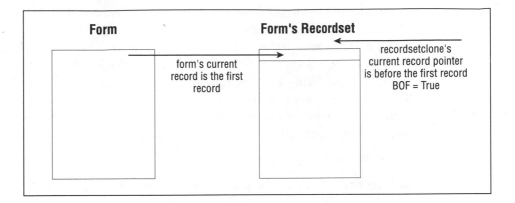

**Passing the Form Object as an Argument**   We create the DisableEnable function procedure to disable and enable the navigation buttons; the procedure runs when the form first opens and when you move to a different record (and the form recognizes the Current event). To make the procedure reusable on other forms, we'll pass the form to the procedure as an argument.

The DisableEnable function shown in Listing 16.14 begins by creating the recordsetclone with its separate current record pointer. The procedure can now switch between the form and the recordset using whichever recordset or form property or method it needs. The procedure determines if the current record is the new record by testing the form's NewRecord property. If it is the new record, the Next and New buttons are disabled and the procedure ends. If the current record is not the new record, the procedure determines if the recordset contains any records.

Determining the presence of records is necessary because if we try to move around in a recordset that has no records at all, we cause run-time errors. The procedure uses the recordsetclone's RecordCount property to determine if records exist and disables the First, Previous, Next, and Last buttons if no records are found. If there are records, the next step is to determine where we are in the recordset.

**Using the Bookmark Property to Synchronize the RecordsetClone and the Form**   Determining our location in the recordset is when the recordsetclone becomes important. We'll use the recordsetclone's current record pointer to move around in the recordset and test whether we've moved the recordsetclone's pointer beyond the limits of the recordset. We need a way to synchronize the recordsetclone to the form so that we can start with the recordsetclone and the form pointing to the same record. We use the Bookmark property to do the synchronization. When you open a bound form, Access automatically assigns a unique bookmark to each record in the recordset. Both the form and the recordsetclone have a Bookmark property. The form's Bookmark property returns the value of the bookmark for the record displayed by the form. The recordsetclone's Bookmark property returns the value of the bookmark for its current record, so you can point the recordsetclone at the record displayed in the form by using the assignment statement

```
rstClone.Bookmark = frm.Bookmark
```

**Using the Recordsetclone's BOF and EOF Properties**    The procedure uses the BOF and EOF properties to determine if the current record is the first record or the last record.

The procedure determines if the current record is the first record by using the recordsetclone's MovePrevious method to move the recordsetclone's current record pointer to the previous record and then testing the recordsetclone's BOF property. If the recordsetclone's BOF property is True, then the MovePrevious method has moved us to the current record position before the first record and we must have been at the first record before the move. In this case we disable the First and Previous buttons. If the recordsetclone's BOF property is False, we were not at the first record before the move, so we enable the First and Previous buttons. The procedure resynchronizes the recordsetclone and the form to point to the same record.

The final step is to determine if the current record is the last record by using the recordsetclone's MoveNext method to move the recordsetclone's current record pointer to the next record and then test the recordsetclone's EOF property. If the recordsetclone's EOF property is True, then the MoveNext method has moved us to the current record position after the last record and we must have been at the last record before the move. In this case we disable the Last and Next buttons. If the recordsetClone's EOF property is False, we were not at the last record before the move so we enable the Last and Next buttons.

After finishing the tests, the procedure ends.

### Listing 16.14

```
Public Function DisableEnable(frm As Form)
'To call the function set the form's OnCurrent
'property to =DisableEnable(Form)
```

```
Dim rstClone As Recordset
'Create a clone of the form's recordset to
'move around in without affecting the form's
'recordset
Set rstClone = frm.RecordsetClone
'Determine if the current record is the
'new record and if it is, disable the Next
'and New buttons and then exit.
If frm.NewRecord Then
    frm!cmdFirst.Enabled = True
    frm!cmdNext.Enabled = False
    frm!cmdPrevious.Enabled = True
    frm!cmdLast.Enabled = True
    frm!cmdNew.Enabled = False
    Exit Function
End If
'If the current record is not the new record
' enable the New button
    frm!cmdNew.Enabled = True
'If there are no records, disable all
'other buttons
If rstClone.RecordCount = 0 Then
    frm!cmdFirst.Enabled = False
    frm!cmdNext.Enabled = False
    frm!cmdPrevious.Enabled = False
    frm!cmdLast.Enabled = False
Else
' Synchronize the current record in the clone
'to be the same as the current record displayed
'in the form.
    rstClone.Bookmark = frm.Bookmark
'Move to the previous record in the clone,
'if the clone's BOF is True, the form must be
'at the first record so disable the First and
'Previous buttons, otherwise the form is not
'at the first record so enable the First and
'Previous buttons.
    rstClone.MovePrevious
    If rstClone.BOF Then
        frm!cmdFirst.Enabled = False
        frm!cmdPrevious.Enabled = False
    Else
```

```
            frm!cmdFirst.Enabled = True
            frm!cmdPrevious.Enabled = True
        End If
' Resynchronize the current record in the clone
'to be the same as the current record displayed
'in the form.
rstClone.Bookmark = frm.Bookmark
'Move to the next record in the clone,
'if the clone's EOF is True, the form must be
'at the last record so disable the Next and
'Last buttons, otherwise the form is not
'at the first record so enable the Next and
'Last buttons.
rstClone.MoveNext
    If rstClone.EOF Then
        frm!cmdNext.Enabled = False
        frm!cmdLast.Enabled = False
    Else
        frm!cmdNext.Enabled = True
        frm!cmdLast.Enabled = True
    End If
End If
End Function
```

1. Insert the DisableEnable function procedure in the basNavigationButtons module.

2. Display the Products form in Design view. Click in the form's OnCurrent property and assign the function procedure by typing **= DisableEnable(Form)**

3. Save the form and switch to Form view. Test the buttons. For example, when the first record is the form's current record, the First and Previous buttons are disabled (see Figure 16.7).

**FIGURE 16.7:**

The EnableDisable procedure enables and disables the custom command buttons in order to avoid run-time errors.

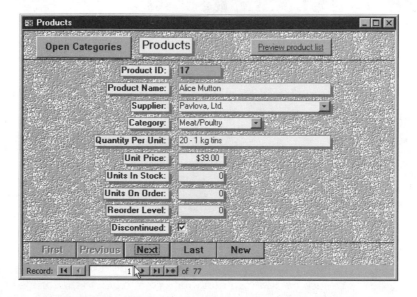

**NOTE**    The RecordCount property returns the total number of records if the recordset is a table-type recordset. If the recordset is a dynaset- or snapshot-type recordset, the RecordCount property returns the number of records that have been accessed. Once the last record in a dynaset- or snapshot-type recordset has been accessed, the RecordCount property returns the total number of records. The only way to guarantee that all records have been accessed is to use the MoveLast method of the recordset object before reading the RecordCount property. However, if all you need to know is whether any records exist, you can use the RecordCount property without using the MoveLast method. If no records are found, the RecordCount property returns 0; otherwise, the property returns an integer greater than 0.

**Not Closing the Clone**    Using a form's RecordsetClone property creates a new reference to the form's existing recordset object. When you are finished using the recordsetclone, you don't use the Close method to attempt to close the recordset object. VBA won't let you close the form's recordset without closing the form and simply ignores any statement that tries to close the recordsetclone. You can set the object variable to Nothing to sever the connection between the variable and the recordsetclone, but normally there isn't much point in doing so.

# Finding a Specific Record

 When you work interactively, you use the Find dialog, available by clicking the Find button in the toolbar or choosing the Find command in the Edit menu (see Figure 16.8). To make the find process faster, you restrict the search to values in a control by selecting the control before displaying the Find dialog.

**FIGURE 16.8:**

When working interactively, you use the Find dialog to find a record with a specified value in a field.

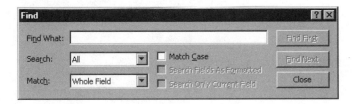

When you automate the search process using either macro or VBA programming, you can avoid displaying the Find dialog and make your application easier to use by adding an unbound combo box to the form's header or footer section and allowing the user to start the search by selecting a specific value from the combo list. Access VBA provides many ways to create an event procedure to find the specific record corresponding to the selected value.

The event procedure runs when the user changes the value in the combo box and the combo box recognizes the AfterUpdate event. We'll look at three ways to find a specific record including using the FindRecord method, the ApplyFilter method of the DoCmd object, and the RecordsetClone property.

To explore the search techniques, open the Employees form in Design view and place an unbound combo box in the header section. Set the combo box properties as follows:

| Property | Setting |
|---|---|
| Name | cboFind |
| RowSourceType | Table/Query |
| RowSource | Employees |
| ColumnCount | 2 |
| ColumnWidths | 0"; 0.75" |
| BoundColumn | 1 |

# Using the FindRecord Method of the DoCmd Object

The simplest approach for finding a specific record is to create an event procedure for the combo box that mirrors each interactive step of the process with a VBA statement. Listing 16.15 shows an event procedure for this approach.

### Listing 16.15

```
Private Sub cboFind_AfterUpdate()
Application.Echo False
EmployeeID.Enabled = True
EmployeeID.SetFocus
DoCmd.FindRecord cboFind
cboFind.SetFocus
EmployeeID.Enabled = False
Application.Echo True
End Sub
```

This procedure begins by turning off screen painting while the procedure runs. In mirroring each interactive step, the procedure must move the focus to the EmployeeID control; however, this control is disabled, so the procedure must first enable the control. After enabling the EmployeeID control, the procedure moves the focus to it and uses the FindRecord command to find the value held in the combo box. After finding the value, the procedure moves the focus back to the combo box, disables the EmployeeID control, turns the screen painting back on, and ends.

**NOTE** By default, screen painting is on, and Access takes the time to update the screen for each statement. The repainting not only takes time but also causes screen flicker as the screen updates after each statement. When you turn off screen painting in a VBA procedure, you must also turn it back on before the procedure ends. When you turn off screen painting in a macro using the Echo macro action, Access automatically turns on screen painting when the macro ends.

# Using the ApplyFilter Method of the DoCmd Object

A more efficient approach uses a filter to select the record directly from the form's recordset. The ApplyFilter method lets you apply a filter to a table, form, or report to restrict or sort the records in the table or in the underlying recordset of the form or report. You can specify a saved query as the filter using the filtername argument, or you can enter an SQL WHERE clause (without the word WHERE) in the wherecondition argument. The ApplyFilter method has two arguments:

| Method Argument | Description |
| --- | --- |
| filtername | A string expression that is the name of a query or a filter saved as a query that restricts or sorts the records. |
| wherecondition | An expression that restricts the records in the form of a valid SQL WHERE clause without the word WHERE. |

You must specify at least one of the arguments; if you specify both arguments, Access first applies the query and then applies the wherecondition to the result of the query. The maximum length of the wherecondition argument is 32,768 characters. (The Where Condition argument for the corresponding ApplyFilter macro action is 256 characters.)

The wherecondition argument to synchronize the form to the value in the combo box is as follows:

```
fieldname=Forms!formname!controlname
```

In this expression, *fieldname* refers to the field in the underlying table or query of the form, and *controlname* refers to the control on the form that contains the value you want to match. For example, to synchronize the Employees form to the value displayed in the cboFind combo box, use the expression

```
[EmployeeID]=Forms![Employees]![cboFind]
```

or use the Me property to refer to the form as follows:

```
[EmployeeID]=Me!cboFind
```

Listing 16.16 shows the event procedure for this approach.

### Listing 16.16

```
Private Sub cboFind_AfterUpdate()
Dim strSQL As String
strSQL = "EmployeeID = " & Me!cboFind
DoCmd.ApplyFilter wherecondition:= strSQL
End Sub
```

## Using the RecordsetClone

The most efficient approach uses the form's RecordsetClone to refer to the form's recordset. The recordset object has methods that you can use to find a specific record. To obtain access to these methods, you can use the form's RecordsetClone property to refer to the form's recordset. The statements

```
Dim rst As Recordset
Set rst = Me.RecordsetClone
```

declare rst as an object variable and assign it to the form's recordset object with its own current record pointer. You can use the FindFirst method of the Recordset object to move the clone's current record pointer to the first record that satisfies a specified criteria. The syntax of the FindFirst method is

```
recordset.FindFirst criteria
```

where *recordset* is a reference for an existing dynaset or snapshot-type recordset object and *criteria* is a string expression that restricts the records in the recordset. The criteria argument is a valid SQL WHERE clause without the word WHERE.

After running the FindFirst method, the recordsetclone points to the found record. However, the current record displayed in the form hasn't changed. The final step is to move the form's current record pointer to the same record that the recordsetclone is pointing to by setting the form's Bookmark property to the recordsetclone's Bookmark property:

```
Me.Bookmark = rst.Bookmark
```

Listing 16.17 shows the event procedure for this approach.

### Listing 16.17

```
Private Sub cboFind_AfterUpdate()
Dim strCriteria As String
Dim rst As Recordset
```

```
Set rst = Me.RecordsetClone
strCriteria = "EmployeeID = " & Me!cboFind
rst.FindFirst strCriteria
Me.Bookmark = rst.Bookmark
End Sub
```

If the sole purpose of the event procedure is to find the record and take no other actions using the variables, you don't need the variables at all and can simplify the procedure as shown in Listing 16.18.

### Listing 16.18

```
Private Sub cboFind_AfterUpdate()
Me.RecordsetClone.FindFirst "EmployeeID = " & Me!cboFind
Me.Bookmark = Me.RecordsetClone.Bookmark
End Sub
```

1.  Open the Employees form in Design view.

2.  Insert the cboFind_AfterUpdate procedure shown in Listing 16.18.

3.  Save the form and switch to Form view. Select an employee in the Lookup combo box (see Figure 16.9). The procedure displays the record of the selected employee.

FIGURE 16.9:

The most efficient search technique uses the FindFirst method of the recordsetclone.

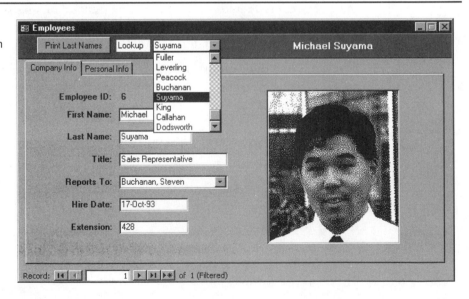

772

# Undoing the Search

After finding a particular record, you may want to undo the search and return to the previously displayed record. In order to undo the search, you need to know which record was displayed last. You can keep track of the previous record by holding the value of its primary key in a module-level variable. You use a module-level variable so that the record's primary key will be available to the procedure that we'll create to undo the search. Modify the procedure that finds a specific record by including a statement to store the current record's primary key value before running the statements that find the specific record. Here are the steps for undoing the search when the search uses the recordsetclone technique:

1.  Enter the following declaration statement in the Declarations section of the form module:

    ```
    Private LastFind
    ```

2.  Modify the cboFind_AfterUpdate() event procedure to set LastFind to the primary key of the current record before any other statement as shown in Listing 16.19.

### Listing 16.19

```
Private Sub cboFind_AfterUpdate()
LastFind = EmployeeID
Me.RecordsetClone.FindFirst "EmployeeID = " & Me!cboFind
Me.Bookmark = Me.RecordsetClone.Bookmark
End Sub
```

3.  Place a command button named cmdUndoFind and with caption Last Lookup in the header of the Employees form and create the event procedure shown in Listing 16.20. The cmdUndoFind_Click event procedure uses the same find technique to find the record matching the value stored in the LastFind variable and then synchronizes the combo box to the displayed record.

### Listing 16.20

```
Private Sub cmdUndoFind_Click()
Me.RecordsetClone.FindFirst "EmployeeID = " & LastFind
Me.Bookmark = Me.RecordsetClone.Bookmark
Me!cboFind = LastFind
End Sub
```

4. Save the form and switch to Form view. Select an employee in the Lookup combo box. Click the Last Lookup button. The previous employee is displayed (see Figure 16.10).

**FIGURE 16.10:**

The Undo Lookup button runs a procedure that uses the value of the EmployeeID stored in a module-level variable to locate the previously found record.

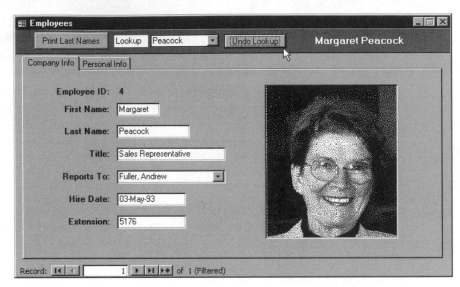

> **NOTE**
>
> If you worked the examples in this chapter, the Employees form has the set of custom navigation buttons for physical navigation from record to record by position and has the combo box and Undo button for logical navigation. You can coordinate the two sets of controls by modifying the procedure for the Previous button so that clicking the Previous button displays the previous record by position regardless of whether that record was selected logically or physically. You should either coordinate the two sets of controls or remove one set.

# Working with the Data in the Tables

In the previous sections of this chapter we worked with records in an open form. We used the form's RecordsetClone property to refer to the form's recordset object so that we could get access to the properties and methods of the recordset object. Another way to work with the records in a recordset object is to open a recordset in memory directly without working with a form at all. Opening and working with recordsets in memory has a distinct performance advantage because Access doesn't have to take time to create the visual representation of the form on the screen.

# Creating Recordset Variables to Work with the Data

A recordset is a set of records of a table or the set of records that results from running a query or an SQL statement that returns records. When you work with data in VBA procedures, you work with recordsets. You use the OpenRecordset method of the Database object to create a new recordset object based on the table, query, or SQL statement. You use the following statements to create a new recordset:

```
Dim rst as Recordset
Set rst = database.OpenRecordset(source, type, options,
   lockedits)
```

where *database* is a reference to an existing Database object and *source* is a string expression specifying the name of a table, query, or an SQL statement that returns records. You use the optional *type*, *options*, and *lockedits* arguments to specify the characteristics of the recordset. See Chapter 11 for more information on the syntax of the OpenRecordset method and for information on the properties and methods of the four types of recordsets.

A recordset created in a procedure exists in memory only while the procedure runs. When the procedure is finished, the recordset object variable ceases to exist and the recordset object is destroyed.

Examples:

1. Create a new standard module named basRecordsets and insert the procedure shown in Listing 16.21. The TableRecordset procedure opens a table-type recordset on the Customers table using the CurrentDB function to represent the database that is open in the Access window. The procedure prints the CustomerID and the CompanyName to the Debug window. Run the procedure in the Debug window by typing **TableRecordset** and pressing Enter.

## Listing 16.21

```
Public Sub TableRecordset()
Dim rst As Recordset
Set rst = CurrentDb.OpenRecordset("Customers", dbOpenTable)
Do Until rst.EOF
    Debug.Print rst(0), rst(1)
    rst.MoveNext
Loop
End Sub
```

2. Insert the DynasetRecordset procedure shown in Listing 16.22. This procedure declares db as an object variable, points the variable to the current database using the CurrentDb function, and then opens a snapshot-type recordset for the customers from Argentina. The procedure uses an SQL statement as the source of the records as follows:

```
strSQL = "SELECT * FROM Customers WHERE Country = 'Argentina'"
```

The procedure prints the CustomerID and the CompanyName (using different syntax) to the Immediate pane. Run the procedure in the Debug window by typing **DynasetRecordset** and pressing Enter.

## Listing 16.22

```
Public Sub DynasetRecordset()
Dim db As Database
Dim rst As Recordset
Dim strSQL As String
strSQL = "SELECT * FROM Customers WHERE Country = 'Argentina'"
Set db = CurrentDb
Set rst = db.OpenRecordset(strSQL, dbOpenSnapShot)
Do Until rst.EOF
    Debug.Print rst("CustomerID"), rst!CompanyName
    rst.MoveNext
Loop
End Sub
```

3. Insert the RecordsetOtherDatabase procedure shown in Listing 16.23. This procedure opens a table-type recordset for the Expense Categories table in the Expenses database. When the table you want to work with is in another database, you have to open the other database in memory first and then open a recordset on the table. To open the other database, you use the

OpenDatabase method of the Workspace object; the procedure uses the default reference for the workspace that is currently open, DBEngine(0). If the other database is in a different folder than the database that is currently open in the Access window, include the path in argument of the OpenDatabase method. (In some cases you may need to use the full path even if expenses.mdb is in the same folder as the current database.) After you open the Expenses database, the procedure opens a table-type recordset on the Expense Categories table and prints the values of the first two fields to the Immediate pane. Run the procedure in the Debug window by typing **RecordsetOtherDatabase** and pressing Enter.

### Listing 16.23

```
Public Sub RecordsetOtherDatabase()
Dim db As Database
Dim rst As Recordset
Set db = DBEngine(0).OpenDatabase("expenses.mdb")
Set rst = db.OpenRecordset("Expense Categories", dbOpenTable)
Do Until rst.EOF
    Debug.Print rst(0), rst(1)
    rst.MoveNext
Loop
End Sub
```

Figure 16.11 shows the results of running the procedures in Listings 16.21, 22, and 23.

## Opening a Recordset on Another Recordset, TableDef, or QueryDef

You can also create a recordset object based on another recordset object, an existing TableDef, or an existing QueryDef object. The Recordset, TableDef, and QueryDef objects all have their own OpenRecordset methods. Use the following statements to open a new recordset on one of these objects:

```
Dim rst as Recordset
Set rst = object.OpenRecordset(type, options, lockedits)
```

where *object* is an existing TableDef, QueryDef, or Recordset object and the optional *type*, *options*, and *lockedits* arguments specify the characteristics of the recordset.

**FIGURE 16.11:**

The results of three procedures that open recordsets and loop through the records, printing values from each record.

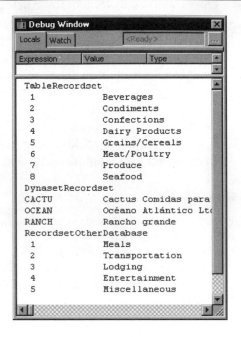

As an example, open a new recordset on the Customers table:

1.  Insert the TableDefRecordset procedure shown in Listing 16.24 in the basRecordsets module. As an existing table, Customers is a TableDef object in the TableDefs collection in the current database. The procedure uses the CurrentDb function to refer to the current database and then uses the OpenRecordset method of the TableDef object to open a recordset on the table. Run the procedure in the Debug window.

### Listing 16.24

```
Public Sub TableDefRecordset()
Dim rst As Recordset
Set rst = CurrentDb.TableDefs("Customers").OpenRecordset
Do Until rst.EOF
    Debug.Print rst!CompanyName
    rst.MoveNext
Loop
End Sub
```

# Recordset Navigation

When you create a recordset object, you are placing rows of data in a memory buffer and pointing to a single record at a time, the current record. You can work only with the current record. You navigate through a recordset by moving the current record pointer to one record after another. (See Chapter 11 for additional information.)

## Move... Methods

You use the four Move... methods of the Recordset object to move the current record pointer so that it points to another record. The syntax for the Move... methods is

```
rst.{MoveFirst | MoveNext | MovePrevious | MoveLast}
```

where *rst* is a reference to an open Recordset object.

>**MoveFirst** makes the first record the current record.
>
>**MoveNext** makes the next record the current record.
>
>**MovePrevious** makes the previous record the current record.
>
>**MoveLast** makes the last record the current record.

You can use the Move method to move the current record pointer a specific number of records forward or backward. The syntax for the Move method is

```
rst.Move rows, start
```

where rows is the (signed) number of records you want to move and the optional start argument is the bookmark that identifies the record you start the move from.

**NOTE**  When the recordset is a forward-only–type recordset, you can only move the current record pointer forward toward the end of the recordset. With this type of recordset you can use only the MoveNext and Move-Last methods and the Move method with a positive number of rows.

**Detecting the Limits of a Recordset**    You use the BOF and EOF properties to detect whether you have moved the current record pointer beyond the limits of the recordset. While the current record pointer points to a record within the limits, both properties have the False value. If the current record is the first record and you use the MovePrevious method, you have moved "ahead" of the first record of the recordset; the BOF property is True, and there is no current record. Similarly, if the current record is the last record and you use the MoveNext method, you have moved beyond the last record of the recordset and the EOF property is True.

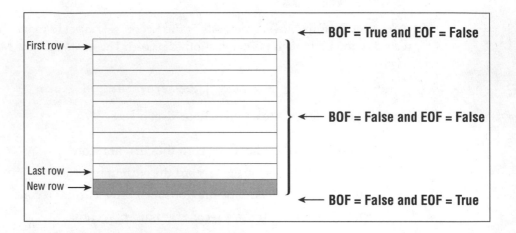

## Reading the Data Values

The Value property of a field in the recordset returns the data value for the field. You can use any of these four references to retrieve a data value:

| | |
|---|---|
| exclamation point | recordsetname!fieldname |
| index by name | recordsetname("fieldname") |
| index by variable | strfield = "fieldname" recordsetname(strfield) |
| index by number | recordsetname(indexnumber) |

## Updating a Recordset

Recordsets have the Requery method that you can use to reexecute the query or reread the table on which the recordset is based. When you use the Requery method, the first record in the recordset becomes the current record. Whether you can update an existing recordset depends on a number of factors, including the options you used when you opened it. You can determine if you can use the Requery method by testing the recordset's Restartable property.

**Restartable Property**  If the recordset's Restartable property is True, you can use the requery method to update the recordset as follows:

```
If rst.Restartable = True Then rst.Requery
```

If the recordset's Restartable property is False, then you need to use the OpenRecordset method to create a new recordset in order to do the update.

---

**NOTE**   The Restartable property for a table-type recordset is always False; if you try to use the Requery method on a table-type recordset, VBA generates a run-time error.

---

## Counting the Records

You use the RecordCount property of the recordset to determine the number of records. The value returned by the property depends on the type of the recordset. For a table-type recordset, the RecordCount property gives the total number of records in the table. For dynaset-type, snapshot-type, and forward-only–type recordsets, the RecordCount property returns the number of records accessed. The RecordCount property does not return the total number of records unless all of the records have been accessed.

If you haven't deleted records, then using the MoveLast method forces the last record to be accessed and the total number of records returned. With rst declared as a Recordset variable and num as an Integer, the following statements return the total number of records:

```
rst.MoveLast
num = rst.RecordCount
```

If others are adding or deleting records, then you need to update the recordset first (assuming that the recordset is updatable) as follows:

```
rst.Requery
rst.MoveLast
num = rst.RecordCount
```

## Walking a Recordset

As shown in Chapter 14, you can use a Do...Loop to loop through each record in a recordset as follows:

```
Do Until rst.EOF
    [statements]
    rst.MoveNext
Loop
```

where rst is an object variable that refers to the recordset. If the recordset has no records, the EOF property has the True value; therefore, the looping condition is true and the loop doesn't execute.

## Testing for an Empty Recordset

It is important to include a test for an empty recordset in any procedure that would fail if the recordset has no records. If rst.RecordCount = 0, no records exist. The following piece of code shows a simple test that you can include immediately after creating a new recordset; it displays a message and exits from the procedure if the recordset is empty and, otherwise, moves the current record pointer to the first record.

```
If rst.RecordCount = 0 Then
    MsgBox "There are no records!"
    rst.Close
    Exit Sub
End If
rst.MoveFirst
```

## Finding the Position of the Current Record

You can use the AbsolutePosition property to determine the position of the current record pointer in a dynaset-type or snapshot-type recordset (but not a table-type or forward-only–type recordset). The AbsolutePosition property value is zero-based, so a setting of 0 refers to the first record in the recordset. If a recordset has no records, the AbsolutePosition property value is a –1.

You can also use the PercentPosition property to determine the position of the current record as a percentage of records accessed when you read the property. In order to base the PercentPosition on the total number of records, you must be sure that all of the records have been accessed, for example, by using the MoveLast method before reading the PercentPosition property.

## Closing a Recordset

When the procedure ends, the recordset variable ceases to exist and the recordset object itself closes unless the recordset is the recordset for an open form. In this case the form's recordset object stays open after the procedure ends and closes only when the form closes.

Normally, it is not necessary to explicitly close a recordset object at all. But if you are finished with it before the end of the procedure and want to reclaim the memory, you can use the Close method to close the recordset.

```
rst.Close
```

Follow the next sequence of steps to explore some of these concepts:

1. Insert the RecordsetNavigation procedure shown in Listing 16.25 into the basRecordsets module. The procedure opens a snapshot-type recordset on the Customers table and displays the current record position. (When you first open a recordset, the current record is the first record.) The procedure moves the current record pointer to the end of the recordset, back to the beginning, and then forward five records. The next statements display the current record position, data values in three fields using different reference syntax, and the total number of records. The next statements determine if the recordset allows the Requery method; if the recordset allows, the procedure runs the Requery method to update the recordset and displays the current record position. The next statement moves the current record pointer backward by one record and tests the BOF property. Finally, the procedure closes the recordset.

### Listing 16.25

```
Public Sub RecordsetNavigation()
Dim rst As Recordset
Set rst = CurrentDb.OpenRecordset("Customers", dbOpenSnapshot)
MsgBox "The current record is " & rst.AbsolutePosition + 1 &
➥"which is " & rst.PercentPosition & " % "
rst.MoveLast
rst.MoveFirst
rst.Move 5
MsgBox "The current record is " & rst.AbsolutePosition + 1 &
➥" which is " & rst.PercentPosition & " % "
MsgBox rst!CompanyName & rst("ContactName") & rst(3)
```

```
MsgBox "The number of records is " & rst.RecordCount
'Can you use the Requery method?
If rst.Restartable Then
    rst.Requery
    MsgBox "The recordset has been requeried."
    MsgBox "The current record is " & rst.AbsolutePosition + 1 &
    ➥"which is " & rst.PercentPosition & " % "
Else
    MsgBox "Can't requery the recordset."
End If
rst.MovePrevious
If rst.BOF Then
    MsgBox "Moved before the first record. There is no current
    ➥record."
End If
rst.Close
End Sub
```

2. Run the procedure in the Debug window by typing **RecordsetNavigation** and pressing Enter. Figure 16.12 shows the messages that indicate progress through the procedure.

**FIGURE 16.12:**

The RecordsetNavigation procedure displays messages to indicate progress through the procedure.

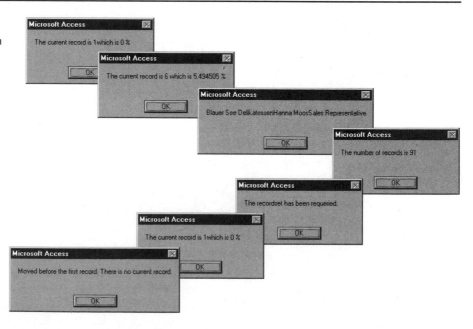

# Finding a Specific Record

You find a specific record in a recordset by specifying a search condition that you want a record to satisfy and using one of the techniques that the Jet database engine provides to move the current record pointer to the "first" record that satisfies the condition. You use different techniques to find records, depending on the type of recordset you create:

- The Find methods are used with dynaset-type and snapshot-type recordsets

- The Seek method is used with table-type recordsets.

In addition to these data access object techniques, you can use the OpenRecordset method directly to find the records that satisfy a search condition as follows: use the source argument of the OpenRecordset method to specify an SQL statement instead of the name of a table or query and include the search condition as part of the SQL statement. When you run the OpenRecordset method, VBA creates a new recordset object that contains only the records that satisfy the search condition.

This section describes both the data access and the SQL techniques for finding a record. Also see Chapter 11 for additional information on finding records.

## Using the Find Methods

Which of the four Find... methods you use depends on where you want to start your search (at the beginning or end of the recordset or at the current record) and the direction in which you want to search (downwards or upwards):

**FindFirst** starts at the beginning of the recordset and searches downwards.

**FindLast** starts at the end of the recordset and searches upwards.

**FindNext** starts at the current record and searches downwards.

**FindPrevious** starts at the current record and searches upwards.

The syntax is similar for all four methods. For example, the syntax for the FindFirst method is

```
recordset.FindFirst criteria
```

where *recordset* is the name of an existing recordset and *criteria* is a string expression used to locate the record. Here are some examples of criteria expressions:

```
"OrderDate > #5-30-96# And RequiredDate <#11-30-96#"
"Country = 'Germany'"
"CompanyName Like 'B*'"
```

**Using the NoMatch Property**    Each of the Find... methods moves the current record pointer to the first record that satisfies the search condition. If no record is found, the current record pointer is left in limbo; with no record to point to, its state is undefined. You can use the NoMatch property to determine whether the search has been successful. If the NoMatch property is True, no record was found; otherwise, a record was found. When no record is found, you should set the current record pointer to a valid record. You can set the pointer back to the record it was pointing to before the search by using a bookmark to save your place before searching and then returning to the saved place.

Let's explore these concepts:

1. Create a new module named basFindingRecords. Insert the FindRecord procedure as shown in Listing 16.26. The procedure creates a dynaset-type recordset on the Customers table, uses the FindFirst method to find the first customer from Norway, and sets a bookmark for the found record. The procedure uses the FindNext method to find the next customer from Norway. When a second customer isn't found, the procedure displays a message, returns the pointer to the first customer, and displays the company name; otherwise, the procedure displays a message with the company name for the second customer.

### Listing 16.26

```
Public Sub FindRecord()
Dim db As Database
Dim rst As Recordset
Dim strFound As String, strCriteria as String
Set db = CurrentDB
Set rst = db.OpenRecordset("Customers",dbOpenDynaset)
strCriteria = "Country = 'Norway'"
rst.FindFirst strCriteria
strFound = rst.Bookmark
rst.FindNext strCriteria
If rst.NoMatch Then
```

```
        MsgBox "There is no second record. Go back to the first
        ➥record found."
        rst.Bookmark = strFound
        MsgBox "The first customer is " & rst!CompanyName
   Else
        MsgBox "The second customer is " & rst("CompanyName")
   End If
   rst.Close
   End Sub
```

2. Run the procedure in the Debug window by typing **FindRecord** and pressing Enter. The procedure finds a single customer from Norway. Figure 16.13 shows the messages displayed.

**FIGURE 16.13:**

The messages displayed by the FindRecord procedure

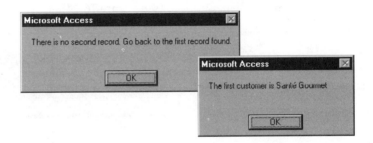

3. Create the FindAll procedure shown in Listing 16.27. This procedure uses the FindFirst method to locate the first customer from Argentina. If no customer is found, the procedure displays a message and terminates. If a customer is found, the procedures uses the FindNext method in a Do...Loop to find all additional records. The Do...Loop uses the NoMatch property as the looping condition; the loop continues to execute until the the FindNext method fails to find a record and NoMatch property is True. Each pass of the loop displays the company name for the current record and finds the next record that satisfies the search criteria.

### Listing 16.27

```
   Public Sub FindAll()
   Dim db As Database
   Dim rst As Recordset
   Dim strCriteria
   Set db = CurrentDB
```

```
Set rst = db.OpenRecordset("Customers",dbOpenDynaset)
strCriteria = "Country = 'Argentina'"
rst.FindFirst strCriteria
If rst.NoMatch Then
    MsgBox "There are no customers from Argentina."
Else
    Do Until rst.NoMatch
        Debug.Print rst("CompanyName")
        rst.FindNext strCriteria
    Loop
End If
End Sub
```

4.  Run the procedure in the Debug window by typing **FindAll** and pressing Enter. The names of the three customers from Argentina are printed to the Immediate window (see Figure 16.14).

**FIGURE 16.14:**

The FindAll procedure uses a loop with the FindNext method to find all of the records that satisfy the search criteria.

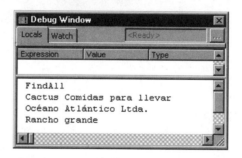

## Using the Seek Method for a Table-Type Recordset

When the recordset is a table-type recordset, the Find... methods don't apply and you must use the Seek method. Seek works only when you are searching in a table field that is indexed. You must either set the index in table Design view by setting the table field's Indexed property to Yes (Duplicates OK) or No (No Duplicates) or create the index for the field as part of the VBA procedure. (See Chapter 19 "Creating and Modifying Database Objects" for information on creating an index programmatically.) Seek uses the index to perform the search; therefore, a Seek search is faster a Find search. The syntax for Seek contains two statements: The first statement sets the current index for the search to the name of the index you are using for the search, and the second statement performs the search using the current index.

```
tablerecordset.Index = indexname
tablerecordset.Seek comparison, key1, key2...
```

where

> *tablerecordset* is the name of an existing table-type recordset that has *indexname* as an existing index.
>
> *indexname* is the string expression that is the name of the index.
>
> *comparison* is one of the following string expressions "<", "<=", "=", ">", ">="
>
> *key1*, *key2*, are the values corresponding to fields in the current index.

**NOTE**   The comma between the comparison and the search values is a required part of the syntax.

Examples:

1. To use the Seek technique to find the first customer from Argentina, first create an index for the Country field by setting the field's Indexed property to Yes (Duplicates OK) in table Design view (see Figure 16.15). In the procedure, create a table-type recordset on the Customers table and then use the statements below to set the current index to the Country index and run the Seek method.

    ```
    rst.Index = "Country"
    rst.Seek "=", "Argentina"
    ```

2. To use the Seek technique to find the first employee with a specified first and last name, you can create a multiple field index in table Design view. Figure 16.16 shows the Indexes window with the FullName index having the LastName and FirstName fields. In the procedure, create a table-type recordset on the Employees table and then use the statements below to set the current index to the FullName index and run the Seek method.

    ```
    rst.Index = "FullName"
    rst.Seek "=", "Peacock", "Margaret"
    ```

FIGURE 16.15:

You can create an index in table Design view.

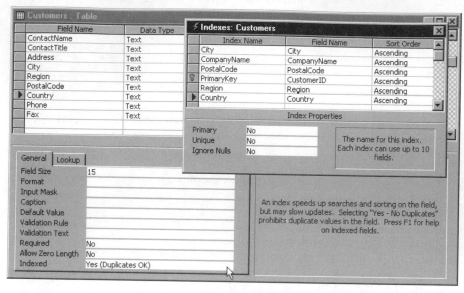

FIGURE 16.16:

You can create a multiple index for search fields in the Indexes dialog of table Design view.

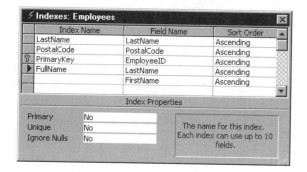

3. To use the Seek technique on the primary key index, you can identify the index with the string "PrimaryKey". For example, to use the Seek technique to find the first order with OrderID greater than 11040, create a table-type recordset on the Orders table and then use the statements below to set the current index to the primary key index and run the Seek method.

```
rst.Index = "PrimaryKey"
rst.Seek ">", 11040
```

In the Seek technique, the search takes place in the index. (See Chapter 11 for more information on indexes.) The comparison argument is used to locate the first record whose indexed field satisfies the comparison. In the first example above, Access searches in the Country index for the first time Argentina appears in the index lookup table and then uses the index lookup table to locate the corresponding table record and makes it the current record. If no record is found, the current record pointer is in limbo and the current record is undefined. You use the NoMatch property to determine whether the Seek technique was successful; the NoMatch property has the value True if no record was found and False otherwise.

To explore the Seek method:

1. Open the Customers table in Design view and set the Indexed property of the Country field in the Customers table to Yes (Duplicates OK).

2. Insert the SeekAll procedure in Listing 16.28 in the basFindingRecords module. The procedure opens a recordset on the Customers table. (When you open a recordset on a table in the current database without specifying the recordset type, Access creates a table-type recordset.) The next statements set the current index to the (indexed) Country field and search in the index for the first customer from Argentina. The procedure uses the NoMatch property to determine if the search was successful and prints the results of the test.

### Listing 16.28

```
Public Sub SeekAll()
Dim rst As Recordset
Set rst = CurrentDb.OpenRecordset("Customers")
rst.Index = "Country"
rst.Seek "=", "Argentina"
If rst.NoMatch Then
    MsgBox "There are no customers from Argentina."
Else
    MsgBox "The first customer from Argentina is " &
    ➥rst!CompanyName
End If
End Sub
```

3. Type **SeekAll** in the Immediate pane and press Enter.

> **NOTE**  There is no SeekNext method; the Seek method finds only the first record satisfying the search criteria.

**Using the Seek Method with a Table in Another Database**   A table-type recordset can be opened only on a table in an open database. Therefore, you cannot open a table-type recordset on a linked table in another .mdb database from the current database or on a linked ODBC table (such as an attached Excel table). However, you can use the Seek technique on a table in another .mdb database, whether the table is linked or not, by first opening the other database in the procedure. Once the other database is open, you can use the OpenRecordset method of that database to open a table-type recordset on one of its tables. As an example, we use the Seek method to search a table in the Expenses database (created in Chapter 1).

1.  Insert the SeekOtherDatabase procedure shown in Listing 16.29 in the basFindingRecords module. The procedure opens the Expenses database using the OpenDatabase method of the Workspace object. (You may need to include the path information particularly if the database file is not in the folder that contains the database that is currently open in the Access window.) After opening the Expenses database in memory, the procedure uses the OpenRecordset method on the Expenses database object to open a table-type recordset on the Expense Categories table. ExpenseCategoryID is the primary key of this table. The procedure sets the current index to the primary key index and then uses the Seek method to find the record with the ID of 3. The next statements determine whether the search is successful and prints the result of the search in the Debug window.

### Listing 16.29

```
Public Sub SeekOtherDatabase
Dim ws As Workspace
Dim db As Database, rst As Recordset
Set ws = DBEngine(0)
Set db = ws.OpenDatabase("expenses.mdb")
Set rst = db.OpenRecordset("Expense Categories")
rst.Index = "Primarykey"
rst.Seek "=", 3
```

```
If rst. NoMatch Then
    MsgBox "There is no such category."
Else
    MsgBox "The category is " & rst!ExpenseCategory
End If
End Sub
```

2. Type **SeekOtherDatabase** in the Immediate pane and press Enter. The search is successful. (See Figure 16.17.)

---

**FIGURE 16.17:**

The result of the search of a table in another .mdb database, using the Seek method

## Using an SQL String with Search Criteria

Often the fastest way to find records is to use SQL techniques instead of the Find... or Seek methods. To find a record using SQL, you simply open the recordset, using an SQL statement to specify the recordset as the argument of the OpenRecordset method, instead of the name of a table or query. For example, the SQL statement to find the customers from Argentina is

```
SELECT * FROM Customers WHERE Country = "Argentina"
```

If you don't know SQL, you can use query Design view to create the query, switch to SQL view, copy the equivalent SQL statement, and paste the result into your code. The hardest part is converting the SQL statement to a string that Jet will accept. When the SQL statement contains a string, as in this example, the source argument of the OpenRecordset method is a string expression that contains a string. You must identify the inner string within the outer string expression with symbols other than double-quotes because double-quotes are already being used to indicate the outer string expression. (See Chapter 8 for more information.) The double-quotes that enclose Argentina can be replaced either with single quotes (apostrophes) or with pairs of double quotes. Either of the following expressions work.

```
strSQL = "SELECT * FROM Customers WHERE Country = ""Argentina"""
strSQL = "SELECT * FROM Customers WHERE Country = 'Argentina'"
```

1. Enter the SQLRecords procedure in the basFindingRecords module as shown in Listing 16.30. The procedure opens a recordset that contains only the customers from Argentina and uses a Do...Loop to print the company names in the Debug window.

### Listing 16.30

```
Public Sub SQLRecords()
Dim rst As Recordset
Dim strSQL As String
strSQL = "SELECT * FROM Customers WHERE Country = 'Argentina' "
Set rst = CurrentDb.OpenRecordset(strSQL)
Do Until rst.EOF
    Debug.Print rst!CompanyName
    rst.MoveNext
Loop
End Sub
```

## Deciding Which Search Technique to Use

The search technique that you should use depends on several factors. If you need only the records that satisfy a search condition, the SQL technique often gives the best performance. However, if you need all of the records returned by a table or query, whether or not they satisfy the search condition, then you'll need to create recordsets to return all of the records anyway; using the Find or Seek techniques to locate the specific record may give the best overall performance.

If you've already located a specific record by any of the techniques and plan to return to the record later in the procedure, the fastest way to return to the record is to use a bookmark.

To find a record for the first time, the general rule is that the Seek method is the fastest (but is limited to table-type recordsets), the SQL method is next, and the Find methods are the slowest. The more records you have to search, the greater the performance difference between the SQL and Find methods.

> **TIP**
>
> In deciding which search technique gives the best performance, use the Timer function to time the procedure. (See Chapter 14 for more information on using the Timer function.)

# Using Clones

Sometimes you need to work with more than one record at a time. For example, suppose you want to compare the values in two records. A recordset has a single current record, and you can work only with the single record; one workaround is to create a second recordset with its own current record. For example, the following statements open two recordset objects on the Customers table:

```
Set rst1 = CurrentDB.OpenRecordset("Customers")
Set rst2 = CurrentDB.OpenRecordset("Customers")
```

Another solution is to use the Clone method of the Recordset object. The Clone method creates a new recordset object that is identical to the original recordset object with an important difference: The new recordset object, called a *clone* of the original, has its own independent current record pointer. The Clone method has the syntax

```
Set clone = original.Clone
```

where *original* is the object variable pointing to the recordset object and *clone* is the object variable pointing to the new recordset object. Creating a clone is faster than creating a new recordset object using the OpenRecordset method. The features of the Clone method are:

- The bookmarks are interchangeable between the original and the clone recordset objects.

- The clone doesn't have a current record defined when you first create it.

- If the recordset is a table-type recordset, the clone does not inherit the current index (the Index property setting).

- You cannot create a clone for a forward-only–type recordset.

- If you use close the original or the clone recordset object using the Close method, the other recordset object does not close.

To explore using a clone, we'll create a procedure that compares the values in the Country field for two consecutive customer records.

1. Insert the Duplicates procedure shown in Listing 16.31 in the basFindingRecords module. The procedure opens a table-type recordset on the Customers table and moves the current record pointer 20 rows forward

to the 21st record. The procedure creates a clone and synchronizes the clone's current record pointer to the same record. The MovePrevious method moves the clone's current record pointer to the clone's previous record. The procedure compares the values in the Country field for the original (record 21) and the clone (record 20) and displays the results of the comparison and the values in the two records. The next statements close both recordset objects.

### Listing 16.31

```
Public Sub Duplicates()
Dim db As Database, rst As Recordset
Dim rstClone As Recordset
Set db = CurrentDB
Set rst = db.OpenRecordset("Customers")
rst.Move 20
Set rstClone = rst.Clone
rstClone.Bookmark = rst.Bookmark
rstClone.MovePrevious
If rstClone!Country = rst!Country Then
    MsgBox "The previous record has the same value for Country."
Else
    MsgBox " The previous record does not have the same value for
    ➥Country."
End If
MsgBox "Previous record value: " & rstClone!Country & "Current
➥record value: " & rst!Country
rst.Close
rstClone.Close
End Sub
```

2. Type **Duplicates** in the Immediate pane and press Enter. The values in the two records are displayed in a message box. (See Figure 16.18.)

**FIGURE 16.18:**

When a procedure needs to work with more than one record at a time, use the Clone method to create a duplicate recordset with its own current record pointer.

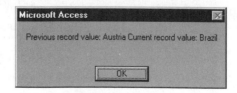

> **NOTE**
>
> Don't let the use of the word "clone" confuse you. When you use the Clone method on a recordset object, you are creating a new recordset object, which is the duplicate of the original recordset object but with an independent current record pointer. By contrast, when you use the RecordsetClone property of a form, you are creating a new object variable that refers to the form's recordset object; you are not creating a separate recordset object. The recordsetclone also has an independent current record pointer.

> **NOTE**
>
> When you create a clone of an existing recordset object using the Clone method, the clone and the original recordset objects have the same bookmarks. Two recordset objects created by any other means have different sets of bookmarks even when they are based on the same table, query, or SQL statement. You cannot synchronize their current records using bookmarks. For example, if you open a form based on a table and then use the OpenRecordset method to open a recordset on the same table, the two recordset objects have separate sets of bookmarks.

## Reading Table Data into an Array

When you don't need to change the data, creating a forward-only–type recordset is the fastest way to retrieve a set of records. As the name implies, you can only move forward through a forward-only–type recordset. You can use only the MoveNext or the Move method to move the current record pointer forward. You can use only the FindFirst and FindNext methods to find specific records because these methods move the current record pointer forward.

If you don't need to change the data but you do need random access to the data, the forward-only–type recordset is no longer the solution. Instead, you can create an array to hold the data in memory. (See Chapter 13.) After you read the data from the recordset into an array, you can close the recordset and release the tables for others to use. (If you are working in a multiuser environment, using arrays minimizes record-locking conflicts.)

You use the GetRows method of the Recordset object to copy rows from a recordset object into a two-dimensional variant array. The syntax is

```
varArray = recordset.GetRows(number)
```

In this syntax,

> *recordset* is any type of recordset.
>
> *varArray* is a variable of Variant data type.
>
> *number* is the number of rows you want to copy.

The array returned by the GetRows method is a two-dimensional array with the first element identifying the field and the second element identifying the row. As an example, varArray(2,3) is the value of the third field in the fourth row. (Access starts each index at zero.)

If you request more rows than are available, only the available rows are returned. You can use the UBound function to determine the number of fields and rows returned. The UBound function has the syntax

```
UBound(arrayname,dimension)
```

where the optional *dimension* argument is 1 for the first dimension and 2 for the second dimension (inconsistently not zero based). If you omit the dimension, the first dimension is assumed. The UBound function returns the largest index for the specified dimension of the array. To determine the numbers of fields and rows returned, use the statements

```
numFields = UBound(varArray, 1) + 1
numRows = UBound(varArray, 2) + 1
```

Since the field and row indexes begin with zero, the statements add one to the largest indexes to obtain the number of fields and rows.

The GetRows method copies the specified number of records beginning with the current record. After the GetRows method is executed, the current record is the next unread row. All fields of the recordset are returned including memo and binary fields. If you don't want all of the fields to be included, use a query or an SQL statement to restrict the fields in the recordset before using the GetRows method.

To explore these concepts:

1. Create a new module named basArrays and declare the varArray variable in the Declarations section as a public module-level variable using the declaration statement

   ```
   Public varArray As Variant
   ```

You use a module-level variable so that the array continues to exist after the values are read into it by the ArrayRecordset procedure we create in the next step.

2. Enter the ArrayRecordset procedure in a new module named basArrays as shown in Listing 16.32. The procedure opens a dynaset-type recordset on the Customers table, moves 20 rows forward, prints the absolute row position, reads three rows into a variant array, prints the absolute row position again, and closes the recordset. The procedure determines the number of fields and rows actually read into the array and uses a For...Next loop to print out the values in the first two fields of each row in the array.

## Listing 16.32

```
Public Sub ArrayRecordset()
Dim rst As Recordset
Dim numFields As Integer, numRows As Integer
Dim j As Integer
Set rst = CurrentDB.OpenRecordset("Customers", dbOpenDynaset)
rst.Move 20
Debug.Print rst.AbsolutePosition
varArray = rst.GetRows(3)
Debug.Print rst.AbsolutePosition
rst.Close
numFields = UBound(varArray, 1) + 1
numRows = Ubound(varArray, 2) + 1
Debug.Print "Fields: " & numFields & " Rows: " & numRows
For j = 0 To numRows - 1
    Debug.Print varArray(0,j) & " Company Name: " & varArray(1,j)
Next
End Sub
```

3. Run the procedure in the Debug window by typing **ArrayRecordset** and pressing Enter.

4. Because varArray is a public variable, its values are retained until the database closes. The values are available to all modules and to the Debug window. Type **?varArray (1,2)** and press Enter. The value in the second field of the third row is printed (see Figure 16.19).

**FIGURE 16.19:**

The ArrayRecordset procedure uses the GetRows method to read data into an array.

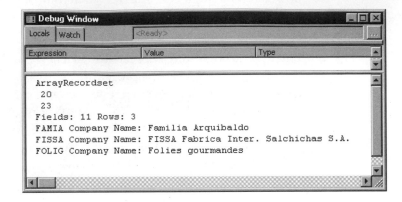

```
ArrayRecordset
  20
  23
Fields: 11 Rows: 3
FAMIA Company Name: Familia Arquibaldo
FISSA Company Name: FISSA Fabrica Inter. Salchichas S.A.
FOLIG Company Name: Folies gourmandes
```

# Summary

This chapter focuses on using VBA procedures to automate navigation in the forms interface and on using VBA to navigate through the data by creating recordset objects in memory without opening forms. The important points follow:

- You can use the methods of the DoCmd object to duplicate the keystrokes, mouse clicks, and menu command selections of the interactive environment.

- While event procedures are useful in creating procedures for navigating in the interface, creating reusable procedures normally requires using function procedures and storing them in standard modules.

- Use the form's RecordsetClone property to create a reference to the form's recordset object that has a current record pointer independent of the form's current record pointer. Using the recordsetclone gives you access to most of the methods and properties of the Recordset object.

- Creating custom navigation buttons to browse through the records involves procedures that move the current record pointer beyond the limits of the recordset. Use the BOF and EOF properties to determine whether you have exceeded the limits.

- You can find a specific record using a form in three ways:
  - The FindRecord method of the DoCmd object duplicates the interactive approach to finding a record.
  - The ApplyFilter method of the DoCmd object applies a filter to the records.
  - The RecordsetClone property allows you to use the Find... methods of the form's recordset object.
- You can work directly with the data without opening a form by creating one of four types of recordset objects in memory. You can base a recordset on a table, a query, or an SQL statement that returns records.
- The key to understanding recordsets is the current record: you can work only with the current record, and you use the Move methods to move the current record pointer from one record to another.
- To work with two records simultaneously, you can open a second recordset or use the Clone method to create a duplicate of the original recordset but with an independent current record pointer.
- To find a specific record using a recordset, do one of the following:
  - Specify the search condition in an SQL statement and create a recordset based on the SQL statement.
  - Create a recordset and then use the Seek method for a table-type recordset when the search condition is based on an index or the Find methods for the other types of recordsets.
- If you don't need to change the data but need random access, you can read data into an array.

# CHAPTER

## SEVENTEEN

# Data Maintenance with Access VBA

- Protecting data using a review mode

- Using procedures for custom data validation

- Modifying procedures created by the Command Button Wizard

- Carrying values forward to a new record

- Maintaining data using a recordset instead of a form

You can use two fundamental approaches to work with the data in your database application: the forms approach and the recordset approach.

In the forms approach, you provide forms that the user can work with to add new records, change data values in fields, and delete existing records. You use VBA procedures to automate data maintenance operations such as displaying a blank record, setting default values for fields in a new record, validating new or changed data in fields, undoing or saving changes to a record, and deleting an existing record.

A problem associated with using forms to change data values is that Access may not automatically update records and display the most current values. (See Chapter 4 for examples.) This chapter shows you how to use VBA procedures to update the sources of data to display the most current data. (See Chapter 8, "Data Maintenance with Macros," for a treatment of several additional data maintenance problems using macro programming.)

In the recordset approach, you are adding, changing, or deleting records without necessarily displaying the records to the user in a form. For example, suppose you want to change the title of your sales representatives to Account Executive. In the recordset approach you create a procedure that opens a recordset on the Employees table and makes the change in memory without ever displaying the records to the user.

In this chapter you learn how to write procedures for both approaches.

> **NOTE**
> For hands-on experience with the techniques described in this chapter, create a new copy of the Northwind sample database named Northwind_Ch17 and work through the steps of the examples.

# Maintaining Data Using Forms

In most database applications you provide a set of forms that allow the user to work with data. The core of many of these applications is a set of data entry forms designed for efficient heads-down entry of new records and modification of existing records. Often you want a data entry form to serve as a review form as well. In data entry mode, the data controls are unlocked and enabled so that the user can change the data at will; in review mode, the data controls are normally locked and disabled so that the user cannot make changes. An important design concept is to use review mode to protect your data against inadvertant changes and include a way, possibly protected by a password, for the user to change the form to data entry mode.

## Toggling a Form between Review and Data Entry Modes

A good strategy for avoiding inadvertant changes to the data is to open the form in review mode and provide a command button for changing the mode between data entry and review. Clicking a command button runs a procedure that loops through the data controls on the form and changes their Locked and Enabled properties. (See Chapter 14 for information on creating loops through collections.) As an example, we'll prepare the Customers form as a dual mode form:

1.  Open the Customers form in Design view. Select all the text boxes and the Country combo box. Set the Enabled property to No and the Locked property to Yes for the multiple selection.

2.  Create a new standard module named basSupport. Insert the LockControls and UnlockControls procedures shown below. Each procedure uses the For Each ... Next loop to loop through each control on the form. If the control is a text box or a combo box, the procedure sets the value of the Locked and Enabled properties.

```
Public Function LockControls()
Dim ctl as Control
For Each ctl in Screen.ActiveForm.Controls
    If TypeOf ctl is TextBox Or TypeOf ctl is ComboBox Then
    With ctl
        .Locked = True
        .Enabled = False
    End With
    End If
Next
End Sub
```

```
Public Function UnLockControls()
Dim ctl as Control
For Each ctl in Screen.ActiveForm.Controls
    If TypeOf ctl is TextBox Or TypeOf ctl is ComboBox Then
      With ctl
          .Locked = False
          .Enabled =True
      End With
      End If
Next
End Sub
```

3.  Place two command buttons in the form's header section. Set the properties of the two buttons as follows:

|  | First Button | Second Button |
| --- | --- | --- |
| Name | cmdLock | cmdUnLock |
| Caption | Review Mode | Data Entry Mode |
| OnClick | =LockControls() | =UnLockControls() |

4.  Save the form and switch to Form view. The form is in review mode with its data controls locked and disabled (see Figure 17.1). Click the Data Entry Mode button and try to change a control.

**FIGURE 17.1:**

Avoid inadvertant changes to data by creating procedures that loop through the data controls and toggle their Locked and Enabled properties.

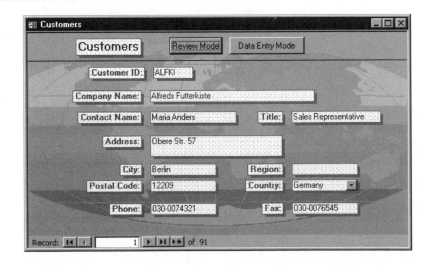

# Using VBA to Validate Data

An important part of designing an application is determining how the application validates new and changed data. Access provides a set of properties that you can use when you create a table to test the data before saving the data to the disk; these properties include the Required, AllowZeroLength, and ValidationRule properties for fields and the ValidationRule property for the table. You can also set a ValidationRule property for controls on forms. You use the ValidationRule properties for a table field, for the table itself, and for a form control to specify requirements that data must satisfy. You use the ValidationText property to specify the text you want Access to display in a message box if the new or changed data doesn't satisfy the ValidationRule setting. Chapter 8 describes the different ways that the Access interface provides for validating data.

As an example, when a new order is placed using the Orders form in the Northwind database, the order date is filled in automatically because the DefaultValue property of the form's OrderDate control is set to =Date(), but the user fills in the required date as part of taking the order. No validation rule has been set for the RequiredDate field. To specify that the required date must be greater than the order date, you can set one of the ValidationRule properties so that Access tests the condition

RequiredDate > OrderDate

and refuses to do the update if the condition is not met. Which ValidationRule should you use? You cannot specify the test using the ValidationRule property for the RequiredDate field (as a field property in table Design view) because the condition refers to the value in another field, but you can use the ValidationRule property for either the table or the RequiredDate control on the Orders form.

The property you choose depends on when you want Access to test the data. Access tests a control's ValidationRule property when you attempt to move the focus out of the control after entering new data or changing existing data in the control. Figure 17.2a shows the ValidationRule for the RequiredDate control, and Figure 17.2b shows the message displayed when you enter an invalid date and tab out of the control.

**FIGURE 17.2:**

Access tests a control's ValidationRule property (a) when you enter or change the data in the control attempt to move the focus out of the control. If the condition is not met, Access displays a default message or the text you specify as the ValidationText property (b).

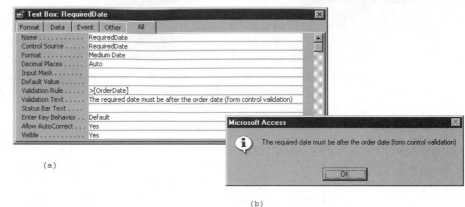

(a)

(b)

By contrast, Access tests the table's ValidationRule property when you attempt to save the record after entering new data or changing existing data; consequently, the user can enter invalid data in a record and not realize that validity problems exist until attempting to save the record. Figure 17.3a shows the ValidationRule for the Orders table, and Figure 17.3b shows the message displayed when you enter an invalid date and attempt to save the record.

**FIGURE 17.3:**

Access tests a table's ValidationRule property (a) when you enter or change data in the record and attempt to save the record. If the condition is not met, Access displays a default message or the text you specify as the ValidationText property(b).

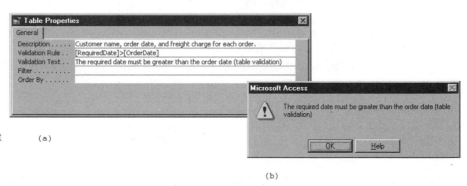

(a)

(b)

**NOTE**

When a form contains a subform, moving the focus to the subform is an attempt to save changes to the record in the main form and triggers testing the ValidationRule for the underlying record source of the main form.

The order of validation for controls on a form and fields in the underlying table is the following:

1. The control's ValidationRule property when you try to update a changed control

2. The underlying field's ValidationRule property when you try to update a changed control

3. The underlying table's ValidationRule property when you try to save a changed record

When you try to save a changed record, in addition to testing the table's ValidationRule property, Access tests the table's integrity rules. If you designated a primary key, Access tests that the primary key fields are not empty and that the primary key is unique (entity integrity). In addition, if the table is in a one-to-many relationship and you checked the referential integrity option for the relationship, Access tests that the changes you made won't create any orphan records.

For many purposes, setting the field, table, and control ValidationRule properties is sufficient to protect your data. When you use a ValidationRule property you are limited to the default behavior: Access tests the rule and either accepts the data or refuses to accept the data and displays a message. When the default behavior is insufficient, you can use macros and VBA procedures to set more complicated validation rules and to control what Access does when the rules are violated. For example, you can use programming when you want to

- Display different messages depending on the value entered

- Ask the user for input on whether to use a validation rule

- Use more than one validation rule to validate a record

- Carry out additional operations depending on the outcome of the validation test

- Change the timing of the validation tests

In the next section, you learn how to change the timing of a validation test.

# Using an Event Procedure to Cancel the Default Behavior

When you use Access VBA to validate data, normally you create an event procedure that includes the conditions you want to test and the operations you want to carry out when one or more conditions are met. The events in Table 17.1 (on the CD under Tables\Chapter17.pdf) are commonly used to trigger a validation event procedure.

When you are able to cancel the default behavior following an event, the event procedure has a Cancel argument. Setting the Cancel argument to True in the procedure cancels the default behavior that follows the event. The default behavior that follows the BeforeUpdate event recognized by a control is that Access updates the changed value in the control buffer to the record buffer. If you use one of the BeforeUpdate events to trigger a validation procedure, you can cancel the update if the data fails the validation test. By contrast, if you use an AfterUpdate event to trigger a validation procedure, Access has already updated the buffer so you can't cancel the update. (There are times when you can use an AfterUpdate event to trigger a validation procedure; for example, if you use the form's AfterUpdate event, you may be able to include instructions to undo the update by deleting the saved record.)

As an example we use the BeforeUpdate event to trigger a validation macro for the RequiredDate text box. Our procedure improves on the ValidationRule by undoing the change so that the user doesn't have to click the Esc key.

1. Choose the Orders form in the Database window and click the Code button in the toolbar. The Orders form opens in Design view and the form module is displayed.

2. Insert the RequiredDate_BeforeUpdate procedure shown in Listing 17.1. If the date in the RequiredDate text box is less than or equal to the value in the OrderDate text box, the procedure displays a message, uses the Undo method of the text box control to undo the change, and then sets the Cancel argument to True to cancel the update to the record buffer. The user must now change the data in the control to a valid date or tab out of the control without making any changes.

**Listing 17.1**

```
Private Sub RequiredDate_BeforeUpdate(Cancel As Integer)
If RequiredDate <=OrderDate Then
    MsgBox "The required date must be greater than the order date."
    Me!RequiredDate.Undo
    Cancel = True
End If
End Sub
```

3. Save the form and switch to Form view. Change the Required Date to a value that is less than the Order Date and press Enter. The procedure displays the message and cancels the update.

# Changing the Timing of a Validation Test

In this section, you use an event procedure to change the timing of the test for uniqueness of the primary key value. By default, Access tests for uniqueness when you try to save the record—you'll create an event procedure to perform the test as soon as you enter a value in the primary key control instead.

When you design a data table, you specify how the primary key is entered. You can use the following methods:

- Automatically assign sequential numbers by using an AutoNumber field as the primary key.

- Create your own expressions to assign unique values automatically.

- Permit the primary key to be entered as part of data entry.

No matter how the value is entered, Access checks for duplicate values when you try to save the record. The most convenient time to test for uniqueness is often as soon as you leave the primary key control, instead of waiting until you enter values in all the data controls and try to save the record. You can create an event procedure to handle the uniqueness test yourself and run the event procedure as soon as you try to update the changed control, that is, when the changed control recognizes the BeforeUpdate event.

## Checking for Duplicate Primary Key Values

As an example of how to check for duplicate primary key values, we will create an event procedure for the CustomerID control on the Customers form that tests for uniqueness of the value entered in the control.

Chapter 8 describes how to use the DCount domain aggregate function to check for duplicate values by counting the number of records in the table with the same primary key value. If a record in the Customers table has the same value as the value entered in the CustomerID control on the form, the function

```
DCount("*","Customers", "CustomerID =
Forms!Customers!CustomerID")
```

returns a value greater than zero. Listing 17.2 shows the VBA version of the primary key validation macro. The procedure uses the ActiveForm property of the Screen object to refer to the active form. Note that you cannot use the Me property in an argument of the domain aggregate functions.

### Listing 17.2

```
Private Sub CustomerID_BeforeUpdate(Cancel As Integer)
If DCount("*", "Customers", "CustomerID =
Screen.ActiveForm.CustomerID") Then
    MsgBox "There is another customer with the same CustomerID."
    Cancel = True
End If
End Sub
```

If a duplicate record exists, the DCount function returns the value one, so the condition is True; the procedure displays a message and cancels the update.

VBA provides another way to search for the duplicate record that often gives better performance than the DCount function. You can use the Seek method to search for the duplicate record in a table as shown in Listing 17.3.

### Listing 17.3

```
Private Sub CustomerID_BeforeUpdate(Cancel As Integer)
Dim rst As Recordset
Set rst = CurrentDB.OpenRecordset("Customers", dbOpenTable)
rst.Index = "PrimaryKey"
rst.Seek "=", Me!CustomerID
```

```
If Not rst.NoMatch Then
    MsgBox "There is another customer with the same CustomerID."
    Cancel = True
End If
End Sub
```

This procedure begins by opening a table-type recordset on the Customers table. (The recordset must be a table-type recordset in order to use the Seek method.) The procedure sets the current index to the primary key and searches for a record in the table with a primary key matching the value in the CustomerID control on the form. If a record is found, the NoMatch property has the value False and the expression

```
Not rst.NoMatch
```

has the value True; in this case, the procedure displays a message and cancels the subsequent default behavior. If no record is found, the procedure ends without taking further action.

The event procedure in Listing 17.3 uses the OpenRecordset method to create a second recordset object for the Seek operation. The new recordset object exists in addition to the recordset object associated with the Customers form. In this type of situation you can't use the RecordsetClone property to refer to the form's recordset for the following reason. When you use a form's RecordsetClone property to refer to the form's recordset, any indexes that may have been set for the table are not cloned as part of the recordsetclone reference. Therefore, trying to set a current index on the recordsetclone causes a run-time error.

## Using the Command Button Wizard for Data Entry Operations

We'll use the Command Button Wizard to create a set of command buttons for automating the four basic data entry operations that all simple data entry forms need: adding a new record, undoing changes to a record, saving changes, and deleting a record.

1. Open the Customers form in Design view, click the Control Wizard tool in the toolbox to activate the control wizards. Click the Command Button tool and place four command buttons in the form's header section. Use the

Command Button Wizard's Record Operations category to create buttons as follows:

| Action | Button Text (Caption property) | Name |
|---|---|---|
| Add New Record | Add | cmdAdd |
| Undo Record | Undo | cmdUndo |
| Save Record | Save | cmdSave |
| Delete Record | Delete | cmdDelete |

2. Save the form and switch to Form view (see Figure 17.4). Click the Data Entry Mode button (you placed it earlier in the chapter) and test the buttons. Note the following behavior:

| Button | Behavior |
|---|---|
| Add | The first time you click the Add button, Access displays the blank record. If you click again when the blank record is displayed, there is no response. |
| Undo | If you change the value in one of the controls and click the Undo button, the change is undone. If you change the record, click the Save button to save all of the changes to the record, and then click the Undo button, the changes are undone. If you make no change and click the Undo button, a default error message is displayed (see Figure 17.5). |
| Save | If you change the record and click the Save button, the record is saved (provided the change satisfies the validation rules for the record). If you don't change the record, there is no response when you click the Save button. If you click the Add button to display the blank record and then click the Save button, there is no response. |

| Button | Behavior |
| --- | --- |
| Delete | If you click the Delete button for a customer with orders, the default error message shown in Figure 17.6a is displayed and the record is not deleted. In the relationship between Customers and Orders, the Cascade Delete Related Records option is not checked, so you can't delete any customer that has orders. If the customer has no orders, such as the customer with CustomerID FISSA (record 22), the default confirmation message is displayed as shown in Figure 17.6b; if you click No to cancel the deletion, Access displays the default message shown in Figure 17.6c. |

**FIGURE 17.4:**

The Customers form with data entry buttons.

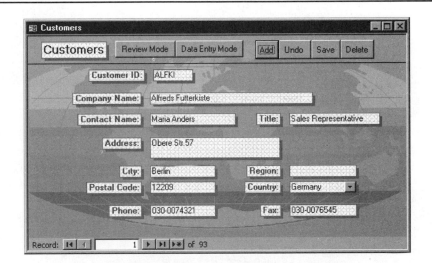

**FIGURE 17.5:**

The default error message when you click the Undo button and there are no changes to undo.

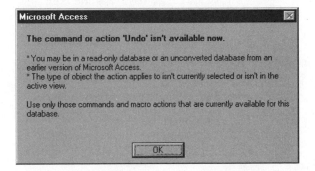

**FIGURE 17.6:**

The default error message when you click the Delete button and the customer has orders (a). The default confirmation message when the customer has no orders (b) and the default error message when you click No to cancel the deletion (c).

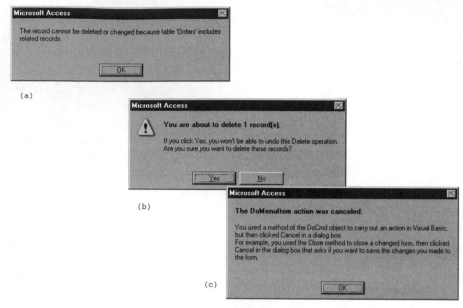

(a)

(b)

(c)

3. Switch to Design view and click the Code button in the toolbar to view the procedures. To view any of the procedures that the wizard created, select the command button from the Object combo list on the left below the module's title bar. Listing 17.4 shows the event procedure that the Command Button Wizard created for the Add button.

## Listing 17.4

```
Sub cmdUndo_Click()
On Error GoTo Err_cmdAdd_Click
    DoCmd.GoToRecord, , acNewRec

Exit_cmdNew_Click:
Exit Sub

Err_cmdNew_Click:
    MsgBox Err.Description
Resume Exit_cmdNew_Click
End Sub
```

For each of the four procedures, the Command Button Wizard includes a generic error handler that displays a default error message and then exits the procedure. For each of the buttons, the wizard runs a method of the DoCmd object. The procedures for the buttons to add a new record and to save the record don't fail.

To add a new record, the wizard runs the GoToRecord method. When the blank record is already displayed, the New Record command on the submenu of the Go To command in the Edit menu is not available; however, like the GoToRecord macro action, the GoToRecord method does not fail if the new record is already displayed.

To save changes, the wizard uses the RunCommand method to run the Save Record command on the Records menu. (At the time of writing this book, the wizard was still using the DoMenuItem method to run menu commands and the released version may have either method.) This command is available for existing records and for the blank record whether or not you have changed the record. If you make changes that do not satisfy the validation rules for the record, Access displays the default message or a custom validation message and does not update the record. The VBA method mimics this behavior.

The procedures for the buttons to undo changes and to delete a record may fail. If the procedure fails, an error message is displayed because VBA cannot run the method. Let's explore the code and modifications you can make to avoid the error messages.

## Modifying the Procedure to Undo a Change

To undo changes to the record, the wizard uses the RunCommand method to run the built-in Undo command (in the final version of Access 97 the wizard may still use the DoMenuItem method instead to run the Undo command in the Edit menu). When you work interactively and have made no changes to a record, this command is grayed out and unavailable. When you try to run the menu command programmatically but have made no changes to the record, the method fails because the command is unavailable. The Undo commands are available only when you have actually made a change to the record. You can use the form's Dirty property to test whether the current record has been changed before issuing the command. The Dirty property has the value True if the current record has been modified since it was last saved; otherwise, it is False. With the modification shown in Listing 17.5 , you get no response if you click the Undo button for an unchanged record. In addition, if you change and save a record, you can no longer use the Undo button to undo the changes to the last saved record.

(After you save the record, the form's Dirty property is False until you change the record again.)

### Listing 17.5

```
Sub cmdUndo_Click()
On Error GoTo Err_cmdNew_Click
If Me.Dirty Then
    RunCommand acCmdUndo
End If
Exit_cmdNew_Click:
Exit Sub
Err_cmdNew_Click:
    MsgBox Err.Description
Resume Exit_cmdNew_Click
End Sub
```

## Modifying the Procedure to Delete a Record

To delete a record, the wizard creates the procedure shown in Listing 17.6.

### Listing 17.6

```
Private Sub cmdDelete_Click()
On Error GoTo Err_cmdDelete_Click
    RunCommand acCmdDeleteRecord

Exit_cmdDelete_Click:
Exit Sub

Err_cmdDelete_Click:
    MsgBox Err.Description
Resume Exit_cmdDelete_Click
End Sub
```

The procedure shown in Listing 17.6 uses the RunCommand method to run the Delete Record command If, as in Access 95, the wizard uses the DoMenuItem method to select the record and then a second DoMenuItem method to run the Delete command, the procedure is shown in Listing 17.6a.

### Listing 17.6a

```
Private Sub cmdDelete_Click()
On Error GoTo Err_cmdDelete_Click
    DoCmd.DoMenuItem acFormBar, acEditMenu,8,,acMenuVer70
    DoCmd.DoMenuItem acFormBar, acEditMenu,6,,acMenuVer70

Exit_cmdDelete_Click:
Exit Sub

Err_cmdDelete_Click:
    MsgBox Err.Description
Resume Exit_cmdDelete_Click
End Sub
```

If deleting a selected record would violate the referential integrity rules and cascade options checked for the relationships between the data table and other tables in the database, Access does not permit the deletion. If the deletion is allowed, Access displays the default confirmation message (see Figure 17.6b); if you cancel the deletion, VBA displays the default error message shown in Figure 17.6c because clicking the No button prevents VBA from carrying out the command to delete the record. You can modify the cmdDelete_Click procedure to suppress the error message as follows:

1. Determine the error code for the default error message in Figure 17.6c by changing the procedure's error handling code to

```
Err_cmdDelete_Click:
    MsgBox Err.Number & Err.Description
Resume Exit_cmdDelete_Click
```

2. Display the customer with CustomerID FISSA. Click the Delete button and click No to cancel the deletion. The message box reveals the error code is 2501. Click OK to close the message box. If you display the blank record, the Delete Record menu command is not available; let's see if Access displays a default error message in this case.

3. Click the Add button to display a new record. Click the Delete button. Access displays the default error message indicating that the error code is 2046 (see Figure 17.7). (If the wizard uses the procedure shown in Listing 17.6a, the error code will be 2501 instead and you don't have to set a trap for the 2046 error.) In the next step we set traps for both of these anticipated errors.

**FIGURE 17.7:**

The default error message when a command is not available has the error code 2046.

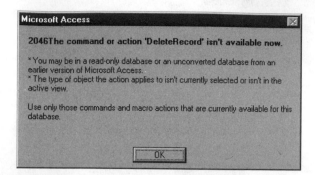

4. Modify the error handling code to test the error code and exit the procedure without displaying the message if the error code equals 2501 or 2046 as shown in Listing 17.7. The Else statements handle the errors that we haven't anticipated.

### Listing 17.7

```
Sub cmdDelete_Click()
On Error GoTo Err_cmdDelete_Click
    RunCommand acCmdDeleteRecord
Exit_cmdDelete_Click:
Exit Sub
Err_cmdDelete_Click:
If Err.Number = 2501 Or Err.Number = 2046 Then
    Exit Sub
Else
    MsgBox Err.Description
    Resume Exit_cmdDelete_Click
End If
End Sub
```

5. Save the module. Test the modified procedure by *displaying* the customer with CustomerID FISSA and clicking the Delete button and then by clicking the Add button and clicking the Delete button. Neither default error message is displayed.

**Deleting a Record When It Has Related Records**    When you try to delete a record from a table using a form that has the AllowDeletions property set to Yes, the response depends on whether the table is related to other tables in a relationship that has referential integrity enforced and whether the record you want to delete actually has related records in another table. For example, the Customers and Orders tables are related and the Enforce Referential Integrity option is checked. When a particular customer has no orders, you can delete the customer record. If the customer has orders, the response depends on whether the Cascade Delete Related records option is checked.

If the Cascade Delete Related Records option is checked, Access allows the simultaneous deletion of both the customer and the related orders. But if the Cascade Delete Related Records option is not checked, Access won't allow you to delete a customer who has related orders. In this case you can use an event procedure like the one shown in Listing 17.8. (You can also use this procedure if you don't want to allow the deletion of a record that has related records regardless of the cascade option.) The procedure uses the DCount function to determine the number of related records for the record displayed in the form. In this example the DCount function determines the number of orders for the current customer. If the customer has no orders, the procedure allows the deletion. If the customer has orders, the procedure displays a message with the number of orders and then the procedure ends.

### Listing 17.8

```
Sub cmdDelete_Click()
Dim intNumber As Integer
On Error GoTo Err_cmdDelete_Click
intNumber = DCount("*", "Orders", "CustomerID =
Screen.ActiveForm.CustomerID")
If intNumber = 0 Then
    RunCommand acCmdDeleteRecord
Else
    MsgBox ("There are " & intNumber &
    ➡" orders so you can't delete this customer.")
End If

Exit_cmdDelete_Click:
Exit Sub

Err_cmdDelete_Click:
If Err.Number = 2501 or Err.Number = 2046 Then
    Exit Sub
Else
```

```
      MsgBox Err.Description
      Resume Exit_cmdDelete_Click
   End If
   End Sub
```

**Cascading the Delete**   When a record has related records, the cascade option is checked, and you want to allow deletions of both the displayed record and all of its related records, you can use an event procedure like the one shown in Listing 17.9. This procedure also begins by determining the number of related records and allowing the deletion if none exist. When the record has related records, the procedure uses the MsgBox function as the condition of an If statement. The MsgBox function displays a message with the number of related records and asks the user for a decision on whether to delete the record and its related records.

Execution of the procedure pauses until the user clicks one of the buttons on the message box. When the user clicks a button, Access can evaluate the MsgBox function and resume execution of the procedure using the value returned by the MsgBox function. If the user clicks the Yes button, the record and its related records are deleted. Otherwise, the procedure ends.

### Listing 17.9

```
Sub cmdDelete_Click()
Dim intNumber As Integer
On Error GoTo Err_cmdDelete_Click
intNumber = DCount("*","Orders", "CustomerID =
Screen.ActiveForm.CustomerID")
If intNumber = 0 Then
    DoCmd.DoMenuItem acFormBar, acEditMenu, 7, , acMenuVer70
Else
    If MsgBox ("This customer has " & intNumber &
    ➡"orders. Do you want to delete the
    ➡customer and the orders?", vbYesNo) = vbYes Then
        RunCommand acCmdDeleteRecord
    End If
End If

Exit_cmdDelete_Click:
Exit Sub
```

```
Err_cmdDelete_Click:
If Err.Number = 2501 or Err.Number = 2046 Then
    Exit Sub
Else
    MsgBox Err.Description
    Resume Exit_cmdDelete_Click
End If
End Sub
```

1. Close the Customer's form, if necessary. Choose the Relationships command in the Tools menu. Double-click the relationship line between the Customers and Orders tables to display the Relationships dialog (see Figure 17.8a). Check the Cascade Delete Related Records option and click OK.

2. Select the Customers form in the Database window and click the Code button in the toolbar. Modify the cmdDelete_Click() event procedure that the Command Wizard created as shown in Listing 17.9.

3. Save the module. With the first customer displayed in the Customers form, click the Delete button. The message box displays provides the choice (see Figure 17.8b).

**FIGURE 17.8:**

Choose the Cascade options in the Relationships dialog (a). The procedure to cascade the delete uses the MsgBox function as the condition of an If...Then decision structure to display a dialog that lets the user make a choice to delete the customer and the orders (b).

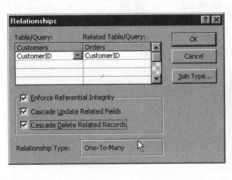

(a)

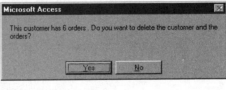

(b)

# Carrying Values Forward to a New Record

Often the data for many fields in a new record is identical to the data in another record. Without automation, the fall-back solution is to manually reenter the duplicate values in the new record. However, you can develop programming techniques to fill in the recurring values and thus reduce your manual labor.

This section describes two techniques for carrying values from another record. The first technique is designed to carry values from the current record to the next new record. The technique sets the DefaultValue property for the controls whose values you want to carry to the next new record. The second method is designed to carry values from some other record (not necessarily the current record) to the next new record. In both techniques, you normally carry forward only some of the values; both techniques use a control's Tag property to indicate whether the control's value is to be carried forward.

## Setting the DefaultValue Property

When you set the DefaultValue property for a field in table Design view or for a control in form Design view, Access automatically enters the value of the DefaultValue property in the control when you display a new record in the form. Setting the DefaultValue property in Design view is useful when you want to use the same value for every new record, or when you want to use the same expression to calculate the value to be inserted in the control for every new record. For example, the DefaultValue property for the OrderDate control on the Orders form is set to =Date() so that each new order displays the current date automatically.

You can also set the DefaultValue property programatically. Suppose you want to carry values forward from the current data entry record to the new record. Carrying values from one record to the next is often a very efficient way to to batch data entry when one or more fields change infrequently.

As an example, suppose you've recently started working with a new supplier who offers many products in one or two categories and you want to add the new products. A convenient way to update your data is to carry forward the values in the SupplierID and CategoryID controls on the Products form (see Figure 17.9a). After you save the data for a new or changed product and click the New button (in the default navigation buttons on the form) to move to a new blank record, the values in these two controls would appear automatically in the new record. Here are the steps to automate the process:

1. Open the Products form in Design view. Select the SupplierID and CategoryID controls and type **Carry** in their Tag property. You can use the Tag property to store any information that you want; here we use the Tag property to mark the controls whose values we want to carry forward.

2. Click the Code button in the toolbar to display the form's module. Insert the event procedure shown in Listing 17.10 below. The two controls have a text value so the procedure must evaluate the text value. The result is a string (" & ctl.Value & ") within a string, so you must use one of the sets of symbols that Access recognizes for delimiting a string within a string. (See Chapter 8 for more information on strings within strings.) This procedure uses pairs of double quotes to indicate the inner string (""" & ctl.Value & """). Finally you enclose the result in double quotes to indicate that the final result is a string ("""" & ctl.Value & """").

### Listing 17.10

```
Private Sub Form_AfterUpdate()
Dim ctl As Control
For Each ctl In Screen.ActiveForm.Controls
    If ctl.Tag = "Carry" Then
        ctl.DefaultValue = """" & ctl.Value & """"
    End If
Next
End Sub
```

3. Switch to Form view to test the procedure: Change any control in the current record, such as the units in stock, and then click the New button. The values for the supplier and the category are carried forward to the new record (see Figure 17.9b).

## Using Custom Default Values

Another technique for faster data entry involves looking up information from some other record and copying data from that record into the new record. For example, suppose that customers placing new orders typically have the order shipped to an address that doesn't change very often. In Northwind, the Orders form is designed so that when you select the customer from the combo box, the shipping name and address are assumed to be the same as the customer name and address. In this case the CustomerID_AfterUpdate event procedure copies the customer's name and address into the corresponding shipping controls. As an example of copying information from another record, we'll change the event procedure so that instead of copying the customer's name and address, VBA looks up the last order placed by the customer and copies the shipping information from that order as the shipping information for the new order.

**FIGURE 17.9:**

You can use the Tag property to mark a control whose value is carried forward and use a procedure to set the DefaultValue property to the current value of the control.

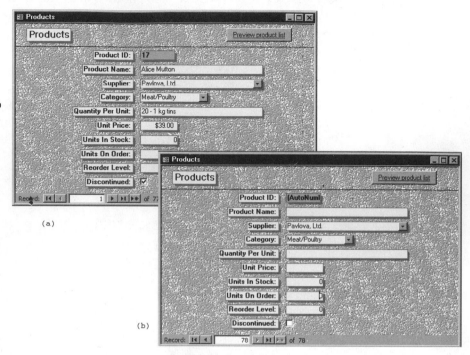

(a)

(b)

1. Open the Orders form in Design view and select the ShipName, ShipAddress, ShipCity, ShipRegion, ShipPostalCode, and ShipCountry controls. Click in the Tag property in the Multiple selection property sheet and type **Carry**. The controls we want to copy are now marked.

2. Click the Code button in the toolbar to display the form's module.

3. Modify the statements of the CustomerID_AfterUpdate event procedure as shown in Listing 17.11. The FindLast method finds the last order for the customer you select in the CustomerID combo box. This combo box contains the value for the search. When you build the string criteria for the FindLast method, you need to force VBA to determine the selected value in the combo box before it can use the search criteria to find the record. In other words, the string criteria for the FindLast method contains an inner string. In this example CustomerID has a text value, so you can use any of

the following three expressions for the criteria. In the third expression Chr$(34) is the ANSI representation for pairs of double quotes.

```
strCriteria = "CustomerID = """ & CustomerID & """"
strCriteria = "CustomerID = '" & CustomerID & "'"
strCriteria = "CustomerID = " & Chr$(34) & CustomerID & Chr$(34)
```

## Listing 17.11

```
Private Sub CustomerID_AfterUpdate()
Dim rst As RecordSet
Dim strCriteria As String
strCriteria = "CustomerID = """ & CustomerID & """"
Set rst = Me.RecordsetClone
rst.FindLast strCriteria
If Not rst.NoMatch Then
    ShipName = rst!ShipName
    ShipAddress = rst!ShipAddress
    ShipCity = rst!ShipCity
    ShipRegion = rst!ShipRegion
    ShipPostalCode = rst!ShipPostalCode
    ShipCountry = rst!ShipCountry
End If
End Sub
```

For each value that is carried forward, the procedure uses an assignment statement to assign the value of a control on the form to the value of the field with the same name in the record for the last order. In other words, each assignment statement matches a control in the form's controls collection with a field in the recordset's fields collection. The match works because the Orders form is designed so that each bound control on the form has the same name as the field it is bound to. The procedure works, but it is rather inelegant because each control has a separate assignment statement. A more elegant procedure loops through all of the controls on the form; on each pass through the loop, the procedure determines if the control's value is to be carried forward and sets the control's value to the corresponding field's value.

### A More Elegant Solution: Looping through the Controls Collection

To achieve the more elegant result, we'll modify the procedure in Listing 17.11 to do the matching of bound controls and fields automatically when the names are the same. Each assignment statement assigns the value of a control to the value in the field with the corresponding name.

As a first step, we recast the assignment statement into a syntax that is more appropriate for looping through a collection. The following two assignment statements are equivalent:

```
ShipAddress = rst!ShipAddress
ShipAddress.Value = rst("ShipAddress")
```

In the second statement, however, the left side explicitly states that the Value property is being set, and the right side uses the parentheses reference for the ShipAddress field. When you use the parenthetical reference for a field, you can replace the string literal for the name of the field with a variable that has the same value. When we create the statements to loop through the controls, we'll need to replace string literals such as "ShipAddress" with an expression that contains the loop counter.

The next part of the explanation is more abstract and is typical of the kind of reasoning you need when you create loops. We are going to set up a For...Next loop to loop through the members of the controls collection, so we need to use a number index to refer to controls on the form.

If frm refers to the form, the number of controls on the form is frm.Count - 1 and the controls collection has index numbers ranging from 0 to frm.Count - 1.

If k is an index number in this range, then

- frm(k) refers to some control on the form.

- frm(k).Value is the value of the control.

- frm(k).Name is the name of the control.

Now let's get specific. Some value of the index number corresponds to, say, the ShipAddress control; in other words, there is some number j for which

- frm(j) refers to the ShipAddress control.

- frm(j).Value is the value of the ShipAddress control.

- frm(j).Name is the name of the control (and is also the name of field the control is bound to).

We can also write the following assignment statement for the ShipAddress control for the particular index number that corresponds to the ShipAddress:

```
frm(j).Value = rst(frm(j).Name)
```

Each control corresponds to a different value of the index number, so as the index numbers range from 0 to the number of controls on the form, each index number corresponds to a different control. In looping through the controls on the form, we first test the control's Tag property. If the Tag property has the value Carry, the procedure sets the control's value to the value of the matching field; otherwise, the procedure moves to the next control without setting a value. Listing 17.12 shows the loop that does the automated matching.

### Listing 17.12

```
Private Sub CustomerID_AfterUpdate()
Dim frm As Form
Dim rst As RecordSet
Dim strCriteria as String, k as Integer
strCriteria = "CustomerID = """ & CustomerID & """"
Set frm = Me
Set rst = frm.RecordsetClone
rst.FindLast strCriteria
If Not rst.NoMatch Then
    For k = 0 To frm.Count-1
        If frm(k).Tag = "Carry" Then
            frm(k).Value = rst(frm(k).Name)
        End If
    Next
End If
End Sub
```

1.  Modify the statments in the CustomerID_AfterUpdate procedure as shown in Listing 17.12. Save the module.

2.  Display the new record. Select a customer such as Around the Horn. The procedure displays the customer's shipping name and address.

3.  Modify the shipping name and address as follows:

    shipping name        Butterfield's Bicycles

    shipping address     2 Southdown Lane

4.  Click the New button and select the Around the Horn in the Bill to combo box. The new record displays the shipping information from the last order for this customer.

# Working with Data in Two Related Forms

You may occasionally need to have two related forms open at the same time. For example, while reviewing orders for an existing customer using the Customer Orders form, you may need to open the Customers form to edit information. With two forms open simultaneously, you need to make sure that the forms display the most current data. When you edit an existing record in a form, Access automatically updates (*refreshes*) the data displayed in the related form as soon as it becomes the active form. However, when you add a new record or delete an existing record, Access does not automatically update these changes. (See Chapter 4.)

## Observing the Automatic Refresh of Edited Data

Before observing the automatic update, we need to automate the Customer Orders form. We place a lookup combo box on the Customer Orders form for selecting and displaying an existing customer in that form and a command button to open and synchronize a second form—the Customers form—to display the record for the selected customer.

1.  Open the Customer Orders form in Design view and set the AllowEdits property to Yes. (You set the AllowEdits property to Yes so that you'll be able to change the values in the lookup combo box.) Choose the Form Header/Footer command from the View menu. We'll place the command button and the lookup combo box in the form header.

2.  Deactivate the Control Wizard tool. Place a command button named cmdCustomer and with the Caption property set to Customer Info in the form header. Insert the event procedure shown below. You can use any of the following arguments for the where condition:

    ```
    strWhere = "CustomerID = Forms![Customer Orders]!CustomerID"
    strWhere = "CustomerID = Screen.ActiveForm.CustomerID"
    strWhere = "CustomerID = """ & Me!CustomerID & """"
    strWhere = "CustomerID = """ & Form.CustomerID & """"
    ```

    In each of the last two expressions, you must concatenate the string variable to produce a string, such as " & Me!CustomerID & " and then use one of the delimiters, such as pairs of double quotes, to mark the beginning and the end of the string within the outer string expression.

```
Private Sub cmdCustomer_Click()
Dim strForm As String, strWhere As String
strForm = "Customers"
strWhere = "CustomerID = """ & Me!CustomerID & """"
DoCmd.OpenForm formname:= strForm, wherecondition:=strWhere
End Sub
```

3. Place a lookup combo box in the form header. Set the Caption property of the label to Lookup Customer and set the combo box properties as follows:

| | |
|---|---|
| Name | cboFind |
| RowSourceType | Table/Query |
| RowSource | Customers |
| ColumnCount | 2 |
| ColumnWidths | 0;1.5 |
| BoundColumn | 1 |
| LimitToList | Yes |
| List Width | 1.5 |

4. Enter the following event procedure.

```
Private Sub cboFind_AfterUpdate()
Dim strCriteria As String
strCriteria = "CustomerID = """ & Me!cboFind & """"
Me.RecordsetClone.FindFirst strCriteria
Me.Bookmark = Me.RecordsetClone.Bookmark
End Sub
```

5. Select an existing customer using the lookup combo box and click the Customer Info button.

6. If you added the Data Entry Mode button in Chapter 16, click the button to change the mode of the Customers form to data entry mode. If you didn't add this button, the form is in data entry mode by default. Change the spelling of the company name and click the Save button or press Shift Enter to save the change. Notice that the changed spelling is displayed automatically in the Customer Orders form (see Figure 17.10).

7. Close the Customers form.

**FIGURE 17.10:**

When you save the change in the Customers form, the Customer Orders form refreshes automatically.

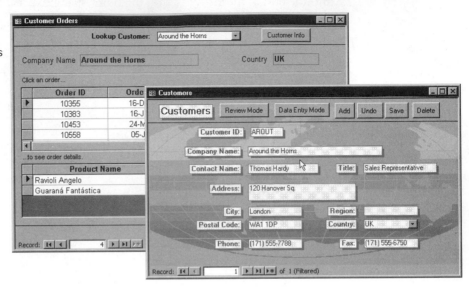

## Using the NotInList Event to Add a New Row to a Combo List

If you type the name of a new customer in the combo box, Access displays the usual error message explaining that you must enter a value in the combo list. We'll modify the Customer Orders form to allow the user to enter the name of the new customer in the combo box. When Access compares the entered text to the names in the combo list and finds the name is not in the list, the combo box recognizes the NotInList event. We'll create an event procedure for the NotInList event.

The declaration statement for the NotInList event procedure has the syntax

```
Private Sub controlname_AfterUpdate(NewData As String, Response
as Integer)
```

where

- *controlname* is the name of the control.
- NewData is the string argument that holds the text that the user typed into the combo box. Access uses the NewData argument to pass the text to the event procedure.

- Response is the intrinsic constant that you set within the procedure to tell Access how to respond to the event. You can set Response to any of three constants as follows:

    **acDataErrDisplay** displays the default error message. Use this constant when you don't want to allow the user to add a new value to the combo list.

    **acDataErrContinue** does not display the default error message. Use this constant to prevent Access from displaying the default error message.

    **acDataErrAdded** does not display the default error message but allows you to add an entry to the combo box list. Use when the event procedure includes statements that add the value to a field in the underlying data source for the combo box. The design of the procedure depends on the RowSourceType and RowSource properties of the combo box. After the entry is added to the list, Access automatically requeries the combo box.

We create the cboFind_NotInList event procedure that starts by displaying a message box asking if you want to enter a new customer. If you click the Yes button, the procedure undoes the entry in the combo box, suppresses the default error message, opens the Customers form ready for data entry with a blank record, and copies the text you typed as the new company name. If you click the No button, the procedure displays a message and undoes the entry in the combo box. Listing 17.13 shows the event procedure. In this procedure

1. Switch to Design view. Click in the Lookup Customer combo box, click in the NotInList event property, and click the Build button at the right of the property box. Create the event procedure shown in Listing 17.13.

### Listing 17.13

```
Private Sub CustomerID_NotInList(NewData As String, Response As
Integer)
Dim intNew As Integer
intNew = MsgBox ("Do you want to add a new customer?", vbYesNo)
If intNew = vbYes Then
    RunCommand acCmdUndo
    Response = acDataErrContinue
    DoCmd.OpenForm formname:="Customers",datamode:= acFormAdd
    Forms!Customers!CompanyName = NewData
Else
```

```
      MsgBox "The company name you entered isn't an existing
   ➡customer."
      RunCommand acCmdUndo
      Response = acDataErrContinue
   End If
   End Sub
```

2. Switch to Form view and type **Denver Delights** as the name of a new customer in the combo list. Click the Yes button in the message box. Access displays a new data entry record in the Customers form with the CompanyName filled in.

3. If you added the Data Entry Mode button in Chapter 16, click the button to change the form to data entry mode; if you didn't add the button, the form is already in data entry mode. Enter **DENVE** as CustomerID, choose USA in the Country combo box, and enter other information for the new customer. Close the Customers form.

4. Click down arrow of the Lookup combo box. The new customer does not appear in the list.

## Refresh Does Not Display New Records

When you add a new record using the Customers form, Access does not automatically display the new record in the Customer Orders form. In order to display the new record, you must requery both the combo box and the form. (See Chapter 8 for details.) We'll create an event procedure that requeries the Customer Orders form and the cboFind combo box just after the new record is saved and the Customers form recognizes the AfterInsert event.

The interesting part of this procedure is that the procedure runs from the Customers form but takes actions on the Customer Orders form. The actions require that the Customer Orders form be open, so the procedure must determine whether the Customer Orders form is open before taking the actions.

The Form_AfterInsert event procedure uses the IsLoaded function to determine if the Customer Orders form is open and terminates if the form isn't open. If the form is open, the procedure uses the SelectObject method of the DoCmd object to select the Customer Orders form and runs the RunCommand method to save the record in the Customer Orders form. (You must save the record before you can run the Requery method; it is not necessary to save the record before using the Requery action in a macro, however.) The procedure requeries the combo box and then the form by running the Requery method of each object. Listing 17.14 shows the event procedure.

### Listing 17.14

```
Private Sub Form_AfterInsert()
Dim frm As Form, cbo As ComboBox
If IsLoaded("Customer Orders") Then
    Set frm = Forms![Customer Orders]
    Set cbo = frm!cboFind
    DoCmd.SelectObject acForm, "Customer Orders"
    RunCommand acCmdSaveRecord
    cbo.Requery
    frm.Requery
End If
End Sub
```

1. Open the Customers form in Design view. Enter the event procedure shown in Listing 17.14. Save and close the form.

2. Enter **Boulder Commissaries** as the name of a new customer in the combo box in the Customer Orders form. Click Yes to enter a new customer.

3. Enter **BOULD** as the CustomerID, choose USA in the Country combo box, and enter other data for a new customer in the Customers form. Close the Customers form.

4. Drop the Lookup Customer combo box on the Customer Orders form. The name of the new customer is in the list. When you select the new customer, the form displays the new customer.

You can automate the process of displaying the new customer in the Customer Orders form by modifying the event procedure shown in Listing 17.14. Enter the following statements after the frm.Requery statement. After requerying the form, the modified procedure sets the combo box to the new CustomerID and then synchronizes the Customer Orders form to the value in the combo box using the recordsetclone method. (See Chapter 16.)

```
cbo = Forms!Customers!CustomerID
frm.RecordsetClone.FindFirst "CustomerID = """ & frm!cboFind & """"
frm.Bookmark = frm.RecordsetClone.Bookmark
```

# Editing Data in a Recordset

Although you generally provide forms in the Access interface so that the user can edit data, sometimes working directly with a recordset is faster than working with a form. In this section you learn how to work with data directly without displaying a form. You'll create a procedure to open a recordset in memory and then use the methods of the Recordset object to add, edit, and delete records.

In Chapter 16 you learned how to navigate in a recordset from one record to another by moving the current record pointer. If the recordset is a table-type or dynaset-type recordset, you may be able to edit existing records, add new records, and delete existing records. This section assumes that you can make changes to the recordset.

> **NOTE**
>
> Your ability to change the data in a recordset depends on a number of factors including the options you set when you created the recordset, the type of query or SQL statement you are using for a dynaset-type recordset, and whether other users have placed locks that prevent you from making changes (if you are working in a multi-user environment). Depending on how the query is designed, you may be able to edit certain fields but not other fields. (See queries, results, and updating in online Help.) You cannot edit recordsets based on crosstab or union queries.

## Changing a Record

The fundamental rule in working with recordsets is that you can work only with the current record. This means that you must move the current record pointer to a record before you can edit it. In learning how to change records, you need to understand that Jet uses a separate location in memory called a *copy buffer* for the contents of a record that is being edited.

Editing the current record and saving the changes is a three-step process:

1. Move a copy of the current record into the copy buffer using the Edit method.

2. Make the changes.

3.  Save the changes you made in the copy buffer to the current record using the Update method. Alternatively, empty the copy buffer without saving the changes using the CancelUpdate method

If you try to edit a record without moving it into the copy buffer with the Edit method, a run-time error is generated. If you move to another record without saving the changes to the current record with the Update method, an error is not generated, but the changes are not copied to the current record. The changes you make in the copy buffer are also lost if you close the recordset, set the bookmark property to another record, or use the Edit or AddNew method again without first using the Update method.

As an example, we create a procedure that finds the record for the Bottom-Dollar Markets customer in the Customers table and changes the contact name.

1.  Create a new standard module named basRecordset. Insert the EditRecordset procedure shown in Listing 17.15. The procedure opens a table-type recordset on the Customers table, sets the current index to the primary key, and uses the Seek method to locate the record for Bottom-Dollar Markets. If the record is not found, the procedure displays a message and terminates. If the record is found, the procedure displays the contact name for the record. The procedure runs the Edit method to copy the record to the copy buffer, changes the contact name, runs the Update method to save the changed record to the table, and displays the changed contact name.

## Listing 17.15

```
Public Sub EditRecordset()
Dim rst As Recordset
Set rst = CurrentDb.OpenRecordset("Customers")
rst.Index = "PrimaryKey"
rst.Seek "=", "BOTTM"
If rst.NoMatch Then
    MsgBox "There is no customer with this CustomerID"
    Exit Sub
Else
    MsgBox "The contact name is " & rst!ContactName
    rst.Edit
    rst!ContactName = "Sara Cherry"
    rst.Update
```

```
        MsgBox "The contact name is " & rst!ContactName
    End If
End Sub
```

2. Press Ctrl+G to display the Debug window. Run the EditRecordset procedure by typing **EditRecordset** in the Immediate window and pressing Enter. The procedure displays message boxes with the current contact name (see Figure 17.11a) and then with the edited contact name (see Figure 17.11b).

**FIGURE 17.11:**

Using a procedure to edit a record by running the Edit and Update methods of a recordset.

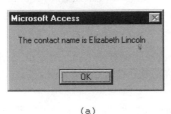

(a)

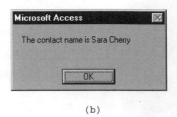

(b)

## Adding a Record

Adding a new record and saving the changes is also a three-step process:

1. Create a new record in the copy buffer and set any default values using the AddNew method. Access sets any default values you have specified in table Design view and sets the values of the fields without default values to Null.

2. Enter the new data.

3. Save the changes made in the copy buffer and add the saved record to the recordset using the Update method. Alternatively, empty the copy buffer without adding the new record using the CancelUpdate method.

The position of the new record in the recordset depends on the type of recordset If you are adding a record to a table-type recordset, the new record is added to the end of the recordset unless you have set the Index property. If you have set the current index using the Index property, the new record is inserted in its proper place in the sort order according to the current index. If you are adding to a dynaset-type recordset, the new record is added to the end of the recordset. In any case the current record pointer continues to point to the record that was current before you added the new record. To make the new record the current record, set the Bookmark property to the LastModified property setting.

> **NOTE**
>
> If you move to another record without saving the changes with the Update method, an error is not generated. However, the new record is not added, and the changes in the copy buffer are lost. The changes you make in the copy buffer are also lost if you close the recordset, set the bookmark property to another record, or use the Edit or AddNew method again without first using the Update method.

As an example, we create a procedure that adds a new record to the Customers table.

1. Insert the AddRecordset procedure shown in Listing 17.16 in the basRecordset module. The procedure opens a table-type recordset on the Customers table and sets the current index to the primary key. The procedure runs the AddNew method to create a new record in the copy buffer, sets the values for the CustomerID, CompanyName, and Country fields, and runs the Update method to save the record to the table. Because the current index has been set, the new record is inserted in primary key order as the first record of the recordset. The procedure sets the Bookmark property to the LastModified property to move current record pointer to the new record. The procedure displays the company name for the new record, moves the current record pointer to the next record, and displays the company name for the next record in the recordset.

### Listing 17.16

```
Public Sub AddRecordset()
Dim rst As Recordset
Set rst = CurrentDb.OpenRecordset("Customers")
rst.Index = "PrimaryKey"
rst.AddNew
rst!CustomerID = "AARDV"
rst!CompanyName = "Aardvark Inc."
rst!Country = "Australia"
rst.Update
rst.Bookmark = rst.LastModified
MsgBox "The company name is " & rst!CompanyName
rst.MoveNext
MsgBox "The company name is " & rst!CompanyName
End Sub
```

2. Type **AddRecordset** in the Immediate pane and press Enter. The procedure adds the record, displays a field from the new record (see Figure 17.12a), and then displays a field from the next record in the recordset (see Figure 17.12b).

**FIGURE 17.12:**

The AddRecordset procedure opens a recordset on the Customers table, adds a new record to the beginning of the recordset (a), and displays the information from the second record (b).

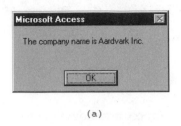

(a)

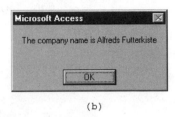

(b)

As another example, we'll add a new category to the category combo list in the Products form without opening the Categories form. The source of the category combo list is the Categories table, so adding a new value to the combo list requires adding a new record to the Categories table. The CategoryID_NotInList event procedure in Listing 17.17 displays a message box asking if the user wants to add a new category. If the user clicks the Yes button, the procedure opens a recordset on the Categories table, requests that the user enter a description for the new category, adds the new product directly to the table, and sets the Response argument to acDataErrAdded to instruct Access to requery the combo list. If the user clicks the No button, the procedure displays a custom message, undoes the entry, and suppresses the default error message.

### Listing 17.17

```
Private Sub CategoryID_NotInList (NewData As String, Response
    ➥As Integer)
Dim intNew As Integer, strDescription As String, rst As Recordset
intNew = MsgBox("Do you want to add a new category?", vbYesNo)
If intNew = vbYes Then
Set rst = CurrentDb.OpenRecordset("Categories")
    rst.AddNew
    rst!Categoryname = NewData
    strDescription = InputBox("Enter a description for the new
    ➥category.")
```

```
        rst!Description = strDescription
        rst.Update
        Response = acDataErrAdded
    Else
        MsgBox "The value you entered is not a valid category"
        RunCommand acCmdUndo
        Response = acDataErrContinue
    End If
End Sub
```

1. Select the Products form in the Database window and click the Code button in the toolbar. Create the procedure shown in Listing 17.17.

2. Save the form and switch to Form view. Click the New button to display a new record.

3. Type **Chocolates** in the Category combo list and press Enter. Click Yes to enter a new category (see Figure 17.13a), type **White and Brown chocolates** in the input box (see Figure 17.13b), and click OK. Access adds the new category to the Categories table, requeries the combo list, and displays the new category.

**FIGURE 17.13:**

Adding a new value to a combo list by adding a record to the table that is the data source of the list.

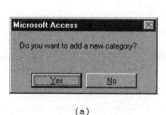

(a)

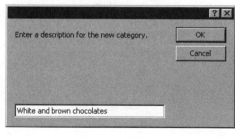

(b)

## Using the EditMode Property

You can use the recordset's EditMode property to determine the status of editing for the current record. The EditMode property returns integer values corresponding to the following states:

- dbEditNone if no editing is in progress

- dbEditInProgress if the Edit method has been executed and a copy of the current record is in the copy buffer

- dbEditAdd if the AddNew method has been executed and the copy buffer contains the data for a new record, which hasn't been saved to the recordset

> **WARNING**
>
> A common error is to forget to execute the Edit method before trying to change the data in a record; fortunately, this mistake causes a run-time error so you are alerted to your mistake. An equally common error is to forget to execute the Update method after you have changed an existing record or entered the data for a new record. This mistake does not cause a run-time error, but the contents of the copy buffer are simply discarded without warning. Without the assistance of a run-time error message, these failure-to-Update errors are much harder to troubleshoot.

## Deleting a Record

Deleting an existing record is a one-step process—you delete the current record using the Delete method. There is no temporary buffer to hold the contents if you change your mind; the deletion is immediate and irreversible. Curiously, the deleted record is still considered to be the current record, even though you can't refer to it. You must move the current record pointer away to a valid current record if you plan to execute any methods that require a valid current record.

As an example, let's delete the record added to the Categories table in the last section.

1. Insert the DeleteRecordset procedure shown in Listing 17.18 in the basRecordset module. The procedure opens a dynaset-type recordset on the Categories table, uses the FindFirst method to move the current record pointer to the record, and runs the Delete method to delete the record

### Listing 17.18

```
Public Sub DeleteRecordset()
Dim rst As Recordset
Set rst = CurrentDb.OpenRecordset("Categories", dbOpenDynaset)
rst.FindFirst "CategoryName = 'Chocolates'"
```

```
MsgBox "The category name of the record to be deleted is " &
    ➥rst!CategoryName
rst.Delete
rst.MovePrevious
MsgBox "The category name of the previous record is " &
    ➥rst!CategoryName
End Sub
```

2. Type **DeleteRecordset** in the Immediate pane and press Enter. The procedure displays the message boxes indicating the record to be deleted (see Figure 17.14a) and the previous record, which became the current record when the procedure ran the MovePrevious method after deleting the record (see Figure 17.14b).

---

**FIGURE 17.14:**

Messages before and after running the Delete and MovePrevious methods.

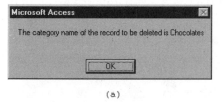

(a)

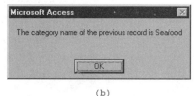

(b)

# Summary

This chapter focuses on using VBA procedures to work with data in two ways. In the forms approach, the user uses forms to work with data. This chapter covers the procedures for automating the processes of adding new records and editing and deleting existing records through a form. In the recordset approach, the user takes actions that run procedures that edit, delete, or add new records directly to a recordset without displaying a form. The important points include

- You can protect data from inadvertant changes by providing a form with command buttons that run procedures to toggle between review and data entry modes.

- You can use procedures to customize data validation, for example, by changing the timing of the validation test.

- You can use the Command Button Wizard to create simple data maintenance procedures and modify the procedures to prevent run-time errors and to suppress default error messages.

- You can make data entry more efficient by arranging to carry values forward to a new record in two ways:

  - Use a procedure to set the DefaultValue property

  - Use a procedure to copy the field values from a specified record to a new record

- You can use the Requery method to display the most current data when Access doesn't update a form automatically.

- You can use the Edit, AddNew, and Delete methods of the Recordset object to work directly with a recordset in memory without opening a form.

# CHAPTER

## EIGHTEEN

**18**

# Working with Groups of Records Using Access VBA

- Sorting and selecting records displayed in a form or report

- Using Query By Form to pass data from a form to a query

- Using the multi-select list box for random selection of records

- Working with a group of records in a recordset

- Running stored queries and SQL statements

- Making bulk changes to a recordset

In the previous two chapters, you've learned how to create procedures for working with a single record using two fundamentally differing approaches: forms and recordsets. In the form approach the user works with forms to navigate between records and controls and to view and modify data, and in the recordset approach actions of the user run procedures that create and manipulate recordsets in memory without a visual representation. This chapter focuses on working with groups of records using the two approaches.

The first part of the chapter uses the form approach. You learn how to

- Automate operations to sort records and to select groups of records that satisfy search criteria using a form or report

- Open a form or report that displays a limited selection of records upon opening

- Change the selection after the form or report is open

- Use a form to collect search criteria and how to pass the criteria to a query (Query By Form)

Many of the VBA techniques are similar to the macro programming techniques described in Chapter 9. The first part of the chapter ends with a discussion of using a multi-select list box to select records.

The second part of the chapter focuses on working with recordsets in VBA procedures. You learn how to use stored queries and SQL statements to sort and select groups of records and how to use action queries to make bulk changes to recordsets.

**NOTE** For hands-on experience with the techniques described in this chapter, create a new copy of the Northwind sample database named Northwind_Ch18 and work through the steps of the examples.

We begin by creating a new form for the Northwind_Ch18 database that we'll use to illustrate procedures for sorting and filtering a form.

- If you worked through the beginning of Chapter 9, "Working with Groups of Records Using Macros," you have already created and saved the form under the name frmOrderStatusClean.

    1. To import the form choose the Get External Data command in the File menu, choose Import from the fly-out menu, locate the NorthwindMacros database you created in Chapter 9, select the frmOrderStatusClean form, and click OK.

    2. After importing the form, select the frmOrderStatusClean form in the Database window, copy and save the form as frmOrderStatus, and open the form.

- If you didn't work through the beginning of Chapter 9, follow the description in the first few pages of Chapter 9 to create the frmOrderStatus form. You should also work through the section, "Sorting Interactively" in Chapter 9 before continuing with this chapter.

# Sorting Records in a Form or Report

You can automate the sorting process for the records in a form or report by setting the OrderBy and the OrderByOn properties of the form or report in a procedure.

## The OrderBy Property

You can use the OrderBy property of a form or report to sort by a single field or to create a complex sort by several fields with some fields in ascending and others in descending order. The OrderBy property is a string expression that consists of the name of the field or fields you want to sort, arranged in the order of the sort and separated by commas; to sort a field in descending order, you type **DESC** after the name of the field. For example, to sort the frmOrderStatus form by customer and then by order date in descending order, you set the form's OrderBy property to

```
Customers.CompanyName, OrderDate DESC
```

Setting the OrderBy property specifies a new sort order, but does not perform the sort.

## Using the OrderByOn Property

You set the OrderByOn property to True or False to apply or remove the sort that you specified. For a form you can set the OrderBy property in the form's property sheet, in a macro, or in a VBA procedure and then use a macro or VBA procedure to apply and remove the sort using the OrderByOn property. For a report you can set both the OrderBy and the OrderByOn properties in the report's property sheet, in a macro, or in a VBA procedure.

## Using a Triple-State Toggle Button

To illustrate these ideas, we'll create a button and an event procedure to sort the records of the Order Status form by customer. We use a toggle button instead of a command button because a toggle button has a value that can be used by the procedure. By default a toggle button has two values, True and False, but setting the TripleState property to Yes gives a third value, Null.

- When the toggle button has the value False, it looks like a command button.

- Clicking the button changes it to the Null state in which the button flattens but still appears raised.

- Clicking the button again changes it to the True state in which the flattened button appears sunken.

We'll create a procedure to test the button's state and remove the sort if the button is in the False state, apply an ascending sort if the button is in the Null state, and apply a descending sort if the button is in the True state. Figure 18.1 shows the three states of the toggle button and the resulting sorts by customer.

1. Switch to Design view, select all the controls in the detail section, and set their Enabled properties to No. The controls don't need to be enabled when you use the OrderBy property for the sort.

**FIGURE 18.1:**

Using a triple-state toggle button to remove a sort when the toggle button is False (a), apply an ascending sort when the toggle button is Null (b), and apply a descending sort when the toggle button is True (c).

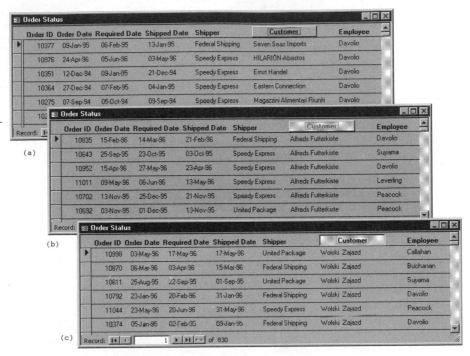

2. Delete the Customer label in the header section and replace it with a toggle button; set the properties as follows:

| | |
|---|---|
| Name | tglCustomer |
| Caption | Customer |
| TripleState | Yes |
| Default Value | False |
| FontWeight | Bold |
| ControlTip Text | Click to toggle no sort, ascending, descending |

3. Click in the OnClick event property and click the Build button at the right of the property box. Insert the event procedure shown in Listing 18.1. The procedure creates the str variable to hold the name of the sort field and the tgl object variable to refer to the toggle button. The event procedure uses the Me property to refer to the form. You can use either the If...Then...Else or the Select Case structure to test the state of the toggle button.

Listing 18.1 uses the Select Case structure.

- If the toggle button has the True value, the form's OrderBy property is set to a descending sort by CompanyName and the form's OrderByOn property is turned on.

- If the toggle button has the False value, the form's OrderByOn property is turned off so that the records are returned to unsorted order.

- If the toggle button is neither True nor False, the form's OrderBy property is set to an ascending sort by CompanyName and the OrderByOn property is turned on.

### Listing 18.1

```
Private Sub tglCustomer_Click()
Dim str As String, tgl As ToggleButton
str = "Customers.CompanyName"
Set tgl = tglCustomer
Select Case tgl.Value
Case True
    Me.OrderBy = str & " DESC"
    Me.OrderByOn = True
Case False
    Me.OrderByOn = False
Case Else
    Me.OrderBy = str
    Me.OrderByOn = True
End Select
End Sub.
```

4. Save the form, switch to Form view, and click the toggle button (see Figure 18.1). As you cycle through the states, the records are sorted by customer name first in ascending order, then in descending order, and then the sort is removed.

Because Access saves the OrderBy and OrderByOn settings that are in effect when you close the form but does not save the state of the toggle button, the three settings can get out of sync with one another when you first open the form. We'll use the event procedure in Listing 18.2 to initialize the sort properties by setting the OrderBy property to the zero-length string and the OrderByOn property to False when the form opens.

## Listing 18.2

```
Private Sub Form_Open(Cancel As Integer)
Me.OrderBy = ""
Me.OrderByOn = False
End Sub
```

1. Switch to Design view, click in the form's OnOpen event property, and click the Build button at the right of the property box. Insert the event procedure shown in Listing 18.2 in the form's module.

2. Save and close the form.

3. Open the form. The two sort property settings are initialized and in sync with the toggle button. As you cycle through the states, the records are sorted by customer name first in ascending order, then in descending order, and then the sort is removed.

## Sort by Any Column

When records are displayed in a tabular form, you can automate sorting the records by specific columns. Replace the label of each column you want to sort by with a triple-state toggle button and create an event procedure to sort the records by a field in the column, such as the one in Listing 18.1. Using this technique, each of the sorts is independent and the last toggle button clicked overrides previous sorts and determines the final sort. For example, if you toggle the Customer button to sort ascending by customer and then toggle the Employee button to sort ascending by employee, the records are sorted in ascending order by employee.

1. Switch to Design view, delete the Employee label, and replace it with a toggle button. Set the Name property to tglEmployee and the Caption property to Employee. Set the other properties to be the same as those you set for the tglCustomer toggle button.

2. Click the Code button in the toolbar to open the form's module. Select the tglCustomer_Click procedure; then copy and paste the procedure. Modify the procedure name to tglEmployee_Click and change the assignment statements for the str and tgl variables to

```
str = "LastName"
Set tgl = tglEmployee
```

3. Save the form and switch to Form view.

4. Click the Customer toggle button and then click the Employee toggle button. Figure 18.2 shows the result; notice that the state of the Customer toggle button is out of sync because the toggle button is in the flattened raised state (to indicate an ascending sort by customer), whereas the records are sorted by employee.

**FIGURE 18.2:**

The state of the Customer toggle is out of sync; the button indicates an ascending sort by customer, but the records do not reflect the customer sort.

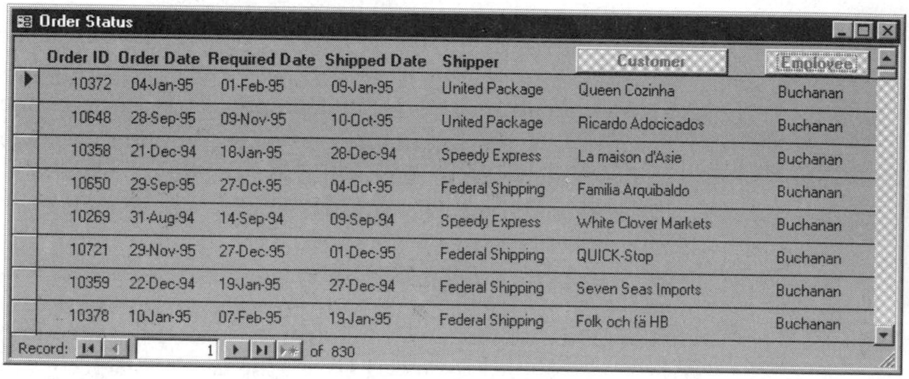

| Order ID | Order Date | Required Date | Shipped Date | Shipper | Customer | Employee |
|---|---|---|---|---|---|---|
| 10372 | 04-Jan-95 | 01-Feb-95 | 09-Jan-95 | United Package | Queen Cozinha | Buchanan |
| 10648 | 28-Sep-95 | 09-Nov-95 | 10-Oct-95 | United Package | Ricardo Adocicados | Buchanan |
| 10358 | 21-Dec-94 | 18-Jan-95 | 28-Dec-94 | Speedy Express | La maison d'Asie | Buchanan |
| 10650 | 29-Sep-95 | 27-Oct-95 | 04-Oct-95 | Federal Shipping | Familia Arquibaldo | Buchanan |
| 10269 | 31-Aug-94 | 14-Sep-94 | 09-Sep-94 | Speedy Express | White Clover Markets | Buchanan |
| 10721 | 29-Nov-95 | 27-Dec-95 | 01-Dec-95 | Federal Shipping | QUICK-Stop | Buchanan |
| 10359 | 22-Dec-94 | 19-Jan-95 | 27-Dec-94 | Federal Shipping | Seven Seas Imports | Buchanan |
| 10378 | 10-Jan-95 | 07-Feb-95 | 19-Jan-95 | Federal Shipping | Folk och fä HB | Buchanan |

Record: 1 of 830

## Event Procedures for a Complex Sort

It is possible to write procedures to keep the toggle buttons in sync with the current sort; these procedures involve the same kind of programming that is required for a complex sort. In complex sorts each subsequent sort on any field takes previous sorts into account. For example, in a complex sort, toggling a sort by customer and then a sort by employee would produce records sorted first by customer and then by employee for each customer.

We'll modify the event procedure to do a complex sort for the Customer and Employee triple-state toggle buttons as shown in Listing 18.3. The modified procedure for the Customer toggle button works by checking the status of the Employee button, checking the status of the Customer button, and then building a sort string by concatenating the Employee sort order with the Customer sort order.

### Listing 18.3

```
Private Sub tglCustomer_Click()
Dim str As String, str0 As String
```

```
Dim tgl As Control, tgl0 As Control
Dim strSort As String
str = "Customers.CompanyName"
str0 = "LastName"
Set tgl = tglCustomer
Set tgl0 = tglEmployee
Select Case tgl0.Value
    Case True
        strSort = str0 & " DESC"
    Case False
        strSort = ""
    Case Else
        strSort = str0
End Select
If Not strSort = "" Then strSort = strSort & ", "

Select Case tgl.Value
    Case True
        strSort = strSort & str & " DESC"
    Case False
        strSort = strSort
    Case Else
    strSort = strSort & str
End Select

If strSort = "" Then
    Me.OrderByOn = False
Else
    Me.OrderBy = strSort
    Me.OrderByOn = True
End If
End Sub
```

The procedure begins by creating variables to store the strings for the Customer sort field (str), the Employee sort field (str0), and the complex sort (strSort) that the procedure builds. The procedure also declares object variables to refer to the Customer toggle button (tgl) and the Employee toggle button (tgl0). When you click the Customer button, the procedure uses the first set of Select Case statements to test the state of the Employee button. The procedure starts building the string for the complex sort by storing the string for the current Employee sort order in the strSort variable. After storing the Employee sort order, the procedure determines whether it is necessary to concatenate a comma to the end of the string as follows:

- If the records are currently sorted by employee, the procedure concatenates a comma to the end of the sort order string in preparation for adding the customer sort order to the end of the string.

- If the records are not currently sorted by employee, the sort order is set to the zero-length string. There is no need to concatenate a comma to the end of the string.

The procedure uses the second set of Select Case statements to test the state of the Customer button and concatenates the Customer sort order corresponding to the current state of the Customer button to the end of the sort order string. After building the string for the complex sort, the procedure tests the final sort order string; if the sort string is the zero-length string, the sort order is turned off; otherwise, the form's OrderBy property is set to the sort string and the sort is turned on.

1. Modify the tglCustomer_Click event procedure as shown in Listing 18.3.

2. Copy all the statements of the event procedure for tglCustomer_Click between the procedure declaration and end statements and paste the statements to the tglEmployee_Click event procedure (replacing the previous statements). Change the variable assignment statements as shown below. The event procedure now works correctly for the tglEmployee toggle button.

```
str0 = "Customers.CompanyName"
str = "LastName"
Set tgl0 = tglCustomer
Set tgl = tglEmployee
```

3. Save the form and switch to Form view.

4. Test the complex sort in the Order Status form. For example, click the Customer button to sort the records by customer and then click the Employee button to sort the records for each customer by employee.

# Selecting Groups of Records in a Form or Report

One of the most common and important operations in a database application is selecting a group of records that satisfy search conditions. For example, in an order entry database, you may want to design a form that displays orders for a specific customer, all orders placed after a specified date, or the orders for a specified customer placed after a specified date and handled by a specified employee. You select records from the entire set of records by specifying search conditions that you use to filter out the records satisfying the conditions. Access provides many techniques for filtering records.

## Search Conditions

The first step in selecting a group of records is to set up the search condition. You can uses these five basic search conditions:

**Comparison test** compares the value of one expression to the value of another expression. For example, OrderDate < #1/1/97# searches for orders in the Orders table placed before 1/1/97.

**Range test** tests whether the value of an expression lies within a range of values. For example, OrderDate Between #9/1/96# And #1/1/97# searches for orders in the specified date range.

**Membership** in a group tests whether the value of an expression matches one of a set of values. For example, Country In ("France", "Germany", "South Africa") searches for customers from one of the three specified countries.

**Pattern matching** tests whether a string value matches a specified pattern. For example, LastName Like "M*" searches for employees whose last name begins with the letter *M*.

**Null value test** tests whether a value has the Null value. For example, RequiredDate Is Null searches for orders without a required date.

*(continued)*

You can create complex searches by combining up to 40 simple search conditions using logical operators, such as AND and OR.

After using one of several techniques to initiate the search, Jet retrieves the records that satisfy the search condition.

The search condition is often referred to as "an SQL WHERE clause without the word WHERE."

The rest of this section describes techniques for opening a form or report with an initial filter that displays a group of selected records and techniques for changing the records displayed after the form is open.

## Opening a Form or Report with Selected Records

To select records when a form or report is first opened, you can do any of the following:

- Use a parameter query as the form's or report's record source

- Set a property such as RecordSource or Filter in a macro or procedure that runs when the form or report opens

- Use one of the macro actions or VBA methods to apply the search condition to the existing record source when the form or report opens

**Parameter Query**    A parameter query is a query that requires additional information before it can run. When you use a parameter query as the record source of a form or report, you can use two techniques to supply the additional information to the query: you can use the default dialog box that Access displays automatically when a query criteria contains a parameter, or you can use controls on another form to collect the information. When a query gets its information from a form, you are using the *Query By Form* technique.

As an example, the Sales By Year report has the Sales By Year parameter query as its record source. If you run the Sales By Year query by selecting it in the Database window and clicking the Open button, Access displays the two default dialogs for the parameters in the query (see Figure 18.3).

FIGURE 18.3:

The default dialogs for the Sales By Year parameter query

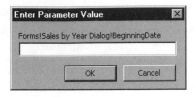 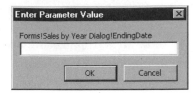

Figure 18.4a shows the two parameters included in the criteria expression for the ShippedDate field. The syntax of the parameter references, such as

```
Forms![Sales by Year Dialog]!BeginningDate
```

indicates that the parameter query is designed to obtain its values from the Sales By Year Dialog form. However, when the form is not open, Access displays the default dialogs to collect the additional information.

If you run the Sales By Year query by opening the Sales By Year report, Access displays the Sales By Year Dialog form (see Figure 18.4b). After you specify the dates and close the form, the Sales By Year query runs, using the information you entered in the form (Query By Form); then the Sales By Year report opens and displays the selected records.

FIGURE 18.4:

A parameter query (a) and the custom dialog form (b) that supplies the values of the parameters

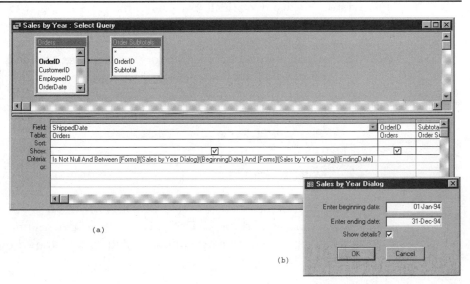

**Setting the Recordsource Property**    You can set the form's or report's RecordSource property by writing a macro or an event procedure triggered by the Open event. You can set the RecordSource property to the name of a stored query or an SQL statement; however, when setting the property in a VBA procedure, you must use a string expression. For example, to display the records for the customers from Argentina in the Customer Labels report

1.  Open the Customer Labels report in Design view, click in the report's OnOpen event property, and click the Build button at the right of the property box. Create the event procedure shown below. The SQL statement selects records for customers from Argentina from the Customers table.

```
Private Sub Report_Open(Cancel As Integer)
Me.RecordSource = "SELECT * FROM Customers WHERE Country =
    ➡'Argentina'"
End Sub
```

2.  Save the report and switch to Print Preview. The Open event is triggered, and the report displays the selected records.

**Setting the Filter Property**    A form or report has a Filter property that you can use to specify records and a FilterOn property that you use to turn a filter on or off. The Filter property is a string expression that is a valid SQL WHERE clause without the word WHERE. You can set the Filter property to select the records in a macro or an event procedure triggered by the form's or report's Open event.

1.  Modify the event procedure for the Open event of the Customer Labels report as follows:

```
Private Sub Report_Open(Cancel As Integer)
Me.Filter = "Country = 'UK'"
Me.FilterOn = True
End Sub
```

2.  Switch to Print Preview. The selected records are displayed.

**Using the OpenForm or OpenReport Method**    The OpenForm and OpenReport methods of the DoCmd object have two arguments that you can use to select records: the wherecondition and the filtername arguments.

The wherecondition argument is a string expression that is a valid SQL WHERE clause without the word WHERE. For example, to open the Customers form displaying customers from Argentina, you use the statement

```
DoCmd.OpenForm formname:="Customers", wherecondition:= "Country =
➥ 'Argentina'"
```

The filtername argument is a string expression that is the name of a stored filter query in the database. You must first create a filter query that filters the form's or report's underlying table or query in order to select records. A filter query must include all the fields in the form's or report's recordset. A filter query can also be a parameter query. We'll create a filter query in the next section.

**Using the ApplyFilter Method**     The ApplyFilter method of the DoCmd object also has the wherecondition and filtername arguments. You can run the ApplyFilter method automatically when the form or report opens by creating an event procedure for the Open event. For example, to select customers from Argentina you can use the following event procedure for the Customers form:

```
Private Sub Form_Open(Cancel As Integer)
DoCmd.ApplyFilter wherecondition:= "Country = 'Argentina'"
End Sub
```

Figure 18.5 shows the result of opening the Customers form and triggering this procedure.

**FIGURE 18.5:**

You can use the ApplyFilter method in a procedure triggered by the form's Open event to filter the records when the form opens.

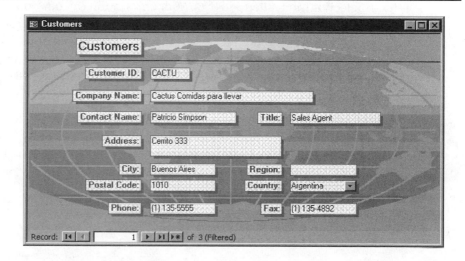

## Changing the Selection in an Open Form or Report

After a form or report is open and displays records, you can use several different techniques to change which records are displayed. These techniques include:

- Using the built-in Filter For command that allows the user to enter filter criteria in a text box in the shortcut menu

- Using the built-in Filter By Selection and Filter By Form filter windows that allow the user to create a filter for an open form

- Changing the RecordSource property of an open form using a macro or procedure

- Running the ApplyFilter action or method to apply a filter to an open form

- Changing the Filter property of an open form or report and then turning the filter on in a macro or procedure

Of the techniques discussed here, only the technique that sets the Filter and FilterOn properties can be used to select records for an open report; the remaining techniques apply only to selecting records in open forms.

**Using Filter For, Filter By Selection, and Filter By Form**     You can use the three built-in filter techniques that Access provides for allowing the user to select and change records displayed in an open form: Filter For, Filter By Selection, and Filter By Form. Your application can offer these techniques if it includes the built-in menu commands or toolbar buttons. For example, to use the new Filter For technique to select records for the Customers form, include the Filter For command in your application so that the user can right-click in a control, type the criteria in the Filter For text box (see Figure 18.6), and press Enter to apply the filter.

  To use the Filter By Form technique to select records for the Customer Orders form, include the Filter By Form command or the Filter By Form toolbar button. Figure 18.7 shows the filter to find the orders placed after 1/1/97 by customers from Argentina. Clicking the Filter button in the toolbar applies the filter.

**FIGURE 18.6:**

Right-click in a control to display the built-in Filter For command.

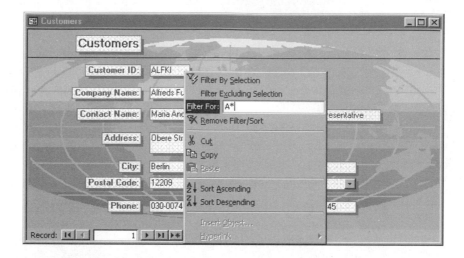

**FIGURE 18.7:**

Using the Filter by Form filter window to create a filter

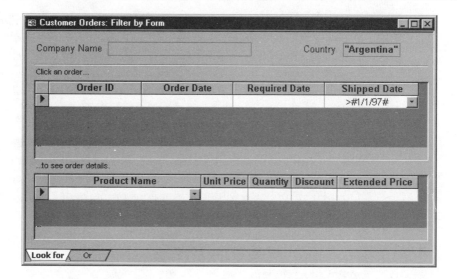

You can also customize the Filter By Form interface. You can create macros or event procedures for a pair of events, the Filter and ApplyFilter events, to customize the process.

A form recognizes the Filter event when you click the Filter By Form button or choose the Filter By Form or Advanced Filter/Sort subcommand in the Filter command in the Records menu. (The Filter event is not recognized when you use the Filter By Selection technique.) Access runs the event procedure before displaying the Filter By Form interface, so you can use the event procedure to modify the default Filter By Form interface or replace it with your own custom filter window. After the event procedure runs, the customized Filter By Form interface is displayed. As an example, if you don't want to display the second subform in the Customers Orders form when the Filter By Form interface is active, you can use the following event procedure to hide the subform:

```
Private Sub Form_Filter(Cancel As Integer, FilterType As Integer)
Me.[Customer Orders Subform2].Visible = False
End Sub
```

Access uses the FilterType argument to tell the event procedure which of the two filter windows the user is trying to open; Access uses the intrinsic constants acFilterbyForm and acFilterAdvanced. You can include statements that determine the value of the FilterType argument and include instructions depending on the filter window the user is trying to open.

A form recognizes the ApplyFilter event when the form detects one of three types of actions: actions to remove the filter, to apply the filter, or to close the filter window. The form recognizes the ApplyFilter event either in response to interactions with the user or in response to macros or procedures. The ApplyFilter event occurs when the user clicks the Apply Filter or Remove Filter button on the toolbar, chooses the Apply Filter/Sort or Remove Filter/Sort command in the Records menu, clicks the Filter By Selection button on the toolbar, or chooses the Filter By Selection subcommand from the Filter command of the Records menu. The ApplyFilter event also occurs when a macro or procedure runs an action or method that applies or removes a filter (such as the ApplyFilter, OpenForm, or ShowAllRecords actions or methods), closes the filter window, or sets the Filter or FilterOn property.

You can create an event procedure to perform different operations depending on which of the three actions triggered the event. The syntax for the ApplyFilter event procedure is

```
Form_ApplyFilter (Cancel As Integer, ApplyType As Integer)
```

You can use the Cancel argument to cancel the default behavior that follows the event (applying the filter, removing the filter, or closing the filter window). Access uses the ApplyType argument to inform the event procedure which action caused the event; Access sets the ApplyType argument to one of the intrinsic constants acShowAllRecords, acApplyFilter, or acCloseFilterWindow. The event procedure can include different sets of statements for each alternative. The procedure runs before the filter is actually applied, before the filter is removed, or after the filter window is closed but before the form is redisplayed. Consequently, you can use the statements of the procedure to

- Modify the filter before it is applied. For example, you can read and change the Filter property.

- Change how the form is displayed when the filter is removed. For example, if you are filtering to select the orders that have been paid, you can hide controls on the Orders form that may be inappropriate for the filter such as the Amount Due.

- Undo or change actions that a macro or procedure took when the Filter event occurred. For example, if you hid controls on the Filter By Form interface when the Filter event occurred, you can show these controls after the filter is applied.

You can redisplay the second subform on the Customers Orders form as follows:

```
Private Sub Form_ApplyFilter(Cancel As Integer, ApplyType As
Integer)
Me.[Customer Orders Subform2].Visible = True
End Sub
```

**Changing the RecordSource Property**    After a form is open, you can change the form's RecordSource property to an SQL statement or a stored query that selects the records. For example:

1. Open the Customers form in Form view.

2. Type **Forms!Customers.RecordSource = "SELECT * FROM Customers WHERE Country = 'Argentina'"** in the Debug window and press Enter. The record source is changed and the selected records are displayed.

You cannot change a report's RecordSource property after the report is opened.

**Using the ApplyFilter Method**    Another way to change the records displayed in an open form, but not an open report, is to run the ApplyFilter method of the DoCmd object. You can use either the filtername argument to specify an existing filter query or the wherecondition argument to specify the records using a string expression that is a valid SQL WHERE clause without the word WHERE. The filter query can be a parameter query that obtains its information from controls on the same form, such as a selection combo box placed in the form's header, or from controls on another form, such as a custom dialog designed to collect selection criteria. The next section includes an example of using a parameter query as the filter query.

**Changing the Filter Property**    A form or report has a Filter property that you can use to specify records and a FilterOn property that you use to turn a filter on or off. The Filter property is a string expression that is a valid SQL WHERE clause without the word WHERE. After a form or report is open, you can set the Filter property to select the records. Set a Form's Filter property and then set the FilterOn property to True.

To explore the Filter property:

1. Open the Products By Category report in report Design view. Observe that the Filter property is blank and the FilterOn property is No. Switch to Print Preview.

2. Type **Reports![Products by Category].Filter = "CategoryName = 'Beverages'"** in the Debug window and press Enter. The Print Preview of the report does not change because the FilterOn property is No. Switch to Design view to note that the Filter property is changed to CategoryName = 'Beverages'.  Switch back to Print Preview.

3. Type **Reports![Products by Category].FilterOn = True** and press Enter. The report window changes to display the filtered records. Switch to Design view to note that the FilterOn property is changed to Yes.

4. Type **Reports![Products by Category].Filter = "CategoryName = 'Condiments'"** The report window changes to display the filtered records. Once the FilterOn property is Yes, you can change the filter simply by setting the Filter property.

5. Close the report. If you close the report without saving it, Access discards both the Filter and the FilterOn settings. If you close the report after saving it, Access discards the Filter setting but not the FilterOn setting.

# Finding a Group of Records Using Query By Form

A basic database operation is selecting a group of records that meet one or more selection criteria. For example, in the Order Status form you may want to display a list of orders for a particular customer, shipper, or employee; or you may want to review all orders taken by an employee after a specific date or all orders to be shipped by a specific shipper before a specified required date. When working interactively, you select a specific group of records by creating and applying a filter. Microsoft Access provides several ways to create filters interactively, including Filter For, Filter By Form, and Filter By Selection. These techniques give the user powerful ad hoc querying abilities. You can also customize these built-in techniques with programming as described in the preceding section. The following section describes another technique called Query By Form that you can use to provide a simple interface for selecting a group of records.

## The Query By Form Technique

The Query By Form technique is basically the same for both macro and VBA programming. Chapter 9 describes the Query By Form technique and automates the technique using macros. Here is a summary of the steps involved. (Refer to Chapter 9 for the specific details.)

- Select the field you want to use for the selection and make sure the field is included in the form's record source. For example, to select records for a customer in the frmOrderStatus form, add the CustomerID field from the Orders table to the form's record source.

- Place a unbound combo box in the form's header or footer that holds the search value for the selection field. Design the combo box to display a list for selecting the search value. For example, create a combo box named cboCustomer with a list that includes CustomerID as the combo box's (hidden) bound column and Company Name as the displayed column. (The user selects a company name and the combo box holds the corresponding customer ID.)

- Create a filter query based on the form's record source that selects records that match the search value held in the combo box. For example, to select orders for a customer in the Order Status form, create a filter query named qfltOrderStatus based on the form's record source and set the criteria for the CustomerID field to Forms!frmOrderStatus!cboCustomer.

- Create an event procedure that uses the ApplyFilter method of the DoCmd object to run the filter query and display the filtered records when the user changes the value in the combo box and the combo box recognizes the AfterUpdate event. For example, Listing 18.4 is the event procedure version of the macro shown in Table 9.4

### Listing 18.4

```
Private Sub cboCustomer_AfterUpdate()
DoCmd.ApplyFilter "qfltOrderStatus"
End Sub
```

When you work interactively, you can remove the filter by choosing the Remove Filter/Sort button in the Records menu. Chapter 9 shows how to automate the removal of the filter by placing a command button in the form header and using a macro to run the Show All Records macro action and then set the combo box value to Null to indicate that no records have been selected. The event procedure for the command button shown in Listing 18.5 is the VBA version of the macro shown in Table 9.5.

### Listing 18.5

```
Private Sub cmdShowAll_Click()
DoCmd.ShowAllRecords
cboCustomer = Null
End Sub
```

Another way to show all the records is to display a null row in the combo list; when the user selects the null row, all of the records are shown. Chapter 9 explains how to create a union query for the RowSource property of the combo box that displays a null row and how to modify the filter query to select all of the records when the user selects the null row in the combo list.

## Using Multiple Criteria to Select a Group of Records

Often you want to use more than one selection criteria. For example, you can use the frmOrderStatus form to find all orders for a customer that are handled by a specific employee. You can place a selection combo box in the form header for each field you want to use to select records, modify the filter query to include the additional criteria for each combo box, create an event procedure for each combo box that applies the filter, or modify the procedure that removes the filter so that the procedure sets all the combo boxes to null (see Figure 18.8). See the section "Using Multiple Criteria to Select a Group of Records" in Chapter 9 to create a selection combo box named cboEmployee and modify the filter query. You'll need to add the EmployeeID field from the Orders table to the form's record source before you can search by employee. The event procedure for the combo box is

```
Private Sub cboEmployee_AfterUpdate()
DoCmd.ApplyFiler "qfltOrderStatus"
End Sub
```

and the event procedure for the command button that removes the filter is

```
Private Sub cmdShowAll_Click()
DoCmd.ShowAllRecords
cboCustomer = Null
cboEmployee = Null
End Sub
```

**FIGURE 18.8:**

The combo boxes for selecting a customer and an employee and the command button for removing the filter.

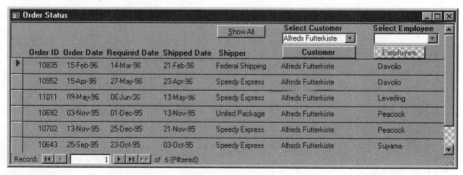

## Synchronizing Two Combo Boxes

When the list displayed in a combo box is long, you can use two combo boxes instead of one and design the pair so that the contents displayed by the second combo box depend on the value you select in the first—that is, *the second combo box is synchronized to the first*. For example, in an orders database, the list of customers typically contains several hundreds or thousands of names, so you can use one combo box to select the first letter (or pair of letters) and a second combo box to display the company names for all of the customers whose names begin with the letter (or combination). Chapter 9 shows how to use macro programming to synchronize two combo boxes for selecting a customer on the Customers form. The technique is the the same when you use VBA procedures. (Refer to Chapter 9 for the details.)

1. Place an unbound combo box named cboFind in the header of the Customers form that uses the event procedure shown in Listing 18.6 to look up a customer. Because the CustomerID has string values, the string expression for the argument of the FindFirst method contains an inner string (" & Me!Find & "); the procedure uses pairs of double quotes to identify the inner string within the outer string.

## Listing 18.6

```
Private Sub cboFind_AfterUpdate
Me.RecordsetClone FindFirst "CustomerID = """ & Me!cboFind & """"
Me.Bookmark = Me.Recordsetclone.Bookmark
End Sub
```

2. Place an unbound combo box named cboFirst in the form's header section that displays a list of the first letter of the customer ID and also displays a null row.

3. Create a new query named qrySecond for the row source for the cboFind combo box so that it displays either the customer names that have a CustomerID beginning with the letter displayed in the first combo box or displays all of the customer names if you haven't selected a letter in the first combo box. The query selects records for the cboFind combo box by using the value displayed in the first combo box on the form as the criteria for selecting records.

4. Create an event procedure that runs after you select a different value in the cboFirst combo box. The cboFirst_ AfterUpdate event procedure synchronizes the cboFind combo box by rerunning its query and then moves the focus to the cboFind combo box (see Figure 18.9). Listing 18.7 shows the event procedure that is analogous to the macro in Table 9.6. The procedure uses methods of the combo box instead of using the methods of the DoCmd object.

**Listing 18.7**

```
Private Sub cboFirst_AfterUpdate()
cboFind.Requery
cboFind.SetFocus
End Sub
```

**FIGURE 18.9:**

When you select a letter in the combo box on the left, an event procedure synchronizes the combo box on the right to display only the customers whose names begin with the selected letter.

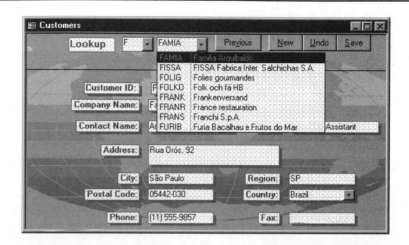

**TIP**

The Requery method of an object or a form is faster than the Requery method of the DoCmd object. When you run the Requery method of the DoCmd object, Access closes the query and then reloads it from the database. However, when you use the Requery method of an object of form, Access reruns the query without reloading it.

# Using a Multi-Select List Box to Filter Records

The selection techniques described in the previous sections are based on selecting records that satisfy a search condition. A fundamentally different technique uses the multi-select list box to display a list of choices and allows the user to choose records at random without using a search condition. This technique is more flexible than the other techniques because you can choose the individual records you want to display.

The standard list box allows you to select a single item from the list. However, you can use the MultiSelect property to choose more than one item. The MultiSelect property has the following values:

**None** to select a single item.

**Simple** to select multiple items by choosing each item separately.

**Extended** to extend the selection of multiple items. Press Shift+click or Shift+Arrow to extend the selection from the previously selected item to the current item.

You click to select an item and Ctrl+click to deselect an item in the list box.

To explore the multi-select list box, we can create a form that displays orders in a multi-select list box. We use a combo box to select an employee and synchronize the list box to the combo box by using an event procedure triggered by the combo box's AfterUpdate event. That event procedure displays orders in the list box corresponding to the value selected in the combo box.

1.  Create a new unbound form named frmAssignOrders. Set the following form properties:

    | | |
    |---|---|
    | Caption | Assign Orders |
    | ScrollBars | Neither |
    | RecordSelectors | No |
    | NavigationButtons | No |
    | MinMaxButtons | None |

2.  Place an unbound combo box named cboCurrent with the following properties

    | | |
    |---|---|
    | ColumnCount | 2 |
    | RowSource | SELECT EmployeeID, LastName & ", " & FirstName As FullName FROM Employees ORDER BY LastName; |
    | BoundColumn | 1 |
    | ColumnWidths | 0";1" |

3. Set the Caption property of the combo box label to Current Salesperson.

4. Create the parameter query named qrySortCountry as shown in Figure 18.10. This query uses the value of the EmployeeID chosen in the cboCurrent combo box to select records (Query By Form). We'll use this query as the row source for the multi-select list box.

**FIGURE 18.10:**

The parameter query for the list box gets its criteria from a combo box on the form.

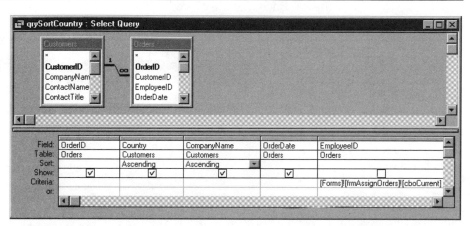

5. Create an unbound list box named lstOrders with the following properties:

| | |
|---|---|
| RowSource | qrySortCountry |
| ColumnCount | 4 |
| ColumnWidths | 0.5; 0.65; 1.5; 0.5 |
| Boundcolumn | 1 |
| MultiSelect | Simple |

6. Set the Caption property of the list box label to Orders assigned to current salesperson.

7. Create the event procedure shown in Listing 18.8. This event procedure requeries the list box when you choose a different employee in the cboCurrent combo box.

### Listing 18.8

```
Private Sub cboCurrent_AfterUpdate
lstOrders.Requery
End Sub
```

8. Save the form and switch to Form view. Select an employee in the Current Salesperson combo box. Figure 18.11 shows the form with the orders for Steven Buchanan displayed.

**FIGURE 18.11:**

The unbound Assign Orders form displays records from the Employees table as the row source of the combo box and records from a query based on the Orders and Customers tables as the row source of the multi-select list box. An event procedure keeps the list box synchronized to the combo box.

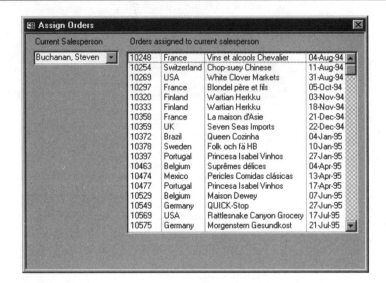

## Sorting List Box Rows by Changing the RowSource

You can make the list box more useful by allowing the user to sort the rows by any of the fields. One way to change the sort order of the rows in a list box or combo box is to change the RowSource property on-the-fly. We'll place a set of four command buttons along the bottom of the list box and use each button to change the list box's RowSource property to a different query.

1. Create the qrySortOrderID, qrySortCompany, and qrySortOrderDate queries as duplicates of qrySortCountry but with the following sort orders.

| Sort Query | OrderID | Country | CompanyName | OrderDate |
|---|---|---|---|---|
| qrySortOrderID | Ascending | | | |
| qrySortCompany | | Ascending | | |
| qrySortOrderDate | | | | Ascending |

2. Place a set of four command buttons named cmdSortOrderID, cmdSortCountry, cmdSortCompany, and cmdSortOrderDate along the bottom edge of the list box, with captions as shown in Figure 18.12.

---

**FIGURE 18.12:**

Changing the sort order by changing the RowSource property on-the-fly

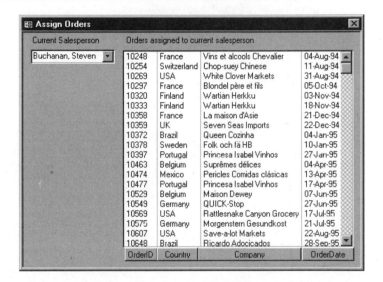

3. Create an event procedure for each command button that sets the RowSource property of the list box to the corresponding query. For example, Listing 18.9 shows the event procedure for the cmdSortOrderID button.

### Listing 18.9

```
Private Sub cmdSortOrderID_Click
Me!lstOrders.RowSource = "qrySortOrderID"
End Sub
```

4. Save the form and switch to Form view. Select Steven Buchanan and test the sorting buttons.

## Exploring the Multi-Select List Box

When you select multiple items in the list, Access creates a collection for the list box called the ItemsSelected collection. Each member of the ItemsSelected collection is an integer that refers to a selected row in the list box or combo box. Even though the members of the ItemsSelected collection are integers, their data type is Variant by default.

When you work with a multi-select list box, a row can have two index numbers: an index number for its position in the list box and another index number (or item number) for its position in the ItemsSelected collection. Both index numbers are zero-based. You can use the ListIndex property of the list box to determine the position of a row in the list box. When you select a row in a multi-select list box, Access automatically assigns it an item number. Since the ItemsSelected collection is also zero-based, the first item selected is referred to as ItemSelected(0), the second item selected is referred to as ItemSelected(1), and so on. If the first item selected is the fourth row of the list (with position number 3), then ItemSelected(0) returns 3.

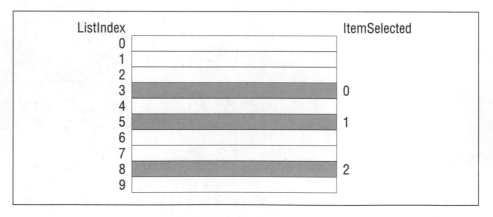

Both the ListIndex property and the ItemsSelected collection return a position number of a row. If you want to return the data in the row, you use the Column property or the ItemData method. You use the ItemData method to return the data in the bound column of a row specified by its position number. You use the Column property to return the data in a specific column of a row specified by its position number. Let's explore these concepts in the Debug window.

1. Select Steven Buchanan and click the OrderID sort button.

2. Open the Debug window by pressing Ctrl+G. Select row 3, row 6, and row 8 (see Figure 18.13a). We'll use the Count property to verify that three items are selected. Type **?Forms!frmAssignOrders!lstOrders.ItemsSelected .Count** and press Enter. The Debug window displays 3.

3. To display the row number corresponding to the second item in the collection, type **?Forms!frmAssignOrders!lstOrders.ItemsSelected(1)** and press enter. The Debug window displays 5. (Row 6 has position number 5.)

4. To display the data in the bound column of the second item in the collection, type **?Forms!frmAssignOrders!lstOrders.ItemData(5)** and press Enter. The Debug window displays the OrderID of the item 10333.

5. To display the data in any column of the second item in the collection, you use the Column property of the list box or combo box. The first argument of the Column property is the number of the column you want to display and the second argument is the number of the row; both are zero-based. So to display the second column of the second item in the collection, type **?Forms!frmAssignOrders!lstOrders.Column(1,5)** and press Enter. The Debug window displays Finland (see Figure 18.13b).

**FIGURE 18.13:**

Three rows selected in the multi-select list box (a). Use the Items-Selected collection to keep track of the selections in the list box and use the ItemData method or the Column property of the list box to display data (b).

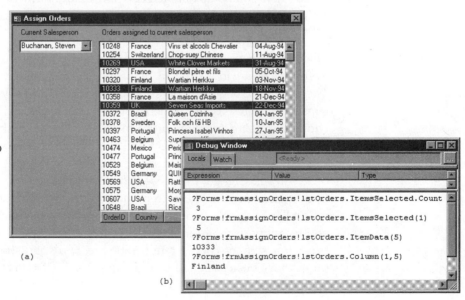

**Reassigning the Orders One at a Time**    Now that we have a way to allow the user to select arbitrary items in a list box, we can put the list box to work. Suppose that a new employee is hired and you want to reassign some orders that are currently assigned to other employees to the new employee. We place a second combo box on the form to display the name of the employee to whom we want to assign the orders and use a command button to perform the reassignments. After you select the orders you want to reassign, clicking the command button runs an event procedure that walks through the collection of selected orders. For each order in the collection, the procedure changes the name in the EmployeeID field to the new employee. When all orders have been re-assigned, the procedure displays all the orders currently assigned to the new employee.

All this work can take place in memory. The procedure opens a recordset on the Orders table. The fastest way to find the order corresponding to an item in the collection is to use the Seek method with the current index set to the OrderID index (that is, the PrimaryKey index). After finding the order, the procedure uses the Edit method to copy the record to the copy buffer, reassigns the employee, and then uses the Update method to save the changes.

1.  Place a new combo box named cboNew on the form. Set the RowSource, ColumnCount, BoundColumn, and ColumnWidths the same as for the cboCurrent combo box.

2.  Place a command button named cmdAssign on the form and create the event procedure in Listing 18.10 for the Click event of the command button. The procedure begins by determining whether current and new salespersons have been selected; it then displays a message and terminates if either choice is missing. Next the procedure determines whether any orders have been selected for reassignment and again displays a message and terminates if there are no selected orders. If there are salespersons selected and orders to be assigned, the procedure opens a table-type recordset on the Orders table and sets the current index to the primary key. The procedure uses a For Each...Next loop to loop through the collection of selected orders and reassigns each order in the collection. After reassigning the orders, the procedure sets the cboCurrent combo box to display the salesperson the orders have been assigned to and requeries the list box to display this person's orders.

## Listing 18.10

```
Private Sub cmdAssign_Click()
Dim db As Database, rst As Recordset, msg As String
Dim varNumber As Variant
If IsNull(cboCurrent) Or IsNull(cboNew) Then
    msg = "You must select a current employee and another"
    msg = msg & " employee you want to reassign orders to."
    MsgBox msg
    Exit Sub
End If
If lstOrders.ItemsSelected.Count = 0 Then
    MsgBox " You must select at least one order to reassign."
    Exit Sub
End If
Set db = CurrentDB
Set rst = db.OpenRecordset("Orders",dbOpenTable)
rst.Index = "PrimaryKey"
'set up the For Each loop through the collection
For Each varNumber In lstOrders.ItemsSelected
    rst.Seek "=", lstOrders.ItemData(varNumber)
    rst.Edit
    rst!EmployeeID = cboNew
    rst.Update
Next
cboCurrent = cboNew
cboNew = Null
lstOrders.Requery
End Sub
```

3. Save the form and switch to Form view. Select Steven Buchanan as the current salesperson and Laura Callahan as the new salesperson. Select orders with OrderIDs of 10649 and 10650 (see Figure 18.1).

4. Click the reassign button. The procedure reassigns the orders and displays Laura Callahan as the current salesperson. Click the OrderID button and verify that the two orders have been assigned to Laura Callahan.

FIGURE 18.14:

Reassigning selected
orders from one
employee to another

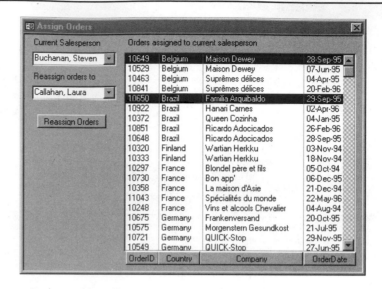

# Navigational Techniques of DAO versus Relational Techniques of SQL

When you want to work with a group of records in VBA procedures, you can use two fundamental sets of techniques: DAO techniques and SQL techniques.

**DAO Techniques**    With DAO techniques you can loop through a recordset and select or change one record at a time. For example, in the last section, we used DAO techniques to loop through the records chosen in a multi-select list box and edit one record at a time. DAO techniques are also called navigational techniques because you navigate through a recordset using a loop to examine a single record at a time.

**SQL Techniques**    SQL techniques are appropriate when you can define the group of records using a query or an SQL statement. You can create a selection query to select records or an action query to modify the group and then run the query in a single VBA statement. SQL techniques are also called relational techniques, or set techniques, because you define a group of records and the end result you want Jet to produce. However, you don't specify how the result is to be accomplished.

The SQL technique is almost always faster than the DAO technique because SQL relies on the built-in code of the Jet engine. Jet has its own optimized techniques for selecting and modifying records. When your VBA procedures use SQL techniques to select and modify records, you allow Jet to use its own optimized ways of producing the result you specify. Normally, you use navigational techniques only when either the group of records or the changes you want to make for each record cannot be readily specified using a query or an SQL statement.

# Using Stored Queries and SQL Statements

Using SQL techniques involves creating stored queries and writing SQL statements.

In Microsoft Access you can create queries in two ways: you can use the design grid in query Design view to create the query graphically, or you can use SQL view to create a query SQL as an *SQL statement*. SQL is the standard database language used by Microsoft Access and every other major database application. You use SQL to write a statement that describes the set of data that you want to retrieve.

SQL is designed to be software independent; in theory, it doesn't matter which software application you are using to actually retrieve the data. In practice, there are several dialects of SQL that are not completely interchangeable. (This book uses Access SQL to refer to the dialect used in Access.) You can use either SQL view or Design view to create and edit most kinds of queries. When you create a query in the design grid, Access creates the equivalent SQL statement. You can observe the SQL statement for a query by choosing View ➤ SQL or by selecting SQL View from the Query View button (on the toolbar when you are in Design view). Figure 18.15 shows the query Design view and the SQL view for the qrySortCompany query. The English language request for the data is

> List the OrderID, country, company name, and order date for all orders currently assigned to the employee chosen in the cboCurrent combo box on the frmAssignOrders form, sorted by company name.

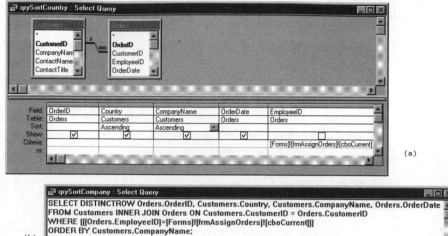

**FIGURE 18.15:**

The design view and SQL view for a query

## The Vocabulary and Grammar of SQL

An SQL statement is a request for data from a relational database. The statement contains the names of the tables and fields holding the data and additional information that defines the search and the action you want taken. SQL has a vocabulary of English words including about 100 special SQL keywords. The Access SQL keywords are usually shown in uppercase in the SQL views, although SQL keywords aren't case sensitive in Access. An SQL statement includes commands, clauses, operators, and group aggregate functions. Table 18.1 shows the seven commands in Access SQL that you can use to request a specific action. Table 18.2 shows the most common SQL keywords. (Both tables are on the disk under Tables\Chapter18.pdf.)

An SQL statement begins with one of the commands and includes one or more clauses that specify the data that the command applies to and provide additional information about the final result you are requesting. Each clause begins with a keyword, such as WHERE, ORDER BY, or FROM, and may include other SQL keywords; built-in functions (but not user-defined functions); field, table, or query names; expressions; constants; and references to controls on forms and reports.

Access SQL uses the punctuation shown in Table 18.3 (on the CD under Tables\Chapter18.pdf).

Although every query you create in the design grid has a corresponding SQL statement, there are some queries, called *SQL queries* or *SQL specific queries*, that you can create only as SQL statements in SQL view; these queries have no Design view equivalents. The SQL queries include the following six types:

**Union queries** are used to combine the results of two or more select queries into a single result when each of the select queries has the same number of columns and corresponding fields have the same data type.

**Non–equi join queries** are used to create joins that are not based on equality.

**Single-record append queries** are used to specify the value of each field in a single new record and then append the record to an existing table or query.

**Data definition queries** are used to create, modify, or delete a table or create or delete an index on a table.

**Subqueries** are used when a query depends on the result of another query.

**Pass-through queries** are used to send commands that retrieve records or change data directly to an SQL database server.

## Stored Queries versus SQL Statements: Performance Considerations

After you create a query in Design or SQL view, you can do one of the following:

- Save it as a *stored* query listed in the Database window and enter the name of the query wherever you need to use it

- Enter the SQL statement directly in a property setting, macro action argument, or VBA statement

Although you can use either a stored query or an SQL statement in any situation that requires a query, in most cases using a stored query gives the best performance. When you store a query as a database object, Access analyzes the query and stores an optimized version. When you run the stored query, you are running an optimized version. If you change the query, Access analyzes it again the next time you run it and stores the newly optimized version. On the other hand, every time you run an SQL statement, Access analyzes the statement and determines the optimal way to execute it. Because the analysis and optimization take time, the SQL statement usually executes more slowly than the equivalent stored query.

## Using Stored Queries and SQL Statements in VBA Procedures

Most VBA procedures involve a mixture of stored queries and SQL statements. Learning to write SQL statements directly is a useful skill. As you continue with your work with relational databases, you will eventually develop SQL skills; however, you don't have to conquer SQL immediately. Instead you can ease into SQL by using the query Design view to create the query (unless you are creating an SQL specific query). After creating the draft, switch to SQL view, copy the SQL statement or clause, switch the the Module window, and paste the SQL statement or clause into the VBA procedure. The hard part is modifying the SQL statement or clause to include VBA variables and then expressing the result as a text string that Jet can understand.

# Creating New Stored Queries in VBA Procedures

A query is a set of instructions or definitions for retrieving and modifying data. When you work interactively, you create a new query and save it as a Database window object in the current database. When you work with queries directly in VBA, you refer to a stored query as a QueryDef object, one of the data access objects that is managed by Jet. As Chapter 11 explains, a QueryDef object is a member of the QueryDefs collection (the collection of all stored queries), and the QueryDefs collection belongs to the Database object in a database created with the Jet database engine. See Chapter 11 for more information on the relationships between the data access objects.

> **NOTE**
>
> A new feature in Access 97 is that you can bypass the Jet engine and work directly with an ODBC database using another database engine such as Microsoft SQL Server. In this case the QueryDefs collection belongs to the Connection object instead of the Database object. This chapter assumes you are using the Jet database engine and makes no further reference to the Connection object.

You can create new stored queries in VBA procedures using the CreateQueryDef method of the Database object. Because this method creates an object, you can declare an object variable to point to the new object. The syntax for declaring the variable and creating a new Querydef object in a database is

```
Dim qdf As QueryDef, db As Database
Set qdf = db.CreateQueryDef(name, sqlstatement)
```

where qdf is an object variable that refers to the new querydef object you are creating, db is an object variable that refers to an open database object that will contain the new querydef, *name* is an optional string expression that identifies (names) the new querydef, and *sqlstatement* is an optional valid SQL statement expressed as a string. If you specify a valid name as the first argument of the method, Access automatically saves the new querydef object as a query in the Database window and appends the object to the QueryDefs collection.

If you omit an argument in the statement that creates the new query, you can use the Name and SQL properties of the QueryDef object to define the query as follows:

```
Set qdf = db.CreateQueryDef()
qdf.Name = name
qdf.SQL = sqlstatement
```

If you omit the *name* argument and use the Name property to define the query, Access doesn't automatically save the new queryDef. You have to append the QueryDef object to the QueryDefs collection as follows:

```
db.QueryDefs.Append qdf.Name
```

You can create a *temporary querydef* object by setting the *name* argument to the zero-length string. Because the zero-length string is not a valid name, the new QueryDef object cannot be saved to the database. Therefore, when the procedure ends, the temporary QueryDef object ceases to exist.

As examples, we'll create a few new stored queries.

**Creating a New Select Query**     We'll create a new select query to find the customers who placed orders after a specified date.

1.  Open a new module named basQueryDefs. We'll design a query in query Design view and paste the SQL statement into a new VBA procedure.

2. Open query Design view and create a query based on the Orders and Customers tables that returns the company name, contact name, and order date for each order placed after 7/1/95. Figure 18.16a shows the Design view for the query. When you create a query in query Design view, Access always includes the table name for each field and may include redundant sets of parentheses in the corresponding SQL statement. The table name is required only when you have fields with the same name in two or more tables (or other nested queries) in the query. In Figure 18.16b the redundant parentheses and optional table names have been eliminated. When you strip out redundant parentheses and table names, switch to SQL view and run the query to make sure the SQL statement is still valid. Copy the SQL statement to the clipboard. Do not close the query window because we'll use this query in the next example.

3. Enter the procedure shown in Listing 18.11 in the basQueryDefs module. We'll name the new stored query qryRecentCustomers. When you paste the SQL statement shown in Figure 18.16b, you'll need to reconnect the three lines into a single line of code. After reconnecting the pieces of the SQL statement, you can rebreak it to make your code more readable. VBA won't let you use the line continuation character to break an SQL statement but you can concatenate the pieces as shown below. After creating the new query, the procedure refreshes the Database window and terminates.

**FIGURE 18.16:**

You can create most SQL statements by creating the query graphically and switching to SQL view.

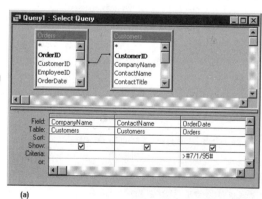

### Listing 18.11

```
Public Sub NewStoredQuery()
Dim db As Database, qdf As QueryDef, strSQL As String
strSQL = "SELECT CompanyName, ContactName, OrderDate FROM "
strSQL = strSQL & "Customers INNER JOIN Orders ON "
strSQL = strSQL & "Customers.CustomerID = Orders.CustomerID "
strSQL = strSQL & "WHERE OrderDate > #4/1/95#;"
Set db = CurrentDB
Set qdf = db.CreateQueryDef("qryRecentCustomers", strSQL)
RefreshDatabaseWindow
End Sub
```

4. Run the procedure in the Debug window by typing **NewStoredQuery** in the Immediate pane and pressing Enter. Switch to the Database window; the qryRecentCustomers query appears in the refreshed list. Select the query and double-click to run it. Figure 18.17 shows the datasheet for the new stored query.

5. Delete the qryRecentCustomers query.

**FIGURE 18.17:**

The datasheet for a query created in a procedure

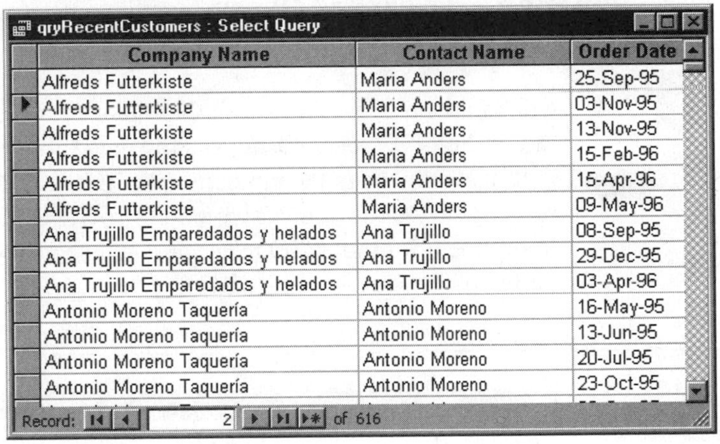

| Company Name | Contact Name | Order Date |
|---|---|---|
| Alfreds Futterkiste | Maria Anders | 25-Sep-95 |
| Alfreds Futterkiste | Maria Anders | 03-Nov-95 |
| Alfreds Futterkiste | Maria Anders | 13-Nov-95 |
| Alfreds Futterkiste | Maria Anders | 15-Feb-96 |
| Alfreds Futterkiste | Maria Anders | 15-Apr-96 |
| Alfreds Futterkiste | Maria Anders | 09-May-96 |
| Ana Trujillo Emparedados y helados | Ana Trujillo | 08-Sep-95 |
| Ana Trujillo Emparedados y helados | Ana Trujillo | 29-Dec-95 |
| Ana Trujillo Emparedados y helados | Ana Trujillo | 03-Apr-96 |
| Antonio Moreno Taquería | Antonio Moreno | 16-May-95 |
| Antonio Moreno Taquería | Antonio Moreno | 13-Jun-95 |
| Antonio Moreno Taquería | Antonio Moreno | 20-Jul-95 |
| Antonio Moreno Taquería | Antonio Moreno | 23-Oct-95 |

qryRecentCustomers : Select Query

Record: 2 of 616

## Breaking SQL Statements in VBA Code

When using SQL statements in VBA code, you can break the statement into pieces to make your code more readable. Assign the first piece of the SQL statement to a string variable, such as strSQL, and then concatenate the second piece to the string variable and assign the result to the string variable, and so on. For example, the SQL statement SELECT * FROM Orders WHERE OrderDate > #7/1/96#; can be written as three lines of code as follows:

```
strSQL = "SELECT * "
srtSQL = strSQL & "FROM Orders "
strSQL = strSQL & "WHERE Order Date > #7/1/96#;"
```

Each piece must include spaces at the beginning or end so that the final concatenated expression reproduces the original SQL statement exactly.

**Creating a New Action Query**    We'll convert the select query we just created to an action query that creates a new table.

1. Click in the query and choose the Make Table command from the Query menu. Enter tblRecentOrders as the new table name. Figure 18.18 shows the SQL view for the make table query with the redundant parenthesis and unnecessary table names stripped out. The SQL statement for a make table query includes the INTO *tablename* clause to specify the name of the new table.

**FIGURE 18.18:**

The SQL statement for Make Table query

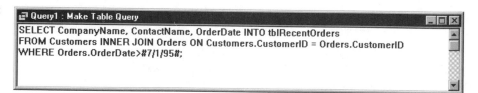

```
Query1 : Make Table Query
SELECT CompanyName, ContactName, OrderDate INTO tblRecentOrders
FROM Customers INNER JOIN Orders ON Customers.CustomerID = Orders.CustomerID
WHERE Orders.OrderDate>#7/1/95#;
```

2. Enter the NewActionQuery() procedure in the basQueryDefs module as shown in Listing 18.12. This procedure creates the new querydef object and then sets the SQL property to the SQL statement.

### Listing 18.12

```
Public Sub NewActionQuery()
Dim db As Database, qdf As QueryDef, strSQL As String
strSQL = "SELECT CompanyName, ContactName, OrderDate "
strSQL = strSQL & "INTO tblRecentOrders "
strSQL = strSQL & "FROM Customers INNER JOIN Orders ON "
strSQL = strSQL & "Customers.CustomerID = Orders.CustomerID "
strSQL = strSQL & "WHERE OrderDate > #5/1/96#;"
Set db = CurrentDB
Set qdf = db.CreateQueryDef("qryRecentCustomers")
qdf.SQL = strSQL
RefreshDatabaseWindow
End Sub
```

3. Run the procedure in the Debug window. Switch to the Database window and note the new action query. Select the new action query and double-click to run it. Access runs the query and creates the table.

4. Delete the new query and table.

**Creating a Temporary Query** We'll create a temporary query that selects records for recent customers. The new query ceases to exist when the procedure ends.

1. Enter the NewTemporaryQuery() shown in Listing 18.13 in the basQueryDefs module. The NewTemporaryQuery is identical to the procedure in the previous example except the zero-length string is used as the name argument for the query.

### Listing 18.13

```
Public Sub NewTemporaryQuery()
Dim db As Database, qdf As QueryDef, strSQL As String
strSQL = "SELECT CompanyName, ContactName, OrderDate "
strSQL = strSQL & "INTO tblRecentOrders "
strSQL = strSQL & "FROM Customers INNER JOIN Orders ON "
strSQL = strSQL & "Customers.CustomerID = Orders.CustomerID "
```

```
strSQL = strSQL & "WHERE OrderDate > #5/1/96#;"
Set db = CurrentDB
Set qdf = db.CreateQueryDef("")
qdf.SQL = strSQL
RefreshDatabaseWindow
End Sub
```

2. Run the procedure in the Debug window. When you run the procedure, VBA creates the new query but can't save it because the name isn't valid. Switch to the Database window and note that the list of queries hasn't changed.

**NOTE**   In the remainder of this chapter, db is an object variable of the Database type that refers to an open database, rst is an object variable of the Recordset Type, and qdf is an object variable of the QueryDef type. Also, sqlstatement represents a valid SQL statement expressed as a string.

# Running Select Queries in VBA Procedures

A select query retrieves data from the database and returns a set of records to memory. By contrast, an action query modifies the data in the database but returns no records to memory. This section describes procedures for running select queries, and the next section describes running action queries.

## Running a Stored Select Query

To run a stored select query you can use either the OpenQuery method of the DoCmd object or the OpenRecordset method.

### Using the OpenQuery Method of the DoCmd Object    Use the OpenQuery method of the DoCmd object when you want to run a select or crosstab query and display a query window in one of its views. The syntax for the OpenQuery method is

```
DoCmd.OpenQuery queryname,view,datamode
```

where *queryname* is a string expression that is the valid name of a query in the current database, *view* is an optional intrinsic constant for specifying the view (acNormal, acDesign, and acPreview), and *datamode* is an optional intrinsic constant for specifying the data mode (acAdd, acEdit, and acReadOnly). The default view is Normal view, and the default data mode is Edit. For example, to run the qryRecentCustomers that the NewStoredQuery procedure creates, add the statement

```
DoCmd.OpenQuery "qryRecentOrders"
```

following the statement that creates the query. When you run the procedure, the procedure creates the new stored query, runs it, and opens the datasheet to display the records.

**Using the OpenRecordset Method**    You use the OpenRecordset method to run a stored select query and return the result as a recordset in memory instead of in a query window. You can use the OpenRecordset method of the Database object as follows:

```
Set rst = db.OpenRecordset(queryname,type,options,lockedits)
```

*queryname* is the name of an existing select query; *type* is an optional intrinsic constant that specifies the type of recordset (dbOpenDynaset, dbOpenSnapshot, dbOpenForwardOnly); *options* is an optional combination of integer constants that you use to specify the characteristics of the recordset such as dbAppendOnly, dbDenyWrite, and dbReadOnly; and *lockedits* is an optional constant that determines the locking for the recordset. (You cannot open a table-type recordset on a query.)

You can also create separate object variables for the query and the recordset and use the OpenRecordset method of the querydef object as follows:

```
Set qdf = db.QueryDefs(queryname)
Set rst = qdf.OpenRecordset(type,options,lockedits)
```

As an example, you can modify the NewStoredQuery procedure to run the qryRecentCustomers query and return the results to memory without displaying a datasheet. To do so, declare rst as an object variable for the recordset object created in memory and add statements to create a recordset as follows:

```
Dim rst As Recordset
Set rst = db.OpenRecordset ("qryRecentCustomers")
```

When you run the procedure, the stored query and the recordset are created. The recordset is destroyed when the procedure finishes.

## Running an SQL Statement

When you don't need to store a select query and you don't need to display a query window, you don't have to create a Querydef at all. In fact, you can just run the SQL statement to create the recordset in memory using the OpenRecordset method of the database object.

To run an SQL statement for a select query, you use the OpenRecordset method of the Database object as follows:

```
Set rst = db.OpenRecordset(sqlstatement)
```

For example, the NewSQLStatement() procedure shown in Listing 18.14 creates a recordset for working with the data for recent customers without creating a querydef object. The procedure prints the order date for each selected record to the Debug window.

### Listing 18.14

```
Public Sub NewSQLStatement()
Dim db As Database, rst As Recordset, strSQL As String
strSQL = "SELECT CompanyName, ContactName, OrderDate "
strSQL = strSQL & "FROM Customers INNER JOIN Orders ON "
strSQL = strSQL & "Customers.CustomerID = Orders.CustomerID "
strSQL = strSQL & "WHERE OrderDate > #6/1/96#;"
Set db = CurrentDB
Set rst = db.OpenRecordset(strSQL)
Do Until rst.EOF
    Debug.Print rst!CompanyName & ": " & rst!OrderDate
    rst.MoveNext
Loop
End Sub
```

1.  Insert the NewSQLStatement procedure in the basQueryDefs module.

2.  Type **NewSQLStatement** in the Immediate pane of the Debug window and press Enter. The results of the SQL statement are printed (see Figure 18.19).

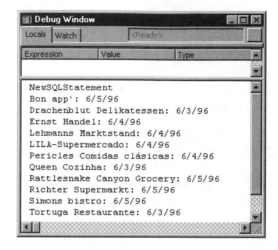

**FIGURE 18.19:**

When you don't need to store a select query and you don't need to display a query window, you can run the SQL statement to create the recordset in memory.

## Sorting and Filtering a Recordset

When you want to sort and filter a recordset, you can use either SQL techniques or the Sort and Filter properties of the recordset.

**Using SQL Techniques to Sort and Filter a Recordset**     If you can define a group of records using an SQL statement, the fastest way to sort or filter the records is to modify the SQL statement to include clauses for the sort and filter and use the modified SQL statement to simultaneously define and sort or filter the records.

As an example, the SQLSortFilter procedure shown in Listing 18.15 uses an SQL statement to select records from the Customers table, filter the records to obtain only the customers from Germany, and then sort the records by company name. The procedure prints the filtered and sorted recordset in the Debug window. You can enter the procedure in a new module named basGroups and run the procedure in the Debug window.

### Listing 18.15

```
Public Sub SQLSortFilter()
Dim db As DATABASE, rst As Recordset
Set db = CurrentDb
Set rst = db.OpenRecordset("SELECT * FROM Customers WHERE Country
➡ = 'Germany' ORDER BY CompanyName")
```

```
Do Until rst.EOF
    Debug.Print rst!CompanyName
    rst.MoveNext
Loop
End Sub
```

1. Create a new module named basGroups and insert the SQLSortFilter procedure.

2. Type **SQLSortFilter** in the Immediate pane of the Debug window and press Enter.

**Using the Sort and Filter Properties of a Recordset**   You can use the Sort and Filter properties to sort and filter an existing recordset. When you use these properties, the existing recordset is not affected and you must create a second recordset based on the first in order to see the effects of the settings.

### Sorting a Dynaset or Snapshot-Type Recordset

You can use the Sort property to sort an existing dynaset or snapshot-type recordset. You set the Sort property to a string expression that is an ORDER BY clause of a valid SQL statement but without the ORDER BY phrase. You cannot use the Sort property to sort a table-type recordset. The DAOSort procedure in Listing 18.16 creates a dynaset-type recordset for the Customers table, sets the Sort property to sort the records by country, and creates a second recordset based on the first that includes the effect of the sort. The procedure uses Do Until loops to print the company names for both the unsorted and the sorted recordsets (see Figure 18.20).

### Listing 18.16

```
Public Sub DAOSort()
Dim rst As Recordset, rstSort As Recordset
Set rst = CurrentDb.OpenRecordset("Employees", dbOpenDynaset)
rst.Sort = "City"
Set rstSort = rst.OpenRecordset()
Debug.Print "Unsorted list:"
Do Until rst.EOF
    Debug.Print rst!LastName
    rst.MoveNext
Loop
Debug.Print "Sorted by City:"
Do Until rstSort.EOF
```

```
        Debug.Print rstSort!LastName
        rstSort.MoveNext
    Loop
    End Sub
```

**FIGURE 18.20:**

When you use the Sort property of a recordset, you have to create a second recordset based on the first to see the effect of the Sort.

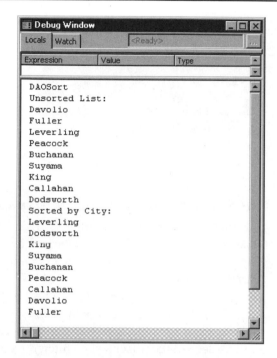

## Using the Index Property to Sort a Table-Type Recordset

You sort a table-type recordset by setting its Index property to an existing index for the table. You must use the Index property to sort a table-type recordset, and you can't use the Sort property. The DAOSortTable procedure in Listing 18.17 begins by creating a table-type recordset for the Customers table and printing the city and company name in primary key order. The procedure sets the current index to sort the records by city (one of the existing indexes for the table), moves the current record pointer back to the first record, and prints the city and company names for the sorted recordsets in the Debug window.

### Listing 18.17

```
Public Sub DAOSortTable()
Dim rst As Recordset, rstSort As Recordset
Set rst = CurrentDb.OpenRecordset("Customers", dbOpenTable)
Debug.Print "Sorted by Primary Key:"
Do Until rst.EOF
    Debug.Print rst!City & " " & rst!CompanyName
    rst.MoveNext
Looprst.Index = "City"
rst.MoveFirst

Debug.Print "Sorted by City:"Do Until rst.EOF
    Debug.Print rst!City & " " & rst!CompanyName
    rst.MoveNext
Loop
End Sub
```

### Filtering a Dynaset or Snapshot-Type Recordset

You use the Filter property to filter the records in a dynaset- or snapshot-type recordset. You cannot filter the records of a table-type recordset. Set the Filter property of the recordset to a string expression that is the WHERE clause of a valid SQL statement without the word *WHERE*. After setting the Filter property you must create a second recordset object based on the first to see the effect of the filter. The DAOFilter procedure in Listing 18.18 opens a dynaset-type recordset on the Employees table, sets the filter to select employees from London, and then creates a second recordset for the filtered records. The procedure prints the last name for records from the unfiltered and the filtered recordsets (see Figure 18.21).

### Listing 18.18

```
Public Sub DAOFilter()
Dim rst As Recordset, rstFilter As Recordset
Set rst = CurrentDb.OpenRecordset("Employees", dbOpenDynaset)
rst.Filter = "City = 'London'"
Set rstFilter = rst.OpenRecordset()
Debug.Print " Unfiltered recordset: All employees"
Do Until rst.EOF
    Debug.Print rst!LastName & ":   " & rst!City
    rst.MoveNext
```

```
Loop
Debug.Print "Filtered recordset: Employees from London"
Do Until rstFilter.EOF
    Debug.Print rstFilter!LastName & ":    " & rstFilter!City
    rstFilter.MoveNext
Loop
End Sub
```

**FIGURE 18.21:**

When you use the Filter property of a recordset, you must create a new recordset based on the original recordset to see the effect of the filter.

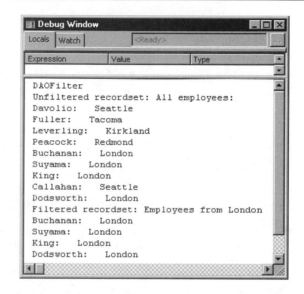

The procedures in Listings 18.16, 18.17, and 18.18 create a second object variable for the sorted or filtered recordset so that both the original and the sorted or filtered recordsets can be used in the procedure, for example, for printing to the Debug window. If you don't need to work with both recordsets, you can avoid the memory burden of two recordsets by reusing the object variable. The following code snippet reuses the rst object variable and also shows how you can combine sorting and filtering:

```
Set rst = db.OpenRecordset(sqlstatement)
rst.Sort = strSortCondition
rst.Filter = strFilterCondition
Set rst = rst.OpenRecordset()
```

# Making Bulk Changes to a Recordset with Action Queries

When you run an action query or a data definition query, records are not produced in a datasheet or in memory. (See the next section for more information on data definition queries.)

## Running a Stored Action Query

To run a stored action query in a VBA procedure you can use either the OpenQuery method of the DoCmd object or the Execute method.

### Using the OpenQuery Method of the DoCmd Object    The syntax for
the OpenQuery method for running an action query is

```
DoCmd.OpenQuery queryname
```

where *queryname* is a string expression for the name of a stored action query in the current database.

For example, you can run the qryRecentCustomers make-table query created in the NewActionQuery example by adding the following statement after the statements that define the query:

```
DoCmd.OpenQuery "qryRecentCustomers"
```

When you run the modified procedure, both the stored make-table query and the table are created.

> **NOTE**   If you don't want to display the default confirmation messages that Access displays when you run an action query, use the SetWarnings method of the DoCmd object to suppress system messages. Set the warningson argument to False to turn off the messages before you run the action query. When you turn off system warnings in a procedure, you must turn them back on by setting the warningson argument to True. By contrast, when you turn off system warnings in a macro, Access turns the warnings back on automatically when the macro terminates.

**Using the Execute Method**    Both the QueryDef and the Database objects have Execute methods that you can use to run a stored action query. The syntax for the Execute method of the QueryDef object is

```
qdf.Execute options
```

and of the Database object is

```
db.Execute source, options
```

where *source* is a string expression that is the name of the stored action query (or an SQL statement). In either statement, the *options* argument is an optional integer constant that specifies the characteristics of the query, including

| Options Constant | Description |
| --- | --- |
| dbDenyWrite | Denies write permission to other users. |
| dbInconsistent | Executes inconsistent updates. |
| dbConsistent | Executes consistent updates. |
| dbSQLPassThrough | Causes the SQL statement to be passed to an ODBC database for processing. |
| dbFailOnError | Rolls back updates if an error occurs. |
| dbSeeChanges | Generates an error if another user changes the data you are editing. |
| dbRunAsync | Executes the query asynchronously (for ODBCDirect only). |
| dbExecDirect | Executes the statement without first calling the SQLPrepare function (ODBCDirect only). |

> **WARNING**    If any records are locked when you run the Execute method for an update or delete query, the method will not update or delete the records that are locked. Nevertheless, the Execute method does not fail, and there is no indication of the locked records. To avoid the data inconsistencies caused by locked records, always use the dbFailOnError option for an update or delete query to roll back all successful changes if any of the records affected by the action query are locked.

For example, we'll use the Execute method to run a make-table query.

1.  Modify the NewActionQuery procedure (see Listing 18.12) as shown in Listing 18.19.

### Listing 18.19

```
Public Sub NewActionQuery()
Dim db As Database, qdf As QueryDef, strSQL As String
strSQL = "SELECT CompanyName, ContactName, OrderDate "
strSQL = strSQL & "INTO tblRecentOrders "
strSQL = strSQL & "FROM Customers INNER JOIN Orders ON "
strSQL = strSQL & "Customers.CustomerID = Orders.CustomerID "
strSQL = strSQL & "WHERE OrderDate > #4/1/95#;"
Set db = CurrentDB
Set qdf = db.CreateQueryDef("qryRecentCustomers")
qdf.SQL = strSQL
qdf.Execute dbFailOnError
RefreshDatabaseWindow
End Sub
```

2.  Switch to the Database window and delete qryRecentCustomers and tblRecentOrders, if necessary, and then run the procedure in the Debug window.

> **NOTE**  Use the RecordsAffected property of the QueryDef or Database object to determine the number of records affected by the Execute method.

## Running an SQL Statement for an Action or Data Definition Query

You can create SQL statements for action queries and for data definition queries.

**SQL Statements for Action Queries**    You can create SQL statements for the four kinds of action queries that modify tables by designing the query in query Design view and switching to SQL view. Table 18.4 (on the CD under Tables\Chapter18.pdf) shows the SQL commands and examples for the four action queries. The table also includes an example for the SQL-specific query for appending a single record. The SQL commands for action queries are called the *data manipulation language* (DML) commands.

### SQL Statements for Data Definition Queries

You can also use SQL statements to create SQL-specific queries for defining and modifying new tables, fields, and indexes. These queries are called data-definition queries and use commands called the *data definition language* (DDL) commands. Table 18.5 (on the CD under Tables\Chapter18.pdf) shows the commands and examples. The data definition queries do not produce recordsets, so you run them the same way that you run SQL statements for action queries.

> **NOTE**
>
> When you want to delete all of the records from a table, you can use a DELETE query or a DROP TABLE statement. When you use a DELETE query, only the data is deleted and the table definition remains. However, when you use a DROP TABLE statement, the table definition is removed from the database.

Access SQL has its own data types, which are shown in Table 18.6 (on the CD under Tables\Chapter18.pdf).

### Using the RunSQL Method of the DoCmd Object

You can run an SQL statement for an action or data definition query, using the RunSQL method of the DoCmd object. The syntax is

```
DoCmd.RunSQL sqlstatement
```

where *sqlstatement* is a string expression that is a valid SQL statement. The maximum length of the sqlstatement string is 32,768 characters (in contrast to the 256-character maximum length for the corresponding RunSQL macro action).

For example, Listing 18.20 shows a procedure to alter a table by adding a Salary field with the Currency data type to the Employees table.

### Listing 18.20

```
Public Sub DDLAlterTable()
Dim strSQL As String
```

```
strSQL = "ALTER TABLE Employees ADD COLUMN Salary CURRENCY;"
DoCmd.RunSQL strSQL
End Sub
```

1. Insert the DDLAfterTable procedure in the basGroups module.

2. Run the procedure in the Debug window. Open the Employees table and note the new Salary field.

**Using the Execute Method of the Database Object**    You can use the Execute method of the Database object to run an SQL statement for an action or data definition query as follows:

```
db.Execute sqlstatement, options
```

*sqlstatement* is a string expression for the SQL statement, and *options* is an optional combination of constants that determine the data integrity of the query. For example, you can delete the records in the tblRecentCustomers tables by using the DeleteRecords procedure in Listing 18.21.

### Listing 18.21

```
Public Sub DeleteRecords()
Dim db As Database
Set db = CurrentDB
db.Execute "DELETE * FROM tblRecentCustomers;"
End Sub
```

You can remove a table from the database by using the procedure shown in Listing 18.22.

### Listing 18.22

```
Public Sub DDLDropTable()
Dim db As Database
Set db = CurrentDB
db.Execute "DROP TABLE tblRecentCustomers"
End Sub
```

## Reassigning a Group of Records

We'll use these techniques to modify the frmAssignOrders form created in the section "Using a Multi-Select List Box to Filter Records." This time we are adding the capability to reassign all an employee's orders to another employee. The procedure begins by testing the employee combo boxes; it displays a message and ends if either combo box is empty. If both employees have been selected, the procedure runs an SQL statement to change the EmployeeID field for the orders displayed in the list box from the current to the new employee. After running the SQL statement, the procedure displays the set of all orders for the new employee by setting the current combo box to the new employee, setting the new employee combo box to null, and requerying the list box.

1. Open the frmAssignOrders form in Design view and add a command button named cmdAssignAll.

2. Enter the event procedure shown in Listing 18.23.

### Listing 18.23

```
Private Sub cmdAssignAll_Click()
Dim db As Database, rst As Recordset
Dim varNumber As Variant, strSQL As String, str As String
If IsNull(cboCurrent) Or IsNull(cboNew) Then
    str = "You must select a current employee and another"
    str = str & "employee you want to reassign orders to."
    MsgBox str
    Exit Sub
End If
Set db = CurrentDB
strSQL = "UPDATE Orders SET EmployeeID = " & cboNew
strSQL = strSQL & " WHERE EmployeeID = " & cboCurrent
db.Execute strSQL, dbFailOnError
cboCurrent = cboNew
cboNew = Null
lstOrders.Requery
End Sub
```

3. Save the form and switch to Form view. Choose Robert King as the current salesperson and Margaret Peacock as the new salesperson (see Figure 18.22). Click the Assign All Orders button. All of Robert King's orders are reassigned to Margaret Peacock.

FIGURE 18.22:

The Reassign All Orders
button executes an SQL
statement to reassign
Mr. King's orders to
Ms. Peacock.

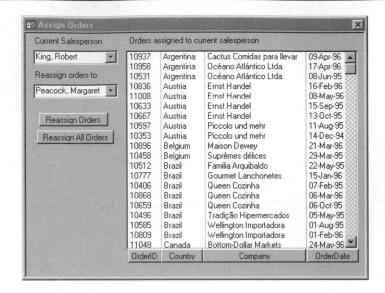

# Transactions

A *transaction* is a group of changes that you want to treat as a single operation.
When you define a transaction, the Jet engine keeps track of the changes made,
storing the changes in a temporary database in memory until all of the transaction's changes have been made. (If enough memory isn't available, Jet creates the
temporary database on your computer's hard disk.) If an error occurs while the
group of changes is being processed, none of the changes are updated to the database. If an error does not occur, when the last change is made, the entire group of
changes is updated to the current database. Transactions are an important way to
maintain the integrity of your data when you are making a series of changes to
your data. For example, in an archive process, old records are appended to
archive tables and then deleted from current tables. If a power failure occurs
between the two queries, old records exist in both the archive and current tables.
By running the queries inside a transaction, you can avoid this kind of data
inconsistency.

## Implicit and Explicit Transactions

Jet uses two kinds of transactions: implicit and explicit. When you run a single
query either as a stored query or an SQL statement, Jet runs the query and makes

all the necessary changes in a temporary database in memory as an *implicit transaction*. When all changes have been made, Jet updates the tables involved. If the power fails while a query is running, when you next open the database Access may inform you that the database needs to be repaired. When you repair the database, Jet undoes any partial updates that may have occurred when the power failed. By contrast, when you want to run more than one query or several statements as a transaction, you must use statements that define an explicit transaction. You can define an *explicit transaction* only in VBA, not in macro programming.

> **NOTE**
>
> The new UseTransaction property in Access 97 lets you specify whether Jet runs a single action query as an implicit transaction. By default, the UseTransaction property setting is Yes, or True, and the action query is run as an implicit transaction. If the action query is a delete or update query, Jet must lock a large number of records until all the changes have been made. Setting the UseTransaction property to No in the query's property sheet, or to False in a VBA procedure, may result in a substantial performance improvement because Jet doesn't have to store the intermediate results in a temporary database and doesn't have to lock a large number of records. UseTransaction is an application-defined property (see Chapter 19 for information on such properties) and applies only to action queries.

Chapter 11 describes Jet's Workspace object as the data access object that manages transactions. You can use methods of the Workspace object to begin and end a transaction as follows:

- The BeginTrans method begins a new transaction

- The CommitTrans method ends the current transaction and saves the changes to the database

- The Rollback method ends the current transaction and restores the database to the state it was in when the transaction started.

To explore transactions, we'll modify one of the procedures for assigning orders from one employee to another. An important use of transactions is to give the user the option to undo the deletion of records.

1. Modify the cmdAssignAll procedure that assigns all of an employee's orders to another employee (see Listing 18.23) as shown in Listing 18.24. The modified procedure in Listing 18.24 creates ws as an object variable that points to the default workspace. The transaction begins just before the statement that executes the SQL statement to update the records. Because of the ws.BeginTrans statement, the changes required by the SQL statement are retained in memory and are not written to the database. The Msgbox asks if you want to save the changes. If you click the Yes button, the CommitTrans method saves the changes to the database; otherwise, the Rollback method discards the changes.

## Listing 18.24

```
Private Sub cmdAssignAll_Click()
Dim db As Database, rst As Recordset, strSQL As String
Dim ws As Workspace, msg As String
If IsNull(cboCurrent) Or IsNull(cboNew) Then
    msg = "You must select a current employee and another"
    msg = msg & "employee you want to reassign orders to."
    MsgBox msg

    Exit Sub
End If
Set db = CurrentDB
Set ws = DBEngine.Workspaces(0)
strSQL = "UPDATE Orders SET EmployeeID = " & cboNew
strSQL = strSQL & " WHERE EmployeeID = " & cboCurrent
ws.BeginTrans
db.Execute strSQL, dbFailOnError
msg = "Are you sure you want to reassign these orders?"
If MsgBox (msg, vbQuestion + vbYesNo) = vbYes Then
    ws.CommitTrans
    cboCurrent = cboNew
    cboNew = Null
    lstOrders.Requery
Else
    ws.Rollback
End If
End Sub
```

2.  Select a current and a new salesperson and click the Assign All Orders command button (see Figure 18.23). Click No to roll back the changes.

**FIGURE 18.23:**

Use methods of the Workspace object to create a transaction and provide the user with the option to undo changes.

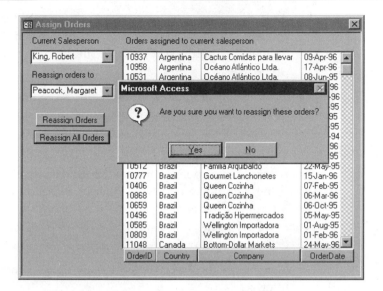

> **NOTE**
>
> Not all databases allow transactions to be defined. For example, you can't use transactions on a recordset based on a Paradox table. If a database object or a recordset doesn't allow transactions, the BeginTrans, CommitTrans, and Rollback methods fail silently without generating a run-time error. Because of the silent failure you should test the value of the Transactions property of the database or recordset object before using the BeginTrans method. If the database or recordset object allows transactions, the value of the Transactions property is True; otherwise, the value is False.

# Summary

This chapter introduces many of the VBA techniques for working with groups of records using the form approach and the recordset approach. The first half of the chapter deals with techniques for sorting and selecting records to be displayed in a form or report. The second half deals with using stored queries and SQL statements to select groups of records in memory without necessarily displaying the results in a datasheet, form, or report. The important points follow.

- As with macro programming, you can use the OrderBy and OrderByOn properties to sort the records of a form or report. However, using a variable to hold and build a sort string facilitates doing complex sorts with VBA procedures.

- You can open a form or report with selected records by using a parameter query as the record source; by using a procedure or macro to set the RecordSource or the Filter property; and by running the OpenForm, OpenReport, or ApplyFilter methods or macro actions.

- After a form is open, you can change the selection of displayed records by using the built-in Filter For, Filter By Selection, and Filter By Form techniques; by using a procedure or macro to change the RecordSource or Filter properties of the form; and by running the OpenForm, OpenReport, or ApplyFilter methods.

- You can use the Query By Form technique to create a simple custom search interface.

- The multi-select list box allows you to select records at random, instead of records, that satisfy a search condition.

- You can use DAO techniques or SQL techniques to work with a group of records in a recordset.

- DAO techniques use methods of the Recordset object to navigate through the group and operate on one record at a time.

- SQL techniques use stored queries and SQL statements to define a selection or to define the modifications you want the Jet database engine to make. SQL techniques rely on built-in code of the Jet engine and are almost always faster than the corresponding DAO techniques.

- You can create new queries (stored or temporary) in VBA procedures using the CreateQueryDef method.

- You can run stored select queries using the OpenQuery method when you want to display the results in a datasheet or using the OpenRecordset method when you need only work with the results in memory. You can also use the OpenRecordset method to run an SQL statement when you don't need to store the query or display the results.

- You can sort and filter a recordset using an SQL statement to define the sorted and filtered recordset or use the Sort and Filter properties of the recordset object. You have to create a new recordset based on the original recordset to see the effect of the sort or filter.

- You can run stored action queries using the OpenQuery and Execute methods and run SQL statements for action queries using the RunSQL and Execute methods.

- The transaction methods, available only in VBA, allow you to run a set of queries or statements as a group.

# Creating and Modifying Database Objects

- Creating a new table programmatically

- Linking to an external table

- Creating a new form programmatically

- Creating a new event procedure programmatically

- Creating custom properties for a data access object

- Creating custom properties for a form or report

- Displaying multiple instances of a form

In most applications you create the tables, queries, forms, and reports interactively in their respective Design views as part of the application design process. In building the application, you also create the macros and VBA procedures interactively that manipulate these existing objects when the user runs the application. Nevertheless, Access VBA provides techniques for creating and modifying most of the Database window objects programmatically.

This chapter shows you how to create and modify tables, queries, forms, reports, and modules using VBA procedures. (You cannot create or modify macros in a procedure.) You will also learn how to create custom properties and methods for these objects.

The objects we'll be working with come from the two components of Access: the Access Application objects, including forms, reports, and modules, and the Jet database engine's data access objects, which include the tables and queries. The object model for each component has a unique technique for creating and modifying its objects, as well as for creating custom properties and methods (because each model is created by a different team of Microsoft developers).

As it evolves in each version, Access VBA provides more object-oriented approaches to programming. The chapter ends with a discussion of one of these object-oriented features: the ability to define a form or report blueprint and generate multiple form objects or report objects from the blueprint.

> **NOTE**　For hands-on experience with the techniques described in this chapter, create a copy of the Northwind sample database named Northwind_Ch19 and work through the steps in the examples.

# Understanding How Access and Jet Create Objects

The Access Application and the Jet database engine are separate software applications working together in an intimate partnership that the interactive user is oblivious to. As a user, you work directly with the Access application.

# The Basic Elements and Features of Object-Oriented Programming

In object-oriented programming, similar objects are grouped into classes by definition. All the objects in a class share the same properties and methods. A specific object belonging to a class is called an instance of the class. The four basic elements of an object-oriented programming system are:

**Abstraction**     The formation of a model for an object that includes those properties and methods relevant to its purpose and ignores other aspects.

**Encapsulation**     The packaging of the properties and methods as internal components of an object.

**Inheritance**     The ability of objects in a child class to automatically reuse the properties and methods of their parent class.

**Polymorphism**     The ability of two or more classes to have methods that share the same name and purpose but have different instructions for implementation, such as the Requery methods for the DoCmd, Form, and Control objects.

While Visual Basic is not truly an object-oriented programming language because it lacks inheritance, it does provide most of the features needed for object-oriented design, including the ability to create blueprints (class modules) for new objects (as instances of the class). In creating a definition for new objects, you can create custom properties (property procedures) and methods (public methods).

In Access VBA, form and report modules are class modules. A new feature in Access 97 is the ability to create class modules that are independent from a form or report.

The internal programming of the Access application includes all the programming connections to Jet. As you work with the Access interface opening and closing tables, queries, forms, reports, macros, and modules, Jet is working behind the scenes creating and destroying objects in memory and saving some objects to the database file. The objects that are included in either the Access application object model or the Data Access Objects object model have predefined properties and methods, so you can manipulate the objects programmatically. The objects that are not included in either object model, such as macros, cannot be manipulated programmatically. With the two applications running simultaneously, each with its own object model, it is easy to get confused about which application is producing the results you see on the screen. Let's review what happens as you work with the Access interface and note the programming objects that are created and destroyed automatically. (You may want to refer to the object models discussed in Chapter 3.)

When you start Access, Jet starts automatically and creates a new DBEngine object and a default Workspace object as temporary objects, which will be destroyed when you close the Access window. When you open an existing database, Jet creates a Database object to represent the current database displayed in the Access window; you can refer to the current database using either Jet's DBEngine(0)(0) or Access's CurrentDB function. Jet keeps track of the Database window objects you've created for the database using Document objects. When you first open a database, Jet also creates Document objects for every saved object in the current database and Container objects for each category of saved object in the current database, including

| Container Name | Contains Information For |
| --- | --- |
| Tables | saved tables and queries |
| Relations | saved relationships |
| Forms | saved forms |
| Reports | saved reports |
| Scripts | saved macros |
| Modules | saved modules |

Each Container object holds administrative information about its category, such as who created the category and who has permission to use it. The Container object for a category holds the Document objects with similar administrative information for each saved object in the category. Jet creates the Database, Container, and Document objects as temporary objects to represent the saved database and its saved objects; it makes these objects available while the database is open so that you can manipulate them programmatically. When you close the database, Jet destroys the Database, Container, and Document objects.

**NOTE**

Unfortunately the Container objects' names may lead to confusion because three of them are identical to the names of three Access collection objects. The Jet Container object named Forms holds administrative information about all the saved forms in the database, while the Access collection object named Forms holds the Form objects that represent the currently open forms (even any open forms that haven't been saved). Similarly, the Reports Container object holds administrative information about all the saved reports while the Reports collection contains Report objects for the open reports. The Jet Container object named Modules holds administrative information about all the saved modules in the database, including standard modules, class modules associated with forms and reports, and class modules that are independent of forms and reports, while the Access collection object named Modules holds the Module objects that represent the modules that are currently open.

The Database window displays the saved Database window objects. When you open and close these objects, Access and Jet create and destroy temporary objects as follows:

For each table listed in the Tables pane, Jet stores a TableDef object and a QueryDef object for each query listed in the Queries pane. When you select and open one of these objects, Jet uses the instructions stored in the TableDef or the QueryDef object to retrieve the stored data and create a Recordset object. Access then displays the Datasheet view as a visual representation of the Recordset object. When you close the table or query, Jet destroys the recordset.

For each form listed in the Forms pane and for each report listed in the Reports pane, Access stores a corresponding set of instructions in the database file. When you open a form, Access creates the Form object and adds it to the Forms collection, while Jet creates and opens any underlying recordsets required by the form either as a recordsource or as the data sources for controls (such as row sources for combo boxes and list boxes). Access creates and displays the form visually and displays the data from the recordset in the form's controls. When you close the form, the corresponding Form and Recordset objects are destroyed. A similar sequence occurs when you open a report.

For each standard module and each independent class module not associated with a form or report listed in the Modules pane, Access stores a corresponding set of instructions in the database file. When you open a module listed in the

Database window, Access displays the Module window and also creates a Module object, adding it to the Modules collection. When you close the module, the corresponding Module object is destroyed. If a form or report has a module, you can open the associated module, provided the form or report is open. Access then processes the opening of these modules in the same manner as with the standard and independent class modules: it displays the Module window, creates a Module object, and adds it to the Modules collection. When you close the form or report module, or when you close the form or report, the Module object for the associated module is destroyed.

For each macro listed in the Macros pane, Access stores a corresponding set of instructions in the database file. When you open a macro, Access displays the Macro window but does not create a corresponding object that you can manipulate using a VBA procedure.

Thus, as you work with an open database, Access and Jet create programming objects in memory that correspond to the physical objects displayed on the screen, as well as other programming objects that do not have visual representations. You can use VBA procedures to manipulate any of the available programming objects, and you can use macro programming to manipulate some of them.

Using VBA you can also create new objects (or instances) using any of the blueprints or definitions of object types (or classes), that Access and Jet make available. Jet and Access have their own techniques for creating new instances. The next two sections describe these techniques.

# Creating Data Access Objects

Using VBA you can create and modify databases, tables, fields, and indexes; you can create and modify relationships between the tables and even link tables from external databases; you can also make new queries to retrieve data from the database and to make bulk changes to them; and you can also define new users and groups for security purposes.

You use one of the Create... methods of a data access object to create a new child object, and you use the OpenRecordset method to create a recordset. Table 19.1 (on the CD under Tables\Chapter19.pdf) lists the data access objects that have methods for creating properties for themselves and for creating child objects.

The general steps for creating a new data access object are:

1. Use one of the Create... methods of a parent object to create the child object.

2. Define the new object's characteristics by setting its properties. In some cases, before the object is complete, you have to create child objects for it. For example, when you create a table, you must also create at least one field and append the field to the table's Fields collection before the TableDef object is defined. This is analogous to creating a table interactively; Access won't let you save a new table until you've defined at least one field.

3. Add the new object to the corresponding collection belonging to the parent using the collection's Append method. You can only append a new object if it is complete.

To remove a saved (persistent) data access object from the database, you generally use the Delete method to delete the object from its collection. To remove a temporary (non-persistent) data access object, including the Database, Workspace, and Recordset objects, apply the object's Close method to close the object instead of deleting it.

It is important to keep in mind that each data access object has its own variations of the steps for creating it, adding it to a collection, and removing it from the database. In Chapter 16 you learned how to create and destroy Recordset objects, and in Chapter 18 you learned how to create and store new QueryDef objects. See Chapter 11 for more information on creating the other types of data access objects.

To illustrate the steps for creating a new data access object in a VBA procedure, we'll create a table, complete with an index and a relationship to an existing table, in the next section.

# Creating and Deleting Database Window Objects

Access VBA provides techniques for creating tables and queries as data access objects and for creating forms, reports, and controls as application objects. In this section we define a table using both the data access object (DAO) techniques and

SQL techniques. Once the table exists, we create a form based on it using the VBA functions for defining application objects.

# Creating a Table

There are two techniques for creating a table: the data access object techniques available only in VBA, and the SQL techniques available in both VBA and macro programming.

## Using Data Access Objects Techniques to Create a Table

This section demonstrates the data access objects (DAO) techniques for creating a new table, creating and adding an index, and creating a relationship between two tables in a database. We'll be using several Create... methods. The arguments of a Create... method correspond to the properties of the object you are creating. Since most of the arguments are optional in the method's syntax, you can omit them when executing the method. However, one or more of the properties are required for appending the new object to its collection; for example, you can't append a new table until you give the table a valid name. If you omit one or more optional arguments when you use the Create... method, you can set the corresponding property with an assignment statement before you append the object to its collection. After you append an object, many of properties become read-only and you can't change their settings. (If you do need to change a read-only property for an object, you'll have to delete the object and create another one.)

**NOTE**   To create tables using the data access objects techniques, you must be working in a Jet workspace; that is, Access must work with the Jet database engine. If you are in an ODBCDirect workspace with Access using another database engine, such as SQL Server, you can't use the data access objects techniques to create or modify tables in your database. In fact, the ODBCDirect object model doesn't have a TableDefs object. However, you can use the Data Definition Language commands of SQL to create and modify tables in an ODBCDirect workspace.

When you create a table, you must also create at least one field for the table.

## CreateTableDef

You use the CreateTableDef method to create a table in your database or to create a link to a table in an external database. (You establish a link to a table in an external database by creating a TableDef object to represent the linked table in the database you are working in.) The syntax for creating a new TableDef object is

```
Set tdf = db.CreateTableDef(name, attributes, source, connect)
```

where tdf is an object variable of the TableDef type that represents the new table you are creating, db is a reference to an open database that will house the new table, *name* is an optional string variable that names the new table, *attributes* is an optional long integer that is the sum of the intrinsic constants for specifying the characteristics of the new table, *source* is the optional name of the table in an external database that you want to create a link to, and *connect* is an optional string containing information about the database type and path for a linked table and information to be passed to ODBC and certain ISAM database drivers. Although all the arguments are optional, set the Name property of the new TableDef object before you append the object; the name must be a unique string in the TableDefs collection and can have up to 64 characters. For example, to create a table named tblEmployeeExpenses in the current database, use the statement

```
Set tdf = CurrentDB.CreateTableDef("tblEmployeeExpenses")
```

or the pair of statements

```
Set tdf = CurrentDB.CreateTableDef
tdf.Name = "tblEmployeeExpenses"
```

> **NOTE**
> After you append a new TableDef object to the TableDefs collection, the Name property continues to be a read/write property. You can remove the TableDef object using the TableDefs collection's Delete method.

## CreateField

You use a table's CreateField method to add a field to it. The syntax is

```
Set fld = tdf.CreateField(name, type, size)
```

where fld is an object variable of the Field type representing the field you are creating, tdf refers to the specific table, *name* is an optional string variable that uniquely identifies the new field, *type* is an optional intrinsic constant that identifies the data type of the new field, and *size* is an optional integer that specifies the maximum size for a field object that contains text. You must set the Name and Type properties before appending a new field to its collection. As with table names, the Name property requires a unique string up to 64 characters in length. (When naming fields, remember that two fields in the table's Field collection can't have the same name.) Set the Type property to a valid intrinsic constant (search Type in online Help for a list of the valid settings). For a data type other than Text, the Type property setting determines the Size property so you don't need to specify a size. If the data type is Text, you can set the Size property to an integer smaller than 255 or omit the setting to accept the default setting for the database.

**NOTE**  After you append a Field object to its Fields collection, the Name property continues to be read/write (except for a linked table's Fields collection), but the Type property becomes read-only. You can remove a Field object from its Fields collection using the Delete method of the collection. However, if you included the field in an index, you can't delete the field unless you first delete the index.

We'll create a new table for tracking employee expenses in the Northwind_Ch19 database.

1. Open a new standard module named basNewTable and enter the procedure shown in Listing 19.1. The NewTable procedure adds a table to the current database named tblEmployeesExpenses. The procedure creates four fields: ExpenseID, EmployeeID, ExpenseType, and Amount, sets their properties, and then appends the fields to the new table's Fields collection. With the table definition now complete, the procedure appends the new table to the TableDefs collection and refreshes the database window.

## Listing 19.1

```
Public Sub NewTable()
Dim db As Database, tdf As TableDef
Dim fld1 As Field, fld2 As Field, fld3 As Field, fld4 As Field
Set db = CurrentDB
Set tdf = db.CreateTableDef("tblEmployeeExpenses")
Set fld1 = tdf.CreateField("ExpenseID",dbLong)
```

```
fld1.Required = True
'To increment the value for new records
fld1.Attributes = dbAutoIncrField
Set fld2 = tdf.CreateField("EmployeeID",dbLong)
fld2.Required = True
Set fld3 = tdf.CreateField
With fld3
    .Name = "ExpenseType"
    .Required = True
    .Type = dbText
    .Size = 30
End With
Set fld4 = tdf.CreateField("Amount",dbCurrency)
With tdf.Fields
    .Append fld1
    .Append fld2
    .Append fld3
    .Append fld4
End With
db.TableDefs.Append tdf
RefreshDatabaseWindow
End Sub
```

2. Run the NewTable procedure in the Debug window.

3. Click in the Database window and observe the new table. Figure 19.1 presents the new table in Design view.

**NOTE**   You cannot designate an AutoNumber data type directly when you create a field using the CreateField method because Jet does not recognize the AutoNumber data type. Instead, set the data type to dbLong and then set the field's Attribute property to the intrinsic constant dbAutoIncrField to automatically increment the field value for new records. (The dbAutoIncrField setting applies only to tables in an .mdb database.)

It is interesting to note that most of the field properties that you set in table Design view, such as Description, Caption, and InputMask, are not built-in properties of the Field object. You'll learn how to set these properties for a new field in the section "Adding Application-Defined Properties to Data Access Objects" later in this chapter.

**FIGURE 19.1:**

Use the CreateTable method to set up a new table and the CreateField method to add a field to the new table.

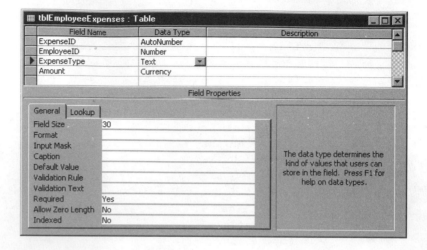

> **NOTE**
>
> Description, Caption, and InputMask are examples of properties that are not built-in DAO properties of the Field object. These are examples of application-defined properties used by the Access application and are not recognized automatically by Jet.

**Creating an Index** When you create a new index for a table, you must also create at least one field for the index.

### CreateIndex

Use the CreateIndex method of the specific table to define and name a new index for the table. The syntax is

```
Set idx = tdf.CreateIndex(name)
```

where idx is an object variable of the Index type that represents the index you are creating, tdf refers to the table, and *name* is an optional string variable that uniquely identifies the new index. As with tables and fields, set the Name property before appending the new index, specifying a unique string up to 64 characters in length.

NOTE After appending the new index, you can change the Name property only for a local table, not a linked table. You can remove an index from a table using the Indexes collection's Delete method.

## CreateField

You use the CreateField method of the specific index you are creating to add a field to it. The syntax is

```
Set fld = idx.CreateField(name)
```

where fld is an object variable of the Field type for the index field you are creating, idx refers to the specific index, and *name* is a string that uniquely identifies the new field in the index but refers to an existing field in the table. Although you use this statement to create a field in the index, you are not adding a new field to the table; you are actually using the statement to create an index field based on an existing table field. After creating index fields, append them to the Fields collection of the new index and then append the new index to the table's Indexes collection.

As an example, we'll create a new primary index that contains the ExpenseID field for the tblEmployeeExpenses table we created in the NewTable procedure in Listing 19.1.

1. Enter the procedure in Listing 19.2. The procedure creates an index named Primary for the tblEmployeeExpenses table and sets the Primary property to True. The procedure uses the index's CreateField method to add a new index field based on the existing EmployeeID table field, appends the index field to the index's Fields collection, and then appends the new index to the Indexes collection of the table.

## Listing 19.2

```
Public Sub NewIndex()
Dim db As Database, tdf As Tabledef
Dim idx As Index, fld As Field
Set db = CurrentDB
Set tdf = db.TableDefs("tblEmployeeExpenses")
Set idx = tdf.CreateIndex("Primary")
idx.Primary = True
```

```
Set fld = idx.CreateField("ExpenseID")
idx.Fields.Append fld
tdf.Indexes.Append idx
End Sub
```

2.  Run the NewIndex procedure in the Debug window.

3.  Open the tblEmployeeExpenses table in Design view and observe that ExpenseID is now the primary key (see Figure 19.2).

**FIGURE 19.2:**

Use the CreateIndex method to create an index and the CreateField method to create an index field based on an existing table field.

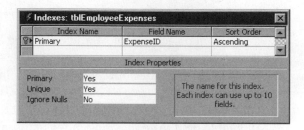

The Primary, Unique, and IgnoreNulls properties that you can set in Design view are also properties of the Index object, so you can set them in a VBA procedure. In addition to the properties listed in Design view, Jet defines other properties of the Index object (see Chapter 11 for more information). For example, the order of records returned depends on the Attributes property of each field in the index; by default, the index field is sorted in ascending order, but you can set the Attributes property to the intrinsic constant dbDescending to sort the field in descending order.

**Creating a Relationship**   When you create a new Relation object to represent a new relationship for two existing tables or queries, you must also create at least one relation field for the relation based on an existing field in the primary table or query, and you must specify the name of the corresponding matching field in the existing foreign table or query.

### CreateRelation

Use the database's CreateRelation method to create and name a new relation between a primary table or query and a foreign table or query, respectively. The syntax is

```
Set rel = db.CreateRelation(name, table, foreigntable, attributes)
```

where rel is an object variable of the Relation type that represents the new relationship, db refers to the database in which you are defining the new relationship, *name* is an optional string variable that uniquely names the new relation, *table* is an optional string variable that names the existing primary table or query, *foreigntable* is an optional string variable that names the foreign table or query, and *attributes* is an optional Long variable that contains intrinsic constants to specify information about the relationship. Include the arguments in the CreateRelation statement or use assignment statements to set the properties. Set the properties before appending the relation; none of the properties can be changed after you append the relation to the database's Relations collection. If you want to modify an existing relation, you must delete it from the Relations collection using the collection's Delete method, and then create a new relationship.

### CreateField

You use the CreateField method of the specific relation you are creating to create a new field. The syntax is

```
Set fld = rel.CreateField(name)
```

where fld is an object variable of the Field type that represents the relation field, rel refers to the specific relation, and *name* is a string that uniquely identifies the new relation field. As is the case with index fields, this statement does not create a new field in the table; instead, it defines a new relationship field that must be based on an existing table field.

As an example, because an employee can have many expense records, we'll create a relationship between the new tblEmployeeExpenses table (as the foreign table) and the Employees table (as the primary table).

1. Enter the NewRelation procedure shown in Listing 19.3. The procedure creates a new relationship named ExpenseRelation, using the Employees table as the primary table and the tblEmployeeExpenses table as the foreign table. The procedure creates a relation field based on the EmployeeID table field in the primary table and specifies the name of the matching field in the foreign table (also EmployeeID). After defining the relation field, the procedure appends the new relation field to the relationship's Fields collection, and then appends the new relationship to the database's Relations collection.

## Listing 19.3

```
Public Sub NewRelation()
Dim db As Database, rel As Relation, fld As Field
Set db = CurrentDB
Set rel = db.CreateRelation("ExpenseRelation")
rel.Table = "Employees"
rel.ForeignTable = "tblEmployeeExpenses"
Set fld = rel.CreateField ("EmployeeID")
fld.ForeignName = "EmployeeID"
rel.Fields.Append fld
db.Relations.Append rel

End Sub
```

2. Run the procedure in the Debug window.

3. Choose the Relationships command from the Tools menu. The relationships layout is displayed. Click the Show Table button in the toolbar, select tblEmployeeExpenses, and click OK. Access adds the tblEmployeeExpenses table to the layout and displays the relationship (see Figure 19.3).

**FIGURE 19.3:**

Use the CreateRelation method to define a new relationship between two tables and the CreateField method to add a relation field based on an existing field in the primary table.

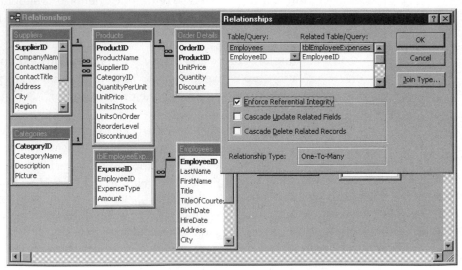

> **NOTE** By default, when you create a relation between two tables in the current database, Access enforces referential integrity and does not cascade updates or deletes; you must specify these settings with the Attributes property of the Relation object before appending the relation to the Relations collection. Search Attributes in online Help for a list of intrinsic constants for the Relation object.

## Using SQL Techniques to Create a Table

When you use the SQL techniques to create objects, you create *data-definition queries* that can be run by both macros and VBA procedures. A data-definition

query is an SQL-specific query that begins with one of the commands listed in Table 19.2 (on the CD under Tables\Chapter19.pdf). Use the data-definition queries to create tables and indexes, to modify tables by adding or removing columns, to modify tables by adding or removing an index, and to define relations and enforce referential integrity. You can save a data-definition query as a stored query, or you can run the SQL statement directly using the same techniques for running an action query or SQL statement in a macro or VBA procedure.

> **NOTE** You can use the data-definition language to create and modify tables only in a Jet database(.mdb). To create or modify tables in a non-Jet database, you have to use the data access objects techniques.

The syntax for a data-definition query that creates a table is

```
CREATE TABLE tablename (field1 type (size), field2 type (size), ...)
```

where *tablename* is the name of the table to be created, *field1*, *field2*, ... are the names of the fields you are creating with the statement (you must create at least one field), *type* is the data type for the new field, and *size* is the field size in characters (you specify the size only for Text and Binary fields). You can also include CONSTRAINT clauses to define one or more indexes at the same time that you define the new table (search CONSTRAINT clause in online Help for more information).

Listing 19.4 shows the SQLNewTable procedure that creates the tblEmployeeExpenses table. The procedure executes the SQL statement for a data-definition query that uses the CREATE TABLE command to create a table containing four fields.

### Listing 19.4

```
Public Sub SQLNewTable()
Dim db As Database, strSQL As String
strSQL = "Create Table tblEmployeeExpenses "
strSQL = strSQL & "(ExpenseID COUNTER, EmployeeID LONG,
ExpenseType TEXT(30), Amount CURRENCY);"
Set db = CurrentDB
db.Execute strSQL
RefreshDatabaseWindow
End Sub
```

Access SQL has the COUNTER data type, so you can create an AutoNumber field directly. (By contrast, when you use DAO techniques, you create a dbLong field and set its Attributes property to dbAutoIncrField to increment the field's value for new records.)

You can use the ALTER TABLE command to add or drop a single field or add or drop a single index from an existing table. The ALTER TABLE data definition query to add or drop a field has the syntax

```
ALTER TABLE tablename {ADD COLUMN field type (size) |DROP COLUMN field}
```

where *tablename* is the name of the table you are changing and *field* is the name of the field you are adding or dropping. If you are adding a field, *type* is the data type of the new field and *size* is the field size if the new field is the Text or Binary data type.

To modify a field, you must first delete it and then add a new field of the same name. Listing 19.5 show the SQLModifyTable procedure that modifies the ExpenseType field to increase its field size from 30 to 40 characters.

### Listing 19.5

```
Public Sub SQLModifyTable
Dim db AS Database, strDROP As String, strADD As String
strDROP = "ALTER TABLE tblEmployeeExpenses "
strDROP = strDROP & "DROP COLUMN ExpenseType;"
```

```
strADD = "ALTER TABLE tblEmployeeExpenses "
strADD = strADD & "ADD COLUMN ExpenseType TEXT (40);"
Set db = CurrentDB
db.Execute strDROP
db.Execute strADD
End Sub
```

**Creating an Index**     There are three ways to create an index for a table:

- using the CREATE TABLE command when you create the table,
- using the ALTER TABLE command to add a field to an existing table,
- and using the CREATE INDEX command to add a field to an existing table.

The three techniques do not have the same result: if you want to define relations and enforce referential integrity, you must use either the CREATE TABLE or ALTER TABLE commands.

The CREATE INDEX data-definition query has the syntax

```
CREATE [UNIQUE] INDEX indexname ON tablename (field1
[ASC|DESC], field1 [ASC | DESC], ...) [WITH {PRIMARY | DISALLOW
NULL | IGNORE NULL}]
```

where *indexname* is the name of the index you are creating, and *field1, field2, ...* are the names of the fields you are creating the index on. Use the UNIQUE key word to prohibit duplicate values in the indexed field or fields. Use the DISALLOW NULL option to prohibit null entries in the indexed field or fields of new records. Use the IGNORE NULL option to prevent records with null values in the indexed field or fields from being included in the index. (Recall that the index is a separate table that Jet creates and uses for finding records; by setting this option the index is smaller and the search is faster.) Use the PRIMARY key word to specify the indexed field or fields as the primary key for the table.

Listing 19.6 shows a procedure that uses the CREATE INDEX command to add an index to the ExpenseType field and specifies the WITH DISALLOW NULL clause to require an entry in the field.

### Listing 19.6

```
Public Sub SQLCreateIndex()
Dim db AS Database, strIndex As String
```

```
strIndex = "CREATE INDEX IndexExpenseType ON tblEmployeeExpenses
StrIndex = strIndex & "(ExpenseType) WITH DISALLOW NULL;"
Set db = CurrentDB
db.Execute strIndex
End Sub
```

To explore the SQL techniques, follow these steps:

1.  Open the Relationships window and delete the relationship between the Employees and the tblEmployeeExpenses tables. Close the window and delete the tblEmployeeExpenses table.

2.  Insert the SQLNewTable, SQLModifyTable, and the SQLCreateIndex procedures in Listings 19.4, 5, and 6 in the basNewTable module.

3.  Run the three procedures in the Debug window in the order listed in Step 2.

4.  Open the new tblEmployeeExpenses table in Design view. Observe the change in the size of the ExpenseType field and the new index (see Figure 19.4).

---

**FIGURE 19.4:**

Use data-definition queries to create a table, modify a field, and create an index.

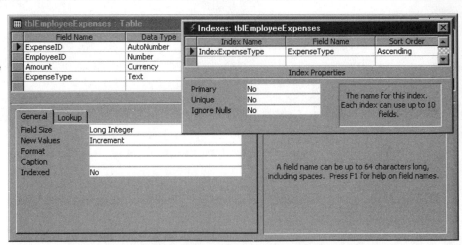

---

**Creating a Relationship**   You can create a relation between two tables or queries using data-definition queries based on the CREATE TABLE or the ALTER TABLE commands. The CREATE TABLE and the ALTER TABLE commands use a CONSTRAINT clause to define primary and foreign keys and to create relations and enforce referential integrity. A *constraint* is a limitation on the values that can be entered into a field. You use a CONSTRAINT clause in a CREATE TABLE or an ALTER TABLE statement in two situations: to create or delete an index, or to create or delete a relationship.

There are two versions of CONSTRAINT clauses, depending on whether you are creating a constraint on a single field or a constraint on more than one field. To illustrate, the syntax for the CONSTRAINT clause for creating a constraint on a single field and creating a relationship is

```
CONSTRAINT constraintname FOREIGN KEY (ref) REFERENCES foreigntable
➥foreignfield
```

where *constraintname* is the name of the constraint you are creating, *ref* is the name of the matching field in the primary table, *foreigntable* is the name of the foreign table and *foreignfield* is the name of the matching field in the foreign table. Use the FOREIGN KEY reserved word to specify a field as a foreign key.

Specifically, the CONSTRAINT clause to designate EmployeeID as the foreign key for the tblEmployeeExpenses table and create a relationship with the Employees table is

```
CONSTRAINT IndexEmployee FOREIGN KEY (EmployeeID) REFERENCES
➥Employees (EmployeeID)
```

Listing 19.7 shows the corresponding SQLNewRelation procedure that creates the relationship between the Employees and the tblEmployeeExpenses tables. The procedure adds a relationship to the tblEmployeeExpenses table, specifying the Employees table as the foreign table for the relationship.

### Listing 19.7

```
Public Sub SQLNewRelation()
Dim db AS Database, strRel As String
strRel = "ALTER TABLE tblEmployeeExpenses "
strRel = strRel & "ADD CONSTRAINT IndexEmployee "
strRel = strRel & "FOREIGN KEY (EmployeeID) REFERENCES"
strRel = strRel & "Employees (EmployeeID);"
Set db = CurrentDB
db.Execute strRel
End Sub
```

1. Insert the SQLNewRelation procedure in the basNewTable module.

2. Run the procedure in the Debug window.

3. Open the Relationships window and note the new relationship.

## Linking to an External Table

Working interactively, you can link to a table in another database by choosing the Get External Data and the Link Tables command in the File menu. Once an external table has been linked, you can refer to it the same way you refer to a local table in the current database. For example, if Expense Categories is a linked table in the current database, you can create an object variable using the assignment statement

```
Set tdf = CurrentDB.TableDefs("Expense Categories")
```

In this section you learn how to create the link to an external table using a VBA procedure.

### The Connect Property

The key to working with external tables is the Connect property. To create a link to a table in another database, you use the syntax

```
Set tdf = db.CreateTableDef(name, attributes, source, connect)
```

where *name* is an optional string variable that is the name you use in the current database to represent the linked table, *attributes* is an optional long integer for specifying the characteristics of the table, *source* is the string expression for the name of the external database's table, and *connect* is the optional string containing information about the database type, the path for the linked table, and information to be passed to ODBC and certain ISAM database drivers.

The Connect property of the TableDef object includes the database type and the path to the database that contains the linked table (see Table 19.3 on the CD under Tables\Chapter19.pdf). After you specify the connection to the database as the Connect property, you use the SourceTableName property of the TableDef object to specify the name of the external database's table that you want to link to.

## Linking to the Table

Listing 19.8 shows a procedure that links a new table in the current database to the Expense Categories table in the Expenses.mdb database (created in Chapter 1).

1.  Insert the LinkTable procedure in Listing 19.8. The procedure uses the CreateTableDef method to create a TableDef object in the current database. The procedure also sets the properties for the new TableDef object to create the link to the Expense Categories table in the expenses.mdb database. You may need to change the path to the expenses.mdb database on your computer. The procedure saves the link by appending the new TableDef object to the current database's TableDefs collection.

### Listing 19.8

```
Public Sub LinkTable()
Dim db As Database, tdf As TableDef
Set db = CurrentDB
Set tdf = db.CreateTableDef("Expense Categories")
tdf.Connect = ";DATABASE=c:\Sybex\expenses.mdb"
tdf.SourceTableName = "Expense Categories"
db.TableDefs.Append tdf
RefreshDatabaseWindow
End Sub
```

2.  Run the LinkTable procedure in the Debug window. Click in the Database window. The Expense Categories table is now linked.

# Creating a Form or Report

Access VBA provides a set of functions for creating forms, reports, and controls. These functions are particularly useful when you are creating a custom wizard that builds a new form or report according to the user's specifications gathered in wizard screens. Table 19.4 (on the CD under Tables\Chapter19.pdf) describes the built-in Access functions used to create forms, reports, controls, and report group levels and the statements for deleting controls; you can think of these functions and statements as methods of the Application object.

The CreateForm function creates a minimized form in Design view using the syntax

```
Set frm = CreateForm(database, formtemplate)
```

where frm is an object variable that represents the form object you are creating, *database* is a string identifying the name of the database that contains the form template you are using, and *formtemplate* is a string identifying the name of the form you are using as a template to define the new form. If you omit the first argument, the current database is used; if you omit the second argument, the form is based on the template specified in the Forms/Reports tab of the Options dialog, available by choosing the Options command in the Tools menu.

The CreateControl function has the syntax

```
Set ctl = CreateControl(formname, controltype, section, parent,
➥columnname, left, top, width, height)
```

where *formname* is a string identifying the name of the open form to which you are adding the new control, *controltype* is an intrinsic constant identifying the new control's type, *section* is an intrinsic constant specifying the form section that will contain the new control, *parent* is a string identifying the name of the parent control for a label, check box, option button, or a toggle button control (if the control you are creating does not have a parent control, use a zero-length string for this argument), *columnname* is the name of the field that the control will be bound to (if you are creating an unbound control, use a zero-length string for this argument), *left, top* are numeric expressions in twips indicating the coordinates of the upper-left corner of the control you are creating, and *width, height* are numeric expressions in twips indicating the width and height of the control.

The DeleteControl statement has the syntax

```
DeleteControl formname, controlname
```

where *formname* is a string expression identifying the form containing the control and *controlname* is a string expression specifying the control you want to delete.

To illustrate these functions, we'll create a simple form for the Shippers table in Northwind_Ch19. We'll use the CreateForm and the CreateControl functions to create the objects and the DeleteControl statement to delete one of the new controls.

1. Create a new module named basNewForm and insert the procedure in Listing 19.9. The procedure creates a new minimized form bound to the Shippers table and initializes the Top variable to 100 twips (Top is the distance in twips between the top of the form and the top of the next label–text box pair to be created).The procedure loops through the fields of the

Shippers table. For each field in the table, the procedure uses the CreateControl function to create label and text box controls and sets the label's Caption property and the text box's ControlSource property to the name of the field. The procedure increases the Top variable by 400 twips so that the next label–text box pair is located 400 twips below the previous pair. The procedure also creates a command button. After creating the controls, the procedure restores the form, uses the OpenForm method to switch to Form view, and then runs the built-in command to size the form. The procedure saves the form as frmNewForm.

## Listing 19.9

```
Public Sub NewForm()
Dim db As Database, frm As Form
Dim lbl As Label, txt As TextBox, cmd As CommandButton
Dim Top As Integer, var As Variant
Set db = CurrentDB
Set frm= CreateForm
With frm
    .RecordSource = "Shippers"
    .Width = 2.5
End With
Top = 100
For Each var in db.TableDefs("Shippers").Fields
    Set lbl = CreateControl(frm.Name,acLabel,acDetail, ,
    ➥,300,Top,1500,230)
    Set txt = CreateControl(frm.Name,acTextBox,acDetail, ,
    ➥,1600,Top,1500,230)
    lbl.Caption = var.Name
    txt.ControlSource = var.Name
    Top = Top + 400
Next
Set cmd = CreateControl(frm.Name,acCommandButton,acDetail, ,
➥,2000,Top)
cmd.Caption = "Push me!"
cmd.Name = "cmdPush"
cmd.SizeToFit
'insert modification here
With DoCmd
    .Restore
    .OpenForm frm.Name
```

```
        .RunCommand acCmdSizeToFitForm
    End With
    SendKeys "frmNewForm", False
    SendKeys "{Enter}", False
    RunCommand acCmdSaveAs
    End Sub
```

2.  Run the procedure in the Debug window. The form is shown in Figure 19.5.

**FIGURE 19.5:**

Use the CreateForm and
CreateControl functions
to create a form in a VBA
procedure.

> **NOTE**
>
> When you run the Save As command in a procedure using the statement RunCommand acCmdSaveAs, Access displays the Save As dialog and pauses until you enter the name of the new object and click OK or press Enter. You can use the SendKeys statement to send the keystrokes for the name and for closing the dialog. When you use the SendKeys statements before running the Save As command, Access stores the keystrokes in a buffer until needed by the Save As dialog. Set the Wait argument to False to return control to the procedure immediately after sending the keystrokes.

## Creating a Module

Access 97 provides the new Module object together with properties and methods so that you can define new modules and modify existing modules programmatically. See Chapter 10 for more information on the Module object.

As an example, we modify the NewForm procedure to create a form module for the new form. The statement

Set mdl = frm.Module

where mdl is an object variable of the Module type and frm refers to the form, uses the Module property of the form to create the module, and returns a reference to the new module.

## Creating an Event Procedure

You can use the CreateEventProc method of the module object to define a new event procedure in an existing module. The CreateEventProc method creates the code template for an event procedure for a specified event, as well as a specified object, and returns the line number of the first line of the event procedure. The syntax of the method is

*lngReturn* = mdl.CreateEventProc(*eventname*, *objectname*)

where *lngReturn* is a variable that represents the line number of the first line of the event procedure, *eventname* is a string expression indicating the name of an event, and *objectname* is a string expression specifying the name of an object.

After creating the code template, use the InsertLines method of the module object to insert the text for the event procedure. The syntax for the InsertLines method is

mdl.InsertLines *line*, *string*

where *line* is the number of the line where you want to start inserting code (the existing code moves down) and *string* is the text that you want to insert in the procedure. To add multiple lines of code, use the instrinsic constant vbCrLf to break a line and start a new line (the vbCrLf constant is equivalent to pressing Enter at the end of a line of code) and use the intrinsic constant vbTab to insert a tab.

We modify the NewForm procedure in Listing 19.8 to create an event procedure for the Click event of the command button that displays a message asking whether to delete the button. If the user clicks Yes, the event procedure switches the form to Design view, deletes the command button, and switches back to Form view. Here is the event procedure that the modified NewForm procedure will create:

```
Private Sub cmdPush_Click()
Dim intResponse As Integer
```

```
intResponse = MsgBox("Do you want to delete the command button?",
➡vbYesNo)
If intResponse = vbYes Then
    DoCmd.OpenForm Me.Name, acDesign
    DeleteControl "frmNewForm", "cmdPush"
    DoCmd.OpenForm "frmNewForm"
End If
End Sub
```

1. Close the frmNewForm form. Select frmNewForm in the Database window and press Delete to delete the form.

2. Insert the following lines of code in the NewForm procedure at the line marked with the "insert modification here" comment. The modification declares the variables needed for the new code, creates the new form module, and inserts the code template for the new cmdPush_Click event procedure. The procedure builds the string expression for the lines of the event procedure. Several lines of the code require embedding a string within a string; the procedure uses pairs of double quotes to mark the beginning and the end of each string within the string expression. After building the str variable containing the text for the event procedure, the procedure uses the module's InsertLines method to insert the text starting at the line following the first line of the code template.

```
Dim mdl As Module, lngReturn As Long, str As String
'create a form module and return a reference to the module
Set mdl = frm.Module
'create an event procedure for the command button's Click event
lngReturn = mdl.CreateEventProc("Click", "cmdPush")
str = "Dim intResponse as Integer" & vbCrLf
str = str & "intResponse = MsgBox(""Delete the
➡button?"",vbYesNo)" & vbCrLf
str = str & "If intResponse = vbYes Then" & vbCrLf
str = str&vbTab&"DoCmd.OpenForm Me.Name, acDesign"&vbCrLf
str = str&vbTab&"DeleteControl ""frmNewForm"", ""cmdPush"""&vbCrLf
str = str&vbTab&"DoCmd.OpenForm ""frmNewForm"""&vbCrLf
str = str & "End If"
mdl.InsertLines lngReturn + 1, str
```

3. Run the modified NewForm procedure. The procedure creates the frmNewForm form and creates the form module with the event procedure (see Figure 19.6).

4. Click the Push Me button on the new form and then click Yes. The event procedure deletes the command button and displays the form without the command button.

**FIGURE 19.6:**

Use the CreateEventProc method to create an event procedure and the InsertLines method to insert the code for the procedure.

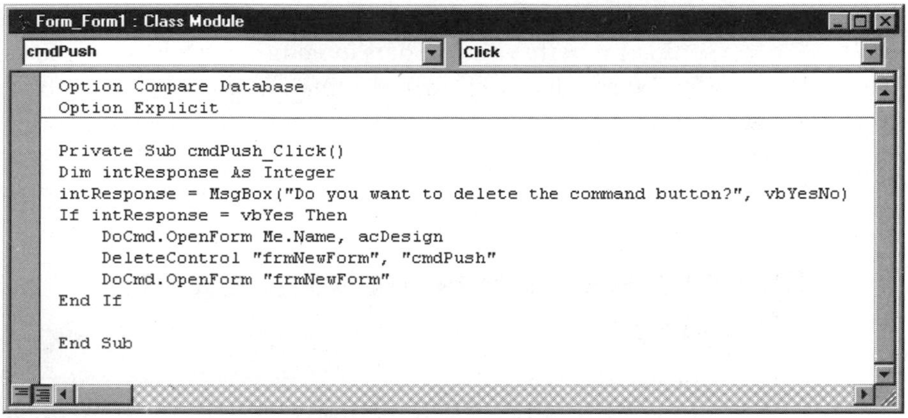

```
Form_Form1 : Class Module

cmdPush                                      Click

Option Compare Database
Option Explicit

Private Sub cmdPush_Click()
Dim intResponse As Integer
intResponse = MsgBox("Do you want to delete the command button?", vbYesNo)
If intResponse = vbYes Then
    DoCmd.OpenForm Me.Name, acDesign
    DeleteControl "frmNewForm", "cmdPush"
    DoCmd.OpenForm "frmNewForm"
End If

End Sub
```

## Deleting a Database Window Object

You use the DeleteObject method of the DoCmd object to delete a database window object. The syntax is

DoCmd.DeleteObject *objecttype, objectname*

where *objecttype* is an optional intrinsic constant indicating the type of the object you want to delete and *objectname* is an optional string expression indicating the name of the object. To delete an object selected in the Database window, you can omit both arguments.

For example, to delete the frmNewForm form:

1. Close the frmNewForm form.

2. Type **DoCmd.DeleteObject acForm, "frmNewForm"** in the Immediate pane of the Debug window and press Enter.

# Creating Your Own Properties

All Access application objects and data access objects have built-in properties that describe their characteristics. Each object has a Properties collection containing its built-in properties. Throughout various chapters of this book you have learned how to read property settings and how to set the values of read/write properties. You can't change or delete the built-in properties themselves, only their values. Much of the object manipulation you've learned about involves manipulation by setting property values. There are times when it is convenient to customize objects by creating your own custom properties. In this section, you'll learn techniques for creating properties for data access objects, and you'll learn how to create new properties for the Access application objects. You'll discover that Jet and Access take entirely different approaches to custom properties.

## Custom Properties for Data Access Objects

You can create a custom property for a data access object and add the custom property to the object's Properties collection. The simplest way to create a custom property for a data access object involves three steps as follows:

1. Use the CreateProperty method of the data access object to create a Property object with a unique name.

2. Set the Type and Value properties of the new Property object.

3. Use the Append method of the Properties collection to add the new property to the Properties collection of the data access object.

### Using the CreateProperty Method

The CreateProperty method has the syntax

```
Set prp = object.CreateProperty(name, type, value, DDL)
```

where *prp* is an object variable that represents the Property object you are creating, *object* is a reference to the object you are creating the property for, *name* is an optional string that uniquely names the new property, *type* is an optional constant that identifies the data type of the new property, *value* is an optional Variant containing the initial value for the property, and DDL is True or False indicating whether the property is a Data Definition language (SQL) object.

As an example, we'll create an all-purpose Tag property for the Customers table. Most of the Access application objects have a Tag that you can use to store information (see the section, "Using the Tag Property" later in the chapter), but the data access objects don't have the Tag property. We'll specify the Type as dbText to hold text values. When you create a user-defined property, you must specify an initial value before you can add the property to the Properties collection. For a form, report, or control, the built-in Tag property has the zero-length string ("")as the default value, however, you can't use the zero-length string for a user-defined property, so we'll set the initial value to "My tag"

1.  Open a new module named basProperties and enter the procedure shown in Listing 19.10. We include our own error handling in this procedure because if you try to append a property that has already been appended, a run-time error (code 3367) is generated. The procedure traps for this error; if the property has already been appended, the statement that runs the Append method generates the error and the Resume Next statement allows the procedure to continue without executing the Append method. If an error with another error code occurs, a message box displays the error information and the procedure ends.

### Listing 19.10

```
Public Sub TableTag()
Dim db As Database, tdf as TableDef, prp As Property
On Error GoTo Error_TableTag
Set db = CurrentDB
Set tdf = db.TableDefs("Customers")
Set prp = tdf.CreateProperty("Tag")
prp.Type = dbText
prp.Value = "My tag"
tdf.Properties.Append prp

Exit_TableTag:
Exit Sub

Error_TableTag:
If Err = 3367 Then
'The property has already been appended to the collection.
```

```
        Resume Next
    Else
        MsgBox Err.Number & Err.Description
        Resume Exit_TableTag
    End If
End Sub
```

2. Make sure the Customers table is closed and run the TableTag procedure in the Debug window.

When you run the TableTag procedure, the Tag property is created, is saved to the disk, and becomes a permanent property of the table. New, user-defined properties do not appear in property sheets so you can't set them interactively.

**NOTE** You must append a user-defined property to the Properties collection of the data access object before the property can be saved to the database. If the procedure ends without appending the property, the property is discarded.

## Referring to a User-Defined Property

When you refer to a user-defined property in a procedure, you must include an explicit reference to the Properties collection and you must use the property's name in the syntax. You can use either the exclamation point or the parentheses syntax as follows:

*object*.Properties!*propertyname*

*object*.Properties("*propertyname*")

**NOTE** When referring to a user-defined property you cannot use either the abbreviated *object.propertyname* syntax or the reference by index number *object*.Properties(n) syntax.

For example, to refer to the Tag property of the Customers table

1. Type **?CurrentDB("Customers").Properties("Tag").Value** in the Debug window and press Enter. The Debug window prints My tag.

2. Type **CurrentDB("Customers").Properties!Tag.Value = "Change tag"** and press Enter. The value of the custom Tag property is changed.

3. Type **?CurrentDB("Customers").Properties("Tag").Value** in the Debug window and press Enter. The Debug window prints Change tag.

## Deleting a User-Defined Property

You can delete a user-defined property by running the Delete method of the Properties collection of the data access object. For example, we can delete the custom Tag property for the Customers table as follows:

1. Type **CurrentDB("Customers").Properties.Delete "Tag"** in the Debug window and press Enter. The custom Tag property is deleted.

2. Type **CurrentDB("Customers").Properties!Tag.Value = "Change tag"** and press Enter. An error is generated because the Tag property no longer exists (see Figure 19.7).

**FIGURE 19.7:**

The error message that appears when you refer to a user-defined property that doesn't exist

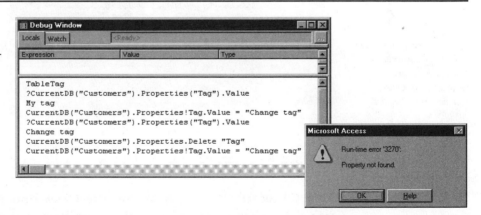

## Adding Application-Defined Properties to Data Access Objects

The application-defined property is a special kind of user-defined property. As explained in Chapter 11, when an application such as Microsoft Access defines a property for a data access object, the property is called an application-defined property. The Jet engine doesn't automatically recognize application-defined properties. Table 19.5 (on the CD under Tables\Chapter19.pdf) lists examples of the application-defined properties that Microsoft Access defines.

There are two ways to have Jet recognize an application-defined property. The first way is to set the property's value for the first time in the user interface; the second way is to set the property's value for the first time in VBA code.

**Setting an Application-Defined Property in the Interface**    When you create a table interactively, you can set the table's Description property in table Design view. If you enter a value for the Description property in the property sheet, Jet automatically adds the Description property to the table's Properties collection. Subsequently, you can set or get the value using the syntax for a user-defined property. Figure 19.8 shows the Table Properties property sheet for the Customers table with an initial setting for the table's Description property.

**FIGURE 19.8:**

When you set an application-defined property in the property sheet of an object, Jet automatically adds the property to the object's Properties collection.

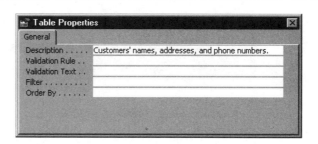

To explore how Jet handles the Description property when you enter a value interactively and when you do not:

1. Type **?CurrentDB("Customers").Properties("Description").Value** and press Enter. The current setting for the Description property is displayed.

2. Type **CurrentDB("Customers").Properties("Description").Value = "Customers of Northwind Traders"** and press Enter. Then type **?CurrentDB("Customers").Properties("Description").Value** and press Enter. The Debug window displays the current value of the property.

3. Open the Customers table in Design view and display the Table Properties property sheet. The Description property displays the changed setting.

4. Create a new table named tblNoDescription with a single field. Type **?CurrentDB("tblNoDescription").Properties("Description").Value** and press Enter. Jet doesn't recognize the Description property for the new table and displays the error message (see Figure 19.9).

**FIGURE 19.9:**

The error message that appears when Jet does not recognize an application-defined property

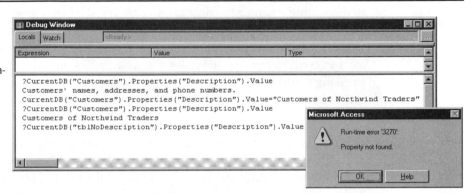

**Setting an Application-Defined Property in Code** When you want to set an application-defined property for an object for the first time in code, you have to first create the property and append it to the Properties collection. For example, the procedure shown in Listing 19.11 creates the Description property for the tblNoDescription table.

### Listing 19.11

```
Public Sub ApplicationProperty()
Dim db As Database, tdf As TableDef, prp As Property
Set db = CurrentDB
Set tdf = db.TableDefs("tblNoDescription")
Set prp = tdf.CreateProperty("Description")
prp.Type = dbText
prp.Value = "There is a Description"
tdf.Properties.Append prp
Debug.Print tdf.Properties!Description
End Sub
```

1. Enter the ApplicationProperty procedure in the basProperties module.

2. Run the procedure in the Debug window. The procedure creates the Description property for the tblNoDescription table. The Debug window displays the new setting for the property.

**Setting Startup Options Programmatically**   When an application-defined property cannot be set in the interface, the only alternative is to set it for the first time in VBA code. An important property in this category is the Allow-BypassKey property of the Database. The AllowBypassKey property allows you to determine whether the user can bypass the startup options and the AutoExec startup macro you have set for your application. When AllowBypassKey has the value True (the default value), pressing the Shift key on startup bypasses the startup condition; when the AllowBypassKey has the value False, the effect of pressing the Shift key on startup is disabled. This property is not available in the Startup option dialog.

You can use the procedure in Listing 19.12 to set the value of the AllowBypass-Key property. The procedure uses error handling to determine if the property has already been appended to the Properties collection. This procedure is an example of generating an error deliberately as part of the logic of the procedure. The procedure begins by attempting to set the AllowBypassKey property. If the property has already been added to the database, the statement to assign the property value is executed and the procedure ends. If the property has not been added to the database, the assignment statement fails, the error (code 3270) is generated, and the error-handling code takes over. The error-handling code creates the property, sets its value , and appends the property to the Properties collection of the database.

To use the procedure, call the procedure and specify the argument as False (if you want to disable the Shift key as a bypass of the startup conditions) or as True (if you want to enable the Shift key as a bypass).

### Listing 19.12

```
Public Sub SetByPass(booByPass As Boolean)
Dim db As Database, prp As Property
On Error GoTo Error_SetByPass
Set db = CurrentDB
db.Properties!AllowBypassKey = booByPass

Exit_SetByPass:
Exit Sub
```

```
Error_SetByPass:
If Err = 3270 Then
'The Property does not exist and needs to be created
    Set prp = db.CreateProperty("AllowBypassKey")
    prp.Type = dbBoolean
    prp.Value = booByPass
    db.Properties Append.prp
    Resume Next
Else
    MsgBox Err.Number & Err.Description
    Resume Exit_SetByPass
End If
End Sub
```

1. Enter the SetBypass procedure in the basProperties module.

2. Switch to the Database window, choose the Startup command in the Tools menu, and set the Application Title to Testing the ByPass. When you close the Startup dialog, the title bar displays the new title.

3. To disable the bypass effect of the Shift key on start up, type **SetByPass(False)** in the Debug window and press Enter. The AllowBypassKey property has been added to the database and the effect of the Shift key on startup has been disabled.

4. Close the database. Press the Shift key and start up the database; the title bar continues to display Testing the ByPass. Enable the bypass effect of the Shift key on startup by typing **SetByPass(True)** in the Debug window and pressing Enter. This time, when you close the database and press the Shift key while starting up the database, the startup options are disabled and the title bar displays the words "Microsoft Access."

# Custom Properties for Forms, Reports, and Controls

There is no way to add custom properties to the Properties collection for a form, report, or control. However, there are two ways you can create custom properties for these Access application objects. The simplest way to create a custom property for a form, report, or control is to use the Tag property. The second way, available only for forms and reports, is to use property procedures. This section describes both techniques.

## Using the Tag Property

You can create custom properties for forms, reports, and controls using the Tag property. Forms, form sections, reports, report sections, and controls all have a Tag property which you can use to store a string expression. The default setting is the zero-length string(""), but you can store any string expression up to 2048 characters in length. The Tag property can be set in the property sheet, in a macro, or in a VBA procedure.

We used a form's Tag property in Chapters 5 and 15 to keep track of how a form was opened. If the form was opened by clicking a button on a form other than the main switchboard, we stored the name of the form with the opener button. Macros and procedures for closing the form used the Tag property to decide whether to unhide switchboard. In those examples, we used the Tag property as a custom "FormOpener" property.

### Using the Tag Property to Store Multiple Custom Properties

You can store several custom properties in the Tag property; you just need a way to identify the values. A useful structure is proposed in the *Access 97 Developer's Handbook* by Paul Litwin, Ken Getz, and Mike Gilbert (Sybex, 1997). The proposed syntax is:

TagName1=TagValue1;TagName2=TagValue2;...;TagNameN=TagValueN

In this structure, names and values are separated by an equal sign (=), pairs are separated by a semicolon (;), there are no spaces, and you cannot use the semicolon in any values. To use a structure like this one, you need to create string manipulation procedures that can read the Tag property setting, search for a specified custom property name, and read its corresponding value. For more information, see the *Access 97 Developer's Handbook* by Paul Litwin, Ken Getz, and Mike Gilbert (Sybex, 1997).

# Custom Properties for Forms and Reports

Chapter 12 introduced the three kinds of procedures: function procedures, sub procedures, and property procedures. You use property procedures to create custom properties for forms and reports and for the new objects you create using independent class modules.

Property procedures normally come in pairs: Property Let procedure creates a property whose value you can assign, and a Property Get procedure creates a property whose value you can read.

When you create a custom property that you set by referring to an object instead of by assigning a value, use a Property Set procedure to create the property that you set and a Property Get procedure to create a property that returns a reference to an object. These custom properties are analogous to the Form, Report, RecordsetClone, and Module properties that return objects instead of values.

## Using the Property Let Statement

To create a custom property for a form or report, you use the Property Let statement to create a property procedure in the form's or report's module. In the simplest case, the syntax is

```
Public Property Let propertyname (propertyvalue As datatype)
[statements]
End Property
```

where *propertyname* is the name of the custom property you want to create and *propertyvalue* represents the value of the custom property. When the object is defined using an independent class module, you create the Property Let procedure in the module.

As an example, suppose you want to create a custom property for a form called the LockedForm property that is analogous to the Locked property of a control. You design the LockedForm property so that when you set its value to True, all of the data controls on the form are locked and when you set the LockedForm property to False the data controls are unlocked. You create the Property Let procedure in the form's module using the syntax

```
Public Property Let LockedForm (booLock As Boolean)
[statements]
End Property
```

where the statements lock the data controls on the form if you set the LockedForm property to True and unlock the data controls otherwise.

**Calling a Property Procedure**    You run a Property Let procedure by including the procedure name as a property in an assignment statement that assigns a value to the property. For example, the LockedForm Property Let procedure runs whenever you set the value using an assignment statement such as

```
Forms!Suppliers.LockedForm = True
```

Normally, you create the property procedure as a Public procedure stored in the form's module. If you want the custom property to behave like a built-in form property, it must be public so that it can be called from macros or from procedures in other modules.

**NOTE**    A form's custom property does not appear in the form's property sheet, so you can't set a custom property in Design mode. You can, however, set the property in a macro or a VBA procedure (if it is a public procedure).

**Creating a BrowseMode Property**    As an example, we'll create Locked-Form as a custom property for the Suppliers form. We'll create the property so that when we set the value of the LockedForm property to True, the data controls on the form are locked and when we set the value of the LockedForm property to False, the data controls on the form are unlocked. (For simplicity, we create the procedure for text box controls only, but you can modify the procedure to lock or unlock any type of data control.) The value of the LockedForm property is True or False and has the Boolean data type.

1.  Select the Suppliers form in the Database window and click the Code button in the toolbar.

2.  Choose the Procedure command in the Insert menu and select the Property option in the Insert Procedure dialog (see Figure 19.10a). VBA automatically inserts code templates for both the Property Let and Property Get procedures (see Figure 19.10b)

3.  Insert the property procedure shown in Listing 19.13. The value of the property is passed as an argument to the procedure. The procedure determines if the value is True or False. In either case, the procedure uses a For Each...Next structure to loop through the controls on the form. We can refer to the

**FIGURE 19.10:**

Create a custom form property by inserting property procedures (a). VBA creates a pair of code templates for the new Property Let and Property Get procedures (b).

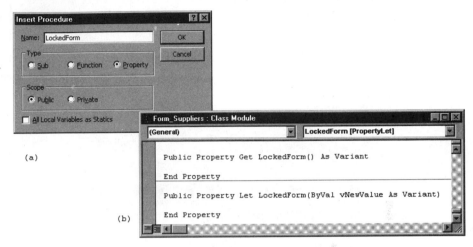

(a)

(b)

Controls collection as Me.Controls or simply as Me because the Controls collection is the default collection of the form. When you set the LockedForm property to True, the property procedure first tests to determine if there are any unsaved changes to the records, saves the changes if there are any, and then locks all of the text box controls. When you set the LockedForm property to False, the procedure unlocks the controls.

## Listing 19.13

```
Public Property Let LockedForm(booLock As Boolean)
Dim ctl As Control
Select Case booLock
Case True
    If Me.Dirty = True Then
        Runcommand acCmdSaveRecord
    End If
    For Each ctl In Me
        If TypeOf ctl Is TextBox Then ctl.Locked = True
    Next
Case False
For Each ctl In Me
        If TypeOf ctl Is TextBox Then ctl.Locked = False
    Next
End Select
End Property
```

4. In the code template for the LockedForm Property Get procedure change the data type of the procedure's return value from Variant to Boolean. We'll create the procedure later but the data types must match to avoid a run-time error.

5. Save the module and switch to Form view. Run the procedure by typing **Forms!Suppliers.LockedForm = True** in the Debug window and pressing Enter. Confirm that the data controls are locked.

6. Type **Forms!Suppliers.LockedForm = False** and press Enter. Confirm that the data controls are unlocked.

## Using the Property Get Statement

The LockedForm property procedure we created with the Property Let statement is a write-only property. If you try to read its value in the usual way, by typing **? Forms!Suppliers.LockedForm** and pressing Enter in the Debug window, there is no response. To make the LockedForm property readable, we'll use the Property Get statement to create the other member of the property procedure pair.

When you create a write-only custom property named *propertyname* using a Property Let procedure, you can also create a Property Get procedure with the same name that returns the value of the property. In the simplest case the syntax is

```
Public Property Get propertyname As datatype
[statements]
propertyname = expression
End Property
```

where the datatype returned by the Property Get procedure must be the same as the datatype of the argument passed to the Property Let procedure. In other words, if you set a property to a value with a specific data type, you can only read a value with the same data type. A Property Get procedure runs whenever you try to read the value of the property in a macro or a VBA procedure.

We'll create a Property Get procedure for the LockedForm property; the LockedForm Property Get procedure returns the value True or False with the Boolean data type.

1. Insert the property procedure shown in Listing 19.14 in the Suppliers form module. The procedure tests the locked property of a data control on the

form. If the Locked property of a data control is True, then the form is in browse mode and the procedure returns the value True. Otherwise, if the control is unlocked, the procedure returns the value False. To return a value from a Property Get procedure, you set the name of the procedure to the value you want to return (just as you do with a function procedure).

### Listing 19.14

```
Public Property Get LockedForm() As Boolean
LockedForm = Me.CompanyName.Locked
End Property
```

2.   Save the module and switch to Form view. Type
     **? Forms!Suppliers.Lockedform** in the Debug window and press Enter. The
     Debug window prints True or False depending on the mode you left the
     form in.

After creating the Property Let (or Set) and Property Get paired procedures for a custom property in a form's module, you use the custom property in the same way you use a built-in form property (except that you can't set or view its value in a property sheet). For example, when doing data entry for a product, you can provide browsing of the corresponding supplier by opening the Suppliers form and setting its LockedForm property as follows:

1.   Open the Products form in Design view and place a button named
     cmdSupplier on the form.

2.   Enter the event procedure shown below for the button's Click event. The
     procedure uses the OpenForm method of the DoCmd object to open the
     Suppliers form and synchronizes it to the Products form. The opened form
     is the active form, so the procedure uses the Screen object to refer to the
     Suppliers form when setting the LockedForm property to True.

```
Private Sub cmdSupplier_Click
Dim strWhere As String
strWhere = "SupplierID = Screen.ActiveForm.SupplierID"
DoCmd.OpenForm formname:= "Suppliers", wherecondition:= strWhere
Screen.ActiveForm.LockedForm = True
End Sub
```

3. Save the form and switch to Form view. Click the button. The Suppliers form opens synchronized and with locked data controls.

> **NOTE**
>
> When you create a custom property for a form or report using the Property Let and Property Get procedures, you create the procedures as public procedures in the form's or report's module. If you want another form or report to have the same property, you must copy the property procedures to the other form's or report's module. In the LockedForm example, the Property Let procedure shown in Listing 19.13 is reusable as is and can be copied to another form's module; however, the Property Get procedure shown in Listing 19.14 refers to a specific control on the Suppliers form and is not reusable without modification.

## Creating Custom Methods for a Form or Report

You can create a custom method for a form or report by entering a public procedure in the form's or report's module. For example, you can create a custom method called LockControls that locks the data controls on a form as shown in Listing 19.15

### Listing 19.15

```
Public Sub LockControls()
Dim ctl As Control
If Me.Dirty = True Then
    Runcommand acCmdSaveRecord
End If
For Each ctl In Me
      If TypeOf ctl Is TextBox Then ctl.Locked = True
    Next
End Sub
```

and a custom method called UnlockControls that unlocks the data controls as shown in Listing 19.16.

### Listing 19.16

```
Public Sub UnLockControls()
Dim ctl As Control
For Each ctl In Me
        If TypeOf ctl Is TextBox Then ctl.Locked = False
    Next
End Sub
```

After creating a custom method for a form by entering a public procedure in the form's module, you use the custom method the same way you use a built-in method.

For example,

1. Insert the LockControls and UnlockControls procedures shown in Listing 19.15 and 19.16 in the Suppliers form module.

2. Save the module and the form and switch to Form view.

3. Run the method to lock the controls by typing **Forms!Suppliers.LockControls** in the Debug window and pressing Enter. The controls are locked.

4. Type **Forms!Suppliers.UnlockControls** and press Enter. The controls are unlocked.

**NOTE**  You can create a custom method for an object defined by an independent class module by entering a public procedure in the calling module.

# Displaying Multiple Instances of a Form

When you create a new form by placing controls and setting properties in form Design view and by creating procedures in the form's module, you create a blueprint or a set of directions for generating a specific form object. When you save the blueprint, its name is listed in the Forms pane in the Database window. In object-oriented programming terminology, the blueprint is called a *class*. When you select the name in the Database window and double-click, or when you use the OpenForm macro action or method, Access uses the blueprint to create and display a form object. In object-oriented programming terminology, the form object displayed is the *default instance* of the class.

Access VBA provides a way to create more than one form object for the blueprint as additional instances of the class; this means that you could take orders for two customers by displaying two copies of the Orders form (see Figure 19.11), or if you are reviewing products in the Products List form, you could display product information forms for several products at the same time (see Figure 19.12). Each of the form objects based on the blueprint is a separate instance of the class. Access VBA provides a special object called the Collection object as a way to keep track of the separate instances of a class.

**FIGURE 19.11:**

You can create separate instances of Orders and take two orders at the same time.

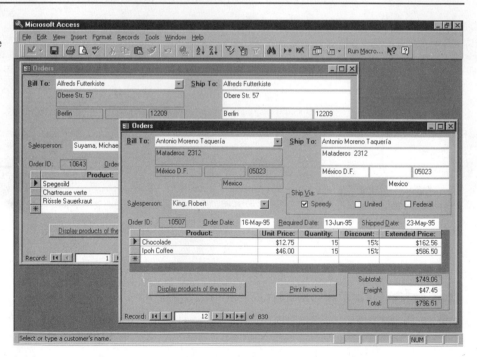

FIGURE 19.12:

You can create separate instances of Products and display product information for several products simultaneously.

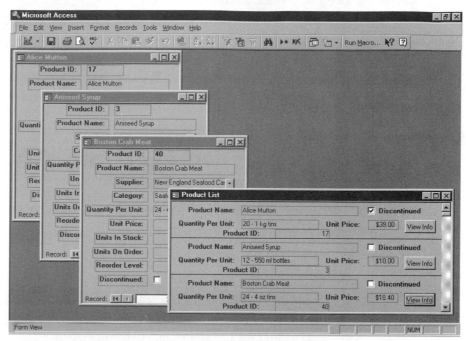

# Referring to a Closed Form in VBA

You refer to an open form in VBA using any of the familiar references Forms!formname, Forms("formname"), or Forms(n). Access VBA provides a way to refer to a closed form. To refer to a closed form named *formname*, use the syntax

Form_*formname*

For example, working in the Debug window, you can set the value a property of a closed form using an assignment statement such as Form_Customers .Caption = "My customers", and you can determine information about a closed form such as ?Form_Customers.RecordSource. When you refer to a closed form using the Form_*formname* syntax, VBA opens and hides the form. The reference to a closed form is also a reference to the form's module.

## Using the Collection Object

Access VBA allows you to create your own collections of objects and variables using the built-in Collection object to hold a set of objects of any type. We'll define a new Collection object to contain the new form objects that we'll be creating for the blueprint. Access VBA uses the New keyword to indicate new instances in two different ways: in declaration statements and in object variable assignment statements.

## Using the New Keyword in a Declaration Statement

You can use the New keyword in the declaration statement for an object variable as follows:

Dim *varname* As New *type*

where *varname* is the object variable you are declaring and *type* is the object type.

Without the New keyword, the declaration statement declares an object variable of the specified object type but doesn't create the object; you must use the Set statement to point the object variable to the object (and create the object if it doesn't already exist). For example, when you include the New keyword in the declaration statement

```
Dim CollectForms As New Collection
```

VBA automatically assigns a new Collection object the first time a procedure calls a property or method of the CollectForms object variable; this means that you don't need to use the Set statement to assign a new object to the object variable. When you include the New keyword in the declaration statement for an object, you are *implicitly creating* the object. For example, the declaration statement

```
Dim tdf As New TableDef
```

implicitly creates tdf as an object variable and automatically creates the TableDef object in the first statement in the procedure that assigns a property or runs a method for the object.

# Using the New Keyword in an Assignment Statement

The simplest Set statement has the syntax

Set *objvariable* = *objectexpression*

where *objvariable* is the object variable you are assigning and *objectexpression* is a reference to an object, another object variable of the same object type, or a function, property, or method that returns an object of the same object type. Examples of the simplest Set statement are

```
Dim frm As Form, rst As Recordset
Set frm = Forms!Customers
Set rst = Forms!Customers.RecordsetClone
```

The simple Set statement assigns an object to an object variable (and creates the object if it doesn't already exist). You can point several object variables at the same object using Set statements. For example, if the Orders form is closed, you can use the following statements to create and point the frm1 and frm2 object variables at the Orders form

```
Set frm1 = Form_Orders
Set frm2 = Form_Orders
```

In this case, the frm1 and frm2 object variables point to the same object.

1. Type **Set frm1 = Form_Orders** in the Debug window and press Enter. VBA has opened and hidden the form. Verify by choosing the Unhide command from the Window menu; leave the form hidden.

2. Type **Set frm2 = Form_Orders** in the Debug window and press Enter (see Figure 19.13a). This statement points the frm2 object variable at the hidden form. Choose the Unhide command in the Window menu (see Figure 19.13b). Click OK to unhide the single instance of the Orders form.

3. Close the Orders form.

You can use the New keyword in a Set statement to create new instances; the syntax is

```
Set objvariable = New objectexpression
```

where *objectexpression* is the name of an object, another object variable of the same object type, or a function or method that returns an object of the same object type.

**FIGURE 19.13:**

Without the New keyword, each assignment statement in the Debug window (a) assigns an object variable to the same object (b).

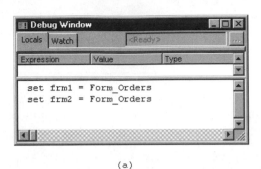

(a)                                                            (b)

When you include the New keyword, the Set statement creates a separate instance of the object. For example, you can use the following statments to create separate form objects

```
Set frm1 = New Form_Customers
Set frm2 = New Form_Customers
```

When you include the New keyword, frm1 and frm2 object variables point to different objects.

1. Type **Set frm1 = New Form_Orders** in the Debug window and press Enter. VBA has opened and hidden an instance of the form. Verify by choosing the Unhide command from the Window menu; leave the form hidden.

2. Type **Set frm2 = New Form_Orders** in the Debug window and press Enter (see Figure 19.14a). VBA opens and hides a second instance of the form. To verify, choose the Unhide command in the Window menu (see Figure 19.14b); Orders is listed for each separate instance. Click OK to unhide each instance of the Orders form. Figure 19.15 shows the two instances.

3. Using the navigation buttons, browse the recordset of each instance. Note that each instance has its own current record pointer. When you create multiple instances of a form, each instance has its own current record pointer and may have its own properties except for its name. Every instance of a form blueprint has the same name; this means that you cannot refer to a specific instance using its name. When you create a new instance, Access does add a member to the Forms collection so you can refer to an instance by its index number in the Forms collection.

4. Close all forms except the two instances of the Orders form. Type **Forms(0).Caption = "First"** in the Debug window and press Enter. The caption for one of the instances changes to First. Type **Forms(1).Caption = "Second"** and press Enter. The caption for the other instance changes to Second. Close both instances.

**FIGURE 19.14:**

When you include the New keyword, each assignment statement in the Debug window (a) creates a new instance and assigns it an object variable (b).

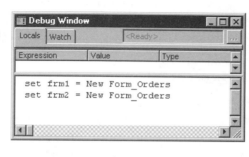

(a)                    (b)

**FIGURE 19.15:**

Two instances of the Orders form

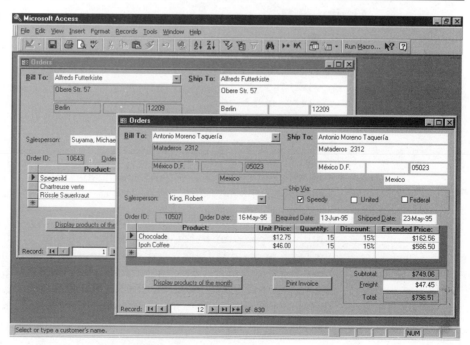

## Creating Multiple Instances

You can explore the process of displaying multiple instances of a form as follows:

1. Open a new standard module named basMultipleInstances. Create an object variable for a new Collection object by entering the following statement in the Declarations section of the module. This statement implicitly creates a new collection object to hold the form objects. By entering the declaration statement in the Declarations section of the module, you are declaring a module-level variable that continues to exist as long as the database is open. (You'll see the significance of declaring CollectForms at the module-level shortly.)

   ```
   Dim CollectForms As New Collection
   ```

2. Insert the Multiples procedure shown in Listing 19.17. The procedure declares frm as an object variable. The assignment statement uses the New keyword to create a new hidden instance of the Orders form. The procedure unhides the instance and then uses the Add method to add the instance to the CollectForms collection.

### Listing 19.17

```
Public Sub Multiples()
Dim frm As Form
Set frm = New Form_Orders
frm.Visible = True
CollectForms.Add frm
End Sub
```

3. Save the module. Run the Multiples procedure in the Debug window. An instance of the Orders form is created, displayed, and added to the CollectForms collection. You investigate the purpose of the CollectForms collection in the next step.

4. Place an apostrophe in front of the Collectforms.Add frm statement in the Multiples procedure to comment out the statement. Run the procedure in the Debug window. The procedure creates the instance and displays it for a brief moment, but this time, when the procedure ends, the frm object variable ceases to exist. With no variable pointing to it the instance is destroyed. By adding the instance to the CollectForms collection, there is a reference to the instance in the collection so the instance continues to exist as long as the

collection exists. By declaring the CollectForms object variable as a module level variable, we guarantee that the collection and therefore that the new instances of the Orders form will continue to exist after the Multiples procedure ends.

5. Delete the apostrophe, save and close the module. Run the Multiples procedures in the Debug window several times; each time you run the procedure, a new instance of the Orders form is created, displayed, and added to the collection (see Figure 19.16).

**FIGURE 19.16:**

Creating multiple instances of the Orders form by adding the instances to the module-level CollectForms collection object

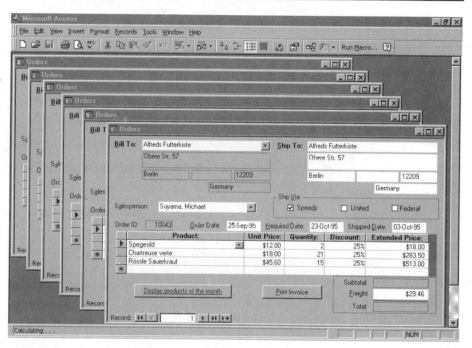

# Example: The Product List and Viewing Product Information

To illustrate how to include multiple instances in an application, we'll add a command button to the Product List form that runs a procedure that creates and displays a new instance of a form that displays product information.

1. Create a copy of the Products form named frmViewProduct and modify the copy as shown in Figure 19.17. Close the frmViewProduct form.

**FIGURE 19.17:**

The frmViewProduct form

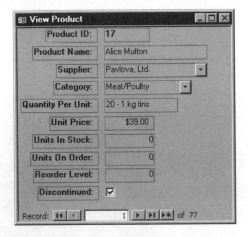

2. Open the Product List form in Design view and set the PopUp property to No. Place a command button named cmdView in the Detail section and set Caption property to View Info.

3. Click the Code button in the toolbar. Implicitly create the CollectForms collection by entering the following statement in the Declarations section

```
Dim CollectForms As New Collection
```

4. Enter the event procedure shown in Listing 19.18. The procedure creates the frm object variable, creates a new instance of the frmViewProducts form, and adds it to the CollectForms collection. The procedure uses the With structure to set the Filter property to synchronize the new instance to the product selected in the Product List form, and to set the FilterOn property to apply the filter. The With structure also includes statements to set the Caption and the Visible properties.

## Listing 19.18

```
Private Sub cmdView_click()
Dim frm As Form
Set frm = New Form_frmViewProduct
CollectForms.Add frm
```

```
With frm
    .Filter = "ProductID = " & Forms![Product List]!ProductID
    .FilterOn = True
    .Caption = ProductName
    .Visible = True
End With
End Sub
```

5. Save the Product List form and switch to Form view. Select a product and click the View Info button. An instance of the frmViewProduct form opens for the product you selected. Select another product and click its View Info button. A second instance of the frmViewProduct form opens for the second product. Figure 19.18 shows the result of displaying several instances of the frmViewProduct form.

**FIGURE 19.18:**

Displaying several instances of a form, each synchronized to a selected product

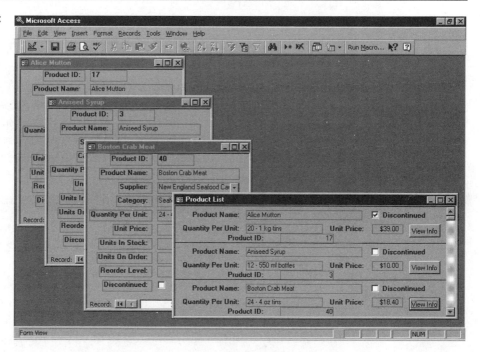

# Summary

This chapter has introduced you to techniques for creating and modifying new objects programmatically. Because the Access application and the Jet database engine have been created by different Microsoft developers, the two object models use different techniques for creating and deleting objects and for creating new object properties and methods. The chapter gives you a glimpse of these advanced VBA topics.

- In most cases, you use the Create... method of a data access object to create a child object. Normally, you must create a complete child object with required properties and often with its own required child object before you can save the child object. For example, to create a TableDef object you must give the object a valid name and create at least one Field object with a Name and Type property.

- You create a custom property for a data access object by using the object's CreateProperty method and appending the new Property object to the object's Properties collection.

- An application such as Access that acts as a host for the Jet database engine may create application-defined properties for a data access object. Jet is unaware of an application-defined property until you either set the property in the application's interface or create a Property object for the property and append the new Property object to the Properties collection of the data access object.

- Access VBA provides a set of built-in functions that you can use to create new forms, reports, and controls programmatically.

- Access 97 provides a new Module object with properties and methods that you can use to create and modify modules programmatically.

- You create a custom property for a form or report by creating a pair of public Property Let (or Property Set for a property that returns an object) and Property Get procedures in the form's or report's module. You set the custom property using an assignment statement in a macro or procedure and you read the value of the custom property by referring to the custom property in a macro or procedure.

- You create a custom method for a form or report by creating a public function or sub procedure in the form's or report's module.

- Access 97 provides a new independent class module that you can use to create new objects not associated with a form or report. Create custom properties for the class by creating Property Let (or Property Set) and Property Get property procedures and create methods by creating public function or sub procedures and storing the procedures in the class module.

- When you create a new form or report, you are creating a blueprint or class that Access uses to create individual form or report objects. When you open a form, Access creates the default instance. You can use the blueprint to create separate instances using the New keyword in assignment statements. You can create a module-level Collection object to keep track of the multiple instances.

# CHAPTER

## TWENTY

# Expanding
# Access

- Converting macros to VBA procedures

- Creating a library database

- Introducing dynamic-link libraries

- Using ActiveX controls

- Understanding remote control using Automation

This final chapter is an overview of a few advanced topics available with VBA programming. This chapter is neither comprehensive in the range of features nor completely thorough in its treatment of these topics. The purpose of this chapter is to give you a glimpse of the landscape surrounding Access should you decide to venture forth.

Because many of the advanced features of Access require VBA programming, the chapter begins with a discussion of converting macros to VBA procedures. Macro programming is an excellent way to learn how to automate an Access database. If you find you need to include any of the VBA-only features discussed throughout Part III, you can leverage your work with macros by converting them to VBA procedures complete with simple error handling.

The chapter continues with discussions of several ways to expand the world your database lives in. The chapter explains how to create a database as a custom library in which you can store VBA procedures. Custom libraries will allow you to easily reuse VBA procedures in your other databases. You'll learn how to create these library databases and how to gain access to them from another database. You also will learn about dynamic-link libraries that store code written and thoroughly debugged by other developers. One of the most important dynamic-link libraries is one that Windows makes available, called the Windows API. By borrowing and using library code, you can expand the abilities of your application beyond those of Microsoft Access.

After discussing how to expand a database application using libraries, the chapter's focus shifts to explain how to use two components of ActiveX to enrich a database. ActiveX is a set of technologies developed by Microsoft to allow communication between computers, applications, and objects. In the first ActiveX technique you will add new controls, called ActiveX controls, to Access. ActiveX controls behave like the familiar toolbox controls, but provide capabilities that Access doesn't provide— such as the ability to display an interactive calendar or play a sound or video file. In the second ActiveX technique you will write programs in Access VBA. These programs control the objects of another application, such as Excel or Word, in the same way you control the Access Application and Jet database objects. The technology that allows you to control another application programmatically is called Automation.

**NOTE** The word "application" is used in this chapter to refer to off-the-shelf programs such as Access, Excel, Word, Visio, and Visual Basic. This chapter uses the word "project" to refer to the set of Visual Basic procedures you've written for a particular file created using one of these programs. For example, in Access, a project is the set of all the standard, form, report, and independent class modules in an Access .mdb file. Earlier chapters referred to the file you were creating as your "application"; in this chapter we'll call the file your "project" to avoid overuse and confusion.

**NOTE** For hands-on experience with the techniques described in this chapter, create a fresh copy of Northwind and name it Northwind_Ch20.

# Converting Macros to VBA Procedures

Part II showed you how to use macro programming to automate a database. You learned how to write macros to navigate through the database, automate data entry, and work with groups of records. You also learned how to avoid macro errors by testing conditions before executing macro actions that could fail.

In Part III you learned how to use VBA programming to automate many database tasks. You also learned how to use additional VBA powers, such as the ability to detect errors, write instructions to handle an error, create new objects, and run a set of instructions in an all-or-nothing unit called a transaction. You can build fully automated, complex projects entirely with macros. However, even the simplest project may require some VBA procedures if you want to include any of the VBA-only features described in Part III. Both the nature of the task you try to automate and who will use the custom application determine whether VBA is required. Here are some reasons for using VBA procedures instead of macros:

**To create custom functions** Access includes a large set of built-in functions that you can use with operators to create complex expressions. Sometimes an expression you need to use in several places is long and complex. Rather than retyping a complex expression, you can create your own custom function. You can use custom functions the same way you use the Access built-in functions.

**To handle more complex decisions**   The built-in decision functions, conditions in macros, and the RunMacro action for repeated operations provide convenient ways to handle simple decisions. If you need more complex decision structures, you may still be able to use macros. But using the powerful and efficient control structures of Visual Basic often results in a solution that is faster and easier to create and that runs faster than the equivalent macro-control structure.

**To trap errors**   Because of limited error handling in macro programming, the approach we adopted in Part II is to avoid most errors by anticipating them. We used a simple Visual Basic error handler to suppress default error messages when macros alone were insufficient. As unanticipated errors occur, you can often troubleshoot and modify the application by using macros. This will help you avoid future occurrences. Nevertheless, external events that you can't prevent or anticipate may occur: a file may be deleted, the power may shut down while a macro is running, or a network connection may be lost. The most important reason for including Visual Basic in your application is that it has the ability to handle unanticipated errors. With Visual Basic, you can include error handling in two ways: in an individual procedure to handle VBA errors that occur when the procedure runs, and in the event procedure for a form's or report's Error event to handle interface and Jet database engine errors that occur when the form or report is active.

**To provide hard-copy documentation**   The documentation for macros that is created by the Database Documenter is not as convenient to use as a printout of Visual Basic code. For large or complicated applications, easy-to-use hard-copy documentation is essential.

**To create and manipulate objects**   In most cases you can create and manipulate objects interactively (that is, in the object's Design view). There are times, however, when it is useful to define or modify an object automatically when the application is running. For example, the wizards create objects to your specifications: the Form Wizard creates forms and the Combo Box Wizard creates combo boxes. The built-in wizards are written in Visual Basic. You may want to create a custom wizard that is specific to your application. You can use data definition language queries of Access SQL to create and modify tables, to create and delete indexes, and to create relationships between tables. You can run data definition queries using either macros or VBA procedures. However, the data definition language of Access SQL is limited compared to the capabilities of the data access objects available only through VBA. With VBA, you can create and manipulate any of the objects in the database, as well as the database itself.

**To perform actions not available with macros** There are some actions that cannot be carried out efficiently, or at all, with macros alone. An important example is *transaction processing*. Transaction processing is available only in VBA. In a Visual Basic transaction, all of the operations of the transaction are run in memory; if an operation fails, the transaction is aborted, leaving the data tables as they were before the transaction began. If all operations are successful, the results of the transaction are updated to the data tables.

**To pass arguments to your code** With macros, you set the action arguments in the lower pane of the Macro window when you create the macro. You can't change these arguments when the macro is running and you can't use variables in the macro action arguments. These limitations prevented certain macros from being reusable. For example, the macros for deleting records that we created in Chapter 8 referred to specific fields and specific tables by name; you have to modify these macros for each data entry form. Other macros that we created are reusable because we used the Screen object instead of references to specific controls and forms. Using the Screen object has the same effect as using a variable. VBA provides additional, more efficient ways to change the arguments in your code when the code is running and to use variables in the arguments.

**To create variables** In macro programming, the only way to create a variable is to use an unbound control on a form to hold the temporary value. While the form is open, the value in the control is available for use by other forms, queries, macros, and VBA procedures. By contrast, VBA provides the ability to create a variable as a named location in memory without using a control on a form. VBA also lets you limit the variable's scope by specifying which other procedures have access to the variable.

**To optimize performance** There are features of Visual Basic, such as optimized methods and compiling, that result in better performance than the corresponding macros-only approaches. For example, Visual Basic provides the Seek method to locate a record in a table, which is significantly faster than the FindRecord action. VBA provides bookmarks to save your place in a recordset so you can quickly return to a record. Transaction processing is typically much faster than running separate operations. Another performance gain is possible because the code you write in Visual Basic is compiled. *Compiling* checks the code for certain types of errors and converts the code into a form that Access can execute more efficiently. In macro programming, the individual macro actions have been designed for optimal performance, but the macros you create are not compiled.

**To work outside microsoft access**    With macros, your work outside Access is extremely limited. You can use the RunApp action to launch another Windows or MS-DOS-based application, but once the application is open you are limited to working interactively with it. This chapter shows you how to use VBA to extend your programming horizons beyond the off-the-shelf Access application. Using Visual Basic, you can automate the other application with *Automation* or *dynamic data exchange (DDE)* and you can write instructions for ActiveX controls (formerly called OLE custom controls) that provide special abilities to your Access project. Using Visual Basic, you can also communicate with the Windows *application programming interface (API)* using functions in the *dynamic-link libraries (DLLs)* provided by Windows. For example, you can check to see if a file exists, determine the display driver, or determine if other applications are running.

Whether you use macro or VBA programming to automate your database is up to you. Many complex projects created in-house for use by coworkers use only macros. By contrast, most professional Access developers creating custom applications for others use only VBA procedures if for no other reason but the error handling capability. Some developers use macro programming to create a prototype in the quickest time possible and then use VBA for the full development of the prototype into a custom application that includes comprehensive error handling, transaction processing, optimal performance, and interactions with Windows or other applications.

**NOTE**    Even VBA-only databases must use macros for two operations: the AutoKeys macro for reassigning keys and the AutoExec macro for carrying out actions when the database starts.

If you decide to rewrite some or all of your macros as VBA procedures, you don't have to start from scratch. Access provides the ability to convert macros to VBA code complete with simple error handling. After converting a macro to a VBA procedure you can modify the error-handling instructions, change the decisions and loop structures to the more efficient control structures available in VBA, and add the features not available in macro programming.

There are two ways to convert macros:

- You can convert all of the event macros for a form or report to a set of event procedures that Access stores in the form's or report's module.

- You can convert all of the macros in a macrosheet to function procedures stored in a new standard module.

**NOTE**    In previous versions of Access, you created custom menu bars or shortcut menus using macros. You can convert the menu macros to Access 97 command bars using the Create Menu From Macros and Create Shortcut Menu From Macros commands in the fly-out menu of the Macros command in the Tools menu. Search "converting macros" in online Help for more information.

## Converting Event Macros to Event Procedures

You can convert all of the event macros for a form or report to event procedures and store them in the form's or report's module. To explore this process, open the Northwind_Ch20 database and take the following steps:

1.  Open the Customers macrosheet. Figure 20.1a shows the two event macros for the Customers form: the ValidateID macro is assigned to the BeforeUpdate event of the CustomerID field and the Update Country List macro is assigned to the form's AfterUpdate event.

2.  Open the Customers form in Design view. Figures 20.1b and 20.1c show the assignments of the macros to event properties. Scroll to the end of the Form properties sheet to observe that the form's HasModule property is set to No, which indicates that the Customers form is a lightweight form without a form module.

**FIGURE 20.1:**

The Customers macrosheet (a) stores macros that are assigned to the BeforeUpdate event of the CustomerID text box (b) and the AfterUpdate event of the form (c).

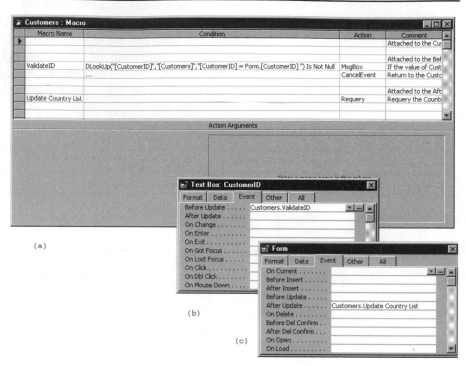

3. In the Tools menu, select the Macros command and then the Convert Form's Macros to Visual Basic command. Figure 20.2a shows the Convert form macros dialog with options to add simple error handling and to include your macro comments as comments in the VBA procedure.

**FIGURE 20.2:**

Use the Convert form macros dialog to add error handling and the macro comments to the new event procedure (a). The message displayed if the conversion is successful (b).

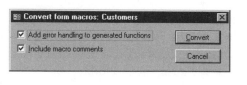

4. With both options checked, click the Convert button. After a few seconds, if the conversion is successful, the message shown in Figure 20.2b is displayed. The property sheets for the form and CustomerID text box indicate that the macro assignments have been replaced with assignments to event procedures, and that the form's HasModule property has been changed to Yes (see Figure 20.3).

**FIGURE 20.3:**

When you convert a form's macros, the macro assignments are replaced with assignments to event procedures (a) and (b) and the form's HasModule property is set to Yes (b).

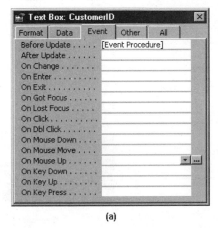

(a)

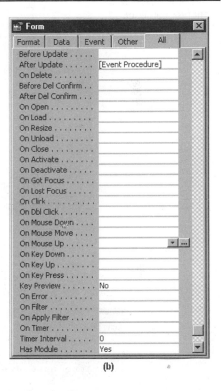

(b)

5. Click the Code button in the toolbar. The ValidateID event macro has been converted to the CustomerID_BeforeUpdate event procedure shown in Figure 20.4a. The Update Country List macro has been converted to the Form_AfterUpdate event procedure shown in Figure 20.4b. The new event procedures include the macros' comments. The new procedures have basic error handling that displays the error code in a message box if a runtime error occurs.

**FIGURE 20.4:**

The ValidateID macro is converted to the CustomerID_BeforeUpdate event procedure (a) and the Update Country List macro is converted to the Form_AfterUpdate event procedure (b).

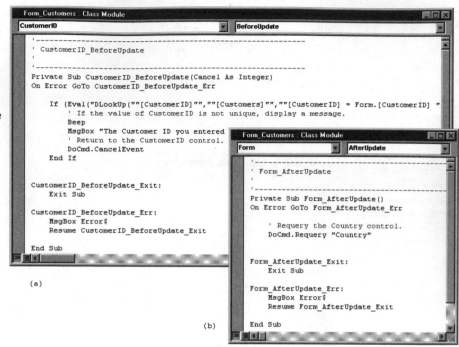

When you convert the event macros for a form or report, Access automatically creates the form or report module (if necessary) and changes the names of the event macros to the corresponding event procedure names using the following syntax:

```
Form_eventname or Report_eventname
controlname_eventname
```

Access automatically assigns the event procedure to the event property. If the form or report module already exists, Access adds the converted event procedures to the module. The macrosheets that stored the event macros continue to exist and are unchanged.

# Converting Macros to Function Procedures

Instead of converting the event macros for a form or report to event procedures, you may opt to convert all the macros stored in a macrosheet to function procedures stored in a new standard module. In this approach, a macro triggered by an event is converted to a function procedure, but the function procedure is not automatically assigned to the event. Rather, the original macro continues to be assigned to the event and you must manually reassign the event property to trigger the function procedure. Also, a macro that is called by another macro using the RunMacro macro action (or by a VBA procedure using the RunMacro method of the DoCmd object) is converted to a function procedure. The macro or procedure that calls the original macro is not automatically modified to call the function procedure. You must manually modify the macro or procedure to call the function procedure.

When you convert macros in a macrosheet to function procedures in a standard module, VBA names the function procedure using the syntax

```
macrosheetname_macroname
```

and replaces spaces in both names with underscore characters (_). The original macrosheet continues to exist, and the original macros continue to be called as they were before you created the function procedures. You must change the properties or statements that call the macros to call the function procedures instead.

1. Open the Customer Phone List macrosheet. The macrosheet (see Figure 20.5a) contains the Alpha Buttons event macro, which is triggered by the AfterUpdate event of the CompanyNameFilters option group on the Customer Phone List form (see Figure 20.5b). Scroll down to observe the Print macro, which is called as a support macro by the ^p macro in the Sample Autokeys macrosheet.

**NOTE**  The Alpha Buttons macro uses the form's RecordsetClone property to refer to the form's recordset, then uses the RecordCount property of the recordset to count the number of records displayed by the form. To refer to a property of the form's recordset in a macro, use the syntax Recordsetclone.*propertyname*.

**FIGURE 20.5:**

The Customer Phone List macro sheet (a) contains the Alpha Buttons event macro assigned to the AfterUpdate event of the option group on the Customer Phone List form (b).

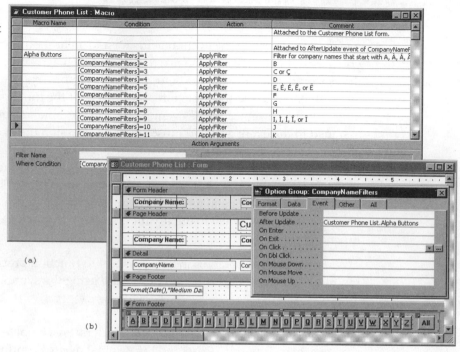

(a)

(b)

2. Choose the Save As/Export command in the File menu. Choose the Save As Visual Basic module in the Save As dialog (see Figure 20.6a) and click OK. Click the options to add error handling and comments in the Convert macro: Customer Phone List dialog shown in Figure 20.6b and click the Convert button. Access creates a new standard module named Converted Macro - Customer Phone List and displays a message to indicate successful conversion.

**FIGURE 20.6:**

Use the Save As dialog to save a macrosheet as a new standard module (a) and the Convert macro dialog to add error handling and comments (b).

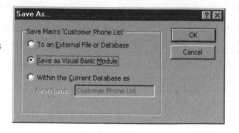

(a)

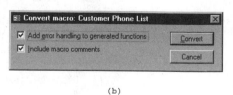

(b)

3. Choose Converted Macro - Customer Phone List in the Modules tab of the Database window and click Design to display the new module. Figure 20.7 shows the Customer_Phone_List_Alpha_Buttons function procedure. Notice that the procedure uses the CodeContextObject property of the Application object to refer to the object that has the focus when the procedure runs.

**FIGURE 20.7:**

When you convert the macros in the Customer Phone List macrosheet using the Save As command, the Alpha Buttons macro is converted to a function procedure and named Customer_Phone _List_Alpha_Buttons. The new function procedures are stored in a new standard module named Converted Macro- Customer Phone List.

```
Converted Macro- Customer Phone List : Module

(General)                                    Customer_Phone_List_Alpha_Buttons

' ------------------------------------------------------------
' Customer_Phone_List_Alpha_Buttons
'
' ------------------------------------------------------------
Function Customer_Phone_List_Alpha_Buttons()
On Error GoTo Customer_Phone_List_Alpha_Buttons_Err

    With CodeContextObject
        ' Attached to the Customer Phone List form.
        ' Attached to AfterUpdate event of CompanyNameFilter option group.
        If (.CompanyNameFilters = 1) Then
            ' Filter for company names that start with A, À, Á, Â, Ã, or Ä.
            DoCmd.ApplyFilter "", "[CompanyName] Like ""[AÀÁÂÃÄ]*"""
        End If
        If (.CompanyNameFilters = 2) Then
            ' B
            DoCmd.ApplyFilter "", "[CompanyName] Like ""B*"""
        End If
        If (.CompanyNameFilters = 3) Then
            ' C or Ç
            DoCmd.ApplyFilter "", "[CompanyName] Like ""[CÇ]*"""
        End If
        If (.CompanyNameFilters = 4) Then
            ' D
            DoCmd.ApplyFilter "", "[CompanyName] Like ""D*"""
```

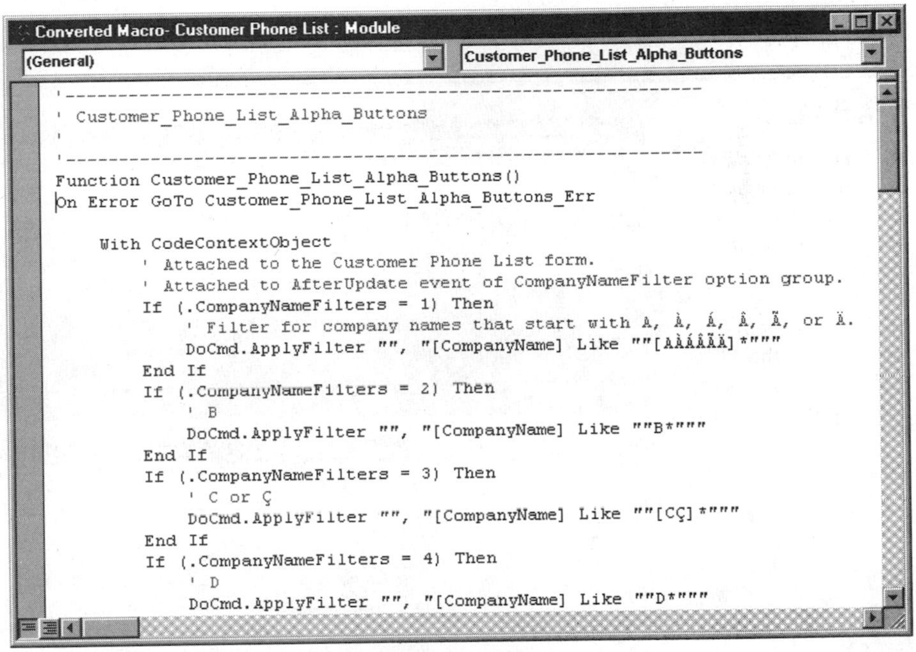

4. Open the Customer Phone List form in Design view. The AfterUpdate property of the CompanyNameFilter option group is still assigned to the event macro. To assign the function procedure instead of the macro, type **= Customer_Phone_List_Alpha_Buttons()** in the AfterUpdate property box.

5. Save the form and switch to Form view. Click one of the buttons in the form's option group.

6. Open the Sample Autokeys macrosheet. The ^p macro uses the RunMacro action to run the Print macro. Change the macro action to RunCode. Type **Customer_Phone_List_Print()** as the Function Name argument

(see Figure 20.8a). Omit the equals sign (=), but you must include the parentheses, even if the function has no arguments. Alternatively, click in the Function Name argument and then click the Build button at the right of the argument box to display the Expression Builder. Click the Functions folder and then click the Northwind_Ch20 folder. The Expression Builder lists the standard modules in the list box in the center and the new function procedures in the list box at the right (see Figure 20.8b). Select Converted Macro-Customer Phone List in the second box and Customer_Phone_List_Print() in the third box, click Paste, and then click OK to close the builder.

**FIGURE 20.8:**

To call the function procedure, change the Run Macro macro action to the Run Code macro action (a). Use the Expression Builder to set the Function Name argument for the RunCode macro action (b).

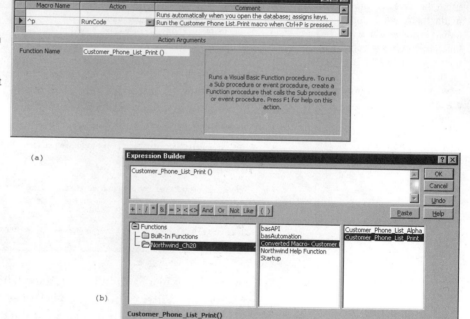

7. Save the macrosheet. Click in the Customer Phone List form, click one of the buttons in the form's option group, and press Ctrl+P. The ^p macro runs the function procedure.

# Understanding Library Databases

When you create generic procedures that you want to reuse in your other Access projects, there are two ways you can make them available: store them in a module and import the module into another project, or create a library database and make the library database available to another project. A *library database* is a collection of procedures objects that you can call from another Access project.

## Creating a Library Database

Creating a library database is exactly the same as creating a regular Access database. However, you normally won't store data in the library database the way you do in a regular database. You can use any valid name for the library. The convention is to use the .mda extension for a library database, but you can use the .mdb extension, too. Here are some guidelines for the macros and VBA procedures in a library database:

**Test thoroughly**   Before you place a macro or a VBA procedure in a library database, you should test it thoroughly. VBA procedures should have error handling to deal with unanticipated errors.

**Program for efficiency**   After a procedure or macro passes your reliability tests, reexamine the program for optimal performance. Here are some suggestions:

- When you have a choice of control structures, make sure you have used the most efficient structure. For example, if you are looping through a collection, use the For Each...Next structure instead of the For...Next structure.

- Avoid the decision functions IIf, Choose, and Switch in favor of If...Then and Select Case decision structures, which usually run faster.

- Use variables with the most specific data types and object data types.

- Use the most efficient options to refer to objects, such as Me to refer to the form in which the code is running.  Use the With...End With structure to set several properties.

- Keep a copy of your macros and procedures and strip out comments from the versions that you place in a library. While each comment in a macro or VBA procedure takes only a fraction of a second to process, the time spent on a comment is wasted. Normally, the time spent processing comments is so small that you should comment freely to make your code more readable. However, a procedure in a library database should be so impervious to errors that readability should no longer be the highest priority. By making a copy, you provide a backup should your procedure need to be changed.

**Compile**   You achieve the fastest VBA code only when you run it in a compiled state. After you have added the procedures to the library, or after you add a new procedure or make any changes to an existing library, you can compile all of the procedures as follows:

1.   Open any module in the library database.

2.   Choose the Compile and Save All Modules command in the Debug menu.

> **NOTE**   A new feature in Access 97 allows you to save a library database (or any other database) as an .mde file. An .mde file compiles the modules, removes the readable source code (leaving only the compiled code), and compacts the database. The size of the .mde file is reduced, and the project uses memory more efficiently and performs better.

## Creating a Reference to a Library Database

Before you can use a library database in an Access project, you have to add a reference to the library in the project. To understand how this works, we'll add a reference to the Solutions.mdb sample database so that we can use it as a library database in the  Northwind_Ch20 database. Whenever you open a database that has a reference to a library database, the library database is available. The first time your project calls a procedure in the library, Access loads the module containing the procedure into memory (Access also loads any other modules that contain procedures that can be called by the procedure you called). You can call the library's procedures as though the procedures were part of the project.

1. Open any module in the current database and choose the References command in the Tools menu to display the References dialog (see Figure 20.9a).

2. Click the Browse button and select Microsoft Access Databases (*.mdb) in the Files of Type combo list of the Add Reference dialog (see Figure 20.9b).

**FIGURE 20.9:**

Use the References dialog to set a reference to another database, another application's type library, or an ActiveX control (a). Use the Add Reference dialog to add a new reference (b).

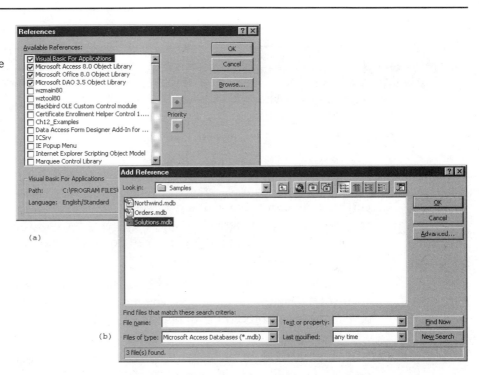

3. Locate the Solutions.mdb file in Program Files\Microsoft Office\Office\Samples directory and click OK. The Solutions.mdb database now appears checked in the References dialog (the References dialog lists the database as either Solution or Solutions). The solutions.mdb database has a module named IsLoadedModule. This module contains the IsLoaded("*formname*") function that returns the value True if the form whose name you pass as a string to the function is open. Otherwise, it returns the value False. The same function appears in the Utility Functions module in Northwind_Ch20. To test the library database, we'll delete the Utility Functions module in Northwind_Ch20.

4. Close the References dialog. Click in the Database window; select and delete the Utility Functions module.

5. Open the Categories form. Press Ctrl+G to display the Debug window, type **?IsLoaded("Categories")** in the Immediate pane, and press Enter. Access locates the IsLoaded function in the Solutions.mdb database, runs the function procedure, and returns the value True.

> **NOTE**
> A new feature in Access 97 allows you to create references programmatically using the new Reference object. Search "Reference object" in online Help for more information.

## Moving a Library Database

If you move or rename a library database, Access may not be able to find it. When you call a procedure in the library database, Access displays an error message and then opens the References dialog displaying the word "MISSING" in front of the name of the library database. You can Browse to find the new location and reset the reference.

If you deselect an item in the References dialog, your database is no longer aware of the item. To avoid errors, you must remove all references in your database to the item's procedures or objects.

## Editing Library Code

You can edit a VBA procedure stored in a library database while you are working in the current project without opening the library database directly. (If you saved the library database as an .mde file, you can't view or edit its procedures.) To display a procedure in a library database:

1. Open the Object Browser and select the library database from the Project/Library combo list. Then select the module in the Classes list box on the left and select the procedure in the Members list box on the right. Figure 20.10a shows the selections in the Object Browser for the IsLoaded function in the Solutions.mdb library database. (The library may be listed as either Solution or Solutions.)

2. Click the View Definition button to display the procedure. Figure 20.10b shows the IsLoaded function procedure, the title bar of the module window displays, and the names of the library and the module. Now you can make changes to the procedure.

**FIGURE 20.10:**

Use the Object Browser to view modules stored in a library database (a). Click the View Definition button to display a procedure (b).

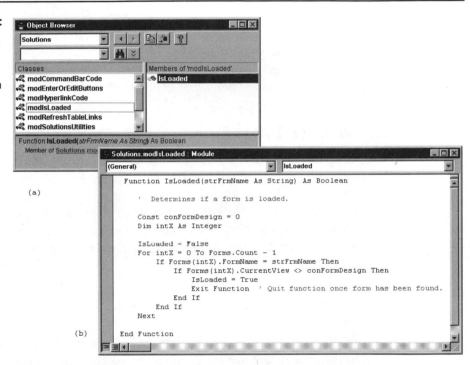

(a)

```
Function IsLoaded(strFrmName As String) As Boolean

    '   Determines if a form is loaded.

    Const conFormDesign = 0
    Dim intX As Integer

    IsLoaded = False
    For intX = 0 To Forms.Count - 1
        If Forms(intX).FormName = strFrmName Then
            If Forms(intX).CurrentView <> conFormDesign Then
                IsLoaded = True
                Exit Function   ' Quit function once form has been found.
            End If
        End If
    Next

End Function
```

(b)

# Understanding Dynamic-Link Libraries

A *dynamic-link library* (DLL) is a library of procedures to which applications such as Access and Excel can link. A dynamic-link library exists in files separately from the applications. Several applications can be linked to and share a single dynamic-link library at the same time. The link to the library is termed *dynamic* because the link is activated only at run-time when a procedure in the library is called. Dynamic-link libraries are usually written in C or C++ in order to provide the optimal performance. They normally have the .dll extension. The Windows operating system uses sets of dynamic-link libraries to house the functions it uses. Windows has procedures stored in several of its dynamic-link libraries that you can use to manipulate files, manage windows, and write entries in the Registry. The Windows operating system automatically loads and unloads dynamic-link libraries as it needs them and as applications such as Access call procedures in them.

There are two kinds of dynamic-link libraries: libraries specified by a type library and those that do not have a type library. In terms of writing VBA procedures, the difference between the two kinds of libraries is significant because you call procedures in the two kinds of libraries in markedly different ways.

## Using a Type Library

A *type library* is a file that is associated with, but separate from, the dynamic-link library. It contains information about the procedures in the library. VBA uses one of the ActiveX technologies called Automation for interacting with a type library (see the next section for a discussion of Automation). A type library usually has a .olb or .tlb extension. When a dynamic-link library has an associated type library, the installation program normally installs and registers the type library in the OLE section of the Windows Registry.

In order to use a dynamic-link library that has a type library in an application such as Access, you may need to add a reference to the type library if the installation program (for Access or the library) hasn't already added the reference. You can add a reference to the type library in Access by opening any module, then selecting the References command from the Tools menu. Add the reference by checking the box to the left of the type library in the list. If the type library doesn't appear in the list, click the Browse button to locate the library in your computer's file system. After adding a reference, you can use the procedures in the dynamic-link library as though they were a built-in part of VBA.

> **NOTE**
>
> An example of a dynamic-link library that uses a type library is the data access objects library. It contains all of the procedures for working with the data access objects. The DAO350.dll file contains both the DAO dynamic-link library and the type library. When you install Access 97, the reference to the type library is added automatically.

# Using a Declare Statement

When a dynamic-link library doesn't have a type library, you have to tell VBA where the library is every time you want to use a procedure in the library. You also have to tell VBA exactly how to call the procedure and what kind of response to expect after running the procedure. If you want to use a DLL procedure in a module, you must place a Declare statement in the module's Declarations section. The Declare statement gives the following information about the procedure:

- The scope of the declaration. In a standard module, you can use the Public keyword if you want the DLL procedure to be available to all procedures modules in the project or the Private keyword if you want the DLL procedure to be available only to procedures in the module. In a form or report module, you can use only the Private keyword.

- The name the procedure has in your module. You can give a custom name to the procedure by using the Alias keyword. If you don't supply an alias, the name the procedure has in your module must be exactly the same as the name the procedure has in the DLL. You use an alias when the DLL procedure has a name that includes an invalid character or has a name that is the same as a VBA keyword.

- The name and path of the DLL. The name of the library is enclosed in quotes and is not case-sensitive.

- The name the procedure has in the DLL. The name the procedure has in the DLL is case-sensitive.

- The number and data types of the arguments. The DLL expects the arguments to be placed in a particular order and to have a certain size. Declaring arguments correctly is the hardest part of using a DLL in VBA. The VBA declaration must be set up correctly to pass arguments by value or by reference exactly as the DLL expects them.

- The data type of the return value if the procedure is a function.

The syntax for the Declare statement for a function procedure in a DLL is

```
[Public|Private] Declare Function procedurename Lib "libraryname"
[Alias "aliasname"][([arglist])][As type]
```

where *procedurename* is the name you are using in your module to identify the procedure, the Lib clause specifies the dynamic-link library that houses the procedure, and *aliasname* is the name that the procedure has in the DLL. The syntax for the Declare statement for a sub procedure is similar, except that the Function keyword is replaced by Sub and there is no return value. An argument in the arglist has the syntax

```
[Optional] [ByVal|ByRef] [ParamArray] varname[()] [As type]
```

where *varname* is the name of the variable and *type* is the variable's data type.

> **WARNING** You must pass to the procedure, in the correct order, precisely the number and data type of arguments that the DLL expects. If you don't do this, the DLL may try to access memory it doesn't have permission to access. The result is a General Protection fault. In other words, Access crashes and you can't save your work.

After declaring a function in the declarations section of the module, you can then call it in a VBA procedure.

## The Windows API DLLs

The best examples of dynamic-link libraries that require Declare statements are the libraries that the Windows operating system makes available. This set of dynamic-link libraries is called the *Windows API* (Application Programming Interface). The API includes more than 1,000 functions that are part of Windows and accessible to Windows applications. The Windows API stores most of the functions in three dynamic-link libraries in the Windows\System directory as follows:

**Kernel32.dll** includes functions for memory management, task management, resource handling, and related operations.

**User32.dll** includes functions related to the management of Windows, such as functions for working with menus, messages, cursors, carets, timers, communications, and other nondisplay operations.

**GDI32.dll** includes the functions related to the graphics display, such as drawing, coordinates, and fonts.

As comprehensive as VBA is in allowing you to automate Access, VBA doesn't include the ability to work with the Windows environment. This is where the Windows API comes in.

Suppose you need some information about how the user interface is set up. For example, you might wonder whether there is a mouse. And, if so, is the mouse right-handed or left-handed? What is the width of the cursor ? There is no way to get answers to these questions using a VBA function. However, there is a function in the Windows API called GetSystemMetrics that you can use for this purpose. It is located in the user32 dynamic-link library. The function takes a long integer as its only argument and returns a long integer. You specify the particular information you want to retrieve using a numeric code. Table 20.1 (on the CD under Tables\Chapter20.pdf) shows examples of the information you can retrieve, the corresponding constants, and their numerical equivalents.

1. Open a new module named basAPI. Enter the Declare statement (below) in the Declarations section. In this example we use the same name for the function in our module as that used in the library function. This allows us to omit the alias part of the declaration statement.

```
Public Declare Function GetSystemMetrics Lib "user32" (ByVal
nIndex As Long) As Long
```

2. In the Declarations section, declare the following constants:

```
Public Const SM_CXSCREEN = 0
Public Const SM_CYSCREEN = 1
Public Const SM_MOUSEPRESENT = 19
Public Const SM_SWAPBUTTON = 23
```

3. Enter the InterfaceInfo procedure shown below.

```
Public Sub InterfaceInfo()
Debug.Print "Screen width = " & GetSystemMetrics(SM_CXSCREEN)
Debug.Print " Screen height = " & GetSystemMetrics(SM_CYSCREEN)
If GetSystemMetrics(SM_MOUSEPRESENT) = 1 Then
    If GetSystemMetrics(SM_SWAPBUTTON) = 1 Then
        Debug.Print "There is a left-handed mouse present"
    Else
        Debug.Print "There is a right-handed mouse present"
    End If
```

```
Else
    Debug.Print "There is no mouse present"
End If
End Sub
```

4. In the Debug window, type **InterfaceInfo** and press Enter. Figure 20.11 shows the result for a computer with 800 by 600 pixels screen resolution and a right-handed mouse.

**FIGURE 20.11:**

Use the Windows API GetSystemMetrics function to retrieve information about the user interface.

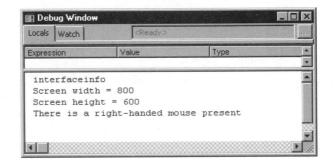

This example is deceptively simple because the GetSystemMetrics function takes only a single argument.

> **WARNING**  One of the difficulties in working with the Windows API functions is that they don't provide protection from mistakes. By declaring an API function incorrectly, you can easily cause a General Protection fault and crash Access—you may even crash Windows 95. Before you test a Windows API function, save all of your objects. Once a General Protection fault occurs, you won't have an opportunity to save anything.

This section has given you a brief glance into the Windows API. The book's CD-ROM includes the Microsoft textfile called win32api.txt with the syntax for the API declarations for Visual Basic. For more information see the *Access 97 Developer's Handbook* by Paul Litwin, Ken Getz, and Mike Gilbert (Sybex, 1997).

# Using ActiveX

ActiveX (formerly called Object Linking and Embedding, or OLE) is the technology that Microsoft provides for allowing applications to communicate with each
other. ActiveX is a set of standards for transferring information in the form of
objects between Windows applications. ActiveX has two basic elements: a model
for objects called the Component Object Model (COM) and a set of ActiveX capabilities. The set includes the following:

**Object Linking and Embedding**   With Object Linking and Embedding
you can place an object created in one application inside a document
created in another application. There are two techniques for storing the
object: linking and embedding. When you link an object, you store a copy
of the object's data and a link to the original file. If you make changes to
the original file, the changes are transmitted to the linked object. When
you embed an object, you store only a copy of the object's data without the
link to the original file. When you embed an object there is no link to the
original file, so changes to the original file are not transmitted to the
embedded object.

**In-place activation**   With In-place activation you can edit an object
embedded in a control from within the boundaries of the control, without
opening a separate instance of the application that created the object. To
edit an embedded object, double-click the control to activate it. Activating
the embedded object causes the application that created it to be grafted
onto the document's application. For example, when you activate an
embedded Word document on an Access form, the Word menus and toolbars replace the Access menus and toolbars that have the same name.
Additional Word menus and toolbar buttons are added as well. After activating the embedded object, you can use the grafted menus to perform
operations on the object just as though you had opened the file directly in
Word. In-place activation is available only for embedded objects. When
you activate a linked object, the application that created the object opens in
a separate window that displays the file.

**Automation**   With Automation (previously called OLE Automation) you
can write procedures in an application that send instructions to another
application and control the objects that the other application can create.
For example, you can write VBA procedures in Access that instruct Excel
to open a new worksheet and copy Access data into the worksheet.

Automation provides the ability to work with objects in another application by remote control.

**ActiveX controls**   An ActiveX control (previously called an OLE control) is a self-contained object that you can add to a document in an application. The object has its own properties and methods and recognizes its own events. After adding an ActiveX control to a document, you can send instructions to the control. For example, you can add a Calendar ActiveX control to an Access form and write VBA procedures to control the Calendar's behavior.

Windows applications differ widely in their compliance with the ActiveX standards. You will have to study an application's documentation and often experiment directly with the application in order to determine the extent of its compliance. Similarly, ActiveX controls differ widely in their compliance with the ActiveX control standards. In addition, applications differ in their ability to work with a specific ActiveX control. For example, an ActiveX control that has a set of properties, methods, and events when used in an application such as Visual Basic may not have the same set of properties, methods, and events when you insert the control on a form in Access.

Access 97 is capable of embedding and linking objects created in other applications. Whether you can use in-place activation for an object you have embedded in an Access form depends on whether the application that created the object complies with the ActiveX standards for in-place activation. In Access 97 you can use VBA to control objects of another application that complies with the Automation standards for making objects available. Furthermore, you can control the objects in Access 97 from another application that complies with the Automation standards for controlling objects. In Access 97 you can embed an ActiveX control in an Access form and use VBA to control the object, if the ActiveX control is one that Access supports.

# Using ActiveX Controls

ActiveX controls are self-contained objects that can give your application new and useful abilities without requiring you to write the code. Examples of ActiveX controls include animated buttons, audio players, video players, marquees, progress bars, and three-dimensional check boxes. Access ships with one ActiveX control, called the Calendar control, so you can learn how to add a custom control to your forms. The controls are tested, debugged and ready for use. ActiveX controls have their own events, properties and methods. In addition to the properties, methods, and events that are specific to the ActiveX control, when you insert the ActiveX control in an Access form, you are inserting the control in an Access frame. As a result, the Access properties, methods, and events of the Access frame also apply to the ActiveX control.

**NOTE**
For years, ActiveX controls have been a part of the Microsoft technology for communication between software components under the name OLE controls or .ocx controls. The emergence of the World Wide Web has spurred the evolution of Microsoft's OLE technology into ActiveX technology, with a new emphasis on small and efficient programs optimized for the Web. These include a set of downloadable ActiveX controls. If you spend much time navigating the Web, you know that Web sites often offer to download ActiveX controls to your computer and register the controls automatically in your Windows registry. Between the web-optimized ActiveX controls and the set of ActiveX controls created for non-Web use, there are more than 1,000 ActiveX controls commercially available.

You can usually set some of the properties in Design view, while other properties must be set in macros or procedures. An ActiveX control has the Access properties listed in Table 20.2 (on the CD under Tables\Chapter20.pdf) and its own set of control-specific properties. Depending on which ActiveX control you are working with, the control-specific properties that you can set in Design view may or may not be listed in the Access property sheet for the control. The control-specific properties may also be listed in the ActiveX control's own custom properties dialog. If an ActiveX control has a custom properties dialog, the Access property sheet contains a property named Custom. You can display the custom properties dialog by clicking the Build button at the right of the Custom property box. As an alternative, you can display the custom properties dialog by right-clicking the ActiveX control, choosing the ...Object command, then choosing the Properties command from the fly-out menu. The Locked and ControlSource properties are available only for ActiveX controls that can be bound to a table field.

An ActiveX control has the following Access events: Enter, Exit, GotFocus, LostFocus, and Updated. These are the only events listed in the Access property sheet. In addition, the ActiveX control has its own specific events that it recognizes. Normally, the control-specific event properties are not listed in either the Access property sheet or the control's custom properties dialog and are available only when you open the form's module.

An ActiveX control has the Access methods SetFocus and SizeToFit. The ActiveX control also has its own control-specific methods. You can learn about the control-specific events, methods, and properties using the Object Browser.

**NOTE**
You can get custom controls from Microsoft and from third-party vendors. Access 97 ships with a single custom control to get you started—the Calendar control. The Access Developers Kit has 12 custom controls. Many of the custom controls that come with Visual Basic 4.0 work with Access. You can get a list of vendors who provide OLE controls for Access at the Access developers' web site at http://www.microsoft.com/accessdev. There is an extensive list of information on OLE controls at the OLE Broker World Wide Web site located at http://www.olebroker.com. You can also create your own ActiveX controls using a number of programming languages, including Visual Basic 5.0.

In this section we'll explore the Calendar control that ships with Access 97. The Calendar control has control-specific properties that you use to determine the control's appearance and to set and read the data in the control. The control has control-specific methods that you use to set the day, month and year, and to update the calendar. The control also has a method for displaying an About box with version and copyright information. The control recognizes control-specific events when the user clicks or double-clicks the control, moves to a new date, or presses a key. The control also recognizes an event when the date changes.

## Installing and Registering an ActiveX Control

An ActiveX control must have the correct entries in the Windows Registry before you can use it. Some controls have an installation program that installs and registers the control automatically. You must register other controls yourself. To view the list of OLE controls registered on your computer:

1. Choose the ActiveX Controls command in the Tools menu to display the ActiveX Controls dialog (see Figure 20.12). ActiveX control files have the .ocx extension. Access 97 ships the Calendar control, so you should find this control on the list. If the Calendar control is not on the list, you'll need to install it from the installation disks. For example, if you installed Access as part of the Office 97 Professional, insert the installation CD-ROM, click Add/Remove in the first installation dialog, select Microsoft Access, and click Change Option in the second dialog. Then select the Calendar Control option in the Microsoft Access dialog (see Figure 20.13). When you install the Calendar control, it is automatically added to the list in the ActiveX Controls dialog.

2. To register a new control installed on your system, click the Register button in the ActiveX Controls dialog. Locate the control's file in the Add ActiveX Control dialog (see Figure 20.14). Normally, custom controls are installed to the Windows\System directory. To unregister a control, click the Unregister button.

When you install and register an ActiveX control, its type library installs automatically. This feature allows you to use the control's properties and methods in your VBA code just as though they were built into Access.

**FIGURE 20.12:**

The ActiveX Controls dialog lists the controls that are registered in the Windows Registry on your computer.

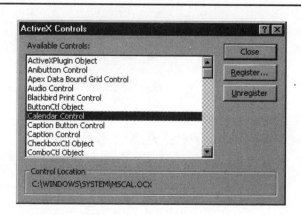

FIGURE 20.13:

If the Calendar Control is not listed in the ActiveX Controls dialog, run the setup program on the Installation disk to install the control.

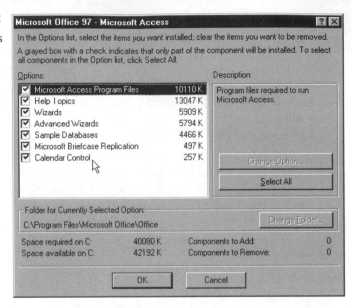

FIGURE 20.14:

Use the Add ActiveX dialog to register an ActiveX control.

## Inserting an ActiveX Control

After you install and register an ActiveX control, there are two ways to place that ActiveX control on a form: use a menu command or add the control to the toolbox.

In the first way, you choose the ActiveX command from the Insert menu.

1.  Open a new blank form in Design view and name it frmCalendar. Choose the ActiveX Control command in the Insert menu. Figure 20.15a shows the Insert ActiveX Control dialog. Select the Calendar control and click OK. The Calendar control is inserted and displays the current date when the form is in Design view.

2.  Switch to Form view (see Figure 20.15b). Select the month and year using the combo boxes and click in a day box to select a day in the displayed month. (In the next section you will learn how to use the selected date.)

3.  Delete the Calendar control.

**FIGURE 20.15:**

Choose the ActiveX Control command in the Insert menu to display a list of registered controls (a). Select the month and year using the combo boxes of the Calendar control and click in a day box to select a day (b).

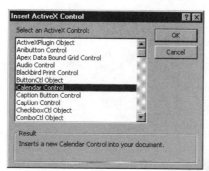

(a)

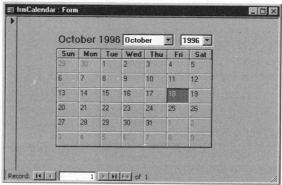

(b)

In the second way, you add a button for the ActiveX control to the toolbox. Then you select the control from the toolbox and drag it to your form, just as you would a built-in control.

1. Right-click the toolbox between two tool buttons and choose the Customize command from the shortcut menu. Click the Commands tab, choose ActiveX Controls in the Categories list box, then choose the Calendar Control in the Objects list box (see Figure 20.16a).

2. Drag the Calendar Control to the toolbox and then close the Customize dialog.

3. Select the Calendar Control tool in the toolbox (see Figure 20.16b), click in the form, and draw the control the size that you want. When you release the mouse button, the Calendar Control is inserted.

**FIGURE 20.16:**

Customize the toolbox by adding an ActiveX control (a). Select the Calendar control, or other controls, in the toolbox (b).

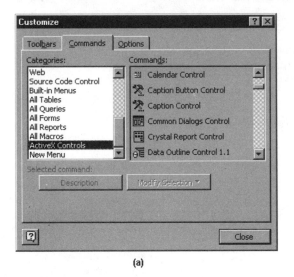

(a)  (b)

When you place an ActiveX control on a form using either technique, two things happen: the control is placed in an unbound object frame, and Access automatically adds a reference to the control's type library to your application. To observe the reference, open a module and then either choose the References command from the Tools menu (see Figure 20.17a), or open the Object Browser and observe the Calendar Control listing in the Project/Library combo box. Select the Calendar Control to display the list of the control-specific properties, methods, and events (see Figure 20.17b).

**NOTE**

The Object Browser lists only the control-specific events, properties, and methods for an ActiveX control. It does not list the Access events, properties, and methods that apply to any ActiveX control inserted in an Access unbound object frame.

**FIGURE 20.17:**

After you place an ActiveX control on a form, Access automatically creates a reference to the control's type library in your database (a). After setting a reference to an ActiveX control, you can observe its control-specific events, properties, and methods (b).

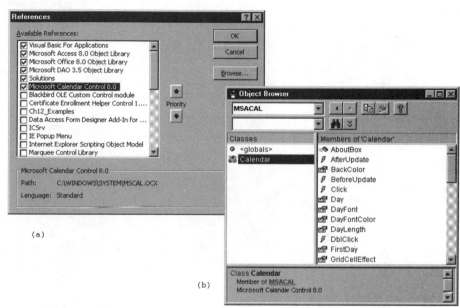

(a)

(b)

## Setting Properties at Design Time

There are two ways to set the control-specific properties when you are working with an ActiveX control in Design view. You can use the control's property sheet or, if the control has a custom property dialog, you can use the dialog.

### Using the Property Sheet

A custom control is placed in an unbound object frame, so when you select the custom control in Design view, the property sheet displays the Access properties for the frame, as well as the control-specific properties. The property sheet does not list event properties for the control-specific events. The property sheet for the

Calendar Control includes both the object frame properties shown in Figure 20.18a and the control-specific properties starting with the Custom property shown in Figure 20.18b.

**FIGURE 20.18:**

The Access property sheet for the Calendar control lists the properties you can set at Design time, including the object frame properties (a) and the control-specific properties starting with the Custom property (b). The property sheet does not include properties for the control-specific events.

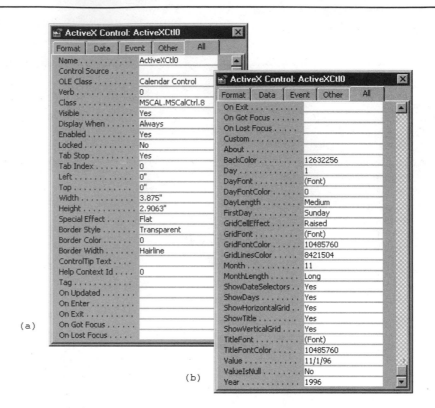

(a)

(b)

You can explore the control-specific properties in the Debug window.

1. Press Ctrl+G to display the Debug window and type **?Forms!frmCalendar!ActiveXCtl1.Value** and press Enter. The Immediate pane prints the current date. You can set the calendar's date when the form is in either Form view or Design view.

2. Type **Forms!frmCalendar!ActiveXCtl1.Value = #2/6/97#** and press Enter. The calendar changes to display the date. You can change the appearance of the calendar by setting properties.

3. Type **Forms!frmCalendar!ActiveXCtl1.ShowTitle = False** and press Enter.

## Using the Custom Property Dialog

Display the custom property dialog by clicking the Build button next to the Custom property listed in the property sheet. Another way to display the dialog is to right-click the control and choose the Calendar Control Object command, then the Properties command from the shortcut menu. You also can display the custom property dialog for the Calendar control by double-clicking in the control. The Calendar control properties dialog includes tabs for setting general properties, colors, and fonts (see Figure 20.19).

**FIGURE 20.19:**

The Calendar Control Properties dialog has tabs for the control-specific properties that you can set at Design time, including the general (a), color (b), and font (c) properties.

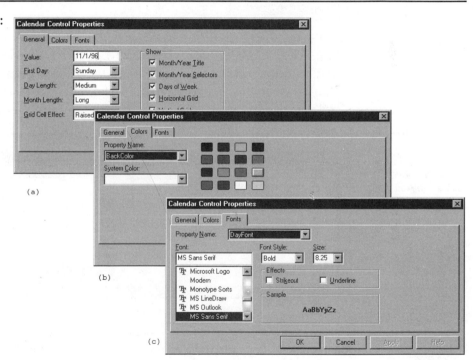

# Using Events

For a built-in control, the events that the control recognizes have corresponding properties that are listed in the Event category of the property sheet. You can use the event for a built-in control to trigger a macro, an event procedure, or a function procedure. For an ActiveX control, the Event category lists only the events that are recognized by the control frame: the Enter, Exit, GotFocus, LostFocus, and Updated events. The control-specific events are not listed in the property sheet and are available only in the form module. After placing a custom control on a form, Access automatically creates code templates for event procedures for each ActiveX control event.

**NOTE**  You can trigger only event procedures—not function procedures or macros—with an ActiveX control-specific event.

1. With the form in Design view, select the Calendar control and click the Code button in the toolbar. Select ActiveXCtl1 in the Object combo box on the left to display the code template for the Updated event. Click the Procedures combo box on the right to view a list of both the Access events that the control's frame recognizes and the control-specific events (see Figure 20.20).

**FIGURE 20.20:**

The Procedures combo box for the ActiveX control lists all of the events for the control, including both the object frame events and the control-specific events.

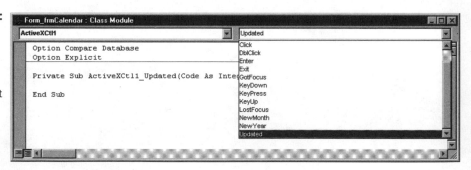

As an example of how to use the Calendar control, we'll add a calendar to the Orders form and bind it to the Required Date control. This allows you to use the calendar to select the date.

1. Open the Orders form in Design view and drag the lower boundary of the Detail section to make room for the calendar.

2. Click the Calendar control in the toolbox, click the RequiredDate in the field list, and drag to the lower part of the form. Change the Name property to ActiveXCalendar, change the ShowTitle property to No, and adjust the size of the calendar control. The Calendar Control is now bound to the

RequiredDate field. Add a label with the Caption property set to Select Required Date.

4. Switch to Form view and browse through the records. The Calendar updates automatically to display the value of the RequiredDate field for the record (see Figure 20.21).

5. Change the required date for an order using the Calendar control. The RequiredDate control does not update automatically. You can update the control interactively by selecting the Refresh command in the Records menu or by pressing F9.

**FIGURE 20.21:**

The Calendar is bound to the RequiredDate field and updates automatically when you browse to another record. However, when you change the date in the Calendar, the RequiredDate control does not update automatically.

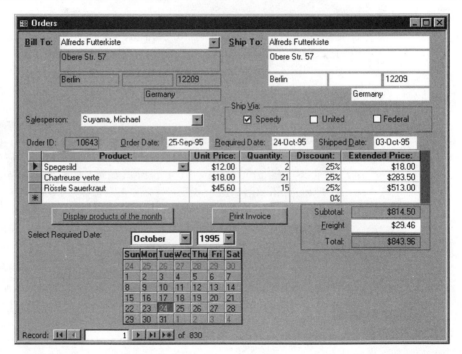

To refresh the form automatically, you can create an event procedure for the AfterUpdate event of the Calendar control. Because AfterUpdate is a control-specific event, a corresponding event property is not listed in the property sheet. Therefore, you must display the form's module by choosing the Code command in the View menu or by clicking the Code button in the toolbar when the form is in Design view.

1. Switch to Form view, select the Calendar control, and click the Code button in the toolbar. Enter the event procedure shown below.

```
Private Sub ActiveXCalendar_AfterUpdate
    Me.Refresh
End Sub
```

2. Save the module and switch to Form view. Change the required date using the Calendar control; observe that the form refreshes automatically.

# Automation

Automation (previously called OLE Automation) is one of the most important features in Microsoft's ActiveX technology for communication between software components. With Automation, you can build mega-applications that have the special abilities of the major applications. In building these mega-applications, you will work with objects from other applications using the same techniques you have learned for working with objects in Access. Specifically, you'll set and get properties and you'll run methods of objects. *Automation* is the process by which the application you are working in sends instructions to another application. Applications that can use objects from another application or that make their own objects available for use by another application are called *ActiveX components*. The application that supplies the objects is called the *Automation server* and the application in which you write the procedures to control those objects is called the *Automation controller*. The objects that are controlled are called *Automation* or *ActiveX objects*.

Each of the Microsoft Office applications is an ActiveX component and has particular strengths packaged, as ActiveX objects, that it shares with any other application that is in compliance with the set of rules called the *standards of Automation*. Access 97 has strengths in storing, retrieving, and updating data; Outlook 97 has strengths in scheduling and contact management; Excel 97 has strong data analysis capabilities; Word 97 has strengths in formatting and reporting data; PowerPoint 97 has strengths in presenting data; and FrontPage 97 has strengths in Web page creation and Web site management. Automation is an open standard. This means that the specifications are publicly available and any vendor can create applications that conform to the standard. For example, Visio

International makes the strengths of Visio, its technical drawing program, available to other applications through Automation.

Each of these applications supplies a set of ActiveX objects so you can use Automation to create an application that uses Access to manage data, Excel to analyze the data, Word to report on the data, Visio to create drawings based on the data, PowerPoint to create a slide presentation of the data, and FrontPage to create a Web page and publish the data on the Web. The advantage of Automation is that you can build the advanced features of several pre-written, debugged, and thoroughly tested off-the-shelf applications into your project using the same skills and techniques that you've learned to create a project using only Access.

Some applications are only Automation servers, providing their objects for control via other applications. Other applications are only Automation controllers, with the ability to send instructions for working with objects provided by others, and do not provide any objects themselves. Some applications can act in both modes. As examples, Access 97, Excel 97, Project 97 and Visual Basic 5 have both modes and use Visual Basic for Applications as the programming language for sending Automation instructions. (ActiveX is an evolving technology. Previous versions of applications may have limited, or may even lack, Automation capabilities). Visio can be only an Automation server, providing objects that can be controlled using VBA, C or C++.

**NOTE**  This chapter assumes that Access is the Automation controller application unless explicitly noted otherwise.

When an application supplies ActiveX objects, what it actually makes available are the blueprints for objects. In object-oriented programming terminology, the blueprints are called *classes* or *object types,* and the objects you create from the blueprints are called *instances* of the class or object type. The class for an object includes its name, the definition of properties and methods, and the events that the object recognizes. An Automation server stores all of the information about its objects in an object library. Typically, when you install an application, its object library and an online help file for the object model install automatically. An object library has either the .olb extension (for object library) or the .tlb extension (for type library), and the library's online help file has the .hlp extension. Some examples follow:

**The Access object model** is provided in the MSACC8.OLB file with help in the Acmain80.hlp file. Both files are installed by default in the \Program Files\Microsoft Office\Office folder.

**The data access objects (DAO) object model** of the Jet database engine is provided by the DAO3032.DLL file, which is installed automatically when you install Access97, Excel 97, Visual Basic 4.0 and Visual C++. The default folder is either \WINDOWS\SYSTEM or \Program Files\Common Files\Microsoft Shared\DAO.

**The Excel object model** is provided in the Excel8.OLB file with help in the Xlmain8.hlp file. Both files are installed by default in the \Program Files\Microsoft Office\Office folder.

**The Visual Basic for Applications** model is provided by the VBA332.DLL file in the \Program Files\Common Files\Microsoft Shared\VBA directory. The help file for Access VBA is Acvba80.hlp. It is installed by default in the \Program Files\Microsoft Office\Office folder, while the help file for the other Office application, VBAoff8.hlp, is installed by default in the \Program Files\Common Files\Microsoft Shared\VBA folder.

## Learning About an Application's Objects

You can learn about another application's Automation objects while you are working in Access by adding the application's object library to the Object Browser. You add an object library to the Object Browser by setting a reference to the library as follows:

1. Open any module in your project.

2. Choose the References command from the Tools menu. Figure 20.22a shows the References dialog. The current Access project has references to the items that are checked. Items without check marks are available for adding to the project. Use the Priority buttons to change the position of an item in the list. If an item is not listed, click the Browse button to display the Add Reference dialog (see Figure 20.22b). Here you can locate the type library on your computer and click the OK button to add the reference.

**FIGURE 20.22:**

The References dialog lists both the references already added and those available to add to the current project (a). If the object library of an installed application isn't in the list, click the Browse button to display the Add Reference dialog (b) and locate the object library.

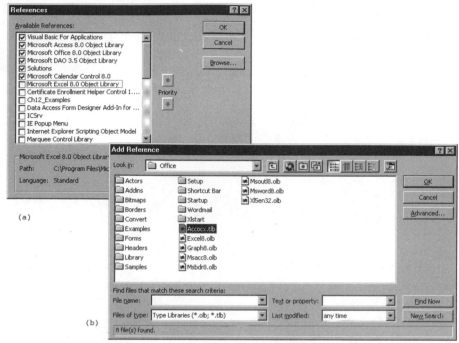

(a)

(b)

3. Check the reference to the Microsoft Excel 8.0 Object Library.

When you add a reference to a type library you are storing the path to the type library in your project. If you move the object library, you will have to create a new reference to the library. The reference is added only for the Access project with which you are currently working. When you add a reference to an object library, VBA recognizes the objects in the object library; you can use them the same way you use the Access and DAO objects.

**NOTE**   This chapter assumes that you have Microsoft Office 97 installed on your computer. If this is so, add a reference to the Microsoft Excel 8.0 and Word 8.0 Object Libraries. If you don't have Office 97 installed, you can add a reference to another Automation server that you have. If you have only Access, you can modify some of the examples and use Access as both an Automation controller and server.

## Using the Object Browser

After adding the reference, you can use the Object Browser to explore the application's objects. Chapter 10 explains how to use the Object Browser. Figure 20.23 shows the properties and methods of the Worksheet object in Excel 8.0 Object Library. When you add the reference, you also add online help for the application's objects.

FIGURE 20.23:

You can use the Object Browser in Access to explore the objects in Excel.

> **NOTE**
>
> Before you can use Automation successfully, you'll need to carefully study the object model of the application you want to control and learn the properties, methods, and events for the objects you want to control. The object models for the other Office 97 applications are substantially more complex than the Access and the Data Access Object models you've learned about in this book. Because ActiveX is an evolving technology, the object models for these applications have changed substantially from version to version. The changes have often required considerable time to update the programs.

## Using the Information in the Object Library

The real benefits of adding a reference to an object library come from the fact that VBA can use information in the object library. When you set a reference to an object library, VBA loads the object library into memory so it can look up information in the library when you compile the module. When you are writing VBA procedures to work with the Automation objects, you can use the information in the library—such as the intrinsic constants and specific object data types—that the other application uses.

**Using Intrinsic Constants**　You can use the intrinsic constants provided by the server application. For example, if you are working with Excel you can use the intrinsic constants with the .xl prefix in your Access procedures. You don't have to use the numeric equivalents and you don't have to redefine these constants.

**Using Object Data Types**　You can declare variables of a specific data type. For example, if you are working with Excel, you can declare object variables of the Worksheet, Chart, and Range object types. When you declare an object variable of a specific data type instead of as the generic Object data type, your code runs significantly faster. This happens because VBA can verify object information once and for all when you compile and save the module.

## Early Binding and Late Binding

The process of verifying that an object exists and that a specified property or method is valid is called *binding*. There are two times when the verification process can take place: during compile time (*early binding*) or run time (*late binding*). When you declare an object variable as a specific data type, you are using early binding so the verification can take place during compile time. When you declare a variable of the generic Object data type, you are using late binding. In this case, VBA must find and verify the object information during execution of any VBA statement that includes a reference to the object or one of its properties or methods.

Applications often have object data types with the same name. For example, all of the Office applications have an Application object. You can qualify an object data type using the name of the application with the syntax *application.objecttype* To determine the name that is used to identify the application in Automation, open the Object Browser and look up the name in the list displayed in the Project/ Library combo box. When you declare an object variable for an Automation object, you can qualify the object data type to prevent VBA from creating the wrong object. To illustrate, the following statements use early binding to declare object variables:

```
Dim appAccess As Access.Application
Dim appExcel As Excel.Application
Dim wine As Excel.Window
Dim winp As Project.Window
```

> **NOTE**
> You don't have to add a reference to an application's object library in order to use the application's Automation objects. If you don't add a reference, then don't use either the application's instrinsic constants or specific data types. Use of either causes a run-time error.

## Using Automation Objects

These are the steps to control an Automation object in a procedure:

1.  Create an object variable for the Automation object.

2.  Create an instance of the Automation object and point the object variable to the new instance.

3.  Control the object in a procedure by setting or getting its properties or by running its methods.

4.  Close the object when you are finished.

### Creating an Instance of an Automation Object

When you want to use an application's Automation objects, you must first gain access to the application. The first step is to create an instance for one of the special objects in the application's object hierarchy that Windows recognizes.

As I discussed in Chapter 11, when you use one of the data access objects, you have to start at the top of the DAO object hierachy with the DBEngine object and traverse the hierarchy to the object you want to work with. In the same way, when you want to work with an Automation object from another application, you must start with one of the objects that the operating system recognizes. Normally, you start with the object at the top of the hierarchy, which is usually called the Application object. When you create a new instance that refers to the Application object, the operating system starts up an instance of the application. With the application started, you can traverse the object hierarchy to the object you want to work with. Some applications have more than one object that the operating system recognizes. As an example, the Windows operating system recognizes the Workbook and Chart objects as well as the Application object for Excel. (In previous versions of Excel, the Worksheet—but not the Workbook object—is one of the special Excel objects that is recognized by Windows.) In this case, when you create a new instance that refers directly to the Workbook or Chart object, Windows starts up an instance of Excel, then creates an instance of the Workbook or Chart object. Then you can begin your traverse from the selected object.

There are three ways you can create an instance of an Automation object. You can use the CreateObject function, the GetObject function, or the New keyword to create the object implicitly. No matter which technique you use, the Automation server typically starts in a hidden window and remains hidden unless you explicitly make the window visible. Sometimes you need only the capabilities of the Automation server and may not need to show the application. For example, when you use the the mathematical functions of Excel to perform calculations on the data in an Access database you don't need to show the Excel window.

**TIP**    Displaying a visual representation takes additional time. Therefore, you shouldn't display the Automation objects unless it is absolutely necessary.

**Using the CreateObject Function**    Use the CreateObject function to create a new instance of one of the special Automation objects that the operating system recognizes, then returns a reference to the object. The CreateObject function has the syntax

```
Set objvar = CreateObject (appname.objecttype)
```

where *objvar* is an object variable, *appname* is the application name as listed in the Object Browser, and *objecttype* is the name of the object type you want to create. For example, to work with Word, declare an object variable and create an object to refer to the Word application as follows:

```
Dim appWord As Word.Application
Set appWord = CreateObject("Word.Application")
```

The CreateObject function starts an instance of the Automation server application. If the server is already running an instance, CreateObject starts another instance, unless the application is a single-instance application. For a single-instance application, only one instance of the application is created no matter how many times you run the CreateObject function.

To illustrate these ideas, we'll use the CreateObject function to create an instance of Word (this example assumes you have Microsoft Word 97 installed). With Word running, we have access to Word's object model and can use the Open method of Word's Documents object to open the Products.doc sample document.

1. Open a new standard module in Access named basAutomation and enter the procedure shown in Listing 20.1.

### Listing 20.1

```
Public Sub LaunchWord()
Dim appWord As Word.Application, strdoc As String
Set appWord = CreateObject ("Word.Application")
MsgBox "Word is running"
appWord.Visible = True
strdoc = "c:\Program Files\Microsoft Office\Office\"
strdoc = strdoc & "Samples\Products.doc"
appWord.Documents.Open (strdoc)
Set appWord = Nothing
End Sub
```

2. Choose the References command in the Tools menu and, if necessary, click the check box for Microsoft Word 8.0 Object Library to set the reference to Word. Click OK to close the dialog.

3. Press Ctrl+G to display the Debug window. Type **LaunchWord** in the Immediate window and press Enter. After launching an instance of Word, the procedure displays the message reporting that an instance of Word is

running. However, Word does not appear in the Task Bar until you set the Visible property to True. After you close the message box, the procedure unhides the window and uses the Open method of the Documents object to open a document. The procedure severs the link between the object variable and the instance of Word by setting the object variable to Nothing. Setting the object variable to nothing does not close Word; when the procedure terminates, Word is running.

> **NOTE**   Automation servers behave differently. Some Automation servers appear in the task list even though they are launched in a hidden window. Others, such as Word and Excel, don't appear in the task list until you unhide them. Some Automation servers, including Access, terminate when you sever all links from any object variables that point to the instance of the Automation server. Word and Excel continue to run unless you explicitly close them in the procedure.

4. Click the Word button in the task bar. The Word window is restored and displays the window for the Products document (see Figure 20.24).

5. Minimize Word. (We'll use the running instance of Word later.)

**Using the GetObject Function**   The GetObject function is more versatile than the CreateObject function. With the GetObject function you can duplicate the effect of the CreateObject function, point an object variable to a running instance of the Automation server object, or open an object that has been saved to a file.

The GetObject function takes two arguments and has the following syntax

```
Set objvar = GetObject(documentname, appname.objecttype)
```

where *objvar* is an object variable, *documentname* is a string that specifies the path of the file containing the object you want to retrieve, and *appname.objecttype* is a string that represents the application and one of the special object types that the operating system recognizes. Both arguments are optional, but you must include at least one of them. You can create a new instance, point to a running instance of the automation server, or open a specific file.

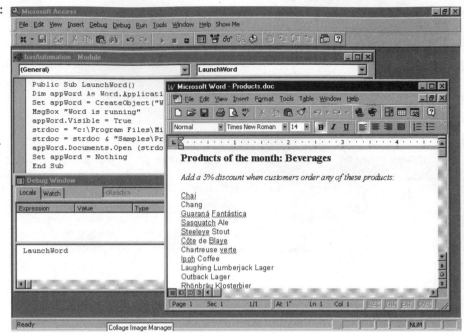

**FIGURE 20.24:**

Use the CreateObject function to open an instance of Word, and then use the Open method of Word's Documents object to open a document. The instance of Word is running when the procedure ends.

## Creating New Instance

If you set the document name to the zero-length string, the GetObject function duplicates the behavior of the CreateObject function by creating a new instance of the specified object type. If you specify the Application object, the GetObject function creates an instance of the server application. If you specify one of the other objects that the operating system recognizes, the GetObject function creates a hidden instance of the server. Then it creates an instance for the specified object and returns a reference to the specified object. As an illustration, the following statements create a new instance of Access:

```
Dim appAccess As Access.Application
Set appAccess = GetObject("","Access.Application")
```

The GetObject function creates a new hidden instance of the Automation server application (unless the server is a single-instance application and there is already an instance running) and returns a reference to the server. Access is a multiple-instance application, so these statements create a new instance of Access.

1. Insert the procedure shown in Listing 20.2 in the basAutomation module.

### Listing 20.2

```
Public Sub GetAccess()
Dim appAccess as Access.Application
Set appAccess = GetObject("","Access.Application")
MsgBox "Access is running"
appAccess.Visible = True
appAccess.NewCurrentDatabase "NewDatabase"
End Sub
```

2. Type **GetAccess** in the Immediate pane and press Enter. The procedure launches a new hidden instance of Access. Note that the Task Bar displays a button for Access even though the application is hidden. After you close the message box, the procedure unhides the Access window and uses the New-CurrentDatabase method to create a new database named NewDatabase. The database window for the new database flashes for an instant. When the procedure ends, the instance of Access terminates. If you want to leave the new instance of Access running in memory when the procedure ends, declare the appAccess object variable in the Declarations section of the module instead of declaring the variable within the procedure.

3. Locate and delete the NewDatabase file. The procedure saves the NewDatabase file in the folder specified as the Default Database Folder in the General tab of the Options dialog, available by choosing the Options command in the Tools menu. You can use the Options dialog to change the default folder for new databases.

4. Modify the GetAccess procedure by cutting the variable declaration statement and pasting the statement in the Declarations section of the module. Run the GetAccess procedure in the Debug window. When the procedure ends, the new database is displayed in the Access window (see Figure 20.25).

5. Close the second instance of Access.

**FIGURE 20.25:**

Use the GetObject function to create a new instance of Access, then use the NewCurrent-Database method to create a new database in the Access window. Declare the object variable for Access in the module's Declaration section if you want to leave the instance of Access running.

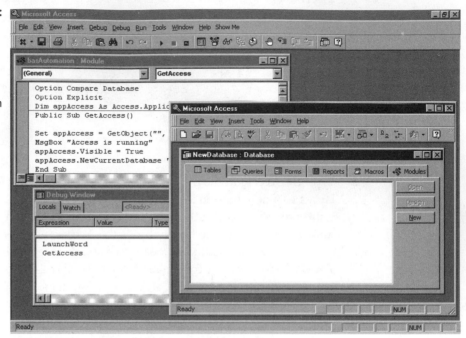

## Pointing to a Running Instance of the Automation Server

If you omit the *documentname* argument in the GetObject function, the GetObject function returns a reference to a running instance of the specified object and does not start up an instance of the Automation server. If the server is not running, the GetObject function returns a run-time error. For example, the statements

```
Dim appVis As Visio.Application
Set appVis = GetObject(,"Visio.Application")
```

return a reference to the Visio application if the application is running; otherwise, they return an error message.

> **NOTE**
>
> When you use the GetObject function to access an Automation server application that is already running, you omit the first argument of the GetObject function entirely. However, you must include the comma as a placeholder.

To illustrate, we'll create a procedure that refers to the running instance of Word and opens a second document.

1. Insert the RunningWord procedure shown in Listing 20.3 in the basAutomation module.

### Listing 20.3

```
Public Sub RunningWord()
Dim appWord As Word.Application, strdoc As String
Set appWord = GetObject(, "Word.Application")
strdoc = "c:\Program Files\Microsoft Office\Office\"
strdoc = strdoc & "Samples\Formaggi.htm"
appWord.Documents.Open (strdoc)
Set appWord = Nothing
End Sub
```

2. Type **RunningWord** in the Immediate pane and press Enter. When the procedure finishes running, restore the Word application. The Word window displays the Formaggi HTML document (see Figure 20.26).

**FIGURE 20.26:**

Use the GetObject function to refer to the running instance of Word. The Running Word procedure opens a second document.

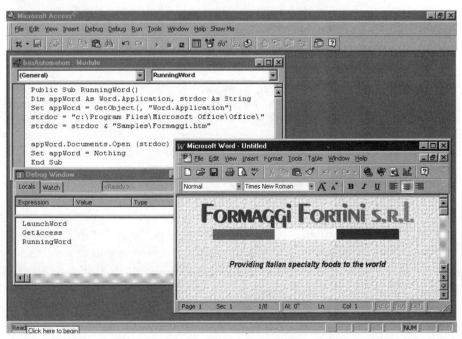

3.   Close the Formaggi document without closing Word. Minimize Word.

## Opening a Specific File

If you specify a document name in the Get Object function, the function creates a new hidden instance of the Automation server based on the document's file extension. The function opens the file and returns the object in the file. For example, the statements

```
Dim objvar As Workbook
Set objvar = GetObject("c:\Excel\updates.xls")
```

open an instance of Excel, open the updates.xls file, and return a reference to the Workbook object. If the application is already running, the GetObject function starts another instance (unless the server is a single-instance application). When a file has more than one object type that the operating system recognizes, you can specify which object you want to create by using both arguments or by declaring an object variable with the specific object type. For example, an Excel file can have both worksheet and chart object types. The statements

```
Dim wksXL As Object
Set wksXL = GetObject("c:\Excel\updates.xls","Excel.Workbook")
```

also create a hidden instance of Excel, open the updates.xls workbook, and return a reference to the workbook.

> **NOTE**   Returning a reference to an object that is lower in the application's object hierarchy is faster than returning a reference to an object that is higher in the hierarchy and traversing down to the object.

**Using the Parent Property to Traverse the Object Hierarchy**   When you open one of the special objects that is lower in the application's object hierarchy, you can traverse the hierarchy of the server's object model in both directions. To traverse up the hierarchy, use the object's Parent property. For example, if you are working with a particular worksheet, you can access the workbook that contains the worksheet by using the Parent property. To access another worksheet, or a chart in the same workbook, you can use the Parent property to traverse up the hierarchy to the workbook and then refer to another object in the workbook.

To illustrate, we'll create a procedure that uses the GetObject function to open an Excel spreadsheet.

1. Insert the GetSpreadsheet procedure shown in Listing 20.4 in the basAutomation module.

### Listing 20.4

```
Public Sub GetSpreadsheet()
Dim wks as Workbook, strwks as String
strwks = "c:\Program Files\Microsoft Office\Office\"
strwks = strwks & "Examples\samples.xls"
Set wks = GetObject(strwks)
wks.Parent.Visible = True
wks.Windows(1).Visible = True
wks.Worksheets("Worksheet Functions").Select
Set wks = Nothing
End Sub
```

2. Make sure Excel is not running. Type **GetSpreadsheet** in the Immediate pane and press Enter. The procedure uses the GetObject function to open a hidden instance of Excel. Click Yes in the Excel message to allow Excel to run the macros in the workbook. Excel opens a hidden instance of the sample.xls workbook. (The GetObject function knows to open Excel because of the file extension .xls.) The procedure uses the Parent property to traverse the object hierarchy upwards to refer to the Excel application and unhides the application window. While the Excel instance is now visible, the window containing the file is not. To make the worksheet visible, you must make the workbook visible. In Excel, the Workbook object doesn't have a Visible property. However, you can use the Windows method of the Workbook object to refer to the window containing the workbook (as the first window in the Windows collection), then use the Visible property of the Window object to unhide the window. After making the workbook's window visible, the procedure refers to the Worksheet Functions worksheet and uses the Select method to make it the active worksheet (see Figure 20.27).

3. Minimize the running instance of Excel.

**FIGURE 20.27:**

Use the GetObject function to refer directly to an Excel workbook and the Parent property to traverse up the Excel object hierarchy.

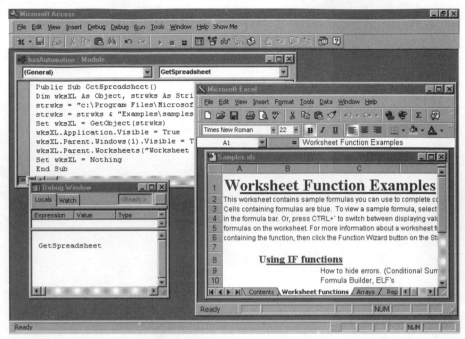

### Using the GetObject Function to Determine Whether an Application Is Running

You can use the GetObject function to determine whether there is already an instance of an application running and to make sure that only one instance runs. Listing 20.5 turns on error handling and then uses the version of the GetObject function that omits the document name to launch Excel. If Excel is not running, a run-time error is generated and the procedure uses the CreateObject function to open Excel and unhide its window. If Excel is running, the procedure ends without taking any action.

1. Insert the TestInstance procedure shown in Listing 20.5 in the basAutomation module.

### Listing 20.5

```
Public Sub TestInstance()
Dim appXL As Excel.Application
On Error Resume Next
'If the application is not running, an error occurs
```

```
Set appXL = GetObject(,"Excel.Application")
If Err.Number<>0 Then
    Set appXL = CreateObject("Excel.Application")
    appExcel.Visible = True
    MsgBox "Excel is running"
End If
End Sub
```

2.  Type **TestInstance** in the Immediate pane and press Enter. The procedure detects the running instance of Excel, an error does not occur, and the procedure terminates.

3.  Close the running instance of Excel and run the TestInstance procedure again. This time the GetObject function generates an error because the Excel application is not running. The procedure creates and unhides a new instance of Excel. The message dialog is hidden behind the window displaying the new instance of Excel. When you close the message dialog, the procedure ends and the instance of Excel is destroyed.

**Using the New Keyword to Create an Object Implicitly**    You can also create a new instance of an ActiveX object by using the New keyword when you declare the object variable. The New keyword creates an instance of the ActiveX object and assigns a reference to the object variable you are declaring. You can use the New keyword only for applications that support it, such as Access and Visual Basic. VBA starts up a new instance of the application each time you use the New keyword (unless the application is a single-instance application).

For example, the procedure in Listing 20.6 opens another hidden instance of Access and unhides the window.

1.  Enter the NewAccess procedure shown in Listing 20.6 in the basAutomation module.

### Listing 20.6

```
Public Sub NewAccess()
Dim applAccess As New Access.Application
Dim strfile as String
applAccess.Visible = True
strfile = "c:\Program Files\Microsoft Office\Office\Samples\"
strfile = strfile & "Northwind.mdb"
applAccess.OpenCurrentDatabase strfile
```

```
MsgBox "Access is running"
End Sub
```

2.  Run the procedure in the Debug window. The Access window opens and the Northwind database is displayed in the Access window. (The path in Listing 20.6 assumes the default installation of Microsoft Office 97. If you installed Access 97 to another folder, you'll have to change the path.) The Access window remains open as long as the procedure runs. The message dialog is behind the window displaying the new instance of Access. When you close the message dialog, the procedure ends. When the procedure ends, the appAccess object variable and the instance of Access created by the procedure are destroyed.

## Releasing the Object

When your VBA procedure uses the ActiveX objects of an Automation server application, your procedure is responsible for both opening and closing the object. When you are finished with the object, you should close the object and exit the object application. You can sever the link between the object variable and the object by setting the object variable to Nothing using the statement

```
Set objvar = Nothing
```

However, when VBA runs this statement, only the link to the object is severed. The object itself may continue to exist. Applications have differing behavior in this regard. For example, Excel, PowerPoint, and Word all continue to run after an object variable that refers to the application is set to Nothing, or is destroyed when the procedure ends. By contrast, destroying an object variable in Access causes the instance to terminate only if the application was launched using Automation. All applications have a method, typically Close or Exit, that you can use to exit the application. Most ActiveX objects have a Close method that allows you to close the object. For example, if you are working with Excel, you first use Excel's Quit method to close the application and then set the object variable to release the reference as follows:

```
appExcel.Quit
Set appExcel = Nothing
```

This section has shown you the basic mechanics of working with Automation server applications. We've covered how to open and close them, and how to create and destroy ActiveX objects. Writing instructions to manipulate the ActiveX objects of another application requires intimate knowledge of the application's object model, including the properties, methods, and events for its objects.

# Summary

This chapter gives you a glimpse of several advanced topics that require VBA programming. The chapter begins with a discussion of converting macros to procedures which will enable you to leverage your effort in creating a macro, as well as use the VBA-only features described in this chapter and throughout Part III. The chapter then introduces you to techniques for expanding the functionality of Access by including features from other sources, such as library databases, other code libraries, ActiveX controls, and ActiveX objects provided by other applications (ActiveX components). The chapter's important points are as follows:

- You can create library databases of useful procedures and make them available to other databases.

- You can use functions and procedures stored in dynamic-link libraries.

- If the dynamic-link library has a type library, you can set a reference to it and use the procedures the same way you use the procedures in your application.

- If there is no type library, you must declare the procedure in a module that follows the specific syntax required by the library.

- You can add functionality to your project by adding ActiveX controls to forms. ActiveX controls have their own properties, methods, and events.

- You can use Access VBA to control another application, such as Excel or Word, by remotely using Automation.

Congratulations! You've come to the end of this book. With practice, you'll be able to master and use the techniques described throughout the book to create complex automated custom applications. In addition to teaching you the basics of Access macro and VBA programming, this book has given you a brief introduction to a few of the more advanced topics that lie ahead.

# INDEX

Note to the Reader: Throughout this index **boldface** page numbers indicate primary discussions of a topic. *Italic* page numbers indicate illustrations or tables.

## SYMBOLS

# (number sign)

    for conditional compilation constant, 700

    in hyperlink data, 29

    for literal date, 532

& (ampersand)

    for concatenation, 533–534

    for keyboard combination in Caption property, 246

… (ellipsis), in Condition cell, 253

+ operator, 533–534

:= (colon equals) assignment operator, to pass argument by name, 447–448, 617

= (equal sign)

    as assignment operator to set property, 442

    for calculated control, 164

    in Expression argument of SetValue, 212

? (question mark), to evaluate expression in Debug window, 283, 444

@ (at symbol), for sections of message box, 218

' (apostrophe), for comments, 563

. (dot) operator

    in data access object reference, 491

    and execution speed, 595

    in macro reference, 227

    in object names, 130

    in property reference, 131

    when calling method, 446

! (exclamation point) operator

    in data access object reference, 491

    and execution speed, 595

    in object name, 130, 462

[ ] (square brackets)

    in Item argument of SetValue macro action, 210

    for object names including spaces, 130

| (vertical bars), for order of operations, 407

## A

AbsolutePosition property, 782

abstraction, 913

acApplyFilter constant, 865

Access, 62

    built-in library databases, 117

    environmental options for, **80–83**

    help with errors, 690, *723*

    hyperlink subaddress file syntax, *28*

    SysCmd function to return information about, **683**

    tools in, 4

    update process, **97**

Access 97, strengths, 1006

Access application object model, **123–127**, **464–477**, 914. *See also* specific object names

    Access Visual Basic objects, **476–477**

        Collection object, **477**

        Debug object, **477**

        Err object, **476**

    Application object, **123**, **464**

    collections, **466**

    Control object, **124–126**, **468–472**

        combo box and list box controls, **469–470**

        Hyperlink object, **471**

        Tab control, **471–472**, *472*

Controls collection object, **124**, 466

DoCmd object, **473–474**

Form object, **124**, 466

forms collection object, **123**, 466

Microsoft Office shared objects, **477**

Module object, **466–468**

Modules collection objects, 466

properties collection, **474**

property objects, **475**

Reference object, **476**

References collection, **475–476**

Report object, **124**, 466

Reports collection object, **123**, 466

Screen object, **126**, 473

VBA-only application objects, 126

Access components, **116–122**

Application layer, **116–117**

Jet database engine, **118–120**

Access Developers Kit, ActiveX controls, 996

Access interface, 512

macro error management, 720

access intrinsic constants, 632

access key, 246

Access object model, 1008

Access programming model

basic concepts, 438

as event-driven, **93–94**

Access project, in Object browser, 481–482

Access type library, *480*, 480–481

Access VBA compiler, **694–701**

automatic compiling, **695–698**

Compile on Demand option, **696–698**

conditional compilation, **700–701**

explicit compiling, **699**

Access VBA object hierarchy, *121*

Access VBA programming, vs. macro programming, **61–62**

Access VBA programming environment, **556–571**. *See also* module view

compiler, **569–571**

programming style, **568–569**

syntax checking, **567**

Access Visual Basic objects, **476–477**

acCloseFilterWindow constant, 865

acCmdRefresh constant, 632

acDataErrAdded constant, 833

acDataErrContinue constant, 833

acDataErrDisplay constant, 833

acFilterAdvanced constant, 864

acFilterbyForm constant, 864

acForm constant, 632

Acmain80.hlp file, 1008

acPreview constant, 632

acPrevious constant, 632

acShowAllRecords constant, 865

acSysCmdInitMeter intrinsic constant, 684

acSysCmdUpdateMeter intrinsic constant, 684

action argument, 205. *See also* arguments for macro actions

Action column, 202, 229

Action Failed dialog, *217*, 217, *276*, **277**, 294

action queries

bulk changes to recordsets with, **898–903**

creating, *888*, 888–889

OpenQuery action to run, **426–431**

running stored, **898–900**

SQL statement for, 900–901

to modify group of records, 426

actions, 61, 200

Activate event, 99, 171

active control, 89

ActiveControl property, 77, 91

active Database window object, property to determine name, 77

active error handler, 727

active form, 89

macro to move to specific control on, **299–300**

macro to move to specific control on subform, **301**

moving to record on, **305–307**

moving to record on subform of, **307–308**

moving to specific control, **753–758**

reference to controls on, **137–138**

ActiveForm property, of Screen object, 91, 444, 461, 665

active object, Screen object to refer to, 126, **138–139**

active report, reference to controls on, **137–138**

ActiveReport property, of Screen object, 461

active window
    current data on, 168
    running macro from, **230–231**
ActiveX, **993–994**
ActiveX category, in Customize dialog, 50
ActiveX components, 1006
ActiveX controls, 125, 488, **994–1006**
    Access events for, 995–996
    binding to field, 1004–1005, *1005*
    custom property dialog for, **1003**, *1003*
    events, **1003–1006**
    how to use, 1004–1006
    inserting, **998–1000**
    installing and registering, **996–998**, *998*
    Procedures combo box for, *1004*
    setting properties at design time, **1001–1003**
    setup program to install, *998*
ActiveX Controls dialog, *997*, 997
ActiveX objects, 1006
    releasing, **1024**
Add button
    creating, 814
    event procedure for, 816
adding records, methods for, 512–513
add-ins, 117–118
AddNew method, 512, 513, 839
AddRecordset procedure, 839–840, *840*
Add Reference dialog, 617, *985*, 985, 1008, *1009*
Add Watch dialog, 713, *715*
AfterUpdate event, 96, 97, 98, 238, 625
    event procedure for, 38
    macro to apply filter, 392
AfterUpdate property, 981
aggregate function, in calculated control, 166
Alias keyword, for DLL procedure, 989
AllowAdditions property, 307, 379
AllowByPassKey property, 79, 495, 946
AllowDeletions property, 361, 820–822
AllowEdits property, 830
    vs. Locked property, 379
AllowZeroLength property, 807
AllRecords setting, for Cycle property, 308

ALTER TABLE statement, 931
ampersand (&)
    for concatenation, 533–534
    for keyboard combination in Caption property, 246
AND logical operator, 858
ANSI character set, 95
apostrophe ('), for comments, 563
Append method, 499, 516, 917, 940
append queries, 883
    for data entry, 428, *429*
application-defined properties
    for data access objects, **494–495**, **944–947**
    setting in code, **945–946**
Application layer, **116–117**
Application object, 111, 120, **123**, **464**, 1013
    GetOption method, 447
    manipulating, **450–453**
Application operations, from Command Button Wizard, 24
ApplicationProperty procedure, 945–946
applications, 971
    calling procedures from other, **581**
    communication with user, 680–681
    learning about objects, **1008–1012**
    VBA to manipulate objects in other, 475
ApplyFilter action, **313–315**, *314*, *315*, 394
ApplyFilter event, form recognition of, 864
ApplyFilter event procedure, 864–865
ApplyFilter method
    of DoCmd object, **770–771**, *861*, 861
    to change record display on open form, **865–866**
    to run filter query, 868
archive process, 60
argument list, variables declared in, **606**
arguments
    arrays as, **643**
    custom data types as, **645**
    declaration of data type, 591
    for dynamic link library, 989
    for macro actions, **205–209**
    named, **617**
    optional, **623–624**
    passing form as, 622

passing form object as, 763

passing indefinite number, **622–623**

passing Me property as, **621**

passing objects as, **620–622**

passing to methods, **446–448**

for procedures, 539, 745

in reusable procedures, **590–591**

run-time errors from missing, 624

variables as, 597, 606–608

variant, **618–620**

Visual Basic to pass, 973

arithmetic calculations, on Variant variables, 533

Array function, **639**

ArrayFunction procedure, 639

ArrayRecordset procedure, 799, *800*

arrays, **636–643**

as arguments, **643**

bounds for, 637

creating based on values in list, **639**

dynamic, **640–643**

reading table data into, **797–799**

assignment operator

(=) to set property, 442

:= (colon equals) to pass argument by name, 447–448, 617

assignment statement, 595, 601, 605

New keyword in, **959–961**, *961*

at (@) symbol, for sections of message box, 218

Attribute property, 522, 921

audit trail, record deletions and, 361

AutoExec macro, 974

bypassing, 946

AutoExec macrosheet, 234, *336*, 336

AutoKeys macro, 974

reassigning key with, 369

AutoKeys macro group, *234*, 234

AutoLookup queries, **160–161**, *161*

automated Access application, **58–60**

automated database application, 4

automatic compiling, **695–698**

automatic refresh, of edited data, **830–831**, *832*

Automation, 974, 993–994, **1006–1024**

and DCmd object, **450–451**

and Jet database engine, **488–489**

learning about application's objects, **1008–1012**

standards of, 1006

Automation client, 524

Automation controllers, 488, 1006, 1007

Automation objects, 488, **1012–1024**

creating instance, **1012–1015**

using CreateObject function, **1013–1015**, *1016*

using GetObject function, **1015**, 1016, *1018*

Automation servers, 488, 1006, 1007

behavior of, 1015

in-process, 489

pointing to running instance, **1018–1019**, *1019*

AutoNumber data type, 921

AutoNumber field, 928

as primary key, 811

AutoReport: Tabular Wizard, 418

Average function, 643

avoidable errors, **691–692**. *See also* errors

# B

back-end database, 571

background

color as visual cue for form mode, 674

setting by code type, 562–563

bang (!) operator, *See* exclamation point (!) operator

base name, 26

BaseName, in Hungarian naming style, 70

Beep action, 205

Beep argument, for MsgBox action, 218

BeforeUpdate event, 38, 96, 97, 98, 238, 345, 625

default behavior for, 101

to trigger validation procedure, 810

Beginning of File (BOF) property, 507, 762, 764, 779–780, *780*

testing, 307

BeginTrans method, of Workspace object, 905, 907

binding

control to table field, 162

early or late, **1011**

bitmaps for reports, 9, *11*

Black Moshannon Systems, Speed Ferret, 73

blank primary key error, 723

blank rows, in macrosheet, 229

BOF (Beginning of File) property, 507, 762, 764, 779–780, *780*

   testing, 307

Bookmark property, 76, 459, 771

   setting to LastModified property setting, 838

   to synchronize recordsetclone and form, **763–764**

bookmarks, **459–461**

   Clone method and, 514

   from Jet, **507–508**

   for new records, 512

   of original and clone recordset objects, 795

   setting in procedure, *565*, 565

   to move to new record, 513

Boolean values, in method arguments, 452

BoundColumn property, 311

   for combo box, 179, 393

bound control, **156**

   pushing data from combo box into, **182**

   SetValue macro action for value, 211

bound form, 155

   opening, 740

bound report, 155

bounds for array, 637

   for dynamic array, 641

break mode, 702

   Debug window in, **711–714**, *712*

   entering and leaving, **703–705**, *703*

   executing group of statements in, **709**

   Quick Watch in, 714, *715*

   testing in, **706**

breakpoints, **279**, 703, 716

   setting and removing, **706–708**, *707*

BrowseMode property, creating, **950–952**

buffer. *See also* copy buffer

   control, 97

   for data changes, 162

   delete, 513

   record, 97, 162

   temporary, 316

bugs, *See* errors

Build button, for expression in macro argument, 207

builders, 118

built-in programs, 86

built-in properties, for data access objects, **493**

Buttons argument, for MsgBox() function, 260–261

button sets, for MsgBox() function, 259

buttons on switchboard, instructions for, 8

ByRef keyword, 614

ByVal keyword, 614


## C

calculated controls, 156–157, 214

   aggregate function in, 166

   on form, **164–175**

calculated query fields, **163**, *164*

calculations

   in queries, 153

   saving to database, **177–178**

Calendar control, 995, *999*

   how to use, 1004–1006

called macro, 231, 265

called procedures, 553

   errors in, **734**

   VBA search for, 554

calling macro, 231, 265

calling methods, **446–449**

   in Debug window, **448–449**, *449*

calling procedures, **542–543**, *543*, **572–584**

   from another application, **581**

   from macros, 580, *581*

   from procedure in another module, 578

   from procedure in same module, **577–578**

   function procedures, **572–581**

   triggering by event, **579–580**

calling property procedure, **950**

calling sub procedures, **581–584**

   and expressions, 584

   from another procedure, **584**

   trigger by event for, **581–583**

Call keyword, for function procedure, 575, 577

CallMultiply procedure, 618–619

calls box, **715–716**, *716*

call tree, 606–607, 696

Cancel argument, for event procedure, 810

CancelDelete method, lack of, 513

CancelEvent action, 345

CancelUpdate method, 512

Caption property, 31, 593, 922

    assigning keyboard combination in, 246

    assignment statement to set, 549

    for hypertext description, 31

carriage return with line feed, constant for, 642

carrying values forward to new record, **823–829**

Cascade Delete Related Records, 366, 821, 823

cascade options, for relationship, 522

cascading deletions, **366–367**, *367*, *368*, **822–823**

case sensitivity

    of passwords, 47

    in sort order, 562

CategoryID_NotInList event procedure, 840–841

cboCustomer_AfterUpdate macro, *394*

cboFind_AfterUpdate event procedure, 769, 771–772, 773

cboFind_AfterUpdate macro, *312, 314, 317–318*

cboFind_AfterUpdate procedure, 870

cboFirst_AfterUpdate macro, *408*

ChangeCaption function, 620–621

changed records, Requery action to display, 224

Change event, 96

Change procedure, 594

Chart control, 124

child objects, 500

Choose Builder dialog, *144*, 258, 548, *549*, 560

Choose() function, **262–263**, *263*, 983

    vs. Switch() function, 264

class definitions, 488

classes, **112–113**, 956, 1007

Classes list box, in Object Browser, 478

class modules, 92, 467, **544**

clickable image, for hyperlink, **32–33**, *33, 34*

Click event, 20, 95, 98, 243, 245, 625

    default behavior for, 101

    for synchronizing forms, 185, *187*

    for triggering macros, 237

clicking command button, sequence of events for, **95**

clipboard, to copy and paste for macro creation, 228

Clone method, **514–515**, 795, 797

clones, **795–797**

closed forms, 111

    reference to, **957**

Close macro action, 249, 332

Close method, 498, 753, 917

CloseUnhide procedure, 749

closing

    database, **249–250**

    forms, **246–248**, *247*

        event procedure for, 582

    objects, 603

    recordsetclone, 767

    recordsets, **505**, **783**

    related forms, macro for, **332**, *332*

cmdAssignAll_Click procedure, 903, 906

cmdAssign_Click procedure, 879

cmdCategories_Click macro, *244*

cmdClose_Click macro, *424*

cmdDelete_Click macro, *362, 365, 367*

cmdDelete_Click procedure, **818–823**

cmdDisplayDatabaseWindow_Click macro, *250*

cmdExitDatabase_Click macro, *250*

cmdLoopCount_Click macro, *266*

cmdLoopExpression_Click macro, *269*

cmdMessage_Click macro, *258*

cmdNew_Click macro, 350

cmdNewCustomer_Click macro, *371*

cmdOrders_Click procedure, 745

cmd prefix, 26

cmdPreview_Click macro, *423*

cmdPrevious_Click macro, *318*

cmdPrint_Click macro, *411, 424*

    flow diagram for, *412, 413*

cmdProduct_Click macro, 329

cmdRecordset_Click() event procedure, 741

cmdReturn_Click macro, *247*

cmdReturn_Click() procedure, 727

cmdReviewCustomer_Click macro, *326*

cmdSave_Click macro, *430–431*

cmdSave_Click procedure, 694

cmdSetControl_Click procedure, 756

cmdSetControlOnSubform_Click procedure, 756

cmdSetOtherFormControl_Click procedure, 756

cmdShowAll_Click macro, *396*

cmdSortOrderID_Click procedure, 875

cmdToControl_Click procedure, 754

cmdToControlOnSubform_Click procedure, 754

cmdToOtherFormControl_Click procedure, 754–755

cmdUndo_Click macro, 352

cmdUnDo_Click procedure, 818

cmdUndoFind_Click event procedure, 773

cmdView_click event procedure, 964–965

cmdViewCustomer_Click event procedure, 751

Code Builder, 548, 551

    eliminating use, *564*

Code button (toolbar), 544, 977

code template, 549, 551

    for Error event, 289

Coding options, 563

coercing variant variable, 600

Collection objects, **477**, **516–517**, 956, **958**

    assigning, 958

    creating object variable for, 962

collections, 111, **466**

    appending new objects to, 499

    indexing by number, **463–464**

    in Jet, 491

    references to objects in, **462–464**

    using For… with, **663–664**

    zero-based indexes, 463

colon equals (:=) assignment operator, to pass argument by name, 447–448, 617

color, setting by code type, 562–563

Column property, 412, 469–470

    to pull data from combo box list into unbound control, **181–182**, *182*

    to return data in multi-select list box, 876, 877

columns

    sorting by, **385**

    width in macrosheet, 228

ColumnWidths property, 179

combo box control, 157, *158*, **469–470**

    pulling data into unbound control from, **181–182**, *182*

    pushing data into bound control from, **182**

    sequence of events for text changes in, **95–96**

    to look up information, **178–182**, *180*

combo boxes

    macro to requery, 356, 408

    Query By Form to synchronize, **405–406**

    query criteria to return records for all values of empty, **398–399**

    for selection on forms, **392–393**

    setting value to Null, 396, 400

    synchronizing, **405–409**, *405*, **869–871**, *871*

    to create second selection, **397–398**

Combo Box Wizard, **35–38**, *36*, *37*, 59, 310

combo list

    adding null row for selection, **400–404**, *403*

    process when value is not in, **316**

    for search process, 768

command bars. *See also* menus; shortcut menus; toolbars

    customizing, **51–52**

    running macros from, **232–233**

command buttons

    appearance of, 24, *25*

    Caption property of, 593

    on custom dialog, **421–422**

        macros for, **423–424**

    for data entry operations, **349**, *349*

    event properties for, *20*

    on forms for interface navigation, 743

    Hyperlink property, 471

    for hyperlinks, **33–34**, *34*

    names of, 24, *25*

    procedures for, **19–22**

    sequence of events for clicking, **95**

    to call procedure, 553

Command Button tool, *23*, 23, 246

Command Button Wizard, **22–25**, *23*, 59, 726, 739

    for data entry operations, **813–823**, *815*

    operations automated with, *24*

commands

    adding to shortcut menu, 56

adding to toolbar, 57

dimmed, 216

macro actions to duplicate built-in, **214–217**

removing from command bar, 51

Command Wizard, error handlers from, 728

comments

color setting for, 563

and error avoidance, 293, **718**

in macros, *240*, 240

and performance, 983–984

in program code, 568

Comments column, of Macro window, 202

CommitTrans method, of Workspace object, 905, 906, 907

compacting database, 699

comparison test, for record selection, 857

compiled state, 569

Compile Loaded Modules button (toolbar), 699

compiler, **569–571**. *See also* Access VBA compiler

compiler directive, 700

compile-time errors, 569, 690, 691

typical messages, *695*, 695

compiling, 974

complex sort, **854–856**

macros for, **385–389**, *388*

Component Object Model (COM), 993

Concatenate function, 577, 606

Concatenate procedure, 617

concatenating field values, 163, *164*

conditional compilation, **700–701**

conditional compilation constant, 700

conditional macros, 251, **252–258**

decision functions, **262–264**

Choose() function, **262–263**, *263*

immediate If function, **262**, *262*

Switch() function, **263–264**, *264*

flow diagram for, *252*, 253

loops, **264–270**

counted loop, **265–267**, *266*

running loop, **269–270**, *269*

tested loop, 265, **268**, *268*, *269*

MsgBox() function as condition in, **257–259**, *258*, *259*

with one alternative, **253–254**, *254*

opposite condition in, **255–257**

with two alternatives, **254–257**, *256*

when condition is true, 253

Condition cell, ellipsis (…) in, 253

Condition column, of Macro window, 202

conditions testing, **651–659**

If…Then…Else, **653–656**, *655*, 725, 851

If…Then decision structure, **651–653**, *652*, 983

Select Case decision structure, **657–660**, *659*, 983

to test toggle button state, 851–852

to trap errors, 725, 729

Typeof…Is, **656–657**, 660

confirmation box, suppressing default, 365–366

Connect property, of TableDef object, **932**

constants, **631–635**

creating, **634–635**

custom, **596**

declaration statement, 596

displaying in Object Browser, 633

from server application, 1011

intrinsic, **632**

naming, **599**

scope of, 599

use in procedures, 596

CONSTRAINT clause, 927, 931

constraints, 931

Container object, **524**, 914–915

to track permission, 85

container relationships, hierarchy of, 113–114, *115*, *116*

Continue button (toolbar), 704

control buffer, 97

Control Name argument, for GoToControl macro action, 299

Control objects, **124–126**, **468–472**

Requery method for, 465

control properties

for hyperlink, 31

With…End With structure to change, 675

Control Properties dialog, 52, *53*

controls

calculated, 156–157, 214

communication between fields and, **162–178**

ControlSource property for, **156–157**

copying and pasting, 583

default property for, 125

DefaultValue property for, 427

determining type, 656

Enabled property of, 89

on forms,

    calculated, **164–175**

    events for, **99**

macro to move to specific on active form, **299–300**

moving to specific in other open form, **302**

name change and event procedure, 583

navigation between, **753–758**

for navigation with macros, **298–303**, *300*

Parent property of, 135

pasting reusable, **247–248**

procedure to change font color, 665–666

procedure to change properties, 594

references to, **133–134**

reference to properties, **134**, *135*

reference to those on active form or report, **137–138**

relating to data, **151–158**

sequence of events for tabbing between, 98

with two data sources, **157**, **178–182**

ValidationRule property of, 342, *343*, *808*

Visible property of, 89

without ControlSource property, **158**, *159*

controls collection, looping through, **827–829**

Controls collection object, **124**

ControlSource property, **156–157**, 178

    blank, 176

    of calculated control, DLookup() function in, 171–172

    calling function in expression for, 551–552, *552*

    for combo box, 179, 393

    controls without, **158**, *159*

    for data control, 125

    data sources for calculation, 165

    domain aggregate functions in, 174–175

    expression referring to different open form, 169–170, *170*

control structures, 650

    nesting in VBA, **672–673**

Control Wizards button, *23*, 23, *36*, 36

Control Wizard tool, 813

Convert form macros dialog, *976*, 976

copy buffer, 511, 836

    creating new record in, 838

    loss of changes, 837, 839

copying

    command between command bars, 52

    rows in macrosheet, 244

copy and paste

    for controls, 583

    in Module view, 566

counted loops, **265–267**, *266*

COUNTER data type, 928

counter variable, for For…Next loop, 661

Counting procedure, 663

counting records, **781**

Count property, 77, 476, 516

Create… methods, 916–917, 918

CreateArray procedure, 638–639

CreateControl function, 934, 935

CreateDatabase method, of Workspace object, 499–500

CreateEventProc method, of module object, 937, *939*

CreateField method, 500, **919–921**, *922*, **923–924**, 925–926, *926*

CreateForm function, 933–934

CREATE INDEX data-definition query, 929

CreateIndex method, **922**, *924*

CreateObject function, **1013–1015**, *1016*

CreateProperty method, of data access object, **940–942**

CreateQueryDef method, of Database object, 499, 501, 885

CreateRelation method, 924–925, *926*

CreateTableDef method, of Database object, 500

CREATE TABLE statement, 931

CreateWorkspace method, of DBEngine object, 499

Criteria cell, in query design grid, 153

crosstab queries, and editing, 836

Ctrl+Break

    for Break mode, 703

    to stop endless loop, 671

Ctrl key, to copy commands between command bars, 52

currency literals, 532

current data

    displaying, **167–169**

    macro to display, **222–225**, *222*

current database, function to refer to, 492
CurrentDb function, 492, 495, 664, 775, 914
Current event, 99, 330, 751
    for synchronizing forms, 186, *187*, *331*
current execution path, 695
current form, printing group of records based on, **410–415**
current index, 509
CurrentObjectName property, 77
CurrentPage setting, for Cycle property, 308
current procedure, 703
current record, 303, 455, 505, 758
    changing, **836–838**
    finding position of, **782**
    setting new record as, 838
    testing for first, 764
    vs. new record, 512
current record pointer
    after deleting record, 842
    creating second, **455–459**, *456*
    determining position of, 782
    Move… methods for, 779
    moving before editing record, 836
    and multiple instances of form, 960
    for recordsetclone, 740–741
    RecordsetClone property to create second, 762, *763*
    setting after Find with no matches, 786
    setting to first record, 741
CurrentRecord property, 77
current records, and disabled navigation buttons, 762
CurrentRecord setting, for Cycle property, 308
current statement, 703
current values
    Debug window to print, **710–711**
    viewing in Module window, *710*, 710
custom constants, **596**
custom database property, 79
custom data type
    as arguments, **645**
    Public keyword for, 645
custom default values, for data entry, **825–829**
custom dialog
    command buttons on, **421–422**

creating, **420–426**, *422*
    macros for command buttons, **423–424**
    to select records, **415–426**
custom dialog form, from wizard, 15, *16*
CustomerID_AfterUpdate procedure, 827, 829
CustomerID_NotInList procedure, 833–834
Customer Labels Dialog form, 416
custom error messages, **722**
CustomersLinked form, from Form Wizard, *185*, 185
custom functions, 971–972
Customize dialog, 49–50, *50*
    Commands tab, 203, *204*
custom libraries, 970
custom menus, 42, **48–58**
custom messages, displaying for data validation, *346*
custom methods, for form or report, **954–955**
custom objects, class module for, 92
custom properties, **940–955**
    for data access objects, 494, **940–947**
    deleting, **943**
    for forms and reports, **947–954**
    procedure to create, 541
    Property Let statement for, **949–952**
    references to, **942–943**
    setting, 953
    Tag property to create, **948**
custom properties dialog, for ActiveX control, 995, **1003**, *1003*
custom toolbars, 42, **48–50**
    creating and displaying, **57–58**
custom user interface, 5
Cycle property, 308

# D

DAO3032.DLL file, 1008
DAO (Data Access Objects) language, 63, 120
    techniques for navigation, **880–881**
DAOFilter procedure, 896–897
DAO properties, types, **493–495**
DAOSort procedure, 894–895

DAOSortTable procedure, 895, 896

data access languages, 62

data access object creation, **498–505**

    QueryDef object, **501–502**

    recordset creation, **502–505**

data access object model, **515–525**, 914, 1008. *See also specific object types*

    collection objects, **516–517**

    Container object, **524**

    database object, **517–518**

    DBEngine object, **516**

    Document object, **524–525**

    Error object, 524

    Field objects, **518**

    Group object, 525

    hierarchy, **489–492**, *490*

    Index object, **519–521**

    Parameter object, **523–524**

    Property object, **524**

    QueryDef object, **523**

    Recordset object, **522–523**

    Relation object, **521–522**

    TableDef object, **518**

    User object, **525**

    Workspace object, **517**

data access objects, 68, 116, **486–527**

    application-defined properties for, **494–495**

        adding, **944–947**

    CreateProperty method, **940–942**

    creating, **916–917**

    custom properties for, **940–947**

    default collections for, **491–492**

    properties, 76

    references for collections, 664

    references to, **491**

    reference to existing, **495–498**

    tags for, **72**

    to create table, **918–926**

    types, **493**

    user-defined properties, **494**

Data Access Objects (DAO) language, 63, 120

data access objects library, 988

database, 4

    closing, **249–250**

    compacting, 699

    encrypting, 48

    front-end and back-end, 571

    hyperlink to form in different, 32–33

    names of files, 499

    opening two simultaneously, **496–498**

    saving calculation to, **177–178**

    setting properties, 78

    statistics on current, 79

database applications, types available from Database Wizard, 6

Database Documenter, to print macros, **279–280**, *280*, *281*

Database object, 495, **517–518**

    Close method of, 498

    CreateQueryDef method of, 499, 501, 885

    CreateTableDef method of, 500

    creating, 499

    Execute method of, **899–900**, 902

    Jet creation of, 914

    OpenRecordset method of, 503

database properties, **79–80**

    custom, 79

Database Properties dialog, 79, *80*

Database To Save As MDE dialog, 570

Database window, 69

    displaying, **248**

    icons in, *558*

    Modules pane, 8

    Modules pane in, 466

    Modules tab, Converted Macro - Customer Phone list, *981*, 981

    procedure statements to redisplay and minimize, 44–45, *46*

    Queries pane, 153

    saving macro object in, 226

    startup properties to hide, 43

Database window objects, 69

    creating, **917–939**

    deleting, **939**

    lifetime of, 85

    list of, 79

    property sheets for, 74, *75*

SysCmd function to return state of, **682**

tags for, 71

Database Wizard, 5, **6–22**, 739

adding fields with, *9*, 9

database description, *9*, 9

event procedures creation, 22

limitations, 59

starting, *8*, 8

styles specified in, *10*

switchboards for navigation path creation, **7–11**

techniques used, **16–22**

data controls, 125

data conversion functions, 534

data definition, Jet database engine to manage, 118

data definition language commands, 901

data definition queries, 883, 927

SQL statements for, 901

data entry

carrying values forward to new record, **823–829**

carrying values forward to next session, **427–431**

Command Button Wizard for, **813–823**, *815*

creating form, 428, *429*

custom default values for, **825–829**

data entry with macros, **340–375**

adding new records, **348–351**

carrying values forward to new record, **357–360**, *360*, *361*

data validation, **341–348**

saving changes, **353–357**

undoing changes, **351–352**

user deletion option, **361–369**

working with data in two open forms, **369–374**, *373*

data entry mode, 805

forms for, 594

visual cue for, 674

DataErr argument, 290–291, 724

data integrity

and form changes by users, 242

Jet database engine to manage, 118

and multiple forms, 748

and one-to-many relationship, 324

data maintenance, with related forms, **830–835**

data manipulation

with Jet engine, 119

in recordset object, **505–515**

data manipulation language commands, 901

data reconciliation, after .mde file creation, 571

data retrieval, Jet engine management of, 119

data sharing, with Jet engine, 119

Datasheet view, recordset for, *154*, 154

data source, of form or report, 155

data in tables, **774–799**

clones, **795–797**

finding specific record, **785–794**

reading into array, **797–799**

recordset navigation, **779–784**

recordset variables to work with, **775–778**

Data Tip, displaying current value as, 710

data types, **531–539**

automatic conversion of, **533–534**

creating, **643–645**

declaring for arguments, 591

and errors, **718**

for function procedure's return value, 591

Hyperlink, 29

literals, **532**

object, **538–539**

summary, 631

for variables, **599–600**

Variant, 531, **532–537**

variant as default, 533

data validation, 60

displaying custom message for, *346*

with macros, **341–348**

timing of, **811–813**

VBA for, **807–809**, *808*

data values

carrying forward to next data entry session, **427–431**

Debug window to assign to forms and reports, **285–286**, *286*

displaying for control in MsgBox action, 231, *232*

editing in recordset, **836–843**

location of, 518

macro to change for form or report, **209–214**

passing to procedure, **612–624**

reading in recordset, **780**

storage of, 502

date literals, 532

date-stamp, for changed record, **353–355**, *355*

date value, in SetValue Expression argument, 212

DAvg() function, 172

dbAppendOnly constant, 891

dbAutoIncrField constant, 921

dbConsistent constant, 899

dbDenyWrite constant, 891, 899

dbEditAdd, 842

dbEditInProgress, 842

dbEditNone, 841

DBEngine object, 85, 111, 120, 489, 492, 914

   CreateWorkspace method of, 499

   as temporary object, 495

dbExecDirect constant, 899

dbFailOnError constant, 899

dbInconsistent constant, 899

DblClick event, 245, 625

dbOpenDynamic recordset object type, 503

dbOpenDynaset constant, 891

dbOpenDynaset recordset object type, 504

dbOpenForwardOnly constant, 891

dbOpenForwardOnly recordset object type, 504

dbOpenSnapshot constant, 891

dbOpenSnapshot recordset object type, 504

dbOpenTable recordset object type, 503

dbReadOnly constant, 891

dbRunAsync constant, 899

dbSeeChanges constant, 899

dbSQLPassThrough constant, 899

DCount() function, 172, 316, 812, 821

   to count related records, 364, 366

   to test for primary key value uniqueness, **344–346**

DDLAlterTable procedure, 901–902

debugging statements, marking for conditional compilation, 700

Debug menu

   Add Watch, 713

   Compile All Modules, 699

   Compile Loaded Modules, 699

   Compile and Save All Modules, 699, 984

   Edit Watch, 714

Debug object, **127–128**, **477**

Debug window, *127*, 127, **441**, **710–715**. *See also* Immediate pane of
   Debug window

   bookmarks in, 460

   in break mode, **711–714**, *712*

   calling methods in, **448–449**, *449*

   calling sub procedures in, **583**

   getting property settings in, **444–445**

   Locals tab, 711, *712*, 712–713

   printing from code to, **716**

   running macros from, **235–236**

   setting properties in, **442–443**, *443*

   to add new record, 513

   to assign values to forms and reports, **285–286**, *286*

   to call procedure, **574–576**

   to delete record, 514

   to display values from forms and reports, **283–284**, *284*

   to evaluate Field properties, 518, 519

   to run macro action or macro, **284–285**

   to run VBA statements, 531

   to test Move methods, 506

   to troubleshoot macro errors, **282–286**, *285*, *286*

   two current record pointers in, 457

   Watch tab, *127*, 127–128, 711–714, *715*

decision functions, **262–264**, 972

decision structures, 264–265, 650

declaration

   of collection object, 962

   of custom constant, 596

   of data type for argument, 591

   of data type for return value from function procedure, 591

   of dynamic-link library, **989–990**

   explicit, 446

   of fixed-size array, 637–638

   implicit, 446

   for module-level dynamic array, 640

   for module-level variable, 625

   in modules, 544–545

   for naming constants or variables, 599

   New keyword in, **958**

   for NotInList event procedure, 832–833

   placement in procedure, 608

   Public keyword in, 547

of recordset object variables, 602

for standard module, 554

statements in procedures, 569

summary, 631

to create constants, **634–635**

of variables, 72, **597–604**

in argument list, **606**

for reusable procedures, 745

to pass to Querydef object, 885

within procedure, **604–605**

Declarations section, of module, *18*, 18, 544–545

decompilation, **699**

default behavior

canceling, **101**

event procedure to cancel, **810–811**

default collections

for data access objects, **491–492**

for object, 133

default confirmation box, suppressing, 365–366

default data type, Variant as, 533

default error handling, 690

for nonfatal errors, 692–693

default error message, *276*

for empty field, *287*

default Form view, command bars, *215*

default instance of class, 956

default message, for Cascade Delete Related Records option, *366*

default processing, interrupting with macros, **238**

default property

for controls, 125

for object, 134

defaults, in object references, 131

Default Type settings, for MsgBox() function, 261

DefaultValue property, 826

for controls, 427

setting, 357–358, **824–825**

default values, custom for data entry, **825–829**

#Default Workspace# object, 517

delete buffer, 513

Delete button

creating, 815

on Switchboard Manager, 40

DeleteControl statement, 934

deleted records, Requery action to remove, 224

Delete key, disabling, 369

Delete method, 516, 917

of Properties collection, 943

DeleteObject method, of DoCmd object, 939

DELETE query, 901

DeleteRecordset procedure, 842–843

deleting

custom property, **943**

Database window objects, **939**

providing as user option, **361–369**

records,

cascading, **366–367**, *367*, *368*, **822–823**

with methods, 513–514

procedure for, **818–823**

and referential integrity, 288

with related records, **82–83**

rows in macrosheet, 228

Description property, 922

for Err object, 729

for query, 494

of table, 944

design time, 20, 702

design-time properties, 74

viewing property sheet for, **74–75**

Design view, 19–20, 116

for queries, 152

destroying

objects, 603

recordset, automatic, 154

variables, 601, 603, **604**

destructive testing, 719

DFirst() function, 172

dialogs

for InputBox function, 681

as property sheets, 78

Dim keyword, 628

vs. Static keyword, 609

dimmed commands, 216

Dim statement, to created fixed-size array, 637

Dirty property, 77
    macro to test, **351–352**
    to test for record changes, 817
DisableEnable function procedure, 763–767
displaying
    current data, **167–169**
    Database window, **248**
    modules, 557
displaytext part of hypertext information, 29
Division by Zero error, 264, 287
Division procedure, 730–733
DLast() function, 172
DLLs (dynamic-link libraries), 489, 544, 629, **987–992**
DLookup() function, 178
    pulling data with, **171–175**
    syntax for, 173–174
    to test reference to field, 141
DMax() function, 172
DMin() function, 172
Do...Loop decision structure, **666–671**
    to walk a recordset, 782
Do...Loop Until decision structure, 668, *669*, 670
Do...Loop While decision structure, **667**, *668*, 670
DoCmd object, 89, *90*, 284, **473–474**
    ApplyFilter method, **770–771**, *861*, 861
    and automation, **450–451**
    Close method, 24
    DeleteObject method, 939
    FindRecord method, **769**
    GoToRecord method, 758
    methods of, **450–453**
    OpenForm method, 744, 860, 953
    OpenQuery method, 890–891, 898
    OpenReport method, 860–861
    Requery method, 465, 871
    and running macro action, 235
    RunSQL method, 901–902
    SelectObject method, 834
    SetWarnings method, 898
documentation
    hard-copy, 972
    of macros, **239–240**

Documenter dialog, *280*, 280
Document object, 68, **524–525**
    to track permissions, 85
DoEvents function, **679–680**
DoEventsLoop procedure, 679–680
DoLoopUntil procedure, 670
DoLoopWhile procedure, 670
domain, 172, 173
domain aggregate functions, **172**, **174–175**
    in Expression argument, 213
DoMenuItem method, 817
dot (.) operator
    in data access object reference, 491
    and execution speed, 595
    in macro reference, 227
    in object names, 130
    in reference to property, 131
    when calling method, 446
double-click time limit, changing, 245
Do Until...Loop decision structure, 668, *669*, 670, 894
DoUntil procedure, 670
Do While...Loop decision structure, **667**, *667*, 669
DoWhile procedure, 669
drag and drop
    lookup field to form, 392–393
    in Module window, 566
    to define macro action to open form, 243
DROP TABLE statement, 901
DStDev() function, 172
DStDevP() function, 172
DSum() function, 172
Duplicates procedure, 795, 796
DVar() function, 172
DVarP() function, 172
DynamicArray procedure, 641–642
dynamic arrays, 636, **640–643**
    setting bounds, 641
dynamic data exchange (DDE), 974
dynamic-link libraries (DLLs), 489, 544, 629, **987–992**
    declaration for, **989–990**
    type libraries, **988**
    Windows API, **990–992**

DynasetRecordset procedure, 776
dynaset-type recordset, 523
    adding new record, 838
    filtering, **896**
    Find methods for, **785–788**
    and locating record, 508–509
    RecordCount property for, 767, 781
    sorting, 894

# E

early binding, **1011**
Echo macro action, 205, 365, 769
Edit button, on Switchboard Manager, 40
Edit Hyperlink dialog, 29, *30*
editing
    automatic refresh of data after, **830–831**, *832*
    data in recordset, **836–843**
    embedded object, 993
    existing records, **370**
    library database code, 986–987
    loss of changes after moving to another record, 837
    in macrosheet, **228–229**
    methods for, 511–512
    in module window, **566–567**
    saving records after, 162
editing mode, F2 to switch to, 228
Edit menu, 565
    Bookmark, 565
    Clear, 566
    Delete Record, 223, *224*, 361
    Find, 309, 506, *768*, 768
    Find or Replace, 566, *567*
    Go To, 305, 758
        New Record, 346, 350
    Replace, 615
    Undoing Current Field/Record, 351
    Undo Typing, 351
Edit method, 511, 837
    and errors, 842
edit mode, F2 to toggle, 303

EditMode property, of recordset, **841–842**
EditRecordset procedure, 837–838
Edit Switchboard Item dialog, *41*, 41
elegant code, 739
ellipsis (…), in Condition cell, 253
empty combo box, query criteria to return records for all values
        of, **398–399**
Empty value, 535–536
Enabled property, 89, 805, *806*
encapsulation, 468, 913
        in VBA, **440–441**
Encrypt/Decrypt Database dialog, 48
encrypting database, 48
End button, 705
End of File (EOF) property, 507, 671, 762, 763, 779–780, *780*
        testing, 307
End If keyword, 653
endless loop, 671
End Property statement, 541
End statement, vs. Stop statement, 704
End Sub keyword, 289
End Sub statement, 540
End Type statement, 644
Enter event, 95, 98, 168
entity, 438
entity integrity, 809
enumerated constants, 632
        displaying in Object Browser, 633
environmental options, for Access, **80–83**
EOF (End of File) property, 507, 671, 762, 763, 779–780, *780*
        testing, 307
equal sign (=)
        for calculated control, 164
        in Expression argument of SetValue, 212
Erase statement, **638–639**
        and dynamic arrays, 643
Err object, **476**, 720, **729**
        Number property of, 727
error codes, **287**
Error event, 100, 289
        event procedure code template for, 723–724
        in form and report modules, **722–726**

error handling, **288**, **289–292**, **690–735**
  for command button procedures, 817
  custom instructions in message boxes, *733*
  for custom navigation buttons, *761*, 761
  dealing with unavoidable errors, **693–694**
  Err object, **476**, 720, **729**
  error codes, **719–722**
  generic error handler, **730–734**
  macros vs. Visual Basic, 972
  On Error statement, **729**
  resuming execution after, 728
  testing, **292**
  troubleshooting tools, **701–716**
error messages
  compile-time, *569*, *695*, 695
  custom, **722**
  default, *276*
    for Delete button, *816*
    for deletion of related record, *363*
    for unavailable command, *820*
    for Undo button click, *815*
  from attempt to display property that refers to object, *445*
  from declaring Public constant in form or report module, *636*
  from failed move to subform control, *301*
  from full identifier in Control Name argument, *299*
  from inappropriate commands, *216*, 216–217, *217*
  from moved library database, 986
  from references using Screen object in Immediate window, *139*, 139
  from reference to nonexistent user-defined property, *943*
  from short reference in Immediate window, *138*
  from syntax checking, 275, 567
  from unrecognized application-defined property, *945*
  from unsuccessful use of private procedure, 555, *556*
  from using Me in event property setting, *622*
  help for, **702**, *703*
  "Type mismatch," *619*, 619
  for value not in combo box list, *315*
  Value property and, *519*
  "Variable not defined," 608
  when evaluating run mode property, 132, *133*
  Write Conflict, *455*

Error objects, 85, 489, 524
errors, 274. *See also* compile-time errors; macro errors; run-time errors
  avoidable and unavoidable, **691–692**
  avoiding, **717–719**
  breakpoints to locate, 708
  in called procedures, **734**
  fatal and nonfatal, **692–693**
  multiple from one action, 720
Errors collection, 489, 720
event-driven programming, 21
  timing in, **99–101**
event function procedure, 93
EventFunction procedure, 579
event handler, 93, 237
event-handling procedures, 542
EventLogger application, 102–105, *103*, *104*, *105*
event macros, 93, 225, 237
  steps in creating, **238–239**
event procedures, 21, 22, 93, 540–541, **548–550**, *550*
  changing to function procedures, **591–594**
  converting macros to, **975–978**
  creating, **937–939**
  creating to close form, 582
  creation with Database Wizard, 22
  form module to store, 291
  public vs. private, 547
  syntax and code building tools, **550–551**
  to cancel default behavior, **810–811**
  to close form, 24, *25*
  triggering, 745
  viewing directly, **560**
  vs. function procedures, 745
event properties, 20, 92
  for forms, 93
  help for, 20–21, *21*
events, 20, 68, **91–105**, 438, 439
  for ActiveX controls, **1003–1006**
  assigning macro to, **239**
  categories of, **94**
  for controls on forms, **99**
  for forms, **100**, 150

for form sections, **100**

hands-on experience with, **101–105**

new in Access 97, **92**

for reports, **100–101**

for report sections, **100–101**

sequences of, **94–96**, **98–99**

Excel8.OLB file, 1008

Excel 97, strengths, 1006

Excel, hyperlink subaddress file syntax, *28*

Excel object model, 1008

exceptional macro actions, **293–294**, *294*

exclamation point (!) operator

in data access object reference, 491

and execution speed, 595

in object name, 130, 462

exclusive mode, for database, 46

executables, 488

Execute method

of Database object, **899–900**, 902

of QueryDef object, **899–900**

execution, suspending, **702–709**

execution control in VBA, **650–686**

conditions testing, **651–659**

loops for repetition, **660–672**

nesting control structures, **672–673**

object reference abbreviations, **674–675**

execution of macros, flow of, **229**

execution time, and hierarchy levels, 590

Exit event, 98, 168

Exit statements, **678**

Exit Sub statements, 733

Exit this database button, on main switchboard, 12

Expenses application, 58–60

explicit compiling, **699**

explicit counter, 267

explicit declaration, 446

explicit transactions, **904–907**

explicit variable declaration, and errors, **717**

expression, value to suspend code execution, 714

Expression argument, for SetValue macro action, **212–213**, 358

Expression Builder, 118, *982*

starting location effect on, 144

to create references, **141–144**, *142*, *143*, *145*

to reduce errors, 275–276

expressions

calling function procedures in, **582–583**, *583*

calling procedures in, 542

and calling sub procedures, 584

Debug window to evaluate, **283**

parsing, 275

external applications, 89

macro execution, 450–451

external tables, links to, **932–933**

# F

False constant, 632

fatal errors, **692–693**

Field objects, **518**, 518

Field property sheet, for Database window object, 74, *75*

fields

adding with Database Wizard, *9*, *9*

adding for hyperlink to employee personal home page, 29

binding ActiveX control to, 1004–1005, *1005*

binding control to, 162

communication between controls and, **162–178**

concatenating values, 163, *164*

General properties of, 74

properties, 807

references to, **139–141**

selecting for Lookup combo box, 36, *37*

SQL statement to restrict input to array, 798

ValidationRule property for, 341, *342*

Fields collection, 140, 491, 518

of Recordset object, 522–523

in TableDef object, 113, *114*

File menu

Close, 249

Database Properties, 79

Get External Data, 487, 849, 932

Link Tables, 932

Open Database, 46

recently opened databases on, 58
Save As/Export, 390, 980
files, GetObject function to open, **1020–1024**
Filter By Form, 389, 862, *863*
Filter By Selection, 389
Filter For technique, 862, *863*
Filter Name argument
    for ApplyFilter action, 313
    for OpenForm macro action, 325
FilterOn property, 860, 866
Filter property
    for form or report, 860, 866
    for recordset, 457, 894, *897*
filter query, 861
    ApplyFilter method to run, 868
    based on Record Source of report, **419–420**
    creating, **391–392**
    creating for report, **418–419**
    criteria for, **422–423**
    for OpenReport Where Condition argument, 418
    setting criteria, **393–394**
    to include combox box value, 397
filters
    automating removal of, **395–396**
    for dynaset-type recordset, **896**
    for recordsets, **893–897**
    removing, 868
    for snapshot-type recordset, **896**
    to change records displayed in open form, 862
    to select record for recordset, 770–771
Find... methods, **510–511**
FindAll procedure, 787–788
Find button (toolbar), 309, 768
Find dialog, 505, 768
Find in Field dialog, 309, *310*
FindFirst method, of Recordset object, 771, *772*, 797
finding
    current record position, **782**
    group of records, with Query By Form, **389–396**
    records to print, **409–415**
    specific records, **309–317, 768–774, 785–794**
        with ApplyFilter method, **770–771**

automating the process, **310–311**, *311*
deciding technique to use, **794**
with RecordsetClone property, **771–772**
undoing search, **773–774**, *774*
using FindRecord method, **769**
FindLast method, 826
Find methods, **785–788**
FindNext method, 787, 797
FindRecord action, 312
FindRecord method, of DoCmd object, **769**
FindRecord procedure, 786–787
Find and Replace (shareware), 73
FirstRecord function procedure, 759
first record, testing for, 764
    in macro, 307
fixed-size array, 636
    Erase to reinitialize elements, **638–639**
fixed-size arrays, **637–638**
flat-file database, 151
flicker, 769
flow diagrams
    for Choose() function, *263*
    for cmdPrint_Click macro, 412, *413*
    for conditional macro, *252*
    for conditional macro with one alternative, *253*
    for determining related record count and delete option, *368*
    to document macros, *240*
    and error prevention, 293
    for IIf() function, *262*
    for loops, *267*
    for macro with pair of one-alternative conditions, *255*
    for nonexecutable macro actions, *294*
    to resynchronize form using Current event, *331*
    for Switch() function, *264*
    for tested loop, *268*
    for testing for open form, *373*
flow of execution, 250. *See also* macro execution flow
    for macros, **229**
    VBA statements to control, 650
focus
    ActiveControl property to refer to, 77
    moving to specific control, 753

moving within record, **757–758**

and Screen object, 462

selecting objects and, **89**

SetFocus method to move, **755–757**

setting when form is opened, 594

folders, in Expression Builder, 141–142

font, for text in modules, 563

FontToRed function procedure, 665–666

For…Next decision structure, **661–664**, *662*, 983

    for controls collection, 828

    using with collection, **663–664**

    vs. For Each…Next, 666

For Each…Next decision structure, **664–666**, *672*, 950, 983

ForeColor property, 665

foreign key, 521

foreign query, 521

foreign table, 521

Form_AfterInsert event procedure, 834–835

Form_AfterInsert macro, *373*

Form_AfterUpdate procedure, 825

Format menu, Change To, 34

Form_BeforeUpdate macro, *355, 360*

Form_Close event procedure, 753

Form_Close macro, 332

form controls

    creating shortcut menu for, 57

    hyperlinks as unbound, **30–35**, *34*

Form_Current event procedure, 751–752

Form_Current macro, *331*

Form_Error procedure, 290–291, *724*, 724, *725, 726*

form macro group, 227

form modules, 8, 467

    creating, 544

    discarding, **250**

    Error event in, **722–726**

    module-level variable visibility when created in, **628–629**

    Module window combo box for, 559, *560*

    Module window for, *558*

    opening, 557

    running function procedure stored in, **576**

    to store event procedures, 291

Form object, **124**, **466**, 915

    automatic implicit reference to, 603

    passing as argument, 763

    Requery method for, 465

Form_Open macro, **384**

Form Operations, from Command Button Wizard, *24*

form properties, references to, **131**

Form property, 77, 622

FormRecordset function, 742–743

forms, 4, **150–195**, **804–829**

    in Access vs. in Jet, 915

    active, 89

    adding hypertext field to, 30

    adding Review button to, **327–328**, *328*

    automating navigation, **747–750**

    calculated controls for, **164–175**

    caption in title bar, 73

    carrying values forward to new record, **823–829**

    closing and unhiding, **246–248**, *247*

    Command Button Wizard for data entry operations, **813–823**, *815*

    creating, **933–936**

    creating command button to close, 23

    creating second current record pointer, **455–459**, *456*

    creating shortcut menu for, 57

    custom methods for, **954–955**

    custom navigation buttons for, **759–767**, *760*

    custom properties for, **947–954**

    and custom user interface, 5

    data maintenance with related, **830–835**

    Debug window to assign values to, **285–286**, *286*

    Debug window to display values form, 283–284, *284*

    displaying multiple instances, **955–965**, *956, 957, 961, 963*

    dragging to Macro window, 243

    event procedures to cancel default behavior, **810–811**

    event procedure to close, 24, *25*, 582

    event properties for, *93*

    events for controls on, **99**

    events for, **100**, 150

    form/subform to synchronize, **189–193**

    global variables, 177

    hiding and unhiding, **748–750**

importing, 849

with logical navigation, removing navigation buttons from, **320**, *320*

macro to change values for, **209–214**

macro to close related, **332**, *332*

macro to save new, *221*, 221

macros to navigate, **242–250**

macro to synchronize report to, **411–415**, *411*

Me property for, **461–462**

NotInList event to add row to combo list, **832–835**

opening with selected records, **858–861**

OrderByOn property for, **381**, **850**

OrderBy property, **381**, 849

passing as argument, 622

pop-up, 327

recognition of Filter event, 863–864

RecordsetClone property, 456

and recordsets, **740–743**, *741*

RecordSource property for, **155**, *155*

record sources and, 178

references to, **130–131**

reference to field in record source of, **140**

reference to one instance out of multiple, 960

relating to data, **151–158**

return path between Main Switchboard and, **23–24**

running macro by trapping events on, **237–238**, *237*

selection combo box on, **392–393**

sequence of events for opening, **98–99**

SetValue macro action for, **211–212**

sorting records in, **849–856**

synchronized, 13

and navigation, **750–758**

with reports, **333–334**, *335*

testing for open, 372, *373*, 752

toggling between review and data entry mode, **805–806**, *806*

in VBA, **453–462**

VBA to validate data, **807–809**, *808*

working with data in multiple open, **369–374**, *373*

Forms collection, 111, *112*, 960

form sections, events for, **100**

form's module, discarding, **250**

Forms switchboard, 13, *15*

form/subform, to synchronize two forms, **189–193**

Form view, setting property value in, 443

Form view menu bar, reduced, *44*

Form View Title Bar, 56

Form Wizard, 325, 378, 739

for one-to-many-to-many forms, *193*, 193, *194*

starting, 184

to synchronize forms, 183, **184–186**, *184*, *186–188*

to synchronize subforms, **190–193**

forward-only-type recordset

for data retrieval, 797

Edit method and, 512

RecordCount property for, 781

frmOrderStatus form, 378

front-end database, 571

FrontPage 97, strengths, 1006

full identifier

in Control Name argument, and error message, *299*

for macro, 228

Full Module view, *18*, 18

fully qualified reference, 138

for procedure, 545

functional testing, 719

function keys

F2 to toggle editing and navigation modes, 228, 303

F5 to leave break mode, 707

F6 to toggle between window panes, 563

F8 for Step Into, 708

F9 to refresh, 167, 168

F9 to toggle breakpoint, 706

function procedures, 93, **539–540**, **551–552**

calling, **572–581**

changing event procedure to, **591–594**

converting macros to, **979–982**

passing variables by reference and, 616

vs. event procedures, 745

functions, 453

# G

GDI32.dll, 990

General option, for database sort, 561

general procedure, *543*, 543

General properties, of fields, 74

General Protection fault

from API functions, 992

from incorrect arguments to DLL, 990

GetAccess procedure, 1017

GetLocal procedure, 607

GetObject function, **1015**, 1016, *1018*

to determine if application is running, **1022–1023**

to open specific file, **1020–1024**

to return reference to running instance of Automation server, **1018–1019**, *1019*

GetOption method, 447

GetReturnValue function, 577

GetRows method, of Recordset object, 797–798

GetSpreadsheet procedure, 1021

GetSystemMetrics Windows API function, 991, *992*

getting properties, 442, **443–446**

in Debug window, **444–445**

GetVariableByRef procedure, 614

Global Code module, *18*, 18

global macros, creating, **246–247**

global macrosheet, 246

global menu bar, 53–55, *54*

as startup property, 55, 57

global shortcut menu, creating, *56*, 56–57

global toolbar, creating, 57–58

global variables, 626

unbound control as, 175

global variables form, 177

Go/Continue button (toolbar), 707

GotFocus event, 95, 98, 99, 168

GoToControl macro action, 299, 301, 312, 452

GoToControl method, 91, 452

to move focus, 754

GoToPage method, 447

GoToRecord macro action, 305, 307, 308, 350

GoToRecord method, 758, 817

graphical query design, 152

graphics, clickable as hyperlink, **32–33**, *33*, *34*

grayed commands, 216

grouping objects, **111**

Group object, 525

groups of records

macros and, **378–433**

modifying, **426–431**

printing based on current form, **410–415**

Query By Form to find, **389–396**

reassigning, **902–903**, *904*

selecting, **857–879**

automating process, **392–396**

changes in, **862–866**

custom dialog for, **415–426**

interactive process, **390–392**, *391*

multiple criteria for, **394–404**, **868–869**, *869*

multi-select list box for, **871–879**, *874*

using Query by Form, **867–871**

sorting, **379–389**

by column, **853–854**

in form or report, **849–856**

group of statements, executing while in break mode, **709**

# H

hard-coded values, 591

hard-copy documentation, 972

hard typing, 600

HasData property, 77

HasModule property, 250, 544, 592, 975, 977

height of rows, in macrosheet, 228

help, **702**, *703*

displaying from Object Browser, 526

for event property, 20–21, *21*

Events and Event Properties Reference, *100*

for macro actions, 205–206, *206*, *207*

statements reference, *676*, 676

trappable errors lists, 720, *721*

helpers, 4

hidden text box, unbound, 317, *319*

hiding

    forms, **748–750**

    objects, 243

    procedures, **555**

    shortcut menus, 43

    toolbars, 43, 57

HKEY_CURRENT_USERS key, *82*

.hlp extension, 1008

HomePage text box control, hyperlink field in, 30, *31*

horizontal bar, adding to menu, 52

host application, 120

HTML document, hyperlink subaddress file syntax, *28*

Hungarian naming style, 69–70

hyperlink address, 27

HyperlinkAddress property, 31, 33, 471

Hyperlink data type, 29

Hyperlink objects, 469, **471**

hyperlinks, **26–35**

    changing control type, **34**

    clickable image for, **32–33**, *33*, *34*

    command button for, **33–34**, *34*

    history list of, 35

    label control as, **31–32**, *34*

    storing as data in table, **28–30**

    to web page, **33–34**

    as unbound form control, **30–35**, *34*

    uses in Access, 27

hyperlink subaddress, 27

    syntax, *28*

HyperlinkSubAddress property, 31, 33, 471

Hyperlink toolbar button, 29

I

icon

    in message box, 218

    for MsgBox() function, 261

identifiers. *See also* references

    avoiding errors, 275

If…Then decision structure, **651–653**, *652*, 983

If…Then…Else decision structure, **653–656**, *655*

    to test toggle button state, 851

    to trap errors, 725

If Typeof…Then…Else decision structure, 672

IgnoreNulls property, of Index object, 924

IIf() function, **262**, *262*, 983

Image control

    Hyperlink property, 471

    Picture property, 34

immediate If function, **262**, *262*

Immediate pane in Debug window, *127*, 127, 235, *236*, 282

    in break mode, 712

    navigating, **711**

    statement execution in, 711

    to create recordsets, 504

    to evaluate object property, **131–132**, *132*

    to print current values, **710–711**

    to set and get properties, *445*

    to test Move method, 508

implicit counter, for macro loops, 266, *267*

implicit declaration

    and errors from misspellings, 597

    of variable, 446

implicit transactions, **904–907**

importing, forms, 849

indent, in program code, *568*, 568

independent class modules, 92, **467–468**, 544

    icons for, *558*

    Module window for, *558*

    opening, 557, *558*

index

    for array, 636

    by name, 462–463

    by position, **463–464**

    by variable, 463

    for controls collection, 828

    creating for tables, 922–923, **929–930**

    for Seek method, *509*, 509, 788, 789, *790*

    term defined, *520*

Indexed property, of table field, for Seek method, 788

Indexed Sequential Access Method (ISAM), 119

Indexes collection, in TableDef object, 113, *114*

index number, in multi-select list box, 876

Index objects, 500, **519–521**

    Fields collection, 518

    properties of, 924

Index property, 509, 838

    to sort table-type recordset, **895–896**

Index property sheet, for Database window object, 74, *75*

inheritance, 440, 913

Initialize event, 92, 625

in-place activation, 993

in-process Automation server, 489

InputBox function, **680–681**, *681*

InputMask property, 211, 922

Insert ActiveX Control dialog, *999*, 999

Insert Hyperlink button (toolbar), 33

Insert Hyperlink dialog, 31, *33*, 33

inserting

    ActiveX controls, **998–1000**

    rows in macrosheet, 228

InsertLines method, of module object, 937, 938

Insert menu

    ActiveX, 999

    Class Module, 557

    Module, 557

    Picture, 32

    Procedure, 551, 583, 950

Insert Module button (toolbar), 557

Insert Picture dialog, 32

Insert Procedure dialog, 551, *552*, 950, *951*

    All Local Variables as Static, *611*

instances, 92, **112–113**

    of ActiveX object, New keyword to create, 1023–1024

    of application, GetObject function to determine if running, **1022–1023**

    of Automation object, creating, **1012–1015**

    of class, 1007

    of form,

        creating multiple, **962–963**, *963*

        example of multiple, **963–965**, *965*

        reference to one of multiple, 960

interactive database, 4

interface errors, and Jet database engine, **722–726**

InterfaceInfo procedure, 991–992, *992*

interface navigation, **743–758**

Internet

    direct access to, 471

    hyperlinks for files on, 27

Internet Explorer, 34

interrupting default processing, with macros, **238**

intrinsic constants, **632–633**

    in method arguments, 452

IsDate function, 533

IsEmpty function, 536

IsLoaded function, 372, 540, 752, 834, 985

    to avoid errors, 692

IsLoadedModule module, 985

IsLoaded procedure, *19*, 19

IsMissing function, 624

IsNull function, 534, 535

IsNumeric function, 533

IsObject function, 538

ItemAdded event, 92, 476

Item argument, for SetValue macro action, **210–212**

ItemData method, 469

    to return data in multi-select list box, 876

ItemRemoved event, 92, 476

ItemsSelected collection

    of list box controls, **470**

    for multi-select list box, **876–879**, *877*

# J

Jet data access objects, 116. *See also* data access objects

Jet database engine, 62, 68, 72, 83, **118–120**

    to access data, 516

    and application-defined properties, 494

    and automation, **488–489**

    bookmarks for, **507–508**

    creation of form's recordset object, *454*, 454

    database management services from, 486–487

    DBEngine object to represent, 111

error management, 719

evolution of, **119–120**

hierarchy, *122*

index maintenance by, 520

and interface errors, **722–726**

intrinsic constants, **632–633**

logical navigation with, **508–511**

and record selection and modification, 881

recordset created by, 152

starting Access and, 517

join control, communication between Lookup controls and, 162

join field, unique index for, 160

join queries, 883

# K

Kernel32.dll, 990

keyboard combination, assigning in button Caption property, 246

keyboard shortcuts, macros for, 61

Key Combinations, disabling with Startup dialog, 43

KeyDown event, 95

KeyPress event, 95

keys in Registry, 80–82

keystrokes

automating navigation with, **303**

macro actions to send, **219–222**

passing control to Windows for processing, 679

sending programmatically, 96

Keystrokes argument, for SendKey action, 220

KeyUp event, 96

keywords in Visual Basic, 289

keyword text, color for, 563

# L

label control

hyperlink as, **31–32**, *34*

Hyperlink property, 471

labels

Parent property of, 135

for switchboard buttons, editing, *41*, 41

LastModified property, 512, 838

last record, testing to determine if current record is, 764

LastRecord function procedure, 759

late binding, **1011**

LaunchWord procedure, 1014

Left() function, 406

Let assignment statement, 448

Let keyword, 444

libraries

custom, 970

object, **1011–1012**

library databases, 117, **983–987**

creating, **983–984**

editing code, **986–987**

moving, **986**

references to, **984–987**

life cycle, of object variables, **602–603**

lifetime

of module-level variables, **629–630**, *631*

of objects, **85**

of procedure-level variables, **609–612**

of unbound control variable, 175

of variables, 599

LifetimeModule procedure, 630, *631*

lightweight form, 250, 557

Like operator, 407

LimitToList property, 96, 286, 311, 316

line continuation character, 569

line labels, in VBA error handlers, 726–728

LinkChildFields property, 190

for subform control, 189

LinkMasterFields property, 190, 192

for subform control, 189

links, to external tables, **932–933**

LinkTable procedure, 933

list box

displaying column data in, *877*, 877

multi-select, **871–879**, *874*, *877*

sorting rows, **874–875**, *875*

walking through selection to change data, 878–879, *880*

list box controls, 157, **469–470**
  ItemsSelected collection of, **470**
ListIndex property, 876
literals, **532**
  editing in property sheet, 591
  passing to called procedure, 612–613, *613*
  replacing with variable, 744
  and reusable procedures, **590–591**
loaded modules, compiling, 699
Load event, 98, 186, *188*, 625
Locals pane in Debug window, *127*, 127–128
LocalVariable procedure, 607
local variables, 597
  automatically destroyed, 604
  creating, 598
LockControls method, 954
LockControls procedure, 673, 805–806
LockedForm property, creating, 950
LockedForm property procedure, 952
Locked property, 805, *806*
  vs. AllowEdits property, 379
locking
  pessimistic or optimistic, 119
  records, **455**
logical expression, for conditional execution flow, 251
logical navigation among records, **309–323**, 505–506
  adding to another form, **321–323**, *323*
  with Jet, **508–511**
  testing, 319
logic errors, **277**, 692
Long data type, 596
lookup combo box, 35–38, *39*
  to automate search, 310
Lookup controls, communication between join control and, 162
lookup table, for Choose() function, 262
LoopCount macro, *266*
LoopExpression macro, *269*
LoopRecordset procedure, 672
loop structures, 251, **264–270**, 650
  for controls collection, **827–829**
  endless, 671
  with recordset, 507, **671–672**, *673*

in VBA, **660–672**
  Do…Loop, **666–671**
  Do…Loop Until, 668, *669*, 670
  Do…Loop While, **667**, *668*, 670
  Do Until…Loop, 668, *669*, 670
  Do While…Loop, **667**, *667*, 669
  For…Next, **661–664**, *662*
  For Each…Next, **664–666**, 672
  While…Wend, 671
LostFocus event, 98, 168
lower bound for array, 637

# M

macro actions, 87, **205–225**, *440*
  arguments for, **205–209**
  and corresponding DoCmd object method, 452
  Debug window to run, **284–285**
  displaying current data, **222–225**, *222*
  duplicating built-in commands, **214–217**
  exceptional, **293–294**, *294*
  flow diagrams for nonexecutable, *294*
  help for, 205–206, *206*, *207*
  vs. method of DoCmd object, 474
  sending keystrokes, **219–222**
  sending messages, **217–219**, *218*, *219*
  setting values, **209–214**
  vs. Visual Basic methods, 284
Macro button (toolbar), 230, 298
macro conversion, **971–982**
  event macros converted to event procedures, **975–978**
  to function procedures, **979–982**
macro creation, **225–230**
  editing in macrosheet, **228–229**
  flow of macro execution, **229**
  storing macros, **226–228**
  using macro flow diagrams, **225–226**, *226*
macro errors, **274–295**
  Access management of, 720
  from delete operation when related records exist, **364–365**, *365*

designing to avoid, **292–293**

logic errors, **277**

run-time errors, **275–277**

syntax errors, **274–275**

troubleshooting tools, **278–286**

    breakpoints, **279**

    Debug window, **282–286**, *285, 286*

    MsgBox action, **281**, *282*

    printing macros, **279–280**, *280, 281*

    single stepping, **278–279**

macro execution flow, **229**, 250–270

    conditional pattern, 251, **252–258**

    looping pattern, 251

    sequential pattern, 251

macro flow diagrams, **225–226**, *226*

macro group, 227

Macro Name argument, for RunMacro action, 265

Macro Name column, 229

    of Macro window, 202

macro objects, vs. VBA objects, 439, *440*

macro programming, **128**

    goal of, 200

    run-time properties in, **75–76**

    vs. VBA programming, **61–62**, 743

macros, 4, 86, 916. *See also* data entry with macros; navigation
    with macros; running macros

    to apply selection filter, **394–395**, *394, 395*

    calling procedures from, **580**, *581*

    to close related forms, **332**, *332*

    comments in, *240*, 240

    for complex sort, **385–389**, *388*

    for counted loop, *266*

    Debug window to run, **284–285**

    defined, 200

    documenting, **239–240**

    and error codes, 287

    events to trigger, 745

    to fill new record with data from previous record, *430*,
        430–431, *432*

    to find record, **312–315**, *312*

    forms navigation with, **242–250**

    full identifier for, 228

global, **246–247**

and groups of records, **378–433**

to interrupt default processing, **238**

to keep forms synchronized, **330–332**, *331*

names for, **227**

for NoData event, **425–426**

for object manipulation, **87–88**, *87*, **241–250**

to open task form and hide switchboard, *244*

preventing execution of specific action in, 279

printing, 240, **279–280**, *280, 281*

references to those in groups, **227–228**

to remove filters, 395–396, *396*

to requery to match synchronized combo boxes, 408

running macro from other, **231–232**, *231*

to save new form, *221*, 221

to set validation rules, 343

startup, **335–336**

storing in groups, **226–228**

and sub procedures, 584

to synchronize report to form, **411–415**, *411*

    with filter query, **333–334**, *335*

testing, 221–222, **239**, **244–245**

vs. toolbars, 48–49

macrosheets, 200, *201*, 226–227

    AutoExec, 234

    blank rows in, 229

    copying row in, 244

    editing in, **228–229**

    global, 246

    for startup conditions, *336*, 336

Macro window, 200–202, *201, 202*

    columns in, 200

    dragging table, query, form or report to, 243

    running macro from, **230**

    toolbar, *203*, 203

main form, 136, 189

main switchboard, 7, **11–12**, *12*

    Exit this database button, 12

    return path between forms and, **23–24**

Make Default button, on Switchboard Manager, 40

many-to-many relationship, 6

.mda file extension, 117, 983

.mdb file extension, 85, 493, 499, 524

.mde file extensions, 117, 570, 696, 984

    restrictions to saving database as, 571

.mdw file extension, 493

.mdz file extension, 8

membership, for record selection, 857

memory

    data type and, 599

    loading modules into, 629

    for object variable and object, 602

    for variables, 595

    and Variant variable, 537

menu add-ins, 118

menu bar

    adding menu to, 55

    creating custom, **53–55**, *54*

    customizing, 49

    on default Form view, *215*

    global, 53–55, *54*

        as startup property, 55, 57

    Startup options, 123

Menu Builder, 49

menus

    adding horizontal bar to, 52

    custom, 42, **48–58**

    in module Design view, 565

    removing commands from, 54

Me property, 77, 91, 439, **590**

    for form or report, **461–462**

    passing as argument, **621**

    and screen objects, **461–462**

    and standard module, 592

    to refer to form, 742

Message argument, for MsgBox action, 218

message box

    custom error-handling instructions in, *733*

    from error handler, 729

    macro action to display, 217

messages

    default for Cascade Delete Related Records option, *366*

    passing control to Windows for, 679

Meter procedure, 684

methods, 61, 86, 88, 89, 235, 439

    assigning result of, **448**

    calling, **446–449**

    of DoCmd object, **450–453**

        vs. macro actions, 474

    passing arguments to, **446–448**

    of Recordset object, access to, 456

    to manipulate objects, *90*, 90

mini-datasheet, 178

Miscellaneous operations, from Command Button Wizard, *24*

misspellings, 567

    and run-time errors, 275

Modal property, 326, 327, 329

Modal Type settings, for MsgBox() function, 261

Module Design toolbar, customizing, *707*

module Design view, menus in, 565

module-level code, 545

module-level constants, creating, **635**

module-level variables, 597, **625–630**

    creating, 598

    declaring private, 628

    lifetime of, **629–630**, *631*

    memory use by, 604

    visibility when created in form or report module, **628–629**

Module objects, **466–468**, 915

    CreateEventProc method of, 937

    InsertLines method of, 937

modules, 4, **543–545**, 915–916. *See also* form modules; report modules; standard modules

    compiling loaded, 699

    creating, **936–939**

    custom data types defined in, 644

    Declarations section, *18*, 18

    layout of, 544–545, *545*

    loading into memory, 629

    states of, 702

    Visual Basic for, 19

Modules pane, in Database window, 466

module toolbar, *565*, 565

module view, **557–565**

Module window, *558*

    combo boxes, 558–559, *559*

    default view of, 19

displaying, 18

editing in, **566–567**

and macros, 230

and Object Browser, 478

title bar of, 22

viewing current values in, *710*, 710

mouse button click, sequence of events for, **95**

MouseDown event, 95

   help for, *21*

MouseUp event, 95

   help for, *21*

Move… methods, of Recordset object, 457–458, *458*, 506, 779

MoveFirst method, 741

MoveLast method, and counting records, 781

Move method, 508, 797

MoveNext method, 671, 764, 797

MovePrevious method, 764, 796

moving. *See also* navigation; navigation with macros

   command on command bar, 52

   library databases, **986**

   rows in macrosheet, 229

   to another record, and loss of editing changes, 837

   to new record using Bookmark property, 513

MSACC8.OLB file, 1008

MsgBox function, 366, **680–681**

   for cascading deletes, 822

   to collect user input, **259–261**

   in conditional macros, **257–259**, *258*, *259*

   as troubleshooting tool, 574

MsgBox macro action, 217

   to troubleshoot macro errors, **281**, *282*

multi-criteria selection process, **397–404**

multiple field index, for Seek technique, 789, *790*

multiple instances

   displaying for form, **955–965**, *956*, *957*, *961*, *963*

   example, **963–965**, *965*

Multiples procedure, 962

Multiply function, 618

multi-select list box, **871–879**, *874*, **876–879**, *877*

MultiSelect property, 470, 872

**N**

#Name? error message, 166

NameEachTable procedure, 664–665, *665*

NameForms procedure, 663–664

Name property

   for fields, 920

   for primary key control, 340

   for QueryDef object, 885

   for TableDef object, 919

names

   for arguments, **617**

   of command buttons, 24, *25*

   conflicts in, and errors, **718**

   of database file, 499

   index to refer to object, 462–463

   of macros, **227**

   of objects, **26**

      changing, **73**

      spaces in, 130

   in Visual Basic, **71–72**, **546**

naming conventions, 26, **69–71**, 568

   and error prevention, 293

navigating mode, 228

navigation

   automating for forms, **747–750**

   between controls, **753–758**

   custom button creation, **759–767**, *760*

   with DAO, vs. SQL relational techniques, **880–881**

   error handling for custom buttons, *761*, 761

   and form synchronization, **750–758**

   in interface, **743–758**

   of recordsets, **779–784**

   smart buttons for, **762–767**

navigation buttons, removing from form, 320, *320*

navigation with macros, **298–337**

   logical navigation among records, **309–323**

   physical navigation between records, **303–308**

   return to previous record, **317–319**, *318*

   synchronizing two forms, **323–334**, *324*, *326*

   through controls, **298–303**, *300*

navigation mode, F2 to toggle, 303

navigation path, switchboards to create, **7–11**

nested procedures, 553

    calls box to troubleshoot, **715–716**, *716*

nesting control structures, in VBA, **672–673**

NewActionQuery procedure, 889, 900

New button, on Switchboard Manager, 40

New dialog, Databases tab, *8*, 8

NewForm procedure, 934–936, 937–938

NewIndex procedure, 923–924, *924*

New keyword, 605

    in assignment statement, **959–961**, *961*

    in declaration statement, **958**

    to create instance of ActiveX object, 1023–1024

New Object button (toolbar), 200, 554, 557

NewRec function procedure, 759

NewRecord property, 762, 763

    testing value of, 306–307

new records

    adding, **370–373**, *371*

    carrying values forward to, **823–829**

    requery to display, 371–372, *373*, **834–835**

    vs. current record, 512

new record table, creating, **427–428**

NewRelation procedure, 925–926

NewSQLStatement procedure, 892

NewStoredQuery procedure, 887, 891

NewTable procedure, 920–921

NewTemporaryQuery procedure, 889–890

New Toolbar dialog, 53

No constant, 632

NoData event

    macros for, **425–426**

    of report, 412

NoInList event, 288

NoMatch property, 791, 813

    for Find… methods, **786**

    as looping condition, 787

    of Recordset object, 509

non-equi join queries, 883

nonfatal errors, **692–693**

non-persistent objects, 85, **493**

Nothing value, for Object data type, **538**

NotInList event, 96, 624

    to add row to combo list, **832–835**

Not operator, 255

    to toggle property, 677–678

Now() function, 212, 355

Null constant, 632

null row

    adding to selection combo list, **400–404**, *403*

    SQL statement to display, *406*, 406

Null state, for toggle button, 381, 382

NullToZero procedure, 652

Null value, 534

    in combo box, 396

        and filter query, 398

    from domain aggregate function, 175

    and query, 535

    for TripleState property, 850

null value test, for record selection, 857

NumberGame procedure, 658–659

Number property, of Err object, 727, 729

number sign (#)

    for conditional compilation constant, 700

    in hyperlink data, 29

    for literal date, 532

# 0

Object Browser, **478–482**, *479*, *481*, **525**, *526*

    pasting code into module from, 479

    to view Excel objects, *1010*, 1010

    to view intrinsic constants, **633–634**

    to view modules in library database, 986–987, *987*

Object Browser button (toolbar), 478, 525, 633

Object Browser dialog, 633, *634*

object code, 694

object data types, **538–539**, 600

    Automation and, **1011–1012**

object-enabled approach, 90

object hierarchy, **120–122**, *121*

    Parent property to move through, **1020–1021**

object library, **1011–1012**

object linking and embedding, 993

object manipulation, **86–91**

    macros for, **87–88**, *87*, **241–250**

    with Visual Basic, **89–91**, 972–973

object-oriented model, 440

object-oriented programming, elements and features, **913**

object relationships, **110–115**

    grouping similar objects, **111**

    objects containing objects, **113–115**

objects, **68–86**, 438. *See also* Automation objects

    closing, 603

    in collections, references to, **462–464**

    containing objects, **113–115**

    creating,

        in Access vs. Jet, **912–916**

        reusable, 246

    default collection for, 133

    hiding, 243

    as hyperlink target, 27–28

    independent class module to define, 468

    learning about application's, **1008–1012**

    lifetime of, **85**

    macro programming environment use of, 128

    multiple actions on single, **674–675**

    names for, **26**, **69–71**

        changing, **73**

    object variable and, 602

    passing as arguments, **620–622**

    properties of, **74–77**. *See also* properties

        default, 134

    properties representing other, **135**

    property sheet of, 20

    reference by name, **129–130**

    selection and focus, **89**

    singular, 111

    state of, 20, 91

    temporary, 85, 915

    in VBA, vs. macro objects, 439, *440*

    in VBA programming, 438, **439**

object types, 1007

    Typeof…Is to determine, **656–657**

object variables, 72, 444, 497

    for Collection object, 962

    life cycle of, **602–603**

    New keyword for declaring, **958**

    Set assignment statement to assign method result to, 448

ODBC database

    errors in, 720

    working directly with, 884

ODBCDirect, 120, 516, 918

    object model for opening connection with, 121

Off constant, 632

Office Assistant, 477

Office shared objects, **477**

.olb extension, 988, 1007

OLE, *See* ActiveX

OLE automation, 450, 488. *See also* Automation

OLE Broker World Wide Web site, 996

On…GoSub statements, 660

On…GoTo statements, 660

OnClick event, default behavior for, 101

OnClick property, 245, 258, 334, 548, 622

    for triple-state toggle button, 851

On constant, 632

OnCurrent Property, 331

one form-one record source model, **159–160**

OnError property, 724

    for form, 289

On Error statement, 727, **729**

one-to-many relationship

    Attribute property and, 522

    and AutoLookup query, 160

    and data integrity, 324

    form/subform technique to display, 190, *191*

    primary key for, 520

one-to-many-to-many form, *191*, **191–192**

one-to-one relationship, Attribute property and, 522

one-way path, from switchboard to reports, *14*

OnMouseDown event property, 20

OnOpen property, for switchboard, 45

OnUnLoad event property, 652

OpenAForm procedure, 591–593

open database, object to represent, 517

OpenDatabase method, of Workspace object, 496–497, 792

Open dialog, *47*

Open event, 91, 98

open form, 111

    macro to move to control in another, **302**

    moving to record on different, 308

    pulling data from different, **169–171**

    reference to control on, 133

    testing for, 752

OpenForm macro action, 205, 235–236, *236*, 325, 330, 467, 956

    arguments for, 206–208, *208*

OpenForm method, 91, 452, 453

    of DoCmd object, 744, 860, 953

OpenForms function, 540, *541*

OpenHide event function, 748, *749*

opening

    files, GetObject function for, **1020–1024**

    forms,

        command button for, 744

        defining macro action for, 243

        with selected records, **858–861**

        sequence of events for, **98–99**

    reports, with selected records, **858–861**

    two databases simultaneously, **496–498**

OpenQuery macro action, 209

    to run action query, **426–431**

    vs. RunSQL macro action, 426

OpenQuery method, of DoCmd object, 890–891, 898

OpenRecordset method, 499, 503, 505, 672, 775, 777, 792, 813, 916

    SQL statement in source argument of, 793–794

    to create recordset in memory, 892

    to run stored select query, 891

OpenReport macro action, 417–418, 467

OpenReport method, 452, 453

    of DoCmd object, 860–861

opposite condition, in conditional macros, **255–257**

optimistic locking, 119

optional arguments, **623–624**

Optional keyword, 623

Option Compare Database statement, 548, 561–562

Option Explicit statement, 548, 597–598, 695, 717

option group, sequence of events for value checking, 98

Option Private Module statement, 628

Options dialog, 80, *81*, 561

    Advanced tab, Conditional Compilation Arguments, 701

    Forms/Reports tab, Always Use Event Procedures, *563*, 563, 588

    General tab, *561*

    Modules tab, AutoSyntax Check, 717

    Module tab, 19, **562–563**, *562*

        Auto Data Tip, 710

        automatic compile levels, 696–698, *697*

        Auto Syntax Check, 567

    record-locking options, 455

    Require Variable Declaration, 598

    View tab, 200, *201*

OptionValue property, 158

Or cell, in query design grid, 153

ORDER BY clause, 403, *404*

OrderByOn property, **381**, 384, **850**, 852

OrderBy property, **381**, 384, 849, 852

OrdersLinked form, from Form Wizard, *185*, 185

Order Status report, from Report Wizard, *411*

ordinary array, 636

OR logical operator, 858

orphan records, 535

OtherPublic procedure, 626

Outlook 97, strengths, 1006

out-of-process Automation server, 488–489

OutputAllFields property, 419, 420

# P

Page Break control, 471, *472*

Page object, 471–472

Pages collection, 471

Painting property, 76

ParamArray keyword, 643

Parameter object, **523–524**

parameter query

    for list box, *873*

    to select records, 417, 858–859, *859*

parent and child relationship, 113

parentheses, syntax error from missing, 275

Parent property, 135

    to move through object hierarchy, **1020–1021**

parsing expression, 275

passing arguments to methods, **446–448**

    by name, 447–448, 617

    by order, 447, 617

passing data to procedures, **612–624**

    event procedures, **624–625**

    indefinite number of arguments, **622–623**

    Me as argument, **621**

    named arguments, **617**

    objects as arguments, **620–622**

    optional arguments, **623–624**

    variable by reference or by value, **613–616**

    variant arguments, **618–620**

PassingVariableByRef procedure, 614

passing variables by reference, and function procedure vs. subprocedure, 616

pass-through queries, 883

password

    limits of protection, 48, 59

    removing, 48

    to protect user interface, 42, **46–48**

    to restrict database access, 42

Password Required dialog, *47*, 47, 58–59

pasting

    code into module from Object Browser, 479

    reusable control, **247–248**

path to files, as hyperlink, 27

pattern matching, for record selection, 857

PercentPosition property, 782

performance

    and library database procedures, 983–984

    macros vs. VBA, 973–974

    Me property and, **590**

    stored queries vs. SQL statements, **883**

    variables in procedures and, **594–596**

    Variant data type impact, 600

permissions

    dialog to assign, *84*

    and workgroup security, 83

persistent objects, 85, **493**

pessimistic locking, 119

physical navigation, 505, **506–508**

    between records, **303–308**

    removing default navigation buttons for, 320

    through records of form, **758–767**

Picture property, 126

    of image control, 34

planning, to avoid errors, 717

polymorphism, 913

pop-up form, 327

PopUp property, 327, 329, 420, 964

position, index to refer to object, **463–464**

pound sign (#), *See* number sign (#)

PowerPoint 97, strengths, 1006

PowerPoint, hyperlink subaddress file syntax, *28*

precondition, testing, 292

Prefix, in Hungarian naming style, 70

prefixes

    cmd, 26

    for VBA variables, **72**

Preserve keyword, 641

Previous Control property, of Screen object, 656

PreviousControlType function, 656

previous record, maintaining track of, 773

PreviousRecord function procedure, 759, 761

PrimaryID_BeforeUpdate macro, *345*, *348*

primary key

    checking for duplicate values, **344–346**, *345*

    data entry of, 811

    displaying violation form, **346–348**, *347*, *348*

    and form/subform links, 190

    holding value for previous record, 317, *319*

    for reusable macros, 340

    for searching for specific record, 311

    storing for previous record, 773

    timing of test for value uniqueness, 811

primary key fields, testing, 809

primary key index, 520

    Seek technique for, 790

PRIMARY keyword, 929

Primary property, of Index object, 924

primary query, 521
primary table, 521
Print button, macro for, 424
printing
  current values using Debug window, **710–711**
  errors table, 722, *723*
  finding records for, **409–415**
  macro definition, 240
  macros, **279–280**, *280*, *281*
Print Macro Definition dialog, 240, *241*
Print method, for Debug object, 441, 477
Print Preview button, macro for, 423
private functions, running in Debug window, 575–576
Private keyword, 289, 547, 555
  for DLL procedure, 989
  for module-level variables, 625
private procedures, 86
  vs. public, 86, **547**
PrivateScoping procedure, 627
procedure-level constants, creating, 635
procedure-level variables, 597, **604–625**
  automatically destroyed, 604
  creating, 598
  lifetime of, **609–612**
  visibility of, **606–608**
procedures, 19, 86, 531, **539–556**. *See also* reusable procedures;
    variables
  calling, **542–543**, *543*
  for command buttons, **19–22**
  converting macros to, **971–982**
  copying and pasting, 583
  declaration placement in, 608
  event, 93, 540–541
  fully qualified reference for, 545
  function, 93, **539–540**
  for Lookup combo box, 38
  modules to store, **543–545**
  naming conflicts and, 718
  for object manipulation, **89–91**
  passing data to, **612–624**
  property, 541
  public vs. private, 86, **547**

references to, **545–546**
reusable, 553
running macro from, 237
running select queries in, **890–897**
setting bookmarks in, *565*, 565
to set validation rules, 343
simple examples, **548–556**
  event procedure, **548–550**, *550*
  function procedure, **551–552**
  hiding procedure, **555**
  running another procedure in module, **553**
  running procedure in another module, **554–555**
statement to create variable in, 595
stored queries created in, **884–890**
stored queries and SQL statements in, **884**
sub, **540–541**
  for synchronizing forms, 38
use of variables, **596**
visibility of, 547
procedure separator, 549
Procedure View, *18*, 18
process, 488
Product function procedure, 623
programming style, **568–569**
programs, 21, 86
  storage of, 86
progress meter, SysCmd function to display, **683–684**, *685*
projects, 625, 971
Prompt argument, for MsgBox() function, 260
propagation of Null values, 534
properties, **74–77**, 439. *See also* custom properties
  for ActiveX controls, 995, **1001–1003**
  available only in VBA, 76
  calling procedures to set, 542
  of controls, reference to, **134**, *135*
  DAO, **493–495**
  for database, **79–80**
  default for controls, 125
  design-time vs. run-time, 74
  of Form object vs. Recordset object, 740
  of forms, 466
    references to, **131**

getting, **443–446**

Immediate pane in Debug window to evaluate, **131–132**, *132*

Not operator to toggle, 677–678

permanent change in, 443

reading value in VBA, 442

read-only, **77**

of Recordset object, access to, 456

reference by name, 129

of reports, references to, **131**

representing other objects, **135**

of Screen object, 340

for security, **83–85**

setting in Debug window, 442–443, *443*

setting in VBA, **442–443**

SetValue macro action to change, 210

of subform control, **189–190**

that represent objects, 444

Properties collection, 122, **474**, 491

appending user-defined property to, 942

Append method, 940

Delete method, 943

for objects, 494

in TableDef object, 113, *114*

Property Get procedure, as reusable procedure, 954

Property Get statement, 541, **952–954**

Property Let procedure, as reusable procedure, 954

Property Let statement, 541, **949–952**

Property objects, **475**, **524**

property procedures, 541

calling, **950**

Property Get statement to read, **952–954**

Property Set statement, 541

property sheets

for ActiveX controls, **1001–1002**, *1002*

after macro conversion, *977*, *977*

assigning event macros in, *237*

dialogs as, 78

editing literal in, 591

of Report form, 20

viewing design-time properties in, **74–75**

viewing event procedure from, 560

protection of database, disabling, 59

pseudocode, 694

public constants, 597

public function procedure, calling from another module, 578

Public keyword, 547, 554

for array shared among all procedures, 638

for custom data type, 645

for DLL procedure, 989

public module-level variables, *627*, *628*

public procedures, 86

property procedure as, 950

vs. private, 86, **547**

PublicScoping procedure, 626

public variables, 597

pulling data

with DLookup() function, **171–175**

from different open form, **169–171**

from same form, **165–168**

into unbound controls, **176–177**, *176*

using Column property, **181–182**, *182*

pushing data

from combo box control into bound control, **182**

into unbound controls, **176–177**, *176*

# Q

queries, 4. *See also* SQL statement

AutoLookup, **160–161**, *161*

calculated fields, 153, **163**, *164*

and custom user interface, 5

Description property for, 494

dragging to Macro window, 243

and Jet, 487

and Null value, 535

and Recordset object, 522

recordset returned by, 454

references to fields in, **140–141**

relationship between fields in, 521

Requery action to rerun, 224

retrieving value of field in, 173

stored, 153

and SQL statements, **881–884**

stored definition of, 523

temporary relationships for, 152

timer for, 678–679

to join data in multiple tables, 152

Query Builder, 179, *180*, 390, *390*

Query By Form, 15, 393, 858–859

  to find group of records, **389–396**, **867–871**

  to select record, *333, 334*

  to synchronize combo boxes, **405–406**

  use by wizard, 17

QueryDef object, **523**, 884, 915

  creating, 499

  creating Recordset object based on existing, 504

  Execute method of, **899–900**

  Fields collection, 518

  Name property, 885

  opening recordset on, **777–778**

  SQL property, 885

QueryDefs collection, 884

  appending QueryDef object to, 885

query Design view, 142, 793, 881, *882*

Query menu, Make Table, 888

QueryRunTime procedure, 678

question mark (?)

  to display property setting in Immediate pane, 444

  to evaluate expression in Debug window, 283

Quick Watch, in break mode, 714, *715*

quotation marks

  for literal strings, 532

  to identify strings within strings, 359

# R

random access to data, 797

range test, for record selection, 857

read-only access, opening database in, 497

read-only properties, **77**

read/write access, opening database in, 497

reassigning groups of records, **902–903**, *904*

recalculation of controls, 169

record buffer, 97, 162

RecordCount property, 456, 763, 767, 781

Record Navigation operations, from Command Button Wizard, *24*

Record Operations, from Command Button Wizard, *24*

records. *See also* groups of records

  adding new, **370–373**, *371*

    macro for, **348–351**

  adding to recordset, **838–842**

  counting, **781**

  deleting, and referential integrity, 288

  determining if selection contains, 412

  editing existing, **370**

  finding specific, **309–317**, **768–774**

    macro for, **312–315**, *312*

  finding those to print, **409–415**

  locking, **455**

  logical navigation among, **309–323**

  methods for editing and updating, 511–512

  methods to delete, 513–514

  moving focus within, **757–758**

  moving to on active form, **305–307**

  moving to on different open form, 308

  moving to last on subform, 304

  moving to specific on subform of active form, **307–308**

  moving within, **302–303**

  new vs. current, 512

  physical navigation between, **303–308**, **758–767**

  problems testing for first in macro, 307

  return to previous, **317–319**, *318*

  saving after editing, 162

  saving new, **356–357**

  selecting with Query By Form, *333, 334*

  tabbing to next, **308**

  testing for presence, 412, 763

  undoing changes to, **817**

  ValidationRule property for, 341, *342*

recordset, EditMode property of, **841–842**

recordsetclone, 456, 740

  bookmarks for, 460–461

  closing, 767

  creation in DisableEnable function, 763

RecordsetClone property, 456, 515, 767

    of form, 740

    and indexes, 813

    to find specific records, **771–772**

    to test record position, 762, *763*

Recordset data access object, 502

    types, 503

RecordsetNavigation procedure, 783–784

Recordset object, 85, 454, **522–523**

    access to properties and methods, 456

    Clone method to duplicate, 514–515, 795, 797

    creating, 499

    data manipulation in, **505–515**

    Fields collection, 518

    Filter property of, 457

    FindFirst method of, 771

    GetRows method of, 797–798

    Move methods of, 457–458, *458*

    NoMatch property of, 509

    Sort property, 457

recordset object variables, declaring, 602

RecordsetOtherDatabase procedure, 776–777

recordsets, **152–155**

    automatic destruction, 154

    bulk changes with action queries, **898–903**

    closing, **505**, **783**

    for combo box or list box, 157

    counting records in, **781**

    creating, **502–505**, 775

    creating variables to work with data, **775–778**

    detecting limits, 307, 779–780, *780*

    editing data, **836–843**

        adding records, **838–842**

        changing record, **836–838**

        deleting records, **842–843**

    and forms, **740–743**, *741*

    looping through with VBA, **671–672**, *673*

    navigation of, **779–784**

    opening on another recordset object, 777–778

    reading data values in, **780**

    Restartable property of, 781

    run-time error from attempt to move beyond limits, 760

    sorting and filtering, **893–897**

    testing for empty, 412, 763, **782**

    tracking records in, 459

    updating, **780–781**

    in VBA, 438, **454–462**

Records menu

    Apply Filter/Sort, 380, 864

    Filter, Advanced Filter/Sort, 390

    Refresh, 167, 168–169, 171, 193, 222

    Remove Filter/Sort, 864, 868

    Save Record, 353, 817

record source of form, reference to field in, **140**

RecordSource property, 157, 159, 454

    changing, 865

    filter query based on, **419–420**

    for form or report, **155**, *155*, 860

    SQL statements in, 18, 153

Redim statement, 640, 641, 642

Reference object, **476**

references

    abbreviations for objects, **674–675**

    to active object using Screen object, 126, **138–139**

    adding to another database, 617, *618*

    to closed forms, **957**

    to controls, **133–134**

        on active form or report, **137–138**

    to control's properties, **134**, *135*

    to data access objects, **491**, **495–498**

    Expression Builder to create, **141–144**, *142, 143, 145*

    to fields, **139–141**

        in table or query, **140–141**

    to form properties, **131**

    to forms, **130–131**, **461–462**

        with Me property, 742

    to library databases, **984–987**

    to macro in macro group, **227–228**

    to objects by name, **129–130**

    to objects in collections, **462–464**

    to procedures, **545–546**

    to properties by name, 129

    to report properties, **131**

to reports, **130–131**

    with Me property, **461–462**

to subforms, **135–137**, *137*

to user-defined property, **942–943**

unqualified vs. fully qualified, 138

References collection, **475–476**

References dialog, *475*, 475, *985*, 985, 1008, *1009*

References object, 92

referential integrity, 341

    deleting records and, 288, 819

    enforcing, 152

    index for, 520

    and Jet, 486

    for relationship, 522

refresh

    automatic, for edited data, **830–831**, *832*

    and new records, **371**

Refresh Current Page button (Web toolbar), *35*

refreshing data display, 167, 168

Refresh method, 516–517

RefreshTableLinks standard module, 544

Registry Editor (regedit.exe), 80, *81*

Registry (Windows 95), 80–82

reinitializing

    code, **706**

    variables, 601, 602–603, 706

related forms, synchronizing, **183–193**

Relation objects, 500, **521–522**, **924**

    Fields collection, 518

Relationships dialog, *363*, 363–364, *823*

relationship table, for Database Wizard, 7

releasing, ActiveX objects, **1024**

Remove Filter/Sort command (shortcut menu), 380

removing

    command from command bar, 51

    commands from menus, 54

    password, 48

RepaintObject action, 223, 224

Repeat Count argument, for RunMacro action, 265

Repeat Expression argument, for RunMacro action, 265

Replace dialog box, *615*

report

    caption in title bar, 73

    creating shortcut menu for, 57

Report_Close macro, *423*

Report Date Range form, 18

Report form, property sheet of, 20

report macro group, 227

report modules, 8, 467

    creating, 544

    Error event in, **722–726**

    module-level variable visibility when created in, **628–629**

    Module window combo box for, 559, *560*

    opening, 557

    running function procedure stored in, **576**

Report_NoData macro, 412, *414*, 425

Report object, **124**, **466**

Report Operations, from Command Button Wizard, *24*

report properties, references to, **131**

reports, 4

    automating record selection for, **409–415**

    bitmaps for, 9, *11*

    creating, **933–936**

    creating filter query for, **418–419**

    custom methods for, **954–955**

    custom properties for, **947–954**

    and custom user interface, 5

    Debug window to assign values to, **285–286**, *286*

    Debug window to display values from, **283–284**, *284*

    dragging to Macro window, 243

    events for, **100–101**

    macro to change values for, **209–214**

    macro to synchronize to form, **411–415**, *411*

    Me property for, **461–462**

    opening with selected records, **858–861**

    OrderByOn property for, **850**

    OrderBy property, 849

    RecordSource property for, **155**, *155*

    references to, **130–131**

    running macro by trapping events on, **237–238**, *237*

    setting data values with SetValue macro action, 212

    sorting records in, **849–856**

    synchronizing to form, **333–334**, *335*

testing for data, **334**

in VBA, **453–462**

Reports container object, 915

report sections, events for, **100–101**

Report Wizard, for tabular report, 410, *411*

requeries, 169

for new record display, 371–372, *373*

to display new records, 371–372, *373*, **834–835**

Requery macro action, 223, 224, 356

Requery method

of object, vs. DoCmd object, 871

for recordsets, 780

in VBA, **465**

RequiredDate_BeforeUpdate procedure, 810–811

Required property, 807

Reset button (toolbar), 611

Resize event, 99

Response argument

for Error event, 724

for Form_Error procedure, 290–291

Restartable property, of recordset, 781

Resume statement, after error handler, 732

returned value, for function procedure, 539

return path, between form and Main Switchboard, **23–24**

return value

data type for, 591

using from function, 577

reusable control, pasting, **247–248**

reusable objects, creating, 246

reusable procedures, 553

argument instead of literal, **590–591**

creating, **744–747**

guidelines for, **747**

variables to create, **589–594**

to walk through form's recordset, 742–743

review mode, 805

forms for, 594

visual cue for, 674

ReviewMode procedure, 675

Rollback method, of Workspace object, 905, 907

row height, in macrosheet, 228

rows

in combo list, NotInList event to add, **832–835**

in query, limiting and sorting, 153

selecting in macrosheet, 228

RowSource property, 157, 179

for combo box or list box, 178

sorting list box rows by changing, **874–875**, *875*

SQL statements in, 18

to select rows matching value in other combo box, 407

RunCode macro action, 580, 584

RunCommand macro action, 205, 217, 220, 351

for DeleteRecord command, 362

to save record, 353

RunCommand method, 817

RunMacro action, 231

repeating actions in, 265

Run Macro button, adding to toolbar, 203, *204*

Run Macro dialog, 298

Run menu

Clear All Breakpoints, 706

Compile Loaded Modules, 291

Continue, 703, 705, 707

Go/Continue, 704

Reset, 706

Run, 230

for macros, 203

Run to Cursor, **709**

Set Next Statement command, 709

Single Step, 278

Step Into, 708

Step Over, 708

Toggle Breakpoint, 706

Run method, 584

run mode property, error message when evaluating, 132, *133*

running. *See also* calling procedures

running macros, **230–238**

by trapping event on form or report, **237–238**, *237*

from active window, **230–231**

from another macro, **231–232**, *231*

from command bar, **232–233**

from Debug window, **235–236**

from Macro window, **230**

from shortcut keys, **233–234**

from VBA procedure, 237

as startup, **234–235**

suppressing screen updates while, 366

RunningWord procedure, *1019*, 1019

RunSQL macro action, 209

vs. OpenQuery macro action, 426

RunSQL method, of DoCmd object, 901–902

run time, 702

run-time error dialog, 704–705, *705*

run-time error message, for fatal error, *693*

run-time errors, **275–277**, 690, 691

arithmetic calculations and, 533

and break mode, 703

checking variable data type to avoid, 600

disabling navigation button to prevent, 762

from attempt to move beyond recordset limits, 760

from missing argument, 624

from referring to deleted record, 513

from running function in form module in Debug window, *576*

and macro programming, **288**

in macros, 293

vs. Visual Basic, **286–292**

traps for, 289

in VBA, 476, **726–734**

VBA management, 720

run-time properties, 74

in macro and VBA programming, **75–76**

Run to Cursor command (shortcut menu), 709

# S

Sales by Year dialog, 416, *417*

Sales Reports dialog, 416, *417*

SamePrivate procedure, 627

SamePublic procedure, 626

Save As dialog, *220*, *980*, 980

Save As Visual Basic module, 980

Save button, creating, 814

saving

calculation to database, **177–178**

database without source code, **570–571**, *571*

independent class module, 557

new records, **356–357**

records after editing, 162

saving editing changes, with macros, **353–357**

saving records, options for, 353

scope

of constant, 599

of module-level variable, 625

of procedures, 547

of variables, 72

and errors, 718

screen

suppressing updates while running macros, 366

turning painting on and off, 769

Screen object, **126**, **473**, 595, 749

ActiveForm property of, 444, 461

ActiveReport property, 461

advantage of, 327

for function procedures in standard modules, 592

for Item argument in SetValue macro action, 211

and Me property, **461–462**

Previous Control property of, 656

properties in ControlSource expression of unbound control, 166

properties of, 340

using to reference active object, **138–139**

vs. Me, 462

search conditions, **857–858**

searching, *See* finding

Search Text combo box, in Object Browser, 478

Search the Web button (Web toolbar), *35*

security, 570

from Jet engine, 119

.mde files and, 696

passwords for, 42

security properties, **83–85**

SeekAll procedure, 791

Seek method, **509–510**, **788–793**, 837, 878

for table in another database, **792–793**

to search for duplicate record, 812–813

SeekOther Database procedure, 792–793

Select Case decision structure, **657–660**, *659*, 983

    to test toggle button state, 851–852

    to trap errors, 725, 729

Selected property, 76

selecting. *See also* groups of records, selecting

    objects, and focus, **89**

    records using custom dialog, **415–426**

    records using Query By Form, *333*, *334*

    row in macrosheet, 228

selection-centricity

    of macro, 88

    in VBA procedures, 90–91

selection combo box, on forms, **392–393**

selection combo list, adding null row to, **400–404**, *403*

selection criteria, for group of records, 389

Select Location dialog, *32*, 32

SelectObject macro action, 205, 248, 249

SelectObject method, 91

    of DoCmd object, 834

select query

    creating, 885–887, *886*

    running in VBA procedures, **890–897**

self-documenting names, 69

SendKeys macro action, 96, 205, **219–222**, 302

SendKeys queue, 679

SendKeys statement, 96, 757–758, 936

sequence of events, **94–96**, **98–99**

    for checking value of option group, **98**

    for clicking command button, **95**

    for mouse button click, **95**

    for opening forms, **98–99**

    for tabbing between controls, 98

    for text changes in text box or combo box, **95–96**

sequential flow pattern, 229, 650

    for macro execution, 251

session, 516, 517

Set assignment statement, to assign method result to object variable, 448

SetByPass procedure, 946–947

Set Database Password dialog, 46, *47*

SetFocus method

    for ActiveX control, 996

    to move focus, **755–757**

Set keyword, 444

Set Next Statement command, 709

Set statement, 958

    New keyword in, 959–960

setup program

    for Microsoft Access, 83

    to install ActiveX control, *998*

SetValue macro action, 87, **209–214**, 243, 357–358

    Expression argument for, **212–213**

    to hold temporary values, **213–214**

SetWarnings macro action, 365

SetWarnings method, of DoCmd object, 898

shared array declarations, 638

Shift key

    enabling for Startup properties bypass, 495

    to bypass startup property settings, 42, 45

        disabling, 79, 946–947

    to extend selection in list box, 470

shortcut keys

    running macro from, **233–234**

    for troubleshooting, 709

shortcut menu

    Build, 141

    Customize, 56

    Hyperlink, 30

    Remove Filter/Sort, 380

    Sort Ascending, 379

    Sort Descending, 379

ShortcutMenuBar property, 57

shortcut menus, 49

    adding commands to, 56

    creating, **55–57**, *56*

    in Customize dialog, 50, *51*

    customizing, 49

    hiding, 43

    startup options, 123

    for subform, *215*

Shortcut Menus menu bar, 56

shortcut menu for toolbar, Customize, 49, 232

short syntax, 138

Show All Records macro action, 868

Show Only Web Toolbar button, *35*

Show Table button (toolbar), 926

Simonyi, Charles, 69

single-record append queries, 883

Single Step button (toolbar), 278

Single Step dialog, *278*, 278–279

single stepping, **278–279**

singular objects, 111

size of font, for text in modules, 563

SizeMode property, 32

Size property, for fields, 920

SizeToFit method, for ActiveX control, 996

smart navigation buttons, **762–767**

snapshot-type recordset

    Edit method and, 512

    filtering, **896**

    Find methods for, **785–788**

    and locating record, 508–509

    RecordCount property for, 767, 781

    sorting, 894

sorting

    by columns, **385, 853–854**

    complex, **854–856**

    groups of records, **379–389**

        interactively, **380–381**

    list box rows by changing RowSource property, **874–875**, *875*

    macros for complex, **385–389**, *388*

    recordsets, **893–897**

    records in form or report, **849–856**

    rows in query, 153

sort order, for comparing string expressions, 561

Sort property, of Recordset object, 457, 894, 895

source code, 569, 694, 696

SourceDoc property, 126

SourceObject property, 126

    for subform control, 189

soure code, saving database without, **570–571**, *571*

spaces, in object names, 130

Speed Ferret (Black Moshannon Systems), 73

SQL (Structured Query Language), 62

    navigation techniques, **880–881**

    vocabulary and grammar, **882–883**

SQLCreateIndex procedure, 929–930

SQLModifyTable procedure, 928–929

SQLNewRelation procedure, 931

SQLNewTable procedure, 928

SQL property, of QueryDef object, 885

SQLRecords procedure, 794

SQLSortFilter procedure, 893–894

SQL specific queries, 153, 883

SQL statement

    for action queries, 900–901

    breaking in VBA code, **888**

    to create tables, **927–932**, *930*

    for data definition queries, 901

    to display null row, *406*, 406

    domain aggregate function as, 175

    to modify group of records, 426

    performance vs. stored queries, **883**

    for queries, 501–502, 881

    in query Design view, 153, *154*

    and Recordset object, 522

    recordset returned by, 454

    running, **892**, *893*

    setting RecordSource property to, 860

    to sort and filter recordset, 893–894

    and stored queries, **881–884**

    table name in, 886

    for union query, *404*

    use by wizard, 18

SQL view, 153, *154*, *882*

    union query in, 401

square brackets ([ ])

    in Item argument of SetValue macro action, 210

    for object names including spaces, 130

standard modules, 8, 466, 544, *545*

    converting macros to function procedures in, 979

    creating, 554

    icons for, *558*

    Module window for, *558*

    opening, 557

    for reusable procedures, 745

    running function procedure stored in, 574–576

    to store function procedure, 592

standards of Automation, 1006

starting Access, and Jet, 517

Start Page button (Web toolbar), *35*

startup, running macros at, **234–235**

Startup dialog, *43*, *45*, *78*, *335*

    Menu Bar options, 123

    Shortcut Menu Bar options, 123

startup macro, **335–336**

startup options, VBA code for, 946–947

startup properties, 42, **78**, *78*, **495**

    global menu bar as, 55, 57

    Shift key to bypass settings, 42, 45

        disabling, 79

statements, 453, 530

    Debug window to run, 531

statements reference, *676*, 676

state of object, 20, 91

Static keyword, **609–612**

Static statement, to created fixed-size array, 637

static variables, 609–612, *611*

statistics, on current database, 79

Step Into button (toolbar), 708

Step Out command, 708

Step Over button (toolbar), 708

stepping through code, **708–709**

StillThere procedure, 630

Stop Current Jump button (Web toolbar), *35*

StopMacro action, 256–257

Stop statement, 703

    vs. End statement, 704

storage of data, Jet engine management of, 119

stored queries, 153

    creating in VBA procedures, **884–890**

    performance vs. SQL statements, **883**

    running, **898–900**

    running select, **890–891**

    and SQL statements, **881–884**

string delimiters, 359

string literals, 532

strings, within strings, **359**, 825

string value, in SetValue Expression argument, 212

string variable, as SetValue Expression argument, 358

stub, 549, 551

for Error event, 289

styles, specifying in Database Wizard, *10*

subcontrol, 158

subform controls, 126

    properties of, **189–190**

subforms

    on active form, moving to record on, **307–308**

    in Expression Builder, *142*, 142

    macro to move to specific control on, **301**, **302**

    moving focus, and data validation, 808

    moving to last record on, **304**

    references to, **135–137**, *137*

Subform/Subreport Linker, 189, *190*

subkeys, 81

Sub keyword, 289

sub procedures, 93, **540–541**

    calling, **581–584**

    calling in Debug window, **583**

    and macros, 584

subqueries, 883

subreport controls, 126

Sub statement, 540

Suffix, in Hungarian naming style, 70

SummaryInfo Document object, 79

support macros, 979

support procedure, 186, *187*, *543*, 543

suspending execution, **702–709**

switchboard, unhiding, 244

switchboard buttons, editing label, *41*, 41

Switchboard form, 589

    editing, 40

    multiple forms from, 16–17, *17*

Switchboard Items table, 17, *18*

Switchboard Manager, 5, **39–41**, *39*, 59, 739

switchboards, *7. See also* main switchboard

    instructions for buttons, 8

    macro action to hide, *244*

    for navigation path creation, **7–11**

    OnOpen property for, 45

Switch() function, **263–264**, *264*, 983

synchronized forms, 13

synchronizing
    combo boxes, **405–409**, *405*, **869–871**, *871*
    reports to form, **333–334**, *335*
    toggle buttons with sort, **854–856**
synchronizing forms, **183–193**, **323–334**, *324*, *326*
    form/subform technique for, **189–193**
    with Form Wizard, **190–193**
    maintaining synchronization, **328–330**, *329*, *330*
        macro for, **330–332**, *331*
    procedure for, **38**
syntax checking, **567**, **717**
syntax errors, **274–275**
SysCmd function, **682–684**, *685*
    to display progress meter, **683–684**, *685*
system-defined constants, **632**
system information, SysCmd function to return, **683**
system.mdw file, 83, 118
system messages, suppressing, 898

# T

tabbing
    between controls, sequence of events for, 98
    to next record, **308**
Tab control, 124, **471–472**, *472*
table creation, **918–932**
    Data Access objects technique, **918–926**
        CreateField method, **919–921**, *922*, **923–924**
        CreateIndex method, **922**, *924*
        CreateTableDef method, 919, *922*
        relationships, **924–925**, *926*
    links to external tables, **932–933**
    SQL techniques, **927–932**, *930*
        index creation, **929–930**
        relationships, **930–392**
TableDef object, 68, **518**, 915
    collections in, 113, *114*
    Connect property of, **932**
    CreateField method of, 500
    creating, 500, 919

creating Recordset object based on existing, 504
    Fields collection, 518
    opening recordset on, **777–778**
TableDefRecordset procedure, 778
TableDefs collection, 491
table Design view, index in, 788, 789, *790*
table fields, macro programming to change, 209
table name, in SQL statement, 886
Table Properties property sheet, *944*, 944
Table property sheet, for Database window object, 74, *75*
TableRecordset procedure, 775, *776*
tables, 4
    and custom user interface, 5
    Description property of, 944
    dragging to Macro window, 243
    references to fields in, **140–141**
    relationship between fields in, 521
    retrieving value of field in, 173
    storing hyperlinks as data in, **28–30**
    ValidationRule property, 807
TableTag procedure, 941–942
table-type recordset, 813
    adding record to, 838
    Index property to sort, **895–896**
    and locating record, 508
    RecordCount property for, 767, 781
    Restartable property for, 781
    Seek method for, **788–793**
Tab Order for command buttons, 594
tabular report, Report Wizard for, 410, *411*
Tag property, 748, 824, *826*
    of control, 829
    creating, 941
    for open form, 749
    to create custom properties, **948**
tags, 26
    for data access objects, **72**
    in Hungarian naming style, 70
    for VBA object variables, **72**
task flow diagram, 12, *13*
template files, 8
temporary control buffer, for value in text box, 316

temporary objects, 85, 915

temporary query, creating, 889–890

temporary querydef object, 885

temporary values, SetValue action to hold, **213–214**

Terminate event, 92, 625

tested loops, 265, **268**, *268*, *269*

testing, **719**

    in break mode, **706**

    for empty recordset, 412, 763, **782**

    logical navigation controls, 319

    macros, 221–222, **239**, **244–245**

    multi-criteria selection process, **398**

    NewRecord property value, 306–307

    for open form, 372, *373*, 752

    precondition, 292

    for report data, **334**

    Visual Basic error handler, **292**

TestInstance procedure, 1022–1023

text box

    Parent property of, 135

    sequence of events for text changes in, **95–96**

TextBox object data type, 595

text changes, in text box or combo box, sequence of events for, **95–96**

Text property, 76, 134

tglCustomer_Click event procedure, 854–855

tglCustomer_Click macro, *382*, *386–387*

tglCustomer_Click procedure, 852

Then keyword, 653

tight loop, 671

Timer events, 100

Timer function, **678–679**, *679*

timing

    of data validation, **811–813**

    of data validation tests, 60

    in event-driven programming model, **99–101**

Title argument

    for MsgBox action, 218

    for MsgBox() function, 261

title bar

    form or report caption in, 73

    of Module window, 22

    Startup dialog to customize, 44–45

.tlb extension, 988, 1007

ToControl macro, *300*

ToControlOnSubform macro, *300*

Toggle Breakpoint button (toolbar), 706

toggle buttons

    Null state for, 381, 382

    procedures to synchronize with sort, **854–856**

    for synchronized form, 186

    synchronizing with current sort, **385–389**, *386–387*

    triple-state, **381–382**, *383*. *See also* triple-state toggle button

ToggleMode procedure, 677–678

toggle statement, 677

ToHiddenRecord macro, *305*

ToLastControlRecord macro, *304*

ToLastRecord macro, *304*, 305–306

ToLastSubformRecord macro, *304*

ToNextControl macro, *300*

ToNextRecord macro, *304*, 305–306

Toolbar Properties dialog, 54, *58*, 58

    and menu bar changes, 55

toolbars

    adding vertical bar to, 42

    custom, 42, **48–58**

    custom button for macro, 232

    on default Form view, *215*

    global, 57–58

    hiding, 43, 57

    Hyperlink button, 29

    vs. macros, 48–49

    Web, **35**, *35*

toolbox

    adding ActiveX control, *1000*, 1000

    built-in controls, *125*

Tools menu

    ActiveX Controls, 997

    Add-ins, 118

    Analyze, 280

    Database Utilities,

        CompactDatabase, 516

        Make MDE File, 570

        RepairDatabase, 516

Macros,
  Convert Form's Macros to Visual Basic, 976
  Create Menu From Macros, 975
  Create Shortcut Menu From Macros, 975
  Options, 19, 80, 561
  References, 985, 1000, 1001, 1008, 1014
  Relationships, 363, 823
  Security, 46, 48
    User and Group Accounts, 83
  Startup, 43, 78, 335
tooltip, for custom toolbar button, *233*, 233
ToOtherFormControl macro, *300*
ToOtherFormControlOnSubform macro, *300*
tracing statements, 708
transactions, 517, **904–907**
  implicit and explicit, **904–907**
  processing, 60, 973
trappable errors, 720
trapping errors, 693, 727
trapping events, 94
  on form or report, running macro by, **237–238**, *237*
triggering function call
  by event, **579–580**
    for sub procedure, **581–583**
triggering macro, 237
  events for, 745
triggering program, 93
  selecting event for, 99
TripleState property, 381
triple-state toggle button, **381–382**, *383*
  and complex sort, 386
  to sort records, **850–853**, *850*, *851*
troubleshooting *See* macro errors, troubleshooting tools
troubleshooting tools in VBA, **701–716**. *See also* Debug window
  calls box, **715–716**, *716*
  help, **702**, *703*, 723
  printing to Debug window from code, **716**
  setting next statement for execution, **709**
  shortcut keys, 709
  stepping through code, **708–709**
  suspending execution, **702–709**
  viewing current values in Module window, *710*, 710

True constant, 632
two-way path, between switchboards and reports, 23
Type argument, for MsgBox action, 218
type-declaration character, 532
type libraries, **988**
type library, 92
"Type mismatch" error message, *619*, 619
Typeof...Is decision structure, **656–657**, 660
Type property, for fields, 920
Type statement, 644

# U

UBound function, 798
unanticipated errors
  error-handling code for, 728
  handling with Visual Basic, 972
unavoidable errors, **692**
  dealing with, **693–694**
unbound controls, **156–157**
  combo box for record search, 311, 867
  pulling data into, **165–168**
  pulling and pushing data into, **176–177**, *176*
  SetValue macro action for value, 211
  to store temporary value, 214
  updating, 167
  as variable, **175–177**
unbound form, 155
unbound form control, hyperlinks as, **30–35**, *34*
unbound hidden text box, 317, *319*
unbound report, 155
unbound text box, for explicit counter, 268
Undo button, creating, 814
undoing
  changes to records, **817**
  command bar changes, 52
  data entry changes with macros, **351–352**
  record search, **773–774**, *774*
unhiding
  dialog, macro for, 423

forms, **246–248**, *247*, **748–750**

switchboard, 244

Uniform Resource Locator (URL), 27

UNION ALL operator, 401

UNION operator, 401

union query, **400–401**, 883

adding null row with, **400–402**

combined list as, **403**

and editing, 836

SQL statement for, *404*

UNIQUE keyword, 929

Unique property, of Index object, 924

UniqueValues property, 406

universal naming convention, 27

Unload event, 186, *188*, 625

UnLockControls method, 955

UnlockControls procedure, 805, 806

unqualified reference, 138

Update method, 512, 837, 842

update query, for data entry, 428, *429*

updating, **97**

methods for, 511–512

recordsets, **780–781**

upper bound for array, 637

URL (Uniform Resource Locator), 27

usability testing, 719

User32.dll, 990

user

communication with application, 680–681

MsgBox() function to collect input, **259–261**

and workgroup security, 83

user account, 525

user control, in interactive database, 4

user-defined constants, 631

user-defined data types, 645. *See also* custom data types

UserDefined Document object, 79

user-defined properties, *See* custom properties

User and Group Accounts dialog, 83–84, *84*

User and Group Permissions dialog, *84*

user interface, 5

API function for information about, 991

protection, **42–58**

custom menus and toolbars, 42, **48–58**

disabling, 59

password, 42, **46–48**

startup properties, 42, **43–45**

user-level security, 48

User object, **525**

UseTransaction property, 905

utilities, for object name changes, 73

utility.mda, 117

# V

validation of data, 60. *See also* data validation

ValidationRule property, 211, **341–343**, 807

of controls, 342, *343*, *808*

order of testing, 809

ValidationText property, 341, 807

value entries, in Registry, 81

Value property, 76, 134, 828

of field in recordset, 780

values *See* data values

variable declaration statement, 595

variables, **588–596**. *See also* procedure-level variables

assigning method result to, 448

assigning property value to, 444

data types for, 531, **599–600**

declaration of, 72, **597–604**

implicit or explicit, 446

within argument list, **606**

destroying, 601, 603, **604**

for faster code, **594–596**

index to refer to object, 463

life cycle, **601–604**

lifetime of, 599

in macros vs. VBA code, 973

memory for, 595

module-level, 597, **625–630**. *See also* module-level variables

naming, **599**

passed as argument, 606–608

reinitializing, 601

replacing literals with, 744

for reusable procedures, **589–594**, 747

scope of, 72

and errors, 718

to set startup property, 495

statement in procedure to create, 595

as temporary memory storage, 72

term definition, 588

unbound controls as, **175–177**

use in procedures, **596**

in VBA programming, 438

variant arguments, **618–620**

Variant data type, 531, **532–537**, 591

advantages and disadvantages of variables, **537**

for array, 636

as default, 533

reasons to avoid, 600

VarType function, **536–537**

VBA332.DLL file, 1008

VBA

index in, 520–521

page manipulation with, 471

vbAbort constant, 632

VBA event procedure, replacing with event macro, *245*

VBA intrinsic constants, 632

VBA object variables, tags for, **72**

VBA-only application objects, 126

VBA run-time error, 476

VBA *See* Visual Basic for Applications (VBA)

VBA variables, prefixes for, **72**

vbCancel constant, 632

vbCrLf constant, 642, 937

vbQuestion constant, 632

vbTab constant, 937

vertical bar

adding to toolbar, 42

for order of operations, 407

View menu

Code, 544, 551

Form Header/Footer, 322, 830

Object Browser, 478, 525, 633

Properties, 419

Toolbar, 53

ViewOrder procedure, 644

visibility

of procedure-level variables, **606–608**

of procedures, 547

Visible property, 214, 243

of control, 89

Visual Basic for Applications model, 1008

Visual Basic for Applications (VBA), 19, 530. *See also* error handling in VBA; execution control in VBA; VBA…

breaking SQL statements in, **888**

data types, **531–539**

for data validation, **807–809**, *808*

entering code, 291

error handler in, **289–292**

testing, **292**

identifying strings within strings, 359

keywords in, 289

names in, **71–72**, 546

procedures, **539–556**

run-time properties in, **75–76**

for startup options, 946–947

statements and functions, **676–684**

DoEvents function, **679–680**

Exit statement, 678

InputBox function, **680–681**, *681*

MsgBox function, **680–681**

SysCmd function, **682–684**, *685*

Timer function, **678–679**, *679*

stored queries and SQL statements in procedures, **884**

suggestions and corrections by, 549

vs. macro programming, 743

Visual Basic for Application (VBA)

advantage of, 487

error handling code, **288**

to set environmental options, 82

Visual Basic methods, vs. running macro action, 284

Visual Basic object model, **127–128**

visual cues, for form in review mode, vs. data entry mode, 674

# W

Wait argument, for SendKey action, 220

Watch tab in Debug window, *127*, 127–128, 711–712, 713–714, *715*

Web toolbar, **35**, *35*

WHERE clause (SQL), 770

Where Condition argument

    for ApplyFilter action, 313

    for OpenForm macro action, 325–326

While…Wend decision structure, 671

width of columns, in macrosheet, 228

Window menu

    Size to Fit, 422

    Split Window, *563*, 563

    Unhide, 244

Windows 95, keystroke combinations and custom key combinations, 234

Windows 95 Control Panel, Mouse option, Buttons tab, 245

Windows

    dynamic-link libraries in, 988

    passing control to for messages and key processing, 679

Windows API dynamic-link libraries (DLLs), **990–992**

window settings, 563

Windows messages, and Access processes, 679

Windows Registry, 80–82

    ActiveX control in, 996–997

    type library registered in OLE section, 988

With…End With block structure, **674–675**

wizards, 4, 117

    learning from, **739**

    limitations of, **59–60**

Word 97, strengths, 1006

word wrapping, 569

workgroup in Access, 83

workgroup information file, 83, 118

workgroup security model, 83

Workspace object, 85, 495, **517**, 905, 914

    CreateDatabase method of, 499–500

    creating, 499

    OpenDatabase method of, 496–497, 792

World Wide Web, 995

    command button for link to, 33–34

Write Conflict, *455*

wzcnf80.mda, 117

wzlib80.mde, 117

wzmain80.mde, 117

wztool80.mde, 117

# X

.xls files, 524

# Y

Yes constant, 632

# Z

zero-based collection indexes, 463

Zoom Box, for editing macrosheet, 228

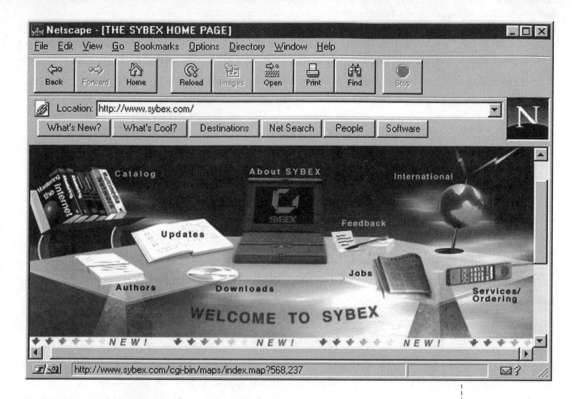

# Using the Companion CD-ROM

## Folders

**Solutions**    The Solutions folder includes the answer databases for the book's chapters and the image and other files required by the Northwind database.

Work through the hands-on exercises in the book and use these files as a check of your work. You can leave the database files on the CD-ROM and run them directly from the CD. Alternatively, you can copy the database files to the MacroVBAHandbook folder you created to store your work (see the Introduction).

| | |
|---|---|
| **Expenses.mdb** | This is the semi-automated database that the Database Wizard creates and that we modify using the other built-in Access tools in Chapter 1. Chapters 2, 3, and 4 also refer to this database. |
| **Northwind_Ch4.mdb** | This is the copy of the Northwind database used in Chapter 4. |
| **NorthwindMacros.mdb** | This is the copy of the Northwind sample database that you create and use throughout Part II. |
| **Ch12_Examples.mdb** | This is the solutions file you create from scratch in Chapter 12. |
| **Northwind_Ch13.mdb** | This is the copy of the Northwind database used in Chapter 13. |
| **Northwind_Ch14.mdb** | This is the copy of the Northwind database used in Chapter 14. |
| **Ch15_Examples.mdb** | This is the solutions file you create from scratch in Chapter 15. |
| **Northwind_Ch16.mdb** | This is the copy of the Northwind database used in Chapter 16. |
| **Northwind_Ch17.mdb** | This is the copy of the Northwind database used in Chapter 17. |
| **Northwind_Ch18.mdb** | This is the copy of the Northwind database used in Chapter 18. |
| **Northwind_Ch19.mdb** | This is the copy of the Northwind database used in Chapter 19. |
| **Northwind_Ch20.mdb** | This is the copy of the Northwind database used in Chapter 20. |

**Tables**    The Tables folder contains the tables referred to in the book. Most of these tables are comprehensive reference tables that you'll want to have available as you write your programs.

**Appendixes**    AppendixA.pdf, "Macro Actions and DoCmd Methods," is an alphabetical list of the 49 macro actions, their action arguments, whether there is a corresponding DoCmd method, additional method arguments, and a description of the action/method. AppendixB.pdf, "Glossary," is a list of the terms used in the book and their definitions.

**Event Logger**    The Event Logger database application (eventlogger.mdb) is used in Chapter 2 for hands-on experience with events. This application was created by the authors of Microsoft Access 97 Developer's Handbook who have kindly given permission to include this excellent tutorial database in this book and on the CD-ROM. You can run the Event Logger from the CD-ROM or copy it to your hard disk.

## And Finally

The file Wind32api.txt is a Microsoft text file that describes the declaration statements required to use procedures in the Dynamic Link Libraries of the Windows Application Programming Interface (API). Chapter 20 refers to this file.

## Installation

As you work through the exercises in the book, you will find instructions for the files on the CD-ROM. For more information, refer to the readme file on the book's CD.